Chicago Architecture

Histories, Revisions, Alternatives

Edited by Charles Waldheim and Katerina Rüedi Ray

University of Chicago Press / Chicago and London

KATHERINA RÜEDI RAY is professor in and director of the School of Art at Bowling Green State University. She is the coauthor of *The Portfolio: An Architecture Student's Handbook* and *Practical Experience: An Architecture Student's Handbook for Internship and the Year Out.*

CHARLES WALDHEIM is associate professor of architecture and director of the Master of Landscape Architecture Program at the University of Toronto. He works as an architect in private practice and is the author of *Constructed Ground: The Millenium Garden Design Competition.*

The University of Chicago Press, Chicago 60637
The University of Chicago Press, Ltd., London

Published 2005
Printed in the United States of America
14 13 12 11 10 09 08 07 06 05   1 2 3 4 5

ISBN: 0–226–87038–3 (cloth)

Library of Congress Cataloging-in-Publication Data

Chicago architecture : histories, revisions, alternatives / edited by Charles Waldheim and Katerina Rüedi Ray.
p. cm. — (Chicago architecture and urbanism)
Outgrowth of a symposium, Chicago is history, held in the fall of 2001.
Includes bibliographical references and index.
ISBN 0-226-87038-3 (cloth : alk. paper)
1. Architecture—Illinois—Chicago. 2. Architecture and society—Illinois—Chicago. 3. Chicago (Ill.)—Buildings, structures, etc. I. Waldheim, Charles. II.Rüedi, Katerina. III. Series.
NA735.C4C3757 2005
720'.9773'11—dc22

2004005113

∞ The paper used in this publication meets the minimum requirements of the American National Standard for Information Sciences—Permanence of Paper for Printed Library Materials, ANSI Z39.48–1992.

The publication of this book was supported by a grant from the Graham Foundation for Advanced Studies in the Fine Arts.

Contents

Foreword

Richard Solomon

In attempting to resolve the conflict between the duty to honor the bride and the duty to tell the truth when confronted with a plain woman, a Hassidic rabbi declared, "*Every* bride is beautiful on her wedding day." Similarly, I suspect everyone is allowed to believe that their hometown is special. I am certainly no exception. I have lived my entire life in Chicago, and I believe that Chicago is a special place.

Later in this book, Daniel Bluestone recalls a program organized by Richard J. Daley in 1958 called Chicago Dynamic Week. I remember that week, although it was nearly fifty years ago. I especially like the pairing of the words in the title: "Chicago" and "Dynamic." *Dyna-* is the Greek root for power, and it calls up a notion of electrical or fluid energy; dynamism; and an energy of flow and flux. A sense, as my dictionary points out, of forces *not* in equilibrium. I think this constitutes a very appropriate way of thinking about Chicago. It is indeed a dynamic city. A city concerned with, and organized by, the exercise of power—power that is not in equilibrium.

This has certainly been the case historically. In the late nineteenth century, the stockyards, the railroads, the steel mills, gave rise not only to an extraordinarily powerful commercial class but also to an extraordinarily militant working class. Both engendered a system of city government and a system of civic organizations of equivalent potency.

It is within this social, cultural, and political matrix that architecture in Chicago has flourished: the Columbian Exposition of 1893—a watershed in American architectural history—was virtually coincidental with the Pullman Strike of 1894 and the Haymarket Riot of 1896, which certainly constitute watersheds in American labor history.

Similar parallels abound through battles for social, racial, and political justice. Housing in Chicago was never merely about residential design. Rather it carried, and continues to carry, resonance from the realms of race and class, wealth and poverty. Design in Chicago has always been informed by struggle. It is here that a group of architectural radicals and a group of political radicals take the same name—the Chicago Seven.

Chicago's dynamism has resulted in a city that has been extraordinarily fecund—its history is rich in "Chicago schools" and "Chicago styles": economics, sociology, theater, psychoanalysis, blues, art, literature—even pizza and hot dogs.

Within each of these schools, the focus has tended to be local to their concerns. Some might say myopically so. They tend to see themselves as formed by the forces within their own borders, nurtured only by the mythic prairie. Thus those involved in the

Chicago schools of architecture and those who consider the history of these schools are often concerned only with the stuff of architecture and the stories of architects. But as the essays in this book make clear, Chicago architecture, like this city, is *dynamic*. It is an architecture that cannot be separated from the social and cultural context—from the power matrix—in which it is embedded.

Indeed, architecture in Chicago has often been a nexus of these contending forces. Mediated by civic involvement; by academic consideration; by its own intellectual, artistic, and cultural dimensions; often formed by acts of extraordinary individual genius, the built environment is still, ultimately, the built manifestation of a power equation. It is the physical consequence of decisions that determine who gets to decide what happens, where it happens, what it looks like, how it is made, and who it serves.

This book grew out of an attempt to investigate one of the recent moments in the fluid alignments of those power equations. In 2001, a symposium sponsored jointly by the Robert Wislow Foundation, the Graham Foundation, the Chicago Development Council, and the University of Illinois at Chicago took as its text the forces that had promoted innovation in Chicago architecture, and as its subtext the question of who should control design.

The symposium was notable for three reasons:

First, because it reilluminated the often obscured but virtually self-evident fact that different interest groups (in this case, commercial developers, the City of Chicago, and representative community groups) have a stake in the way the built environment is organized, that their legitimate positions may be meaningfully divergent, that the positions need to be resolved, and that the resolution will have consequences.

Second, because it represented a happy partnership. An occasion when the academic community, represented by the College of Architecture and the Arts at University of Illinois at Chicago, the commercial community, represented by the Chicago Development Council, and the civic community, represented by the Graham Foundation and the Robert Wislow Foundation, were able to work together toward an informed and informing discussion.

And third, of course, it was notable because it resulted in this book.

This book goes beyond—well beyond—the objectives of the conference and focuses precisely on the dynamics that construct and inform architecture. In so doing it re-presents Chicago and Chicago architecture. It reconceptualizes a local architectural history and social history as a consequence of dynamic forces.

Interestingly, this book is itself a dynamic interpretation. The multiple voices contained in this volume and skillfully orchestrated by Charles Waldheim and Katerina Rüedi Ray allow us to understand this matrix of forces in a fresh way and to see multiple facets and multiple views of a complex reality. In so doing, we are able to reconstruct histories that are more nuanced in their interpretation and more inclusive in their exposition.

Finally, the editors invite us, through the essays in this volume, to consider another aspect of Chicago; that it is and always has been a *paradigmatic* city. This book, although focused on a particular place in the American Midwest, is not a local history. Rather, it is about how architecture works in an urban context. These are essays about architecture, its history, and its historiography. The dynamic forces that determined the built environment in Chicago are active everywhere. The interpretations that are specific to Chicago in this volume are applicable to similar issues in many other places.

In this book, Chicago is emblematic—it is itself and it is more.

My kind of town.

Acknowledgments

Chicago Architecture is the work of many authors. Not only the writers who wrote its twenty-eight essays, not only the photographers who produced its three-hundred-plus photographs, but also the many others who helped shape this final object you hold in your hands. Their work, both on center stage and behind the scenes, made possible the book's birth, development, crafting, and publication. We wish to thank the many members of this community, for without them the book would not have happened.

First, we want to acknowledge the fundamentally important role of the initiators of the *Chicago Architecture* project: Robert Wislow, chairman and CEO of U.S. Equities Realty, Inc.; Richard Solomon, director of the Graham Foundation for Advanced Studies in the Fine Arts; and Roberta M. Feldman, professor in the School of Architecture at the University of Illinois at Chicago (UIC) and director of the City Design Center; all are members of the Board of Trustees of the Graham Foundation. This trio came to the UIC School of Architecture with the idea of organizing a symposium that would unite the educational, philanthropic, civic, and commercial communities in a discussion of the past, present, and future potential of Chicago architecture and urbanism. Those beginnings led to an international symposium in the fall of 2001 titled "Chicago Is History" and later, to this book. We extend our enormous gratitude to these visionary cultural leaders.

A further group of individuals were critical to the success of the symposium. Judith Russi Kirshner, dean of the College of Architecture and the Arts at the University of Illinois at Chicago, Bill Bornhoff, director and vice president of the Chicago Development Council, and Jack Guthman, attorney-at-law and leading cultural patron, gave the project their support at a very early stage and remained staunch advocates throughout. Jane Saks, director of advancement at the College of Architecture and the Arts, and Meghan Brown of U.S. Equities, special assistant to the project, were also involved from the very beginning.

The symposium itself was made possible through generous support of the Robert and Susan Wislow Foundation, the Chicago Development Council, the Graham Foundation, and the UIC College of Architecture and the Arts and School of Architecture. Additional supporting organizations and individuals included the Art Institute of Chicago, the Chicago Architecture Foundation, the Chicago Historical Society, Skidmore, Owings & Merrill, Bank One, and Jack and Sandra Guthman, as well as several anonymous donors. Much needed administrative support came from Carissa Kowalski at the UIC School of Architecture and the Arts, from Meghan Brown at U.S. Equities, and from Tasneem A. Chowdhury at the UIC City Design Center. Many other individuals from the above organizations were involved, and we thank them also.

The book itself emerged out of the symposium and quickly grew in scope and scale. Robert Bruegmann, chair of the Department of Art History at UIC, was an early supporter and critic, and we thank him for his advice and support as well as for leading us to the University of Chicago Press. At the University of Chicago Press we thank our editors, Susan Bielstein, Robert Devens, Elizabeth Branch Dyson, and Maia Rigas, paragons of professionalism as well as a real pleasure to work with. Renate Gokl, graphic designer, made the book a pleasure to behold.

Key organizations that played a part in the symposium also played a major part in the book. The Chicago Historical Society and the Burnham Library of the Art Institute of Chicago, in particular, quickly emerged as two key repositories of images and texts about Chicago history, and they received the brunt of our endless enquiries. In particular, we wish to thank Rob Medina at the Chicago Historical Society and Mary Woolever at the Burnham Library for their help.

There is, however, one individual who, above all others, made this book possible. Richard Solomon, director of the Graham Foundation, saw at the very earliest moment the potential of the symposium project to lead to a significant contribution to scholarship on Chicago architectural and urban history. His vision for and advocacy of the book project itself has made the breadth, depth, and quality of this volume possible.

Marina City, Bertrand Goldberg Associates (1959–67).

Introduction

Chicago Is History

Charles Waldheim and Katerina Rüedi Ray

The *Chicago Architecture* project came to life as the result of a conference titled "Chicago Is History," from which this book has taken inspiration. A product of a broad alliance between academic, commercial, and civic communities, the conference tried to counter Chicago's current conservative architectural culture by examining new visions for contemporary architectural and urban futures. As conference planning progressed, it became increasingly clear to us, the authors, that the institutionalization of a normative Chicago history formed one of the key obstacles to envisioning Chicago's futures. A critical historical analysis of Chicago's architecture and urbanism therefore became an essential step in breaking the spell of the past on all sides of the debate; the identification of this "straw" Chicago "ready for burning" became the main aim of this book.

To historicize history means to both acknowledge and fracture its mythology. Such a revision of the architectural history of Chicago is a critical historical task. It expands the terms through which Chicago's past, present, and future may be understood, and so displaces the singular, homogenous history associated with modernism. This, we set ourselves as the task of this book.

No single city has played such a pivotal role in the history of modern architecture as Chicago. Between 1870 and 1970, the history of Chicago architecture formed the foundational myth for European and later North American architectural modernism. In the modernist imagination Chicago became, and for many architects still is, the city where the future is always better than the past; where an independent rugged pragmatism, half engineering and half individual force of will, focused on a symbolically endless gridded horizon and brought forth an unfettered new architecture, a lusty child that went on to conquer the world. Images of Chicago excised and reassembled by Giedion, Gropius, and Le Corbusier formed the allegorical bedrock of this heroic modernist architectural story. The words of Condit, Giedion, Gropius, Hitchcock, Johnson, Mumford, and Pevsner among many others played further homage to Chicago as modernism's New Jerusalem, with Louis Sullivan, Frank Lloyd Wright, and Ludwig Mies van der Rohe as its hero-prophets. For many architects today their images and words form a canonized Chicago, a historical construct and global institution invoked in every architectural history class and venerated as flesh through the pilgrimages of architectural tourism. Modernism's temple, Chicago's architecture is truly the bedrock of history.

Chicago is also history in another sense. Architectural modernism emerged in parallel with the global expansion of industrial capitalism in the era now known as Fordism. In this tale the city of Chicago too holds a canonical position. The lusty child, hog butcher of the world, spawned slaughterhouses that inspired the production line and the self-made emperor-prince of industrial capital, Henry Ford, after whom Fordism is named. The works of Upton Sinclair and Theodore Dreiser paid homage to Chicago's animal, human, urban, and financial jungle, and described the maelstrom of bodies and commodities fueling the explosive youth of the city. Fed from within by post–Civil War migration, and from without by wave after wave of European immigrants, in this tale modern Chicago's unbridled urban growth and social unrest formed a dialectical opposite to the clean instrumental logic of its idealized architectural counterpart. Moreover, unlike the history of Chicago architectural modernism, which ceased to have new prophets and apostles as Fordism waned, the broader history of Chicago's modernity has continued and mutated. The oil shocks of the 1970s, the transformation of Fordist monopoly capital into post-Fordist multinational capital, and the associated globalization of industrial production have changed Chicago's population, economy, and culture. Today the steel mills of Gary, Indiana, struggle to compete with those in the Far East and fallow railway land is becoming Beaux-Arts–inspired parkland; Mexicans, Puerto Ricans, Poles, and Asians are among the new immigrants forming neighborhood patterns internalizing global spatial divisions at the level of the city; and Chicago has become a heritage destination where modern architecture forms only one part of a plethora of urban cultural identities. Among these multiple new "children," the once-lusty singular child of Fordism has become a respectable, even elderly adult, who today tends her small urban garden, embraced and protected by a wrought-iron fence, in one of New Urbanism's mushrooming neighborhoods marked by flag or gateway identifiers and cast-iron lamps; she travels to a downtown replete with conventioneers and tourists enjoying outdoor art amid colorful planters, traditional festivals, firework displays, and an eclectic range of architectural tours. No longer modernism's temple, here Chicago architecture is history in a more poignant sense, its singular paradigmatic status truly a thing of the past.

Chicago is the product of history in yet another, third sense. As Chicago's civic identity has come to stand for multiple cultures, economies, and political constituencies, so other architectural histories are emerging. These celebrate and legitimize spatial representations, agencies, and practices hitherto excluded from the modernist master narrative and promise a richer if more contradictory picture of Chicago's architectural history. Canonical Chicago's white, mainly Anglo-Saxon and heterosexual middle-class male architectural prophets and apostles are being joined, albeit slowly, by a much more colorful, complex, and cacophonous community, embracing multiple trajectories of race, class, gender, sexuality, nationhood, and age, among others. The new children of post-Fordist Chicago carry their modernist heritage as only one of many other pasts. A global and paradigmatic city, Chicago is many architectural histories.

Finally, Chicago is history in a final and more worrying sense. In the 1960s, earlier than many other first world cities, Chicago recognized the value of its modern architecture, passing landmark legislation that preserved many of the city's prophetic modern buildings. The alliance of politicians and historians was all too successful, so that today landmark legislation fosters a culture of historicism generating a deep collective anxiety about progressive visions of the future. The elderly adult in her garden remains, unable to do much else than tend to her personal space and look backwards with nostalgia at a past whose political, economic, and social violence has been smoothed over and made into tableaus for leisure consumption. The lusty babe unafraid to hurtle into the future appears to have been thrown out with its modernist bathwater. Here Chicago is history in the most melancholy sense of the word. No longer a city where the past is only one foundation for the future, it has no public forum where its newly repackaged history may be historicized so that the unknown future becomes more compelling than the false safety of a mythified past.

The enormity of Chicago's impact on the history of modern architecture demands that those shaping and inhabiting the built environment in Chicago today take up positions that recognize as well as challenge the weight of Chicago's constructed past. Beyond Chicago the canonical role of the city's architecture in the history of modernism is undergoing similar scrutiny. The intention of this volume is to assist in this process, through a kind of critical delamination, a stripping away of sedimentary layers of mythology, a freeing of the many cultural strata forming the city's urban, architectural, and artistic landscape. From this might then come the important critical work of fashioning another, more complex and contradictory past; one that contrasts the cohesive narrative of modernism and affirms the multiple origins from which new speculations on contemporary cultural conditions can spring.

This book of essays is an offering to those speculations. It presents revisions and alternatives to the canonical texts of Chicago's architectural history—to first loosen (but not lose) the hold of the city's modernist architectural history on the process of urban and architectural development and, second, to provide space for other histories to emerge—in order, most importantly, to allow new and unknown futures to be envisioned.

This project is not, of course, the first attempt to come to terms with the city's modernist history. The first generation of postmodernists, perhaps most vocally represented by the Chicago Seven that included Thomas Beeby, Larry Booth, Stuart Cohen, James Freed, James Nagle, Stanley Tigerman, and Ben Weese, who through exhibitions, symposia, teaching, and building worked to construct viable alternatives to the then still oppressive hegemony of Chicago's modernist legacy. Led by Tigerman, theirs was an ambitious opposition to institutionalized modernism through an inversion of architectural style and the deployment of semantic devices intended for a broader audience. Despite the reliance on form, sometimes ironic and sometimes nostalgic, this was the first broadly conceptualized alternative to Chicago's modernist architectural canon. Our work today would be not be possible in precisely the same terms without this oppositional impulse. The work of Tigerman, his colleagues, and coconspirators opened interest in and legitimized research on histories outside the canon. Several of these appear in this anthology in various forms, having first appeared in the now defunct journal *Threshold,* founded by Tigerman at the University of Illinois at Chicago. Perhaps more important, the work of this group opened a space for a multiplicity of voices from within and without Chicago's architectural culture. These voices have continued to grow in subsequent debates and publications within and beyond the city; some of these are also included in this anthology.

In the wake of that project, a second, still ongoing, project must be mentioned. This is the reappraisal and critical reevaluation of the Miesian legacy within and beyond Chicago. Evidenced in the past several years by exhibitions, competitions, conferences, and publications on the topic, this work has been produced by various authors and agents, at varying degrees of quality. At best, this line of inquiry represents an essential critical operation, revealing multiple historical layers within what had been constructed as a singular Miesian oeuvre. At worst this project threatens to condemn Mies to the kind of cultural commodification now visible in much of the work of Frank Lloyd Wright, where once progressive architectural works are packaged for distracted consumption by a culturally conservative mass market. This normalizing tendency is evident in the broad market for "design" in Chicago as a kind of recreation, or destination tourism. Here modern architecture becomes inoculated, an optional excursion from the exurban consumer cacophony in which most of us live.

While acknowledging these two lines of inquiry, this project offers other alternatives, a diverse and potentially incongruous array of voices, each a narrative fashioning multiple relationships to contemporary architectural culture in Chicago and beyond. Yet within this plethora of voices three main concerns guided the inclusion of the essays in this volume. First is a concern with representations—the reproduction and dissemination of images of Chicago architecture, including the role of publicity and promotion in the shaping of received ideas of the "modern." Second is a concern with agencies—the role of real estate developers, finance and insurance sectors, speculative capital markets, as well as the role played by public funding and networks of public patronage, consumer markets, community-based constituencies, and other user groups. The third is a concern with practices—underrepresented architectural and urban practices pursued by individuals or groups whose work did not fit and was excluded from the dominant narrative. These three themes weave in and out of most of the essays, though many essays privilege one of these above other issues.

The organization and structure of the volume in part reflect the dual ambition of the book; first, to revise and offer alternative readings for Chicago canonical architectural history; and second, to identify broader forces beyond architectural and engineered form that shaped these histories. The primary organization of the book therefore consists of two parts, "Revisions" and "Alternatives," which respectively critique and move beyond the modernist history of Chicago's architecture. Part 1, "Revisions," consists of critiques that show the historical construction of Chicago's modernist architectural history. Part 2, "Alternatives," is layered to show the multiple other histories excluded from Chicago's modernist architectural narrative. In this second part the book's concern with multiple cultures, representations, agents, and agencies is foregrounded through clustering thematically similar essays in a quadripartite organization: diversity of practices; forms of representation; role of agents; and impact of agencies—broad forces shaping the city's past and present. In critiquing, expanding, and enriching Chicago's architectural history, the volume assumes an underlying conception of Chicago as a city with tremendous social, economic, cultural, and architectural differences, tensions, and contradictions, rather than as the single-minded city portrayed by modernist mythology.

Within the book's linear form of organization, both text and photo essays are used to explore Chicago architectural history. The text essays principally construct historical narratives, and their illustrations play a subservient role to the text, although other narrative forms (a play, and a first-person account of living in a modernist building) are also included. The photo essays form small folios of photographs or other images with modest supporting texts, reversing the relationship between image and word. The book thus tries to more consciously frame the role of the image/text relationship in the formation of historical knowledge.

Part 1 reexamines the dominant Chicago school myths and thus acts as a series of rereadings of the canonical history of Chicago modernism. Responding to the erasure of difference within canonical modernist histories, this section begins with the question of race. Joanna Merwood's essay outlines the role of natural law and nineteenth-century racial theories in shaping the specific theoretical project of a regional architecture as evidenced in the annals of *Inland Architect*. Robert Bruegmann's "Myth of the

Chicago School" debunks long-cherished myths on the status of commercial architecture at the end of the nineteenth century, using a close reading of the Marquette Building. David Van Zanten chronicles the role of the Columbian Exposition, not as a fiercely debated referendum on the future of modernism as popularly received in architectural history, but rather as the first mass-market dissemination of Chicago design culture enjoying broad professional support from a range of architects practicing in the city. Reuben M. Rainey's essay focuses on the history of the Chicago parks, and the "other" face of William Le Baron Jenney as pioneer of the Chicago landscape. Sidney K. Robinson cannily puts forward the proposition that Frank Lloyd Wright might not, properly speaking, be considered a Chicago architect at all. Daniel Bluestone documents the corollary of that history in Chicago's curious alliance of historic preservation and modern architecture that effectively protected an image of the city as fundamentally modernist in style, while sacrificing many of the impressive architectural achievements of previous eras. Eric Mumford's chronicle of modernist market-rate housing in the pre-Miesian era effectively challenges the idea that Mies van der Rohe was the first architect to introduce modernism to Chicago. The last two essays in this section focus on 860/880 Lake Shore Drive and are striking accounts of the project, not from the conventional perspective of architectural form and structure, but from the perspectives of real estate development, marketing, and a personal narrative of domestic life inside the canonical project. David Dunster reveals the impact of finance and real estate development practice on design decisions, focusing on the complex and fruitful professional relationship between developer Herbert Greenwald and the Mies van der Rohe office. Janet Abrams offers her first-person account of living at 860/880 Lake Shore Drive, looking out of the modernist icon; a perspective that is curiously absent in most accounts of modernist housing in Chicago and beyond.

Part 2, "Alternatives," addresses hitherto marginalized histories. It begins with a cluster of five essays that focus on practices. These consider issues of identity and difference, specifically those of class, race, ethnicity, gender, and sexuality. The cluster begins with Julia Fish's paintings, the first photo essay of the volume, describing the architectural surfaces of a "typical" working-class building on Chicago's Near Northwest Side at 1614 North Hermitage. Lee Bey's essay accounts the failed attempt to include a progressive African pavilion in the 1933 World's Fair in Chicago, a plan that was rejected by fair organizers in favor of stereotypical racist images of Africans. Susan F. King's "Only Girl Architect Lonely" outlines the history of women architects in Chicago and, in particular, their persistent and successful efforts to form long-standing professional associations and informal networks that today still characterize architectural practice in the city. Pamela Hill's essay documents the work of Marion Mahoney Griffin after her return to Chicago from Australia, in her own practice under her own name, thus attempting to evade the shadows cast by her previous professional associations with well-known male architects (Frank Lloyd Wright and Walter Burley Griffin). Christopher Reed's essay explores the role of sexual orientation and ethnicity in the contemporary practice of identifying neighborhoods with gateways, stylized arches, and other urban iconography deemed appropriate for and relevant to particular resident/interest groups. His account spins the city's decision to equate sexual orientation with ethnicity by installing urban "identifiers"—art deco–style phallic markers around Chicago's "Boys Town" neighborhood—following similar "themed" urban "gateways" in ethnic neighborhoods. The group ends with another photo essay, Jane Wolff's documentation of Chicago parks as spaces of "naturalization" of working-class ethnic immigrants as middle-class Americans through the programming of sport, education, and public spectacle. Here tableaus of nature become culture in the profoundest sense, "natural" representations of paternalistic spaces of cultivation and social improvement.

The second cluster of essays in this section deals with the role of representations. It begins with Robert Sobieszek's essay documenting the central role of the architectural photography firm Hedrich-Blessing in the symbolic construction and international dissemination of Chicago's modernist architecture. Ranging from the family firm's initial "theatrical documentary" style and sharp light and shadow effects to the eventual severity of line and elegance of form and the "neutral" light effects employed for postwar modernist architecture, the essay affirms the power of the photographer in the construction of mythical architectural representations. Mitchell Schwarzer's essay on the archetypal Chicago grid follows, taking on the prosaic underpinnings of one of Chicago's most powerful representation within urban culture: its coordinate grid system of street numbering and placement. Contrasting the conventional spectral image of the city from the air, a series of terrestrial images reveals the urban implications for way-finding and place-making based on a system that reproduces virtually the same urban and architectural conditions in endless repetition over an inert topography. Last, the cluster ends with an essay on representations of Chicago architecture through popular images during the periods of the first and second Chicago schools—its picture postcards. The postcards examined here by Igor Marjanović point to another Chicago legacy. Taken from the collection of Alvin Boyarsky, former associate dean at the University of Illinois at Chicago and subsequent chairman of the Architectural Association in London, the postcards are used to argue for a potentially more subversive agenda through representation.

The third group of essays address the work of three modernist architects in Chicago, each in their own way neglected by the historical construction of the second Chicago school: Bertrand Goldberg, Walter Netsch, and Harry Weese. Geoffrey Goldberg offers a photo essay of selected works by his father, Bertrand, and Katerina Rüedi Ray's three-act play, "Making Marina City: Money, Masquerade, and Modernity," dramatizes the role of development and finance in Goldberg's most popularly known work. Sarah Dunn and Martin Felsen offer a photo essay on Walter Netsch and his development of "field theory" as a planning and programming practice for large institutional projects. David Goodman further illuminates that topic with an essay titled "Systematic Genius: Walter Netsch and the Architecture of Bureaucracy," arguing that Netsch's work cannot be explained by the traditional accounts of the lone genius working in the atelier producing original work. Rather, Goodman argues, Netsch developed a model of practice and a body of work that could only be produced by the kind of architectural bureaucracy of a professional services firm, such as Skidmore, Owings & Merrill, that the second Chicago school perfected. Finally, Leah Ray offers a photo essay on the urban concerns of another overlooked Chicago modernist, Harry Weese. Taken together, these three architects have been unfairly regarded as simply offering formal responses to the modernist Miesian legacy; Goldberg playing with circles, Netsch with rotated squares, and Weese with triangles. Yet Goldberg's work reveals an uncanny knack for mobilizing marketing and people to form visionary coalitions of public and private funding in support of the city as a complex social, architectural, and urban enterprise. Netsch's work is most seriously understood as an appropriate response to programming the ever-larger governmental and educational institutions that came to typify postwar public modernism in the United States. Weese's projects reveal a proto-postmodernist sensitivity to the relationships between buildings and public spaces. Occupying a clear civic realm, as well as subtly introducing material presence and quality of light, his work counters what has otherwise often become understood as the undifferentiated and rigidly reproduced placelessness of the modernist city. The work of Goldberg, Netsch, and Weese thus stands as a critique of the cultural hegemony of Chicago modernism. This may be why all three have been unfairly marginalized in the broader narration of Chicago's modernist history.

The penultimate cluster of essays in part 2 addresses the role of powerful agencies in shaping Chicago's history, including those of politics, finance, and globalization. The group begins with a pairing of a photo and a text essay that forms a critical reappraisal of modernist housing in Chicago. D. Bradford Hunt's contemporary reevaluation of the failure of modernist public housing in Chicago is paired with Janet L. Smith's images of the construction and demolition of the infamous towers of modern public housing projects in Chicago. Hunt's essay describes the central role of federal funding restrictions that, against the recommendations of the Chicago Housing Authority, created high-rise superblocks that were unable to accommodate family patterns and prevent the deepening ghettoization of Chicago's low-income African Americans. Smith's photo essay suggests that the current policy of "visible demolition" parallels the erasures of previous eras, once again without the economic and social policies in place to address the underlying causes of "housing failure." Sarah Whiting's essay, "Bas-Relief Urbanism: Chicago's Figured Field," offers an array of images revealing the extent to which the superblock informed Chicago's modernist project and illustrates the economic, social, and political aspects of land-use policy in the modern era. The final pair of essays examines the shift from Chicago as a site of industrial production to its contemporary recasting as a site for consumption in the form of travel tourism and recreation. Charles Waldheim's essay on O'Hare International Airport chronicles the impact of consumer markets, deregulation, and brand identity on the internationally known center of Chicago's transportation network. C. Greig Crysler's concluding essay traces the ironic transformation of Chicago's identity from city as slaughterhouse to city as museum. Crysler's travelogue narrative organizes a "bloody" tour of the city beginning with the site of the infamous Chicago stockyards, steeped in the blood of millions of very real cows, and ending with the recent installation of fiberglass cows across the city as works of public art. Together these essays affirm the transformation of Chicago from an industrial megalopolis into a postmodern center for consumption through differentiation in consumer markets, competition for tourism, and, in the process, the erasure of difficult and uncomfortable histories and identities.

The volume proposes a far more complex history for Chicago's present than modernist accounts of the first and second Chicago schools can sustain. While the spectrum of essays, themes, and concerns in this volume is broad, many areas are still underdeveloped or missing altogether. These include: first, the impact of economic change on the professional structures of architectural practice, and on architectural education processes in Chicago; second, the relationship of the politics of immigration and race to Chicago's urban and architectural form; third, the function of Chicago architecture and urbanism within Chicago's natural ecologies; and finally, coming full circle, the role played in Chicago history by the Chicago Seven. Each of these topics is deserving of a book in its own right. In addition, in the sections dealing with identity and difference, this volume barely touches on the richness of architectures produced by the ethnic, religious, and national communities of the city. In particular, histories of Native American Chicago, of the impact of post–Civil War and Jim Crow eras on architecture by and for African Americans, and the histories of Latino architecture in the city are missing. These areas are only now emerging in Chicago architectural scholarship.

We also need to add a short note about the contributors to this volume. One of the remarkable aspects of working on this book has been the deepening professional relationship that we, the editors, have forged with the volume's contributors. The contributors range from practicing architects, architectural administrators, curators, and politicians in this country and abroad, many writing and doing archival research in their spare time, to distinguished scholars in the fields of architecture, planning, and landscape, as well as architectural and art history, for whom the writing of history is more than a full-time professional occupation. The community of architectural history represented here is made of more kinds of "history workers" than many conventional architectural history anthologies; as the project of Chicago histories expands, the community of "history workers" will hopefully become yet more diverse. We, the editors, have also come from different parts of the world. Playing our part in the global flow of human capital that is the very bedrock of cities like Chicago, and having spent fundamentally important years in Chicago, we have both moved on to other cities. For us, this introduction's title, "Chicago Is History," and this publication now have a particular personal poignancy, mixed with tremendous pride in this project and a deep ongoing commitment to the city we both love.

It is the deep commitment to the city of Chicago shared by all the contributors that underpins the production of this book. It is a commitment that is, in part, shaped by the powerful architectural history of the city, leading each of the contributors to recognize, even as they critique, Chicago's significance for the disciplines of the built environment. Yet, over the course of the past several decades, the city has lost some of that significance. Like many cities with roots in the nineteenth century, it is increasingly a city whose identity is bound up in competition for destination tourism, recreation, and leisure. In this sense, Chicago is increasingly dependent upon maintaining its heritage of modern design as a form of cultural capital generating tourism, education, and entertainment dollars. Rather than producing its own genuine architectural culture, much of contemporary Chicago is packaging its architectural past as a marketable identity differentiating it from dozens of other postindustrial cities, in a global system of mildly differentiated historical representation. Most distressingly, this trend has recently taken the form of zoning "reform" and similar efforts at freezing an image of the city circa pre-Depression boom times in the 1920s, with certain exceptions made for canonical modernist works of the 1950s,'60s, and '70s. This return to architecture as Chicago's brand identity makes the possibility of an actual, authentic architectural culture increasingly challenging. Founded on a cryogenized mythical past whose ubiquity suffers from the same universality as the ahistoricism of the first and second Chicago schools, the return to "history" makes the publication of the many histories collected here even more important to the critical practice of architecture in Chicago and beyond. Only when such histories cease to be commodified myths, "empty signifiers of the bloody history they displaced," and instead illuminate the economic, social, and cultural conditions linking the city's present to the past, can the city begin to construct urban futures where Chicago architecture is not history.

1

Revisions

1

Western Architecture: Regionalism and Race in the *Inland Architect*

Joanna Merwood

In recent years architectural historians have dispelled the modernist myth that the architects of late nineteenth-century Chicago were pragmatists who did not theorize their own work. Louis Sullivan is no longer presented as their lone intellectual voice.[1] Numerous studies of individual architects, along with reinterpretations of Chicago's architectural history, have recovered the previously ignored writings of his teachers and colleagues.[2] These texts, the products of endless speeches, numerous conferences, and thousands of meetings, were published in the professional journal the *Inland Architect,* founded in 1883.[3] However, the magazine remains relatively unexamined except as the source of factual information, perhaps because it complicates the established definition of the "Chicago school" as a practical and spontaneous eruption of a native style.[4] In his canonical *Chicago School of Architecture* (1964), Carl Condit, under the sway of Sigfried Giedion's "anonymous history," quotes freely from the *Inland Architect,* using it as a primary source of information without discussing it as an independent medium.[5] Within more recent scholarship, when the magazine is discussed directly emphasis is placed on its role in forming and maintaining the profession.[6] I would like to expand this attention to include the particular theory of architecture it adopted and encouraged, recognizing the importance of the region's first architectural journal in forming an intellectual basis for design and building in modern America.

The *Inland Architect* was not only a documentary record of practice but also a venue for theoretical writing aimed at reconciling local architecture with a wider history. The magazine promoted a regionalist understanding, arguing for the independence of what it called "western architecture." (Although the American frontier had reached California by the 1880s, Chicago marked its edge, and its citizens called themselves "westerners"). The belief that this western architecture would lead the way to the formation of a new American style depended on an analogy between architectural and natural forms according to which architecture was imagined capable of adapting itself to its environment. A close reading of the *Inland Architect* reveals that theories of architectural evolution and adaptation in the Midwest were formed by the rhetoric of racial expansion and colonization. Chicago borrowed from European theory a new way of understanding architecture in terms of ethnography, as a symbol of the racially determined progress of human civilization. Through their professional journal, William Le Baron Jenney, Peter B. Wight, John Root, Daniel Burnham, Henry Van Brunt, Frederick Baumann, Dankmar Adler, William W. Boyington, Louis Sullivan, and Irving and Allen Pond searched for a style reflecting a new American character. This search took place in a city overwhelmed by violent ethnic and class conflicts, fueled by the rapid increase in immigration. These conflicts must be understood as central to any argument over the establishment of a national identity, whether architectural or political.

Chicago simultaneously bemoaned and reveled in the freedom generated by provincialism. While trying to reduce its distance from Boston, New York, and Philadelphia, its architects upheld the city's lack of intellectual tradition as a positive attribute. When the Chicago architect climbed up the steel tower he had built, he saw himself in the middle of a thriving city, in the center of a young country but also at the leading edge of Europe's extent, looking out towards the West and the future. The authors of the magazine cast themselves as men of action, unencumbered by the morass of historicism choking Europe. In the nineteenth century, critics from Europe and the East Coast of America condemned Chicago architecture as brutish, ugly, and uncultured, arguing that the new forms developed there (particularly the steel-framed skyscraper) were created by economic and environmental conditions rather than by the creative efforts of the architects themselves.[7] For example, in an 1894 review of Chicago building, the French architect Jacques Hermant wrote dismissively that Burnham & Root's Monadnock was "no longer the work of an artist responding to particular needs with intelligence and drawing from them all of the possible consequences. It is the work of a laborer who, without the slightest study, superimposes 15 strictly identical stories to make a block then stops when he finds the block high enough."[8] Much of the commercial work seemed so alien that it was sometimes hard to conceive of it as architecture at all. Giving his opinion of the new Chicago construction in an 1896 survey of the buildings of Burnham's company, the New York critic Montgomery Schuyler wrote, "In the buildings in which the construction is really followed and the wall is omitted, even at the base, the highest success that has thus far been attained amounts rather to a statement of the problem than to a solution of it."[9] In reaction to this negative criticism, the *Inland Architect* attempted to rewrite architectural history so that these new forms might be placed firmly within the tradition, not as a marginalized offshoot but as its culmination, its strongest and most progressive branch.

The story of the Chicago architect as frontiersman was largely fictional. By 1880, the separation between the architect and the builder was nearly complete. The rapidly growing city had welcomed a large number of architects with diverse and sophisticated educations. Chicago architects were trained in East Coast offices like those of Richard Morris Hunt and Frank Furness or at the Massachusetts Institute of Technology. Some had studied in Paris at the École des Beaux-Arts or at the German polytechnics. Influenced by German pedagogy, the University of Illinois established its own program in architecture in 1893, and the University of Michigan was experimenting with one at the same time.[10] Professional accreditation for architects was established by the state of Illinois in 1897. But this professionalism was shrouded in romantic stories of independent and resourceful inventiveness. "The originality of American architecture rests to a great degree upon the basis of studying the necessities of labor and life, and meeting them without hesitancy or prejudice," wrote George W. Maher in the *Inland Architect,* and this pragmatism quickly became theorized as the primary characteristic of western architecture.[11] The magazine encouraged men thoroughly assimilated into the education and practices of architecture to construct a new and modern image of themselves as both pragmatic and objective. However fictitious, this self-constructed myth was extremely useful. The view of the Chicago architect as a builder, as an engineer, and as a maker but never as a writer has remained remarkably dominant in histories of American architecture.[12]

The European architects and historians Eugéne Emmanuel Viollet-le-Duc, James Fergusson, and Gottfried Semper provided the theoretical scheme within which Chicago understood its own work. While John Ruskin continued to inform the writing of a few authors, this period marks the waning of his influence on America and the beginnings of a search for a new scientific understanding. The images of Viollet-le-Duc's work published in the *Inland Architect* are not the famous adaptation of iron to Gothic structure (this eccentric idea of iron construction seemed to hold little interest for Chicagoans), but his sketches of the primitive hut, which was used to support the evolution of a new American style in the West (imagined as a new ethnographic region) out of industrial materials and building processes.[13] Architects eagerly read Viollet-le-Duc's "Habitations of Man" (1875), excerpted in the *American Architect and Building News* in 1876, and studied illustrations of the exhibition of the same name at the 1889 Paris Exposition, published in Chicago's *Building Budget* in 1888.[14] Such a comparative analysis provided a method of categorizing building by region and race rather than by the development of styles, which might allow American architecture to be accommodated into architectural history on an equal footing. The *Inland Architect* reveals how heavily Chicago architects were indebted to Viollet-le-Duc's comparative approach.[15]

In the first theoretical writing published in the *Inland Architect* in 1883, William Le Baron Jenney (who may have heard Viollet-le-Duc lecture while studying in Paris during the 1850s) incorporated the American house into Viollet-le-Duc's system of classification.[16] He presented the "Wig Wam" alongside Sudanese houses and other versions of primitive dwellings as another example of architecture obeying the "great principle . . . that the form of the building grows out of the requirements modified by the material at hand, and the degree of civilization of the builders."[17] An unwieldy collage of fragments from Viollet-le-Duc and Fergusson, Jenney's article, originally a set of lectures delivered at the University of Michigan, is based on the premise that architecture should be studied as a branch of ethnography (figs. 1.1 and 1.2). This ethnography was that of the nineteenth century, in which the four principle races were believed to be, in Jenney's words, "the Turanians, Semitics, Celts and Aryans."[18] Each was a dis-

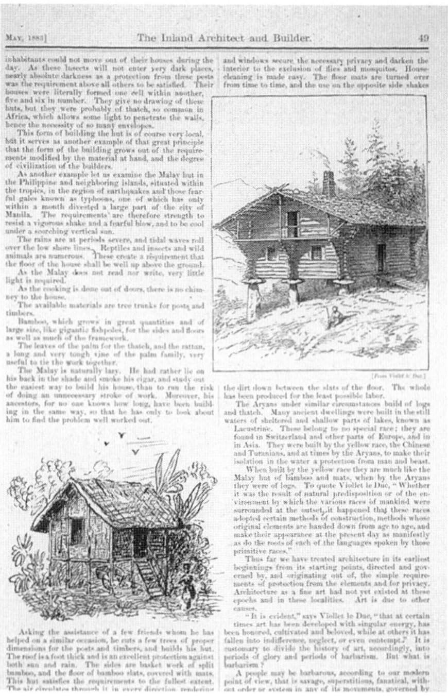

May, 1883] The Inland Architect and Builder. 49

inhabitants could not move out of their houses during the day. As these insects will not enter very dark places, nearly absolute darkness as a protection from these pests was the requirement above all others to be satisfied. Their houses were literally formed one cell within another, five and six in number. They give no drawing of these huts, but they were probably of thatch, so common in Africa, which allows some light to penetrate the walls, hence the necessity of so many envelopes.

This form of building the hut is of course very local, but it serves as another example of that great principle that the form of the building grows out of the requirements modified by the material at hand, and the degree of civilization of the builders.

As another example let us examine the Malay hut in the Philippine and neighboring islands, situated within the tropics, in the region of earthquakes and those fearful gales known as typhoons, one of which has only within a month divested a large part of the city of Manila. The requirements are therefore strength to resist a vigorous shake and a fearful blow, and to be cool under a scorching vertical sun.

The rains are at periods severe, and tidal waves roll over the low shore lines. Reptiles and insects and wild animals are numerous. These create a requirement that the floor of the house shall be well up above the ground.

As the Malay does not read nor write, very little light is required.

As the cooking is done out of doors, there is no chimney to the house.

The available materials are tree trunks for posts and timbers.

Bamboo, which grows in great quantities and of large size, like gigantic fishpoles, for the sides and floors as well as much of the framework.

The leaves of the palm for the thatch, and the rattan, a long and very tough vine of the palm family, very useful to tie the work together.

The Malay is naturally lazy. He had rather lie on his back in the shade and smoke his cigar, and study out the easiest way to build his house, than to run the risk of doing an unnecessary stroke of work. Moreover, his ancestors, for no one knows how long, have been building in the same way, so that he has only to look about him to find the problem well worked out.

Asking the assistance of a few friends whom he has helped on a similar occasion, he cuts a few trees of proper dimensions for the posts and timbers, and builds his hut. The roof is a foot thick and is an excellent protection against both sun and rain. The sides are basket work of split bamboo, and the floor of bamboo slats, covered with mats. This hut satisfies the requirements to the fullest extent.

and windows secure the necessary privacy and darken the interior to the exclusion of flies and mosquitos. House-cleaning is made easy. The floor mats are turned over from time to time, and the use on the opposite side shakes

[From Viollet le Duc.]

the dirt down between the slats of the floor. The whole has been produced for the least possible labor.

The Aryans under similar circumstances build of logs and thatch. Many ancient dwellings were built in the still waters of sheltered and shallow parts of lakes, known as Lacustrine. These belong to no special race; they are found in Switzerland and other parts of Europe, and in in Asia. They were built by the yellow race, the Chinese and Turanians, and at times by the Aryans, to make their isolation in the water a protection from man and beast.

When built by the yellow race they are much like the Malay hut of bamboo and mats, when by the Aryans they were of logs. To quote Viollet le Duc, "Whether it was the result of natural predisposition or of the environment by which the various races of mankind were surrounded at the outset, it happened that these races adopted certain methods of construction, methods whose original elements are handed down from age to age, and make their appearance at the present day as manifestly as do the roots of each of the languages spoken by those primitive races."

Thus far we have treated architecture in its earliest beginnings from its starting points, directed and governed by, and originating out of, the simple requirements of protection from the elements and for privacy. Architecture as a fine art had not yet existed at these epochs and in these localities. Art is due to other causes.

"It is evident," says Viollet le Duc, "that at certain times art has been developed with singular energy, has been honored, cultivated and beloved, while at others it has fallen into indifference, neglect, or even contempt." It is customary to divide the history of art, accordingly, into periods of glory and periods of barbarism. But what is barbarism?

A people may be barbarous, according to our modern point of view, that is savage, superstitious, fanatical, without order or system in any of its movements, governed by

1.1

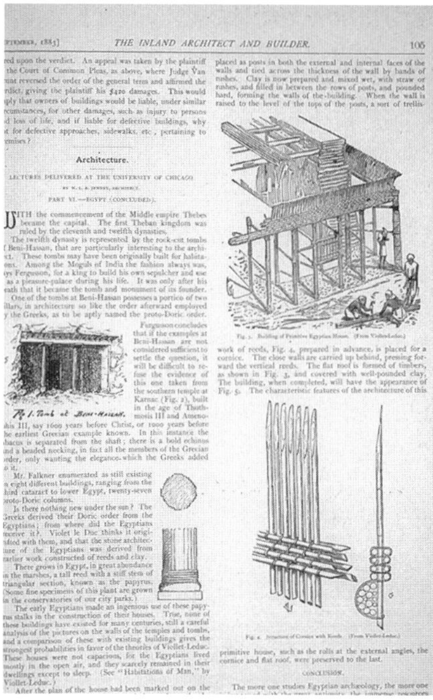

[September, 1883] THE INLAND ARCHITECT AND BUILDER. 105

red upon the verdict. An appeal was taken by the plaintiff the Court of Common Pleas, as above, where Judge Van unt reversed the order of the general term and affirmed the rdict, giving the plaintiff his $420 damages. This would ply that owners of buildings would be liable, under similar rcumstances, for other damages, such as injury to persons d loss of life, and if liable for defective buildings, why t for defective approaches, sidewalks, etc., pertaining to emises?

Architecture.

LECTURES DELIVERED AT THE UNIVERSITY OF CHICAGO

BY W. L. B. JENNEY, ARCHITECT.

PART VI.—EGYPT (CONCLUDED).

WITH the commencement of the Middle empire Thebes became the capital. The first Theban kingdom was ruled by the eleventh and twelfth dynasties.

The twelfth dynasty is represented by the rock-cut tombs f Beni-Hassan, that are particularly interesting to the archi-ct. These tombs may have been originally built for habita-ons. Among the Moguls of India the fashion always was, ys Fergusson, for a king to build his own sepulcher and use as a pleasure-palace during his life. It was only after his eath that it became the tomb and monument of its founder.

One of the tombs at Beni-Hassan possesses a portico of two illars, in architecture so like the order afterward employed y the Greeks, as to be aptly named the proto-Doric order.

Fig. 1. Tomb at Beni-Hassan.

Fergusson concludes that if the examples at Beni-Hassan are not considered sufficient to settle the question, it will be difficult to refuse the evidence of this one taken from the southern temple at Karnac (Fig. 2), built in the age of Thothmosis III and Amenophis III, say 1600 years before Christ, or 1000 years before he earliest Grecian example known. In this instance the bacus is separated from the shaft; there is a bold echinus nd a beaded necking, in fact all the members of the Grecian rder, only wanting the elegance which the Greeks added o it.

Mr. Falkner enumerated as still existing n eight different buildings, ranging from the hird cataract to lower Egypt, twenty-seven proto-Doric columns.

Is there nothing new under the sun? The Greeks derived their Doric order from the Egyptians; from where did the Egyptians receive it? Violet le Duc thinks it originated with them, and that the stone architecture of the Egyptians was derived from earlier work constructed of reeds and clay.

There grows in Egypt, in great abundance in the marshes, a tall reed with a stiff stem of triangular section, known as the papyrus. (Some fine specimens of this plant are grown in the conservatories of our city parks.)

The early Egyptians made an ingenious use of these papyrus stalks in the construction of their houses. True, none of these buildings have existed for many centuries, still a careful analysis of the pictures on the walls of the temples and tombs, and a comparison of these with existing buildings gives the strongest probabilities in favor of the theories of Viollet-Leduc. These houses were not capacious, for the Egyptians lived mostly in the open air, and they scarcely remained in their dwellings except to sleep. (See "Habitations of Man," by Viollet-Leduc.)

After the plan of the house had been marked out on the

placed as posts in both the external and internal faces of the walls and tied across the thickness of the wall by bands of rushes. Clay is now prepared and mixed wet, with straw or rushes, and filled in between the rows of posts, and pounded hard, forming the walls of the building. When the wall is raised to the level of the tops of the posts, a sort of trellis-

Fig. 3. Building of Primitive Egyptian House. (From Viollet-Leduc.)

work of reeds, Fig. 4, prepared in advance, is placed for a cornice. The close walls are carried up behind, pressing forward the vertical reeds. The flat roof is formed of timbers, as shown in Fig. 3, and covered with well-pounded clay. The building, when completed, will have the appearance of Fig. 5. The characteristic features of the architecture of this

Fig. 4. Structure of Cornice with Reeds. (From Viollet-Leduc.)

primitive house, such as the rolls at the external angles, the cornice and flat roof, were preserved to the last.

CONCLUSION.

The more one studies Egyptian archæology, the more one

1.2

1.1 William Le Baron Jenney, "Architecture," *Inland Architect* 1 (May 1883): 49. The upper image is taken directly from Viollet-le-Duc.

1.2 William Le Baron Jenney, "Architecture," *Inland Architect* 2 (September 1883): 105.

tinct race with its own system of religion and government and also its own sensibility toward built form. The Turanians, ruled by despots and worshipping an animate world, exhibited a "lower state of civilization," he believed, but excelled at monumental architecture, like the pyramids. As a nomadic people, he continued, the Semitics had little appreciation for permanent architectural form, emphasizing surface decoration instead of structure. In turn, the Aryans were defined by their "practical common sense" and the plainness and simplicity of their architecture. For Jenney, as for Viollet-le-Duc, the history of architecture was the history of civilization, which was, in turn, the history of race and racial expansion. Jenney's writing supported the idea of American expansion later popularized by Theodore Roosevelt in his book *The Winning of the West* (1889).[19] Echoing the popular mythology that related American westward expansion to a supposed ancient and perpetual "great movement" on the part of the original "Germanic" peoples, Jenney explicitly characterized the people of the United States as present-day Aryans, who are, he wrote, "again migrating westward and spreading themselves over the United States from the gulf of Mexico to Canada and the Pacific to produce a new center of civilization."[20]

Introduced to Chicago by German-educated architects, Gottfried Semper was another source for a scientific understanding of architectural origins and development. Recent scholarly interest has been concerned with the possible influence of Semper's theory of cladding on the design of terra-cotta–clad steel-framed buildings in Chicago.[21] However, on the evidence of the *Inland Architect,* it seems that Semper's ideas were valued more generally as providing a scientific model of architectural development based on architectural and racial types and the climate they inhabited. In his *Four Elements of Architecture* (1851) and *Style in the Technical and Tectonic Arts* (1860–63), Semper drew on contemporary archaeological and ethnographic studies to argue for a strict relationship between handcrafts (which he described as the first architectural products), climate, race, and human development.[22] His emphasis on material and technique seemed particularly suited to Chicago, where new technologies appeared to be exhausting the possibilities of historic forms. His writing attracted the interest of the architect Frederick Baumann, who had immigrated to Chicago from Germany in 1851 and was well established in practice by the 1870s. While Baumann's writing on the design of a system of isolated pier foundations is well known, his intellectual importance has only been recently rediscovered. During the 1880s and 1890s he gave many lectures, and published a number of articles in the *Inland Architect* based on Semper's teaching.[23] Under Baumann's influence, John Root made a translation of Semper's 1869 essay, "Über Baustile," which he titled "Development of Architectural Style."[24] The first translation of the German architect's work in America, it was published in the *Inland Architect* in serial parts from December 1889 to March 1890.[25] This translation introduced Chicago readers to Semper's contention that building styles "are not invented, but develop in various departures from a few positive types, according to the laws of natural breeding, of transmission and adoption. Thus the development is similar to the evolutions in the province of organic creation."[26] While Semper's examples came from the ancient world, the stage was set for a similar ethnographic understanding of the American architecture of the Midwest.

It is difficult to overstate the importance of ethnography in nineteenth-century histories of architecture. As Georges Teyssot has noted, the Victorian classification of architecture into types based on race had little to do with the architectural typologies of the eighteenth century.[27] As the designers of the ethnographic displays at the World's Columbian Exposition recognized, architecture was a vital signal of difference and a necessary tool for self-identification. The idea of an architectural history of America written from an ethnographic perspective was still new but seemed to offer great possibilities, not least the legitimacy of science. Viollet-le-Duc's and Semper's ideas were used to support the evolution of a new American style in the West (imagined as a new ethnographic region) constructed from industrial materials and building processes. Out

1.3 Holabird & Roche, "Hunter's Cabin," World's Columbian Exposition, Chicago, 1893.

of this belief in environmental determinism, in an architecture based on ethnic, regional, and material specificity, sprang a whole genre of articles in the *Inland Architect* devoted to the category of "western architecture." Just as the designers of the "Hunter's Cabin" exhibit at the World's Columbian Exposition (fig. 1.3) used the myth of the West to create a sense of common identity, in these essays the same myth was voiced in relation to architectural theory.[28] The category of "Western Architecture" is synonymous with other "Romantic regionalisms" being constructed at the same time in Germany, England, and Scandinavia, each seeking an architectural identity based in "authentic" vernacular building forms.[29]

The perceived absence of American history meant that a western vernacular was created out of the landscape itself. In 1884, the *Inland Architect* helped found the Western Association of Architects, a new professional association. At the banquet celebrating the event, the magazine's editor, Robert Craik McLean, offered a parable of the natural development of Chicago architecture, in which the first "inland architect" was not a man but a nest-building bird. The next "architects" were beavers and muskrats. They were succeeded, in turn, by the Native American Indians. Then came the white settlers who (inevitably) "constructed the log hut after the plan of the ancient Arians."[30] Here, as in many other narratives, the American Indian represented the link between the "natural" and the "constructed" western worlds.

Perhaps the most articulate of the articles on the subject is Henry Van Brunt's "Architecture in the West," published in 1889.[31] Van Brunt had established a successful practice in Boston before moving to Kansas City in 1885 as architect to the Union Pacific Railroad Company. In this essay he described the country as a whole as an ever westward-expanding frontier, and the architecture being built there as the frontier of a new kind of art. Like Jenney, he claimed the architectural theory of Viollet-le-Duc as that which would best serve America, since it was based on "rational" principles rather than history. Van Brunt criticized the crude emulation of European models he saw around him. He reserved his harshest words for the Queen Anne style introduced by Richard Morris Hunt and popularized by popular journals and pattern books. The Queen Anne style was constantly attacked in the *Inland Architect* for its fashionableness and flimsiness, for its lack of adherence to true building principles. John Root described the body of western architecture as that of a young child, and the Queen Anne as a dangerous disease from which it had only recently recovered.[32] A borrowed history was inadequate for the new country, where the only true model for architecture was nature. A truly western architecture would emerge out of the literal evolution of forms.

Both animal and architectural evolution were seen in racial terms. To consider architecture a result of environment, claimed Root, "is as obvious as to say that a man's exterior form shall be the result of his interior structure, that his skin and hair shall be colored by the climate where he lives."[33] By the 1880s, the idea that a new race of Americans was being formed at the western frontier was already entrenched in the popular imagination. What were the consequences when nineteenth-century race thinking was applied to architectural theory? How could racial, and therefore architectural, identity be determined in this particular environment? Chicago architects did not seem to find any problem in defining a common ethnographic background for their frontier city. On the surface, the story of race as it was told in the *Inland Architect* was invariably positive. Where contemporary races were mentioned, it was in relation to their rapid assimilation into Americans (fig. 1.4). The model of evolution and adaptation, to which both architectural and human form was thought subject, provided the basis for a healthy new style. Architecture shared the same characteristics as the new American. It and he were independent, strong, and masculine.[34] This claim was reinforced by counterexamples of inadequately assimilated forms like the Queen Anne, described as alien, weak, and diseased.

1.4 "Chicago's Great Railway Station," ***Appleton's Magazine*****, c. 1875.**

Writing of the consequences of inadequate or unnatural assimilation, Allen Pond applied the doctrine of the "survival of the fittest" to architectural form. "Time unerring destroys the freak and the abnormal being," he wrote, "and only the normal creation, that which is in harmony with itself and its environment, that which fulfills the laws of the type, prevails against the destructive forces of nature and persists."[35] In the *Inland Architect,* Pond and his brother Irving drew clear parallels between architectural and bodily pathologies. Indeed, they appear to have shared an almost eugenicist approach to the development of architectural form.[36] In a series of articles (including one called "Architectural Kinships"), Irving K. Pond explicitly linked architecture to the racial physiognomy of its builders (figs. 1.5–1.7).

Chicago architects initially agreed that the evolution of a native form would be a process of very gradual and collective change, arising out of slow cultural shifts, not just the inventive power of a few men.[37] Louis Sullivan provided the only dissenting opinion, claiming that certain men contained within themselves the "impulse" of a new style. Such men should not be limited to the slow adaptation of historical forms, he argued, but should heed that inner impulse. Despite the fact that his was a lone voice, architectural histories of this period, including those published in the *Inland Architect,* tended to follow Sullivan's Nietzschean model of progress. Nathan Clifford Ricker, professor of architecture at the University of Illinois, supported the idea of a gradual evolution but was willing to admit it could be bypassed. "If the requisite conditions exist," he wrote, "one man may impart an impulse which may turn the current into a new channel, re-

22 THE INLAND ARCHITECT AND NEWS RECORD. [Vol. XVII. No. 2

Architectural Kinships.

1.5

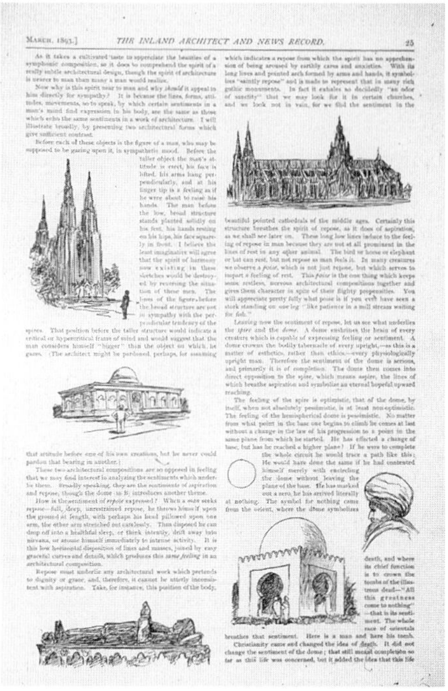
March, 1893.] THE INLAND ARCHITECT AND NEWS RECORD. 25

1.6

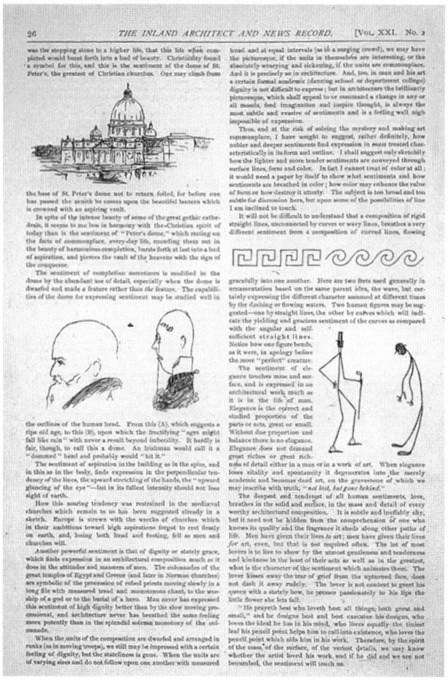
26 THE INLAND ARCHITECT AND NEWS RECORD. [Vol. XXI. No. 2

1.7

1.5 Irving K. Pond, "Architectural Kinships," *Inland Architect* 17, no. 2 (March 1891): 22.

1.6 Irving K. Pond, "Architectural Kinships," *Inland Architect* 17, no. 2 (March 1891): 25.

1.7 Irving K. Pond, "Man and His Art," *Inland Architect* 21, no. 2 (March 1893): 26.

sulting in the development of a new style."[38] Like many others, Ricker proposed not a native of Chicago or the West to do this, but instead an architect who visited from his home in Massachusetts, H. H. Richardson.

The *Inland Architect,* along with other publications such as the *American Architect and Building News,* was instrumental in creating the myth of Richardson as a man with superhuman creative powers.[39] In terms of Roosevelt's theory of racial development through strong bloodlines, Richardson was the architectural frontiersman whose hearty strain must not be allowed to die out, and in the years following his death in 1886, architectural histories would trace a heroic lineage from Richardson, through Root and Sullivan, to Frank Lloyd Wright. Richardson was credited with creating a vibrant new national style out of an imperfect and impure medieval form, using what Root called the "great vigor and masculinity of his genius."[40] Drawing on the popular discourse on evolution, the "bold" and "vital" Richardsonian Romanesque was described as the "cure" for the delicacy and weakness of the diseased Queen Anne style. In this way, its creator had hastened the natural process of architectural evolution, correcting and healing the horrifying mutations of the past.

Despite claims for the vitality and naturalness of the western landscape, its occupants, and its architecture, critics from the northeastern United States were not convinced of its benevolence. In the late nineteenth century all industrial cities were subject to harsh criticism, but the view of Chicago from afar was particularly narrow. Three topics dominated the *New York Times*'s coverage of the city during the period: epidemics of typhoid and cholera, labor unrest, and the bribery of aldermen and officials.[41] The atmosphere of the city seemed rotten in every way. In the *Inland Architect,* fears of various forms of corruption were expressed most directly in articles on sanitation, which operated as thinly disguised metaphors for broader issues of social well-being. Their central claim was that the architect must be continually vigilant in protecting the native environment from attack by alien forces. At the most literal level, the cunning invaders able to infiltrate the home and destroy it from within were bacteria. In this vision of homeland insecurity, architects enlisted the new profession of sanitary engineering to guard against marauding microbes.

In other articles, the metaphor of the alien was not so subtly applied to organized labor. During Chicago's labor disputes of the 1880s, daily newspapers came down strongly against the striking workers. In its anonymous editorial comments, the *Inland Architect* did too. Labor protests were intimately connected to the architect's work, as a large number of the strikers were members of the building trades, particularly bricklayers and carpenters. During the period of the worst conflict, from spring 1885 until late 1888, the

Inland Architect continually voiced its criticism of the organized labor movements. The editors were of the opinion that "labor blames capital for that which it is itself most to blame."[42] Years of strikes demanding an eight-hour workday and protests over the hiring of nonunion labor came to a head in 1886 with the infamous Haymarket bombing, in which seven policemen and an unknown number of protesters were killed. Despite heated national interest in the affair, the *Inland Architect* made no direct mention of the bombing or the subsequent trial. In unsigned editorials, it continued to oppose the striking workers' demands.

The irony of the rustic Romanesque favored by the *Inland Architect* is that conditions of production were far from medieval in this western metropolis, where traditional building crafts were quickly being superseded by industrial technologies. While leaders of the labor movement saw Ruskin and William Morris as firm allies, frequently quoting them in the *Alarm,* Chicago's English-language Socialist weekly (Morris's "The March of the Workers" was reprinted there in 1885, and his "The Tables Turned," in 1888),[43] the nostalgic idea of a return to medieval methods of production held little practical relevance to workers in Chicago's factories and building sites. Labor leaders argued not for a return to craft but for safer and more equitable working conditions. Industrialization had increased the productive power of labor tenfold, they argued, but wages seemed to stagnate and hours grew longer. They compared themselves to automatons asked to perform backbreaking repetitive tasks. In answer to these dehumanizing conditions, to their immanent assimilation into rationalized processes of building production, workers wielded their only weapon, the strike.

Architects had a vested interest in opposing this resistance, since labor disputes disrupted their own work and prevented their clients (business owners and real estate developers) from doing theirs. To cite only one example, the construction of Richardson's Marshall Field Wholesale Store was disrupted for six months due to strikes by building laborers.[44] Beyond financial interests, the architectural theory of the *Inland Architect* linked the appearance of new architectural forms to the continued stability of the state. The architecture of a society is determined by and is a reflection of the way it is governed, wrote Jenney. In Chicago there was a genuine fear that the strikes and associated anarchist activity would disrupt the city to the point where recently reestablished national unity would again be tested.[45] Repeating the same argument made by the popular press, the *Inland Architect* claimed that the more committed labor organizers were isolated and dangerous foreign elements from whom the majority of workers must be protected. This corrupting force was identified with German-born activists like August Spies, editor of the *Arbeiter-Zeitung,* who was hung for his supposed involvement in the Haymarket bombing.[46] In this story the labor agitator was not a "native" but an unwelcome foreign influence. He must be purged in order to maintain the healthy functioning of society. Architecture was used to put down this threatening incursion. Built between the slums of the South Side and the mansions still remaining there, Burnham & Root's First Regiment Armory contained Gatling guns intended to "command both Sixteenth St. and Michigan Ave. in case of riots or in times of disturbance."[47]

However it was not only architects who invoked architecture to argue their cause. The *Alarm* tried to co-opt the sympathies of the "mechanic" by persuading him that effort expended in building "jails, courthouses, custom houses, state houses, law and insurance offices" was an ultimately useless form of production benefiting only property owners.[48] But such passive persuasion was less effective than direct action against those same property owners. The *Alarm* actively promoted the use of explosives in the interests of class warfare. The editors described dynamite as the gift of modern science to the workingman and printed detailed recipes for its manufacture and use in articles such as "Explosives: A Practical Lesson in Popular Chemistry. The Manufacture of Dynamite Made Easy."[49] Architecture was property, and for the anarchists well versed in the writing of Paul Prudhoun, property was theft. With his hands each individual laborer had the ability to make only a small part of any building. With a bomb he had the ability to destroy at a scale usually controlled only by the architect.[50]

Richardson's transmutation of stone into art, of lead into gold, found its opposite in the anarchist's ability to shatter it, to turn that stone back into dust. In a widely distributed manifesto called "Word to Tramps" (1884) the labor activist Lucy Parsons, whose dramatic language and powerful imagery enlivened the otherwise repetitive and didactic tone of the *Alarm,* advised homeless workers considering suicide to blow themselves up in front of the new mansions lining Prairie Avenue.

"Stroll you down the avenues of the rich and look through the magnificent plate glass windows into their voluptuous homes who have despoiled you and yours. Then let your tragedy be enacted here. Awaken them from their wanton sports at your expense. Then send forth your petition and let them read it by the red glare of destruction. Thus when you cast one lingering look behind, you can be assured that you have spoken to these robbers in the only language which they have ever been able to understand, for they have never yet deigned to notice any petition from their slaves that they were not compelled to read by the red glare bursting from the mouths of the cannon, or that was not handed to them on the point of a sword . . . Each of you hungry tramps who read these lines, avail yourselves of those little methods off warfare which Science has placed in the hands of the poor man, and you will become a power in this or any other land. Learn the use of explosives!"[51]

In this vividly painted fantasy Parsons noted that the new transparency of architecture allowed the inequity between those inside and outside to be revealed. Further, she wanted to reverse the gaze through an act of violent human destruction, to transform the longing look inward into the horrified view out. But Marshall Field's architect had perhaps anticipated the threat to his wealthy patrons, and acted against it in advance. A suicide bomb would have been ineffective against Richardson's Glessner House (1885–87) on South Prairie Avenue. The monolithic stone house turned its heavily fortified back to the street, and opened up only to the security of a private internal courtyard.[52] In form, this monument to domestic security, intended as a "naturalistic" spectacle, simulates the solidity and strength of a mythical American landscape standing fast against alien invaders of all kinds.

In direct response to contemporary criticism of Chicago as a dangerous and unnatural place, controlled by a morally questionable economic system, unchecked by cultural feeling, and fraught with social disruption, the *Inland Architect* constructed a counter image of the city as the thoroughly natural result of its beneficent environment. Borrowing from European theory, it viewed architecture in relation to the new science of ethnography and placed itself at the forefront of both racial and architectural progress. A narrative of western architecture was supported by the popular myth of the continuous western movement of the supposed original European race, imagined as a natural and organic operation. The architecture of the West was constructed as a natural outgrowth of the land, the only form possible according to the laws of adaptation and natural selection. This deterministic view was used to support the interests of architects and their patrons in the social and political battles dividing Chicago. The *Inland Architect* was ultimately successful in its aims, at its own expense. The regional identity it created would come to be seen by later writers as the universal basis for modern architecture. From its origins on the periphery, Chicago came to occupy a central position. As the city without history, it would become the paradigm for all future cities. Early twentieth-century historians taught us that the modern was born there, in an entirely natural and unselfconscious process of spontaneous creation. While photographs of the skyscraper rising above the lake and the prairie reinforce this view, the wider ideology in which the story was created deserves more attention if we are to understand the intellectual basis of the concepts of organic adaptation and regionalism in architecture and, in this way, the roots of modernism itself.

Myth of the Chicago School

Robert Bruegmann

This essay was originally written in the late 1980s and appeared in 1991 in Threshold, *a student journal produced by the School of Architecture at the University of Illinois at Chicago during the heady years that Stanley Tigerman was at the helm. Like many magazines of this type,* Threshold *had a small and somewhat erratic distribution. Nevertheless this piece achieved a considerable notoriety as the first important statement on the inadequacy of what was then accepted wisdom surrounding the use of the term "Chicago school." Since that time I have written a great deal more on this topic, notably the chapters on the Tacoma and Marquette buildings in* The Architects and The City: Holabird & Roche of Chicago, 1880–1918 *(Chicago: University of Chicago Press, 1997). In addition, a good many other scholars, notably Joseph Siry, Daniel Bluestone, Sarah Bradford Landau, and Joanna Merwood have followed up on aspects of this line of research so that, by now, this essay has itself become an historical artifact. Certainly the major conclusions will no longer be surprising to most readers, and many can even be said to have become today's accepted wisdom, at least among scholars. Still, I believe that this short piece remains the most complete history of this important term, and I am pleased to see it reprinted in this volume where it might reach a wider audience. I was tempted to bring it up-to-date, incorporating all of the fruitful work of scholars since it was published, but, given the importance of this essay in the historiography of this subject, I finally decided to leave it largely unaltered except for some quite minor modifications to rectify errors that had crept into the original text and a few phrases to explain some of the references. The reader should be warned that some of the bibliography is now out-of-date and that there are several references in the text that are no longer current, most notably a description of the present state of the Marquette building with its cornice removed. A new cornice, closely echoing the appearance of the original but constructed in lightweight concrete, was installed in 2003.*

The checkered history of the term "Chicago school" provides compelling testimony to the power of language. Although born of polemics and from the first vague and contradictory, this phrase has played a major role in shaping the way the city has been seen and, particularly, in the post–World War II period, has influenced the shaping of the city itself. In recent years, as perspectives in architecture and history have shifted, the term seems a curious anachronism from the "modernist era," destined to play a minor role in scholarly footnotes. But once put into currency, terms have a curious life of their own, and it remains to be seen whether "Chicago school" will fall out of use, will lose its modernist overtones to become a standard term in architectural history, or will somehow emerge once again reinvigorated with yet another set of polemical overtones.[1]

The "Chicago School" Is Born

The term "Chicago school" apparently first appeared in a significant way in an essay by author and critic William Dean Howells in 1903. He used it to describe a group of Chicago writers who, he argued, captured the flavor of America's large cities better than their more genteel counterparts on the nation's eastern seaboard.[2] Howells was an eminent literary figure, and it was almost certainly his use of the term that inspired Chicago architect Thomas Tallmadge in 1908 to apply it, by analogy, to the residential work of Louis Sullivan and certain of his colleagues such as Frank Lloyd Wright and George Maher.[3] The term as defined by Tallmadge was much used in the 1910s, but it gradually fell out of use after World War I, as the idea that there should be a distinctive architecture for the Midwest apparently lost favor. The idea was never quite forgotten, however, and the term as used in this way did occasionally appear in print as late as 1964 when a book by Mark Peisch entitled *The Chicago School* was devoted primarily to Midwestern house designs. Since the 1972 publication of H. Allan Brooks *The Prairie School: Frank Lloyd Wright and His Midwest Contemporaries,* however, the work referred to by Tallmadge and Peisch has generally been grouped under the heading "Prairie School."[4]

In the meantime a very different use of the phrase "Chicago school" had gained ascendancy. The term as generally used today was the creation of the European architectural avant-garde of the 1920s. Throughout the 1920s, pictures of American engineering works and utilitarian buildings, primarily industrial structures but also Chicago office buildings from the 1880s and 1890s, appeared in the pages of the books and magazines published by avant-garde architects such as the German architect Walter Gropius and the Swiss designer Le Corbusier. Because these buildings had been largely forgotten by American architects and because the Europeans had little firsthand knowledge about them, the descriptions and illustrations were, as often as not, inaccurate and misleading. This did not trouble the authors, because their intent was not to write history but to create a polemic. This polemic was based on a longstanding myth about the United States as a place unfettered by history and the artificial dictates of artistic good taste, a place where the practical demands of modern life could bring into being new and largely unselfconscious cityscapes.[5]

When the American advocates of the European avant-garde learned about the pilgrimage their European colleagues were making to the soot-covered relics of late nineteenth-century Chicago, they lost no time taking the train to the Midwest. Among them was the great American social and architectural critic Lewis Mumford. Although Mumford became the first American to describe late nineteenth-century Chicago commercial buildings in European modernist terms, it was architectural historian Henry-Russell Hitchcock and Philip Johnson, at that time an architectural historian, critic and curator, who explicitly promoted the term "Chicago school" in their catalog for the show Early Modern Architecture: Chicago, 1870–1910 at the Museum of Modern Art in New York in 1933.[6] Hitchcock and Johnson had probably heard the term "Chicago school" in the context of its earlier uses in literature and architecture and they may have been aware of the "Chicago school of sociology," a term that had been coined to describe the extremely influential work of urban sociologists like Robert Park and Ernst Burgess at the University of Chicago, but they gave no indication that they were concerned how it had been used in the past.[7] It is more likely that, given their background in art history and connoisseurship at Harvard, they appreciated the scholarly sound of the term and its resemblance to labels like the "French school" or "Dutch school" often seen in museums and appropriated it for their own uses.[8] In any event, when Hitchcock and Johnson used "Chicago school" they meant a set of large commercial buildings in Chicago built in the late nineteenth century designed by major Chicago architects like William Le Baron Jenney, Burnham and Root, Adler and Sullivan, and Holabird & Roche. Their basic definition, the one that, with several substantial variations, became standard in the post years was that Louis Sullivan was the prime mover and that a group of architects inspired by him including Jenney, Burnham and Root, and Holabird and Roche survived until about 1910, "when the stylistic revivalism which had made its first striking appearance in Chicago with the World's Fair of 1893 vitiated its force."[9]

Hitchcock and Johnson provided only a sketch, however. It was the great Swiss architectural historian Sigfried Giedion, who, first in his Charles Eliot Norton Lectures at Harvard in 1937–38 and later in a book that grew out of these lectures, *Space, Time, and Architecture,* initially published in 1941 and reissued many times thereafter, fleshed out the historical research on the architects and their buildings. In his work Giedion drew from the tradition of German idealist philosophy and the kind of art history practiced by his teacher Heinrich Wolfflin to provide a sweeping historical framework in which to place them.[10] Giedion felt that the Chicago buildings of the kind that appeared in the MOMA show repudiated the heavily ornamented, historically derived architecture of the nineteenth century that Giedion and the rest of the avant-garde so disliked and showed certain affinities with the stripped-down, ahistorical buildings that Gropius and Le Corbusier were creating in his own day. He therefore considered the Chicago buildings to represent "constituent facts" of architectural history, while with few exceptions, almost everything else in nineteenth-century architecture was a "transitory fact" and could be ignored. Giedion also had the idea of juxtaposing photographs of the Chicago buildings with photos of recent European work, for example, presenting the Second Leiter Building by Jenney on one page with the Maison Clarté by Le Corbusier in Geneva on the facing page, as a way of suggesting a deep affinity if not a cause-and-effect relationship.

For Hitchcock, Johnson, and Giedion the goal was in part to signal work that they thought was good but forgotten. Resurrecting these buildings also served another function, however, providing a kind of historical pedigree and thus vindication for work of their avant-garde colleagues who were often criticized as having turned their backs on history. This kind of polemical operation was by no means unprecedented or even unusual in the history of art. The term "Renaissance," for example, was coined to link a new movement in art back to a previous golden age. At the same time, the term "Gothic," referring quite anachronistically to the nomadic tribe that overran Rome a millennium before, was used to castigate the architecture of the previous centuries. In each of these cases these terms eventually managed to transcend their polemical origins to become standard terms in art history to such an extent that today few people who use a term like "Gothic" are even aware of the negative associations that spawned it.[11]

In the vision of the "school" advanced by Hitchcock, Johnson, and Giedion, one that European, especially Marxist, writers have by and large continued to accept, the Chicagoans were primarily engineers creating utilitarian works devoid of conscious art. The buildings were viewed as objects similar to the grain elevators, bridges, and dams that dotted the American landscape. For these writers the glory of the Chicago school was the brutally simple north half of the Monadnock Building by Burnham and Root, or Holabird & Roche's Tacoma Building, which they regarded as inspired engineering, created by masters of the technical aspects of buildings but with few artistic pretensions.[12] These authors have tended to see these buildings as the inevitable result of a laissez-faire capitalist system that left developers free to extract every possible square inch of land from the site at the least possible cost.[13]

The "Chicago School" after World War II

After World War II, American writers took up the Chicago school theme. The most important figure was the architectural historian and Northwestern University professor Carl Condit, who took the term from Giedion for use in his 1948 article "The Chicago School and the Modern Movement in Architecture"[14] and for his book, *The Rise of the Skyscraper,* published in 1952. By the time of the latter publication, Condit had expanded on Giedion's comparison of work in Chicago with European modernist work by suggesting that the work of the "Chicago School" had directly influenced some of the work that was then going on in the city, notably structures by Ludwig Mies van der Rohe like the recently erected apartment buildings at 860/880 Lake Shore Drive. The term "second Chicago school" soon appeared in the architectural press.[15] Condit himself used this term in an expanded revision of *The Rise of the Skyscraper,* the classic 1964 volume, *The Chicago School.* This book has been so influential that it still serves as the basis for much of the information in survey texts, newspaper stories, and popular magazine articles on late-nineteenth-century Chicago architecture.[16]

Condit was quite forthright in acknowledging his fundamental debt to Giedion for the book's basic historical framework, but because of his training as a historian of technology, he laid particular stress on the development of structure, especially the invention of skeletal framing. And, perhaps because he was an American living in the Chicago area, he was very ready to credit a Chicago architect, William Le Baron Jenney, with the creation of the first metal skeleton office building despite what had already become a considerable weight of opposing evidence.[17] Condit also refused to accept the European judgment that the Chicagoans were naïve engineers. He insisted that Jenney and his fellow architects of the late nineteenth century were, instead, sophisticated artists who were consciously attempting to create a new art, free from the past, based on the expression of the new steel frame. For Condit the simple, straightforward treatment of the steel frame seen in structures like Holabird & Roche's Marquette or McClurg buildings became more important than the brutal simplicity of the Monadnock, which had masonry-bearing walls rather than a full metal frame.

This modernist perspective on history appeared quite convincing from the vantage point of the decades after World War II when the work of Mies and the minimal modernism of steel-and-glass skyscrapers was in the ascendancy. It also appealed to a perpetually strong sense of Chicagoan civic pride, and it fit perfectly with a postwar wave of national sentiment that the United States, having taken a leading military and economic position in the world, should likewise play an important role in the arts. This, in turn, led to an obsession with the discovery of what was peculiarly American about American culture and an outpouring of literature that attempted to locate fields of endeavor in which Americans had excelled or had been innovators.[18]

Chicago architects themselves took up the challenge and consciously attempted to create new buildings in what they considered to be the Chicago school tradition. The Brunswick Building, designed by Skidmore, Owings & Merrill, for example, with its simple concrete frame and flaring base, was described as an attempt to echo the Monadnock Building down the street.[19] Chicago architects prided themselves on a simplicity, even austerity, in their work, seeing it as a direct legacy from the "Chicago school" days.

This viewpoint even entered public policy. After the passage of the City's landmarks legislation in 1968, one of the major arguments given at the hearings for or against designation was how well any given building conformed to the principles of the "Chicago school." A building featured prominently in Condit got a great boost in landmark hearings. Buildings unpublished or criticized by writers on the Chicago school faced an uphill battle. Published criticisms of the ornamental top of Louis Sullivan's Troescher Building, for example, or the absence of Frost and Granger's monumental North Western Station from books on the "Chicago school," helped to doom these structures.

2.1 Exterior of Marquette Building, Barnes-Crosby photograph, c. 1900. Courtesy of Chicago Historical Society, ICHi-19052.

The Chicago school idea did not go unchallenged, even in its heyday. One architectural historian, Winston Weisman of Pennsylvania State University, spent much of his career trying to dispel the myth of the Chicago school. Weisman convincingly demonstrated the contradictions inherent in the use of the term, and he pointed to buildings in many other U.S. cities that had the same features as Chicago buildings, often preceding the Chicago structures in date.[20] But Weisman fell into the trap of trying to argue on the same grounds as his opponents. Rather than challenging basic premises, he merely wanted to prove that there was not as much uniformity in Chicago as had been suggested and that individuals other than Chicagoans had played leading roles in the development of modern architecture. He stated that the "Chicago school" did not exist because it did not fit the facts as he saw them. But denying the "Chicago school" was like denying the existence of the "Gothic." Both terms were historical artifacts in themselves. One could argue that they were inappropriate or internally contradictory, but the desire to banish them did not take into account the deeply conservative nature of language or the emotional satisfactions that the concept provided.

The Marquette Building as a "Chicago School" Building

The degree to which modernist aesthetic ideas affected the viewpoint of historians can be illustrated by looking at a description of a single building, the Marquette, a speculative office building at the northwest corner of Adams and Dearborn streets. Commissioned by the Marquette Building Company, a corporation controlled by Peter C. Brooks of Boston, it was designed by Holabird & Roche in 1891–92 and built 1893–94 at a cost of $1,367,000.[21]

According to Condit, the Holabird & Roche firm "most completely represented the purpose and the achievement of the mainstream of the Chicago School," and he considered the Marquette Building to be one of its most typical works. In this judgment, he again echoed Giedion, who called the Marquette the "typical office building of the 1890s," praising it as "exceptionally well-proportioned, imposing in its simplicity and its wide expanse of 'Chicago windows.'"[22] In *The Chicago School* Condit described something of the program of the building and its plan but spent most of his time describing the exterior treatment, which he characterized as being composed of a straightforward grid of horizontals and verticals. Condit did have several criticisms, however. He noted that the building was divided vertically into a base, a shaft, and a top, and that the two sides were emphasized by rustication at the corners. These were, he felt, "lingering elements of misguided traditionalism" that obscured the basic unity of the building. But these were minor complaints, he added, compared to the building's great virtues. Condit concluded,

The whole quality of the building is impressive: the wide, smooth expanse of glass transforms the big elevations into graceful patterns of light; the openings are perfectly scaled and proportioned; the deep reveals give a powerful statement to the steel cage on which the walls are carried. The Marquette is a striking integration of technical necessities with their aesthetic statement.[23]

The description clearly reveals several of the most important concerns of modernist architectural history. First, it exhibits a modernist tendency to view architecture, like painting and sculpture, in a highly abstract way. Buildings are described in "formal" terms, that is, as a composition of solids and voids, lines, planes, and color rather than in terms of what the architect intended the buildings to mean or what the viewers thought the buildings meant. This method, called "formal analysis" by art historians and analogous to the "new criticism" in literature, enjoyed an unprecedented boom in the postwar years. Although any piece of art can be described in purely formal terms, it seemed especially appropriate for twentieth-century modern art, which consciously intended to be abstract. Condit undoubtedly also felt justified in using this kind of description for the Marquette because, he believed, "Chicago school" architects such as Holabird & Roche were intent on overthrowing the existing historic styles to create a new, ahistorical modern architecture.

The Condit description also clearly indicates that he felt that structure was the prime element that Holabird & Roche wished to express. Based primarily on nineteenth-century French architectural theorists such as Eugéne Emmanuel Viollet-le-Duc, the doctrine of truthful structural expression was considered by many modernist critics as the single overwhelming moral imperative, eclipsing other possible goals advocated by nineteenth-century architects such as the expression of the building's client, its use, the nature of its site, its city, or its country. Thus, in the case of the Marquette, Condit only noted in passing the rich program of sculpture and mosaic work, which memorialized the history of the region, particularly its discovery by European explorers. Finally, the references to the "lingering elements of monumental architecture" reveal an essentially teleological view of architectural history: that architectural development is the story of innovations in technical means and their use toward a specific artistic end, in this case, the fully developed modernist aesthetic of the postwar steel-and-glass skyscraper. The Marquette's three-part facade organization, because it did not look forward to European modernism, was considered a digression.

The "Chicago School" in the Postmodern Era

Viewpoints on architectural history have changed since Condit wrote *The Chicago School*. Studies undermining many of the notions lying behind the formulation of the term have continued since Weisman, if anything, increasing in intensity as scholars in other places have reasserted the claims of their own cities. Much of the new scholarship on Chicago architecture itself has turned away from the monuments associated with the Chicago school and other canonical "modernist" monuments. Condit himself, in a pair of books dealing with Chicago architecture between 1910 and 1970, discussed sympathetically the work of many architects not connected with any of the various versions of the "Chicago school," and in articles he even had praise for the ornamentation of the buildings of the 1880s and '90s.[24] In fact, there seems to exist a special interest today in designers and buildings that are perceived to be at the opposite pole from the "Chicago school." Benjamin Marshall and Howard Van Doren Shaw, for example, are much appreciated, as are the city's major classical monuments such as the Chicago Public Library, the Art Institute, the Field Museum, the Shedd Aquarium, Union Station, and the great stepped-back skyscrapers of the late 1920s such as the Board of Trade, the Civic Opera and Field (LaSalle National Bank) buildings.[25]

This change in viewpoint has also affected the way we think about buildings described as being part of the "Chicago school." Now that their work and writings have become better known, it has become apparent how much architects such as John Root, Daniel Burnham, and Louis Sullivan differed among themselves. The buildings themselves, moreover, as they have been cleaned and restored, testify not only to their extraordinary diversity but to the powerful decorative impulse that went into them.

Looking today at the Marquette Building we can see a different structure from the one Condit saw in the 1960s. It is not that the building itself has changed very much. Restoration work has removed distracting later additions and replaced some of the lost cladding, but otherwise the building appears much as it did in Condit's day. Yet it is hard today to see the Marquette Building as he did, as a minimal grid of horizontals and verticals. Part of the reason for this is the Marquette's changing context. Where earlier historians were obliged to juxtapose photographs of the building with images of European modernist architecture in order to show how similar they were, today the viewer standing on the plaza of Mies van der Rohe's Federal Center across the street hardly needs to turn his head to make this comparison. What might have looked convincing in fuzzy photographs is harder to accept on the street. Unlike the smooth steel cladding of the Federal Center buildings, the Marquette's terra-cotta looks thick and heavy. As Condit himself noted, the two sides of the street facades are emphasized by the use of "rustication," a device used on classical buildings in which the blocks of stone have a rough face and recessed joints in order to give them a greater feel of weight and solidity. In the Marquette, as in many classical buildings, rustication is used to strengthen visually the corners and articulate the facade into a satisfying three-part rhythm. The architects did

2.2 Detail of terra-cotta block from the first floor of Marquette Building. Photograph by Robert Bruegmann, 1988.

2.3 Detail of torus molding above granite base. Photograph by Robert Bruegmann, 1988.

2.4 Transition between terra-cotta wall and entry porch. Photograph by Robert Bruegmann, 1988.

2.2

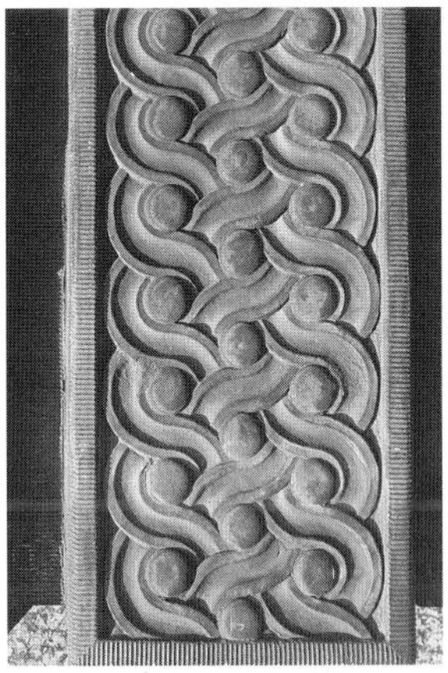

2.3

2.4

exactly the same at the top and bottom, creating the classical base-shaft-top motif that is still apparent despite the addition of an extra bay in 1905–6 and the unfortunate removal of the great classical cornice.

Approaching the building at closer range, it becomes apparent that Holabird & Roche's attempts at creating a classical configuration on the large scale are systematically reinforced by the detail of the decorative treatment. From the sidewalk, for example, the most striking thing about the Marquette is how much the base looks like deeply cut, richly textured brown sandstone despite the fact it is made of terra-cotta, a fired clay material that could have been molded in any pattern. The depth of the door and the window openings and the feeling of solidity created by the use of robust moldings and classical ornamental patterns deliberately contradict any impression that the building was constructed with a metal skeleton and a relatively thin facing. Directly at eye level, the viewer comes face to face with what appears to be great blocks whose heaviness is underscored by a guilloche pattern of the kind usually found on classical torus moldings. Here it is used to give the same kind of textural effect that classical architects achieved using a spaghetti-like random pattern called vermiculation. The desire to make the terra-cotta look like stone is confirmed in a striking fashion by the appearance of small striations on the edges of the blocks. These undeniably suggest chisel marks called "marginal drafting" that were used to create a finished edge on cut stone but which, with terra-cotta, were obviously completely superfluous in any practical sense. Just above grade level the rusticated blocks stop at a thick torus molding articulated with a conventional and beautifully detailed band of bound laurel leaves. Above eye level, the second story is capped with a heavy entablature composed of a series of moldings and decorative devices all derived from classical architecture.

To anyone even slightly conversant with the canons of classical ornament, it will be immediately apparent that Holabird & Roche occasionally used these classical features in a most unclassical way. This fact is probably explained in part by a simple lack of familiarity with the grammar of classical ornament. Expectations about the situation and scale of ornamental motifs are upset at every turn, occasionally producing really awkward passages, as for example, at the transition between the wall plane and the reveal of the recessed central doorway. In fact, the most literal of all the classical elements, the projecting Ionic portico at the entrance, was truly grotesque. Standing in front of the rest of the facade and only loosely tied back to it, the portico would probably have seemed awkward under the best of circumstances, but the peculiarly exaggerated entasis of the column shafts, the placement of a column at the center of the axis where a void would have been expected, and the unfortunate use of guttae below the Marquette inscription, out of place in the Ionic order to begin with and poorly positioned in relationship to the columns, created one of the crudest passages in any building by the firm. The early and skillful removal of this portico, perhaps because it encroached on the public sidewalk, probably had a good deal to do with the high reputation the building has subsequently enjoyed.

If inexperience with the classical vocabulary played a role in some of the deviations from classical norms, this does not appear to have been the chief factor in most of the liberties the architects took. More important was the necessity of creating bold new measures to bring the classical tradition into line with the visual needs of a building of unprecedented scale. For the most part, Holabird & Roche's work shows that they were equal to the task. Even a short study of the Marquette from the sidewalk confirms that the architects fully succeeded in creating the appearance of a thick and richly decorated classical wall sitting on a substantial base that brings the huge structure down to human scale at the sidewalk. In fact, from the perspective of the pedestrian what the building most resembles is one of the great Florentine palazzi of the Renaissance.

After discussing the exterior at some length, Condit devoted only one sentence in *The Chicago School* to the lobby, telling us that it had a balcony decorated with scenes from Chicago history. This reticence is probably due to the fact that for him the lobby represented another backward-looking element in an otherwise forward-looking building. Today, especially after the lobby's restoration, however, the visitor is likely to agree with writers at the time of the building's construction who believed that the lobby was the most notable and praiseworthy feature of the entire structure. Half of a hexagon in plan, the lobby resembles a portion of one of the polygonal chapter houses of medieval Britain, but it is decorated with a lavish classical ornamental treatment. The central feature is an elegant Doric column of Carrara marble. This column is echoed by similar but smaller columns that articulate the outside wall of the space on two levels. From the rotunda a pair of marble stairs with classical balusters and handrails unites these two levels by sweeping from the ground floor up to the balcony with its classical panels framed by pedimented, bracketed surrounds.

2.5

2.5 Original entrance portico. From *The Legend and Legacy of Père Marquette*, c. 1894.

2.6

2.6 Marquette Building, lobby. From *The Legend and Legacy of Père Marquette*, c. 1894.

2.7

2.7 Stairway leading from lobby to mezzanine, Marquette Building. Photograph by Robert Bruegmann, 1988.

2.8 Panther head door panels by Edward Kerneys, Marquette Building. Photograph by Robert Bruegmann, 1988.

In the entranceway and lobby the architects coordinated a highly ambitious cycle of historical depictions in metal and mosaic. Above the doors of the main entrance bronze panels illustrate incidents in the life of Père Marquette and his explorations in what later became the state of Illinois. Inscriptions below the panels were taken from Marquette's diary. The door plates are embellished with panther heads by the sculptor Edward Kerneys, who was also responsible for much of the public sculpture at the nearly contemporary Columbian Exposition in nearby Jackson Park.

In the lobby itself Kerneys executed a number of bronze portrait plaques depicting noted Indian chiefs who were connected in one way or another with the discovery and settlement of the Mississippi Valley. By far the most spectacular piece of the decorative program, however, was the series of mosaics on the ceiling and balcony executed by J. A. Holzer of the Tiffany firm in New York. Now illuminated with a rather harsh direct light, these mosaics were originally lit indirectly by the light that filtered into the building through open elevator cages. The glass and gold surfaces gleaming in the unevenly lit space must have produced an almost ecclesiastical effect. On the balcony parapet three large panels showing scenes from the life of Marquette alternate with panels in which portrait medallions are flanked by elaborate classical trophies ingeniously composed of elements derived from the history of the American West arranged in such a way that a European motif like an ecclesiastical vestment is paired with a belt of wampam, a helmet with an Indian headdress, and so on.[26] The composition as a whole is treated like a Roman frieze with panels framed in vertical elements resembling pilasters. It is the climax in a carefully orchestrated program that attempts to connect the building to the history of the city and the region.

Taken as a whole, the building we behold today is one that was clearly not the product of architects trying to overturn all architectural precedents. It is instead marked by an attempt to tame a new building type of unprecedented size and scale, to use classical ornament to make it relate to a specific place and time, and

2.8

to give it, as much as program and budget would allow, classical proportions and articulation. We can recognize this problem as the same one faced by architects since antiquity when dealing with utilitarian buildings of unprecedented scale. The designers of the great warehouses and aqueducts of antiquity, Renaissance and baroque hospitals and fortifications, nineteenth-century railroad stations and exhibition buildings, almost all used the same solutions. They satisfied the programmatic requirements with as much economy and grace as possible, then lavished inscriptions and sculpture to express the purpose and aspirations of the patron, and they added applied ornament at the most critical points, often transmogrified and vastly enlarged in scale from established canons, to celebrate the place, to commemorate the institutions responsible for the work, and to allow the structure to transcend mere building to become architecture with a capital A.

It would be unfair to say that the vision I have just provided of the Marquette is any more true than the one seen by Condit in the 1960s. It is simply based on a different perspective. One of the interesting consequences of this vision of the building, however, is how much closer it brings us to the way the building was perceived in its own day. In a typical description of the building published in the 1890s, the exterior was described as in the style of the "Italian Renaissance . . . which combines size and solidity with beauty and dignity."[27] The most extended description of the building, found in a rental brochure put out by the leasing agents, lavishes far more space on the building's decorative features, its "classic lines," and its sculptural embellishment than it does on the improvements in engineering.[28] In fact, almost every writer of the day allotted the vast majority of space to the "rotunda" and its artistic effects.

Seeing the Marquette as an attempt to adapt classical forms to a new building type also helps explain the widespread shift toward more academically "correct" classical forms in the 1890s by architects and firms who modernist historians supposed were antagonistic to classical architecture. The fact that H. H. Richardson in his Marshall Field Wholesale Store had already by the mid-1880s created a building that was as much a Renaissance palazzo as a simple warehouse helps to explain why his successors Shepley, Rutan, and Coolidge could so easily turn to a more academic classicism for public buildings like the Chicago Public Library in the 1890s. Likewise, Louis Sullivan in his Wainwright Building, as different as it is in some ways from the Marquette, shared with Holabird & Roche the same desire to use classical forms to tame what was perceived as an urban environment made chaotic by too many individualistic experiments.

This vision of the Marquette's place also helps us to put developments in Chicago more into line with what is already known about similar phenomena in New York and other cities at the same time. The example of the Marquette suggests that the modernist vision of the "Chicago school" as a group of architects interested in creating a new ahistorical architecture primarily based on the expression of structure is too reductivist.

From the vantage point of the 1990s, both architecture and architectural history look quite different from the way they did in the 1960s. Does this mean that the term Chicago school itself is useless and should be abandoned? Not necessarily. The term has already had a number of different and internally contradictory meanings. Labels, moreover, have extraordinary tenacity, as Weisman's apparently logical but frustrated efforts prove. Terms like "Gothic" or "baroque" were equally freighted with the negative polemics of one era but have survived either by being overlaid with other kinds of polemics or by gradually losing their negative overtones to become standard art historical terms.

It is this latter course that appears to be underway in the use of "Chicago school." In some recent publications it has come to be used to mean virtually all Chicago buildings built before the First World War.[29] On the one hand, this has reduced dramatically its usefulness in defining a single style, point of view, or group of buildings. On the other hand, this loose definition has the great advantage of avoiding most of the modernist polemic that makes it seem out-of-date today. It still carries vague overtones of moral rectitude and irrefutable aesthetic logic but without the inconvenience of being too closely pinned down to any specific buildings or theoretical point of view.

In this way, "Chicago school" might well survive as a term that includes not just the modernist, ahistorical Marquette building of the gridded structural expression but also the more recently rediscovered Marquette, with its richly ornamented walls of simulated classical masonry. It is an improbable transition but no less improbable than the vicissitudes that the term has already undergone. It has almost died several times, but it has always returned to life. The Chicago school is dead. Long live the Chicago school.

The Centrality of the Columbian Exposition in the History of Chicago Architecture

David Van Zanten

IN MEMORY OF ANN LORENZ

3.1 "Court of Honor," World's Columbian Exposition, 1893. Photograph by Charles Dudley Arnold. Courtesy of the Chicago Historical Society, ICHi-2316.

Thomas Tallmadge, the turn-of-the-century Prairie architect and historian of the "Chicago school," commences both his celebrated article "The 'Chicago School'" (1908) and his chapter "Louis Sullivan and the Lost Cause" in his *Story of Architecture in America* (1927) with the image of the "Golden Door" of Sullivan's Transportation Building at the World's Columbian Exposition of 1893. This is a commanding image: huge, emphatic, embracing, completely unexpected and new in its ornamental style, seeming to usher the visitor into some mysterious and wonderful world of the future through its tiny tripartite door. In the memories of those who, like Tallmadge, had witnessed it, with flecks of red, green, and blue, it must have been unforgettable. For Tallmadge this was the symbol of the new Chicago architecture, the summation of Sullivan's contribution and the banner of the younger Prairie designers, Frank Lloyd Wright, Walter Burley Griffin, and himself.

This is not, however, the image usually chosen by the historians of Chicago progressive architecture who have followed Hugh Morrison's 1935 selection of the Wainwright Building in St. Louis or Sigfried Giedion's 1941 choice of the Carson Pirie Scott Building as the quintessential expressions of Sullivan's contribution: the Wainwright because it was the first of his steel-framed skyscrapers, Carson Pirie Scott because it was the most minimally clad. They were establishing his reputation as a functionalist, as the most rational and honest designer of steel-framed skyscrapers, and found these designs most conducive to that preconception. And they hated the Columbian Exposition with its consistently classical Court of Honor (see fig. 3.1 above), close to Sullivan's pavilion only in physical proximity, which gave rise to the turn-of-the-century monumental classicism that Lewis Mumford had already dubbed "The Imperial Façade."[1]

Why this split between the image of a participant's memory and those of later analytical historians? In this case, in part because of the very words of the two men most concerned: Sullivan's damning depiction of the fair as a "Dark dim cloud, more like a fog" setting back architecture fifty years in his *Autobiography of an Idea* of 1924 and Frank Lloyd Wright's famous scene of repulsing the blandishments of Daniel Burnham in his *Autobiography* of 1932. Both of these, however, were written long after 1893 and are both of a literary genre, the autobiography, which imposes its own structures and standards.

The historian today accepts Sullivan's claim that Burnham was his opponent and the fair, a mortal blow to progressive architecture. Yet another early Chicago architect-historian—and one with impeccable moralizing credentials as one of the founders of the Ruskinian movement in America—Peter B. Wight, could respectfully summarize Burnham's contribution thus: "For the practice and profession of architecture, he did this: he made it known and respected by millions who had never heard of an architect in all their lives."[2] One could say the same of Burnham's fair: it was an architectural event that suddenly placed Chicago in the public mind and did so in terms of building. Previous to the opening of the exposition gates on May 1, 1893, Chicago was not especially different from St. Louis or Cincinnati in the public mind, and its architecture was no particular accomplishment of America in general. But on that day the fondest (and also most megalomaniac) dreams of the architects were realized, and for a moment a new place clad in a new and glorious raiment of building stood before them and amazed an applauding public. In 1915, the local writer Vachel Lindsay published his extraordinary *Art of the Moving Picture,* visioning America architecturally on a new scale:

Let the architect appropriate the photoplay as his means of propaganda and begin. From its intrinsic genius it can give his profession a start beyond all others in dominating this land. . . .

The photoplay can speak the language of the man who has a mind World's Fair size. That we are going to have successive generations of such builders may be reasonably implied from past expositions. . . . Let us enlarge this proclivity into a national mission in as definite a movement, as thoroughly thought out as the evolution of the public school system, the formation of the Steel Trust, and the like. After duly weighing all the world's fairs, let our architects set about making the whole of the United States into a permanent one. . . .

The architects would send forth publicity films which are not only delineations of a future Cincinnati, Cleveland or St. Louis, but whole counties, states and groups of states could be planned at one time, with the development of their natural fauna, flora, and forestry. Wherever nature has been rendered desolate by industry, or mere haste, there let the architect and park-architect proclaim the plan. . . .

. . . Why not erect our new America and move into it?[3]

Very much as it did for L. Frank Baum imagining the Emerald City in his *Wonderful Wizard of Oz* of 1900, the impact of the fair transformed Lindsay's idea of what architecture could do and how it could remake the environment.

No Chicago architect—least of all Burnham, Sullivan, or Wright—objected to that. It was precisely what they sought. But they wanted that glorious image to be in the form *they* would give it. Down to the completion of the Auditorium Building in December 1889, Sullivan had been essentially a theater architect, designing fabulous fantasy interiors in this traditional genre. It was at this moment, in the winter of 1890–91, that he turned his decorative skill into an architectural crusade with the simultaneous design of the Wainwright and the Transportation buildings. He presented the latter structure as an "architectural exhibit," an example of what the architecture of the future should be.

Sullivan's solution differed from that of the Court of Honor, but many people felt that Sullivan's example had prevailed, and it was in response to the Transportation Building that the progressive school began to coalesce around 1893, the year Wright went out on his own designing the Winslow House and that Robert Spencer executed his competition design for the Milwaukee public museum and library. The Columbian Exposition not only founded the neoclassical movement, but Tallmadge's "Chicago school" as well. This raises a fundamental question: did Burnham at the outset see his conception of the fair as antithetical to Sullivan's? And, in response, did the younger "Chicago school" take something from Burnham's ideas of the fair?

Burnham was neither a designer nor a trained architect. He was John Root's business partner until the latter's death in the midst of the fair planning in January 1891, and subsequently the employer of other designers. During the crisis of the fair, he employed Dwight Perkins to run his Loop office and Charles Atwood to head design at the exposition. Atwood then functioned as his design partner from 1893 to 1895. After Atwood died in 1895, Burnham offered design partnerships to Frank Lloyd Wright and Cass Gilbert, both of whom declined, and finally set up with Pierce Anderson. A man who could contemplate sharing his practice with Perkins and Wright as well as with Atwood, Gilbert, and Anderson—evidently with equal enthusiasm—was not a blind proponent of a specific style. And this is borne out in the firm's work, which includes the Reliance Building of 1895 as well as the Marshall Field Annex (1891–93) and the Ellicott Square Building in Buffalo (1893–95); the Railway Exchange (1903) as well as the Washington, D.C., Union Terminal (1908) and Continental Bank Building (1912). Some secondary industrial designs are vintage "Progressive functionalism." Burnham clearly was a patron, someone who felt it his job to mobilize talent, not to avoid it. As he is quoted as saying after the death of his brilliant partner Root: "I have worked, I have schemed and dreamed to make us the greatest architects in the world. I have made him see it and kept him at it—and now he dies—damn! damn! damn!"[4]

The monumental effect of the Columbian Exposition was important to the younger architects of Sullivan's circle. Only Griffin ever faced a problem of similar scale in his plan for Canberra of 1911–12, but he admitted freely that his inspiration was the fair. He laid the city out around a triplet of lakes, which he called the "Court of Honor," lined up the public institutions and parks on one side and the government buildings on the other, the latter culminating in a great open pyramid for ceremonies like the Festival Hall at the St. Louis Fair of 1904. He confided to Australian friends that his interest in architecture was first aroused by visits to the Columbian Exposition of 1893. The relative ease with which Griffin's buildings exist in the monumental tableaux of his Canberra reminds us that Sullivan's art was essentially symmetrical and monumental, classical in composition if original in decorative detail.

What, then, was the problem? If Burnham was seeking talented designers; if his monumental classicism was sympathetic with the innovations of Sullivan, Wright, and Griffin; if the whole enterprise of the Columbian Exposition gave Chicago architecture a sense of self and purpose, how did his work come to be depicted as the nemesis of architectural progressivism?

As I have mentioned, in their autobiographies both Sullivan and Wright delineate their objections with great vividness and literary effect. Sullivan:

The future looked bright [in 1890]. The flag was in the breeze. Yet a small white cloud no bigger than a man's head was soon to appear above the horizon. The name of this cloud was eighteen hundred and ninety-three. Following the little white cloud was a dark dim cloud, more like a fog. The name of that second cloud was Baring Brothers.

During this period there was well under way the formation of mergers, combinations and trusts in the industrial world. The only architect in Chicago to catch the significance of this movement was Daniel Burnham, for in its tendency towards bigness, organization, delegation, and intense commercialism, he sensed the reciprocal workings of his own mind.[5]

Wright:

Sitting there, handsome, jovial, splendidly convincing, was "Uncle Dan." To be brief, he would take care of my wife and children if I would go to Paris, four years of the Beaux-Arts. Then Rome—two years. Expenses all paid. A job with him when I came back.

It was more than generous. It was splendid.

But I was frightened. I sat, embarrassed, not knowing what to say.

"Another year and it will be too late, Frank," said Uncle Dan.

That was my cue.

"Yes, too late, Uncle Dan—it's too late now, I'm afraid. I am spoiled already."

I've been too close to Mr. Sullivan. He has helped spoil the Beaux Arts for me, or spoiled me for the Beaux Arts, I guess I mean.

"He told me things too, and I think he regrets the time he spent there himself." . . .

"The Fair, Frank, is going to have a great influence in our country. The American people have seen the 'Classics' on a grand scale for the first time. You have seen the success of the Fair and it should mean something to you too. We should take advantage of the Fair."

He went on: "Atwood's Fine Arts Building, Beman's Merchant Tailor's Building, McKim's Building—all beautiful! Beautiful! I can see all America constructed along the lines of the Fair, in noble 'dignified' classical style. The great men of the day all feel that way about it—all of them." . . .

"I know, yes—I know, Uncle Dan, you may be quite right but somehow it just strikes on my heart like . . . jail . . . Like something awful. I couldn't bear it, I believe. All that discipline and time wasted again waiting for something to happen, that never could happen. I just can't see it as living. Somehow—it scares me."[6]

It was not simply white disciplined classical style that they objected to, it was "Baring Brothers"—the "bigness, organization, delegation and intense commercialism" of Burnham's office, his effort to transform talent through six years of European study into a component of his mechanism. Burnham's reorganization of the practice of architecture to produce on a corporate scale, however, was the price Chicago architecture had to pay in order to accomplish the Columbian Exposition and to come into a sense of itself. The contracts that all the fair architects signed early in 1891 stipulated that they would provide designs only with execution left entirely in the hands of Burnham as chief of construction. Here Sullivan, Hunt, McKim, and Atwood had all already been transformed into mere specialists, facade artists. In this light and from the subsequent experiences of Atwood and Anderson, we see the price Burnham exacted from his collaborators and why, in the end, there was a fundamental contradiction in the whole Chicago architectural enterprise. The problem with Burnham's architecture was not that it was fundamentally classical but that it was not: that it implied no fundamental commitment to any style except that which could be expeditiously plugged into the great corporate mechanism Burnham oversaw.

This leads us finally back to Sigfried Giedion. In his *Space, Time and Architecture*, the Charles Eliot Norton lectures given at Harvard in 1938–39 and published in 1941. Here this Swiss art historian—a student of Heinrich Wolfflin and associate of Le Corbusier—resuscitated the idea of a "Chicago school" transformed into his own terms. His definitions have maintained their authority through the twentieth century. What Giedion proposed was that Chicago was the locus of something like a "natural force" that produced frank, functional construction, starting with the "balloon frame" invented here in the 1830s (which he was the first historian to define and document) and culminating in the steel-framed skyscraper. He mentioned names—that of George Washington Snow for the "balloon frame"; of Jenney, Root, Sullivan for the skyscraper—but gave personalities significance only insofar as they contributed to what he saw as the common enterprise, the creation of a transparently functional architecture. His most memorable lines are, in fact, a quotation from another European looking at Chicago in the 1890s, Paul Bourget in his *Outre-Mer*: "There is so little caprice and fancy in these monuments and these streets that they seem to be the work of some impersonal power, irresistible, unconscious, like a force of nature, in the service of which man has been but a docile instrument."[7] Not only was Giedion blind to the ornamental ambitions that distinguished Sullivan's skyscrapers from those of Jenney and Holabird, but he was also unappreciative of the organizing skill that enabled Burnham to transform ornamental ambitions into riveting popular hallucination in the fair. Giedion proclaimed himself a functionalist, but why was he so oblivious to the functional efficiency of Burnham's accomplishment? One must conclude that his conception of function was very narrow and traditional. To him it meant efficient fabrication, well-making in the oldest sense. It was the modest craftsman's functionalism. The great Chicago architects were not modest craftsmen. They were all leaders, prophets, practicing an art meant to galvanize purpose and to astonish in one way or another. I think that it was the Columbian Exposition that made them so.

Thus Giedion wrote events and intentions out of the history—Burnham's effort to give Chicago an image with the Columbian Exposition; Sullivan's to create a "new style" with his ornament. With a fundamentally European, Wolfflinian insensitivity to the worries, hopes, and fantasies of these white men abandoned on the American prairie, Giedion did not see people, only an abstract evolution. As a consequence he saw the frame—whether wood or steel—binding the forms of Chicago together while today, perhaps, we are coming to sense the great human event that really gave it unity: the Columbian Exposition and Chicago's presentation of itself as a place and as one producing new ideas, whether those of Sullivan with his followers Wright and Griffin or of Burnham with his subordinates Atwood and Anderson. These were all ideas about art as much as about technique, however naïve and fantastic they might have seemed.

William Le Baron Jenney and Chicago's West Parks: From Prairies to Pleasure-Grounds

Reuben M. Rainey

4.1 William Le Baron Jenney. Courtesy of the Chicago Historical Society, ICHi-19760.

William Le Baron Jenney's distinguished reputation as an architect and cofounder of the Chicago school is well established; both Louis Sullivan and Daniel Burnham trained in his office. Jenney's talent for structural innovation is supremely evident in such works as the Home Insurance Building (1884) and the second Leiter Building. But his important projects in landscape architecture are almost forgotten, as is the fact that the prominent Midwestern landscape architect O. C. Simonds, trained under him. His brilliant West Parks system, planned before the Chicago Fire of 1871 but built for the most part after it, and often attributed to Frederick Law Olmsted Sr., is Jenney's major achievement in landscape architectural design (fig. 4.1).[1]

Jenney's legacy of park design is clearly visible to the air traveler on the final approach to Chicago's Midway or O'Hare airport. About four miles west of the Loop's orchard of skyscrapers, three polygons of lush greenery emerge from the dull gray urban grid. These three fragments of forest and lawn pivoting around their central lakes are joined by faint green threads, the remnants of once-majestic boulevards. The West Parks, a small but distinguished component of Jenney's work, exemplify one of the finest traditions of nineteenth-century American urbanism, the creation of parks and boulevards as an armature of order and respite from the burgeoning industrial city.

Jenney's were quintessentially nineteenth-century American parks. Combining lofty visions of social reform with the sobering realities of real estate economics, they were landscapes constructed from scratch to enhance the physical and psychic health of all classes of citizens in America's most rapidly expanding city. At the same time, they served as a pragmatic real estate venture to promote the development of the West Side and to nourish Chicago's overall tax base.

Jenney's original plans for the West Parks also manifest a sophisticated grasp of spatial organization, site engineering, use of water, planting design, circulation systems, and treatment of architectural elements. Only partially realized, they reveal that Jenney was one of the more gifted American park designers of the nineteenth century, worthy of inclusion in the ranks of Frederick Law Olmsted Sr., Calvert Vaux, Horace Cleveland, William Hammond Hall, and Jacob Weidenmann. The West Parks system represented an intelligent synthesis of the leading American park design ideas with those advanced by France's Adolphe Alphand and Britain's William Robinson. These concepts were skillfully adapted to Chicago's challenging prairie landscape—a terrain Jenney viewed as a flat, treeless, poorly drained tabula rasa that offered the designer few clues.

William Le Baron Jenney (1802–1907) was born in Fairhaven, Massachusetts, into a prosperous merchant's family. As a young man he foundered in his early attempts to find a career until he settled on engineering. Disappointed with Harvard's fledgling program, Jenney went to Paris in 1853 to study architecture at the École Centrale des Arts et Manufactures for three years under Louis-Charles Mary. Mary's commonsense rationalism stressed the subordination of ornament to structure, the primacy of "fitness," and the functional articulation of building plans and facades generated by the *papier quadrille*, or grid paper, method of J. N. L. Durand, Mary's former teacher. Jenney's curriculum also included site engineering courses in grading and drainage. While a student, he was able to observe firsthand much of the construction of Alphand's Paris park system, the most brilliant open space concept of its day.

During the Civil War, Jenney's formal education was honed in the field by designing and building earthwork fortifications and bridges under Generals Grant and later Sherman. Jenney also met Olmsted during the war, and he later applied for a job in the Olmsted and Vaux office when they were beginning the design for Brooklyn's Prospect Park. Instead of joining that firm, however, Jenney moved to Chicago in 1867 and there began his professional career.

Jenney's West Parks system belonged to the same nineteenth-century urban middle-class reform movement that had so fervently supported the construction of the great parks in many eastern cities. The reformers—cosmopolitan in outlook, with strong ties to England and France, intensely preoccupied with national identity and cultural self-definition, increasingly self-assured and assertive, and possessed of an abiding faith in the capacity of the built environment to shape human character for good or ill—envisioned an American urbanism that would address the daunting problems of the rapidly emerging industrial city. Many of them, like Jenney, Olmsted, and Cleveland, had roots in New England Protestant culture. They were intent on dealing decisively with a new kind of American city profoundly shaped by the railroad. It was a city that separated work and residence, created special nodes of commerce and industry, and built enormous "process spaces" such as the Chicago stockyards at the end of trunk lines;[2] a city with a web of arteries that converged on a central commercial and cultural district growing at an unprecedented rate; a city with vast and diverse immigrant populations, polarities of wealth and poverty, and acute problems in public health.

The construction of parks and park systems was seen as one way to address some of the problems of the protean industrial city, and Chicago's reformers demanded parks for the same reasons their counterparts did in New York, Brooklyn, Boston, Richmond, and San Francisco. They believed that parks promoted public health by facilitating beneficial exercise in air purified by leaves that filtered out pollutants. Parks relieved urban stress by providing an experience of landscape that soothed the nerves, supplying a

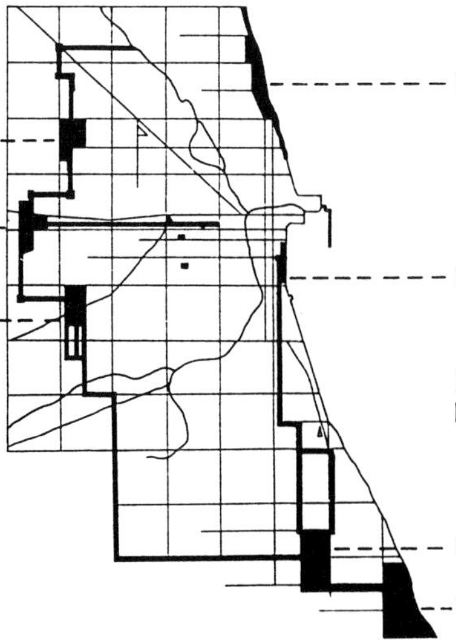

4.2 Plan for the Chicago park system. Redrawn by author and John Meder from West Chicago Park reports, 1879–80, in the libraries of the Chicago Historical Society and the Chicago Parks Department.

counterpoint to hard urban materials, noise, and restricted views. In addition, parks helped to defuse social tension by bringing together individuals of different economic status and ethnic origin in a shared context of lighthearted recreation or more serious civic ritual such as military parades or patriotic holidays. Parks also augmented city revenues (not to mention the individual fortunes of real estate developers), by attracting prime development to their perimeters. Finally, parks could house museums and other didactic exhibits that would further the education of the city's citizens, especially its schoolchildren. Olmsted and Vaux's masterwork, Central Park in New York, and their evolving concept of park systems had established a strong parks tradition as city after city sought to emulate and surpass the achievements of New York. Alphand's brilliant work in Paris of the 1850s, to which Olmsted and Vaux owed a deep debt, established a powerful international precedent.[3]

In 1858, when New York's Central Park was just beginning to take shape and Alphand's work was well under way, Dr. John Rauch and other reformers advocated parks for Chicago to purify the air from miasmas in the rapidly growing population (which surged from 100,000 in 1830 to 300,000 in 1867). The Common Council, the elected body of aldermen of Chicago, submitted a bill to the state legislature in 1868, which passed in 1869, to create an elaborate integrated system of parks and boulevards establishing a greenbelt around the city that would provide a coherent structure to Chicago's potentially chaotic expansion (fig. 4.2). To facilitate construction and administration of this extensive system, the city defined three separate divisions to be headed by teams of appointed commissioners: the North, South, and West park districts. The commissioners sought the top design talent of the day, hiring Olmsted and Vaux for the South Park system and Jenney for the West Parks.[4]

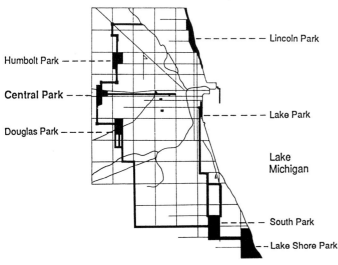

The seven West Park District commissioners took an active role in the design process and schooled themselves in the best precedents of the day. They took pains to observe firsthand the work in progress at the new suburban development at Riverside, designed by Olmsted and Vaux, and appropriated funds to travel to

4.3 Plan of Douglas Park, 1871. Courtesy of the Chicago Park District Special Collections.

4.4 Plan of Humboldt Park, 1871. Courtesy of the Chicago Park District Special Collections.

distant cities to study various efforts—New York's Central Park likely headed the list. No detailed records of Jenney's discussions with the commissioners are available, but one recorded episode suggests that they did not hesitate to critique his designs and, in at least one case, change them.[5]

As Jenney envisioned them, the three West Parks would create a "chain of verdure" and connect the adjacent South and North park systems.[6] The complex would be oriented around three major open spaces of nearly equal size: Douglas Park at the south end, Humboldt Park at the north, and Central Park between them (figs. 4.3–4.5). (Central Park was renamed Garfield Park in 1887 to honor the assassinated president.) An eight-mile network of boulevards would connect the three, establishing an extensive drive on the perimeter of the then-undeveloped western portion of the city. The boulevards would be extensions of the parks and laid out to conform to the city's expanding grid structure. These elegant thoroughfares typically comprised a commercial highway in the center flanked by pleasure drives, bridle paths, and walks, which were separated from each other by allées of trees or strips of lawn. Where a boulevard changed direction at a right angle on the grid, Jenney proposed a small square to serve the surrounding neighborhood. Intersections would sometimes be marked by fountains, groves, arbors, or elaborate floral displays. In the northern portion of the complex, the formal allées would often be replaced by irregular masses of trees grouped into undulating lines to give a more "picturesque" effect (fig. 4.6).

Jenney faced multiple challenges in designing the West Parks, including the necessity to provide facilities for such disparate activities as competitive sports, civic rituals, concerts, therapeutic contemplation of landscape scenery, children's play, family picnics, and education in natural history. In response, he designed a clearly defined ensemble of linked spaces that separated potentially conflicting uses. Each of the three parks would have an individual character, yet a similar treatment of water, structures, and planting throughout would unify then into a "harmonious, consistent, and complete" ensemble. His sophisticated planting plans structured those spaces and transfigured the "wild," treeless prairie into a verdant counterpoint of exotic semitropical plants and hardy native vegetation—a variant to the stock-in-trade "pastoral-picturesque" planting schemes of many large nineteenth-century American urban parks. His work reveals some of the richness and variety of this era's park design, which derives some of its principles from those expressed by Olmsted and Vaux's 1858 plan for New York's Central Park.

In fact, Jenney contacted Olmsted for advice and received a "long and highly instructive letter," which has, unfortunately, been lost. However, if we look at Olmsted's surviving letters to Jenney's colleagues, such as William Hammond Hall and Horace

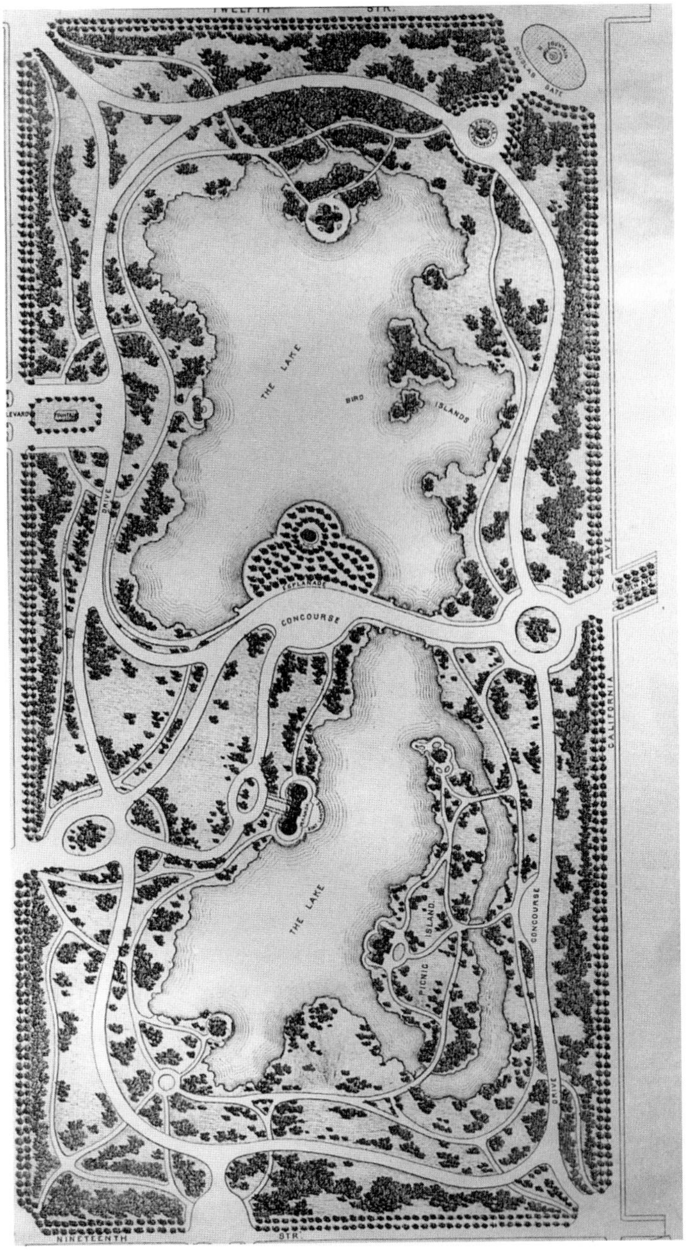
TWELFTH STR.
THE LAKE
BIRD ISLANDS
CONCOURSE
THE LAKE
PICNIC ISLAND
CALIFORNIA AVE
NINETEENTH STR.

4·3

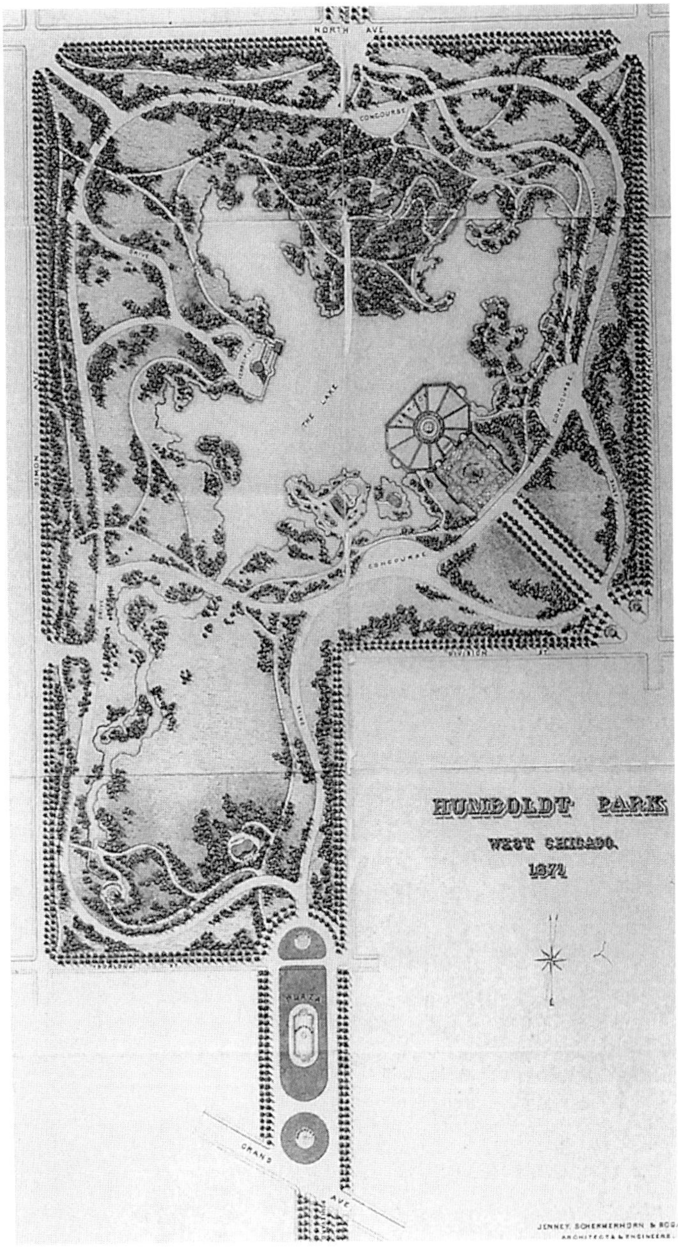
NORTH AVE
CONCOURSE
THE LAKE
HUMBOLDT PARK
WEST CHICAGO.
1874
GRAND AVE
JENNEY, SCHERMERHORN & BOGA
ARCHITECTS & ENGINEERS

4·4

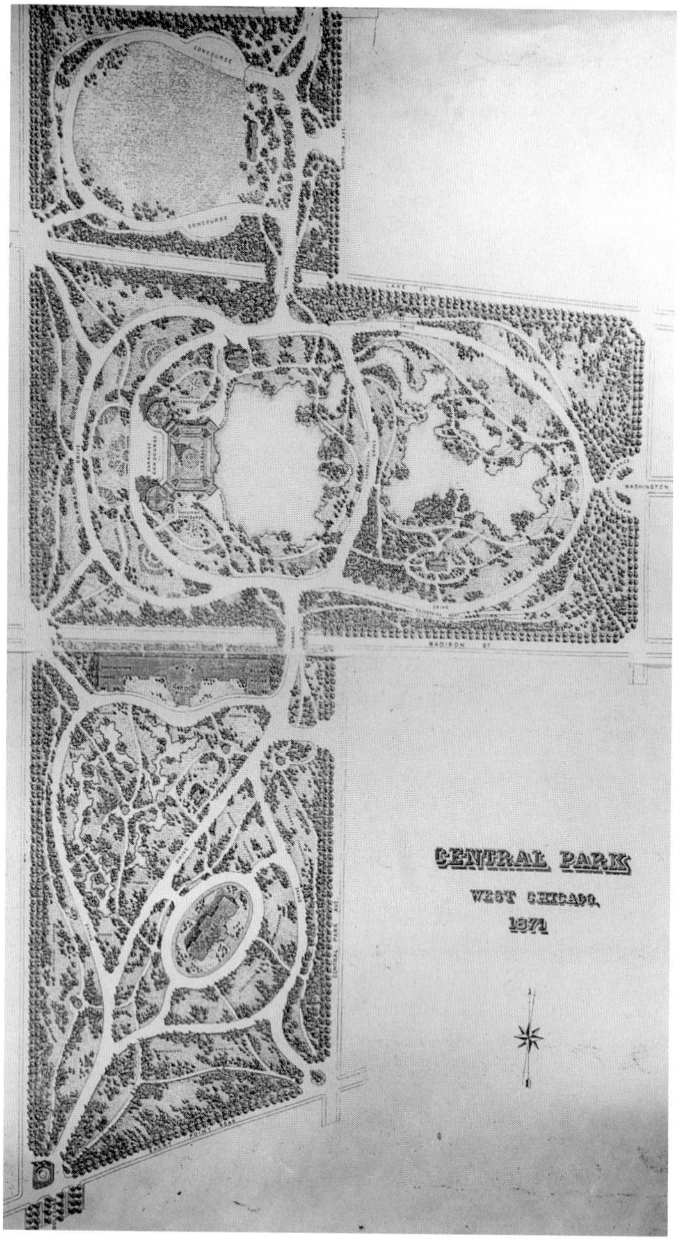

4.5

4.5 Plan of Central Park, 1871. Courtesy of the Chicago Park District Special Collections.

4.6

4.6 View of Grand Boulevard showing allées and median strips. Reprinted from *Picturesque Chicago*, 3d ed. (Chicago, 1882).

Cleveland, and other documents, we can surmise that he would have told Jenney to read Alphand's great work on the Paris park system, *Les Promenades de Paris* (1867–73), and Robinson's critique of those parks in *The Parks and Gardens of Paris* (1869).[7] Olmsted would also likely have advised Jenney first to solve the acute drainage problem of the flat site and then design the park around this structural solution. The West Parks were much smaller than Olmsted and Vaux's urban parks—Douglas and Central, at 171 acres each, and Humboldt, though somewhat larger at 193 acres, were small compared with the 844 acres of New York's Central Park or the 1,055 acres of Chicago's own South Park (later renamed Jackson Park)—and had a rich and complex program envisioned for them. Thus they required the development of an intermediate-scale design, one that was functionally and typologically somewhere between a small neighborhood park of 5 to 10 acres and a large urban park of 800 to 1,000 acres. As opposed to the sweeping lawns and pastoral scenery of large parks, smaller sites called for what Olmsted and Vaux characterized as a "plaisance" treatment. Such scenery is managed in a "more garden like way." It consists of "lawn, shrubbery underwood and brooding trees" but is treated in an architectonic fashion, like the "kept grounds" or "pleasure-grounds" immediately adjacent to an English country house, where one finds strong symmetry in planting beds and path systems. In contrast to large parks where they can be hidden by the landscape scenery, buildings are featured as focal points and used to enhance vistas. In addition, Olmsted likely reminded Jenney that the parks had to accommodate both "exertive" recreation, involving conscious mental or physical activity (baseball, military parades, chess, and so forth) and "receptive" recreation, which soothes without conscious exertion (picnicking, concerts, solitary walks). Where space had to be provided for potentially conflicting activities side by side, separate precincts should be created, marked by different landscape treatments. Finally, Olmsted would have suggested adding interest to the flat terrain by doubling it in the reflection of large bodies of water.[8]

Jenney set to work with a firm commitment to Olmsted and Vaux's concept of an urban park and the specific kinds of recreation it should provide. He expressed his vision in the commission's annual report:

A park is designed for pleasure and healthful recreation. Within its limits, the man of business can forget the anxieties of the counting house, and rest an overworked brain. The laborer and artisan can forget his toil. The family picnic party can enjoy all the necessary privacy in the grounds allotted to that purpose; can spread their cloth and empty their baskets under the trees amid pleasing surrounding of broad lawns, shady nooks, and glimpses of lakes; with a playhouse nearby for children affording shelter for all in case of a sudden storm.

4.7 Central Park topography. Drawn by the author and John Meder from information at the Chicago Historical Society.

4.8 Central Park cut and fill. Drawn by the author and John Meder based on the annual report of the West Chicago Park Commission, 1879, 1880. Chicago Historical Society.

The invalid and convalescent may seek repose and healthful air under the vine covered arbors; or enjoy the quiet to be found in its groves.

The traffic-road, with its hay-wagons, small carts, lumbering teams, droves of cattle, and the accompanying dust and dirt, is antagonistic to the use and primary object of a park, which is to give relief for a while from all intercourse with the toil and humdrum of life, and afford pleasant and healthful recreation for both mind and body.[9]

Jenney created plans for three individual yet related parks that would offer the visitor a variety of landscape experiences. Douglas Park provides the opportunity to become more absorbed in the lush landscape through a series of lakeside promenades with a changing series of water views. Humboldt is dominated by an elegant esplanade terminating in a terrace thrust forward into the central lake; the architectonic peninsula lends an air of urbanity to the park, which surrounds the terrace almost as an English park frames a stately country house. Central Park is the most diverse in program and facilities, containing athletic fields, a recreational lake, a large conservatory, an arboretum, and zoological gardens.[10]

During the first five years of construction, the West Parks and their boulevards were developed substantially according to Jenney's original 1871 plan; however, budget cuts after the Great Fire, the financial panic of 1873, and mismanagement of funds late in the decade necessitated a scaling back. The principal victims of this fiscal attrition were the elegant buildings and terraces for education and recreation, the memorial to the Great Fire, the elaborate planting plans, and the zoological and botanical gardens. Then, in the early twentieth century, Jens Jensen significantly altered Jenney's vision of the parks. Working primarily in the numerous uncompleted areas of the system, Jensen introduced large numbers of hardy native plants along with abstractions of certain features typical of the regional landscape, such as his "Prairie River" in Humboldt Park. Radically altered concepts of the function of urban parks and inadequate maintenance have more recently obliterated all but faint traces of Jenney's work. As Julia Sniderman Bachrach, Mary O'Shaughnessy, and William Tippens have shown, about all that now remain of Jenney's artistry are the original park boundaries, portions of the original lakes' edges, traces of major road alignments (mostly on the perimeters), and segments of the original grading—rather meager skeletal remnants of the rich and vibrant organism envisioned in 1871 and subsequently approved for construction.

A closer look at the development of Central Park is revealing of Jenney's design process. As is often the case, the landscape architect had no say in the site selection; it was cho-

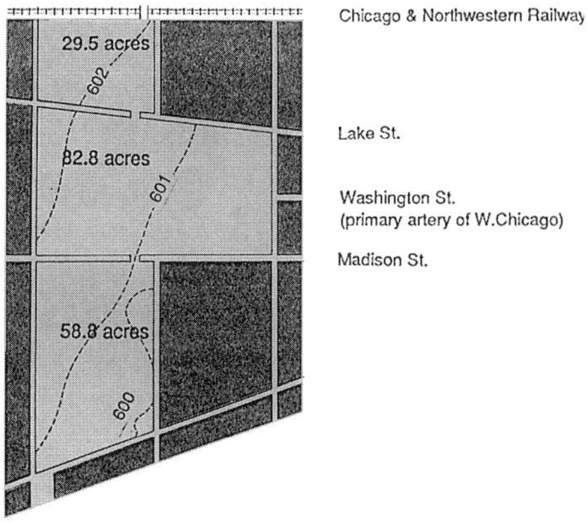

4.7

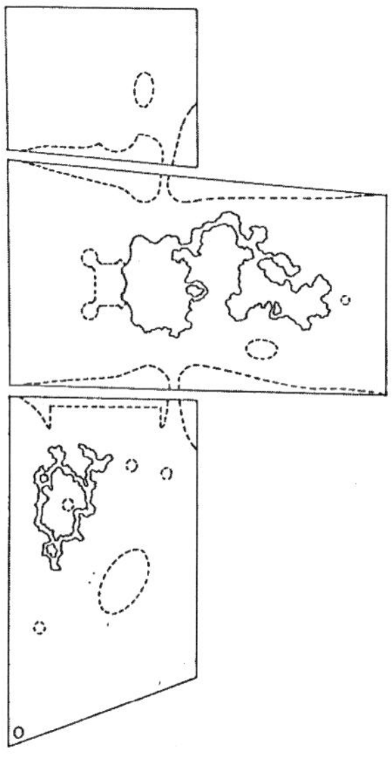
4.8

sen by the commissioners. Although the Central Park site had many strengths, it also posed formidable problems. The 171.1-acre parcel included three rectilinear areas bounded by the north-south grid of the city's street pattern. The northernmost parcel was 29.5 acres, the central, 82.8, and the southern, 58.8. The park was well integrated with the major streets of West Chicago. Washington Street, the major east-west artery, terminated in the center of the eastern boundary of the park's midsection. Jenney took advantage of the connection by proposing first a statue of Washington and then, in 1872, the Fire Memorial on axis with a view toward the park down Washington Street—in the best Hausmannian fashion. Lake and Madison streets—both major east-west thoroughfares—defined the north and south boundaries of the central section and provided ready access by carriage and foot. The proposed boulevards intersecting the northeast and southwest corners of the site connected it to Humboldt and Douglas parks to the north and south, thus completing the central link in the West Parks' "chain of verdure." Access by public transport was also good. The Chicago and Northwestern Railway ran along the northern boundary and provided frequent connections with the city's downtown, some 4.5 miles to the east.

The natural features of the site, however, were far less promising. It was poorly drained and almost flat. The change in elevation from the northwest corner to the southeast corner, a distance of 1,000 yards, was only about 2.5 feet. To make matters worse, the site was nearly devoid of attractive vegetation, suggesting the appearance of a landscape victimized by the scorched-earth policy of some marauding army. Also, the relatively small size of the barren parcel made it exceedingly difficult for Jenney to create the long vistas across lush turf bordered by majestic trees which were the quintessential expression of the therapeutic landscape. These interrelated constraints—the pressing need to solve the drainage problem, the necessity of keeping Lake and Madison, the east-west city streets running through the park, open at all times, and the restrictions of the small size—were decisive factors in Jenney's design (fig. 4.7).

The drainage problem was obviously critical, for unless it was solved the flat site would not support vegetation or permit extensive recreational use. In the tradition of his teacher, L.C. Mary, Jenney opted for the construction of a large 11.1-acre lake fed by artesian wells in the center of the park, to store surface runoff. He also planned a smaller streamlike body of water in the southern section both to deal with drainage and to provide a water supply for the herds of deer and farm animals in the zoological garden. Creation of the lake profoundly affected the park's design, since it occupied the very center of the middle section (fig. 4.8).

The mandate to keep the city streets open was also critical. To keep the park a separate precinct apart from the noise and bustle of the city, Jenney had the major roads heavily bermed with the earth excavated for the lake. Thickly planted, the berms created strong visual barriers that made it impossible to see from one section of the park into another; viaducts bridged the three divisions (fig. 4.9).[11]

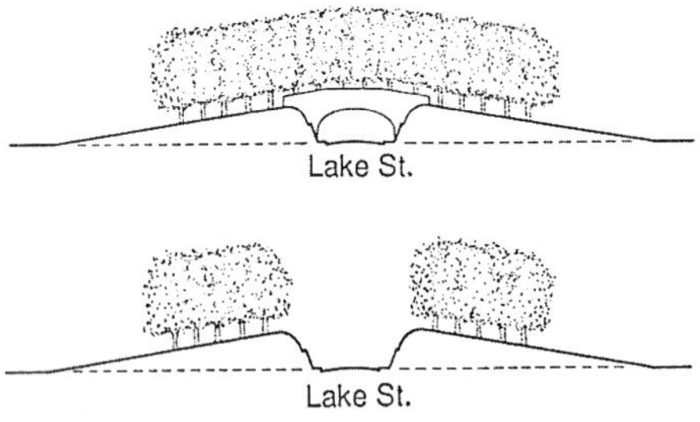

4.9

Having derived the architectural structure of his park from functional necessity, Jenney proceeded to fit the various elements of the program into the three separate sections of his plan. (The plan he generated appears to follow closely the procedure for park design outlined by Alphand in his *Promenades de Paris*.)[12]

It is not known precisely who generated Central Park's program, but it most likely reflected the joint efforts of Jenney and the commissioners, with some input from the public and city officials. (One element, the Fire Memorial, was suggested by the Chicago press.) There were no neighborhood residents to appease, since the whole West Parks system was being constructed on land that was mostly undeveloped. One thing is certain: the park as envisioned in the plan of 1871 was a space for all seasons, permitting a vast range of recreational pursuits—had not budget cuts kept the rich program from complete realization.[13]

Jenney provided clearly defined zones to separate potentially conflicting activities. The necessity of breaking the park into three parts to keep the city streets open was thus turned to the park's advantage. The northern part was used for military parades and active team sports. The western section of the middle part was devoted to concerts, promenades, and other social activities at a music concourse fronting on the lake, while the eastern section was devoted to family picnic areas and special play facilities for children, such as the hoops course, where they could roll iron hoops propelled by a stick around a curving track. It also contained the Fire Memorial. In the southern part were the large conservatory with its winter garden, a natural history museum, and the zoological and botanical gardens (fig. 4.10).[14]

Jenney's highly rational zoning of program requirements is reminiscent of mid-nineteenth-century residential plans which allocate rooms for specific domestic functions (dining room, parlor, library, reception hall, etc.). Indeed, his precise zoning of the park recalls the plan of Jenney's Forsythe residence (ca. 1868; fig. 4.11).[15] The Cartesian rationality of this tripartite scheme may reflect Jenney's training under Mary in Paris, which stressed function, symmetry, and correctness of proportion. The clarity of Central Park's tripartite division and the almost bilateral symmetry of the northern and

4.9 Central Park schematic sections through the principal roadway showing berms and viaduct bridge. Drawn by author and John Meder based on the annual reports of the West Chicago Park Commission, 1879, 1880. Chicago Historical Society.

4.10 Central Park zones of activity. Drawn by the author and John Meder based on the annual report of the West Chicago Park Commission, 1871, 1872. Chicago Historical Society.

4.11 Jenney and Loring's plan for the John Forsythe residence, c. 1868. Redrawn by the author and John Meder from Jenney and Loring, *Principles and Practice of Architecture* [Chicago, 1869], example C, plate Z.

4.12 Examples of *papier quadrille* building plans, based on lectures of Louis Charles Mary, 1852–53. Redrawn by the author and John Meder from Theodore Turak, *William Le Baron Jenney: A Pioneer of Modern Architecture* (Ann Arbor: UMI Research Press, 1986), 51.

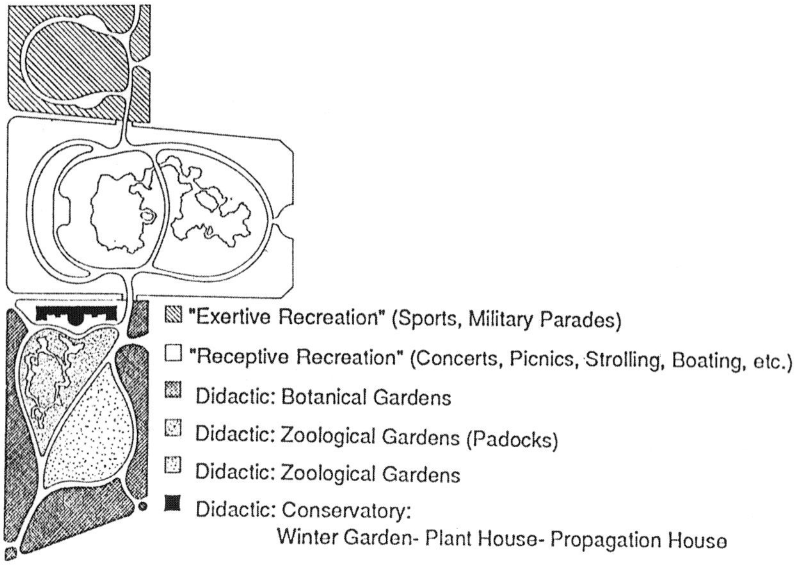

4.10

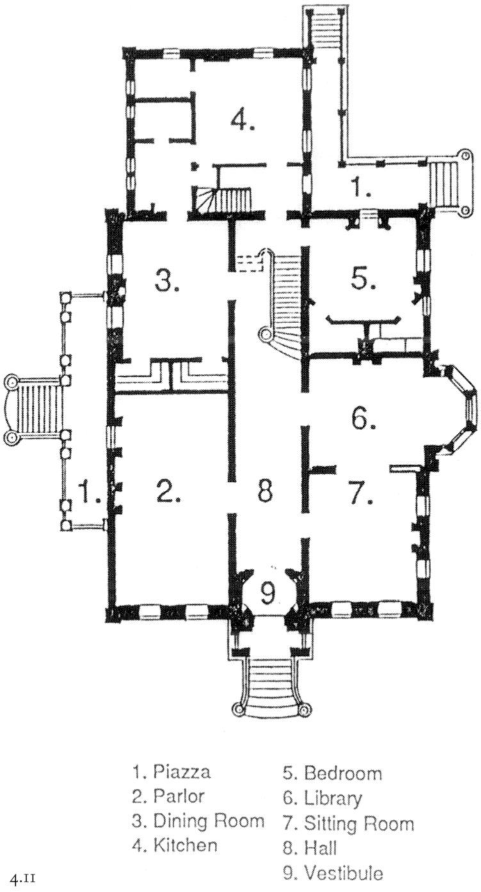

4.11

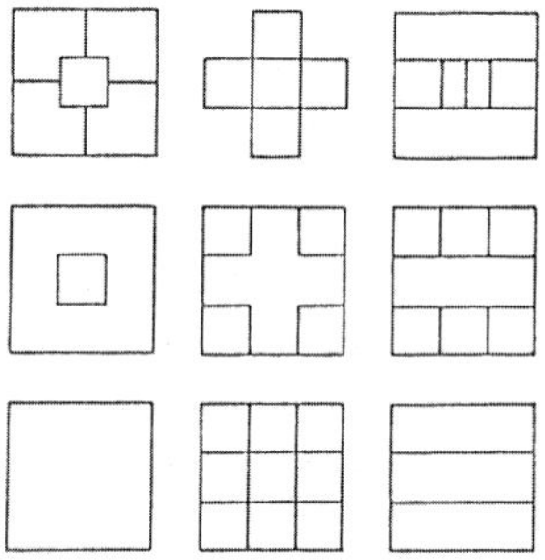

4.12

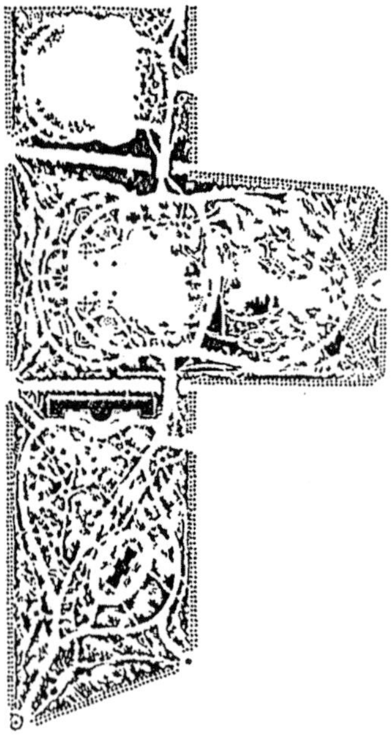

4.13 Central Park figure-ground study. Drawn by the author and John Meder based on the annual reports of the West Chicago Park Commission, 1871, 1872. Chicago Historical Society.

southern parts are quite reminiscent of Mary's methods (fig. 4.12).[16] Indeed, so architectonic is Jenney's park that it appears almost as three adjacent roofless buildings separated by two major streets, with walls of berms and trees rather than masonry. And like the facades of Chicago's streetscapes, each is different in character.

The layout of drives and walks in Central Park is elegant and functional. Like Olmsted and Vaux's design for New York's Central Park, circulation is organized into three separate but interrelated systems of varying widths: fifty-foot carriage drives, fifteen-foot pedestrian paths, and twenty-foot equestrian trails. (However, the flat terrain and limited budget did not allow Jenney to separate these systems by bridges and overpasses.) The three systems are carefully orchestrated to provide the visitor with a wide variety of scenic vistas.[17]

A figure-ground study of the plan (fig. 4.13) reveals the park to be organized into a clear hierarchy of well-defined spaces, appropriately scaled to the activities they were to accommodate. All three sections of the park were surrounded by a wall of trees—some 2.6 miles of American elms that provided shade for promenading. Within this wall, spatial organization varied. The northern section was essentially one large outdoor room of greensward stretching before the concession building, which was centrally sited on its eastern edge like a country house. Nearly bilaterally symmetrical carriage drives and pedestrian walkways encircled the borders of the space. On the eastern perimeter, small bosques (dense groupings of trees) formed a series of small outdoor rooms. The central section was ordered by a central east-west axis defined by the bandstand, a small island near the eastern shore of the upper lake, and the Fire Memorial column. The ground plane was dominated by the 11.1-acre lake. Numerous bosques in the lawn formed a complex network of linked spaces. A large grove of trees just south of the transverse carriage drive, in the vicinity of the children's hoops course, provided a heavily canopied room for shaded picnics. On the northern side of the eastern (or lower) lake, a 1,000-foot corridor of space wove its way in an easterly direction before swinging abruptly toward the northeast corner of the park. Its sinuously curving edge obscured its true dimensions and gave the illusion of a much larger space. The layered spaces created by the bosques broke up the views across the lawn and absorbed large crowds, providing an impression that the park was uncongested.

The southernmost section of the park featured many closely spaced bosques that broke up the space into a plethora of small linked rooms. Into these were tucked the botanical garden, the conservatory, the museum, and various animal paddocks. The diagonal central carriage drive sliced the space into two almost equal portions. One half contained the museum; the other, the animal paddocks and conservatory. The botanical garden wrapped around the southern and western portions of the site and tied the two halves together.[18]

The tripartite circulation network and lucid, straightforward spatial definition were the park's strongest assets. Without this carefully integrated system, the conflicting needs of boisterous crowds of baseball spectators, quiet strollers, and picnickers could never have been accommodated at the same time (fig. 4.14).

Jenney's plantings transformed the site into a lush landscape contrasting with both the spacious "wild" prairie surrounding it and the limited vistas and hard surfaces of the city itself. The use of exotic, large-leafed subtropical understory vegetation, such as *Musa, Artemisia,* and *Dracaena,* was reminiscent of the great urban parks of London or Paris. In contrast to the Prairie school landscape architects who followed, Jenney wanted to transform the native landscape into a lush pleasure-ground.[19]

It is unlikely that Jenney was just trying to be au courant with the latest landscape fashions of Britain and Europe. Rather, he probably agreed with Olmsted's notion that "tropical effects" in planting provided one of the most powerful contrasts to the city environment, while awakening in the beholder "a profound sense of the creator's bountifulness."[20] However, Jenney and Olmsted differed on how to achieve these tropical effects. Olmsted preferred to use hardy native and exotic plants, which would not require costly maintenance and wintering indoors, planted close together to mimic the lushness of tropical scenery or pruned to resemble the habit of tropical plants. Jenney's preference was for real subtropical species, which would have to have been wintered in his proposed conservatory and then bedded out in the spring.

Jenney used plants in three basic ways: they structured spaces of the park; they created prospects and vignettes of varying character; and they provided instruction in the beauty and order of nature, especially in the botanic garden. His diverse plant palette emphasized seasonal color and variety of form (fig. 4.15).

Sustaining order in a planting plan of great variety is always a challenge. Jenney solved the problem by using one dominant vocabulary and playing the others off against it. About 59 percent of the park is lawn and bosque; the rest is forest (8 percent), botanical garden (10 percent), perimeter allées (7 percent), lawn (5 percent), and ornamental planting beds (5 percent), with the remaining 6 percent a lake. The predominance of lawn and bosque in its smaller-scale "plaisance" treatment suggests an Olmstedian em-

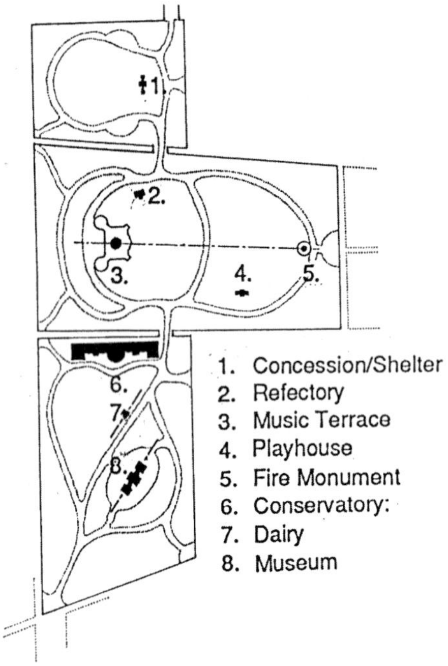

4.14

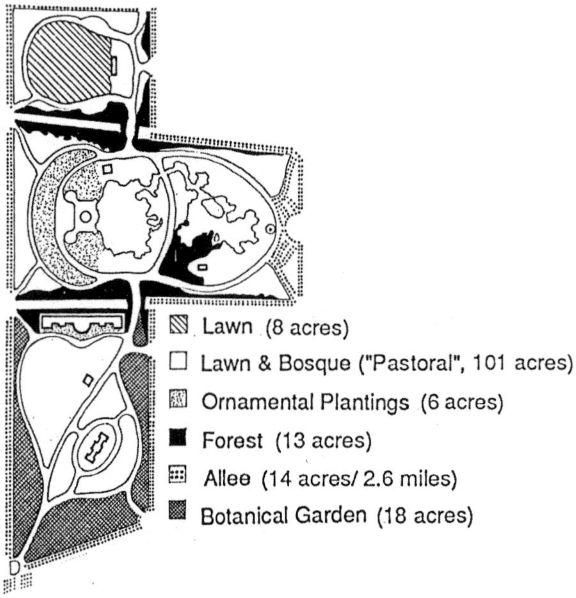

4.15

4.16

4.14 Location of principal buildings in Central Park. Drawn by the author and John Meder based on the annual reports of the West Chicago Park Commission, 1871, 1872. Chicago Historical Society.

4.15 Central Park planting plan diagram. Drawn by the author and John Meder based on the annual reports of the West Chicago Park Commission, 1871, 1872. Chicago Historical Society.

4.16 View of the lake in the middle section of Central Park, with the proposed Fire Memorial in the background. Reprinted from *Picturesque Chicago*, 3d ed. (Chicago, 1882).

phasis on the special therapeutic properties of this type of scenery above all others. Forest was used to buffer the edges of the park along Lake and Madison streets and to create the picnic grove in the center section.[21]

Jenney's buildings were prominent in the park's vistas and carefully integrated with the character of the landscape. The upper park's concession building and the music terrace of the middle section established the central axes for their respective spaces. The planned "imposing" Byzantine music pavilion, gilded and ornate, was to be set atop a massive cut stone parapet and complemented by colorful, fan-shaped flower beds set in emerald green turf flanked by clusters of trees. In contrast, the "rustic" shelters, bridges, and children's playground buildings of the east and central sections were "simple and rural" as befits the "pastoral character" of their settings.[22]

In Jenney's envisioned park, on a summer afternoon Chicagoans could watch a baseball game between neighborhood teams, observe a parade of the city militia, listen to an edifying oration from the bandstand on the music terrace, or dine with friends in the lakeside refectory. They could also contemplate the courage and resiliency of their fellow citizens celebrated by the Fire Memorial, row on the lake, or picnic under the trees with their family. Children of the city could race around the special hoops course or contemplate the wonders of nature in the natural history museum, botanical garden, and 725-foot-long conservatory. Farmers could inspect the herds of fine breeding stock on display in the zoological garden or observe the prancing deer. The harried counting-house clerks could take a refreshing solitary walk through tree-lined lawns, while the scions of industry could detour on their way home for a soothing horseback ride through the verdant landscape. In the dead of winter, the inhabitants of the city's congested districts could ride out on the railroad to stroll in the lush oasis of tropical plants housed in the conservatory, or in summer enjoy the cool shade of the groves while the surrounding prairies were scorched brown by the unrelenting summer sun. Free city concerts of carefully selected, soothing music would draw large crowds, who afterward could linger and promenade the park's tree-lined perimeters or ride in their carriages to other parks in the system (fig. 4.16).

Nineteenth-century Chicago is an example of a typical American "open city" produced by industrialization in a democratic society. Such a city is pluralistic, "a forum for the freedom of choice." Its primary structuring element is an ever-expanding grid of streets without definite ends or limits, a fitting expression of dynamic opportunity and change. Such a city has no well-defined center but is structured instead around a series of nodes of activity, allowing for a wide range of choices. Its eclectic architecture is yet another expression of an emphasis on freedom of choice within a pluralistic milieu.[23]

Jenney's West Parks clearly manifest many of the characteristics of the "open city." Visitors are allowed movement within, or they can venture onto an eight-mile network of parks and boulevards, affording ever-changing panoramas and choice of routes. Their buildings are eclectic, drawing from the glories of Byzantium (a lighthearted note of fantasy and exoticism) and rustic, rural buildings of a decidedly Alpine flavor, perhaps like those in the Bois de Boulogne. There exists a clear reciprocity between the city and these parks. Their spatial organization and circulation system reflect elements of the urban armature that encloses them.

Efficient differentiation of space allows highly contrasting activities to occur simultaneously with the same smoothness and efficiency as that of the new industrial plants or "process spaces" that were beginning to cluster along the city's rail lines—whether to move cattle through stockyards or to sort out mail orders at Montgomery Ward. In attempting to bring together citizens of all ethnic and economic groups and provide them with a wide range of recreational and educational pursuits structured around a rational system of circulation, the West Parks both mirrored and engendered the democratic values of the open city.

Before he was hired by the West Chicago Park Commission, the young Jenney, seeking employment with Olmsted, wrote in 1865, "There is no situation that I can imagine where I should derive more pleasure from the work I might be called upon to perform as one in which Architecture, Gardening and Engineering were associated, and I most earnestly desire and hope that some such position be within my reach."[24] In his masterful vision for the West Parks system, that hope came to fruition. Despite later compromises and cutbacks during construction, the citizens of Chicago were the great beneficiaries of that vision.

5 Does Frank Lloyd Wright Belong in Chicago's Architectural History?

Sidney K. Robinson

Of course Frank Lloyd Wright worked in Chicago, got his first architectural job in Chicago (1887), and found a mentor in Chicago (Louis Sullivan, 1888). But he kept leaving it: first to Oak Park (1893), then to Europe (1909), then back to ancestral (one Welsh immigrant generation!) land in Wisconsin (1911). He learned something in Chicago, but it was not the lesson the city's architectural history came to think it was teaching. Instead, Frank Lloyd Wright used it to launch very anti-Chicago ideals.

What was Chicago's lesson for a young, aspiring architect in 1887? Historians, including Donald Miller in *The City of the Century*, have identified two salient frameworks for Chicago's growth in the latter half of the nineteenth century: the grid of the streets and the balloon frame.[1] For architectural historians, a comparable structural grid is the steel frame that raised the Loop's speculative office buildings to heights and an urban density heretofore unknown.

The "speculative grid," as Miller calls it, facilitated the division of land for quick sale and profit. "In Chicago, the use of the grid represented the transformation of land into a mere commodity—real estate—without sacred or civic significance."[2] Wright's rejection of such repetitive patterns can be seen in his layout for a housing development for C. E. Roberts in 1900. He broke the regularly spaced streets with clusters of four single-family houses in his Quadruple Block Plan. At one scale, this departed from the repetitive grid through its figural grouping; if one steps back to take in a large tract of this pattern, one discovers a secondary grid whose intersections are marked by the housing clusters. Whether the division of the land by Jefferson's Northwest Territories Ordinance produced the Prairie house plan or Wright's geometric alternatives reinterpreted it is an open question.

This early example of a "grid on a grid" is surely a form of what Richard MacCormac called the "tartan grid" in his 1968 essay, "Anatomy of Wright's Aesthetic."[3] Taking up the Froebel Block gifts given to Wright when he was a child (but not a kindergartner!), MacCormac shows how the blocks themselves produced a "unit system," to use Wright's later description. Major and minor axes, primary and secondary sequences seem to grow naturally from the blocks' patterns. H. Allen Brooks emphasizes their significance in his introduction to MacCormac's essay: "The tartan effect results from the fact that certain lines in the grid, due to Wright' alignment of major and minor elements in the design, receive more emphasis than others."[4] While such emphasis on the figural group instead of the repetitive series does not completely obscure the grid, it avoids distributing elements evenly by establishing locations of greater significance.

Wright's subsequent use of various geometric "grids" is significantly different from the structural discipline of the Chicago grid: street or steel. His initial "unit system" was orthogonal, following on a long tradition of laying out buildings using the discipline of a regular module to draw plans. Just one example is Thomas Jefferson's use of gridded paper to lay out structures. It is a technique long used to transfer figural drawings as well. Wright's subsequent search for greater continuity and greater freedom led him to begin his exploration of triangular (hexagonal) and circular units in the 1920s and 1930s. Every step in the exploration of these modules retained the distinction of major and minor in the way that spaces were shaped and walls were located. For Wright continuity never meant equality, and democracy never compromised the freedom to be uncommon. The herd mentality, characterized by city dwellers, according to Wright, finds refuge in equal, indistinguishable increments.

Colin Rowe's important 1956 essay, "The Chicago Frame," points out how the Chicago use of the steel frame differed from both European and Frank Lloyd Wright's "use," or more accurately, rejection.[5] In this insightful investigation, Rowe's primary concern is to show how Americans and Europeans interpreted the structural frame or cage differently. I am indebted to this essay but wish to put a different emphasis on some of its observations by turning aside from the European comparisons made by Rowe. Even when characterizing Wright's difference from the Chicago frame with terms like "dynamic" rather than "static," his discussion of plan development, and the independence of structure and space-forming elements in Le Corbusier and Ludwig Mies van der Rohe, Rowe does not pursue how Wright sought to fuse structure and space. Nor does he explore Wright's structural exploration that interpreted structure as plane rather than line or frame. And this difference is what sets Wright apart from everything that turn-of-the-twentieth-century Chicago architecture was about.

It certainly is possible that one of the reasons Wright felt some sympathy with Mies van der Rohe (before Mies's arrival in Chicago and his embrace of the steel frame) stems from his realization that Mies had achieved something similar in the German Pavilion at Barcelona in 1929. The Barcelona Pavilion can be seen as a universal grid set up by the travertine paving that provides for the placement of a group of figural objects: columns, planes of glass, and marble, whose centerlines or axes are aligned with the floor joints. The location of these elements is strikingly not determined by the grid; they seem to be displaced or to fall short of it. But when one imagines the walls as figures with axes, one discovers that their centerlines are on the grid. The uninflected lines are transformed into axes as they approach the figural objects and then, having passed through them, return to their universal, abstract character.

Surely the most compelling development in Chicago architecture in the decade of the '90s, when Wright left Adler & Sullivan, was the tall office building framed in steel. As an aspiring young architect, Wright could have made a fine career, rising within the prominent offices of Chicago, taking Daniel Burnham up on his offer to send him to Paris, and designing "important" communal and commercial structures using steel. But Wright rejected this way of thinking about structure, spatial arrangement, and social organization. He used it, for lack of any alternative, in the Larkin Building and the Abraham Lincoln Center in Chicago for his uncle, Jenkin Lloyd Jones, but when he found that reinforced concrete could achieve his structural/spatial goals of continuity, the steel frame disappeared.

When Wright went to work for Louis Sullivan, he attached himself to a prominent practitioner of the commercial world, but he also drew close to someone whose thoughts and words ranged far beyond business calculation. Louis Sullivan's buildings were part of commerce, part of the development of the Chicago frame in the 1890s, of course, but his writings expressed a nature-based ideal coming out of Whitman and Emerson. His acquiescence to the frame, which he decorated brilliantly, made him part of commercial Chicago, even as his American romanticism seemed to be directed somewhere else. It could be argued that only the later small banks in midwestern farm towns merged rhetoric and architecture. These banks were not frames either in structure or image. Their singular volumes were the closest Sullivan came to building his ornament; the element of his architecture that Wright specifically admired and interpreted as a basis of "organic architecture."

One could even utter the heresy that the Columbian Exposition buildings of 1893, much maligned by Sullivan, were very like the steel-framed office buildings downtown. Both sets of structures demonstrated how to make buildings using detachable cladding and framed structure. The only difference was in the patterns on the surfaces.

Did Wright reject the frame because he did not like its formal consequences or because he did not like what happened to people when "framed?" This question can be answered one way by those who believe him to have been primarily in search of form, and in another way by those who think he was a significant commentator on social and economic matters. The real possibility that he saw them as connected is surely one of the reasons why Wright is so interesting. Wright's foray into planning through the Broadacre City projects, begun in 1932, has been cited as evidence of his social concerns. (But surely, this is just another architect taking on the design of the whole world, if anyone would give him the commission!) However, the pattern recognition an architect develops can extend to the relationships of social "parts and wholes" and to the correlative patterns

5.1 Frank Lloyd Wright, Broadacre City (1935). Reproduced courtesy The Frank Lloyd Wright Archives, Scottsdale, AZ.

that buildings and their groupings can take. It seems reasonable that this architect, someone whose greatest satisfaction came in making formal patterns as and for buildings, would use his chosen milieu to illustrate social ideals. The preference for form came first.

Wright's attachment to "democracy" and its emphasis on the individual could be one explanation for his embrace of residential construction rather than conventional communal building types requiring steel structure. (Of course the scale of commissions open to a young architect is another.) While the structural steel frame, so prominent in advanced architectural activity while Wright was in Chicago, can be seen as a smaller version of the repetitive pattern of the street grid, it is significantly different from the way wood is distributed in the balloon frame used in houses. The very term "frame," when applied to the wooden structure of closely spaced, thin, dimensional lumber, is misleading. The whole point of the balloon frame is that it does not require the larger, heavier members of a real frame. And its ubiquitous nails replace the elaborate jointing of heavy timber frames. The traditional wooden frame construction, harkening back to the Middle Ages, consisted of heavy timbers with surfaces of infill. The lighter balloon "frame" cut up those heavy members and distributed them evenly over a wall plane (or floor or roof) so that structure and surface began to merge. The wooden members no longer mark out a frame, but take on the new role of contributing to a structural element that has become a sheathed and plastered plane. This structural interpretation becomes central for Wright.

The balloon frame was not the subject of professional attention in the Loop. It did not feature in large commercial development; it did not solve the steel manufacturers' need for new markets when railroads slowed their demand for steel. It was nearly invisible, as vernacular activity usually is, to higher, more self-conscious urban concentrations of power and money. The balloon frame was much more adaptable to the creation of an architectural artifact that merged parts rather than separated them for easy calculation. The large surfaces produced by the interaction of studs, sheathing, and diagonal plaster lath achieve a continuity of parts.

Wright uses steel, of course, in places like the Robie House in Hyde Park, but there it produces a significant spatial emphasis, passing, as it does, along the change in ceiling height and extending the cantilevered surfaces marking the terminals of terrace and court. When he uses steel, not for structural emphasis but as a system, as in the All Steel housing project of 1938, the closely spaced members formed from sheet metal approximate a wooden balloon frame model. This unusual foray into steel construction makes clear how Wright turned the material associated with the frame into a series of structural elements that merge into whole walls acting like structural planes, just as he had interpreted the balloon frame to produce the same structural/spatial continuity.

Wright's preferred clientele in the Oak Park years were businessmen who valued integrity; a particular kind of businessman who made things. As Leonard Eaton's groundbreaking book, *Two Chicago Architects,* reveals, Wright's clients believed in the integrity of the made thing.[6] They were not bureaucrats or "moneymen." They would not submit to residing in a cage.

The houses Wright built for this clientele appropriated formality with major and minor axes and clear base/shaft/capital elevations. The "classicism" of the Prairie house has even been associated with Wright's dreaded Palladio by both being subjects of computer programs that enable drawing one's own Palladian villas or Prairie houses. They can both be developed from a clear hierarchy of formal principles. Such a system or pattern is the antithesis of the repetitiveness of, say, Paxton's 1851 Crystal Palace in London. Wright's Prairie houses rely rather on a traditional hierarchy whose absence was specifically attacked by opponents of the Crystal Palace. This tradition was based on the fact that some things were more important than others, whether in location, volume, ornament, or structure. The Prairie house's culmination in massing and plan of its substantial chimney, focused by the intersection of major axes that are clearly indicated in various presentation plans, provide unmistakable evidence of how much Wright had absorbed beaux-arts conventions. Working with Louis Sullivan would not have impressed these conventions on Wright through the plans of the commercial buildings, but they are clearly evident in Sullivan's ornament, the most important lesson Wright learned from his "lieber Meister."

When Wright retreated to the hills of southwestern Wisconsin and built his Taliesin home and studio (1911, '14, '25, '39), he continued the exploration of structure as surface in plaster-sheathed "balloon frame," which he extended in later projects using reinforced concrete. When Wright drew the connection between Taliesin and Fallingwater (1936), it is clearly because they share the common element of structural planes. Taliesin shows increasing evidence that the planes, both solid plaster and with window openings, were acting as large "beams," or "trusses," transferring loads, cantilevering, acting in tension as well as compression so that volume, spatial formation, and structure were being accomplished with the same architectural element. No other demonstration so forcefully represents what that elusive word "organic" can mean. Taliesin in 1911 was much more conventional in its structural materials, but in the 1930s Wright, with the counsel of structural engineers Mendel Glickman, who worked on Fallingwater, and his new apprentice William Wesley Peters, began to experiment with structure seen as surfaces defining space in ways he had only hinted at earlier. The Usonian houses, developed in this period, are probably the most advanced expression of planar structure with their folded, plywood walls and continuous roof "slab" of three layers of two-by-fours.

An important early expression of Wright working out the distinction he was drawing from the lessons of Chicago was his 1901 Hull House talk, "The Art and Craft of the Machine."[7] Rather than accentuating the contrast between the arts and crafts and the industrial basis for Chicago's new architecture, he tried to draw them together in a new way. In this presentation, Wright sets up the distinction between the old and the new art identifying the structural, jointed practice of the old and the plastic continuity of the new. He tries to position the steel frame as the natural product of the machine, which provided the support for the "plastic" cladding he clearly saw as his mentor Sullivan's major contribution. When Wright identifies the frame with both the old art and with the machine, he introduces a new, alternative category of plasticity, which he recognizes but cannot yet clearly define. In fact, the machine has relevance to plasticity, too, not just as a more efficient way to reproduce the old art of joinery. This early formulation is not fully worked out by the thirty-four-year-old Wright as he tries to build on what he has seen in Chicago, even as he is laying the basis for its rejection. What is more obviously a structure assembled of joined parts than a steel frame? Its independence from what is hung on its exterior could not be clearer. It is this disintegration that Wright would work to overcome or supplant by a new way of thinking about a continuity of structure and spatial/volumetric arrangement that he came to identify as "organic."

Wright never saw commercial activity with its abstract measurement based on money as anything he wanted to have as an origin for architecture. When he focused on the office building, he tried to change commerce into an expression of social unity in the familylike hierarchy of the Larkin (1904) and the Johnson's Wax (1936) buildings. The columns in the Johnson's Wax Building workroom did not create cages but cantilevered centers around which one could gather, like the central atrium of light and greenery of the Larkin Building. This pattern recalls the clustering of the quadruple block plan for residential development in 1900.

The 1924 insurance office projects for Chicago are the closest interpretation of the commercial structures Wright had rejected. They are curious because, although they are concrete cantilever structures, that fact is almost unreadable from the outside. Only in section drawings is the difference evident. The "textile" curtain wall hanging without structural emphasis was one way to show how the floors were not supported at their extremities. During this period, Wright's proposals to create the continuity of structure and spatial enclosure by means of the widely differing "textile block" and curtain wall show how he was continuing to search for the way to resolve his alternative to the Chicago frame. In the later Saint Mark's on the Bouwerie, modified and finally constructed as the Price Tower in Oklahoma, and the Johnson's Wax Research Tower, exposing the core at ground level also allowed the structural means to be understood. It was always equal repetition and the separation of structure and enclosure, which is at the heart of steel frame, that challenged Wright.

Frank Lloyd Wright's later "de-centered," or sliding spatial conception was not an extension of the universal grid of Chicago land and structure. He simply went beyond it after the "tartan grid" interpretation of the Oak Park Studio years. Around 1930 he developed a "reflex" geometry that leapfrogged the orthogonal, incremental framework appropriated by nineteenth-century Chicago from seventeenth-century mathematical models to something some people now associate with fractals. His introduction of the 30/60 triangle opened up spatial possibilities that the right angle alone could not provide. An example of this is the desert camp called Ocotilla of 1928, outside Phoenix, where the compound's walls and buildings are arranged on a sequence of thirty-degree cranks with orthogonal zones of enclosed spaces. Associations with mathematical practice are metaphorical, of course, not derived from an understanding of the mathematical operations, but they are momentarily useful to dramatize distinctions on a very simple, formal level. (We must remember Alexander Rosenblueth and Norbert Weiner's caution: "The price of metaphor is eternal vigilance.")[8]

Wright's ultimate rejection of Chicago can be seen in his outrageous Mile High Building of 1956. In a stunning monument to the cupidity that fueled the "skyscrapers" of the late nineteenth century, the Mile High raises such motivation to new heights even as its nonframe, cantilevered structure contradicts them structurally. In the absence of support for his thinly spread Broadacre City from the interests that built and sustained places like Chicago, such a building would serve as the answer to those human desires Wright could not overcome. It made Broadacre possible by siphoning off, and almost quarantining, motivations Wright found profoundly antithetical to his vision of architecture.[9] It is almost as if Wright were saying at the end of his life, you want aggregated, commercial space, rapacious Chicago, take this! Rather than simply being the folly of an old man, it is a last poke in the eye, an ironic gesture he knew would be misread by those to whom it was directed and who had not really been paying attention for the last six decades.

The relation of Wright and Chicago has many dimensions. His response to its stimulus was selective because he was not trying to "understand" Chicago, just use it to further his own development. And Wright's response to Chicago does not exhaust the sources of his architecture. But as the initial setting for his ideas of what architecture can be, Chicago stimulated some very important responses. Wright rejected Chicago both because its repetitive abstraction undermined more hierarchical traditions of architecture and because he sought another kind of architectural "fluidity" bypassing its incremental subdivision of land and structure. For Wright, Chicago was obliterating architecture's past and misdirecting its future. As a result, Wright can be considered part of Chicago's history only in the sense that it contributed to his own architectural development much as Chicago's mud contributed to the skyscraper: by posing obstacles to be overcome.

6 Preservation and Renewal in Post–World War II Chicago

Daniel Bluestone

This essay analyzes how the critical, academic, and popular construction of the Chicago school narrative shaped the Chicago preservation and renewal movements of the 1950s and 1960s. Historically, preservationists have often staked out a position in opposition to the market and modern development. However, in Chicago the narrow focus on the monuments of the so-called Chicago school provided the basis for an unusual coalition between modernists and preservationists in support of both landmark preservation and modern urban renewal.

Preservation's claim to public support lies in large part in its ability to spatialize history, making the past more palpable, more memorable. Nevertheless, the actual buildings, landscapes, and districts that are preserved are often rather mute. Their historical meaning is gathered apart from the places themselves, either through prior education and experience or through current interpretation. This has held true for sites possessing associational importance as well as for buildings and places recognized aesthetically for their architectural and urban character. Following the lead of other institutionalized efforts at public history, preservation needs to examine more critically the perspective and content of the historical narratives it preserves and promotes. Preservationists could usefully ask: What history is preserved, what ideology is fostered, in historic preservation?[1]

Like other fields of history, preservation has privileged certain points of view and historical narratives. Recently, the challenge to canonical views has led to considerable ferment over the teaching of history. Writing history and preserving buildings clearly reinforce particular histories while ignoring others. However, unlike academic historians, preservationists work in a world in which the traces of histories that they choose to ignore often disappear. In valuing certain buildings, preservationists devalue others. Carried to its extreme, this process of devaluation leads to destruction and fosters a historic landscape that increasingly conforms to and confirms the privileged narrative. As a result of this process, people interested in exploring alternate versions of social and architectural experience find it increasingly difficult to harness the power of actual buildings to make their histories palpable.

This essay analyzes the relationship between the construction of the Chicago school narrative by architectural historians and critics and its role in Chicago renewal and preservation in the two decades following World War II. During this period, an extraordinary coalition between two unlikely partners supported Chicago preservation. Civic leaders and modernist architects, committed to a massive rebuilding of the city with all of the attendant destruction, supported preservationists who campaigned to save Chicago buildings and buttress a historic sense of place. The critical and historiographical concept of the Chicago school of architecture provided the common ground between preservationists and modernists. It fostered a preservation practice based largely on aesthetics. However, a limited historical view of the city's architecture supported only a modest preservation program in what turned out to be the most destructive period in Chicago since the Chicago Fire of 1871.

Recent historians have seriously challenged the critical and historiographical concept of a Chicago school.[2] There is little evidence that the architects of late nineteenth-century Chicago skyscrapers conceived of themselves or worked as a school self-consciously attempting to create a modern, structurally expressive style. One of the earliest chroniclers of their work, the anonymous editors of *Industrial Chicago*, argued that the "commercial style" was "largely technic." They wrote, "A gigantic skeleton or box structure of steel is ornamented with columns, pilasters, piers, capitals, bandcourses, arches, panellings, gables, moldings, etc., gathered from every nation of the earth and from every chronological cycle." In the 1890s, observers considered the style eclectic. Skeleton construction and predominant height more than a shared style characterized the early Chicago skyscrapers.[3]

The term *Chicago school* first appeared around the turn of the century in reference to literature. People who applied the term to architecture used it with imprecision, often in relation to domestic architecture. What became the dominant canonical concept of the Chicago school gained particular power in the 1920s and 1930s in the wake of an emerging American and European interest in modernism. The development appeared in many venues—from university lectures to critical and scholarly writing to museum exhibitions.[4]

The Museum of Modern Art's 1933 display of thirty-three photographs in an exhibition titled Early Modern Architecture: Chicago, 1870–1910, for example, clearly contributed to the canonization of the Chicago school in the 1930s. The Modern's typescript catalog and text on each photograph narrowed the interpretation of significant Chicago architecture to focus primarily on skyscrapers. The catalog included biographies of William Le Baron Jenney; Henry Hobson Richardson; Adler & Sullivan; Frank Lloyd Wright; Burnham & Root; and Holabird & Roche. The two central sections surveyed the technical and aesthetic development of the skyscraper, then set out what became a standard historical trajectory; it linked Richardson to Louis Sullivan to Wright and included an end point of 1910: "The Marshall Field Wholesale Store provided for the young Chicago architects an aesthetic discipline of regularity and simplicity from which Sullivan rapidly created a new personal style. The influence of Sullivan's style was so great that it attracted a group of young architects who formed under his leadership the

Chicago school. The free nontraditional architecture of the Chicago school retained its vigor until about 1910 when the stylistic revivalism which had made its first striking appearance in Chicago with the World's Fair of 1893, vitiated its force."[5]

The Museum of Modern Art exhibition asserted the existence of a distinct school as well as a "Chicago formula of skyscraper design." To reinforce this judgment, the exhibition included a photograph of George B. Post's domed Pulitzer skyscraper in New York (1889), calling it "progressive neither in structure nor design." In contrasting Chicago with the East and in setting out an architectural genealogy, the Early Modern exhibition considerably distorted the form and meaning of Chicago skyscrapers. In late nineteenth-century Chicago, architects did not share a consensus on style or ornament or a design formula except within the production of single firms.

Even at the center of curatorial and scholarly work on the Chicago school, considerable tentativeness persisted through the 1930s. Hugh Morrison's 1935 book, *Louis Sullivan, Prophet of Modern Architecture*, insisted that "until the work of the Chicago school is better known than it is at present . . . it will be impossible to estimate correctly the real force and character of Sullivan's direct practical influence in this country."[6] Such hedging disappeared in the works of historians Sigfried Giedion and Carl Condit, which bracketed World War II. Their writing, framed in strong sympathy with and enthusiasm for stylistic modernism, gave depth and foundation to the myth of Chicago school modernism as laid out in the Museum of Modern Art exhibition.[7]

Work by museum curators and historians and critics of modern architecture in the 1930s and 1940s established the terms and configuration of the Chicago school. This work undoubtedly won some popular adherence from a broad museum-going and journal-reading public. However, to appreciate the tenacity and pervasiveness of the Chicago school construct, it is important to focus less on academic discourse and more on Chicago itself as it stood in the 1950s and 1960s—the time when the canonical view gained its greatest currency in popular culture and when it profoundly shaped Chicago's historic preservation movement. This analysis focuses on the meaning that the Chicago school carried for architects, civic and business leaders, and the general public during this period.

In the context of postwar urbanism, the Chicago school construct operated both as a polemic concerning style and, perhaps more important, as an ideology promoting both the definition and the redevelopment of the city. Although preservationists focused more on the definition of the city and architects were primarily concerned with redevelopment, there were overlaps between the two groups and a commonly held belief in

6.1 Editorial cartoon by Jacob Burck, *Chicago Sun-Times*, 1953. Reprinted with special permission from the *Chicago Sun-Times.*

the exclusive importance of the Chicago school line. Strong civic boosterism promoted the widespread popular diffusion of the Chicago school construct. Postwar enthusiasm for the Chicago school must be understood in the context of the economic and social condition of postwar Chicago. Building interests confronted a socially and economically troubled city in the postwar period. An aging stock of buildings occupied a landscape that had stagnated through a decade of depression and a decade of war and dislocation. Despite the full employment and prosperity of the war years, the Chicago economy appeared threatened by decentralization, suburbanization, and growing cities in the southern and western United States. The city's preeminence in meatpacking, for example, declined precipitously in the 1950s. In 1959, both Swift and Armour announced the closing of their Chicago plants. *Newsweek* reported this news under the headline "The Shrinking Giant."[8]

The aspirations of nineteenth-century Chicago leaders toward primacy within the United States urban system disappeared in the twentieth century. After World War II, the future seemed fraught with dangers of decline rather than boundless possibilities for growth. Adopting a racist urban vision, the city's political and business leaders lamented the city's changing demography. Between 1940 and 1956, a period in which Chicago's resident white population declined slightly, the African American population boomed. Fueled largely by the migration of poor residents from the South who were attracted to the city's industrial jobs, Chicago's African American population climbed from 278,000 in 1940 to 682,000 in 1956, from 8 percent of the population to 18 percent.

Planning and redevelopment literature portrayed the residential neighborhoods where African Americans came to reside, almost by definition, as slums. More troubling for Chicago leaders than the existence of slums was that they impinged on the downtown area. In an article titled "An Encroaching Menace," *Life* magazine reported, "The slums of Chicago each year have pushed closer to the heart of the city. Some of the worst come only six blocks from the glittering skyscrapers. But a newly aroused and desperate city stopped them. But elsewhere in the metropolis, every month, new slums are being born."[9] In the nineteenth century, Chicago had developed a skyscraper downtown that had effectively narrowed, purified, and reformulated images of work and commerce in the city. People increasingly looked to the city's downtown and tall buildings to judge its commerce. This way of viewing cities persisted into the twentieth century and presented considerable problems for Chicago's politicians and business leaders when they saw slums encircling the downtown (fig. 6.1).

Adding to the problem of redevelopment, the downtown remained stagnant in the years immediately following World War II. In 1962, *Architectural Forum* reported that "the major reason why Chicago seemed not to be doing and building after World War II was that there was almost no activity in its aging central business area." The downtown area, the same area that so strongly projected images of a booming economy and metropolis in the late nineteenth century, seemed after World War II to be "asleep," "as dead as prohibition." Chicago's leaders appeared "especially defensive" that the city lagged far behind New York in its postwar office construction.[10]

In the face of such difficulties, history and an invented tradition of the Chicago school seemed especially reassuring: by looking back, many builders in Chicago discovered hope for a more promising future. Chicago's nineteenth-century skyscrapers had testified to the city's commercial vitality and growing economic prominence. Boosterism pervaded their development and promotion. In the mid-1950s, as the city's business and political leaders organized a Central Area Committee to promote massive downtown redevelopment, they invoked the name of the Chicago school to give them a sense of historic mission and, even, destiny.

Similarly, in 1957, history and boosterism pervaded the introduction of the new journal published by the Chicago chapter of the American Institute of Architects (AIA). Titled *Inland Architect*, the journal assumed the name of the nineteenth-century Chicago journal that had chronicled early skyscraper development. The journal helped explore the instrumental utility of invoking a Chicago school in the architectural and planning discourse of the 1950s. The cover of the first issue showed an etching of the portal of Sullivan's Transportation Building at the Columbian Exposition and a photograph of Harry Weese's apartment building at 227 Walton Street with its Chicago windows. The caption read, "Chicago Builds 1893 and Today." The journal's introduction recalled the "strength and stature," the "pioneering" work, and the "bold brash builders of the Chicago School."[11]

Inland Architect offered no mere reverie in past glories. The editors pointed to past successes in the hopes of inspiring people to take up present challenges rather than abandon a troubled city. "The vision of men such as Sullivan, Burnham, Jenney, Root, and Adler brought to the city buildings and plans where necessity became a new kind of beauty. . . . The spirit of the Chicago school was a powerful potential never yet wholly realized. . . . Here is our heritage and our challenge more than ever we are not building for today. Everything we do is an opportunity to do it with vision. Chicago is our opportunity now."[12] Although historical promotion focused on the supposed stylistic innovations and boldness of Chicago school architects, there was no masking the enthusiasm and even wistful nostalgia for the massive capital investment and accumulation represented by earlier skyscraper development. Preservationists should perhaps have greeted efforts to invoke Burnham's name and the 1909 Chicago Plan with some suspicion. Burnham had willingly promoted an urban "re-formation" that anticipated the demolition of nearly all his leading nineteenth-century skyscrapers and the shifting of the visual center of the city from the historic commercial core to the Congress axis linking civic and cultural institutions. For Burnham, the 1909 plan could be implemented without any regrets, loss, or sacrifice because the city had no "buildings possessing either historical or picturesque value."[13]

Architects were not alone in having a lot to gain from a historically inspired postwar building boom. Nor did they stand alone in their enthusiasm for harnessing the Chicago school myth as boosterism for a building campaign. One of the important crystallizing points for such an effort came in 1957 during Chicago Dynamic Week, an event sponsored by U.S. Steel and other business groups. Mayor Richard J. Daley proclaimed Chicago Dynamic Week in August 1957, only a few weeks after clashes between blacks and whites in Calumet Park sparked one of the city's worst race riots in many years. Mayor Daley's proclamation rang with boosterism and local pride: "WHEREAS, Chicago is the birthplace of American architecture, the curtain wall building, which ushered in the age of the skyscraper; and WHEREAS, Chicago today is concerned with the continued use of the newest building forms, materials and techniques to make Chicago a better place in which to live and work; and WHEREAS, the Chicago Dynamic Committee comprising our community's business and civic leaders has been organized to honor the sound building and far-sighted planning of Chicago, the world's most dynamic city . . . I, Richard J. Daley, Mayor of the City of Chicago, do hereby proclaim the week of October 27 through November 2, as 'Chicago Dynamic Week.'"

Edward C. Logelin, vice president of U.S. Steel Corporation and chair of the Chicago Dynamic committee, insisted that the week would bring people capable of recognizing the "possibilities" of the city, leaders who might give direction and form to the city's "billion-dollar rebuilding." Calling attention to Chicago's "great architectural and building tradition," Logelin sought a continuum between past and present: "We have enormous talent, unused power, and we must begin to use it now. We must think about our city building problems, about our creative, life-enriching, unknown art known as architecture, and keep doing something about it. For, as Sullivan said, 'Chicago can pull itself down and rebuild itself in a generation.'"[14]

When Chicago Dynamic Week arrived, reveling in history was more than merely rhetorical. The committee commissioned seventy-nine-year-old Carl Sandburg to return to Chicago to report his view of the nascent Chicago renaissance. Sandburg's earlier poetry had portrayed a tough, sprawling, commercial, and industrial Chicago; in 1957, he

6.2 Frank Lloyd Wright, Alistair Cooke, and Carl Sandburg during a Chicago Dynamic Week television appearance. *Chicago Sun-Times,* October 31, 1957. Reprinted with special permission from the *Chicago Sun-Times.*

obliged his sponsors by simply updating his earlier vision. Chicago, said Sandburg, "has elements of toil, combat, risk taking chances, departing from the known into the unknown. In this spirit during an earlier Chicago Dynamic the skyscraper was born. Today's Chicago Dynamic has cut loose from old traditions and begun to make new ones. Yesterday's skyscrapers are overtowered by steel clad structures rising far taller and with ease and grace."[15]

Frank Lloyd Wright also returned to complete the link to the past but failed to match Sandburg's sanguine boosterism and his enthusiasm for the skyscraper. In a televised session moderated by Alistair Cooke, Wright debated Sandburg on issues ranging from the political character of Lincoln and Jefferson to *Sputnik* to skyscrapers and urban form (fig. 6.2). Wright's Chicago Dynamic hosts were clearly anxious about the suburban challenge to the central city; nevertheless, Wright declared that skyscraper construction was "pushing the city to its end. They have no business in the city—they belong in the country where they can cast shadows on their own ground. Decentralize the entire affair and send people back to scenery."[16] He also ventured the opinion that "in another 15 years this city will be on its way out."[17] Developer Arthur Rubloff and the board chairman of Sears, Roebuck & Company were quick to challenge Wright. Rubloff insisted that Chicago had the greatest opportunity for resurgence and renaissance of "any major city on earth." Besides dinners and radio and television appearances, participants in Chicago Dynamic Week took part in a workshop on curtain-wall construction, placed Carl Sandburg's writing on Chicago in the cornerstone of the new, modern-style Mutual Trust Building designed by Perkins & Will, and held a conference on the question, "Can Good Architecture 'Pay Off'?"[18]

For Chicago's architects of modern curtain-wall buildings, the Chicago Dynamic Week emphasis on local architectural heritage could steer new commissions to a circle of local firms, effectively barring competition from firms based in other cities. In Chicago, architects jockeyed for the mantle of the Chicago school. Historians and critics proved quite willing to construct a connection

6.3 In 1957, the Chicago Theological Seminary planned to demolish Frank Lloyd Wright's Robie House, 1906–9. Photograph by Richard Nickel. Chicago Historical Society, ICHi-21070.

between local architects and the origins of modernism. They established a clear lineage between the First and Second Chicago school; they set the mantle of the Chicago school successor on the shoulders of Ludwig Mies van der Rohe. In 1963, George Danforth reported, "It seems natural that Mies should be asked to come here, because in his every work is the essence of the spirit of the Chicago School of architecture so long gone unrealized."[19]

In March 1957, prior to his participation in Chicago Dynamic Week, Wright had used a visit to Chicago to preserve and promote his own claim to the mantle of Chicago modernism. In doing so, he fueled one of the first major preservation battles in 1950s Chicago. This came when the Chicago Theological Seminary, located in Hyde Park, announced plans to demolish Wright's Robie House to make way for a student dormitory. Wright visited the house and denounced the plans to the local press. He argued that the Robie was "a cornerstone of American architecture" and that "to wreck it would be like destroying a fine piece of sculpture or a beautiful painting" (fig. 6.3).[20]

Wright found ready allies among local architects and residents of Hyde Park. In 1956, a small group had started preliminary discussions of the preservation of Chicago's "architectural wonders."[21] These people included Hyde Park resident Thomas B. Stauffer, a writer and a history and philosophy teacher in the city college system, the Hyde Park independent alderman Leon Despres, and Chicago architects Leo Weissenborn and Earl H. Reed. Reed served as the chair of the national AIA's Committee on the Preservation of Historic Buildings. Chicago modern architect and Hyde Park resident George Fred Keck also joined the campaign to save the Robie House. Initially, those interested in preservation aimed to move the house, which the seminary offered to donate to anyone who would take it. Despite the intervention of the National Trust for Historic Preservation, in their first campaign to save a twentieth-century structure, the Robie House was nearly demolished in July. Various fundraising efforts lagged, and the future looked bleak until William Zeckendorf purchased the building and the lot for $125,000. Zeckendorf's firm of Webb & Knapp had recently joined the city in an ambitious urban renewal of Hyde Park, home to the Robie House and the University of Chicago. Here, according to Zeckendorf, Chicago could have its history and its renewal, too. Zeckendorf's newspaper advertisement of its purchase put the issues succinctly: "Our Christmas Gift to Hyde Park, to Chicago, to Posterity: Robie House, Hyde Park's World Famous Monument. The Heritage of the Past. The Headquarters of the Future. Acting as Guardian of Great Architecture Webb & Knapp is purchasing Robie House to be used for their headquarters during the development of Hyde Park A and B."[22]

A certain irony pervaded the embrace of history in the context of a local urban renewal project that involved the demolition of more than 880 buildings in the neighborhood surrounding the Robie House. However, Zeckendorf's sense of history was shared by a large number of local residents. The Hyde Park–Kenwood Community Conference, a local citizens' group that had sought a major urban renewal program for the area, had in fact conducted a historical survey of all of the buildings charted for demolition. It identified forty-three structures worth photographing and with the help of the urban renewal agency it salvaged interior and exterior ornaments from about fifteen of them. The conference's survey committee could not identify even a single targeted structure worth preserving. The conference even endorsed the removal of "good" buildings because without such action "any urban renewal planning would be defeated."[23] The broader planning effort aimed to "preserve" the university's community as a viable middle-class housing area by demolishing the buildings that housed poor, working-class, and largely African American residents. The opposition to the urban renewal plans turned more on questions of fair housing and social equity than on issues of historic value.[24]

The concern with the future of Hyde Park conspired to submerge most local histories. Viewing the landscape through a prism of class and race contributed to the devaluing of neighborhood architectural history. *Segments of the Past*, the Conference's booklet on its survey project, addressed this sense of a departed history. It asserted that a "once gracious old mansion which has long since been converted into living quarters for thirty families . . . and which has not been maintained is no longer an asset, and usually has to be removed."[25] The idea that some history was no longer historic or worthy of chronicling or preserving was common in Chicago. Considering the potential of Chicago landmarks in 1965, Ruth Moore reported that "changing times, changing neighborhoods" had "all but destroyed the usefulness" of many landmarks.[26] Present use and changed neighborhoods should not necessarily block historic engagement with a structure, but in Chicago, in neighborhood after neighborhood, demographic change somehow pushed buildings beyond the reach and interest of many preservationists. In 1956, the Historic American Building Survey inventory form for the house that Louis Sullivan designed and lived in during the World's Columbian Exposition, just north of Hyde

Park–Kenwood, reported under the entry "Historical Significance and Description" that the house had been subdivided and that the "neighborhood is now predominated by colored occupants."[27] Just as the recording wandered from the facts of significance and description, preservation interest wavered. Photographer Richard Nickel, one of the most devoted of the Chicago school preservationists, gave up his plans to purchase the house when family, friends, and local police convinced him that the neighborhood was too dangerous. Like many other Sullivan residential designs, the house was eventually abandoned, picked clean of its ornament, and demolished.[28] In Hyde Park, history came in fragments, "segmented" or separated from both the historic cityscape and from many residents of the community.

Beyond the Robie House campaign and Wright and Sandburg's personification of history during Chicago Dynamic Week, the first formal public recognition of Chicago landmarks came in 1957. In January, the Chicago City Council unanimously passed an ordinance sponsored by Alderman Despres establishing the Commission on Chicago Architectural Landmarks. The ordinance called attention to Chicago's "internationally important monuments of architectural engineering and style" and cited six buildings as examples: Richardson's Glessner House; Sullivan's World's Fair residence, his Carson Pirie Scott Building, and his Auditorium Theater; Wright's Robie House, and Burnham & Root's Monadnock Building. The ordinance also called attention to the need for landmark preservation by pointing to the earlier demolition of Richardson's Marshall Field Warehouse and Wright's Midway Gardens. The council charged the commission with designating Chicago's architectural landmarks, identifying and marking them, educating the public about their importance, and developing policies for their preservation.[29]

Like the juxtaposition of heritage and contemporary visions for architecture and city building that characterized Chicago Dynamic programs, the first official list of architectural landmarks included both historic and contemporary structures. The six major Chicago school monuments featured on a special architectural tour during Chicago Dynamic Week—the Rookery, the Monadnock Building, the Leiter Building, the Auditorium Building, the Carson Pirie Scott store, and the Reliance—were among the fourteen structures singled out for special recognition on the commission's initial list of thirty-nine landmark buildings. The list, drawn up by a committee of architectural historians, architects, and commission members, included numerous structures by Adler & Sullivan and Burnham & Root in addition to other buildings considered to have a role in the local modernist genealogy. Then, to complete the links to the present, the commission designated such buildings as George Fred and William Keck's University Avenue residence (1937), Mies's Illinois Institute of Technology campus (1947) and Lake Shore Drive apartments (1951), and SOM's Inland Steel Building (1957). The commission's

6.4 A 1962 ceremony naming a major Chicago urban renewal project after Carl Sandburg. Pictured from left to right: George Dovenmuehle and Arthur Rubloff, developers; John G. Duba, commissioner of urban renewal; Carl Sandburg; D. E. Mackelman, deputy commissioner of urban renewal; Louis R. Solomon, architect; and Albert Robin, builder. Photograph from author's collection.

designation offered no protection for the landmarks, but it established architectural "merit," "structure," and "planning" as the criteria for a new aesthetically based landmarks program.

For post–World War II city planners, the clean, crisp lines of modernism had an obvious allure in an otherwise stagnant cityscape. The difference between Chicago and most other U.S. cities is that in Chicago planners and builders incorporated history and a sense of architectural heritage into a broader program of redevelopment. Given this rhetorical commitment of history, the fate of historic buildings and landscapes in the context of renewal merits some attention. There was abundant potential for conflict. However, adherence to the Chicago school's rather narrow canon of architectural significance, which located history within the bounds of a limited number of city lots, helped minimize the possibility that the values of history and modernism would clash directly.

The Robie House preservation, coupled with local patterns of urban renewal demolition, pointed to the extreme unevenness of neighborhood and residential preservation in the 1950s. The Chicago school canon did little to foster preservation of Chicago's diverse stock of domestic architecture. Between 1947 and 1962, Chicago urban renewal officials cleared nearly one thousand acres of urban land for redevelopment projects ranging from Sandburg Village on the north (fig. 6.4) to Lake Meadows on the south to the University of Illinois at Chicago (UIC) Circle Campus on the west. History generally failed to levy a claim on these areas. In fact, the new buildings of Mies van der Rohe, SOM, I. M. Pei, and others that filled Chicago's various urban renewal sites seemed, in the view of many architects and planners, to have much more to do with historic Chicago than the old buildings they replaced.

The issues of preservation and destruction played out in residential neighborhoods mirrored those played out in downtown Chicago in the 1950s and 1960s. Here again, the myth of the Chicago school raised preservation interest in the cases of only a handful of structures while many other buildings were de-

6.5 Columbus Memorial Building, architect W. W. Boyington, 1891. Building demolished in 1959. Chicago Historical Society, ICHi-22331.

6.6 Central light court, Masonic Temple Building, Burnham & Root, architects, 1891–92. Building demolished in 1939. Avery Architectural and Fine Arts Library, Columbia University.

6.7 This view along Randolph "Street was a favored one for people picturing Chicago in the 1890s and early 1900s. Today, only a single low-rise building remains from all of those recorded in this photograph. In the distance with the peaked gable is the Masonic Temple Building, Burnham & Root, 1891–92. The Schiller Theatre Building (renamed the Garrick), Adler & Sullivan, 1891–92, is in the middle ground behind the Ashland Block, Burnham & Root, 1891–92. The City Hall and Courthouse, J. J. Egan, 1873–85, is at the right.

stroyed. In 1956, Earl H. Reed, the Chicago architect who headed the AIA's Committee on the Preservation of Historic Buildings, wrote, "Our historic structures melt away like snow in the summer sun."[30] Reed wrote this in the wake of the 1956 demolition of Solon S. Beman's Pullman Building. In his 1882 building, George Pullman carried his fetish for the sleeping arrangements of Americans off of his sleeping cars, out of his company town, and into the skyscraper. The building provided the extraordinary skyscraper combination of office space for the Pullman Company and apartment space planned for Pullman's middle managers. Stylistically, the building, with its prominent corner turret, its rusticated base, and its deeply modeled window surrounds and entrance arches, did not fit the supposed ahistorical, structurally expressive model of the true Chicago style. The building disappeared in 1956 almost naturally, like melting snow, and without any great surprise or protest; a local newspaper simply assured readers that the building would "remain as legends in the pages of the city's history."[31] With only slightly more notice, Beman's monumental Grand Central Station was demolished in 1971.

The lack of a narrative of Chicago history apart from the Chicago school line made the understanding, appreciation, and preservation of Chicago buildings extremely difficult. One can sense the problem in reading the Historic American Building Survey inventory cards from the 1950s. Paragraphs on structural expression filled the forms of the buildings that seemed to fit the Chicago school pattern, but when surveyors confronted a building like W. W. Boyington's 1892 Columbus Memorial Building, they could only manage a pithy entry on significance: "It commemorates the World's Columbian Exposition; Notable features: Bronze Statue of Columbus and use of ornamental metal in its structure" (fig. 6.5). The building had indeed appropriated civic life as part of its monumental expression, incorporating what contemporaries appreciated as some of the most dramatic ornamental bronze and mosaic work in Chicago. Yet the building was demolished in 1959 without public protest.

In the 1950s and 1960s, concerns over stagnation clearly held in check many claims of history and memory. This had been the case for years. In 1927, for example, the *Engineering News-Record* published a hard-headed account of the obsolescence of Burnham & Root's 1890 Woman's Temple Building. The steel frame was in great shape, but the dormers on the dramatically pitched roof leaked during heavy storms. More important, the building's sloped roof and thick walls and floors did not permit the owner to maximize rental income; the journal calculated that a more efficient building of the same height would bring in an additional $32,000 a year. In an unusual contemporary call for preservation, the *Western Architect* in 1922 evoked the "romanticism" of the Woman's

6.5

6.6

6.7

Temple in a plea for saving the structure. Nevertheless, the building's destruction, "an archaeological disaster," seemed inevitable because the "god" of money blotted from people's minds "all appreciation of historical value and pride in preserving the monuments of past achievement." The appeal to "romantic spirit" failed in the 1920s and certainly did not comport with 1950s visions of the Chicago school rationalism and engineering expression.[32]

In the 1930s, possibilities for profit eclipsed historic values and propelled the destruction of Burnham & Root's Masonic Temple Building, which had been the tallest building in the world when it opened in 1892. The Masonic Temple's central atrium more vividly recalled the concern for and innovation surrounding provision of light and air in Chicago's early skyscrapers than most facades filled with Chicago windows (fig. 6.6). Tearing the building down and replacing it with a two-story building, the owners reduced their 1939 tax bill on a building sparsely occupied in the midst of the Great Depression. Yet local papers interpreted the destruction not as a Depression-era tragedy but rather as a testament to the presence of more modern buildings in the downtown area. The *Daily News*, for example, showed a view of the destruction under the headline, "Early Skyscraper Falls in the Shadow of Modern Giants."[33] The ideals of progress proved to be infertile ground for preservation claims (fig. 6.7).

The picketing, lobbying, public debates, and court challenges that greeted the 1960 plan for demolishing Adler & Sullivan's 1891–92 Schiller Theatre Building (later renamed the Garrick) contrasted sharply with the uncontested demolition of the Pullman, Columbus Memorial, and other Loop buildings. The owners of the Balaban & Katz theater chain wanted to replace the Garrick with a parking garage. Sullivan and the Garrick occupied a dominant position in the Chicago school canon, and demolition plans provoked considerable fury. The Garrick campaign, which ended in demolition of the building in 1961, derived its greatest support from the critical and professional circles supporting modern architecture. People associated with the Illinois Institute of Technology, where Mies was a teacher and where the Institute of Design modeled its education along the lines of the Bauhaus, provided a strong core of support. The Institute had for many years studied, photographed, and revered Louis Sullivan and his buildings as modern forerunners of their own modernist forms and philosophy. When Nickel, a photography graduate of the Institute of Design who had written a thesis on Louis Sullivan, formed a picket line, students, former students, and professors from the Illinois Institute of Technology dominated the group (fig. 6.8).[34] John Vinci, a graduate of the institute, left his drafting table at SOM to join other institute students, including David Norris, on the picket line. Mies, who was said to be ill and unable to join the picket line, sent word that he was "'100 percent' for saving the Garrick." When Le Cor-

6.8 Richard Nickel leading a picket line at the Garrick, *Chicago Sun-Times*, 9 June 1960. Reprinted with permission from the *Chicago Sun-Times*.

busier wrote to Mayor Daley on behalf of the Garrick and he helped authenticate the genealogical links to modernism asserted as part of the movement. He explained the "birth of machinism" to Daley and called it a "sacrilege" that the Garrick might be demolished. He concluded, "The buildings of Sullivan and his School must be saved, even if it means that some streets must be turned aside."[35]

The *Chicago Sun-Times* reported the protest under the headline, "Culture Walks the Picket Line." Stauffer helped Nickel organize the protest. Cultural historian Hugh Duncan presented a picket line brief for preservation that affirmed both history and progress: "I'm imbued with a deep belief in the future of this city. We have such a reputation for gangsterism. But this city is one of the few in the world's history to have created a whole order of architecture, like Gothic or Classical, not just a style but an order . . . The three great American architects of the twentieth century are all Chicagoans—Frank Lloyd Wright, Sullivan, and Ludwig Mies van der Rohe. Do we care?" The preservationists staked their claim entirely on the Chicago school canon and set this heritage and the claims of memory in opposition to the popular memory of gangsters.[36]

Opponents of preservation labeled the campaign an "egghead protest." One letter to the editor urged the preservationists to give up on the Garrick and to save the Art Institute: "These so-called abstract paintings are monstrosities." High culture did undoubtedly raise the stakes in the Garrick campaign. Numerous arts groups joined the preservation coalition in the hopes that the building could be converted into an arts center, with studio space taking over the office floors and the theater offering an important site in the Loop for performances. Cultural politics turned to electoral politics when Alderman Despres declared his support for preserving the Garrick. At the same time, Alderman Paddy Bauler opposed the movement, declaring, "Tear it down! Tear it down before it falls down!" Editorial writers at the *Chicago Sun-Times* suggested that Alderman Bauler might be an authority on "the durability of a head on a glass of beer" but that he best defer to the experts in matters of the Garrick's structural integrity. The politicians and the courts could hold up the demolition by refusing to issue a demolition permit.[37] Initially, the Chicago court found that beauty and architectural heritage provided a substantial basis for preventing the demolition. However, the courts also came to insist that if the city or their parties wished to preserve the building, they would have to buy it. The owners had already rejected pleas from the National Trust for Historic Preservation to renovate the building and attract new tenants at higher rents. Richard H. Howland, president of the National Trust, insisted that the idea to preserve the building idea came not from "mere antiquarians suggesting that the building be preserved intact as an architectural monument," but rather from "realists in today's world."[38]

Mayor Daley, for his part, proved equivocal in his support. He appointed a committee to study the problem, and preservationists increasingly pinned their hopes for the Garrick on the possibility that the city would modify plans for an adjacent civic center to include the Garrick. When Daley rejected this solution, the building was slated for demolition. The preservation campaign then quickly shifted from saving the building to saving its fragments. With $10,000 contributed by the Garrick owners as well as other private funds, Richard Nickel, David Norris, and John Vinci salvaged ornament from the building and distributed it—along with the fame of the Chicago school—to museums, universities, and individual collectors around the world.

The collecting of architectural fragments started to institutionalize the ongoing private efforts of Nickel, who had devoted considerable time to both photographing and salvaging ornament form Sullivan's buildings.[39] In comparison to fully preserved buildings, collected fragments provided a severely constricted link to the architectural past. In the case of Chicago buildings, they also presented something of a conundrum; buildings revered by Chicago school enthusiasts for their supposed structural expression and stylistic modernity were now preserved for posterity through a collection of ornament. Nevertheless, the fragments did permit preservationists to dramatically assert and commemorate their historical priorities in a way that left the real estate market relatively unfettered. Preservation through the collection of fragments also helped shore up the coalition of preservationists and their modernist allies. The city could both remember and build.

Despite the collection of ornament, the years following the Garrick campaign did highlight some of the tensions within the preservation coalition. In 1962, for example, Norman Ross underscored the need for Chicago preservation by objecting to the modernist forms: "What one wishes for, in the rising jungle of sterile steel, glass and concrete, of stark, straight lines are a few rambling, extravagant old buildings that seem to have roots in the soil on which they are built."[40] Steel, glass, and concrete were the precious materials of modern rebuilding. This implicit critique of modern rootlessness simply reinforced the modernists' interest in a local modern lineage that worked against an alienated sense of placelessness in the modern city. During the Garrick debate, one letter to the editor wondered, "What sort of history will we leave our children besides parking lots, superhighways and a nondescript, anonymous and insignificant architecture?" (fig. 6.9).[41] Even the narrowest interpretation of the Chicago school as constituting only architectural monuments could not hide from view the obvious fracture lines between the builders of modern buildings and the preservers of historic buildings. Nevertheless, many Chicagoans did emerge from the campaign with "a new appreciative interest

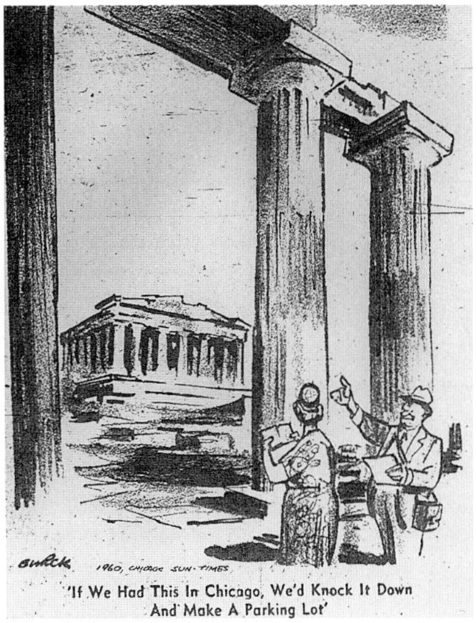

6.9 Editorial cartoon by Jacob Burck, *Chicago Sun-Times*, June 23, 1960. Reprinted with permission from the *Chicago Sun-Times*.

in . . . architectural heritage."[42] The Chicago Heritage Committee, a loose coalition of historians, architects, and preservationists led by Stauffer, Nickel, Despres, Ben Weese, and Duncan and formed in the midst of the Garrick campaign, continued energetically, if selectively, to press claims for history and preservation.

The publicity generated by the Chicago Heritage Committee over the demolition of the Garrick undoubtedly spurred greater vigilance concerning the buildings within the historiographical canon of the Chicago school. The campaign to preserve and restore Adler & Sullivan's Auditorium Theater and Richardson's Glessner House, for example, gained support and credibility from the climate of urgency that developed around the destruction of the Garrick and other Sullivan buildings.

Despite some progress in Chicago preservation, many buildings proposed for demolition in the center of Chicago fell outside of the narrative of architectural significance adhered to by the Chicago Heritage Committee and the Commission on Chicago Architectural Landmarks. As a group, these buildings fared very poorly indeed in relation to those standing in the critical orbit of the Garrick. The case of Henry Ives Cobb's domed, Corinthian-order Federal Building, built between 1896 and 1905, offers a good illustration (fig. 6.10). One plan after another in the postwar period anticipated the demolition of the Federal Building. Increasingly, proponents of Chicago renewal looked to local and federal governments to set an example for the private sector by rebuilding and redeveloping their downtown buildings. Plans called for government not only to rebuild but also to do so along modernist lines with tall buildings sited on wide open plazas. Government could thus boldly renew an aging, cluttered, and stagnant downtown. The Central Area Committee's plan looked to these plans as cornerstones to private rebuilding. The Federal Center would "open up downtown Chicago, providing greenery, a striking urban scene, a place to sit and enjoy the city." According to the review of the plans, "plazas and skyscrapers would replace nineteenth-century 'eyesores' and . . . open landscaped areas would 'let the sun into the Loop.'" Some people believed that the Federal Building possessed a "certain solidity and classical charm," but it covered its entire city block and created an effect that was one of "overcrowding, of dirtiness, and . . . of an urban backwater."[43]

When the Federal Building was planned in the 1890s, some people had called for the construction of a skyscraper. Rejecting the proposal, the Treasury Department's supervising architect declared, "It would not be dignified to erect a steel-frame building. The government puts up heavy masonry structures and puts them up to stay."[44] Now, as people contemplated the building's demolition and its replacement with a skyscraper, few

6.10

6.10 Chicago Federal Building/U.S. Courthouse, Henry Ives Cobb, architect, 1896–1905. Photograph taken in November 1961 shows the construction site for the first phase of the new Federal Center in the foreground. National Archives.

6.11

6.11 Demolition of the Chicago Federal Building, October 1965. At the left is the new U.S. Courthouse and Office Building, 1961–65, designed by Ludwig Mies van der Rohe; Schmidt Garden & Erikson; C.F. Murphy Associates; and A. Epstein & Son. A second federal high-rise office building, a post office, and an open plaza filled the site of the demolished building. National Archives.

of those who campaigned to save the Garrick argued in favor of preservation. If the building had been built as a skyscraper, it might have ironically enjoyed a different fate in the mid-1960s.

In 1959, attempting to boost the plans for Chicago's central area, Mayor Daley opposed a federal judge's call for the preservation of the Federal Building. Daley insisted that it was "fine to talk about beauty and architecture" but that the convenience and comfort of the people in the central area demanded a new federal center.[45] For his part, Stauffer did not think that the building was "historic" or "distinguished architecture"; however, he privately favored its preservation as "a fully stated expression of the style of the time" and as evidence of the "rich texture of stages in the growth" of the city and its architecture. Stauffer's colleagues on the Chicago Heritage Committee generally stood with Daley and roundly rejected calls to save the Federal Building. Norris, who had salvaged ornament from the Garrick, wrote to Nickel that he thought the building was "juck (a new word)" and promised to "make a big stink" if Stauffer got the committee involved. Members of the committee felt strongly that the building "lacked sufficient merit or interest to deserve a fuss." They also though that the modern plaza proposed for part of the site would provide "a most valuable amenity for the whole Loop area." Furthermore, the fact that Mies van der Rohe was the lead architect for the new Federal Center disposed members of the committee toward a project that they felt would be architecturally "excellent."[46] In 1965, the Federal Building was demolished (fig. 6.11). Fragments were saved for placement in other federal buildings, and some people carried off other pieces of the building as part of a private, non–Chicago school recall of a public building.

Some members of the Chicago Heritage Committee did join the campaign to save Jane Addams's Hull House complex from the West Side clearance done for the UIC Circle Campus; but again, the comprehensive planning of the campus by SOM never accommodated more than a fragment of the building complex. Senator Paul Douglas joined the cause, insisting that "symbols and the embodiments of the noble past help to call forth the best in men and women, and they need to be cherished and not ruthlessly destroyed."[47] Here, however, the appeals met demands for redevelopment and a preservation constituency ill prepared to press architectural appeals outside of Chicago school narrative–and even less equipped to press for preservation premised on cultural as opposed to architectural history.

The Chicago school lineage of course assumed a pattern of harmony between the architecture of the past and the present. However, as the government spurred redevelopment of the downtown, growing numbers of early skyscrapers were replaced. Carl Sandburg even noted this in his Chicago Dynamic Week poem: "When one tall skyscraper is torn down/To make room for a taller one to go up,/Who takes down and puts up those skyscrapers?/Man—the little two-legged joker . . . Man."[48] In 1960, reflecting on the proposed demolition of Holabird & Roche's Republic and Cable buildings, structures rooted firmly in the Chicago school construct, historian Carl Condit sought a mechanism for promoting a "broader scale" of aesthetic preservation. He thought that the new buildings projected for these sites would provide "handsome additions to the Loop area and will greatly improve the economic and civic character of our rather disordered urban core." Condit hoped that building owners and the city's planning, landmarks, and land clearance agencies would cooperate so that "new buildings can be erected on sites now occupied by ugly and obsolete structures while the fine work of the Chicago School is preserved."[49] In the midst of his own impassioned effort to save the Republic Building, Ben Weese proposed a similar solution: declare the entire downtown an urban renewal district so that "low buildings pre-dating the Chicago School" and considered of "minimal cultural value" could be demolished to provide sites for a harmonious modernism. This proposal was entered in a section of Weese's article entitled "History Is Important."[50]

History is indeed important; however, which buildings come to represent history is very much dependent on the historical narratives that preservationists bring to their consideration of the built environment. The narrow focus on the monuments of the so-called Chicago school provided a basis for the cohesion of modernists and preservationists in support of landmark preservation during the 1950s and 1960s. For modernists, preserving the landmarks of the so-called Chicago school fostered a narrative of Chicago history that reinforced contemporary interest in modern urban renewal. Moreover, narrowly conceived preservation simply did not pose a threat to the plans for a massive public and private rebuilding of the city. As renewal and preservation proceeded, the historic city came to look increasingly like the Chicago school narrative; the diversity of the city's nineteenth-century architectural production was either destroyed or overlooked by those who relied on architectural designations to gather their sense of history. For those preservationists who were more concerned with defining and defending a sense of place than with building the city anew, the narrow vision of landmarks also held certain advantages. The ascendancy of aesthetic preservation over a variety of associational narratives encouraged preservationists in their belief that they could locate the essence of the city and its history in a few representative structures of the Chicago school. The absolute priority given to aesthetic over associational landmarks in the 1950s and beyond further restricted the use that citizens could make of history; their efforts to forge a vital sense of neighborhood and community identity based in part on history could only be frustrated by the limitations of the aesthetic model. Recognizing the importance of other buildings and histories would have severely tested the interest of city-building modernists in preservation. At every turn, it would have opened up the urban renewal process to the challenges of histories embedded in the city's other buildings and landscapes.

Preservation served city building well in the peak years of post–World War II renewal. However, the mounting challenges to urban renewal and modernism in the late 1960s and 1970s were paralleled by a general broadening of the basis for recognizing and preserving Chicago landmarks. After serving rather narrow interests, the preservation movement in Chicago proved quite capable of flexibly adapting itself to changing historical times and aesthetic tastes. A constricted model of aesthetic preservation rooted in earlier Chicago school notions of architectural merit continued to frame preservation, but broader Chicago histories and a much broader range of forms and styles and building types came under scrutiny. For example, when a small group of architects, historians, and preservationists set out to preserve Henry Hobson Richardson's Glessner House in the 1960s, they took on the institutional title of the Chicago school of Architecture Foundation. Today, the foundation presides over a broad program of architectural tours that range far beyond its base in Chicago school history and myth. Nevertheless, as historian Carroll Westfall argues, limited notions of history, preservation, and the city have continued to erode Chicago's urban fabric in more recent times.[51] In a sense today, as in the 1950s, preservation is only as good or as useful as the histories it values in the historic landscape. The Chicago case strongly suggests that preservationists need to more self-consciously consider the link between the histories they choose to tell and the active structuring of the contemporary city, both in fact and in memory.

More than Mies: Architecture of Chicago Multifamily Housing, 1935–65

Eric Mumford

One of the great myths of Chicago architecture is that Ludwig Mies van der Rohe single-handedly introduced modern architecture to Chicago after his arrival from Germany in 1938. Connected to this myth was that of the "second Chicago school," which culminated in the early 1970s with the Hancock and Sears towers. This period was understood to be the second phase of the technical and design innovations introduced by the era of the early skyscrapers. Between the two Chicago school eras was what Sigfried Giedion described as a "dismal interval" of "regressive neo-classicism."[1] In the 1990s, historians have challenged this myth and more recent scholarship has tended to emphasize continuities between the first Chicago school and the supposedly regressive period that followed it.[2]

If the myth that Mies and his followers' second Chicago school was the inevitable result of the modernizing forces that created the modern city is rejected—and such a view cannot be supported by even the most superficial historical investigation—then how can we understand the history of Chicago building in this critical period? I will discuss the development of some characteristic twentieth-century Chicago urban housing types and then examine a set of midcentury middle- and upper-income multifamily apartment complexes in both practical terms, having to do with clients, markets, and public involvement, and in terms of the architectural strategies used. My intention is not to suggest that Mies was not important to Chicago architecture, but to examine some parallel midcentury approaches that also shaped the urban patterns of postwar Chicago.

Chicago housing history is a large and complex subject, but in the area of multifamily housing a number of innovations were made locally well before the modernism of the 1930s.[3] During the era of the first Chicago school in the 1880s, middle- and upper-class multiunit housing first began to be built in Chicago. Some projects were high-rise apartment hotels that followed the pattern established by John M. Van Osdel's third Palmer House Hotel (1875, demolished 1925), among the first buildings anywhere to have had electric lighting, elevators, and telephones as standard equipment. Like the high-rise office buildings in the Loop developed in the following decade, these early Chicago apartment buildings began to use new technologies of iron, steel, and eventually reinforced concrete framing in their construction. Built at first in the wealthy residential areas north and south of the Loop, they included ten-story hotels by Clinton J. Warren, most of them now demolished except for his Congress Hotel (1893), across the street from Adler & Sullivan's Auditorium Building. Farther from the Loop, the many examples of the type included the famous Hyde Park Hotel (Theodore Starrett, 1887, demolished 1963), and to the north, the still-surviving Raleigh (1891, architect unknown) and Brewster Apartments (R. H. Turnock, 1893).[4] These buildings were often quite similar in

7.1

7.2

7.1 John Van Bergen, Munyer Apartments, North Linden and West Ontario streets, Oak Park, 1916. Photograph by Eric Mumford.

7.2 Barry Byrne, Kenna Apartments, 2214 East Sixty-ninth Street, 1916. Photograph by Eric Mumford.

form to early office buildings, and they covered most of their lots to a height of ten or twelve stories, using small light wells for ventilation.

The low-rise courtyard apartment house, considered a progressive way of housing a large number of families on a relatively small lot, developed slightly later and quickly became a standard form of middle-class housing in the outlying parts of the city.[5] The three- and six-flat types for smaller lots soon joined this common type. Although elevators were not necessary in these three- or four-story buildings, they usually included other "modern conveniences" ranging from electrical wiring and full indoor plumbing to built-in vacuum cleaning outlets.[6] Although often traditional in style, their arrival occurred at the same time that various forms of "modern architecture" also began to be introduced into Chicago architecture. Good examples of the use of new architectural directions inspired by the work of Sullivan and Wright in three and six flats include John Van Bergen's Munyer Apartments in Oak Park (1916; fig. 7.1) and Barry Byrne's Kenna Apartments in South Shore (1916; fig. 7.2).

Within the dense existing city created by the mix of tenements, old row houses, and newer apartment houses, whose form was based on streetcar and elevated lines, the earliest works clearly related to the modern movement in Europe began to emerge in Chicago. These followed the 1933–34

7.3

7.3 Keck and Keck, three-flat buildling at 5551 South University Street, Hyde Park, 1937. Photograph by Eric Mumford.

7.4 Map of Chicago buildings seven stories and over. From Homer Hoyt, *One Hundred Years of Land Values in Chicago* (Chicago: University of Chicago Press, 1933), 243.

Century of Progress Exposition, which showcased an eclectic variety of modernist approaches.[7] Planned by leading national practitioners who had begun to move toward what is often termed "art deco" and "streamlined moderne" in their work, these directions had some limited and immediate effects on multifamily housing architecture in Chicago, such as the work of Andrew Rebori.[8] At the same time, among the first pre-Miesian examples of modernism in Chicago housing architecture were Keck and Keck's Crystal House and House of Tomorrow at the Century of Progress Exposition, both of which anticipated the engineering-oriented direction of later Chicago architecture.[9] This kind of work was still far from the market mainstream in the early 1930s, but a small three-flat by Keck and Keck in Hyde Park, 5551 South University Avenue (1937), developed by the architects in partnership with a University of Chicago professor, is a permanent example of the firm's early modernist work (fig. 7.3)[10] It was intended to be a model for new three-flat development, although it now appears as the end rather than the start of an era: middle-class three flats had appeared in great numbers around the city about 1910, but after World War II they were supplanted by suburban single-family houses on one hand and by larger apartment houses on the other.

It was in the area of public housing that aspects of modernism as it had developed in Europe began to have the most impact in Chicago.[11] The first of the low-rise superblock public housing projects were built in the mid-1930s and used rigid new standards imposed by the Federal Public Works Administration housing division's chief architect, Horatio Hackett of Chicago.[12] As a result, the first Chicago Housing Authority (CHA) projects, the Jane Addams, Julia Lathrop, and Trumbull Park homes (all 1938), were bleak brick complexes of similar buildings, which covered many cleared blocks. Their large design teams provided employment for some luxury apartment house architects of the 1920s, but these projects were seldom considered to be significant architecture by either traditional or modern architects. Despite their barracks-like design, technologically the standardization and economies of scale used in these projects paved the way for modern housing architecture after the war.[13]

Like many myths, the myth of the "second Chicago school" was effective because it engaged elements of the history of Chicago that made it distinctive among U.S. cities, though not unique. Since the early twentieth century, Chicago had developed a lakefront-oriented environment of high-rise building, something that barely existed outside of the United States before the mid-1930s (fig. 7. 4). Most of this high-rise construction was along the lakeshore north of the downtown, with another pocket in Hyde Park to the south. In the pre-Depression era these buildings were among the most technologically advanced buildings anywhere in the world, and they inspired European modernists in the 1920s. The first postwar additions to this environment were indeed the work of Mies. It is often forgotten, however, that on his Promontory Apartments in Hyde Park (1946) and on the canonical glass and steel 860/880 Lake Shore Drive (1948) Mies worked in association with other firms. At the twenty-two-story Promontory, Mies and his associated architects, Holsman, Holsman, Klekamp & Taylor and Pace Associates, exposed the exterior concrete frame, removing the usual division between structure and surface. The client, Herbert Greenwald, a developer with an interest in modern architecture, had invited Walter Gropius, Eero Saarinen, and Frank Lloyd Wright to submit designs for the Promontory project, but the first two declined and Wright asked for too large an advance. Gropius then suggested Mies, who accepted. Greenwald was unable to get bank financing for the project, and so he offered units to buyers as shares in a cooperative. Demand was sufficient to get the project started, but part of Mies's appeal to Greenwald was his ability to design so that the per square foot construction costs were lower than most Chicago public housing. *Architectural Forum* praised the Promontory Apartments for reaching "new heights of directness." It is "nothing more than pale yellow brick panels and aluminum sash in a concrete frame left uncolored and exposed."[14] The concrete columns became smaller as they rose and as their loads lessened, creating a subtle effect which Peter Blake later likened to "stepped-back buttresses on medieval structures,"[15] an interesting contrast to the more classic geometric forms of 860/880 Lake Shore Drive. In fact, however, Mies had also proposed an all-glass-and-steel curtain wall for the Promontory, which as built was a less expensive version of Mies's ideal-type high rise.

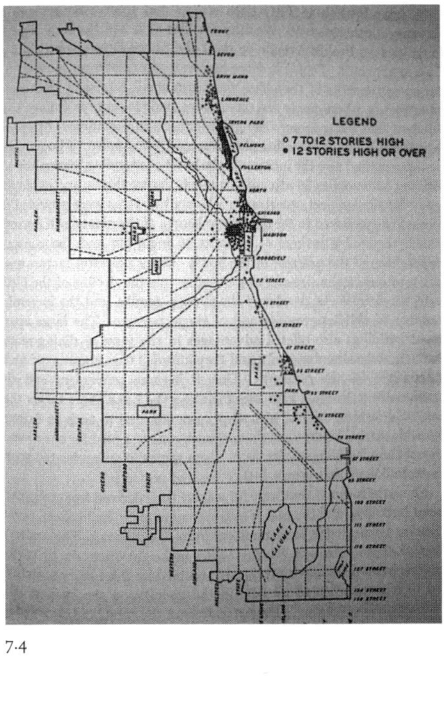

7.4

The construction of Mies's postwar high rises coincided with the remaking of Chicago as a city oriented more toward consumption than manufacturing. While Chicago had suffered through the Depression like most other U.S. cities, in the postwar era it successfully remade itself as a contemporary urban center of service businesses and became a magnet for young professionals. Although Chicago had as much or more "urban renewal" as other cities, it also developed a variety of innovative architectural approaches to middle- and upper-class urban housing, a rarity in the postwar urban environment. A major force in this direction was Herbert Greenwald. He was not only the patron of Mies; he took advantage of the new federal "608" Program, which offered tax breaks to stimulate middle-class urban housing, and commissioned other architects to do similar projects at the same time. At 3100 Lake Shore Drive, Greenwald commissioned Richard Bennett of the firm of Loebl, Schlossmann & Bennett in 1948 to design buildings more luxurious than the experimental Mies projects. Greenwald chose its name, "the Darien," from a Keats sonnet in which the poet likens the vivid sense of Homer's *Iliad* conveyed in a new translation to the Spanish conquistadors' first view of the Pacific Ocean in Panama, "upon a peak in Darien" (fig. 7.5).[16] Bennett, who had taught at Yale between 1940 and 1946, took a completely different approach than

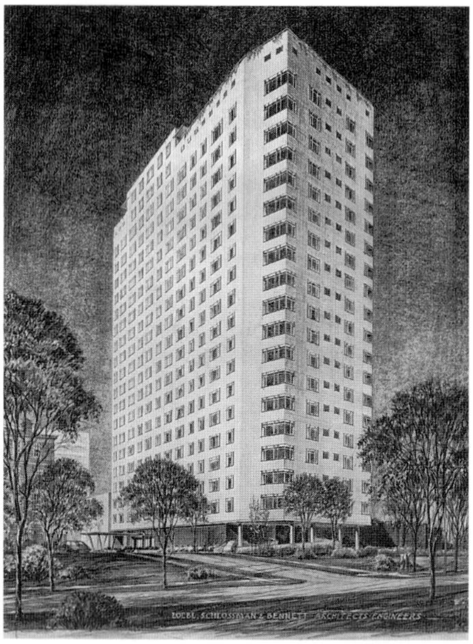

7.5

7.6

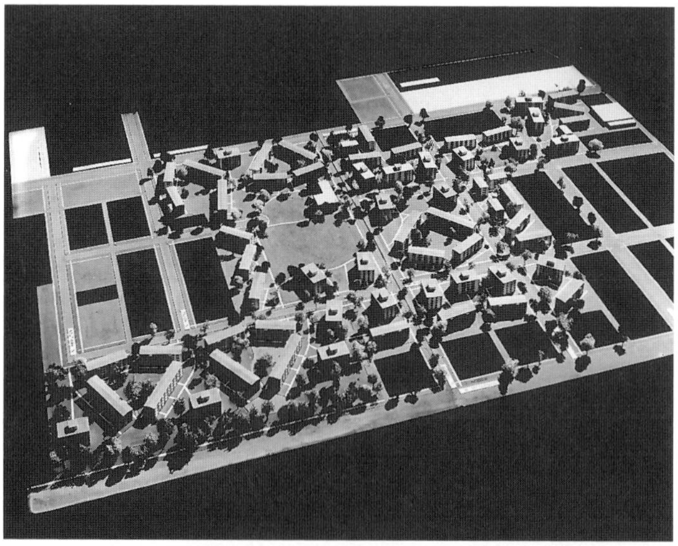

7.7

7.8

7.5 Loebl, Schlossmann & Bennett, the Darien, 3100 North Lake Shore Drive, 1948. Hedrich-Blessing Archive, HB 12339, courtesy of the Chicago Historical Society.

7.6 Loebl, Schlossmann & Bennett, 1350/1360 North Lake Shore Drive, 1948. Photograph by Eric Mumford.

7.7 Holsman, Holsman, Klekamp & Taylor, Winchester–Hood Garden Homes, 1823 West Granville and North Winchester streets, west of Ridge Avenue, 1949–51. Model photograph. Hedrich-Blessing Archive, HB 1318, courtesy of the Chicago Historical Society.

7.8 Holsman, Holsman, Klekamp & Taylor, Winchester–Hood Garden Homes, 1949–51. Photograph by Eric Mumford.

Mies. While the Promontory appears to be an east-facing slab building, it is actually a double T in plan, similar to many prewar high rises. The Darien, on the other hand, is a south-facing slab, one of the first slab apartment buildings in Chicago. While the facade remained a veneer of brick over a concrete frame, as in prewar buildings, the windows became the main patterning element on the exterior. On the north elevation some of the units farthest from the lake had angled Chicago windows, allowing views and introducing a new element into Chicago architecture evocative of the work of Alvar Aalto. The parking and lobby areas also became focuses of architectural attention, suggesting a building raised off the ground on columns as in Le Corbusier's Radiant City schemes. The affinities with Le Corbusier's contemporaneous projects for parklike cities of slab buildings are even clearer in Loebl, Schlossman and Bennett's 1350/1360 North Lake Shore Drive (1948), a pair of Darien-like slabs that replaced the Potter Palmer mansion on the Gold Coast, designed for the development firm of Draper and Kramer (fig. 7.6), and also using the angled windows.

All of these projects were underway as much of the Near South Side was being cleared and redeveloped with government funds and many new projects by the Chicago Housing Authority were being constructed there and elsewhere in Chicago. At all market levels ranging from subsidized public housing to luxury housing, projects were undertaken with the general idea that the city as it existed had to be rebuilt in a new form, one that did away with traditional pedestrian streets and elevated rail lines and replaced them with parklike open spaces, modern limited access highways, and ample parking. While the Chicago Public Housing Authority's projects continued in the same disastrous bureaucratic direction already evident before the war, now extended to high-rise projects, the firm of Holsman, Holsman, Klekamp & Taylor designed several good, large, low-rise superblock projects at the same time. These were based on the same principle of tenant cooperative ownership used by Greenwald at the Promontory Apartments, which had been the basis for buildings designed by the Holsman firm since the 1920s.[17] These were not public housing, but nonprofit, collectively owned, lower-middle-class housing, which paralleled similar efforts in Scandinavia. The projects included Parkway Gardens (1946), Winchester–Hood Garden Homes (1949–51; figs. 7.7, 7.8), and Lunt-Lake Apartments (1949–51). In 1950, they were described by a group of visiting British building industry representatives as the most interesting construction jobs they saw in the United States, although *Architectural Forum* noted the project's many design and construction innovations were "frowned upon by the FHA [Federal Housing Administration]." The Holsman projects were attempts to produce low-rise U.S. modern multifamily housing different from Mies's lakefront projects at a similarly low cost. Floor slabs, steel reinforcement, stair treads and risers, and window sills and trim were prefabricated to reduce costs, and site grading was used to reduce the number of steps in walk-up projects.[18] The projects' complex site plans, which arranged the buildings for good sunlight, and their large angled windows in precast frames set within rowlock bond brickwork, created a different image than the rigidity of either Mies's apartment projects or the bureaucratic blandness of most public housing at the time.

The work of Bennett and the Holsman firm, however, did not become the dominant one in postwar Chicago multifamily housing. In this sense, the second Chicago school myth became an accurate justifying story for postwar Chicago architecture, as firms such as Pace Associates, Skidmore, Owings & Merrill and others began to produce many Miesian projects in Chicago and around the world. In this environment the postwar work of Keck and Keck occupies an anomalous position, Miesian in some ways but also reflecting the brothers' independent and earlier acceptance of modernist ideas in housing. While much of the postwar housing work is not especially distinguished, their Prairie Avenue Courts (1951), a CHA housing project in the South Side urban renewal area, is among the better of such slab projects. It avoided monotony by providing a variety of buildings ranging from two-story row houses to seven- and fourteen-story slab buildings and a variety of unit types, from one to four bedrooms. Another Miesian direction in Chicago architecture of this time is the relatively little known work of Yau C. Wong, who had worked for Mies and who was responsible for the construction documents for the Farnsworth House. Wong looked to Mies's unbuilt courtyard house schemes of the 1930s as the source for such projects as his Atrium Homes (1959) in Hyde Park (fig. 7.9). These eight one-story, 1,500-square-foot, steel-frame houses arranged in two rows of four across a narrow pedestrian walkway are a rare U.S. example of a group of houses of this type. The 20' $\times$ 24' interior courtyards are surrounded on three sides by a band of building 15' deep, with the living and bedrooms facing the courtyard.[19] The eight middle-income owners jointly hired Wong as their architect, but each obtained mortgage financing individually. Despite the extensive urban renewal efforts in the area at the time, the project received no subsidies, and several banks rejected the mortgage applications because the design was not Colonial in style.[20]

In high-rise building and eventually other building types, a new, consciously anti-Miesian approach began to emerge in the work of Harry Weese in the early 1950s, another direction often obscured by the conventional Chicago school mythology. Weese, educated at MIT, Yale, and Cranbrook, was close to Eero Saarinen, the designer of the Gateway Arch in St. Louis and one of the most important American architects of the 1950s. Weese established his firm in Chicago in 1947 and was the first importer there of the furniture of Aalto and other Scandinavian designers. His brick and concrete frame apartment house at 227 East Walton (1954) is an early example of an effort to develop an American urban contextualism, one that uses floor-to-ceiling bay windows

7.9

7.9 Yau C. Wong, Atrium Homes, 1366–1380 East Madison Park, Hyde Park, 1959–61. Hedrich-Blessing Archive, HB 26576, courtesy of the Chicago Historical Society.

7.10 Harry Weese, 227 East Walton, 1954. Hedrich-Blessing Archive, HB 20073, courtesy of the Chicago Historical Society.

7.10

7.11

7.12

7.13

7.11 Harry Weese, Hyde Park row house, 1959. Weese archives, courtesy of Ben Weese.

7.12 Harry Weese with Ben Weese, 235 West Eugenie, 1962. Photograph by Eric Mumford.

7.13 George Schipporeit and John Heinrich, with landscaping by Alfred Caldwell, Lake Point Tower, 1965. Hedrich-Blessing Archive, HB 28204, courtesy of the Chicago Historical Society.

that refer to earlier Chicago buildings within the compositional strategies of mainstream modern architecture (fig. 7.10). In a little-known article published in 1958, "Housing Patterns and What Makes Them," Weese clearly set out the various urban housing options available, ranging from mobile homes and motels to row houses and high rises, and discussed the various code and political reasons why many of these were not being widely used in the United States.[21] Shortly after this Weese, in association with I. M. Pei and Loewenberg and Loewenberg, was given the opportunity to implement a new kind of contextual urban renewal in Hyde Park supported by the University of Chicago.

In this project, developed by William Zeckendorf, Weese and Pei pioneered the urban infill approach that would come to characterize Chicago building after the 1960s. In direct contrast to the clean-slate demolition of earlier urban renewal, Weese related his buildings to specific urban conditions and attempted to strengthen the existing prewar architectural fabric. The most popular units were the four types of row houses, whose simple brick facades pointed the way toward many later infill projects in both Hyde Park and on the Near North Side (fig. 7.11). Unlike Mies's or Wong's atrium houses, Weese revived the basic plan of traditional English and East Coast townhouses, placing the stairs on one side in houses ranging from 15'8" to 27' wide. Less successful were Pei's two more prominent slab buildings that were unconventionally positioned in the middle of East Fifty-fifth Street, a siting intended to reduce traffic speeds.[22] Not long after the Hyde Park row houses, Weese was also among the first postwar architects to design a contextual low-rise apartment house in the Old Town area of the North Side, 235 West Eugenie (1962; fig. 7.12),[23] and he and his younger brother Ben Weese continued to design various types of urban housing throughout their long careers.

Conclusion

While other Mies-influenced architects continued to extend the structurally oriented direction of the second Chicago school in the 1960s with such spectacular projects as Bertrand Goldberg's Marina City Towers (1960), George Schipporeit's and John Heinrich's Lake Point Tower (1965; fig. 7.13), and Skidmore, Owings & Merrill's John Hancock Tower (1969), the less visible and less well-known work of Richard Bennett, the Holsman firm, and Weese still has some relevance to conditions of practice in Chicago housing today. All three firms were concerned with the specific rather than the typical and attempted to adjust their projects to particular site conditions. Instead of heroic structural expression, they concentrated on the economical and intelligent use of materials and on the refinement of existing urban types to reflect changing attitudes about urban living. At the luxury Darien and 1350/1360 North Lake Shore Drive projects, Bennett inflected the brick slabs to respond to the buildings' sites and used angled windows to respond to the desire for lakefront views. At the Holsman firm's various low-rise mutual ownership apartment complexes, the architects used both unconventional site planning and new techniques of prefabrication to provide low-cost urban middle-class housing similar to European projects of the same era. In his many urban projects, Harry Weese developed an influential contextual approach to the existing city well before later postmodernist efforts while retaining a modernist's commitment to producing well-designed, inexpensive housing. By putting these projects back into Chicago's architectural history it is possible to begin to think about Chicago multifamily housing as more than Miesian, to better understand the various responses that emerged to the challenges posed by new technical and social conditions of the twentieth-century metropolis.

Selling Mies

David Dunster

Anyone trying to write about Ludwig Mies van der Rohe faces a hard task. He said little, wrote less, and has been surrounded by a coterie of devotees constantly defending him from all detractors. The purpose of this essay is not to attack Mies at all but to show that, as well as possessing a unique vision, he turned circumstances his way through an approach to his works that was flexible and accommodating. Thus in the first glass-walled high-rise apartments ever constructed, the buildings at 860/880 Lake Shore Drive in Chicago, Mies laid the buildings out to accommodate site constraints, kept costs to a very low per square foot price, and even gave in to objections about the apartment layouts. These are not the accommodations of a stone-faced egomaniac, but of an architect who could be both pragmatic and adaptable. Moreover Mies' approach to this speculative project was deeply sympathetic, and not at all doctrinaire. His defenders however see speculative as a term of abuse. For example:

Promontory was a speculative project whose design was determined largely by economic factors, and as a result many compromises had to be made.

With these words Phyllis Lambert dismisses extra-architectural factors from her excellent discussion of the first tower apartment buildings constructed by Mies van der Rohe in Chicago in the 2001 catalog, *Mies in America*.[1] In this respect, she follows in a long and distinguished tradition of architectural historical writing that treats canonical architects in a finite number of ways.[2] Historians, in discussing the work of architects, tend to focus on the evolution of forms, often merely acknowledging the technological and economic constraints. What buildings are made of and the architect of genius in question are issues that are often given priority over economics.

In the case of Mies, these economic criteria underpinned earlier statements of Mies that glass and steel were the materials of the twentieth century.[3] That glass and steel were to become one of the cheaper materials in a century of increased industrialization also meant that craftsmanship would be decreasingly necessary in the process of construction.

Within the conservative tradition of architectural history, however, what counts more is to show continuity and consistency within an oeuvre. This treatment would dispense with analysis of extraformal factors as mere contingency; its goal is to show how a work fits within a narrative of "capital A" architecture. Mies's best-known works, the Seagram Building in New York and the Farnsworth House in Plano, Illinois, were expensive in both cases at the behest of the client. This possible coincidence between esteem and expense can suggest that cheaper buildings were merely staging posts on the architect's road to the masterpieces preferred by historians of consistency and continuity.

In the epigraph above, three words signal factors—"speculative," "economic," and "compromise"—whose importance can be downplayed if not dismissed in architectural analysis. Equally doubtless, a formalist analysis should not be dismissed for the very reason that architects may sublimate nonformal factors to formal ones during the process of designing. In discussions of the process of design, however, architectural historians and theorists are stymied by the failure of the design methods movement of the 1960s to return to an urgent issue. During that period, nonformal factors were strongly promoted as facts, in the sense that Wittgenstein's philosophy abjures silence in the face of art, and much design resorted to nonformal factors through a crude functionalism. The form of this functionalism—the building looks like this because these were the only bricks/windows, and so on, that the architect could afford—is nothing other than a louche travesty of 1920s theories of functionalism in which the concept of form as function was always present. However, functionalism practiced in this way still produced formal dilemmas whose resolution was dependent on the lowest cost. At the back of Lambert's comment something like these arguments are doubtless present.

Herbert Greenwald, the young developer with whom Mies enjoyed such a fruitful relationship, was indeed a property developer involved, therefore, by definition, in speculation. As to the term "speculative" here it refers not to a branch of philosophy but to real estate development in which the occupants of the building are unknown at the time of design and construction. Lambert implies through her use of the pejorative sense of "speculative" that speculators are merely in the business of profit and that they entertain no high-minded ideal of civic responsibility. Applying this adjective involves subtle and often overly sophisticated differentiations. Herbert Greenwald indeed entered the real estate business because it seemed more lucrative than the other career he was contemplating, that of rabbinical scholar.[4] Greenwald's buildings were speculative. However, because he used Mies van der Rohe as an architect, and perhaps also because they reportedly enjoyed conversations of a philosophical tone, Greenwald cannot be lumped with those "speculators" whose eyes focused solely on the bank balance rather than on higher ideals. In Lambert's terms, while Greenwald had speculative tendencies—which is why she argues that the Promontory is not a great building—at 860/880 Lake Shore Drive the same developer, using the same architect, escapes her stricture. The cost of 860/880 appears only marginally more than the stigmatized Promontory.[5]

Once the building is completed and enters the public realm, the nonformal factors that were accommodated during the building process fade from memory except through the exegeses of architectural historians. Architects consistently downplay such factors in their own presentations, as if these details were exogenous to their reasoning, and historians thereby are forced to promote this notion of architecture as form-giving. In the instance of Mies van der Rohe, historians' interpretations of his works are furthered hindered by his gnomic cast, saying little and writing less. Even as brilliant an historian as Fritz Neumeyer struggles in *The Artless Word* to deduce the philosophical ground from which the taciturn one sprang.[6] Neumeyer's struggle reveals the extent to which historians are dependent on an architect's words for an interpretation of the works. While there is certainly some congruence between the words and the works, anyone with an acquaintance with Freud or Lacan would have trouble with this simplistic intentionalist fallacy.[7] Without going further into these dilemmas, this essay will explore factors other than Mies's continuing and largely internalized process that combined to produce those American works that changed the course of architecture globally. An analysis of these extraformal factors in no way diminishes the stature of Mies's work. On the contrary, his pragmatism and openness to such forces suggests that his "architecture of silence," produced under undoubted economic constraints, strived to avoid polar extremities. Neither the rabblerousing styling of emerging imperial capitalism nor the soi-disant critical architecture of those who would if they could sweep away the structures of power and wealth can be found in the works.

The 860/880 Lake Shore Drive project was speculative, designed within constraints imposed by the site, by market expectations, and by the difficulties of financing and sustaining such a project. The cultural climate within which the project was built should not be underestimated. Following the Great Depression of the thirties and the triumphs of World War II, Chicago appeared to grow out of its earlier downbeat image as, like Cincinnati, a pig city, a porkopolis, bereft of real (read European) culture. As late as 1953, A. J. Liebling attacked the midwestern barbarity of Chicago in his essay, calling it the "Second City."[8] Its reputation as the city that works, whatever the corruption, was well established through the succession of mayors from William Thomson, to Edward Kelly and Richard J. Daley. Boss politics, apparently defeated in New York, reigned supreme inland of the East Coast.[9] Despite the efforts of Daniel Burnham and Edward Bennett in their *Plan of Chicago* (1909), the city ignored many of their recommendations in the twenties when money was abundant. The exceptions were the construction of the Michigan Avenue Bridge, the widening of Pine Street to form Michigan Avenue north of the bridge, and the construction of the east-west section of Wacker Drive from the bridge to Lake Street. After the crash of 1929, tall building construction in Chicago slowed, then stopped. The year 1931 saw the completion of the YMCA,[10] financed by Victor Lawson, the last tall building in Chicago till the completion of 860/880 (1951) and the Prudential Building (1955). The New Deal, however, took off from 1933 with the construction of the Outer Drive, now Lake Shore Drive, and the construction of the subways beneath State and Dearborn streets.

The site upon which Greenwald and Mies constructed the Lake Shore Drive apartments had been in Lake Michigan until the water's edge was hardened during the 1930s by the construction of the Outer Drive. In particular, the area on the lake north of the river, a swamp known as Streeterville, benefited from the Outer Drive project.[11] The lakefront at Grant Park and to the south received more attention than the lakefront to the north prior to 1900. When Potter Palmer moved his family to Lake Shore Drive north of Oak Street in 1882, he ignited the development of the Gold Coast. Large houses were built between State Street and the Drive, while the very wealthy secured sites on the drive itself. What stopped the development south of Oak Street were three factors: the impending construction of the Michigan Avenue Bridge; the widening of Pine Street into Michigan Avenue north of the Loop; and the uncertain status of the land between the widened Pine Street and the lakefront. Events came to a head during and just after World War I. The bridge was completed in 1917, Pine Street widened just after, and squatters' claims to over 180 acres settled in 1920.[12] The lakefront at this point had been pushed east since 1833 to its current position by dumping debris, primarily rubble from the ruins of the Chicago Fire of 1871.[13] The area east of Michigan Avenue was boosted by the construction of Northwestern University Hospital from 1923[14] and the American Furniture Mart. The block between East Lake Shore Drive and Walton grew with apartment buildings of scale for those who could no longer afford a freestanding property in the area, which was now definitively bluebook. In 1920, before North Michigan Avenue had been widened, the Drake Hotel was opened at the corner of this block as the premier hotel of Chicago. Between Walton and Chestnut streets, the Lake Shore Club occupied the site opposite 860/880 in 1924.[15] Owned in large part by grand Chicago families, the McCormicks, the Fields, and the Fairbanks, the whole area grew significantly only during the boom years of the 1920s. Yet it appears from contemporary maps that the lots bounded by Lake Shore Drive and Walton and Chestnut were only built on in two places.

In the '40s and '50s, Chicago embraced modernism through European immigrants and American sponsors. Through the work of Robert Hutchins at the University of Chicago and Walter Paepke at the Container Corporation and the increasing influence of Mies upon Chicago architects, notably Skidmore, Owings & Merrill, Chicago became known, as much as New York, for its embrace of modern attitudes and culture. From its inception in 1916, the Arts Club of Chicago had hosted hard-line modernists and indeed commissioned Mies to convert a building for them that opened in 1951.[16] Through stores like Baldwin Kingrey, teaching initiatives like the Great Books program,[17] and the growth of advertising agencies like Leo Burnett,[18] a knowing and increasingly educated layer of society proved receptive to the products of European modernists, Aalto in furniture, Mies in apartments, and many in typography.[19] To these men and women, the opportunity to live in the Glass House (as 860/880 were dubbed by the local press) spoke of their radicalism in choosing the metropolis rather than the newest suburbs. At exactly the time when returning GIs were offered preferential mortgages in Chicago suburbs like Park Forest, the same costs could give them a place in 860/880. Park Forest involved serious commuting, and the newest version of the Jeffersonian dream sold within libertarian rhetoric; it was to become the locus classicus of William H. Whyte's critique of industrial society *Organization Man*, one of three works that tore apart the postwar dream.[20]

Herbert Greenwald's role as developer of 860/880, and that of his partner, Robert McCormick, in selling the buildings to the buying public emerge from pamphlets produced at the time and later. Initial brochures of the project contain conservative and austere graphics that suggest that a market for the spaces was already known to exist. Later invitations to occupy the buildings took a more elitist tone and also dropped the page-long description of the financial arrangements in the first brochure. While the apartments sold so well that all involved were surprised, they were out of the price range of those working in the office of Mies. Mies, Greenwald, and Genther (the architect-partner of the executive architects, PACE) considered moving in though Mies eventually sold off his options due to cash flow problems in the office. Success encouraged Greenwald to extend the project north to 900/910 Lake Shore Drive, the site for the Esplanade. Crucial to the marketing drive were two things: first, the role of the seven-foot-high model made with bronze mullions (a prefiguration of the facade of Mies's Seagram Building in New York, perhaps) constructed by Ed Duckett[21] and exhibited in a shop window on Michigan Avenue.[22] The second crucial element in the marketing drive was the construction site itself, located, as were most of Greenwald's Chicago projects, adjacent to Lake Shore Drive (north and south), the six-lane New Deal highway that transported commuters between the Loop and the prosperous northern suburbs. The speed of construction and its high visibility contributed to sales. Also contributing to sales was the fact that the site was in a developing area only a few hundred feet from the most expensive and hence prestigious interwar apartment buildings in Chicago—the rich cliff of East Lake Shore Drive.

On Sunday, November 4, 1951, the *Chicago Tribune* ran a full-page story by Edward Barry entitled "People *Do* Live in Glass Houses." This nickname, the "Glass House," took hold such that an eight-page promotional booklet published by the buildings' tenant-owners association in 1957 advertised the buildings using that term. The subtitle of the booklet was "860–880 Lake Shore Drive: A Home for Gracious Living." Inside, the fourth paragraph specified who could call this home. "The 860–880 buildings are now fully occupied by a carefully selected group of tenant-owners. Business executives, attorneys, architects, physicians, and members of many other distinguished professions enjoy the privileges of Glass House living."

It appears that Greenwald selected his sites according to a formula. All his apartment buildings in Chicago—the Promontory, the Algonquin, 860/880 Lake Shore Drive, the Esplanade, the Commonwealth, and the Fullerton—were in close proximity to Lake Michigan, all were located to the edge of already well-established neighborhoods, all were twenty-six stories tall, and none were especially close to the "L." Greenwald's pioneering therefore resides entirely in his choice of architect and in the construction method and planning that the architect had made his own. Certainly, Greenwald's developments elsewhere—Lafayette Park in Detroit; Pavilion and Colonnade Apartments in Newark, New Jersey; and Dominion Square, Montreal—were erected on more complex and inland sites, but in the 1940s and '50s Greenwald changed only one variable within the developer's formula: open-plan apartments in fully glazed towers.

An appealing financing arrangement allowed occupants to pay around $100 per month including hot water, heating, and security, and maintenance, but excluding a garage space. The method was the work of the architects and heating engineers Holsman, Holsman, Klekamp & Taylor, the elder Holsman having been involved since phase one of the Frances Cabrini project, which dealt with design and financing. During his university days Greenwald had also been involved with the public housing project, the River Forest Garden Apartments.[23] The published leaflet for 860/880 (figs. 8.1–8.2) explains lease applications, monthly costs, building management, and the tenant's role as a certificate owner. The text reads:

At the time you apply for an apartment (represented by a Certificate of Beneficial Interest in the Trust) you apply for a lease. Three trustees represent the tenants who participate in the Mutual ownership Plan. All leases must be approved by the Trustees since it is of benefit to all tenants to maintain high standards of tenancy. Your lease when accepted is continuous at your option and cannot be canceled except for cause. Your lease will call for a monthly rental computed at prevailing market rates, LESS THE SAVINGS ACCRUING TO YOU AS AN OWNER AND AS A TAX PAYER. The rental you pay will depend upon the size and location of the apartment you choose. You will, thereby, obtain the maximum in rental value together with an increase in your membership equity each and every month.[24]

Thus a two-part agreement—the certificate of beneficial interest and the separate lease—allowed Greenwald to escape the problem of high costs while requiring the then normal 50 percent down payment. He had used it at the Promontory and Algonquin buildings. It mitigated the Depression's catastrophic effect on high-/medium-rise apart-

8.1

8.1 Marketing brochure for 860/880 Lake Shore Drive, 1957, front cover.

8.2 Marketing brochure, 5.

As the Glass House is a building that "welcomes the present and assimilates the past" in organic structure, its apartments provide a background in which contemporary and traditional furnishings are equally at home.

In the 6-room apartment (top right), floor-to-ceiling picture windows give a breath-taking view of the Lake, while, indoors, veined mirrors reflect a modern setting of elegant simplicity and decor in the mood of the Southwest.

Photograph: Courtesy Tenant-Owner

The masterful combination of distinctive furnishings, richly textured fabrics, rare wood paneling—and a panoramic urban view—offer an invitation to ease and enjoyment in the handsome living room of a 6-room apartment.

Photograph: Courtesy Tenant-Owner

Photograph: Laurence

Rare and treasured pieces often lend drama to Glass House interiors. Above, antique bronze, sconces with exquisite amethyst, baccarat crystal pendants find an appropriate "home" above a piano.

Furniture with a "see-through" appearance, glass-topped tables, light plastic chairs, sofas with slim, tapering legs, gossamer-like draperies help to create an air of unusual spaciousness in this 3½-room apartment, (right). The handsome clear plastic screen, designed by Angelo Testa, is strikingly patterned in black, gold and white, which further accentuates the spacious effect.

Photograph: Idaka

In the 6-room apartment (top right), floor-to-ceiling picture windows give a breath-taking view of the Lake, while, indoors, veined mirrors reflect a modern setting of elegant simplicity and decor in the mood of the Southwest.

Photograph: Courtesy Tenant-Owner

8.2

ment buildings, whereby vacancies resulted in the bankruptcy of the entire building. In order to keep the down payments on a par with suburban homes, Greenwald was also constrained to make 860/880 as cheap to build as possible—around ten dollars per square foot—which was accepted by Mies without question.[25]

Raising money for 860/880 proved especially tricky despite the support of car-dealer Samuel Katzin,[26] with Greenwald at one point paying Mies a minuscule 2 percent design fee in promissory notes (which bounced).[27] McCormick told a story at a seminar in 1980 of failing to find finance in Chicago and New York.[28] Finally Greenwald and Katzin hit upon an insurance company in Cincinnati whose chief executive tested the idea of floor-to-ceiling glazing by taking his wife and daughter to the top of the Allerton Hotel and observing their lack of concern sitting next to the full-height glazing there. It was precisely this feature that frightened other backers, yet within a few years Greenwald and McCormick were promoting the buildings as the "Glass House." In passing it might be worth noting that 860/880 set a pattern for fully glazed apartment buildings in Chicago visible in Montreal, Toronto, and Newark, but which never proved as popular in New York City or most other East Coast cities. In terms of the apartment layouts, McCormick's father refused plans that showed bedrooms on the corners of the buildings, and the Mies office then reworked the layouts, causing the corridors to be lengthened from their more economical early layout.[29] Within the first year of occupation, apartments were already being converted, some by Mies's office, some by others.[30]

Marketing the buildings appears to have been carried out in a subdued and unostentatious fashion. By contrast, as suburbs like Park Forest were under construction, advertising in the Chicago papers was plentiful and exuberant. Not only was price emphasized in these advertisements for suburban homes, but the virtues of family and community were also promoted. The houses that were constructed stretched no imaginations and demanded little alteration in preexisting lifestyles. Hugely successful commercially, Park Forest sits directly within the tradition of suburban buildings.[31] Indeed, the very name conflates settler tradition (*forest*, but also referring no doubt to the wealthiest Chicago suburb, Lake Forest) and civilization, even urbanity in the term *park*. The partial subject of the excoriations of Whyte,[32] Park Forest supplied an almost expressed need and benefited hugely from federal support to returning servicemen. The so-called GI Bill can now be interpreted as a charter to expand suburbs because of the terms in which it offered subsidies to such developments while excluding similar subsidies to urban construction or conversions. Noteworthy too are exclusions of support to black people. In overall respect, however, the solution to the lack of housing was couched in antiurban terms; to discuss the creation of suburbs as if forces were in play of a deeper psychological nature would ignore the evolutionary character of what suburban builders proposed.

Not so Greenwald. His first developments had been close to the University of Chicago, where he studied. Robert Hutchins, president of the university, wanted cheap accommodation for his younger faculty,[33] which had increased due to the postwar bulge of student GIs returning from war armed with university access privileges.[34] Greenwald recognized this market, and the Promontory was his first project to satisfy the university's requirements. Following quickly on its success[35] came the Algonquin buildings designed more by PACE than by Mies, and then the move to North Lake Shore Drive.

What convinced Greenwald to go into partnership with McCormick at 860? Financially, the fact that the McCormick family already owned half the site and that he had found a further financial partner in Katzin. No extensive market research was carried out. Nor were the opinions of real estate men sought—McCormick himself acted as the letting agent. Clearly a substantial market was perceived: a different kind of market than that for Park Forest. Recognizing that the immediate postwar period would become a boom time for residential construction explains only in part the attractions of 860/880. Without doubt the buildings were novel, even experimental. This fact might attract young architects who were returning home; others who might also be attracted were those European immigrants who had already experienced the benefits of apartment living in Berlin, Zurich, or Warsaw.

At this point the character of the buildings, their promise and their threats, merits discussion. If there has been an enigma surrounding the work of Mies, some parameters of the mystery might lie in the formal characteristics of his work. The Smithsons enthused over the control they found in his work, the ways in which technologies were subordinate.[36] The buildings lacked the specific expressiveness that functionalism and classicism might lead an observer to expect. No concessions were made in the undifferentiated grids of the facades as they had been in the Promontory block, to expressing through the size of windows, the kinds of functions which might lay behind the surface. To look at 860/880 no one could sense that one building contained larger apartments than the other did. This aspect later drew adverse comment.[37] Into this anonymity of the facade, prospective tenants therefore had to read themselves, or better had to find a space which attracted them despite its emptiness. Within each apartment, the blankness of the surfaces and their subtle interplay offered few suggestions as to how the apartments should be used; the brochures only hinted at this and no model apartment had been furnished for inspection. Illustrations in a later brochure pictured ways in which older furniture and knickknacks could coexist, but tenants had to discover this for themselves. Would it therefore be too much to suggest that what the buildings offered was an adventure on the theme of home? Despite the still-prevailing idea that a home should satisfy a preconceived desire, these apartments by themselves, ignoring location, value-for-money, and taste, could not by their very nature do this. Instead of providing a comforting promise of normality they offered an unconventional challenge to the very idea of making a home, a family, or a community. The corollary to the urban apartment was the house in the country, a fantasy satirized to great popular acclaim in the novel *Mr. Blandings Builds His Dream House.*[38] In this sense they were structures awaiting inhabitation. If they succeeded, therefore, it was because living there was the antithesis of the advertised American Dream.

The 860/880 apartments were thus constructed and marketed within a situation new to the United States, emerging from the gloom of the Depression and World War II, in a city whose identity excited immigrants yet needed to distance itself from New York. The buildings were built extremely economically, without the air conditioning or added elevators Mies had desired, and sold using a new and affordable financial technique. Greenwald himself from inclination and education tried other architects—Epstein's office, PACE, and Loebl Schlossman, but settled on Mies for reasons that are generally agreed to be a combination of taste and temperament. Mies had come highly recommended by Walter Gropius, had already completed the Promontory apartments for Greenwald, which was a financial success, and had enjoyed a recent one-man show at the Museum of Modern Art in 1947. Greenwald employed Mies at the height of his powers and his office staff at their youngest and most enthusiastic. Through his tenure at the Illinois Institute of Technology, Mies was becoming a figure to the city's press.[39] Together with people interested in modernism in Chicago, the components for a successful project were virtually all in place. That two buildings were proposed by Mies instead of one block is entirely due to divided ownership of the site between the McCormicks and Northwestern University, who happily agreed to the project provided that the site included a view corridor to enable them to construct on their land back of the lake a future apartment building that could boast a lake view. Greenwald's choice of site, typical of his Chicago works, allowed location to do most of the work. Mies's incredibly subtle site planning, the equal of his peers Le Corbusier and Aalto, finally abandoned classical symmetry to contribute significantly to urban development patterns.

9 Inside Mies: Living at 860/880 Lake Shore Drive

Janet Abrams

9.1 Lake Michigan windswept, view from 880 Lake Shore Drive, apartment 22A, 1992. All photographs for this essay © Janet Abrams.

As soon as I stepped inside the apartment, I was a convert. Not that I wasn't already a Mies admirer in the standard architecture school–indoctrinated mold, but this really was different. The impression of these buildings from the outside—from down below, ground level, looking up—is so tight-lipped and parsimonious compared with what lies in store when you open the front door of an individual unit. Particularly in the A tier of apartments looking northeast out over . . . the Beast (fig. 9.1).

I guess it might not be Mies's architecture I fell for, after all, but the lake. The lapping, sometimes growling, all-enveloping creature that lies outside the apartment's windows, expanding my mere eight hundred square feet to infinity. A curiously metamorphic pet, Lake Michigan, whose mood swings are gauged by chameleon changes of surface texture and hue (fig. 9.2). No question but that it is alive. Mies simply had the audacity to domesticate it by creating residential cells that perch like boxes at the opera, a permanent best seat in the house over an ever-changing spectacle. High up, you get a view that ought to be earned only by scaling a cliff, but since the terrain in Chicago is inexorably flat, man stepped in to supply the vantage nature inadvertently forgot (fig. 9.3).

At a certain height, the curve of Lake Shore Drive remains invisible (so sheer is the vertical perspective) until you're standing quite close to the glazed window-walls, looking down. So the water appears—for all intents and purposes—to flow right up to one's floor level. Dinner-cruise boats blithely emerge from the baseboard like slow, dumb beetles; water-skiers casually zoom toward that threshold and summarily disappear. On bright blue Sundays, white sails dot the surface like tiny pocket handkerchiefs or neatly folded serviettes. It's a bit like being on board a ship except that there's no rocking motion and no smell of bilge, apart from those summer days when dead fish get washed up and you have to shut the windows.

The windows, ah, the windows.

Everything that's magic about these buildings (860 and 880 Lake Shore Drive, built between 1948 and 1951, and to a great extent, their "younger" cousins just north, 900 and 910) emanates from the windows. Of course, this is a perverse reading of Mies, so renowned for his relentless celebration of the structural grid, the details of the steel-framed skyscraper. But living here, being on the inside looking out, what captures your attention is not the frame itself, but what's visible through it—a gestalt switcheroo (figs. 9.4, 9.5, 9.6).

What other apartment building makes you want to strip off all your clothes and dance around stark naked as soon as you've shut the front door? There's something distinctly

9.2

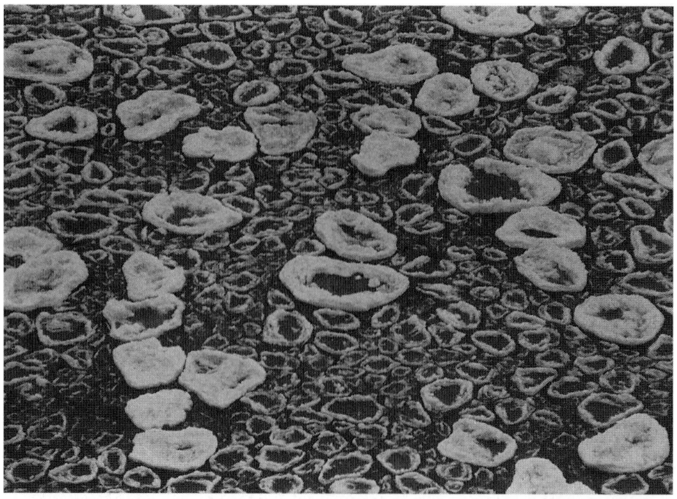

9.4

erotic about all that glazing—the sense of exposure and the proximity to the elements, while being securely "at home" and discreetly out of sight. Nakedness seems the appropriate mode when you're so architecturally "unclad." Nobody tells you, at school, that Mies was a raving scopophiliac. But he must have been. For these buildings are all about viewing and being viewed. (The exhibitionist's idyll is occasionally enhanced by the surprise arrival of the window-cleaning gantry, whose ropes are usually visible outside one or another window, tethered to lampposts down below.)

I love the iceberg glow of the ground floor by night. Management offices, delivery quarters, and mailrooms are all discreetly concealed behind opalescent glass, a core recessed under the body of the building, nestling within the black-painted grid of columns, and illuminated from within. Something sweet and reassuring about that nocturnal glow, decorative in an understated way; an effusion of light under dark crystals, protruding into the night sky; the fire below the rocket just before launch.

You have to make an effort to get inside, even if 880 is your rightful address. Air pressure is a ubiquitous adversary, an invisible but palpable force—whether you're outside struggling to cross the wind-lashed steppes of the podium to the revolving door or, once inside, tugging on doors that resist all normal effort, thanks to internal pressure differentials. Or un-

9.2 Ice "corpuscles" form on the surface of frozen Lake Michigan, February 16, 1992.

9.3 Twilight view up the coast, 1992.

9.4 Ice floes on Lake Michigan, reflected in the windows of 900 Lake Shore Drive, February 16, 1992.

9.5 Twilight view down Lake Shore Drive towards Lake Point Tower, 1992.

9.6 Awash in morning light, the living room at 880 Lake Shore Drive #22A seems to float on Lake Michigan, whose blue waters appear to reach mid-window level.

9.7 Shadows on the drive, 880 and 900 Lake Shore Drive, spring 1992.

9.3

9.5

9.6

9.7

9.8

9.8 Lake Shore Drive traffic superimposed on Lake Michigan: reflections in the window of 880 Lake Shore Drive, apartment 22A, winter 1991–92.

9.9 "Rear Window"—night view of 900 Lake Shore Drive, from bedroom of 880 Lake Shore Drive, apartment 22A reflected in window, 1992.

9.9

latching hopper windows that suddenly hiss and whistle with the Bernoulli effect of a narrow aperture and then, opened a few more millimeters, gust in toward you, delivering a yard of framed glass into your open-armed embrace with nothing (besides a bug screen) between you and the No Parking sign painted in yellow on the curb twenty-two stories below (fig. 9.7).

The tourist down there, leaning backward, trying to frame a canonic view, most likely doesn't register more than the most obvious differences between 860/880 and their younger neighbors. But living here, all sorts of subtle variations make their presence felt: the greater ceiling height, the grid dimensions, the crudeness of the hardware, the fact that no floor-level heating/cooling units block theview. While 900 and 910 have automatic doors that swing open with a characteristic suctiony click at the touch of the doorman's magic button, 860 and 880 are from a more primitive era, all the more authentic in their vintage idiosyncrasies.

In the freight elevator the kick plate declares, reassuringly, "Montgomery Dependable elevators" while the floor-scoreboard is resolutely pre-electronic (backlit translucent numerals in a simple metal plate) and the emergency telephones are the kind of bakelite relics that design magazines once resuscitated for yuppie special offers. Meanwhile, the more orthodox Miesian denizens cherish the suburban blue and orange decor in their tiled bathrooms and gladly put up with work surface–less kitchens where original metal cabinets, in white enamel, proudly bear the Hotpoint brand name. Riding in the curved-corner capsule of the passenger elevator, sad notices periodically announce that "Tenant-Owner X in Apartment Y passed away . . . Memorial Service to be held . . ."—reminders that many of the occupants are venerable creatures themselves, including quite a handful of residents who moved in when the buildings were brand new.

When the morning sun scatters a shoal of golden coins across the lake's placid surface, the air in east-facing apartments gets hot and fluffy and the building audibly "stretches"—creaks that lead invariably to cracks and judicious relocation of one's paintings. You feel all the more like you're on a galleon, high up in the rigging, when the wind lashes and the rain smashes and the snow hurtles past (fig. 9.8) so fast that the place stays bright all night. There is only a few millimeters' protection from the raw elements, just one pane thick, because double-glazing wasn't yet "in." For Christmas, my landlord gave me an ice scraper for the *inside*.

At night, 900 and 860 Lake Shore Drive turn into mesmerizing punch cards, random patches of illumination picked out against the black (fig. 9.9). Mostly the light that seeps out is a kind of amber, or the reflected, flickery blue of the TV screen—a palette

9.10 View of 900 Lake Shore Drive, from 880 Lake Shore Drive, apartment 22A, 1992.

strangely similar to color reproduction in fifties magazines. A table lamp seen glowing one moment will have disappeared the next, extinguished by an invisible hand. Silhouetted figures reach up to garland their windows with holiday lights, caught in a seasonal gesture like characters in a George Segal sculpture. Le Corbusier chaise longues and Mies Barcelona chairs are, seemingly, everywhere, but here and there one spies decor more *retardataire*: chandeliers, gilt-framed pictures on bull's blood walls, *comfy* as opposed to *modern* furniture.

What's so gripping is the sheer miscellany that lurks in these adjacent and, from without, apparently identical cells. Behind the uniform wooden doors along utilitarian gray corridors lies a cacophony of color and tchotchkes and hyperactive houseplants (fig. 9.10).

Like Dave Brubeck's *Take Five* and drip-dry shirts, the Mies apartments belong in my pantheon of mythical Americana, talismans of the huge place across the ocean, a land of meteorological extremes and things quintessentially modern. No matter that they were designed by an émigré German architect; these buildings—especially in their siting—are echt American.

One grows accustomed to encountering architectural landmarks as fossilized specimens of a received history, open alternate Tuesdays, docent provided. When one turns the last corner and sets sight upon the archetype, it's often a letdown. Superimpose a long-cherished fantasy upon an actual place, and illusions are bound to be shattered. So it's a delight to find that not only do the Lake Shore Drive apartments still exist but also that normal people continue to live in them. To come to Chicago no longer a tourist but as a resident and find a home at 880 is to enjoy a rare instance of congruence between the America of my imagination and the modernist idyll of common architectural consensus.

2

Alternatives

10.1 (Opposite) *Grey Sky [Window]*, oil on canvas, 28" × 27", 1993. Private collection; copyright Julia Fish. Photograph by Tom Van Eynde.

1614 North Hermitage Avenue: Painting as Inscription

Julia Fish

In a sequence of works that extended to twenty-nine paintings, begun in 1992 and continuing to 2001, I recorded the experience of looking and living within the space of my home and garden at 1614 North Hermitage Avenue. Step by step, one painting at a time, my attention turned to the visual evidence and structural configurations that indicate this building's history: a brick two-flat storefront that nudges the sidewalk, as a storefront should.[1]

Individually, the paintings re-present the tangible evidence of floors, walls, and windows at one-to-one scale, oriented by point of view, either through the use of a deliberate, slight perspective in relationship to the given subject, or an examination of the paradox of spatial illusion. Collectively, the paintings function as archive: translating the significance of touch, scale, and workmanship characteristic of Chicago's working-class houses and storefronts typical of that time. Irregularities found within the predictable structures and surfaces are key to the history represented here; they signal meaning and condition memory through repeated experience of a specific domestic site and offer an opportunity to reconsider history through the inscription of the painted image.

10.2 *Roof Window,* oil on canvas, 20" × 23", 1995. Private collection; copyright Julia Fish. Photograph by Tom Van Eynde.

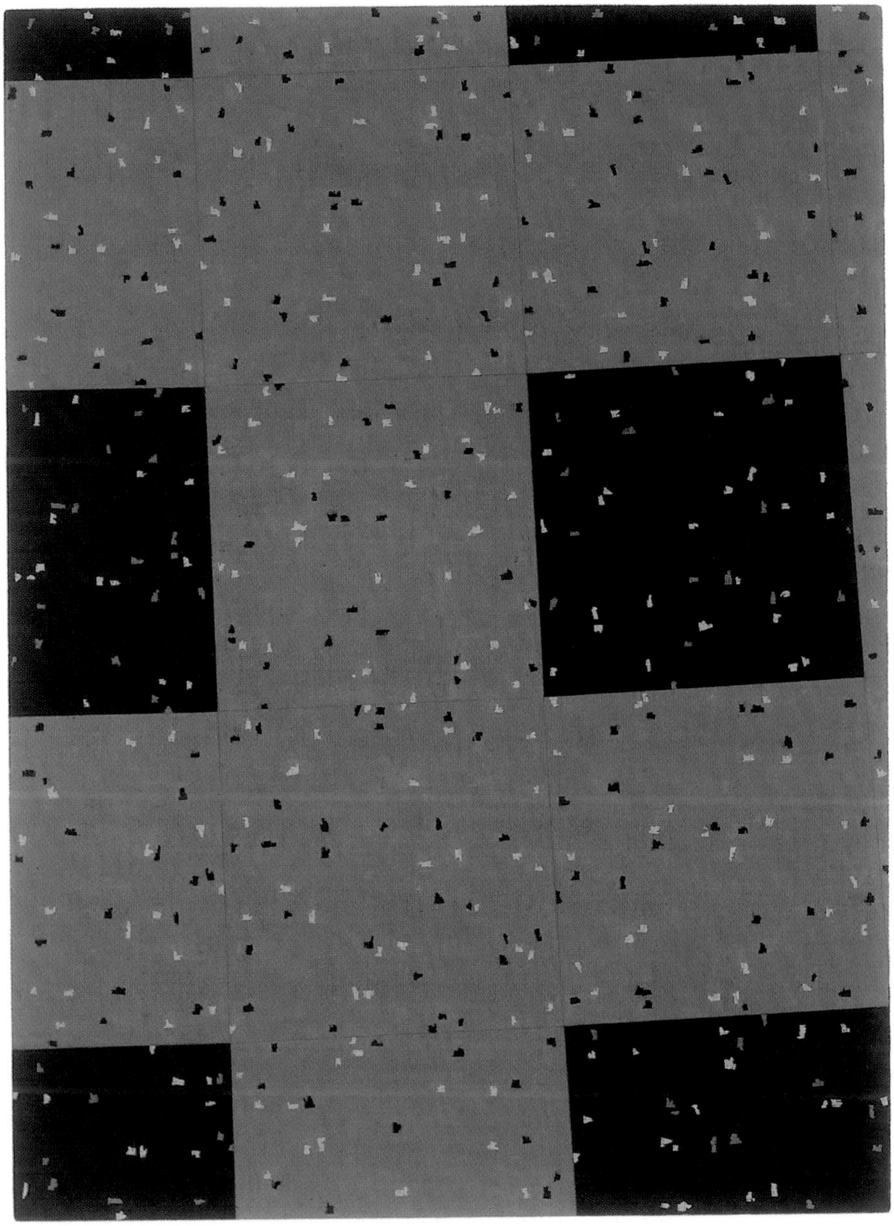

10.3 *Floor II,* oil on canvas, 43" × 32", 1994. Private collection; copyright Julia Fish. Photograph by Tom Van Eynde.

10.4 *Floor,* oil on canvas, 29" × 27", 1993. Private collection; copyright Julia Fish. Photograph by Tom Van Eynde.

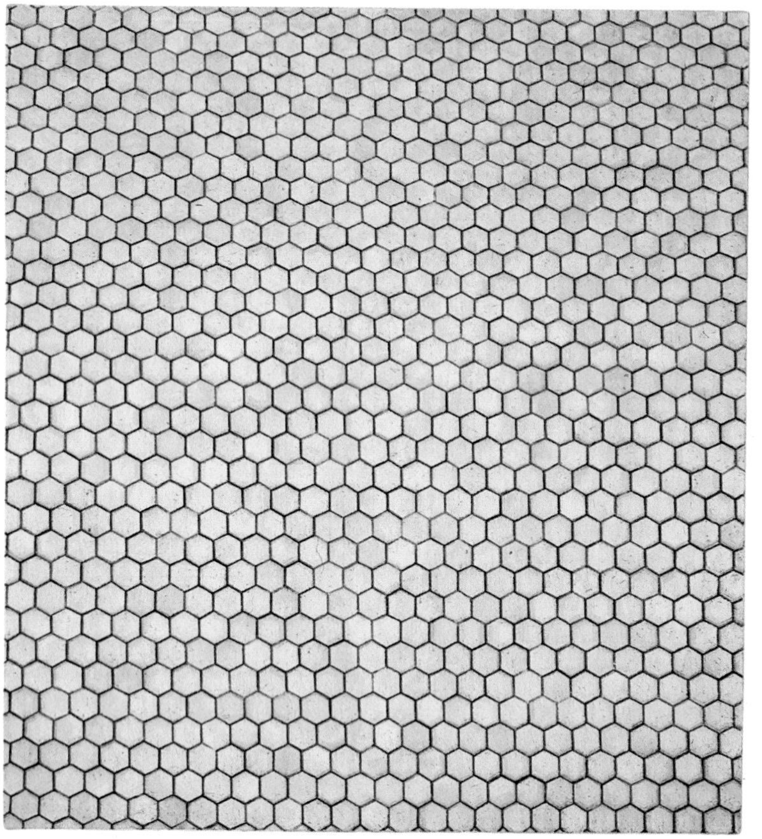

10.5 *Siding*, oil on canvas, 44" × 42", 1994. Private collection; copyright Julia Fish. Photograph by Tom Van Eynde.

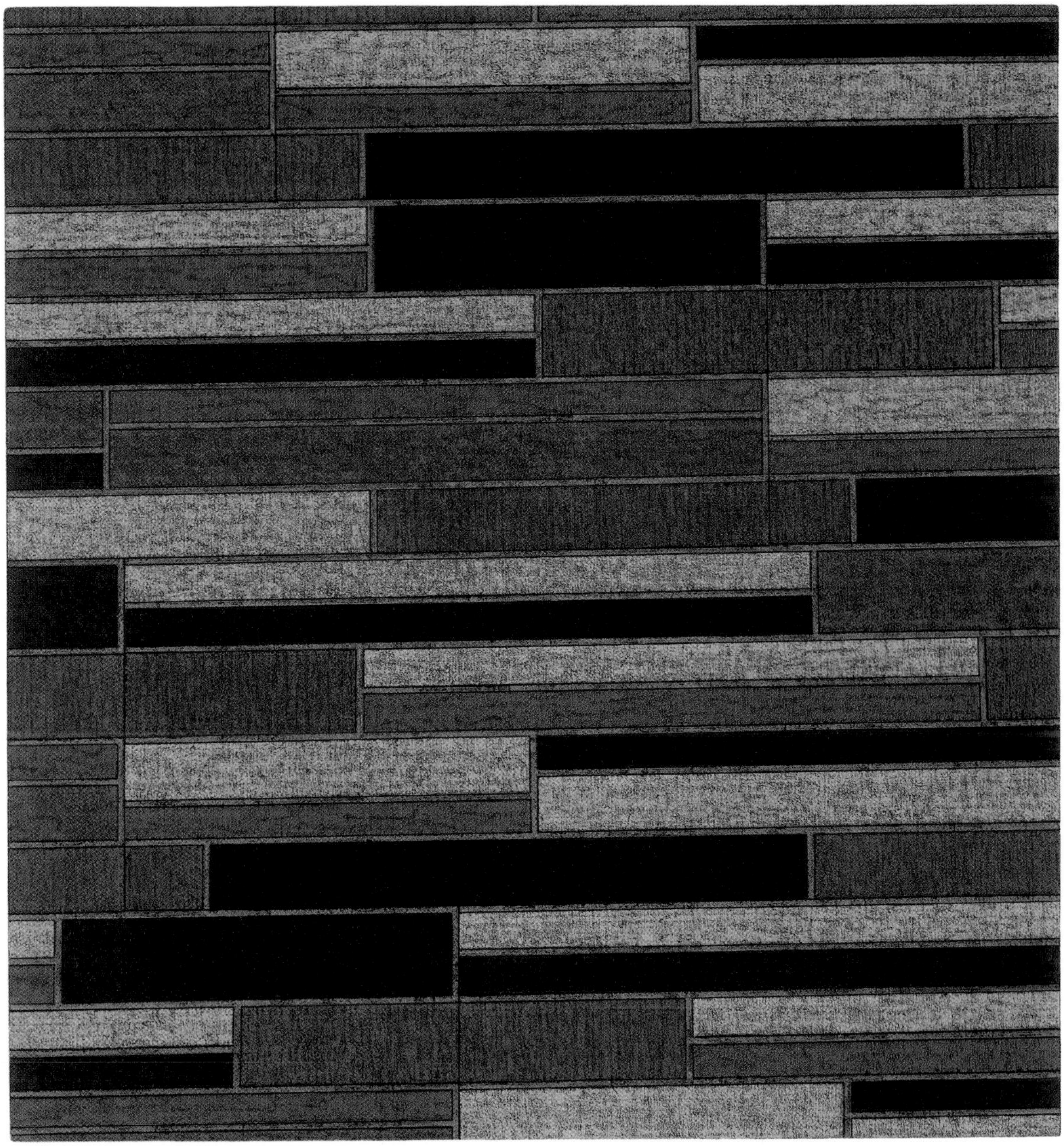

10.6 *Bricks and Siding, North Wall,* oil on canvas, 37" × 36", 1997. Collection of the artist; copyright Julia Fish. Photograph by Tom Van Eynde.

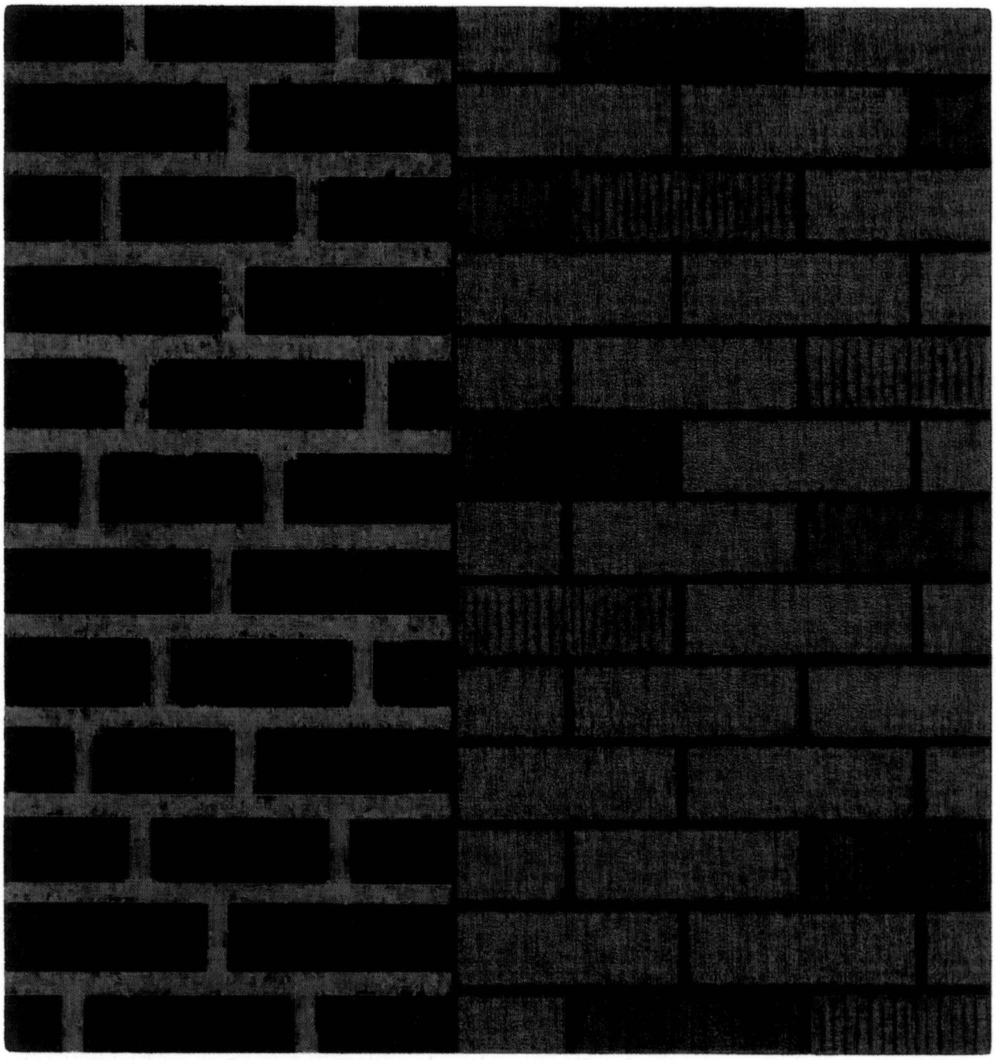

10.7 *Bricks and Siding, South Wall,* oil on canvas, 37" × 36", 1997. Collection of the artist; copyright Julia Fish. Photograph by Tom Van Eynde.

10.8 *Vines Wall,* oil on canvas, 30" × 29", 1995. Private collection; copyright Julia Fish. Photograph by Tom Van Eynde.

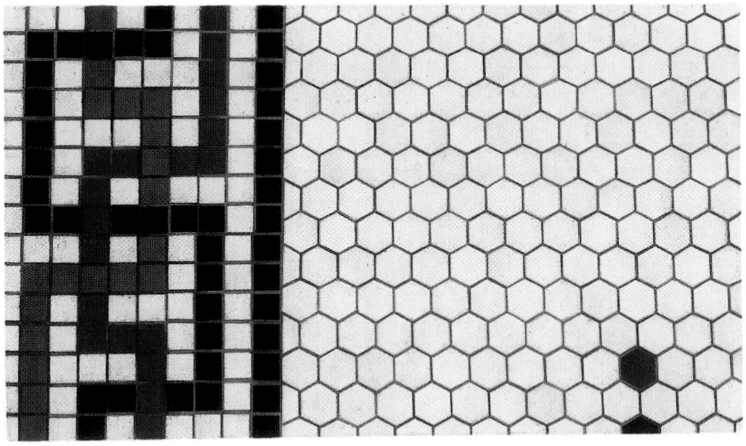

10.9 *Entry [Fragment One],* oil on canvas, 11.5" × 20", 1998. Private collection; copyright Julia Fish. Photograph by Tom Van Eynde.

10.10 *Entry [Fragment Two]*, oil on canvas, 17.25" × 16", 1998. Collection of the artist; copyright Julia Fish. Photograph by Tom Van Eynde.

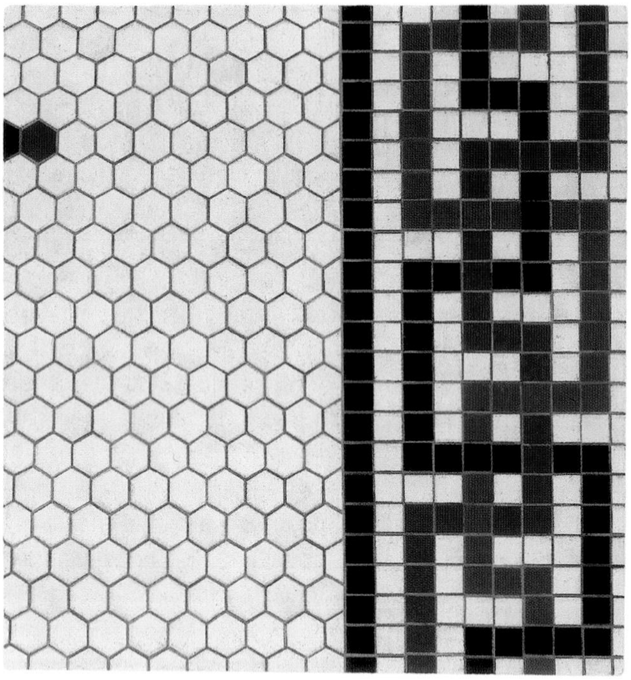

10.11 *[Drawing for] Living Rooms, North—two,* gouache on paper, 25" × 22.5", 2002. Private collection; copyright Julia Fish. Photograph by Tom Van Eynde.

10.12 *[Drawing for] Living Rooms, SouthEast—two,* gouache on paper, 25" × 22.5", 2002. Private collection; copyright Julia Fish. Photograph by Tom Van Eynde.

10.13 1614 N. Hermitage Avenue, 2002. Photograph by Julia Fish.

Notes to the Images

All paintings in oil on canvas translate information at essentially one-to-one scale. *Grey Sky* (fig. 10.1) and *Roof Window* (fig. 10.2) are specific to the dimensions of the pane of glass in south- and north-facing windows. *Floor II* (fig. 10.3) and *Floor* (fig. 10.4) reflect tile measurements at one-to-one scale in the lower register of each canvas. *Siding* (fig. 10.5) depicts a section of the exterior west wall, surfaced with Sears, Roebuck and Company Ranch Stone pattern asphalt siding, first available in 1954. *Bricks and Siding, North Wall* (fig. 10.6) and *Bricks and Siding, South Wall* (fig. 10.7) are one work in two parts, based on identically positioned north and south exterior surfaces of juxtaposed common brick and asphalt siding material; the north wall retains the 1940s Sears, Roebuck asphalt brick siding. *Vines Wall* (fig. 10.8) presents an image of the original garage exterior wall and wintered vines, currently the author's studio. *Entry [Fragment One]* (fig. 10.9) and *Entry [Fragment Two]* (fig. 10.10) are two of four excerpts, oriented as south and north fragments, from the entryway floor. Based upon the plan of the second-floor apartment, the gouache on paper *[Drawing for] Living Rooms, North—two* (fig. 10.11), and *[Drawing for] Living Rooms, SouthEast—two* (fig. 10.12), articulate two of ten rooms and adjoining threshold spaces, oriented on the page as either south- or north-facing at a scale of 1:12 inches.

A Century of Progress: An Alternate Tale

Lee Bey

Architect W. T. Bailey, vacationing at Atlantic City's Hotel Traymore, wrote back home to officials of Chicago's 1933 Century of Progress World's Fair. Bailey's letter to J. C. Mannerood, the fair's assistant director of operations, praised organizers for the exposition's success. In the handwritten note, dated August 2, 1933, and written on hotel stationery, Bailey asks Mannerood to "send me some literature and colored prints" of the fair. Mannerood complied and said in his response: "I appreciate more than I can tell you your interest in our fair."

11.1 Walter Thomas Bailey, n.d. Courtesy of the University of Illinois Archives.

The architect's mannered request for fair trinkets was easy enough to honor. The Century of Progress's publicity machine churned out so many brochures and fair-related tschotchke that scores of it would routinely turn up in resale stores and auctions for the next seventy years. But fair organizers were not as accommodating in 1930, when Bailey pushed to create a Century of Progress pavilion designed to honor the advancement and achievement of the world's black people.

"Booths would show progress of all Africans and descendants," Bailey wrote in a February 12, 1930, letter to the world's fair planning committee. "We are very anxious to teach the world some of the interesting history of the Black People long before the first boat of slaves ever landed in this country." A progressive black exhibit would have been a natural for the 1933 World's Fair. Chicago was seen as the promised land for nearly a million southern migrants seeking to escape the Jim Crow South. The fair was held on Chicago's south lakefront, right on the eastern edge of Bronzeville, a city within a city that became a symbol of black political and economic achievement.

The fair committee's response to the black pavilion: "It does not strike me as offering much of interest and it contains elements of considerable danger," fair organizers wrote in an internal memo to the fair's Exhibits Department. Bailey's request was denied. Fair organizers turned down at least six major proposals and counterproposals to create a black-themed exhibit at the Century of Progress. They ultimately did allow—reluctantly, at first—a replica of Jean Baptist Pointe DuSable's log cabin. But the "Pygmy Village" and other exhibits that featured exploitative and stereotypical depictions of black people largely overshadowed the exhibit. The quest to create a black pavilion is an important part of a larger—and vastly unknown—story set in one of the greatest world's fairs of the twentieth century. Given the fair's international success, an exhibition of black progress and achievement would have—at a relatively early date—placed accomplishments of African descendants on par with their white counterparts.

The Century of Progress was held on more than four hundred acres of lakefront land between Roosevelt and Pershing Road. The fair operated two seasons from May 27,

1933, to October 31, 1934. What better place and time for a black world's fair pavilion than Chicago, 1933? The city had evolved into a promised land for southern black people searching for a new life free of the oppressive neoslavery shackles of Jim Crow legislation. Sharecroppers who had spent generations scratching out a backbreaking existence in the South began new and better lives as wage earners in Chicago's massive steel mills or the Union Stockyards. The more industrious could set up businesses and, if successful, skip the working-class stratum entirely and land among the black middle and upper classes who lived in fine graystones along Grand Boulevard and south Michigan Avenue.

Through racially restrictive covenants, the new arrivals—more than 300,000 by 1933—were largely confined to a patchwork of neighborhoods extending south of downtown. The self-contained city, nicknamed Bronzeville, boasted some of the worst slums in the North. But Bronzeville also contained the biggest black bank in the nation, Binga State Bank at Thirty-fifth and State Streets; the influential *Chicago Defender* newspaper, then located at Thirty-seventh and Indiana, and the North's richest company, Supreme Life Insurance at Thirty-fifth Street and South Parkway (now Martin Luther King Drive). Politically, the area elected the North's first black congressman, Oscar DePriest. Bronzeville launched the careers of jazz trumpeter Louis Armstrong and crusading journalist Ida B. Wells. Bronzeville hosted the mighty South Side NAACP, a branch whose power nearly rivaled that of the civil rights organization's headquarters.

This new and rapidly grown power seemed anxious to flex a little muscle in the early 1930s, and the fair was sizing up to be a good target. And why not? While the previous Chicago world's fair, the 1893 Columbian Exposition, was essentially an architectural and philosophical homage to old Europe, the Century of Progress was designed to celebrate advancement, with its modern, streamlined architecture and its emphasis on the future. The fair was designed to reveal the march of progress and give a glimpse of a better tomorrow. The theme would resonate strongly with black Americans—especially if a black–themed pavilion were built.

In the years leading up to the fair, the Chicago Urban League, the Southside NAACP, and the *Chicago Defender* and other black institutions protested school segregation, resisted racially restrictive covenants, and participated in successful pickets and boycotts of establishments that failed to hire African Americans. These organizations and the fledging black Chicago political establishment began campaigns to make sure African Americans were employed and represented at the fair. Most saw a black-themed exhibit as a crowning jewel of their efforts. Indeed, before the fair even opened, there were three major campaigns for a black exhibit.

11.2 DuSable Cabin, Century of Progress World's Fair. Photograph from "What Buildings Will Be Razed," *Chicago Herald-American Examiner* [Dec. 27, 1934]. Courtesy of the Century of Progress Records, folder 6-48, Department of Special Collections, the University Library, University of Illinois at Chicago.

The Chicago Urban League began advocating in 1928 for DuSable to be honored at the fair. The same year, the National DeSaible Memorial Society—the reasons behind the variant spelling of DuSable's name are not addressed in fair records—took up the cause that same year. The DeSaible Society was led by African American educator Annie E. Oliver. Fair organizers resisted the DeSaible effort for the next four years. But momentum behind it grew as it received the backing of more civic organizations and black professionals. Black structural engineer Charles Sumner Duke—the first black to receive a Harvard engineering degree and credited with the engineering of the Michigan Avenue bridge—loaned his talents to the effort. Oliver would ultimately appeal to the World's Fair president Rufus C. Dawes.

By 1930, Walter Thomas Bailey, a Duke acquaintance and collaborator—the two men would later create a future Chicago landmark, the art moderne–styled First Church of Deliverance at 4313 South Wabash—became interested in a black exhibit. Bailey himself was an example of African American progress. Born in Kewanee, Illinois, in 1882, he had been a star University of Illinois architecture student before becoming the state's first licensed black architect. His office was located in a building he designed: the National Pythian Temple at 3621 South State Street. Built in 1927, the temple building housed offices and the headquarters for the black Knights of Pythias fraternal order.

In the 1930 letter to the fair committee, Bailey envisioned a 75,000-square-foot pavilion "designed in the Egyptian Style of Architecture." He wanted a rectangular building with a central interior court with booths "showing the progress of all Africans and descendants." Black achievement in fields such as education, science, and economics would be heralded. Bailey suggested putting the pavilion between Thirty-first and Thirty-fifth streets along the lake. There the pavilion would be a critical physical link to Bronzeville.

Consider the early 1930s. There were no black studies courses; African American participation was largely ignored in history books and current events. Colonialists were carving up Africa like a freshly killed steer, while books and motion pictures depicted the conquered Africans as primitive, violent savages. To resist this—particularly in a city with a racial history as troubled as Chicago's—with a pavilion that would put black achievement on display before the world was astonishingly progressive; a move of black self-awareness that rivals the best of the civil rights movement thirty years later. The boldness of the plan likely contributed to its undoing—especially given the other pavilion idea that received closer consideration. In 1932, fair organizers appeared to give at least a nod to a proposal to create an "African village" on the fairgrounds. The idea was hatched in part by singer Modoupe Paris, a descendant of a French West African chief, according to fair documents.

"A bit of darkest Africa—with its thatched-roof mud huts, its throbbing war drums, its strange and terrifying tribal dances, its ancient art of working in metal—is planned for Chicago's 1933 World's Fair," said a March 22, 1932, press release issued by the fair. The release also quotes Paris as promising to bring twenty-five "native Africans" to the fair. "They will be dressed in their native loin cloths and live in a semicircle of mud walled, thatched-roof huts," Paris said. The plan had the backing of officials at the University of Chicago and Northwestern University. Paris presented his plans before a community meeting sponsored by the Chicago Urban League at the Appomattox Club at 3632 South Parkway on July 5, 1932. Fair records do not record the results of the gathering. The planned exhibit seemed far from the fair's theme of "progress." Ironically, a year earlier, Paris, Bailey, and Duke had been briefly allied in a plan to produce a progressive black exhibition hall. Paris broke away, according to a 1931 *Chicago Defender* article, because he wanted native Africans, not African Americans, to guide the project.

Paris's plans to contribute to the fair—no matter the form—were never realized. Paris did manage to put together the African and American Negro Exhibition—a kind of black world's fair—at the Bailey-designed Pythian Temple in 1933, just as the Century of Progress opened. The event celebrated an array of African art, design, and history while giving similar honor to African Americans. The Pythian Temple was a good home for the exhibit. The building was billed as the largest building financed, designed, and built by black people—a fact heralded in the structure's architecture; Egyptian motifs, including profiles of a black Cleopatra were molded into the temple's terra cotta. The African and American Negro Exhibition failed to introduce a worldwide audience to the achievements of black people. Located in the heart of Bronzeville two miles west of the world's fair, the exhibition's audience, unlike that of the Century of Progress, was largely local and black.

After the fair, Paris, billed as Prince Modoupe, wound up playing stereotypical African parts in B-grade jungle movies. Among his first was *In Darkest Africa*, made by MGM in 1936. Meanwhile, the DuSable plan was still on the table, due in no small part to Oliver, the Urban League, and other groups. Fair organizers in early 1933 agreed to allow a replica of DuSable's log cabin built on the present-day northeast corner of Wacker and Michigan. Alderman Robert Jackson, a black city council member, raised the construction funds. Bailey surfaced here to help the DuSable cabin's cause. In a May 13, 1933, letter to top fair official Colonel C. W. Fitch, Bailey protested the cabin's siting and complained that it was not easily visible and was in the line of the lake's spray. Fitch responded and had the cabin moved closer to the other fair buildings.

The DuSable cabin was built. The National DeSaible Memorial Committee held an opening ceremony and invited Dawes and other fair dignitaries. Still, some fair officials seemed cool to the cabin—even a year later, in 1934, when fair organizers were assessing the condition of fair buildings, Fitch wrote to a subordinate:

[T]here is another angle in connection with [the cabin] and that is that it represents one of the few distinct contributions of the Negro race to the Exhibition. There was, as you may be aware, considerable feeling last year that the Negroes were not accorded sufficient part in the exhibition. I do not think it was justified, but nevertheless it prevailed.

In the end, the cabin turned out to be a notable attraction at the Century of Progress. But it is remembered as one of the fair's lesser lights; a log cabin undoubtedly would be lost at a fair featuring modernist houses and buildings holding the promise of air conditioning, push-button kitchen appliances, and impervious exteriors. But the importance of the cabin cannot be dismissed. The fair's midway had its share of tawdry entertainment, some of it with a black theme. Bailey and the civic elite surely winced at the mock plantation shows and exhibits of prancing barechested Pygmies. The DuSable cabin had to be something of a balm.

The DeSaible Society's work sparked an interest in DuSable and his role as the city's first settler. The group then began a campaign after the fair to get a school named for DuSable, resulting in the current DuSable High School located in Bronzeville. Aldermen in recent years sought unsuccessfully to get Lake Shore Drive renamed in DuSable's honor. Now the DuSable League is attempting to get a park built in his honor. Yet the failure to build a large-scale pavilion representing black achievement is a loss. The popular fair was a coming-out party for occurrences that became commonplace during the balance of the century: the American fascination with the automobile, prefabricated houses, air conditioning, and the ever-presence of television.

Imagine if black achievement had been invited to the fair as well.

Only Girl Architect Lonely

Susan F. King

Only girl architect lonely. Wanted—to meet all the women architects in Chicago to form a club.

So read Elisabeth Martini's 1921 advertisement in a local newspaper. At that time, she was the only woman architect licensed in private practice in Illinois.[1] Martini was not the first woman to practice architecture in the area, and her want ad underscores an overlooked chapter of Chicago architectural history: women architects practicing and organizing there. Indeed, Martini's want ad led to the organization of the Chicago Women's Drafting Club, which later became the Women's Architectural Club of Chicago (WACC) and then in turn formed the antecedent of Chicago Women in Architecture (CWA), founded in the 1970s and one of the longest-lasting associations of practicing women architects in the nation today.

It is possible to piece together Martini's life and work as an architect (figs. 12.1, 12.2)[2] primarily through the organization she formed. What we know of her now has survived mainly in the form of written correspondence with the network of friends that she met through her club and its' "occasional" publication, the *Architrave* (fig. 12.3). Martini received her architectural training at the Pratt Institute of Design in New York in 1908[3] and arrived in Chicago in 1909 to seek a position in an architect's office. Rejected by ninety firms because of her gender,[4] she turned to business school and quickly landed a secretarial job in an architect's office. From this position she worked her way into the drafting room. When Martini sat for her three-day licensing exam in 1913 she was the only woman of the eighty-six applicants, and she became one of the twenty-eight successful candidates.[5] In May 1914 with license in hand, she opened her own office at 64 West Randolph Street in Chicago,[6] the first woman to become a sole proprietor of an architectural firm in the city. Much of her work consisted of residential projects. The professional path she created for herself allowed her to be independent of employment by men, a path that would be followed by many other women architects.

Martini's ability to sustain a productive architectural practice despite her avowed loneliness is emblematic of the cyclical pattern undergone by women in America of alternating progress and backlash.[7] The history of Chicago women architects and their efforts to organize is important for the history of American women architects because it acts as an example of both the opportunities and limitations available to professional women during different historical periods. The transformation of Chicago women architects from isolated individuals to organized groups, presently with a powerful professional and political presence in the city of Chicago,[8] shows that considerable ground can be covered in four generations. Yet the broader historical picture also reminds us how easily that ground can be lost when economic and social conditions reinforce the unequal economic and political power of women within and beyond the architectural profession. The history of the ebb and flow of the fortunes of women architects as a publicly active and visible force in Chicago architecture is revealed here through two parallel processes: first by their presence in public exhibitions, and second by the formation of women's architectural organizations.

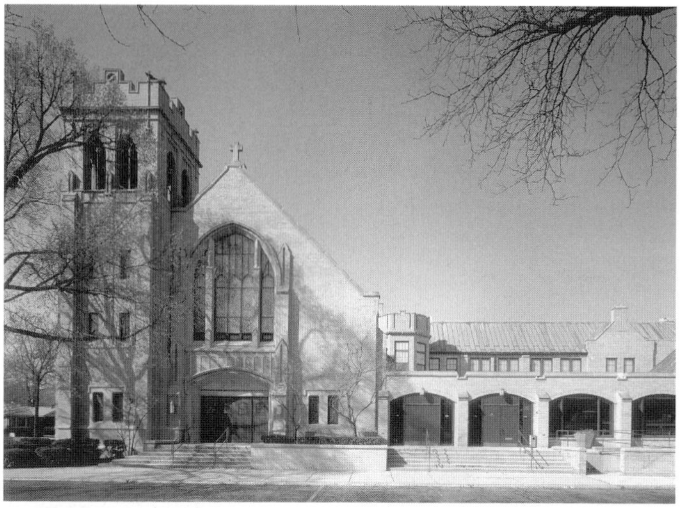
12.1

12.2

The 1893 Columbian Exposition

Changes in the education of architects during the latter part of the nineteenth century spurred women's entry into the architectural profession. Thirty years prior to Martini's admission to the Pratt Institute, formal training became an added requirement to the traditional apprenticeship system for architects. As a result, women architects began to appear more frequently in the profession. One example is Sophia Hayden, the architect for the Women's Building at the Columbian Exposition of 1893 in Chicago.[9] In 1886, she was the first woman to be admitted to the architecture program at MIT (fig. 12.4), and in 1890 she was the first woman to receive its bachelor of architecture, with honors. In 1891, at the urging of some of her friends in Chicago,[10] Hayden entered the competition to design the Women's Building for the upcoming Columbian Exposition, a celebration of the four hundredth anniversary of the discovery of America by Columbus to be held in Chicago in 1893. According to Jeanne Madeline Weimann, author of *The Fair Women,* "On March 25, 1891, Sophia Hayden received a telegram from Daniel

12.1 Exterior view of Saint Luke's Lutheran Church, Park Ridge, Elisabeth A. Martini, architect of record. This was her largest commission. It included both the Church and a three-story educational building. Courtesy of Anthony May Photography.

12.2 Interior view of Saint Luke's Lutheran Church, Park Ridge, Elisabeth A. Martini, architect of record. Courtesy of Anthony May Photography.

12.3 Cover, *Architrave* (1938), the "occasional" publication of the Women's Architectural Club of Chicago. Courtesy of the Art Institute of Chicago, 720-5 W872a, vol. 2–3, 1938–42.

12.4 Sophia Hayden, from class photograph at Massachusetts Institute of Technology. Courtesy of the MIT Museum.

12.3

Burnham telling her that she had won first place in the competition and that she should come to Chicago for a consultation at the expense of the Fair authorities."[11]

Everything about women's involvement in the Columbian Exposition was controversial, including the creation of the Board of Lady Managers and their ensuing decision to hold a competition to select a woman architect to design the Women's Building. The Board of Lady Managers was a women's organization, but not in the sense of Martini's later club. To start with, the members were appointed by men. The idea for the Board of Lady Managers was the result of both the women's club movement that had swept the country during the nineteenth century and the political effects during this period of the heightened activity of the suffragists. Susan B. Anthony, a suffragist leader, had lobbied in Congress for women's representation at the Columbian Exposition and the creation of a Board of Lady Managers, and ultimately the Women's Building was the result of her struggle. However, the Women's Building and the Board of Lady Managers were not what she intended. Anthony had not called for the segregation of women from men in a separate building of their own but for women to serve on the fair's board along *with men*.[12]

Even if Anthony had wanted to serve on the Board of Lady Managers she would not have been selected; her opinions were too controversial.[13] The board was charged with responsibility for the Women's Building, and the women appointed to the board were wealthy and socially prominent. While they were not considered divisive the way Anthony was, they were powerful enough to reject the male architect previously appointed by Daniel Burnham to design the Women's Building, and to instead conduct a national competition to find a woman architect to do the job. Originally Burnham had chosen Richard Morris Hunt of New York to design the Women's Building. Bertha Palmer, wife of the affluent Potter Palmer, was the elected president of the Board of Lady Managers; considered the queen of Chicago's high society, it was she who objected to Hunt's appointment and requested the competition. Palmer felt that a competent, reputable, qualified woman architect existed and would be discovered through the competition.[14]

12.4

Louise Bethune, the first female member of the American Institute of Architects (AIA) and considered America's first professional woman architect, was outraged at the very idea of the competition.[15] She had entered the field through the apprenticeship route. It had been her intent to study at Cornell, but just prior to her application in 1876, she was offered a draftsman position with the Buffalo firm of Richard A. Waite.[16] Bethune took the position with Waite in lieu of the academic path typically followed by women wishing to enter the profession of architecture. As a partner in her own firm, also in Buffalo, since 1881, she could have been awarded the contract for the Women's Building based upon her already established reputation. This would have been consistent with the way in which the other building contracts at the Columbian Exposition were awarded to male architects.[17] Bethune did not compete because she felt it was unethical. She is quoted in the *Inland Architect and News Record* in March 1891 as saying that

> ... The board desires a woman architect, and the chief of construction has issued a circular inviting competition, notwithstanding the fact that competition is an evil against which the entire profession has striven for years and has now nearly vanquished; it is unfortunate that it should be revived in its most objectionable form on this occasion, by women and for women.[18]

Thirteen women entered the competition and received significant press attention, thus achieving the aim set by the Board of Lady Managers to highlight the existence of women architects. First place went to Sophia Hayden. That a formally educated architect won the competition represents a key shift in the architectural professional generally and for women in particular:

> The Exposition found the country Romantic, and left it Classic, and with that change in architectural ideals, schools of architecture automatically assumed a new importance and usefulness. No longer could an architect learn his profession in the drafting room alone. Like Sophia Hayden he must be academically trained; and with Sophia Hayden, he must learn to master the highly technical demands of classic design.[19]

The design of monumental buildings referencing historical forms was at the forefront of an architectural education at MIT. With this training came the watercolor-rendering technique used to capture the imagery of buildings that comprised the Columbian Exposition and would later contribute to its nickname, "the White City" (fig. 12.5). Hayden's thesis design had been a Renaissance museum of fine arts, and with only six weeks in which to prepare her competition sketches, her Women's Building was based on her thesis (fig. 12.6).[20]

Hayden arrived in Chicago in March 1891 with no practical experience in architecture. After graduation, instead of an apprenticeship position with an architectural practice, Hayden had accepted a job teaching mechanical drawing. This fact has been used to prove her level of inexperience concerning the actual construction of buildings. She is slightingly compared with her friend Lois Howe, who had immediately begun practicing architecture upon graduation and had taken second place in the competition.[21] However, Howe, Hayden, and others of this first generation were pioneers, and each had to carve out her own path. It seems harsh to criticize Hayden as inexperienced since in the professional climate of the day it remained difficult for women to obtain work as architects. As Bethune stated at the time, women "meet no serious opposition from the pro-

12.5

12.6

12.5 Exterior view of the Women's Building, Columbian Exposition, 1893, Sophia Hayden, architect. Courtesy of the Chicago Historical Society, ICHi-13864.

12.6 Interior view of the Women's Building, Columbian Exposition, 1893, Sophia Hayden, architect. Courtesy of the Chicago Historical Society, ICHi-17136.

fession nor the public, [but] neither are they warmly welcomed."[22] Sixteen years later, when Martini arrived in Chicago, she too spent months looking for a position in an architectural office and had to take a job teaching mathematics to survive.[23]

The Women's Building was the first building at the exposition to begin construction and the first to be completed.[24] The pressure on Hayden must have been tremendous. Her inexperience makes it probable that she did not realize the difficulty of the task she had undertaken, and she could not have anticipated the personality conflict that appears to have developed between herself and Bertha Palmer. Hayden also indicates in her report to the board that while she knew that she would be required to produce completed construction drawings when she arrived in Chicago, she had not anticipated making major design modifications first and the subsequent negotiations for payment for this additional work. These changes included the addition of a third floor to house a library, an assembly hall, and a rooftop garden. Hayden may not have known that she was paid only one-tenth of the amount the male architects were paid for the design of the other buildings.[25] She received an honorarium of $1,000 plus expenses for her troubles, while it has been estimated that the fee for her completed one-eighth-inch scale working drawings would have been $10,000 (equivalent today to about three hundred thousand dollars)[26] had she been male.[27]

As the construction of the building progressed, much confusion centered on how best to incorporate the numerous international donations by women that were received. Hayden unsuccessfully attempted to contact Palmer regarding this matter, and unfortunately the whole situation took its toll on her. Contemporary sources say that Hayden had a "breakdown" of some sort in Daniel Burnham's office.[28] By this time, Hayden considered the terms under which she had undertaken the work on the Women's Building to be "rather vague,"[29] and in 1894 she wrote that she felt she had been "unduly hurried in the preparation of the drawings."[30] From Enid Yandell, the young artist who sculpted the building's caryatids, and Laura Hayes, Palmer's secretary, we have this description of Hayden:

> **It was generally known around the construction department that no one could change by any amount of persuasion, one of her [Sophia's] plans when she was convinced of its beauty or originality. She was always quiet but generally carried her point.**[31]

It is possible that Hayden's supposed breakdown was a severe case of her "carrying a point"—at the time, being a forceful young woman was neither common nor respected. Whatever the truth of the matter, and in spite of the success of the Women's Building, Hayden never built again, although she lived until 1953.[32]

The Columbian Exposition had provided international visibility for women architects and empowered women to act as significant architectural patrons. However, the harsh political realities of the building's execution prevented Hayden from becoming a role model for future women architects, and the seemingly idealistic competitive process in fact discouraged Chicago women architects from organizing as a group. As Louise Bethune stated regarding the unequal terms of compensation, "It is an unfortunate precedent to establish just now and it may take years to live down its effects."[33]

The 1933 Century of Progress World's Fair

Forty years after the Columbian Exposition, twelve years after Martini's want ad, six years after the formation of the Women's Architectural Club of Chicago (WACC), and four years after the last of the women's world fairs,[34] the Century of Progress World's Fair took place in 1933. In contrast to the Columbian Exposition, the role of women at this second world's fair is more difficult to evaluate. Ironically, this is in part because women were not segregated within their own building. This is not to say that women did not participate in the Century of Progress World's Fair; however, their presence was "minimal."[35] There was a proposal for a Temple of Womanhood, and there are extant drawings prepared by Burnham Brothers[36] of this building among the Century of

Progress papers in the Special Collections Department of the University of Illinois at Chicago Library. A press release on May 8, 1932, announced that "Women's position in the economic and social world has become too important to be isolated in a Woman's Building. All proposals to erect such a structure have been rejected."[37] Susan B. Anthony finally got her wish.

The presence of women at this fair did not cause the stir it did in 1893 for four main reasons. First, the Depression had intensified competition for jobs and significantly reduced interest in supporting the cause of women. The fair itself had to be self-supporting and had no government funding; in fact, only exhibits that were revenue-generating were included.[38] Second, the theme of the fair, "Science and Industry," was unfortunately not an area of strength for women at this time. Third, lack of strong local leadership led to exclusionary tactics. The National Council of Women (NCW), operating from New York City, manipulated the participation of all women's organizations at the fair to their own organization's benefit and to the detriment of women in general. Finally, although Helen Bennett, a reporter for the *Chicago Record-Herald,* built on her experience as the organizer of the four women's world fairs held in the late 1920s to become a key exhibit organizer for the entire exposition, her involvement with the women's exhibits was minimal.

The NCW exhibit, "One Hundred Years of the Progress of Women, 1833–1933," was displayed in the Hall of Social Sciences. Anthony, who had died in 1906, and Palmer, who had died in 1918, were both honored at the NCW's exhibit, the primary focus of which was a sixty-foot mural created by the artist Hildreth Meiere.[39] In addition to the mural, the exhibit included significant artifacts and memorabilia associated with women's history. Anthony's red shawl was included, and Palmer was represented in the form of a wax mannequin in a collection of historically important women.[40] Originally, the women's exhibit was to be a collaborative effort of women's organizations everywhere. Each participating organization was to be given space to display their history and progress. After a year of planning in this direction, the NCW abruptly and unilaterally decided on the unified mural concept. This action led to further infighting among the groups, and some key organizations withdrew.[41]

Martini's reformed club, the WACC, was five years old by then and had gained exhibition experience by participating in previous women's world fairs and by mounting annual exhibits of their own members' works, participated in the Century of Progress World's Fair by sponsoring an international exhibition on the work of women in architecture and the allied arts.[42] WACC was able to work in isolation from the exhibit of the NCW because its exhibit was "technical" in nature, and the NCW's control extended only over those women's organizations that wanted to exhibit their own histories. The WACC exhibit, displayed in the General Exhibits Building, included one hundred entries from women architects all over the world. WACC actually expanded the size of its exhibit and also furnished a women's lounge at the request of the Century of Progress Administration.

The Scheid Residence, designed by WACC member Bertha Yerex Whitman, had won a contest sponsored by *Better Homes* magazine in 1931, and it was probably displayed as part of the WACC exhibit.[43] The written descriptions found in the *Architrave* and in the correspondence between the fair administration and the WACC organization provide the only documentation of the WACC exhibition; no visual record survives. While brochures often accompanied the exhibits, it appears that one was not prepared for the WACC exhibit, most likely due to lack of funding. As mentioned earlier, all exhibits had to be financially self-supporting and, ideally, profit-generating. Economic disempowerment and political dissention therefore combined to weaken women architects' presence at the fair, even as women architects in Chicago were already organized into a coherent and forward-looking organization.

12.7 The offices for Lindberg Engineering at 2450 Hubbard Street, Chicago. The most significant work of WACC's last president, Mary Ann Crawford. Courtesy of the Chicago Historical Society, ICHi-13864.

12.8 Detail of entry to the Lindberg Engineering Offices, Mary Ann Crawford in the foreground. Courtesy of the Chicago Historical Society, ICHi-35828.

12.9 Interior view of the drafting room at the Lindberg Engineering Offices. While the exterior of the building gives a residential impression, the two-story volume of the drafting room projects a modern attitude through the incorporation of what were considered state-of-the-art lighting and mechanical systems. Courtesy of the Chicago Historical Society, ICHi-35829.

Women's Architectural Club of Chicago

The Chicago Women's Drafting Club of 1921 is recognized today by active women's architectural organizations and historians as the earliest organization of practicing women architects in the United States. By the time she wrote her want ad in 1921, Martini had truly been an "Only Girl Architect" for almost a decade. While the Women's Drafting Club, the direct consequence of her ad, only lasted two years, in 1927 local women architects reorganized as the Women's Architectural Club of Chicago (WACC). This second attempt was a result of interest spurred by the series of women's world fairs held in Chicago annually from 1925 to 1928, organized by the previously mentioned Helen Bennett. WACC would sustain itself until the early 1940s.[44] Martini remained a member even after she relocated to Bangor, Michigan, in the early 1930s.

It is worth noting the formation of a student group during this period called Alpha Alpha Gamma (Auksases architektonis meta gunaikum, Greek for the advancement of architecture among women). This organization of women architectural students from Washington University in St. Louis and the University of Minnesota in Minneapolis was formed in 1917.[45] This organization of women students, active in architecture, unfortunately operated in relative isolation from the professional organization of WACC. Ruth Perkins, another practicing architect who had responded to Martini's 1921 ad[46] and later authored the 1938 Historic Overview portion of the *Architrave*, stated, "This Club [WACC] was then [at its formalization in 1927] and is now so far as it is possible to as-

12.7

12.8

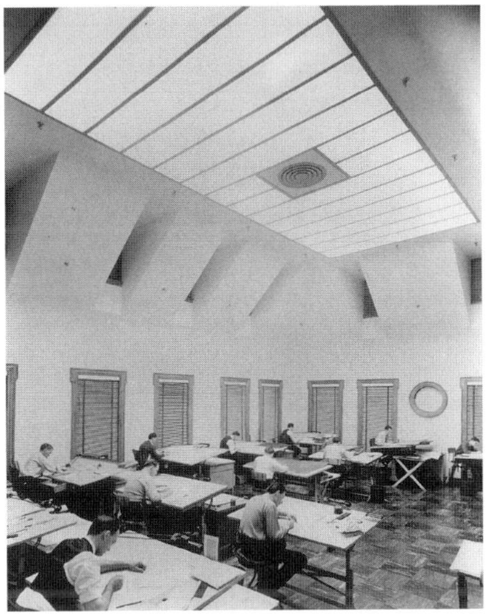

12.9

certain, the only organization of women architects in the United States, except for a college sorority or two."[47]

Sometime during the 1940s WACC itself lost steam. Architect and engineer Mary Ann Crawford was the last known president of the organization, and the last *Architrave* on record is from 1942, the same year she served as president. Crawford was another MIT graduate and received her architecture degree in 1930. It took Crawford eleven years to acquire enough work experience to sit for her licensing exam, which she passed in 1941. In 1943, she also became registered as an engineer.[48] By combining these two professions, Crawford was uniquely poised for the technological revolution that swept the profession in the 1950s and '60s. Crawford's most significant work is the offices for Lindberg Engineering at 2450 Hubbard Street (figs. 12.7, 12.8, and 12.9).

Lack of interest in this type of organization for women was consistent with the post–World War II trend of women leaving the workforce as men returned from war. According to Perkins, who practiced as an architect with Bertram Weber for twenty-five years,[49] even by the time of the 1933 World's Fair most of the women architects in the group had lost their jobs and were no longer practicing architecture. If it was difficult for women to find work under normal economic conditions, the Great Depression compounded the situation, and yet this was the period in which the Women's Architectural Club of

Chicago appears to have been most solid and active. Organizations such as the Society of Women Engineers, which Crawford chaired in the 1950s, remained active after World War II. Possibly through Crawford's efforts, WACC was "persuaded to join with some women engineers and merge into a Women's Division of The Western Society of Engineers." Perkins felt that this was "a disaster as far as our identities as women and as architects were concerned—and soon most of the architects withdrew."[50] The days of WACC were numbered.

Chicago Women in Architecture

Just as Martini represents the second generation, architect Gertrude Lempp Kerbis's career is emblematic of the fourth generation of women architects in Chicago. During the late 1950s and early 1960s, theoretical modernist quests were underway in the large Chicago firms. Project designers such as Kerbis, working in modernist firms like Skidmore, Owings & Merrill (SOM) and Murphy Naess, were searching for the perfectly square steel-framed building and the longest spans. According to local architect Jack Hartray, these quests went beyond firm loyalty, and the designers would meet in the evenings to share their progress. In the end, "Gertrude Kerbis proved to be the most macho of them all, not once, but twice."[51] Hartray was referring to the long span at the Dining Hall for the Air Force Academy in Colorado she designed for SOM in 1958, and to the perfect circular plan at O'Hare's Seven Continents Restaurant which she designed for Murphy Naess in 1963. Yet in 1967, after more then a decade of producing award-winning projects, Kerbis felt she was passed over for the position of designer for the McCormick Place project. At this point, she abandoned the politics and corporate culture of large architectural firms and opened her own practice, Lempp Kerbis Architects. While this action cleared away one set of gender-related issues, another set soon took its place. In a world that was barely ready to employ and promote women as architects, the struggle to obtain the type of client and project she desired as a business owner intensified.[52]

An echo of Martini's call was heard in Chicago when in the winter months of 1973–74 Kerbis "sent out a little note" to all of the women architects that she knew and their friends.[53] Kerbis had no knowledge of the ad that Martini ran in 1921 or of the clubs that had previously existed.[54] The note she sent was an invitation for all of these women to come to her small office on Michigan Avenue. The result was a gathering of more than twenty women, and the first meeting of Chicago Women in Architecture (CWA). While the WACC of the 1920s and '30s had officers like a typical men's club, Kerbis describes the initial CWA group as more a "forum" than an organization.[55] CWA existed without a formal "leader" or president for almost five years. If Martini's club represents the first phase of women's architectural organizations, then Kerbis's represents the second phase. When Kerbis speaks of CWA in her oral history, she discusses the fifth generation of women architects in Chicago as "[t]he next generation, the women who were ten, fifteen, or twenty years younger than me, . . . they became much more effective. But we had to go through this informal process before we got to the formal thing."[56] In 1978, when CWA elected to celebrate its fifth anniversary, the group decided to apply for a grant to assist with funding an exhibition. It was this process that forced CWA to conform to a more traditional format for organizations: in order to apply for the grant, the group was required to have officers. Architect Carol Ross Barney, a representative of this fifth generation and currently a principal of the Chicago firm Ross Barney + Jankowski, was a project designer at the offices of Holabird & Root at the time and was heavily involved with organizing the exhibit. She then became the first president of the group.[57] The grant was accepted, and CWA presented its first exhibit of members' work, Chicago Women in Architecture: Contemporary Directions. It coincided with a national touring exhibit, Women in American Architecture, curated by architect Susana Torre.[58]

CWA differs from WACC in ways that show that progress for women, however slow, has occurred. CWA's membership has always spanned the professional generations, simultaneously focusing energy on female students from the three major universities in the Chicago area while holding onto the founders as honorary members. The end result has been an organization that as it enters its thirtieth year has a diverse membership in terms of experience and staying power. As CWA has grown over the years it has become a mainstay of the Chicago architectural scene. Yet not unlike the WACC of the 1920s and '30s, CWA has had its own ebbs and flows. Its activities increased when opportunities arose, such as local AIA conventions or moments the organization created for itself, beginning with the fifth anniversary and continuing with major events and exhibits at each five-year milestone (1978, 1983, 1988, 1993, and 1998).

Of particular interest is the formation of a splinter group called CARY (short for CARYATIDS or Chicks in Architecture Refuse to Yield to Atavistic Thinking in Design and Society) in the early nineties to address the issues of women architects from a more controversial standpoint. Several of the CARY members were CWA members,[59] and CARY was a task force formed for the purpose of producing an exhibit addressing the issues of women in architecture. CARY's formation can be seen as indicative of the mainstream success of the CWA parent group, which had reached a plateau from which smaller groups could spring.

CARY's plan was to mount the exhibit during the national AIA convention held in Chicago in 1993. The multimedia exhibit, entitled "More than the Sum of Our Body

Parts," was the brainchild of three practicing architects, Carol Crandall, Sally Levine and Kay Janis. It was controversial almost from its inception. The intent of the exhibit was to educate the public about the fact that sexism and discrimination were very much alive in the profession of architecture. During the prosperity of the early 1980s, a veneer of equality for women was established, but when the recession hit, women architects seemed to be among the first laid off.[60] Little had changed since the Great Depression of the 1930s. Anger at this situation fueled the CARY group. Also, the exhibit was conceived during the appointment of Susan Maxman to the office of president of the national AIA, the first woman elected to this position. There was frustration on the part of many professional women, especially in Chicago, who felt that Maxman would not take up the feminist cause against the still-existent inequities between the genders in the profession.[61]

Initially CARY hoped that the exhibit could be mounted at the Chicago Cultural Center, one of the locations for the AIA convention activities. For months CARY was unable to obtain a commitment to a space for the exhibit there. Undaunted, CARY found a home at the Randolph Street Gallery and opened the exhibition with marked success. One of the vignettes, titled *There Were Three Professionals in a Boat . . .*, compared the position of women in architecture to that of women in medicine and law (fig. 12.10). Specifically, the exhibit illuminated the slowness with

12.10

12.11

12.10 *There Were Three Professionals in a Boat,* vignette from the CARY exhibition, Chicago, 1993. Courtesy of Carol Crandall.

12.11 *Water Cooler Wisdom,* a vignette from the CARY exhibition, 1993. In addition to a tape whose script contained inappropriate comments made to women architects by their male coworkers, this display involved a bulletin board on which women could pin up their own encounters with sexist language and attitudes. Courtesy of Carol Crandall.

which the AIA had addressed issues of pay equity, maternity and family leave, and sexual harassment as compared with law (American Bar Association) and medicine (American Medical Association). Humor was a key component to opening a dialog between the sexes. Another favorite was entitled *Water Cooler Wisdom,* which included a talking water cooler, whose script was a tape of actual comments made by male architects to their female coworkers, not twenty or thirty years ago but in the preceding five years (fig. 12.11). The display pointed out that this behavior was in "flagrant violation of the 1964 Civil Rights Act and the AIA Code of Ethics."[62] The exhibit set records in attendance for the Randolph Street Gallery during its two-week time period, and AIA conventioneers were part of the audience. Perhaps more importantly an audience of younger women also attended. Indeed, while CARY disbanded after the exhibit, CWA benefited from its association with CARY by increased membership from women in the next generation who had attended the exhibit.

Today, CWA is credited with supporting and sustaining female leaders in Chicago architecture. The list of past CWA presidents and founding members is a Who's Who of women practicing architecture in the Chicago area. These include Carol Ross Barney, FAIA, principal of Ross Barney + Jankowski; Cynthia Weese, FAIA, dean of the School of Architecture at Washington University and principal of Weese, Langley, Weese; and Linda Searl, FAIA, principal of Searl and Associates and vice chairperson of the Chicago Plan Commission, among others.

CWA has also served an important historical role in recording the work of local women through its five-year anniversaries and its archive at the Chicago Historical Society. A current project in collaboration with the Illinois Chapter of the National Organization of Minority Architects (INOMA) consists of the documentation of Chicago architecture by women and minority architects. The CWA newsletter, the *Muse,* is also an important resource for collating the histories of Chicago women architects as well as the histories of women architects both nationally and internationally. The invitation to speak at the CWA annual brunch has become a coveted honor for both local and national women architects. A lecture series initiated during the twenty-fifth year continues as a forum for promoting the work of women both locally and nationally.

Even as the number of women practicing architecture has radically increased and women are given more opportunities to practice and recognition for their contributions, women still only comprise 19 percent of total professional architectural staff, and only 11 percent of licenced members of the AIA.[63] It is through organizations like CWA that much of women's work in the field continues to be documented. While the 1970s witnessed a burst of interest in the subject, the effort to document and record the history of American women architects, which was spearheaded by Torre in her position as co-founder and coordinator of the first national Archive of Women in Architecture at the Architectural League of New York, has not been surpassed or even maintained.

Indeed, the Architectural League's Archive of Women in Architecture is not, at the time of the writing of this essay, an active archive.[64] The history of women in American architecture is now almost as hard to access as it was thirty years ago. The AIA began to collect gender and racial demographic data in 1983, very late compared with other professions. The importance of these statistical records to tracking the progress of diversity in any profession cannot be overstated.[65] As architects place more emphasis on diversity, the ability of organizations like CWA to record the otherwise unrecoverable early histories of women architects and their organizations takes on increased significance. Awareness of the longevity and persistence of women architects, not only as individual practitioners but also as a continuing collective presence, continues to be an inspiration in Chicago and beyond. Yet, the tale of Chicago women architects is also a cautionary one. While the long perspective affirms the power of women architects to organize and succeed, it also reveals the ground still to be covered in restructuring the profession for women architects to participate equally. As this change occurs the need for women's organizations may diminish, as women architects themselves are able to more easily realize their own histories.

Marion Mahony Griffin: The Chicago Years

Pamela Hill

On February 11, 1937, architect Walter Burley Griffin died unexpectedly in India after a short illness. His wife, architect Marion Mahony Griffin, was at his side. Walter Griffin's sudden death marked the end of an unusual and creative, yet bittersweet, career and the end of one of the most amazing professional partnerships in history.[1] The Griffins' winning of the competition to design the new capital of Canberra is an often-told story. Their work in both Australia and India and Walter Griffin's early work in America are now receiving the attention they rightly deserve. The work of Mahony Griffin and her role in her husband's practice as well as her tenure with Frank Lloyd Wright at the beginning of the century remain problematic. She is considered controversial and continues to pose a dilemma for the architectural historian; one does not know what to make of her. First, she was a woman attempting to participate in a male-dominated profession long before it was common to do so. Second, she was a contemporary, colleague, and employee of Frank Lloyd Wright, the dominant figure of American architectural history. Third, she was an architect who never established an independent practice but spent the majority of her professionally active years working in collaboration with men—Frank Lloyd Wright, Herman von Holst (the architect who took over Wright's practice when he temporarily left the United States for a long sojourn in Europe), and her architect husband, Walter Burley Griffin. The problem is further complicated by the fact that after moving to Australia, Mahony Griffin was no longer a part of the American architectural culture.

One cannot help but be fascinated by Mahony Griffin. Her talents were many; she was an architect, a landscape architect, a designer, an artist, a committed and productive woman. Examined from the perspective of traditional architectural history, one does not know how to evaluate her achievements—she is a "famous" Chicago architect with no Chicago building to her credit. She was as much an artist as an architect, an architect as a planner, and as such she defies classification.

When Mahony Griffin graduated with a degree in architecture from MIT, she was only the second woman to do so; she then quickly became the first woman to be licensed in the state of Illinois and the country.[2] While she claimed "Chicago men welcome women into the profession with open arms,"[3] this was far from the truth. The number of practicing women architects was minimal. While a significant portion of women were becoming college-educated during this time period,[4] Mahony Griffin was one of only a handful to establish a successful career in one of the traditional "male professions." Most college-educated women were entering the newly developed women's professions, such as teaching, nursing, and library and social work. Her first job was with her cousin Dwight Heald Perkins, and it is believed her position with Wright may have been obtained through a friend of her mother's. It is possible that the more casual, homelike atmosphere of the Frank Lloyd Wright Studio, where children ran underfoot and the separation of home and work life was not sharply defined, may have accommodated Mahony Griffin more comfortably than the standard architectural office of the day. In any event, she blossomed during her tenure with Wright, becoming his most senior and valued assistant[5] while helping to produce some of his most significant projects and creating a portfolio that would earn her a reputation as the most gifted renderer of the era.

Yet even as she established a firm footing on the foundation of the architectural profession, the profession was attempting to deny her participation. Herman von Holst claimed sole authorship for her D. M. Amberg House in Grand Rapids, Michigan, in the April 1913 issue of *Western Architect*. Frank Lloyd Wright claimed the Irving House in Decatur as solely his own after returning from his European sojourn. The *Western Architect* featured lengthy coverage of Mahony Griffin and Walter Griffin's work after they won the Canberra competition in 1912, yet the May 1913 issue commented on the lack of women practitioners in the field, in effect dismissing her existence.

The work of all Prairie school architects has suffered in comparison to that of the legendary genius, Frank Lloyd Wright. Although scholarship has attempted to establish the merits of the work of these individuals, they have all had difficulty in stepping out of Wright's shadow. They are considered followers of Wright, and their work is frequently considered derivative and less original than that of Wright.

Architectural history has traditionally been the study of grand monuments and great men. Issues of authorship and attribution are primary. When architects and designers work collaboratively and roles are not clearly defined and separate, these issues are difficult to resolve. Great buildings are generally thought to be the product of one great mind, a lone creative genius. Architecture as a collaborative effort is thus problematic when multiple participants are involved. If one accepts that a great building is created by a single person, then if Mahony Griffin is the designer, Walter Griffin is not. She can be more, only if he is less, and vice versa. This need not be the case, but old patterns of thinking die hard. Given Mahony Griffin's education, talent, personal commitment to her husband, devotion to her work, and her documented presence in her husband's practice, it seems reasonable to assume that her input was more than negligible.

In an attempt to help reestablish the credentials of this often overlooked and dismissed architect, this essay examines a period in Mahony Griffin's life when she did work independently, many years after the time spent in Oak Park with Frank Lloyd Wright and immediately following the decades spent in Australia and India with her husband.

Despite some consideration of staying in India after her husband's death, Mahony Griffin brought their projects to termination and their personal affairs to order, returned briefly to Australia, and then to the United States in 1938, to the home in Rogers Park that she had shared with her mother prior to her marriage.[6] Some historians believe that the stay was to be temporary and that the outbreak of the Second World War intervened and prevented her from ever returning to her adopted country. In any event, she made Chicago her home for the rest of her life until her death in 1961.

Her life during these twilight years in Chicago is vague and not well documented. There are mysteries and contradictions pertaining to her personal life that have not yet been resolved. For instance, despite an extended network of family, she is rumored to have died in poverty and alone. For many years she was buried in an unmarked grave and no record of an obituary or even the simplest memorial service seems to exist.[7] A review of the design work that she produced during this period, however, provides insight into her special abilities and interests as an architect and reveals her as a still vital and important member of the profession.

Despite their lengthy expatriation, the Griffins were not entirely forgotten in their homeland at the time of Walter Burley Griffin's death. Griffin had maintained contact with the Illinois Society of Architects, and they featured a letter from him in their monthly bulletin shortly before his death.[8] In it Griffin describes some of his experiences and projects in India. His death received some notice in local newspapers, and interest in the formative years of the "Prairie school," as it would later be designated, was growing. At a November 1938 meeting of the Illinois Society of Architects, three papers were presented by members of this school: Robert C. Spencer, George S. Elmslie, and Barry Byrne. In his essay Byrne spoke highly of Griffin and "his very talented wife, who is also an architect"[9] and noticed that Griffin's untimely death in India . . . closed a career that was marked both by achievement and the promise of further achievement."[10] Byrne mentioned that Mahony Griffin was again a resident of Chicago and described her as a "person of extraordinary brilliancy."[11] He then went on to say that the "return of Mrs. Walter Burley Griffin to Chicago suggests the interesting possibility of an exhibition of the architectural work of this talented couple. That a prophet should be without honor in his own land is a condition against which honest persons should oppose themselves."[12]

Whether or not Mahony Griffin was in the audience that evening to hear praise of their work is not known. Mahony Griffin did, however, attend the forty-third annual meeting of the Illinois Society of Architects in June of 1940. This was a special event of honor for the architect. A presentation by Mahony Griffin was the highlight of the evening, and it should be noted that Herman von Holst, then retired and living in Florida, had traveled to Chicago to attend. Mahoney Griffin was introduced to the audience by her cousin, architect Lawrence Perkins. The description of the event as appeared in the *Monthly Bulletin* noted that

The program of the evening was, perhaps, an unusual one, given by a lady who, with her husband, had been absent from this country more than a quarter of a century. . . . and through all their married life were partners in the practice of architecture and town planning.

It is significant that she was acknowledged as being a partner with her husband.

Those in attendance had expected Mahoney Griffin to speak

on the subject of "Architecture in Australia," but she changed the subject and only talked momentarily of their efforts in Australia. She took her hearers to other parts of the world, particularly India, where she and her husband had functioned. Before showing many drawings and renderings which she had made of their work, she stated that town planning and architecture must go hand in hand; that one is too dependent upon the other to be carried on independently with success. With diagrams she then launched into the theory of fundamental issues and aspirations in architecture as explained through anthroposophy, a system of science, art, and philosophy, with religion, founded by the late Rudolph Steiner, where the material and spiritual blend.

By prefacing the graphic presentation of her work with an outline of her philosophical beliefs, Mahoney Griffin makes evident the importance of the spiritual component of that work. She also uses this opportunity to comment on the escalating global conflicts of the era by expressing her view

that occidental materialism had reached a state of collapse, as now demonstrated in the struggles of Europe, and that the Orient had much to give the Occident in thought and belief. She said that the conflicting ideas of material and spirit must come together; the East must meet the West. We must understand that matter is real and spirit is real and if we accomplish this, we will have peace in the world.

Mahoney Griffin then proceeded to display some of the Griffins' numerous recent projects.

Mrs. Griffin's drawings were many and beautiful. With an elevation of the library at Lucknow, which was built after designs of the Griffins, she explained the system of deflecting direct sun rays and lighting through reflected light. Insulation and air spaces were dwelt upon. The English

pitched roof transplanted to India she found inappropriate and impractical. The flat roof, in general, fitted conditions of roofing and protection much better. A house with a flat roof, she said, need not be ugly.

The layout of the university grounds were shown and discussed. A student union at this university was shown, as was a house built from their designs at Benares. Stupas were explained, and in this connection she showed a Griffin design for a monument to King George VI in India, square in plan, and like a stepped pyramid in elevation, with approaches to the interior from the four corners. She showed her beautifully drawn decorative details of Indian ornament, pointing out that ornament is as necessary as plane surfaces in order to get emphasis in design.

Designs for the Lucknow exposition buildings covered another roll of drawings. In explaining these Mrs. Griffin touched on the construction of domed roofs, including parabolic curves carried out with bamboo and filled with a sort of mud for temporary buildings.

The question was asked whether all this effort was to be published, illustrated by Mrs. Griffin's splendid drawings. To this she replied that she sought publication, but adequate publication needed financial support, which she was still in search of.[13]

This reporter indeed does not know what to make of "Mrs. Griffin." He seems taken aback that she has dared to change the advertised topic of her talk; he is befuddled by her references to the mystic philosophy anthroposophy,[14] the philosophical movement to which she and her husband were committed devotees. On the other hand, it is obvious that he is impressed by the breadth of her knowledge (structural, aesthetic, and environmental) as well as the beauty of her drawings. Forty-five years after Mahony Griffin's entrance into the profession, it was still highly unusual for a woman to be the highlight of the society's program.[15] The audience expected to hear about the Canberra experience (in the United States, this was the singular accomplishment with which the Griffins were identified), but instead were exposed to the work that the Griffins had done in India; Mahony Griffin was obviously proud of and enthusiastic about that work. Her vibrant presentation must have been somewhat shocking to the "hearers."

One can assume that Mahony Griffin had some expectations of establishing a professional practice upon her return to the States; prior to leaving Australia she had asked her husband's partner, Eric Nichols, to come to the United States with her to continue the practice.[16] Nichols declined. Mahony Griffin did not establish a successful office; however, she remained dedicated to and involved with her profession for a number of years, which is evident in the few known projects that she produced during the decade of the 1940s.

World Fellowship Center, Hills Crystal-Rosary Crystals

Two of the projects that Mahony Griffin produced in the early years of the decade were town planning schemes undertaken for client Lola Maverick Lloyd: the World Fellowship Center in New Hampshire (1942) and Hills Crystal-Rosary Crystals (1943) near Boerne in Lloyd's native Texas.[17] Mahony Griffin and Lloyd's friendship was longstanding. The two women, as well as Lloyd's husband Henry (the son of reformer Henry Demarest Lloyd), were charter members of the Chicago Arts and Crafts Society,[18] founded at Hull House in 1897. Lloyd and Mahony Griffin shared many common interests. Lloyd, a Smith College graduate, had taught college-level mathematics briefly and pursued an interest in archeology and architecture. Both women supported the woman suffrage movement and were pacifists during World War I. Lloyd is in fact primarily known for her activism in the peace movement as well as her advocacy of world government.[19] While Mahony Griffin seems to have had doubts about the practicality of world government, she definitely shared Lloyd's commitment to world peace. In a letter to her husband's mother dated March 12, 1917, she wrote,

> You've no idea I'm sure, how desperately I'm in need of your slender, but capable and sustaining shoulder, to keep on during these days of uncertainty. I think war, war, war morning, noon and night and consequently I row all day long with the Australians on the subject, and have developed into such a termagant that I will be an outcast in my native land when I reach it. None of my erstwhile friends will have anything to do with me . . . I am going home Mrs. Griffin on the next boat which is the Sierra sailing March 21st, and I'm going to do my best to the best of my ability in the interests of peace, disarmament and freedom.[20]

Given their friendship and the Griffins' experience in planning and landscape design, it is not surprising that Lloyd would approach Mahony Griffin to plan the World Fellowship Center. Founded in 1941 by Lloyd and Eugenia and Charles Weller in Albany, New Hampshire, the center was to be located on 290 acres in the White Mountains. A vacation center, it was intended to support the activities of the World Fellowship of Faiths, an interreligious, intercultural peace organization, by providing a peaceful and rustic setting in which persons of diverse backgrounds could meet and share ideas. At the time of its founding, the center's motto was "In time of war, prepare for peace."

The site plan (fig. 13.1) is schematic in nature but indicates Mahony Griffin's ability to work sensitively with the geographic form of the site while superimposing a striking geometric order. "The whole has a formality which makes it comprehensible and gives it distinction."[21] The plan carefully preserves topographic features and indicates indi-

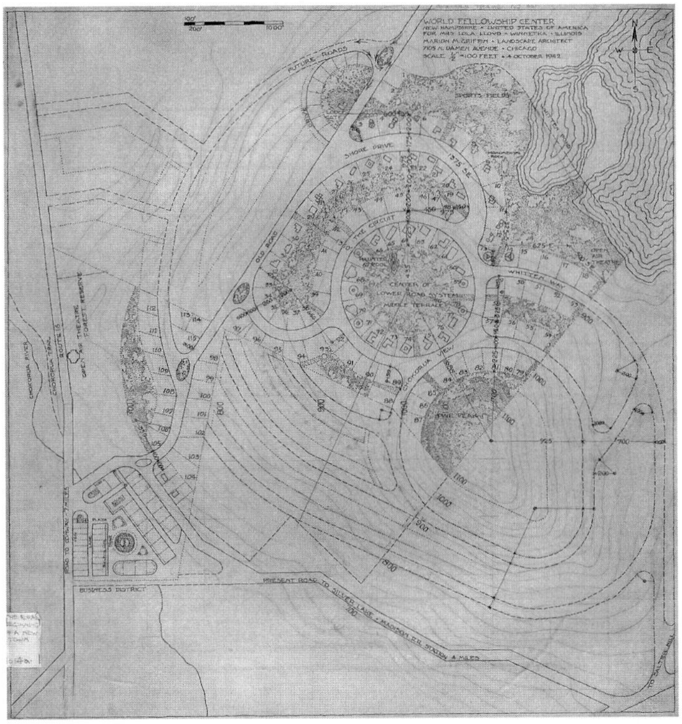

13.1 Site plan, the World Fellowship Center, near Conway, New Hampshire, Marion Mahony Griffin, landscape architect, 1942. Photograph by Greg Williams. Courtesy of the Burnham Library, Art Institute of Chicago.

vidual residential lots with suggested housing configuration, community uses, and future roadways. It was Mahony Griffin's intention that all the houses on the estate should be placed parallel to the Old Road. This orientation is ideal for getting the sunlight in all sides of the house. It also give maximum view of Mount Chokorua. Maintaining this orientation throughout the residential area gives "orderliness and dignity to the district."[22] In general, the roads follow natural contours so that they are level and would require minimum grading to construct. Substantial parklike open areas are set at the interior of each residential "block," an arrangement that Mahony Griffin felt was economically feasible because the parks did not occupy valuable street frontage and the protected green space would add to the value of each lot. "Of course the idea is to keep the whole property as natural as possible. It should be a magnet for nature lovers."[23]

The next project that Mahony Griffin prepared for Lloyd was the town of Hill Crystals and its suburb, Rosary Crystals, in Texas (fig. 13.2). This plan bears some similarity to the plan of the World Fellowship Center, and both embody the principles of planning characteristic of Mahony Griffin's designs.

A basic principle in community planning is to reverence [*sic*] and preserve nature, fixing the development which may continue through time in such a way as to retain the character of

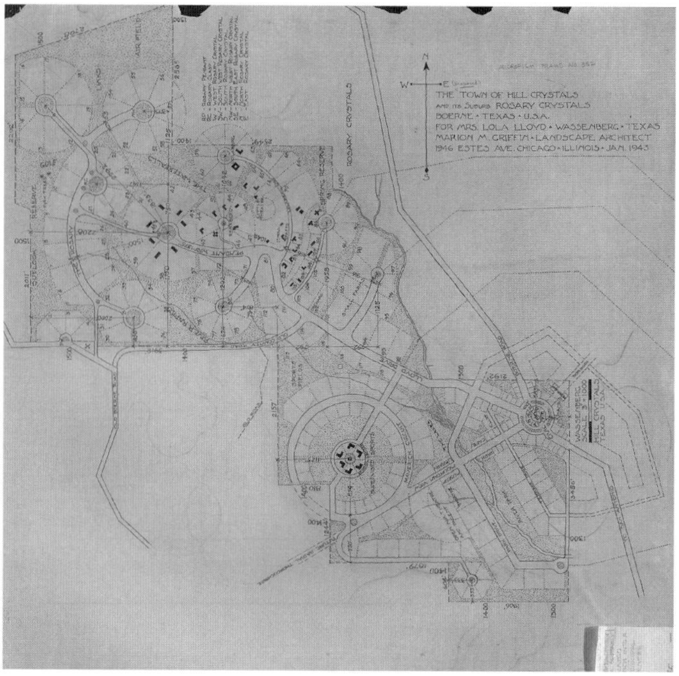

13.2

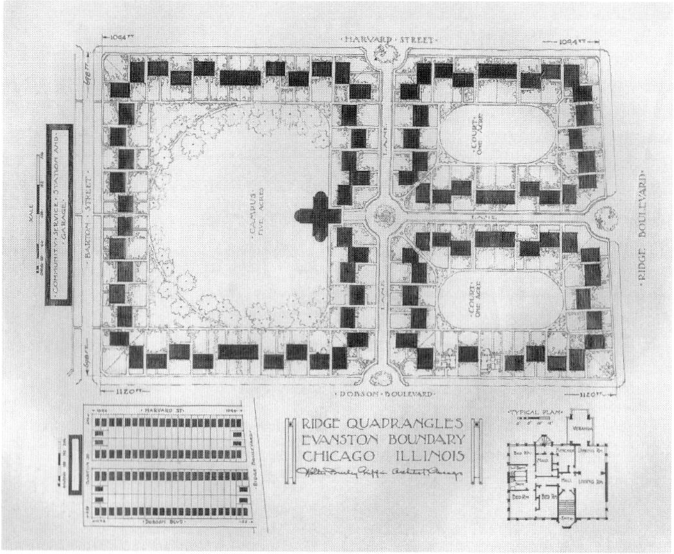

13.3

the district, enhancing but never destroying, so that generations to come may be surrounded by the charms that the creative nature beings [*sic*] have spent the millenniums in bringing about.[24]

Expressing an environmental concern that is relevant yet today, this basic principle succinctly defines the current notion of sustainable development, that is, development that meets the needs of the present without compromising the ability of future generations to meet their own needs. In her description of this project Mahony Griffin goes on to say, "After all it is high time humans changed their policy of destroying nature because of the greed of one generation and made it their task and their joy to save and enhance."[25]

In planning this town and its subdivision, Mahony Griffin carefully placed her roadways, lots, and special uses so that "all the distinctive features" will be "permanently available to everybody."[26] Every lot has both street frontage and park frontage, and paths connect all of the larger green spaces. Residential lots and roadways are aligned so that all houses can be oriented at a forty-five-degree angle to the east-west axis, an orientation that Mahony Griffin felt was ideal "so that all the rooms get the sun and all get the shade."[27]

Another characteristic principle evident in this plan is the disposition of roadways. Major thoroughfares are radial in consideration of the need for direct communication from one center to another; distribu-

13.2 Site plan, the Town of Hill Crystals and its suburb, Rosary Crystals, in Boerne, Texas, Marion Mahony Griffin, landscape architect, 1943. Photograph by Greg Williams. Courtesy of the Burnham Library, Art Institute of Chicago.

13.3 Site plan, Ridge Quadrangles subdivision, Chicago, Illinois, Walter Burley Griffin, architect, c. 1910. Courtesy of the Burnham Library, Art Institute of Chicago.

tive streets are set perpendicular to the major routes. This system establishes a logical location for business and commercial uses that are convenient to, but not intrusive upon, areas of residential development. The particular characteristics of each site are appreciated and maintained.

From their earliest and most modest planning ventures, the Griffins indicated an interest in developing cohesive communities, distinct neighborhoods with common green space as a focal point for housing clusters. This is evident in the Ridge Quadrangles subdivision (Evanston, Ill., c. 1910; fig. 13.3) as well as the Trier Center plan (Winnetka, Ill., 1913). Each of these plans reworked the developers' speculative grid into a more picturesque arrangement, encouraging social interaction and enhancing natural areas. Houses sit at varying distances from the lot line and are varied in plan. The generally flat terrain of the metropolitan Chicago area did not require careful consideration of land formation, but these subdivisions work respectfully with the adjacent superimposed grid. The Ridge Quadrangles plan graphically illustrates that picturesque design can be achieved without sacrificing density of development.

Lloyd's death in 1944 prevented Mahony Griffin from bringing these projects to fruition. Other circumstances, however, would offer Mahony Griffin opportunity to continue to illustrate her planning concepts. By 1945, Chicago and the United States looked to the future. The end of World War II was anticipated, and victory for the Allies appeared imminent. It seemed accepted that life after the war would be different, that change and a new outlook were necessary and that federal funding would be available to be redirected from the war effort to address internal homeland issues. According to H. Evert Kincaid, executive director of the Chicago Plan Commission, urban America was

> awakening to the complexities of the economic and social problems of cities as never before in its history. Almost every sizeable community throughout our country has revitalized its planning commission and the other public bodies charged with the responsibility of providing for the long neglected needs of the people. Newspapers and magazines have found city planning to be first-class news material for their readers. Aspirants to political office have built their platform on "greater city plans." State after state has passed new laws enabling cities to broaden their planning programs, to establish special authorities with vast administrative powers, and to authorize the sale of bonds for purposes never before included within the scope of municipal government. . . .
>
> Yes, our American cities are on the march toward new municipal goals—better transportation—safer highways—greater opportunities for stable employment—more parks and playgrounds—expanded educational opportunities—more homogenous neighborhoods —and adequate homes for the people. It all sums up to one objective—"Better cities in which to live and work."[28]

13.4 Partial site plan of Chicago (northern portion), competition entry for *Chicago Herald American's* "Better Chicago Contest," 1945. Courtesy of the Burnham Library, Art Institute of Chicago.

13.5 Partial site plan of Chicago (southern portion), competition entry for *Chicago Herald American's* "Better Chicago Contest," 1945. Courtesy of the Burnham Library, Art Institute of Chicago.

In that spirit, two of Chicago's newspapers sponsored competitions to address some of the issues facing the postwar city; Mahony Griffin prepared entries for both.

Better Chicago Competition

On April 9, 1945, the *Chicago Herald American* announced the Better Chicago Contest.[29] This competition was the culmination of a series of articles written by William Tell, who had joined the paper in January. Tell's pieces discussed various aspects of urban life that he identified as problematic, such as inadequate and dilapidated housing, filthy streets and unclear air, inappropriate land uses, poor transportation, as well as loss of population and revenue to suburban communities. As Tell described it, "the contest . . . was designed to achieve two objectives: 1) to generate civic interest; and 2) to develop a pattern of living and working by which metropolitan Chicago may shape its postwar future."[30] The competition was open to any interested individual or group of individuals who could compete for the main prize and/or one of six additional individual civic planning problems. The distinguished panel of judges included Lászlo Moholy-Nagy (president of the Institute of Design[31]), Daniel H. Burnham, Jr., John H. Root, and Walter H. Blucher, executive director of the American Society of Planning Officials.[32] Advisor for the competition was Chicago architect Jerrold Loebl. Three main prizes were offered for the plans that suggested the best overall solution for an overall plan of the metropolitan area. Contestants were asked to think of Chicago as a vast area extending beyond its corporate limits and were at liberty and required to determine exactly what constituted Chicago's metropolitan district. Secondary prizes were to be awarded for the following: Neighborhood Community Problem, Political and Administration Problem, Industrial Area Development, Retail Trade and Office Building Area, Railroad Transportation Problem, and Administrative and Cultural Center. Contestants were required to provide drawings and/or diagrams as well as a written synopsis of their ideas.

According to the *Chicago Herald American*, interest in the competition was nationwide, and some of the country's leading architects and planners were expected to participate.[33] The primary task of the designer was to reshape the metropolitan area of Chicago into a unified and livable whole. Mahony Griffin prepared an entry for this competition, a master plan that consisted of two large linen drawings, delineated in black and red ink and graphite (figs. 13.4 and 13.5).[34] The plans encompassed the entire existing incorporated area of metropolitan Chicago, from Devon Avenue on the north, south to 138th Street, and west to the irregular line of the city limits. At first glance it appears that she has superimposed an abstract geometric order over the entire city. Closer examination reveals that careful thought has been given to a holistic transformation of the city from a confused organism to one of order and beauty. Mahony Griffin discusses her vision

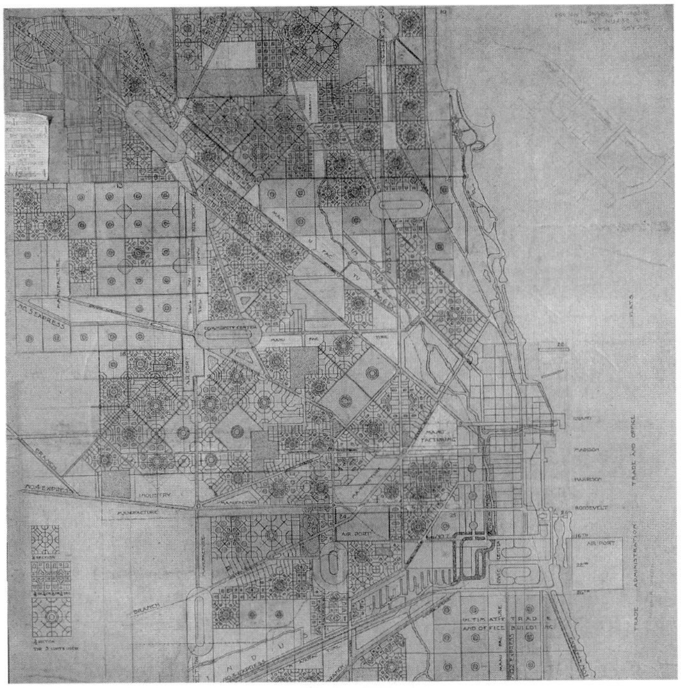

13.4

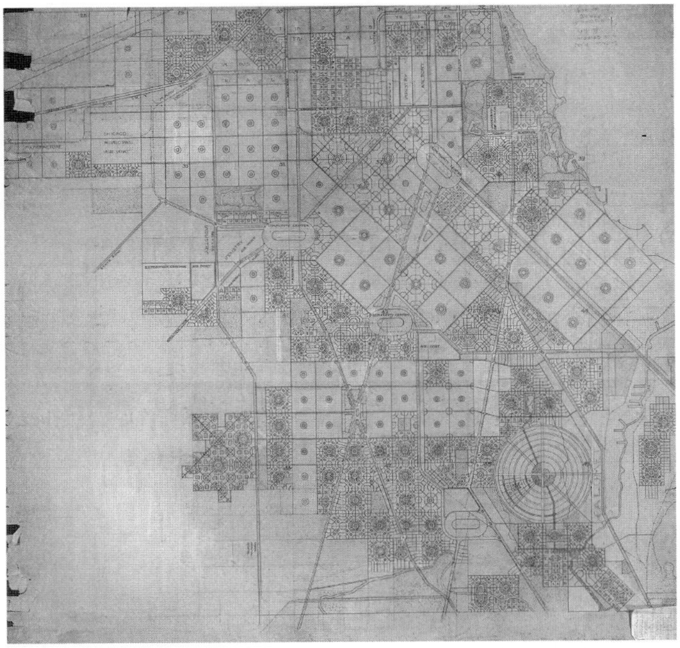

13.5

for the city in detail in her unpublished memoir. Her plan is based on the "mathematical spatial requirement of eliminating all acute angles, and the spiritual requirement of conserving nature."[35]

Mahony Griffin's master plan accepted and retained a number of the major existing elements of the city infrastructure, including the path of its waterways, railroad lines, and major thoroughfares; the established system of parks; major cultural institutions and monumental buildings; the central business district; the intensely occupied "flat" district on the North Side; and the scattering of industry in various locations throughout the city. She then proposed to integrate and organize the whole with a number of modifications. Community centers (indicated as large ovals on the plan) are positioned from one to three miles apart on the plan at locations where railway lines and major thoroughfares intersect. Manufacturing districts are located along through routes; she notes that careful planning of each of these districts would be required so as to ensure that they are not nuisances to the adjacent community. Anticipating the expansion of airways, Mahony Griffin provided a number of smaller airports in locations proximate to the manufacturing and industrial districts as well as convenient to the community centers.

She proposed no revolutionary changes for the central business district, noting that the "original difficulties of the site have been overcome and its location at the confluence of the river with the lake is properly the determining factor of its location."[36] Her only suggestion for this area was that provision should be made for the extension of the district west to Halsted Street. She proposed that a permanent right of way, a promenade, be established on both sides along the Chicago River, from Twenty-fifth Street north to its mouth. She addressed the issue of traffic safety in several ways. First she separated pedestrian traffic from vehicular traffic as much as possible. She recommends that streets be sized according to a hierarchal standard; neighborhood streets should be narrower so through traffic is discouraged. Different modes of transportation are vertically separated: railroads and stations are recessed; airports are located above rail yards. She recommended the elimination of all on-street parking.[37]

Mahony Griffin encouraged the generous planting of trees along all streets to take advantage of their ability to purify the air and dissipate the heat of summer.

The most radical and original of Mahony Griffin's proposals for reshaping her hometown were suggested for several areas on the South Side. Mahony Griffin felt that the "South Side, if properly handled would have a population as profitable to Chicago as the North districts beyond the City limits are."[38] She began with a bold suggestion for transforming the Calumet Harbor District. "Instead of destroying its value for the citizenry as a whole by industrializing Lake Calumet as

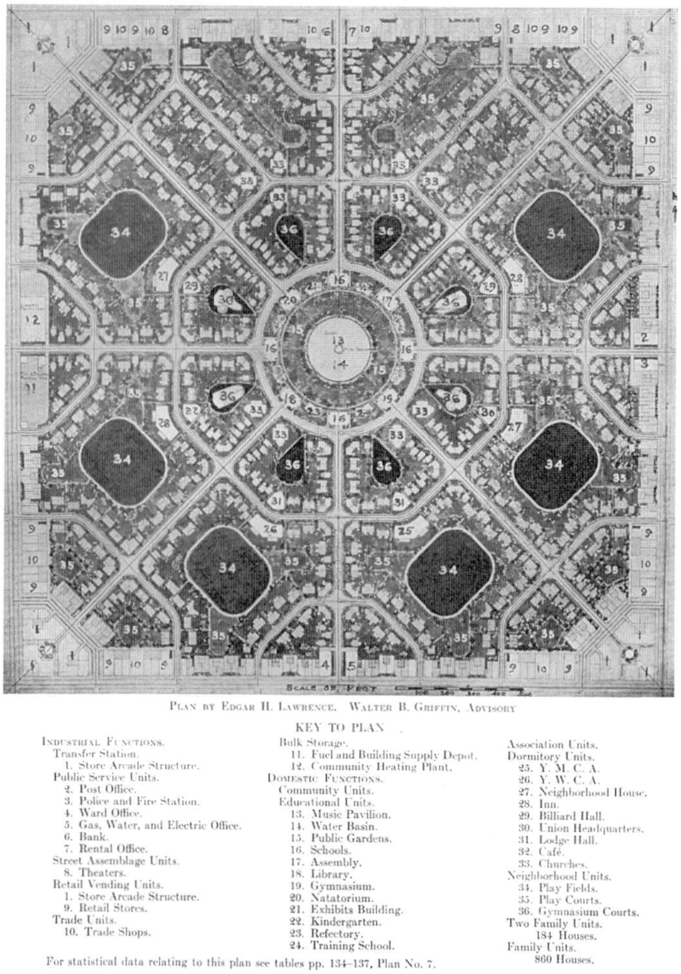

13.6 Site plan for a quarter section of the City of Chicago, plan by Edgar H. Lawrence, Walter B. Griffin, advisor, 1913. Courtesy of the University of Chicago Press.

we have used it," she suggested using the same method of holding back the lake's runoff instead to create a "charming residential community—a New Venice."[39] She proposed creating a new course for the Chicago River, a lock system to form a series of formal reflecting pools and controlled waters for landscaping and architectural effects.

In accordance with her general principal of locating community centers at transportation hubs, Mahony Griffin located the Administrative and Cultural Center where eight major through routes come together, between Halsted Street and Lake Michigan, south of Roosevelt Road and north of Twenty-sixth Street, directly west of the proposed air field at the lake.[40] With characteristic vision, Mahony Griffin noted that this

meeting point of land, water and air transport, if properly handled, should establish a spectacular Architectural Center, a true Urban Cultural Center. A deviation of the river could take freight traffic west of this center. This natural center offers the opportunity for a beautiful expression of the genius of the City as the representative of the present civilization. The construction of this center should not be too hurried. The Field Museum and the Planetarium are already there.[41]

She suggests that this development will spur further development and result in a retail trade and office district comparable to that of the North Side.

The geometry of the individual quarter sections in Mahony Griffin's master plan is strikingly similar to an earlier Griffin project (fig. 13.6).[42] This project was an entry into a 1913 City Club of Chicago competition for the design of a typical quarter section of Chicago. Walter Burley Griffin is believed to have entered this competition anonymously; in the formal publication of the entries produced in 1916 he is listed as advisor to Edgar H. Lawrence. Mahony Griffin's autobiography-memoir includes the plan of this project, the complete synopsis that was included with the competition entry, as well as the "Economic Review of the Plans" by Robert Anderson Pope.

In this plan a typical quarter section is subdivided into four essentially identical quadrants with radial and cross streets terminating at a circular commons area located at the center of the quarter section. Commercial and retail areas are confined to the perimeter streets of the section, and each cluster of residential structures surrounds a play area of a size appropriate to the residential "block." This plan is identical to one of the primary units used in Mahony Griffin's master plan (see fig. 13.4 above). In his review of this plan, Pope praised the fact that the high intensity of development was not obtained at "the sacrifice of park and playground areas, which are situated in such a way as to enhance land values very materially. The arrangement of houses secures for many the maximum possible exposures. Therefore, the intensity has not been established at the expense of sunlight and air."[43] City Club competition winners were announced in March 1913, and the entries were included in the City Club Housing Exhibition held from April 15 to June 1, 1913. Given this time framework, the project was prepared after the Griffins had been informed of winning the Canberra competition and were still working together in the Chicago office.

Within residential neighborhoods, Mahony Griffin recommends the elimination of all alleys and the narrowing of pavements to prevent unnecessary through traffic. Architectural design of buildings is addressed only in general terms, with the exception of the caveat that all buildings, both commercial and residential, have flat roofs to serve as landing pads for helicopters.[44]

While graphically drastic in the breadth of its transformation, Mahony Griffin's plan for a better Chicago was one offering for contemplation of a revitalized city, a city that could enrich and bring joy to all of its many inhabitants. "A city is immortal," she wrote. "All these changes need not therefore entail heavy expenditures but can come with the timely and natural restoration of the properties involved."[45]

As the deadline for the *Herald American* competition neared (July 16, 1945), the paper indicated that the announcement of the winners would take at least an additional month in order to allow time for any overseas entries from servicemen to reach their offices. It was not, however, until December of that year that the paper finally made the announcement[46]—Mahony Griffin was not among the winners.

Chicagoland Prize Home Competition

During the same period that the *Herald American* competition was in progress, another major newspaper conducted a competition of its own. In September 1945 the *Chicago Tribune* announced their "$24,000 Chicagoland Prize Home Competition," which offered twenty-four equal prizes for three specific houses of varying size, with eight prizes in each group. The three problems were as follows: problem no. 1 was for a house of a maximum floor area of 1,100 square feet on a lot 30 × 150 feet and for a family consisting of father, mother, and six-year-old son; problem no. 2 was for a house of 1,400 square on a lot 50 × 150 feet and for a family of parents and two children; problem no. 3 was for a dwelling of not more that 1,700 square feet on a lot 65 × 150 feet for a family of parents, two daughters, and one son. Houses were required to be of one or two stories only, and entries were to include "simple floor plans, perspective, two elevations and appropriate detail of single-family dwellings, without limitation as to period, style or tradition, but consistent with good taste and worthy of recommendation to *Chicago Tribune*

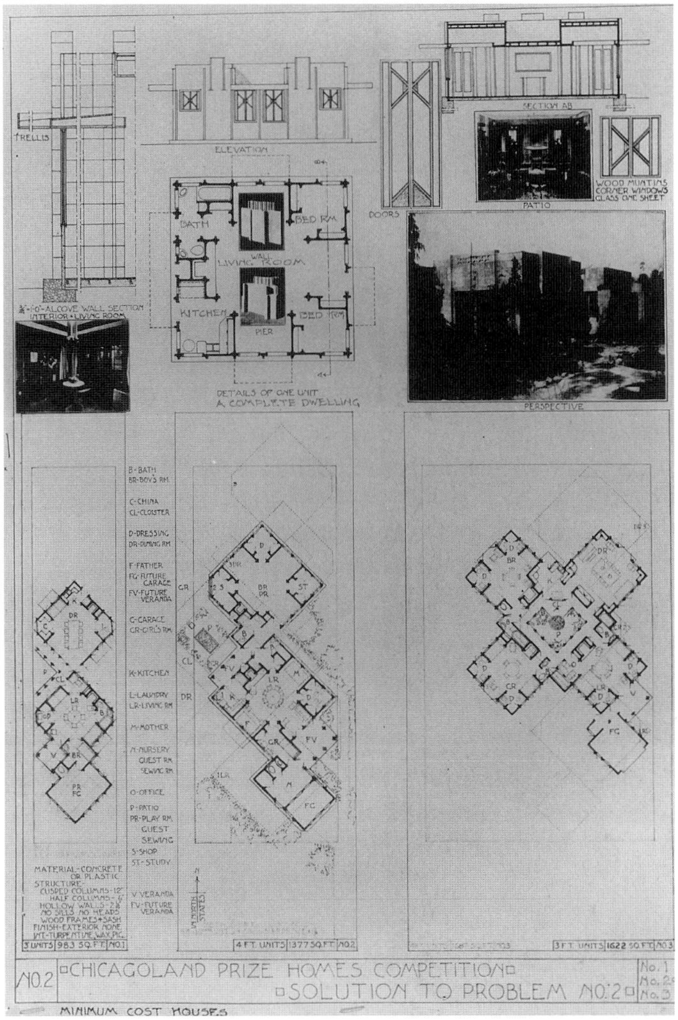

13.7 Chicagoland Prize Home Competition, solution to problem no. 2, Marion Mahoney Griffin, architect, 1945. Negative no. 71994. Courtesy of the collection of the New York Historical Society.

readers as embodying sound and practical principles of design and construction."[47]

The jury consisted of five architects and four builders. The chairman of the jury was Paul Gerhardt, Jr., then president of the Chicago chapter of the American Institute of Architects. Other architect members of the jury included Philip B. Maher, FAIA, John Merill, AIA, and A. N. Rebori.[48]

Mahony Griffin's entry for this competition is titled "Solution to Problem No. 2." The single-board, standard-size entry format (fig. 13.7) includes floor plans across the bottom of the board that addresses each of the three problems. The upper part of the board features drawings (floor plan, elevation, section, wall section, door and window details) almost identical to those produced for the Castlecrag Caretaker's Lodge, designed by Walter Burley Griffin in 1927. It also included photographs of several other earlier Griffin projects. These include an interior photo of Pholiota, the Griffin's own home, an exterior view of the Mower Residence, and a view of the inner courtyard of the Felstead Residence. Reference to these projects as well as the use of Walter Burley Griffin's patented knitlock wall unit as the primary construction system (this is evidenced by the cross-shaped piers, which are an integral part of the wall system) has resulted in this project previously being credited to Mahony Griffin's husband.[49] The three lower-floor plans, labeled 1, 2, and 3, are clearly Mahony Griffin's designs.

All of the plans are sited at a forty-five-degree angle to the north-south grid of the street. This is an orientation seen in several of the Griffins' projects in Australia, including the Cox Residence of the 1930s. Mahony Griffin felt this rotation would provide optimal orientation to both sun and shade for all of the rooms in a house. It is an orientation that she frequently sought in her site planning for residential structures. Each of the plans is based upon the one-room concept first developed for two vacation cottages, Gumnuts and Marnham, and used again for the Castlecrag Caretaker's Lodge and the Griffins' own beloved home, Pholiota.[50] The basic plan includes a central square-shaped living area with fireplace alcove at one end opposite a wall of French doors to the exterior. Perpendicular to the fireplace axis is an axis containing a bed alcove at either end. Service spaces (kitchen, bath, entry, and dressing room) are located in each of the four corners. This one-room floor plan is the basic module upon which each of Mahony Griffin's three individual floor plans are based. This basic living room module occurs in each of the plans and is then repeated and modified to provide additional spaces. In each module a central common area is surrounded by clusters of service areas located in the corners. The concept of developing the plan of a house through the use of intersecting squares had also been used in a number of projects that the Griffins produced while in Australia.

A close examination of these plans reveals both severe impracticalities as well as delightful innovations (fig. 13.8). They contain rather awkward functional arrangements as well as carefully thought-out spaces. In each of the three schemes, the parents' sleeping space are the two separate bed alcoves on either side of the main living room; no private separate bedroom is provided for them. The parents' private dressing room and one bathroom open directly off the living room. In the solution to problem no. 1, the kitchen is exceptionally small and is placed at the back of the house, as remote as possible from the garage and entry; a bathroom opens directly off the living room and access to what could have been the master bedroom is through the small boy's room, which also inconveniently opens directly to the living room. On the other hand, the large dining room, the alcove for china storage and the small desk area tucked in at the top of the living room are rather nice features. In the solution to problem no. 2, the separate guest wing and bath located directly off the entry veranda could be pleasant, and the organization of private areas in one square and living spaces in another is reasonable. However, in this larger house, there is no separate dining room. To reach the large rear module, which is the boy's bedroom, one must walk through the kitchen or bathroom. In the largest house, plan no. 3, the organization of the two children's rooms is clever and extremely workable. Each is designed for two children and provides a recess for the beds, separate dressing rooms for each child, a central play area and study area and access to a bathroom. The dining room is generous and occupies an entire module of its own; it could be a spectacular space. The organization of the four modules around a central courtyard

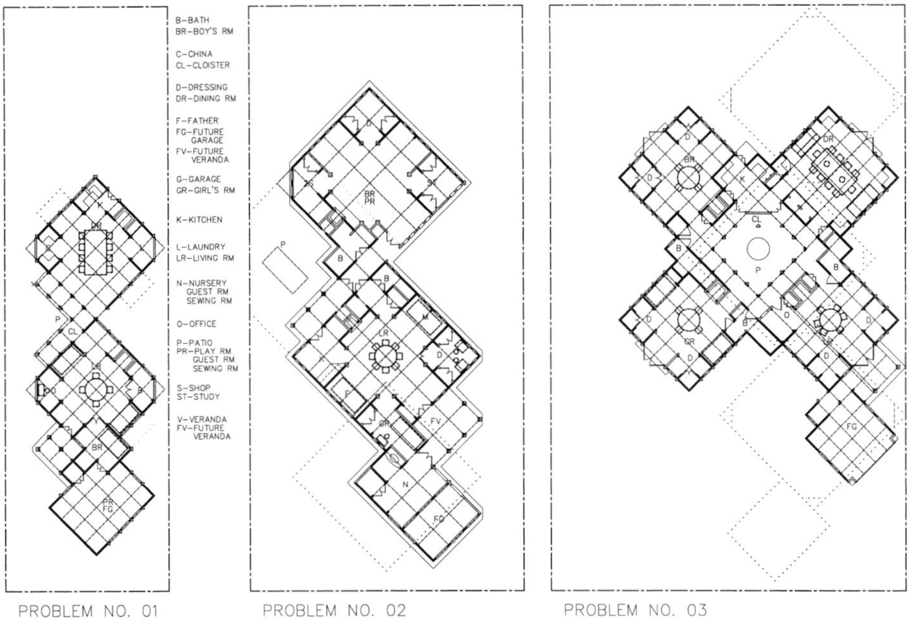

13.8 Detail plans, Chicagoland Prize Home Competition, solution to problem no. 2, Marion Mahoney Griffin, architect, 1945. Redrawn by Pamela Hill.

with pool is exotic but problematic in a northern climate. The bathrooms in all of the plans are eccentric in layout, irregular shapes with fixtures tucked into niches. Yet the entry to all of the homes, through verandas and sheltered from street frontage, provide welcome privacy. The experience of walking from one area of any of the houses to another would be an adventure. In even the smallest house, to traverse from the living room to the dining room one must pass through a glazed gallery with a view to a patio.

A comparison of Mahony Griffin's designs to some of the "winning entries" (fig. 13.9) is illuminating. There are several similarities. First, like Mahony Griffin, most of the entrants envisioned the modern house as a single-story edifice. Also, despite the best efforts of the media to interest the public in the renewal of the city, the architects were not interested in the city; they were designing for the suburbs or at least with no thought to the urban context. Although the lot sizes were based on those typical to the standard urban grid, none of the houses were appropriate in scale or form to an urban site. This was also true of Mahony Griffin's entry. Her one-story concrete house turned forty-five degrees to the street as well as all of the winning entries would have looked out of place on an infill lot of a typical Chicago neighborhood, such as that in which Mahony Griffin herself lived. The judges rejected all traditional entries, deciding that houses of contemporary design best met the requirements of practicality.[51] Mahony Grif-

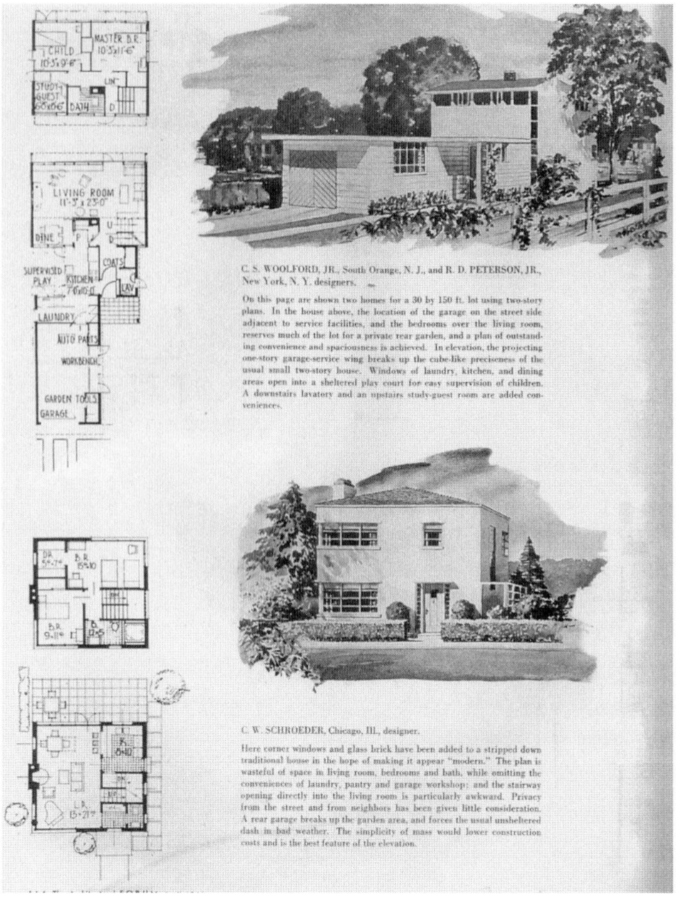

13.9 Winning competition entries, Chicagoland Prize Home Competition, 1945. As published in the *Architectural Forum*, April 1946. Text courtesy of the Chicago Historical Society.

fin's design was in no way traditional, and the winning entries avoided all reference to period styles or historic reference.

The differences between Mahony Griffin's entry and those of the other competitors are striking. Her entry is eccentric and exotic, certainly not the practical solution for which the jury was looking. In some respects her entry was far more "modern." She had rejected the pitched roof that was still associated with the American home, and the suggested use of concrete or plastic as the primary material of construction was radical. The design of the windows and doors, however, with their intricately designed geometric panes of glass, are reminiscent of the Griffin Prairie school–era designs. Her tendency to provide multiple small rooms, with each service function having its own defined space and her separation of living and dining and kitchen areas was contrary to the trend to simplify the plan of the house and combine common spaces into one room.

Despite their many functional shortcomings, there is something evocative and intriguing about Mahony Griffin's entry. Her notion of a house is one of complexity and richness. Overall, there is a confidence and a substance to her design that is totally lacking in the winning designs. In general, the winning entries are stylistically uncertain and unimaginative. It was as if the architects did not really know yet what the "contemporary" American house should be. The two-story entries were particularly homely, with the garage in several cases awkwardly grafted onto the front facade. Inspiration from the California ranch house is obvious in some of the designs, yet to accommodate this popular new house type to the program requirements, the designers had to string the plan out in a linear fashion that is not entirely successful. In the process of experiencing one of the Mahony Griffin houses, there is a sense of mystery and discovery. The plans are not easily comprehended. They lure one back for yet another look; they require study and thought. Most of the plans of the winning competition entries are straightforward and uninspired, boxy and compartmentalized, a series of rooms connected by a long corridor. While the winning entries offered a final resolved solution that could go from drawing board to actual construction, Mahony Griffin's entry suggests possibilities; it does not define an absolute form. One does not know what any of the three houses, presented in plan, would really look like. More work would be required to make them a reality.

In her designs Mahony Griffin was not primarily concerned with the mundane requirements of everyday functions but instead with making spaces to inspire creativity, celebrate nature, and enrich the soul. In the Mahony Griffin plans, the living room is conceived of as quite a different space than that of her competitors. The furniture in the winning designs shows the standard sofa, coffee table, and side chairs; some include a grand piano. Mahony Griffin's living rooms all contain a large round table with chairs, a place for people to gather collectively and interact or engage in a common activity. One can imagine that the judges may have been perplexed by this entry. The proposed plans may not have appealed to or accommodated a typical family of the era or been economically constructed by a contractor. Yet as one contemplates these plans, one can imagine that they were intended to provide refuge and inspiration for a more spiritual way of life than that envisioned by other architects of the era. To Mahony Griffin it was obvious that the design of a house was an intensely personal experience. In discussing her entry, she wrote that a "dwelling is the most important unit in a human community. It is the most complicated problem, the one most difficult to solve in the profession of architecture. The range of possibilities is endless. Other buildings are but incidents in the mass of dwellings."[52]

The competition entries and planning schemes discussed here are the last known Mahony Griffin projects. In reviewing them one is struck most by her sensitivity to the natural world, her belief that architecture and planning can respond to the spiritual needs of humanity and transcend the ordinary. Given any opportunity to practice her craft, she accepted the challenge. One wishes that more opportunities had presented themselves.

In researching Marion Mahony Griffin, one is always hoping to discover long lost, previously unknown projects, and especially, built projects for which she can be fully credited. For those intent upon moving her from her relative obscure place in architectural history to a more prominent one, such evidence would help substantiate her qualifications and abilities as an architect. If one approaches her work from this viewpoint, however, one is bound always to be disappointed. Indeed, Marion Mahony Griffin was an architect, but a very unique architect with a broad range of interests and talents. She was always more than just an architect, but that fact should in no way undermine her status as an architect. One needs to understand more about her as an individual and more about her creative union with her husband. For once Walter Burley Griffin and Marion Mahony Griffin became a couple, her work and that with which her husband is credited are inextricably interwoven. There is no sharp line dividing it, as much as one might like there to be. Her last projects discussed here, completed after the death of her husband, reference many earlier Griffin projects. It will take more years of study to decipher and comprehend her true place in the history of architecture and the cultural history of Chicago and the United States.

The Third Chicago School? Marking Sexual and Ethnic Identity

Christopher Reed

The city of Chicago claims two antagonistic architectural legacies. For much of the twentieth century, the so-called first and second Chicago schools identified the city with forward-looking modernism. In the heyday of modernism, Chicago was hailed as both the birthplace of the skyscraper and the home of the American Bauhaus. From this perspective, references to regional architectures of the past were dismissed as nostalgic atavisms irrelevant to the city's true character and bright future. Louis Sullivan's "form ever follows function" and Ludwig Mies van der Rohe's "less is more" became the shibboleths of an architecture that, under the rubrics of the "International Style" or simply "Modernism," claimed to have discovered the universally applicable template of utopian futurity.

Chicago's venerable association with the architecture of utopian universality contrasts with the city's reputation as an urban jungle (to invoke the title of Upton Sinclair's famous 1906 novel set around the city's stockyards), a tangle of immigrants competing in a primal struggle for survival. This city too had its architecture, and not just tenements in unplanned slums. From the onion domes on Roman Catholic churches in Polish neighborhoods to the Germanic vernacular of numerous brewery-sponsored beer gardens, an architectural rhetoric of ethnic appeal characterized many neighborhoods—and even some downtown monuments.

The 1922 competition that resulted in the construction of the French gothic Tribune Tower, for instance, has long been represented as just the last gasp of atavistic antimodernism without much analysis of what triumphed over the modernists' claims to utopian rationality. Chicago's character as an agglomeration of neighborhoods strongly identified by ethnicity, however, provides a context for the *Chicago Tribune*'s local presentation of the competition through months of weekly features on the potential of the world's regional architectures to provide a template for what it billed as the "world's most beautiful and distinctive office building."[1] When this pageant of ethnicities culminated with the Tribune's selection of French gothic, the solution was presented as a unifying reference to the ideal of civilization that servicemen from across Chicago had recently defended in the Great War. On the exterior of the ground floor, inset stones from Cologne Cathedral, Notre-Dame de Paris, the Colosseum in Rome, Westminster Abbey, the Taj Mahal, and the Great Wall of China—more recently augmented with a rock from the moon—invoke both the universal reach of the newspaper and the contributions of these diverse sources to the fabric of the building and, by implication, to the city it serves. Although modernist consensus condemned the Tribune Tower as backward-looking, its combination of gothic fantasy and pluralist tokenism might be seen as more prescient of Chicago's future than any glass-and-steel box.

14.1 Temple from Greektown project, Chicago, 1996. Elias Pappageorge, architect. Photograph by Christopher Reed.

14.2 Pagoda from Chinatown project, Chicago, 1995. Photograph by Christopher Reed.

14.3 One of the Division Street Gateways (also known as the "Puerto Rican Gates"), Chicago, 1995. De Stefano and Partners, James R. DeStefano and Edward Windhorst, architects. Photograph by Christopher Reed.

Both visually and ideologically, the Tribune Tower's invocation of ethnic identity as a way of situating itself within a narrative of shared multiculturalism offers a paradigm for postmodern Chicago. In an irony rarely noted, during the period of the "second Chicago school" the city was associated architecturally with an enlightened modernism of universal ideals and politically with a growing reputation for ethnic antagonism characterized by competitive ward politics and a rigid, sometimes violent, territoriality.[2] In contrast, postmodern Chicago—which might be dated politically to the 1983 election of Harold Washington, the city's first African American mayor—has been characterized by initiatives to recast the city's racial and ethnic divisions according to an ideal that David Dinkins (another first black mayor of a major U.S. city) christened the "gorgeous mosaic." This visual metaphor has particular importance for architecture and design, for it conceives identity as spectacle, replacing modernism's signifiers of functionalist universality with eclectic signifiers of ethnic specificity that can be resolved in the appreciative vision of the viewer mobile enough to perceive the harmonies of the diverse whole. This ambition is literalized in the decoration of Chicago's new main library, opened in 1991 and named posthumously for Harold Washington. Although critical attention has focused on the exterior of this structure, where Thomas Beeby's overscale historicist decorative elements offer a manifesto of postmodern eclecticism, inside the floor of the central lobby records Washington's exhortations to treasure the urban diversity represented by identity categories (including gay and lesbian) listed in concentric rings of text that one must move around to read.[3]

As evidenced by the library, Harold Washington—unlike Dinkins—has been, since his untimely death in office, canonized as a kind of civic saint who redeemed the city from the most overt forms of ethnic and racial antagonism. The current mayor, Richard M. Daley (son of Mayor Richard J. Daley, who during his quarter-century term came to embody the politics of old-style ethnicity), routinely invokes Washington's ideals, presenting the city to its own citizens, as well as to visitors from its suburbs and beyond, as a "City of Neighborhoods": a permanent World's Fair of diverse cultures, where saint's days and national anniversaries are played out in an extraordinary number of summer festivals and street fairs—more than any other U.S. city—which are publicized by the city as spectacles available to all residents and visitors.[4] By many measures, this strategy has been a success: tourism thrives and, in contrast to many midwestern cities, the number of households quitting the city for the suburbs has fallen below the number moving from the suburbs to the city.

14.3

Appropriately enough for the spectacular metaphor of the mosaic, urban design played an important role in Chicago's project to redefine ethnicity. The city undertook public works projects in its so-called Greektown and Chinatown, as well as a Puerto Rican

14.1

14.2

neighborhood, all of which use architecture and other visual markers to fortify viewers' experience of these areas' ethnic specificity. Both the Greektown and Chinatown projects insert allusions to ethnically specific building types into the urban fabric (figs. 14.1 and 14.2), while the Puerto Rican neighborhood is bracketed with gateway structures that allude to the Puerto Rican flags on shops and cars in the nearby streets (fig. 14.3). The "Puerto Rican Gates," as they are colloquially known, were well received by the local community, commended by the architectural establishment, and published in the national art press.[5] Following this success, the mayor commissioned in the summer of 1997 the architect of the Puerto Rican gates, Edward Windhorst, to design markers for another distinctive Chicago neighborhood.[6] The announcement of a plan to give visual designation to the district that realtors prefer to call Lakeview but that many refer to as Boys Town was both hailed and denounced as the first permanent government-sponsored marker of gay community. The ensuing controversy generated more mail to the city (over seven thousand pieces) than any single issue in Chicago's history and attracted news coverage as far away as New York City, Washington, D.C., San Diego, and London, supplanting (at least for a time) Chicago's reputation as the architectural cradle of modernism with claims to pioneer a postmodern architectural rhetoric of multicultural spectacle.

14.4

14.4 Two pylons at the dedication ceremony for the North Halsted Streetscape Project, Chicago, 14 November 1998. De Stefano and Partners, Edward Windhorst, architect. Photograph by Jason Smith.

14.5 One pylon during the Gay Pride Parade, June 2000. Photograph by Christopher Reed.

Although the City insisted that most of the $3.2 million budget for what was officially called the North Halsted Streetscape Project covered improvements to gutters, curbs, and paving, controversy centered on both the idea of visually designating a section of Halsted Street as gay and on the design of the elements that carried that message: eleven pairs of what the newspapers called "Art Deco style pylons," each twenty-three feet high, illuminated, and ringed with rainbow stripes, intended to flank the street at midblock (fig. 14.4, 14.5). A Department of Transportation prospectus issued to reporters covering the controversy rechristened these elements "identity columns," explaining that they will "rise from the street and climb to a graceful peak, and will contain colored rings which pay tribute to the gay and lesbian community in Chicago and to the rainbow of diversity that has historically been the great strength of the Lakeview community." The awkward ambivalence of this description of the rainbow rings' symbolism (are they about homosexuals or diversity in general?) gave way to more explicit language from the mayor, who released a letter affirming that "the appearance of the street will draw attention to the strong presence of the gay and lesbian community" and framing this in the language of multicultural spectacle: "Years from now we will be taking our grandchildren to North Halsted and other neighborhoods across the city and reminding them that we are all different, yet we are all a community."[7]

The mayor's speech clearly affirmed the equation of sexual and ethnic identity that was implied by the context of the Boys Town project in the Neighborhoods Alive initiative of district markers. This assertion—controversial enough in itself—played out over a symbolically important site. Halsted Street is both the city's longest street and part of the state's longest road, the old Illinois Route 1, which stretches toward Chicago from the hamlet of Cave-in-Rock on the Kentucky border. As such, Halsted Street has been the subject of two documentary films, one in 1931 and a second in 1998, both of which focus on the changing character of the thoroughfare as it passes from the countryside through different ethnically marked urban neighborhoods from African American areas on the South Side through Irish and once-Jewish, now Mexican, districts; then in front of the original Hull House, symbol of the "settlement" movement among new immigrants at the turn of the nineteenth century; from there through the Greek neighborhood with its recently installed tiny temples; along the notorious Cabrini Green public housing projects; and into the now-affluent, formerly Germanic, neighborhoods of Old Town and Boys Town before it finally peters out at an intersection dominated by gas stations, an International House of Pancakes, and parking lots.[8] It was, in part, to redefine Halsted Street's fraying northern terminus that the mayor's streetscape project was proposed, but the implication that a path originating in small-town America and traveling through traditional racial/ethnic urban enclaves should culminate in gay community provoked debates over the construction of subcultural identity both figuratively (in the

14.5

psyche of individuals and the population as a whole) and literally (in the fabric of the city).

To get a sense of these debates, consider the following four quotations from the press coverage. The first comes from a spokesman for the City of Chicago's Department of Planning and Development, reacting defensively to the eruption of controversy about the project: "To me, it was just another local flavor to a neighborhood."[9] The second quotation, from a *Chicago Tribune* editorial supporting the city's plans, endorsed the equation of sexuality with ethnic identity:

Gays seek out big cities like Chicago for much the same reason ethnic and religious minorities once did and still do: Here they find official tolerance and peer-group acceptance.[10]

It is just this analogy that was rejected in the dissenting column of an individual *Tribune* editor the next day:

The city spends money defining many of its neighborhoods, they say, and an ethnic enclave is the cultural equivalent of one based on sexual identity. This claim rings wrong to those of us who don't equate sex with a plate of spanikopita.[11]

The fourth quotation, from Chicago's other daily, the *Sun-Times*, also rejects the reification of gay identity in urban design, sarcastically imagining its complement:

[The city] also needs to celebrate a neighborhood for its heterosexuality. . . . To avoid confusion, though, the kind of twinkling "rainbow rings of lights" that will adorn the tops of the Boys Town pylons will have to go. Replaced I suppose with likenesses of Ozzie and Harriet. Only straight sidewalks would be permitted.[12]

Taken together, these remarks show how the Boys Town proposal plunged discussions of planning and design in Chicago into debates that had animated academic discussions of identity for over a decade, that is, since Steven Epstein's much-discussed 1987 essay, "Gay Politics, Ethnic Identity: The Limits of Social

14.6 Tin Man, Oz Park, Chicago, 1995. Photograph by Christopher Reed.

Constructionism," argued that ethnic and sexual identity had converged. Epstein cited sociological theorization of the "new ethnicity," a term referring to the loosening of traditional forms of ethnic identification among diasporic populations in the United States. Where old ethnicity assumed purity of genetic lineage and immediate experience of immigration, the new ethnicity was defined as a state of mind that allowed, for example, participation by spouses from other backgrounds and relied on the efforts of third- and fourth-generation Americans to retrieve ethnically specific customs abandoned by their parents and grandparents.[13] Self-consciously performative, at least partially volitional, and acquired in adulthood, the new ethnicity paralleled aspects of emerging forms of sexual identity that, concurrently, other sociologists were noting as the basis of new neighborhoods characterized in ways conventionally associated with ethnic districts.

Sociological arguments for the equivalence of ethnic and sexual identity, however, raised problems concerning the architectural signification of gay community. Where the earlier neighborhood projects generated visual vocabulary from the flags and architecture of ethnic homelands, the Boys Town commission raised the question: Where do gays come from? Although the Chrysler Building profile of the pylons hints that we are all from Manhattan, the multicolored rings and over-the-top fantasy of this procession of elements suggests another point of origin:

somewhere over the rainbow, in a land that we've heard of . . . where art deco is the indigenous architectural idiom. And that may not be a bad guess—at least not in a symbolic economy where Chinese Americans come from pagodas, and Greek Americans from Corinthian-columned temples. If, as Chicago's earlier urban markers imply, ethnic identity is constituted in relation to a fantasy/memory of a realm elsewhere, why not choose Oz—and, by inference, the whole glamorous bygone world of midcentury Hollywood—as the gay homeland? Indeed, if Arjun Appadurai is right to argue that traditional forms of ethnic identity have been replaced by "diasporic public spheres" created through electronic media, the location of an originary gay homeland in film confirms the convergence of sexuality and ethnicity as social formations.[14]

Grounding gay identity in Oz may be particularly appropriate to Chicago, moreover. Anticipating the dynamic of the Tribune Tower competition, the historicist architecture of the 1893 Columbian Exposition was for most of the twentieth century seen as another famous local failure to embrace the homegrown modern. But the sequence of ethnic villages, from Dahomean to Teutonic, that lined the Midway leading to the neoclassical White City at the exposition inspired at least one modern American icon: L. Frank Baum's *The Wonderful Wizard of Oz* (the "Wonderful" was dropped after the first edition), a children's story structured as a quest through various foreign cultures toward the towers of the Emerald City. Baum's Chicago connection is celebrated at Oz Park, not far from Boys Town, where a sculpture of the Tin Man stands on a piazza of yellow bricks inscribed with the names of donors, among whom—in an earlier testament to the neighborhood's diversity—are some same-sex couples (fig. 14.6).[15]

Links between gay identity and *The Wizard of Oz* extend far beyond the history of Chicago, however. To be "friends with Dorothy" is a long-standing euphemism for male homosexuality, and I am far from the first to note contemporary gay identity's connection with Judy Garland, Oz, Hollywood musicals, and the whole baggage carried by the elusive term "camp." Notoriously hard to define, "camp" sensibility—characterized by identification with what the dominant culture has displaced from the realms of fashion or propriety—defines gay identity, according to anthropologist Esther Newton, the way "soul" marks Afro-American culture.[16] It is worth, therefore, exploring the implications of *The Wizard of Oz*'s campiness in relation to the parallel structures of ethnic and sexual identity as they are constructed through nostalgia for a homeland.

"There's no place like home!" Dorothy's ambivalent mantra simultaneously asserts and denies the power of home in a pithy encapsulation of the plot of this famous film, in which the heroine's misery in emotionally parched rural America (a condition many queers relate to) is transformed by her fantastical migration to Oz.[17] As she first encounters it, Oz is overtly—if confusingly—ethnicized as the half-African, half-Bavarian Munchkinland, where beehive-shaped, wattle-roofed huts, neatly whitewashed and decorated with gingerbread trim, disgorge miniature inhabitants dressed for an Oktoberfest in what seems an unwitting parody of the parade of ethnic villages along the Midway leading to the White City. For Dorothy, Munchkinland's spectacle of ethnicity originates a quest for the gleaming art deco towers of the Emerald City, where even the horses are rainbow-hued. Dorothy's successful negotiation of Oz's multiculturalism is grounded in her own diasporic nostalgia ("I'm Dorothy Gale, from Kansas!" she informs everyone she meets). Back in Kansas, however, it is her equally powerful nostalgia for Oz that redeems her drab home with roseate—along with all the other hues in the Technicolor spectrum—memories of Oz. "It was a place!" Dorothy exclaims when she wakes up on the farm, "And you, and you, and you, and you were there!"

How campy is Dorothy as she negotiates her way through Oz and is reconciled to Kansas by, in each place, performing wistful memories of the inaccessible other? So too, camp sensibility conjures a passionate nostalgia for artifacts and personalities ignored or displaced by dominant cultural values. And how like Dorothy's Oz are the places sexual minorities construct (or imagine) in order to negotiate identities between memories (or fantasies) of the straight people we were brought up to be and the equally fantastic stereotypes (as horrifying as the Wicked Witch or as fabulous as Glenda in her bubble) that the dominant culture offers as images of gay identity? Looking back on our childhoods from the other side of the life represented by the clubs and shops that line Halsted Street in Boys Town (Oz-like sites of concentrated fantasy), we too may be inclined to reinterpret our origins: "You were there, Mom, and that cute boy in first grade, and the spinster ladies who lived next door. You, and you, and you were there!"[18] Just as ethnic—and particularly "new ethnic"—identity is constituted through memories (or cinematic fantasies) of a homeland that may no longer exist, and certainly no longer exists as it once did in the experience of the emigrant, so gay identity may be structured around the proposition, articulated by Greta Garbo in the title role of another famously campy film, the 1933 *Queen Christina*: "It is possible to feel nostalgia for a place one has never seen."[19]

Ethnic nostalgia can focus on a home country, of course, but recent scholarship urges more attention to the overlooked "third cultures" that expatriates create between their home and host countries, and new-ethnic nostalgia seems at least as likely to center on these "old neighborhoods" of first-generation migrants, with their crowded apartments, specialty shops, festival days, small-circulation newspapers, local bars, and clubs.[20] Such manifestations of the new ethnicity have been largely transient and vicarious: novels, memoirs, films, exhibitions, and in Chicago, endlessly rerun public television programs

14.7 One pylon illuminated at night. Photograph by Christopher Reed.

celebrating the city's individual ethnic groups from the perspective of their assimilated descendants. In contrast, one of the most remarkable accomplishments of sexual minorities in the late twentieth century has been the purposeful reanimation of the spaces and institutions of diasporic urban culture that sociologists and urban planners at mid-century dismissed as doomed to extinction. Refugees from the sex/gender norms of the dominant forms of modern American social organization—the suburb, the small town, the farm—we migrate to the city, where, living in ways associated with the liminality of the recent immigrant, we embody dissent from the heterosexual melting pot.

This move has long been visible in cities like Chicago. In an article some years ago, I suggested a partial catalog of the distinctive visual aspects of gay neighborhoods, citing the graffiti and gardens along a now-demolished stretch of lakefront in the area of Lincoln Park nearest Boys Town.[21] In addition to the accretion of such clear signifiers of sexual identity as rainbow flags and "GAY ZONE" graffiti, I argued, gay neighborhoods are marked by architecture that reflects, first, an appeal to outdated architectural styles and, second, an accommodation to forms of pedestrian culture—especially nighttime strolling—that has largely vanished from other parts of U.S. cities. The latter (dare we call it "pedephilia"?) extends the queer legacy of the nineteenth-century flâneur or dandy as both creator and connoisseur of pedestrian spectacle. The renovation aesthetic likewise engages with history, not to return to the past (that is re*stor*ation), but rather to interpolate the past into the present so that both are simultaneously visible as the image of nostalgia. From this perspective, Chicago's sidewalk parade of bronze-toned, rainbow-striped, art-deco–style pylons, "dramatically uplit from the bottom for nighttime effect, but . . . largely neutral in the daylight" (fig. 14.7), as the city's prospectus put it, seemed to me—at least in theory—an appropriate design response to the formulation of urban gay identity.[22]

But, of course, not everyone agreed. Most of the attacks on the city's plans for Boys Town took the predictable forms of homophobic ranting against any official recognition of gay community and homophobic fretting that heterosexuals might feel marginalized in a designated gay neighborhood.[23] More interesting trends in the arguments over the markers, however, reflect important debates about the nature of gay identity in relation to ethnic models and urban design. Two different, though perhaps complementary, vectors of critique challenge the premise of any project to mark the spaces of gay identity. The first, and most common, argument comes from those who accept the equation of ethnic and sexual identity only to exhort sexual minorities to follow ethnic groups in the drive for unmarked assimilation. Repudiation of what this contingent consistently characterizes as the "gay ghetto" is not new, but it has waxed in proportion with the social formations it condemns. A series of articles promoting the suburbanization of gay men and lesbians, which appeared in a Chicago gay newspaper just before the Boys Town redevelopment project was announced, may have contributed to the tendency for journalists to highlight remarks from person-on-the-street interviews, such as "Ghettoizing the neighborhood doesn't help anyone," and "I have a problem designating any area for anything."[24] Unsurprisingly, the most vehement advocates for assimilation are the already assimilated. A *Chicago Tribune* columnist who identified himself as "a straight, married-with-kids white guy who lives in the suburbs" responded to the Boys Town debates by admonishing gays to choose the "road" of "marital monogamy, sexual restraint and middle-class respectability" over the "dead-end street . . . lined by bathhouses and leather bars, by serial sex and wear-it-on-your-sleeve sensuality."[25] This position claimed its academic adherents as well. The *Washington Post* quoted a professor of city and regional planning at Chicago's Illinois Institute of Technology, who complained that "the ghetto used to be something you wanted to escape from" and that the city's plan "goes against the whole idea of the melting pot."[26]

A second category of critique, though equally suspicious of efforts to mark gay identity, takes the opposite approach, condemning such initiatives not as impediments to assimilation but instead as signs of complicity with the dominant culture's efforts to thwart the radical potential of "queerness" by containing it within fixed geographical boundaries and a limited set of symbols.[27] This critique finds an articulate constituency among theorists who employ poststructuralist ideas to imagine an ideal of subversive "queer space," which, because it is continually in the process of constructing itself in opposition to nonqueer norms, they see as too fluid ever to assume concrete visual form and too subversive to be signaled by a government-sponsored design.[28] This analysis is deficient both as theory and as history, however.

As to theory, it is simply logocentric prejudice to equate the concrete with the visual while asserting the fluidity of verbal expression, as if running up a rainbow flag on a city street is any less a strategic deployment of a polysemic signifier than using the word "queer" in an academic essay (indeed, the rainbow flag and "queer" are analogous signifiers self-consciously conceived to supplant the perceived rigidity of the pink triangle emblem and terms like "gay" and "homosexual" with something more inclusive). Binaries of complicit/radical cannot be mapped onto visual/verbal any more than they fit over the assumed opposition of government and academe as institutional structures. Both are complex systems with complicated and even contradictory relationships to one another and to other forms of power, and academics publishing on "queerness" are no less enmeshed in these dynamics than designers planning the streetscape of a gay neighborhood.

The short history of the Boys Town markers exemplifies some of this complexity. Like Chicago's ethnic neighborhood markers, the Boys Town designs promote a small commercial district. But assumptions that these projects serve monolithic "business interests" are belied by their reception: the Puerto Rican gates—the project on which the Boys Town markers were most closely modeled—were welcomed by local residents as a barrier to gentrification, and the strongest local opposition to the Boys Town markers came from property owners who argued that identifying the neighborhood as gay would lower real estate values.[29] The relationship between economic power and neighborhood marking, in short, is neither straightforwardly subversive nor complicit. By the same token, the spaces of gay sex often privileged by advocates of "queer space"—from public parks to commercial sex clubs—are hardly outside structures of either the law or state-sponsored capitalism.[30]

The divergent lines of objection to the Boys Town markers—the assimilationist and the subversive—spring from a shared fantasy of remaining unmarked. Where the assimiliationists idealize a gay identity totally absorbed into mainstream culture, the subversives imagine a queer outlaw state so marginal as to escape signification altogether. The fantasy of invisibility, however, leads both arguments, despite their claims to enact progressive politics, to slip unwittingly into the uncanny underside of nostalgia: an unacknowledged—and thus uncontrolled—regression toward the pre–Stonewall-era dynamics of the "double life" or the "closet."[31] Would-be subversives ignore the identification of the most marginal spaces of gay sex—especially public bathrooms—with men who are closeted (and often married and politically conservative),[32] while assimilationist objections to the visual signifiers of gay community often fall back on obviously conservative notions of taste and gender. The resident who opposed the Boys Town markers "because he doesn't like labeling neighborhoods" was quoted characterizing the plan as "taking Halsted and putting it in drag"; the same article quoted other complaints that the design was "over the top."[33] By the same token, articles under headlines like "Gay Pride' Street Markers Get a Toning Down" and "Gay Theme Toned Down in Halsted St. Plan," used terms like "more subtle," "less gaudy," and "more refined" to describe changes in the plan following the period of public debate.[34] This attitude is explicit in the remarks of Lorraine Hoffmann, president of two local groups that opposed the Boys Town project with arguments about protecting property values. Explaining her reluctant acceptance of the "toned down" plans, she said: "If you're from Kalamazoo and driving up Halsted, you would think, 'Hmmm, this is pretty.' If you were gay, you might pick up on the symbolism."[35] In this discourse, the repression of the bad gay (the extravagant fairy or drag queen) in favor of the good gay (the embodiment of subtle good taste) replicates the more pernicious dynamics of class and race both within the gay community and among liberal advocates of tolerance in the dominant culture, for whom an aesthetic of expen-

14.8 Halloween parade, Halsted Street, Chicago, 1998. Photograph by Jason Smith.

14.9 Matthew Shepherd vigil and protest, Halsted Street, Chicago, 14 October 1998. Courtesy of the *University of Illinois at Chicago Flame.*

sive tastefulness confers acceptable invisibility on the gay bourgeoisie, while the unignorable extravagance of camp and drag are associated with working-class and racial-minority formulations of gay identity.[36]

But what of the subversives' objections? It can't be denied that the city's plans for Boys Town find a place among other recent manifestations of mainstream interest in the camp signifiers of gay identity: the success of movies like *Priscilla, Queen of the Desert* and *My Best Friend's Wedding*, the television series *Will and Grace*, and the phenomenon that is Ru Paul. Don't these developments lend authority to arguments that camp and nostalgia fail as signifiers of queerness because they are already reified and commodified by the dominant culture? Yes, if your fear is that sexual identity will follow the forms of old-style ethnicity: justified by biology, aspiring to an unmarked assimilation, its distinguishing characteristics reduced to the equivalents of leprechauns on cereal boxes or Chihuahuas advertising tacos. But to fixate on this conception of ethnicity is to ignore the complexity Epstein points to in the "new-ethnic" ideal of loose sociopolitical amalgamations that work to promote the rights of their members and protect them against discrimination while at the same time creating a structure for individuals aspiring, at least to some degree, to "disaggregate" or "de-assimilate" from American social and commercial norms. Those who claim a subversive critique of markers of gay community assume a monolithic idea of the dominant culture, overlooking the tensions and contradictions within its construction of ethnicity where they might find allies in dissent.

Subversive and assimilationist ideologies are linked, ironically, in both their blindness to the dynamism within contemporary constructions of American identity and their belief in individual mobility. Faith in personal mobility underlies the ideal of climbing from the ghetto into the undifferentiated middle class, just as it does the vision of the gay anti-hero—the stealth homosexual—cruising parks and back alleys undetected. Lost between these two extremes is the value of the collective formations indicated by the word "community." It is this idea that emerges in analogies between sexual and ethnic identity and that is affirmed in architectural signifiers of particular neighborhoods as sites of such values.

A collective manifestation of sexual identity: that is both the promise and the threat of a gay neighborhood. Ultimately, it is a potential too vast to be either contained or created by any set of markers. This failure of the signifier to guarantee or become the signified ought to console the opponents of marking on both sides. Perhaps in decades to come, the rainbow pylons will remain, like the German, Polish, and Czech names still visible on some buildings along Halsted Street; these markers did not impede the as-

14.8

14.9

similation of earlier populations of migrants. At the same time, the pylons will also never fully contain or limit the city's queer-identified population. Geographically, another neighborhood, more associated with lesbian identity, is rapidly expanding north of Boys Town. More to the point in this anthology on design, the visual vocabulary of the Boys Town markers has proved a point of departure rather than semiotic closure. Within just a few weeks of their installation, the new street furniture along Halsted Street had been manipulated both in celebration and mourning by the gay community. On Halloween, revelers impersonated the pylons, camping on their ambition to embody the local population (see fig. 14.8). At a vigil for slain gay college student Matthew Shepherd (as on this anniversary in subsequent years), mourners converted the planters installed with the pylons into impromptu altars by tying ribbons to the fretwork and setting candles in the soil (fig. 14.9). Ironically, these trellislike elements were added to the design in response to the controversy as a way of separating the gay-themed commercial street from the residential blocks, but even these supposedly ungay elements became part of the living spectacle of urban gay community. Far from containing or limiting expressions of sexual identity, the Boys Town project has sparked new and unforeseen visual manifestations of queerness in the urban fabric.

These final episodes constitute eloquent arguments for the value of the Boys Town markers on a street—and in a city—rich in symbols of collective identity created by invoking a beloved elsewhere. Elements in the postmodern mosaic of multiculturalism, the Boys Town pylons might also be said to extend a longer legacy of ethnic reference in this city of immigrants, actual and imagined. From this perspective, the first and second Chicago schools—embodied in Sullivan's Moorish fancywork or Mies's equally fanciful exercises in Germanic rationalism—might themselves be seen not as the kind of universal template claimed for modernism but as expressions of their own ethnic and sexual identities.[37]

The Chicago Parks: Tableaus of Naturalization

Jane Wolff

Chicago's parks were built during the same period of time as its most famous architecture, but they are barely discussed in the canonical design histories of the city. The parks don't look like the modernist image of Chicago. In fact, they were products of the transcendentalist idea that direct contact with nature (or at least with an image of rusticity) was morally improving, and they were designed as picturesque and pastoral backgrounds for urban life. However, it would be a mistake to dismiss them as either natural or un-modern. Conceived and developed to make citizens better individually and collectively, the parks belong to the tradition of socially minded design that emerged from the Bauhaus and other sources and that dominated European urbanism for a large part of the twentieth century.

The Chicago parks have complicated relationships to nature and to culture. They were intended as an alternative and antidote to the crowded, toxic physical conditions of the nineteenth-century city, but the iconography of natural remedy was open to discussion. The early landscape parks made use of the picturesque vocabulary that the Olmsteds had developed on the East Coast (fig. 15.1); after the turn of the twentieth century, Jens Jensen advocated a formal language that came from the prairie landscapes of the Midwest (fig. 15.2). All of these illusions of nature were designed and engineered, sometimes at the expense of the less appealing ecology that already existed on a site. A photograph of the construction of Burnham Park, taken when the idealized prairie landscape of Humboldt Park was reaching maturity, shows the dumping of tons of fill along the shore of Lake Michigan (fig. 15.3). The ecology of the marshy edge was destroyed to make the landscape of the park.

The social mission of the parks was also loaded: it was both sincere and paternalistic. The mixing of classes that took place in the rustic parks was supposed to educate immigrants about the mores and manners of American democracy. After the turn of the twentieth century, when Chicago became a center of the Progressive neighborhood parks movement, the parks' didactic programs expanded. The Progressive commitment to improving the physical and intellectual lot of the urban poor made the Chicago parks into highly ordered recreational landscapes and repositories of public institutions from museums to neighborhood field houses. Playgrounds and small parks were built throughout the city, and they were programmed for athletics and other socially oriented activities. Tournaments rewarded cooperation and team spirit as well as athletic ability. The park became an instrument of social improvement analogous to the public library.[1]

In the mid-1930s, the Chicago Park District was formed by the consolidation of numerous smaller agencies, and it quickly began to promote itself as a provider of social benefits. The attractions described in the 1936 *Handbook of Chicago's Parks* ranged from

15.1

15.2

15.3

15.1 A 1914 view of Garfield Park, designed in the Olmsted tradition. Photo: Chicago Park District Special Collection.

15.2 The prairie river at Humboldt Park was part of Jens Jensen's homage to the native Illinois landscape. Photograph: Chicago Park District Special Collection.

15.3 The landfill undertaken for Burnham Park in 1938 completely altered the form and the ecology of Lake Michigan's edge. Photograph: Chicago Park District Special Collection.

large cultural institutions to "excellent opportunity for nature study";[2] visitors could enjoy not only the "picturesque park and play areas"[3] but also the field house recreation programs, which provided "something of vital interest to do for every member of the family . . . young and old, men and women"[4] (fig. 15.4). The Park District even provided instruction on recreational activities at home: it published booklets whose topics ranged from aquariums to board games (fig. 15.5). The booklets tended to promote middle-class goals and values. One of the most normative (and probably the most optimistic) was titled, *You Can Have a Good Lawn* (fig. 15.6).[5]

The Chicago parks seem like democratic institutions not only because of their official agenda for social improvement but also for the idiosyncrasy, spectacle, and freedom of expression they appear to have fostered. They were arenas for public activity, and they were also places where individual citizens expressed their opinions about how the world might be different. Some of those expressions belong to the realm of fantasy. Photographs from the Park District archive depict an amazing range of imaginary landscapes: inside park field houses, Boy Scouts camped among artificial trees (fig. 15.7), vaqueros wrestled bulls in the semiarid mountains (fig. 15.8), and lovers frolicked and sang before a backdrop of rustic green hills (fig. 15.9). Craft projects for the annual Carnival of Lights produced strange juxtapositions like a miniature Taj Mahal on the shores of a lake in Garfield Park (fig. 15.10)

15.4

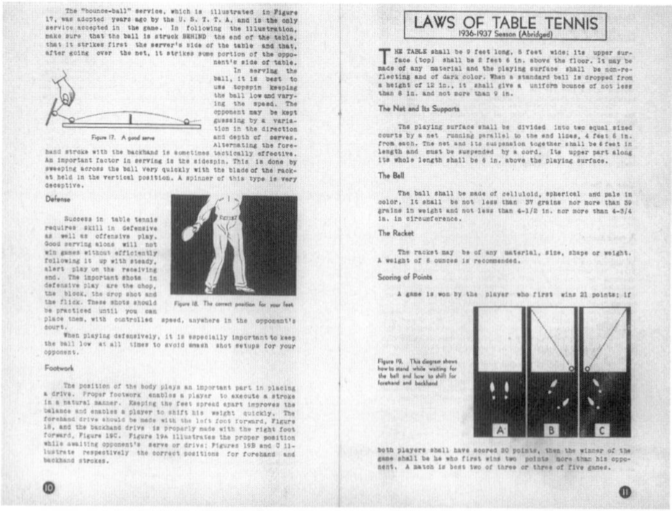

The "bounce-ball" service, which is illustrated in Figure 17, was adopted years ago by the U. S. T. T. A. and is the only service accepted in the game. In following the illustration, make sure that the ball is struck BEHIND the end of the table, that it strikes first the server's side of the table and that, after going over the net, it strikes some portion of the opponent's side of table.

In serving the ball, it is best to use topspin keeping the ball low and varying the speed. The opponent may be kept guessing by a variation in the direction and depth of serves. Alternating the forehand stroke with the backhand is sometimes tactically effective. An important factor in serving is the sidespin. This is done by sweeping across the ball very quickly with the blade of the racket held in the vertical position. A spinner of this type is very deceptive.

Figure 17. A good serve

Defense

Success in table tennis requires skill in defensive as well as offensive play. Good serving alone will not win games without efficiently following it up with steady, alert play on the receiving end. The important shots in defensive play are the chop, the block, the drop shot and the flick. These shots should be practiced until you can place them, with controlled speed, anywhere in the opponent's court.

Figure 18. The correct position for your feet

When playing defensively, it is especially important to keep the ball low at all times to avoid smash shot setups for your opponent.

Footwork

The position of the body plays an important part in placing a drive. Proper footwork enables a player to execute a stroke in a natural manner. Keeping the feet spread apart improves the balance and enables a player to shift his weight quickly. The forehand drive should be made with the left foot forward, Figure 18, and the backhand drive is properly made with the right foot forward, Figure 19C. Figure 19A illustrates the proper position while awaiting opponent's serve or drive; Figures 19B and C illustrate respectively the correct positions for forehand and backhand strokes.

10

LAWS OF TABLE TENNIS
1936-1937 Season (Abridged)

THE TABLE shall be 9 feet long, 5 feet wide; its upper surface (top) shall be 2 feet 6 in. above the floor. It may be made of any material and the playing surface shall be non-reflecting and of dark color. When a standard ball is dropped from a height of 12 in., it shall give a uniform bounce of not less than 8 in. and not more than 9 in.

The Net and Its Supports

The playing surface shall be divided into two equal sized courts by a net running parallel to the end lines, 4 feet 6 in. from each. The net and its suspension together shall be 6 feet in length and must be suspended by a cord. Its upper part along its whole length shall be 6 in. above the playing surface.

The Ball

The ball shall be made of celluloid, spherical and pale in color. It shall be not less than 37 grains nor more than 39 grains in weight and not less than 4-1/2 in. nor more than 4-3/4 in. in circumference.

The Racket

The racket may be of any material, size, shape or weight. A weight of 5 ounces is recommended.

Scoring of Points

A game is won by the player who first wins 21 points; if both players shall have scored 20 points, then the winner of the game shall be he who first wins two points more than his opponent. A match is best two of three or three of five games.

Figure 19. This diagram shows how to stand while waiting for the ball and how to shift for forehand and backhand

A B C

11

15.5

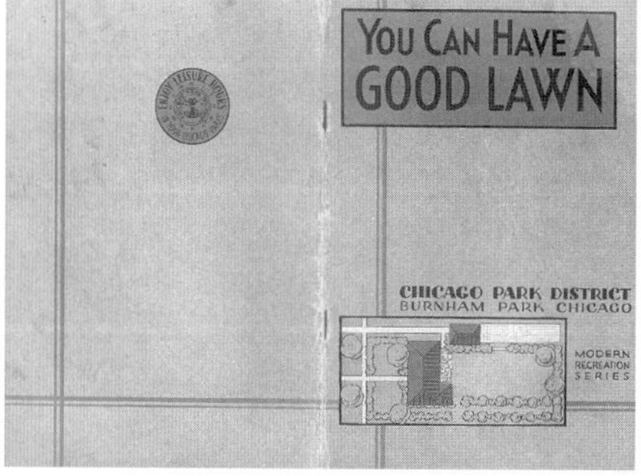

15.6

15.4 Archery practice in the parks, 1930s. Photograph: Chicago Park District Special Collection.

15.5 The style and thoroughness of this instructional booklet on table tennis are typical of pamphlets that the Chicago Park District published on recreation. Photograph: Chicago Park District Special Collection.

15.6 In the 1930s, the Chicago Park District defined recreation broadly enough to include gardening and lawn maintenance. Photo: Chicago Park District Special Collection.

15.7 This field house interior was redefined as a forest so that Boy Scouts could practice for expeditions in the 1930s. Photo: Chicago Park District Special Collection.

15.8 This field house set depicts the Wild West; child actors play not only toreadors but bulls. Photo: Chicago Park District Special Collection.

15.9 Another imaginary field house landscape: a rustic stage set, complete with tree swing. Photo: Chicago Park District Special Collection.

15.10 References in the Carnival of the Lights were as fantastic (and as remote) as the Taj Mahal. Photo: Chicago Park District Special Collection.

15.8

15.7

15.9

15.10

and a dinghy bearing a teepee and cigar store-style Indians (fig. 15.11). After 1968, the Chicago parks were also inextricably linked to political expression and political dissent. The riots in Grant Park were one of the most vivid expressions of unrest in American history. Trucks dispensed tear gas.[6] Policemen wielded clubs against peaceful demonstrators. Protesters mobbed the statue of John Logan, a general in the Civil War and the founder of Memorial Day.[7]

The parks were a kind of stage set for urban life and for the construction of urban identity. Modern in their programmatic and social agendas rather than their forms, they were almost opposite to the Miesian ideal. They were not heroic, they were not monumental, and they were not abstract. They were middle-class, inclusive, domestic, idiosyncratic, and particular. It's precisely those qualities that make the parks so interesting. They allowed for a kind of untidy, open, and varied public life whose expression ranged from the surrealism of a papier-mâché elephant floating on a rowboat (fig. 15.12) to the violence of the 1968 demonstrations (fig. 15.13): they were as free (and as lively) as the rest of the unidealized city of Chicago.

15.11

15.11 An Indian and his teepee become part of the Carnival of the Lights, 1935–36. Photo: Chicago Park District Special Collection.

15.12

15.12 This elephant makes an unlikely but exuberant match with both the park and the rowboat traveling through it. Photo: Chicago Park District Special Collection.

15.13

15.13 Police and rioters in Grant Park, 1969. Photograph by Mary Ellen Mark. Courtesy of Falkland Road, Inc., catalog number 202J-001-23A.

The Architectural Photography of Hedrich-Blessing

Robert A. Sobieszek

In the realm of architectural photography there are images that have as much to do with the art of photography as they do with the art they record. There are bodies of photography that, while documenting some of the more significant monuments of architecture and building, do so with consummate photographic artistry, verve, and authority. Some architectural photography can even come close to defining an entire school, epoch, style, or moment of architectural history. A case in point may well be that of the Chicago-based enterprise Hedrich-Blessing and how this firm's photography has been used for generations in documenting, disseminating, and promoting the international modernism of Chicago architecture.

Hedrich-Blessing's photographs have long been respected by the architecture and design communities, yet similar recognition has not been accorded them by photographic critics and art historians. The reasons behind this shock of unrecognition are fairly clear and center around the same bugaboos of commercialism that have affected much modern photography. There has been little difficulty in ascribing talent and genius to the works of nineteenth- and early twentieth-century photographers like Carleton Watkins or Eugène Atget, all of whom were distinctly commercial. On the other hand, should a contemporary photographer's practice be described as "applied" instead of "art," usually they were critically dismissed. Like many of its illustrious forebears, however, the firm of Hedrich-Blessing has simply made their photographs heedless of any aesthetic or literary categories. And the images it has made over the past seventy years are as breathtakingly powerful and interpretively sensitive as any ever done within the much broader construct of architectural photography.

With the exception of images of human beings, there have been more photographs taken of architecture than any other single subject.[1] Photography was born amidst the first flowering of what is now termed architectural historicism; it was productive during the onslaught of the great nineteenth-century battles between the independents and the Beaux-Arts; and it was fully on hand to document the great urban developments of the last century in Paris, London, and New York. The very first photographers were, partially by necessity because of long exposures, photographers of architecture—Joseph Nicéphore Niépce's 1826 view of the roofs of his outbuildings, Louis-Jacques-Mandé Daguerre's shots of the urban architecture seen from his studio, and William Henry Fox Talbot's calotypes of his abbey at Lacock. Later artists as well as architects like Charles Sheeler and Erich Mendelsohn would find expressive photographic meaning in the abstractions of early modern building and vernacular construction. More recent camera artists such as Lewis Baltz and the team of Bernd and Hilla Becher have continued in this vein and have added greatly to the visual definition of the built environment while fashioning art of the highest order.

16.1

16.1 House of Tomorrow, Chicago Century of Progress International Exposition, Chicago, Illinois, George Fred Keck & William Keck, architects. Photograph by Ken Hedrich, 1933, Hedrich-Blessing Photo. HB-01663A, courtesy of the Hedrich-Blessing Collection, Chicago Historical Society.

16.2 Sears Tower, Chicago, Illinois, Skidmore, Owings & Merrill, architect. Photograph by Jim Hedrich, 1974, Hedrich-Blessing Photo. ICHi-34977aa, courtesy of the Hedrich-Blessing Collection, Chicago Historical Society.

The beginnings and development of photography also paralleled a growth of interest in the preservation of an architectural past—at least the camera was able to "save" those monuments enlightened historical conscience could not. The camera image not only satisfied a need to view the past but also to understand the present. It is by no means insignificant that the first two photographic plates published in César Daly's influential *Revue générale de l'architecture et des travaux publics* [*sic*] in 1856 were of Félix Duban's restoration of a sixteenth-century chateau in the Loire Valley and the construction of Victor Baltard's revolutionary ironwork structure, *Les Halles centrales* in Paris. The "archaeologizing" of historic monuments and the validation of contemporary achievements seem to have been the perennial mandates of architectural photography.

In all of these respects, the firm of Hedrich-Blessing is in keeping with photographic tradition. It has documented classics of modern American architecture such as Louis Sullivan's 30 North LaSalle Building (formerly the Old Chicago Stock Exchange, now destroyed) and George Fred Keck and William Keck's House of Tomorrow (fig. 16.1) from the Chicago Century of Progress International Exposition of 1933 (also destroyed). The firm began its career with photographs of some of the more spectacular Depression-era modern exteriors and interiors in the Chicago area and has continued its role as one of the foremost revealers of modern

16.2

architecture with such images as those of Skidmore, Owings & Merrill's (SOM's) Sears Tower (fig. 16.2). Over the years, Hedrich-Blessing has documented the buildings of many of the greats of modern architecture, including, among many others, Marcel Breuer, R. Buckminster Fuller, Holabird & Root, Albert Kahn, John Portman, both Eero and Eliel Saarinen, Helmut Jahn, Mies van der Rohe, and Frank Lloyd Wright. Where Hedrich-Blessing differs from other architectural photography firms is not only in its precise and dramatic styles but also in the fact that it is, if not the oldest, at least one of the longest lived specialists of the genre.

The firm of Hedrich-Blessing is fundamentally a family business in both an actual and a metaphoric sense. It was founded in late 1929 by Ken Hedrich and Hank Blessing, with Blessing as darkroom manager and Ken as director of sales and chief photographer. Blessing left the partnership within a year of its establishment, but it was agreed that his part of the firm's name would remain since the firm had already attained a certain reputation under the partnership title. Also in 1930, Ed Hedrich joined Ken as bookkeeper, printer, and eventually managing partner. In 1959, before it had a category for photography, the American Institute of Architects (AIA) awarded Ken Hedrich its award for fine arts. Bill Hedrich came into the business as a photographer's assistant in 1931 and was awarded an AIA gold medal in 1967 for his photography. Jack Hedrich, the youngest of the brothers, entered the business in 1953 and became managing partner of the firm in 1976, after the deaths of Ken (1972) and Ed (1976). Ken's son, Jim Hedrich, joined Hedrich-Blessing in 1966, and Bill's daughter, Sandi Hedrich, came on board in 1981 specializing in commercial illustration but has since gone independent. The nonfamilial members of the photographic staff have included a number of exceptionally skilled and talented cameramen, from Giovanni Suter, Hube Henry, and Bill Engdahl in the 1930s and 1940s to the present team, consisting of Nick Merrick, Bob Harr, Jon Miller, Scott McDonald, Steve Hall, Bob Shimer, Chris Barrett, Craig Dugan, Justin Maconochie, and G. Todd Roberts—an extended family of sorts, whose names (intentionally informal, like those of the Hedrichs) appear with the firm's name in its credit lines. The present managing partner is Mike Houlahan, a childhood friend of Jim's.

Considering such an array of individual personalities at work, the photographs of Hedrich-Blessing reflect an overriding spirit, if not a single style. Imprinted with Ken's founding demand for perfection, the firm's images remain a blend of meticulous precision and interpretive resonance along with a fervent, self-conscious pride of craft and art. Family history has it that in the mid-1930s Frank Lloyd Wright was unreasonably demanding, as was his want, about the delivery of some prints Ken was commissioned to make. Hearing that the photographs were as yet not shot because Ken felt it was the wrong season for the best natural light, Wright exclaimed, "Young man, you are just a damned photographer and I am your client!" To which Ken calmly replied, "Sir, you are just a damned architect and I am a photographer."[2] Later, with the sun at a different position in the sky, the photographs were taken, and the firm was informed by Wright's secretary that the architect was quite pleased with the results.

The American photographer Arthur Siegel noted that "when an architect looks at his building he sees the myth in his mind instead. In this situation the photographer who thinks himself an artist cannot cope as well as one who is clairvoyant."[3] The architectural photographer has to be both prescient, if he is to understand what his client (usually an architect) wants, and artistic, if his work is to transcend the immediate needs of the commission and become a notable image. In Hedrich-Blessing's photographs, there is a respect for the subject's integrity coupled with a desire for a fine photographic image, resulting in what critic Nikolaus Pevsner called a "duality of aesthetic qualities—qualities of the originals and qualities of the photographic print, partly the same and partly quite different."[4] The aesthetic features of the architectural work of art are so commingled with those of its most salient photographic print that they are inseparable. The photograph is to a degree invisible and the architecture is clearly apparent; at the same time the building or interior is merely the print's subject and the photograph fully a work of its own pictorial art.

There is also a refinement of aesthetic choices in Hedrich-Blessing's work—choices that involve the most appropriate perspective or viewpoint, the best possible lighting, the least distorting lens or tilt of lens board, the most complementary skyscape to wait for, and many others.[5] Some of the firm's earliest choices and artistic approaches to the photography of architecture were both innovative and highly influential. From their very first years, wrote the architectural photographer Joseph W. Molitor, Hedrich-Blessing "challenged the documentary way of photographing a building. [Ken's] photographs had new and dramatic viewpoints and much bolder techniques, his prints had a sparkle and contrast unheard of at that time, and their impact on the viewer was great."[6] Of course, the vitality of any artistic practice over time depends on the fluidity and resiliency of its creative means, on how it approaches its problems and issues, and what stylistic choices it makes along the way. Over the years, Hedrich-Blessing has found various solutions to interpreting architecture with a camera. In part, these changes are due to shifting cultural attitudes and pictorial tastes. More importanty, many changes are the direct result of confronting new styles and types of architecture. According to Bill Hedrich, "buildings by an architect like Harry Weese are very straightforward, so you show them that way instead of trying to embellish them. With Mies, it was a different ball game. You used the modular approach and a one-point perspective. No two architects are alike. You must interpret their buildings with your camera, but you must be truthful."[7]

That Hedrich-Blessing was founded in Chicago is important when one considers that practically the entire history of modern American architecture can be encountered in that city, from Beaux-Arts and the Prairie school to modernism and postmodernism. That the firm was established around 1930 meant that it could begin its negative files with some impressive, late examples of the Chicago school's "tall buildings," as architect Louis Sullivan so aptly defined them, as well as that city's space-age Century of Progress International Exposition of 1933–34. That exposition was this country's first major manifestation of the European art deco building style, more appropriately labeled this side of the Atlantic as "Depression modern" or "streamlined moderne." While a much older Chicago firm, Kaufmann & Fabry Co., listed themselves as the "official photographers" of the fair, it was Ken Hedrich who was responsible for the most memorable and long-lasting images of the exposition's various pavilions.[8]

What strikes one most about Hedrich-Blessing's photographs of the exposition is the visual exuberance, the flare for the operatic, and the essential spirit of futurism that is shared by both image and building. The exposition featured this country's largest concentration of streamlined moderne building ever assembled. The occasion was the centennial celebration of Chicago's incorporation as a city, but the fair's basic text was, according to an official handbook, "to illustrate the dependence of modern development on scientific research." An obvious subtext to the fair was the unspoken faith in future betterment through scientific advancement—a late manifestation of the nineteenth-century idea of progress. The spirit of the exposition and its sense of futurism were captured precisely by Ken Hedrich in the types of photographic images he created.

If warranted a building might be portrayed clearly and straightforwardly, much as a stage set, because of intricate detailing or fantastic structure. Such an approach is obvious in Ken's photograph of the Travel and Transport Building (fig. 16.3), where its phe-

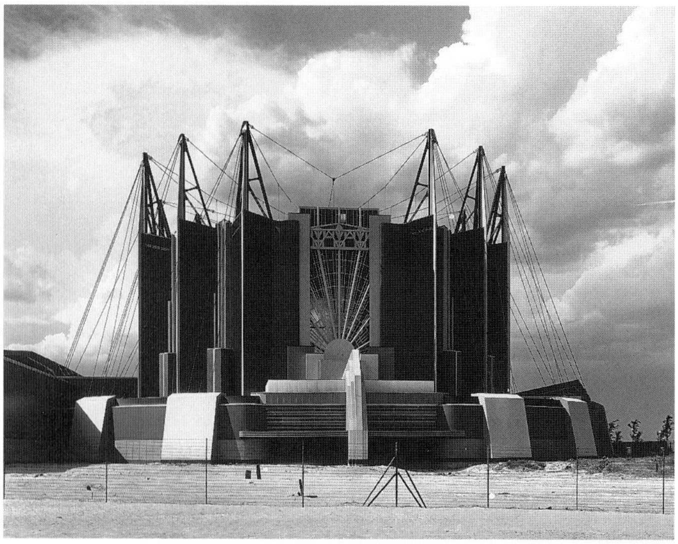

16.3

nomenal Buck Rogers style was so fully dynamic that a more than direct shot would have resulted in a very confusing document. If, on the other hand, a pavilion or its detail could be justifiably interpreted as a very active piece of high theater, it was photographed in a dramatic night shot, replete with banks of spotlights and spectacular water reflections, or with exaggerated, towering perspectives. Ken's night views of Raymond Hood's Electrical Building (fig. 16.4), with its pre–Albert Speer use of searchlights, and Holabird & Root's Chrysler Building (fig. 16.5) are nearly Wagnerian in their operatic bravado and somewhat reminiscent of the manner in which the German architect Karl Friedrich Schinkel treated his stage sets for Mozart's *Magic Flute* in 1816.

Very much a part of the thirties' design sense, this sort of documentary theater was not exclusive to a gala fair or to technologically progressive buildings. The same striving for a dramatic rendition within the bounds of accurate documentation is also found in Bill Hedrich's quintessential presentation of Wright's Kaufmann House ("Fallingwater") four years later (fig. 16.6). According to the photographer, Wright was again, and as usual, displeased with the now famous shot—made while standing in the water below the house and looking up at its looming cantilevered porches and cascading waterfalls—on the grounds that it was much "too acrobatic." Despite the architect's initial reservation, Wright later came to appreciate the image, which has become arguably the single most reproduced and best known architectural photograph of all times. The same urge to document the subject in a kind of theatrical manner can also be found in photographs by Bill Hendrich and Giovanni Suter of both residential and commercial staircases, where the very subject lends itself to a Bauhaus style of pictorial novelty, such as looking straight up or down a spiral run of steps.

During and after World War II, a different spirit in building developed in America, and Hedrich-Blessing's photographs interpreted it in a new manner. Busby Berkeley theatrics were replaced with a marked severity of line and elegance of simplicity that well complemented the beginnings of an Americanized in-

16.3 Travel and Transport Building, Chicago Century of Progress International Exposition, Chicago, Illinois, Edward H. Bennet, Hubert Burnham, & John A. Holabird, architects. Photograph by Ken Hedrich, 1932, Hedrich-Blessing Photo. HB-00770I, courtesy of the Hedrich-Blessing Collection, Chicago Historical Society.

16.4 Electrical Building, Chicago Century of Progress International Exposition, Chicago, Illinois, Raymond Hood, architect, Joseph Urban, lighting designer. Photograph by Ken Hedrich, 1933, Hedrich-Blessing Photo. HB-01763I, courtesy of the Hedrich-Blessing Collection, Chicago Historical Society.

16.5 Chrysler Building, Chicago Century of Progress World's Fair, Chicago, Illinois, Holabird & Root, architects. Photograph by Ken Hedrich, 1933, Hedrich-Blessing Photo. HB-01718, courtesy of the Hedrich-Blessing Collection, Chicago Historical Society.

16.6 Edgar Kaufmann House ("Fallingwater"), Bear Run, Pennsylvania, Frank Lloyd Wright, architect. Photograph by Bill Hedrich, 1937, Hedrich-Blessing Photo. HB-04414 D3, courtesy of the Hedrich-Blessing Collection, Chicago Historical Society.

16.4

16.5

16.6

16.7

16.8

16.7 Buick factory, Melrose Park, Illinois, Albert Kahn, architect. Photograph by Ken Hedrich, 1942, Hedrich-Blessing Photo. HB-06902C, courtesy of Hedrich-Blessing.

16.8 Farnsworth House, Plano, Illinois, Ludwig Mies van der Rohe, architect. Photograph by Bill Hedrich, 1951, Hedrich-Blessing Photo. HB-14490S, courtesy of the Hedrich-Blessing Collection, Chicago Historical Society.

ternational style of architecture consisting mainly of steel and glass. Whether in an industrial, wartime mode of pure efficiency, such as munitions and aircraft factories, or in a more pastoral idiom of domestic residences nestled in woodlands, the photographs display a directness, a quietism, and absolutely judicious placements of forms and elements analogous to their subjects. While there may be a conceptual difference between industrial building and architecture, the movements of architectural styles from the 1930s to the present seem to have brought these functionally dissimilar architectures more closely together than ever before.

Ken Hedrich interpreted Albert Kahn's Buick factory in Buffalo, New York, and its clerestory skylights with much the same feeling and sensitivity that Bill Hedrich approached Mies van der Rohe's ultimate domestic residence, the Farnsworth House of 1951, situated along the banks of the Fox River in suburban Chicago (figs. 16.7, 16.8). No two buildings could be further apart in function, scale, or locale. Yet both images treat their subjects in similar ways and more than adequately record the salient features of the architectures without depicting the entire building. Both present asymmetrical compositions, and both brilliantly play with the pictorial conceit of pars pro toto, in which a detail or portion of the whole is made to stand for the entire complex.

Hedrich-Blessing has remained a vital photographic concern for close to three-quarters of a century. Its techniques, to be sure, and its styles of interpreting architecture have changed appreciably over the years, yet it has never departed from its fundamental pursuit of excellence. New kinds of architecture call for new ideas in documenting them. New kinds of construction and changes in how large buildings and urban locales are developed demand inventive ways of recording and communicating architectural ideas. And new materials available to the photographer lead to new visual possibilities of contributing to the photographic world of architecture. Even changes in the way we think about photography or how we conceptualize its aesthetics can affect the photographer's vision. When someone like Nick Merrick, among others, begins talking about how he does not photograph a building or an interior but rather the subject's "space," he is not only challenging the more traditional expectation of what the proper subject of architectural photography is, he is also describing a new way of looking at and picturing architecture.

If one of the hallmarks of the Hedrich Blessing style during the 1930s was a keen sense of theatrical spotlighting and severe contrasts of light and dark, the firm's lighting styles over the last three decades or so has become nearly the opposite. Principally due to Jim Hedrich, the new style is best characterized by an almost complete lack of dramatic effects, almost a "lightingless" look to the interiors, and a pronounced taste for neutral illumination that is at once "honest" and eloquent. A comparison of an early interior picture and one done later illustrates this point. Giovanni Suter's depiction of a Libby-Owens-Ford showroom display of 1938 (fig. 16.9), with its dreamy backlighting, silhouetted figures arranging flowers, and mirrored reflections, is very different from Bob Porth's utterly white model office of 1981, which is completely austere, reductively minimal, silent, and devoid of human figures (fig. 16.10). Both are essentially the same photograph of a small interior space, but they are totally different expressions. Suter's image is one of reflected translucence appropriate to the client's interest in glass; its aesthetic is that of panache and glitter. Porth's photograph, on the other hand, is all about stilled opacity and rigorous formalism adjusted to the functionalism of the modern office. The mute nonreflectiveness is in keeping with a necessary emphasis on the acoustic ceiling tiles manufactured by the client, U.S. Gypsum Company.

Ken Hedrich's night view of the Chrysler Building at the Century of Progress International Exposition and Bill Hedrich's portrayal of the cantilevered Fallingwater are two of the finest and most arresting images the firm made during the 1930s. A decade and a half later in 1956, Bill Engdahl's depiction of Mies's Crown Hall at dusk is as perfect a summation of the German architect's precision, clarity, and mystery of form as any made of that edifice (fig. 16.11). With its landscape foliage and subtle silhouetting, it humanizes what is really a supremely idealized and starkly conceptual building. Engdahl gracefully romanticizes a structure that could be easily represented as chastely cold and hermetically sterile, which it is not. Bob Shimer's frontally shot, serene view of Schipporeit-Henrich's Lake Point Tower of 1968 (fig. 16.12) is as a fine an architectural photograph as Ken Hedrich's early image of the Chicago Board of Trade Building in 1930. The two images are essentially the same sort of picture. Bill Hedrich's 1969 view of Lake Point Tower (fig. 16.13), however, a vertiginous look up the building's undulating wall, is quite different from anything done in the 1930s. The use of an extreme wide-angle lens for such an exterior shot betrays this image's contemporaneity and is perfectly suited to the facts and form of the building and our experience of them.

In the 1930s, color photography was hardly if ever used by Hedrich-Blessing. Its use expanded slowly during the 1950s until it has become, by now, almost completely the preferred medium. There are certain instances when black-and-white photographs are more pertinent and instructive than color, but today that has become a rare exception. Of course, color has always been a part of architecture—if not always vividly through paint, then at least subtly through hues of granite, sandstone, or marble. Much of the architecture of the 1930s, especially the early international style, is recalled today as essentially noncoloristic, but this has more to do with the black-and-white photographs of it and the proliferation of its monochrome reproductions in magazines than with the

16.9

16.9 Libby-Owens-Ford Showroom, Chicago, Illinois, designer unknown. Photograph by Giovanni Suter, 1938, Hedrich-Blessing Photo. HB-04741A, courtesy of the Hedrich-Blessing Collection, Chicago Historical Society.

16.10

16.10 Office interior (studio setup), Chicago, Illinois, client: U. S. Gypsum. Photograph by Bob Porth, 1981, Hedrich-Blessing Photo. Courtesy of the Hedrich-Blessing Collection, Chicago Historical Society.

16.11

16.13

16.12

16.11 Crown Hall, Illinois Institute of Technology, Chicago, Illinois, Ludwig Mies van der Rohe, architect. Photograph by Bill Engdahl, 1956, Hedrich-Blessing Photo. HB-18506 P4, courtesy of the Hedrich-Blessing Collection, Chicago Historical Society.

16.12 Lake Point Tower, Chicago, Illinois, Schipporeit-Heinrich Associates, architect. Photograph by Bob Shimer, 1969. Hedrich-Blessing Photo, courtesy of Hedrich-Blessing.

16.13 Lake Point Tower, Chicago, Illinois, Schipporeit-Heinrich Associates, architect. Photograph by Bill Hedrich, 1969. Hedrich-Blessing Photo, courtesy of Hedrich-Blessing.

architects' intentions or the actual colors of the architecture. With notable exceptions, buildings today are even more flagrantly colorful than seventy years ago, with their decoratively saturated interiors and their brightly hued, glazed skins of reflective glass. With little wonder, color photography has become essential to the documentation of contemporary architecture and to its publication.

Similarly, with an increasing interest in just how a proposed building will affect a given location—an interest shared by both architectural developers and the general community—a means was needed by which the finished building could be photographically depicted in situ well before construction began. In the late 1970s Hedrich-Blessing, and especially its photographer, Bob Harr, pioneered the application of a technique called "emulsion stripping," which painstakingly conjoined the image of the site with that of the proposed building's scale model. The resulting montage was so skillfully done that the general effect of the full-scale building on its neighborhood was fairly comprehensible. By the end of the 1980s, however, computer-assisted design programs and Photoshop took over, and today computers do such tasks far more easily and convincingly.

Quotations abound in the work of Hedrich-Blessing; references are made to the firm's own work as well as to the history of architectural photography. The diagonally thrusting reach of the Grand

16.14

Hyatt Hotel in New York, as photographed by Bob Harr in 1981, is in essence a reprise of Bill Hedrich's detail of stonework and windows in Wright's Fallingwater of 1937 in that both are shot looking up the side of the architecture from a position fairly close to the structure. The manner in which Harr situates the building in a context—clearly locating it in Manhattan, with the former Pan Am Building at the left and a coy glimpse of William Van Alen's Chrysler Building (1929) at the right—is parallel to Bill Engdahl's 1969 rendition of SOM's John Hancock Tower (fig. 16.14), with its tokens of "placeness" situating it firmly in Chicago—with the old Water Tower at the right and the Playboy Building at the left. From among many other examples, Nick Merrick's photograph of SOM's 33 West Monroe Street building in Chicago (fig. 16.15), done in 1981, is notable in its pictorial referencing of Philip Henry Delamotte's albumen prints of the reconstruction of the Crystal Palace in Sydenham, England, in 1853. And Engdahl's shot of the 101 North Wacker Building by Perkins & Will in Chicago, seen through an open window, is faintly yet persistently reminiscent of Daguerre's 1837 view of a Parisian boulevard pictured from his studio window.

Since Daguerre's time, we have increasingly depended upon the camera to inform us of what is being built around the world. Coincidentally, we also have grown to depend on camera images to show us what edifices we have lost. In no way, however, does the architectural photograph

16.14 John Hancock Center, Chicago, Illinois, Skidmore, Owens & Merrill, architect. Photograph by Bill Engdahl, 1969. Hedrich-Blessing Photo, courtesy of Hedrich-Blessing.

16.15 View of 33 West Monroe Street, Chicago, Illinois, Skidmore, Owens & Merrill, architect. Photograph by Nick Merrick, 1981. Hedrich-Blessing Photo, courtesy of Hedrich-Blessing.

16.15

supplant the architectural experience—the power of size and scale, the relationships of spaces, and the time it takes to pass through them.[9] The architectural photographer offers us interpretations of building that might, when they are just and inspired, reveal new appreciations and understandings of our human-made landscape. The architectural photographer Norman Carver, Jr., wrote that "even though photographs cannot substitute for the actual experience of architecture, certain advantages lie within photography's limitations. In its ability to record only a small segment of the total impression is the advantage of abbreviating to the point of clarity—in pointing out and intensifying the essential of any impression."[10] And, being around long enough, an architectural photography firm can come to literally clarify and define the characteristics of an architectural moment, style, or movement. For all their impressions, interpretations, definitions, and documents, the work of the Chicago firm Hedrich-Blessing and its photographers is to be immensely valued.

Forms of the Grid

Mitchell Schwarzer

1

From 36,000 feet, the far reaches of Chicago come into view more than sixty miles from the downtown. Flying from California to New York on a late January afternoon, I had spent the past couple hours observing a spacing of towns at what I knew to be six-mile intervals, a regular beat that began after Colorado's front range and was interrupted now and then by rivers and small cities. Now, with evening descending over the Chicago metropolis, I saw the squarish formation distort. In its place appeared the creased outlines of subdivisions, grapevine filaments of the East-West and Tri-State tollways, and intermittent megacomplexes like Oak Brook Shopping Center and O'Hare International Airport. The nation's geographic measure had been interrupted. A mesmerizing agrarian world had been replaced by the vaudeville of suburbia. Orthogonals contorted into angles, curves, and scads of geometry-damaged shapes. Yet most intriguing was the equally abrupt return to the orderly grid once I could make out the city proper. Over Chicago, I looked down and saw electric lights of all colors neatly arranged. Below me the city could be read as a scholastic abstraction for the modern era, a Gothic gesture conjuring the similes of illumination and the logics of line and plane. At that moment I understood how Chicago and the American heartland were linked to each other by the straight line, the ninety-degree angle, and their serial configurations.

Since Hippodamus laid out the Greek city of Miletus in the fifth century B.C., grids have been used to order urban and rural land throughout the world. The relationship between Chicago and the agrarian Midwest illustrates some of the most profound and far-reaching aspects of the grid—its engendering of the seemingly contradictory qualities of thickness and dispersion. Much denser than its surroundings, Chicago's fine-grained grid is the finale of the nation's more widely spaced heartland grid. Historically, the city has gathered up the products (and often the lives) of countless farms and hamlets, processing them, selling them, and reimagining them. To this day, this productive energy can be felt on the city's streets and neighborhoods. It is almost as if the quadrants of urban buildings, lots, and blocks are replicated in geometric progression in larger and larger rural units—the chessboards of fields, counties, and even states. Chicago's grid runs far beyond the city's edges, twisting through the suburbs, and merging straight and determined on the endless acres of farmland. Looking down that January evening, Chicago's grid seemed to go on forever, unaccountable to limits or exhaustion. Devon Avenue and Western Avenue stretched far beyond what is sensible for a street. The display of row upon row of crisscrossing lights was compelling. Each neighborhood of the city was wrapped in rectilinear tiers that glowed and radiated skyward. Then, approaching downtown, the illuminated grid issued incredible power. Above the downtown Loop's skyscrapers, I saw even more lights, brighter lights, an ambrosial mob. The

17.1 Near Chicago Avenue and Halsted Street. Photograph by Steve Harp.

downtown was so brilliant I could make out details on individual buildings—flashing rooftops echoing the blazing streets below. Only when the airplane finally crossed over the dark lake waters to the east did the spectacle end.

The word *grid* is derived from *gridiron*, which in earliest Old English usage—*gredire*—meant a cooking utensil formed of parallel bars of iron in a frame used for roasting fish or flesh over a fire. Other definitions establish the word's instrumental character, a grating, grilling, networking of lines for a purpose—which could include support, enclosure, or torture. Wedded to the Latin noun *cadastre*, the gridiron surveys the land and scales for the purposes of establishing ownership and monetary value. Gridding is about limited organization, an activity of platting rather than planning, more an expectation of the future than satisfaction of the present. Despite the geometric connotations of the word, grids do not necessarily lead to a rational organization of land or functional approach to building. The whole that results from a gridiron is less articulated than more rigidly articulated plans that feature forums, boulevards, circles, or crescents. On the plain grid, the outlines are set, but the contents and details are left variable. More often than not, bottom-line economics overshadows purposeful urban design. Sometimes, intentional architectural acts go against the grid's crisp corners and steady grain. The grid is a structuring device that obliterates hierarchical form and encourages the creation of building according to the terms of repetition and formula. Yet, within its cubic dimensions, there is plenty of room for chance.

2

The Land Ordinance of 1785 shaped much of the surface of the United States—from Ohio westward—into six-mile township squares with lines running due north and south and others crossing at right angles. These were further divided into thirty-six sections of one-mile squares (or 640 acres). Roads, farms, and towns across the nation follow these great lines regardless of topography, earlier trade routes, or preexisting settlements. Gridirons in many cities built after this time are aligned to the sections. Even the railroad lines, vehicular roads, and interstate highways, huge builders of space and culture in their own right, are junior partners of the land ordinance's vast experiment in ordination. Culturally speaking, the gridiron laid out by Thomas Jefferson and the Continental Congress was an imposition of geospatial homogeneity that mirrors other foundations of national unity: one has only to think of the English language and Protestant capitalism. Gridding fits perfectly with the American preoccupation with materiality, easing the demarcation, transaction, and development of land as built property. It also accords with the nation's penchant for confining individual expression within fixed bounds.

In 1830, James Thompson platted Chicago's first gridiron south of the Chicago River in the present-day Loop. During its subsequent extensions, the entire city was coordinated with the Land Ordinance of 1785. Whatever street you are walking or driving on in Chicago aligns with far-off country roads, soybean fields, and courthouse squares. Yet since there is neither beginning nor end on the grid, all directions are elusively equivalent. Through the grid's proliferation of commensurate intersections, no single one dominates. Where is Chicago's center? Is it the crossing of State and Madison streets, the base coordinates of the grid? Or is it somewhere on the Michigan Avenue Bridge, where the two Chicago downtowns meet? Or is it next to the Water Tower on fashionable Michigan Avenue, or at the Buckingham Fountain in Grant Park, or within the vortex of the Circle Interchange of expressways? The presence of multiple centers in Chicago—and one could include as well the edge villages of Oakbrook or Schaumburg—encourages flexibility. Matching the region's relentless flatness, the grid imposes a regime of spatial equivalence. Matching the city's entrepreneurial flux, Chicago and its grid are perpetually open for business.

Among American gridirons, Chicago's is remarkable. Unlike New Orleans's contiguous but discrete grids aligned to bends in the Mississippi River or San Francisco's mul-

17.2 Outside Wrigley Field, Sheffield Avenue and Addison Street. Photograph by Steve Harp.

tiple grids charging up hills, Chicago has but one grid without respect to topography. Distinct from William Penn's plan for Philadelphia, there are no regularly spaced parks in the Windy City. And whereas James Oglethorpe's Savannah plan was designed for replication around verdant squares, the streets and avenues of Chicago march straight to meet the prairie. This grid is overloaded with purpose and impatient with digression. Like a sea it covers the entire city. Yet unlike the hidden depths beneath a sea's surface, Chicago's buildings and urban spaces expose the grid's historical influence on architecture and landscape. More than any other American city, Chicago epitomizes the grid's possibilities for structuring urban form. Once laid out, the grid turned the ground plane of the city into an imagined orchard, an illusion of real-estate riches rising into the sky, miscegenation of earth, air, geometry, and money.

When I lived in Chicago during the early nineties I was struck by the grid's ability to inform my sense of place. The grid allowed me to understand any particular site with respect to all other locations. Eight blocks make up a mile; four blocks, a half mile, and so forth. My address, approximately 3600 north and 1200 west, meant I lived four and a half miles north of Madison Street and one and a half miles west of State Street. Anywhere I went, no matter how remote or strange, could be untangled by this quantitative overlay. Numbers translate urban geography in other ways as well. The news radio traffic report every ten minutes grasps distance through intervals of time between key points: thirty minutes from the "Junction" to the "Circle," fifty minutes from "Harlem" to the "Post Office." Unlike many other cities where the traffic report is precariously balanced atop accident and construction delay, Chicago's radiocasting transcends chance for numerical certainty. Nowhere in the world have I experienced so snugly the equation of urban form and geographic measure.

Chicago replicates fractally along the coordinates of the grid. The streets at two-mile intervals tend to be automobile arterials; neon signs of car dealerships and bowling alleys on Cicero Avenue match those on Harlem Avenue or Ninety-fifth Street. Streets at one-mile intervals are the major avenues of pedestrian com-

17.3 From the John Hancock Building, looking west. Photograph by Steve Harp.

merce; at half-mile spacings one finds the minor shopping streets. Whether on Lawrence Avenue to the north, Seventy-fifth Street to the south, or Pulaski Street on the west, roads are passages for the homogenizing actions of the grid. Their one- and two-story brick and stone facades are broken exactly by secondary alleys and streets. Side streets around former Comiskey Park in Bridgeport are reasonable facsimiles of those surrounding Wrigley Field in Lakeview, right down to the generational despair reflected in the beer mugs of sports fans. Despite its imperial scale, much of Chicago is a folio of small, nearly identical parts. There are infrequent surprises across the 230 square miles of city, and few Chicagoans would be able to distinguish—on architectural grounds alone—one area from the next if suddenly dropped into one of them. Everywhere the grid establishes common street widths, lot dimensions, and building profiles—the mile square divided again and again to smaller mathematical modules.

For a city of its size, Chicago has remarkably few rambling mansions and infrequent outbursts of make-belief turrets or balustrades. Even the famous boulevards look solid and nontheatrical. They feature more sumptuous residences than other streets, and occasionally swell into parks and monuments. But their feverish moments (like Palmer Square) are few; the grand routes quickly straighten up, as if embarrassed of any wandering insolence. Within the city grid's system, there is a feeling of restraint, a sense of monumentality more akin to a humming chorus than bravura soloist. Most of the time, Chicago's grid divides land into a common architecture.

3

But not all the time. The grid does something different downtown and along Lake Shore Drive. Counterpoints to the horizontality that prevails in the rest of Chicago, these vertical zones of skyscrapers draw the eyes upward. At the city's eastern edge, buildings seem impatient with the reiterations of the grid accepted further west. They pile up one atop the other, possessed by the possibilities of verticality. On the built shoots that crowd the Loop and stretch along Lake Shore Drive, Frank Lloyd Wright's Prairie style seems a long way off. For Wright, building lines were tamed to the lines of the earth's surface, rock-encrusted foundations and cantilevered eaves discouraging speculation of the heavens. Quite differently, among the residential high rises that form an almost continuous built wall from South Shore to Edgewater (over fifteen miles), hallucinations of Elysium prevail.

Still, is the Chicago skyscraper really a blossom of a different season than the grid? Do the vertical Loop and Lakefront differ all that much from the measured mass of the horizontal city? Seen from the lake or from inside the city, the tall buildings look like a wall of fortifications, regardless of whether they are clothed in weighty masonry or transparent glass and steel. Thus this wall is a synecdoche for the power of the gridiron city, a release from efficiency and obligation. But the wall is also a metaphor for the grid's confinements, a regularly spaced sequence of bastions that lord over and differentiate the land below. To the west of the high-rise wall, the grid dominates and extends to the farthest reaches of the Midwest. To the east, on the sliver of landfill reclaimed from the lake, a different city of parkland and Beaux-Arts museums evokes the civilization to the east and across the Atlantic Ocean.

Downtown Chicago boasts some of the world's tallest buildings: the Sears Tower and John Hancock, and Amoco buildings, built in a short period between the late 1960s and early 1970s. Much earlier, during the booms of the late nineteenth century, such architects as Burnham & Root and Adler & Sullivan constructed the world's first skyscrapers and perfected the development of the skeletal steel frame. The skyscraper is a vertical twin to the horizontal grid of streets. It is no accident that they flowered in Chicago. The steel frame, like the grid, establishes an ordered and completely regularized zone of action. High-rise buildings are containers of measured, equivalent space, much like the city they tower over. Corporations crave large, open spaces that can be divided and subdivided according to their own liking. Indeed, as Rem Koolhaas has noted, the high-rise office is among the least articulated building types the world has known, story after story creating more ambiguous space. From a business point of view, the replicating grids on each floor of the towers are places of desire. As Americans embraced the idea of dividing the land to accomplish great productive feats, so too did they shape the sky into a geometric music of exchange and opportunity. The Chicago skyscraper, traveling high into the sky, continues the city grid and that of the thousands of miles of surrounding farmland. And as much as the farmland itself, the office high rise represents a zone of profitable artifice. The grid brings the land and sky of Chicagoland's immense plain together.

Mies van der Rohe's arrival in Chicago in the late 1930s seems foreordained by the possibilities of the grid. Where else could the architect of gridded steel-frame skyscrapers have experimented with the artistic possibilities of hollowing out the blocklike forms emanating from the grid? Back in 1893, Daniel Burnham's plan for the World's Columbian Exposition famously rejected the full-block city of the gray downtown, carving out lagoons and courtyards and placing an imperial white city around them, a Rome along Lake Michigan. Between the 1940s and 1960s, Mies similarly carved out large blocks from within the grid by which to align his residential lakefront towers, downtown office buildings, and campus structures at IIT. As it had been for Burnham, the grid provided the perfect foil to Mies's experiments in the new spatial geometries that could be construed between tall buildings—the only difference being that Mies's architecture continued the grid's straight and right-angled coordinates. Still, whether working in opposition or in concert, is it accidental that Chicago's grid stimulated the American progenitors of both the City Beautiful and modern movements?

4

Nowadays, after a couple of decades of postmodernism, the grid's impact on Chicago architecture runs a more traditional course. Superblocks and platform towers are out. So too are plazas and other acts of sculpting building shape away from the right-angled coordinates of lot lines. Yet much of the new historicism is skin-deep. Several large housing developments south of the Loop constructed during the 1990s duplicate the row house measure of the prewar grid city within designs more attuned to the isolating land arrangements of suburbia. Indeed, a perusal of urban change anywhere in the city yields a struggle between the historical dimensions favored by the grid and the outsized spatiality of vehicular culture.

Trucks and automobiles, with their own sense of urban rhythm and space, often blithely disregard the grid's exquisite order. For every case where vehicles reinforce the grid—

17.4 Division Street at Elston Avenue. Photograph by Steve Harp.

such as the parking garages arrayed one after the other on residential alleys—more numerous instances of desecration come to mind—the gashes of parking lots, the setback minimalls, the leviathan one-story warehouses and stores that overwhelm grid dimensions of blocks and lots. Driving Chicago's expressways, I especially noticed how the grid city faded from view. Sure, exits mirror the numerical gaps of the grid's arterials. But at high speeds vehicular perception peels away from the city's old cadastral organization. From the Kennedy or Stevenson expressways, one can't make out the bases of buildings or the streets around them. Visual focus and momentum shifts to the roadway infrastructure, the adjacent vehicular-influenced landscape, and far-off landmarks. Similarly, driving to Chicagoland's outskirts and crossing over from the exurbs to the prairie brought me few reminders of the ancestral ties between the urban and rural grids. On the expressways, one could forget that rural Illinois, and much of the Midwest for that matter, is a set of factories on the land, a place once parallel—in terms of function and shape—to the city's factories, offices, and residences. The urban-rural geometric connection so vividly seen from the air doesn't come across in highway perception. Cornfields look like cornfields.

Over the years I lived in Chicago I began to realize that the highway was by no means the first perceptual counterpoint to the grid. The postwar expressways follow off-grid routes reaching back to the founding of the city. Historically, Chicago has been defined as profoundly by radial lines as by gridded ones. The earliest of these off-kilter lines is the Chicago River, which flows from the lake a little over a mile west before separating into north and south branches. Today, the river is murky, saturated with aged effluent. It is soft where the city is hard, slow-flowing where the city is decisive, a supple witness to the redundancy of the past. The urban fabric seen from the river is an outburst of curiosities, a collection of the faded moments of industrial initiative. From early in the nineteenth century, the direction of the river branches, generally southwest and northwest, determined the platting of Chicago's diagonal avenues. Clark Street and Lincoln, Milwaukee, and Archer avenues jut off the gridiron's standard itineraries, stammering out trapezoidal and triangular building

17.5 Armitage Avenue at Ashland Avenue. Photograph by Steve Harp.

sites. Soon after, the railroads (Northwestern, Illinois Central, Burlington Northern) followed these lines, and later still, the expressways widened their corridors. In sequestered or raised channels, these thoroughfares make rapid connections between distant points, and have long skirted the right-angled city in Olympian isolation. For instance, from the "L" at forty miles an hour or so (in good times) the city spreads before the eyes in a long distance panorama of church spires, apartment towers, housing projects, and factories, altogether different from the narrow and repetitive lens imposed on the eyes while observing architecture from within the street grid.

The river and its adjacent corridors once sung productive might. Today, these transforming corridors demonstrate that Chicago's gridded equation of real estate development, urban manufacturing, and agrarian production no longer holds. Gone is the flood of molten iron, the sawing of lumber, the grinding and filing of machine parts, each so precisely honed that they could take the place of any of their counterparts. Gone is the measure of manufacturing, mirrored in the measure of gridded urban development. Skidmore, Owings & Merrill's John Hancock Building (1970) might be the last great architectural synthesis of old Chicago, its diagonal rise from the grid splendidly doubled by giant X bracings (again) contained within grids.

With each passing year, amid the truck and automobile's liberation of industrial positioning, the corridors—like Elston or Clybourn—are becoming an extension of the service-residential city: either mottled by the silence of long-vanished activity or remade by the compulsions of lofts, minimalls and big-box stores. One thinks one can escape the corporate banalities of suburban Lake Cook, but the trunk roads of the city and its periphery are swathed in analogous vehicular motions, building surfaces, and acts of accumulation. If the city's grid and diagonals were once furrowed by agrarian fields and lines of transport, they are now dominated by the urban forms of the suburbs. Today, in place of the geometers' and manufacturers' city emerges a new city of ideas, services, images, and commerce—a city that will approach the grid differently and doubtless exact new forms from it. Yet like those of the past, the buildings and urban designs of the future will be conditioned by the grid's recurring contours and liberated by its repetitious emptiness. The grid's most important characteristic is its staying power, its perseverance beyond the lifespan of people, economies, technologies, and buildings.

5

The grid's legacy to Chicago can only be compared with that of the railroad. The city came into its own in the age of the railroad, whose exactness and power describes the Windy City's bravura. Rail brought with it meticulous schedules but also ceaseless toil. Its revolution was heartless, but billowing and rolling. Most of all, rail was the great counterpart to the grid. Where the grid established an all-around zone of equivalences where anything could happen anywhere, rail recognized the immensities to be gained from hierarchy and concentration. While the grid marked potential, rail opened up clear routes for development. Atop the grid's illusory framework of equivalence was rail's bottom-line economics. From the 1840s to the 1960s, a dialectic of rail and grid was responsible for Chicago's singular urban form and cultural character. The two forces ushered forth a sheer-walled dreamlike metropolis on the American plains. They combined to create a unique brand of pragmatic extravagance—the ordinary extraordinarily propelled. Indeed, the grid-rail city continually superseded itself just by being itself. Over and over again it fancied more spacious limits to necessity. Chicago became historical once the automobile replaced the railroad and cul-de-sac suburbs overpowered the grid's checkerboard.

Chicago has become more historical in recent years as organizations like *Chicago Wilderness* have sought to reverse almost two centuries of land development—caused by grids, industry, railroads, and automobiles. The Chicago metropolis is built atop a set of ecosystems once dominated by tallgrass prairie, oak savannah, and riparian marshland. Yet almost nowhere in the United States have the original ecosystems of an urban region been so massively obliterated. Twenty years ago, virtually no tallgrass prairie or savannah remained. The ideology of the grid as well as that of the Chicago school of architecture is partly to blame. In both cases, the value placed on business and technological innovation overwhelmed nature. Because of the region's flat topography and understated plant communities, the land was regarded as a tabula rasa—fit for total remaking into building, roadway, lawn, and farmland. While Jens Jensen struggled early in the twentieth century to preserve prairie and create prairie gardens in city parks, most architects and landscape architects accepted Chicago's visual future as wholly artificial and modular. Straight lines and ninety-degree angles were the infrastructural myths of a society that had buried its natural history.

Today, as native plant communities are restored throughout Chicagoland, especially in large tracts like that of the Midewin National Tallgrass Prairie near Joliet, we may begin to appreciate the aesthetic attributes of the prairie that Prairie school adherents like Wright and Walter Burley Griffin saw a century ago. The fluctuating horizontal line of the prairie—brown, white, and close to the ground in winter, a riot of color reaching into the sky in summer, a range of drooping browns in autumn—is the long-forgotten counterpart to the grid. Torn up by surveyors and their magnetic needles, this vanished environment once modulated the Midwest's flat horizons. The underground soil infrastructure, in many ways the true heart of the prairie, supported and sustained the rise of the city's agricultural, industrial, and architectural infrastructure. In the future, people might come to see the visual landscape of Chicago underlain not just by the grid but also by the intricate ancestral foundation that lies beneath it and that occasionally softens the rectangles above.

Wish You Were Here: Alvin Boyarsky's Chicago Postcards

Igor Marjanović

A series of anecdotes about a city I lived in and was fascinated by, liberally sprinkled through the photographs will be slides made of early postcards. . . There is a cult of postcards and I succumbed to it while living in Chicago, which is very simple because it was possible to find very unusual material about the history of industry, certainly the history about cities. By going to a junk shop on a Saturday afternoon and pawing through what is there. You will be seeing a lot of postcards, and they indicate a personal taste and a special view which people have of their existence at a moment in time.

Alvin Boyarsky[1]

Chicago Postcards and the Legacy of Alvin Boyarsky

This essay examines the construction of Chicago's urban history through a collection of popular picture postcards. Official architectural history is seldom made of postcards; rather, it builds upon artistic photography and archival photographs as prime historical evidence. This should come as no surprise. Learning from postcards takes the writing of history outside of traditional institutions, such as museums or academia, localizing the complex processes of historical interpretation within a "booster" medium accessible to many audiences. I will argue here that although popular postcards resist privileging forms of "high architecture" visualizations, they still represent an active form of writing history, a complex process of picturing the urban past through careful organization of images into coherent collections. I will examine the postcard collection of Alvin Boyarsky (1928–90), chairman of the Architectural Association in London (1971–90), revealing Chicago's urban history by uncovering the city's economic foundations and suggesting some historical roles for architects in interpreting such layers. Reflective of the city's economic and social context, when postcards are displaced from the context of consumer tourism and placed into architectural discourse through their revalorization, interpretation, and juxtaposition with other types of urban imagery, they generate meaning through the new discourse around them and offer many possibilities for criticism and appropriation. Such popular images are representative not only of the sights they depict, but they also speak through what they leave out. This anonymous yet carefully assembled history is revealed through theoretical narratives of postcard collections and critical reading of postcards in the work of Alvin Boyarsky.

Postcards and Their Collectors

The emergence of tourism in the nineteenth century introduced the concept of time spent away from work and everyday life that is closely related to the postcard as a medium for recording sites of interest. Around the same time, the newly invented art of photography enabled mass reproduction of images used to record various sites/sights—images that could easily be dropped in the mail or pasted into scrapbooks. The art of the postcard was fully defined in 1902 when regulations were changed to allow messages and addresses to occupy one side of the card, leaving the other side for a picture.[2] It is from this time that postcards and tourism form a tentative alliance, augmenting each other in an unusual symbiosis based on mass production (postcards) and mass consumption (tourism). Not to be overlooked are also the roots of postcards in fields other than tourism. In her book *Photomontage,* Dawn Ades refers to "patriotic postcards" as the earliest examples of (photo) montage, a uniquely modern medium based on the use of shocking and sometimes contrasting images displaced from their original context.[3] These early postcards, produced mostly in Europe at the beginning of the twentieth century, collapsed images of kings, national flags, and famous buildings into a single medium. Through the representation of national or regional symbols, postcards contributed to the process of city, region or nation branding. By displaying regional pride and local particularities, postcards also established a link between regional identity and tourism, which heavily relied on the authenticity of a site. In his book *The Tourist: A New Theory of the Leisure Class,* Dean MacCannell writes:

In the establishment of modern society, the individual act of sightseeing is probably less important than the ceremonial ratification of authentic attractions as objects of ultimate value, a ratification at once caused by and resulting in gathering of tourists around an attraction and measurable to a certain degree by the time and distance the tourists travel to reach it. The actual act of communion between tourist and attraction is less important than the *image* or the *idea* of society that the collective act generates.[4]

Furthermore, cultural geographer Mike Crang writes, "We may perhaps note how the practices of picturing become more important than the qualities of the object itself."[5] As a contribution to the nineteenth-century process of nation building, postcards disseminated images that relied on the identity of a particular site. These postcards were careful assemblies of images of places, heroic infrastructural projects, famous people, or animals. Early postcards of Switzerland, for example, display pastoral imagery of a countryside with recognizable Alpine landscape in the background and farmers with their cows in the foreground.[6] While the representation of Swiss landscape conforms to the figural representation of an actual site, the images of cows represent a more complex metaphor, a dialectic of nature embodied in a cow-site (milk production) and a cow-sight (national symbol). Crang defines a process of transition from site to sight as a transformation of urban imagery in which the site itself becomes less important while the image (sight) of that location becomes a historical construct through which we perceive that history.[7] This domination of images is in part based on postcards and their ability to transcend the actual processes that are taking place in a particular site into a representation of places and processes in it.

The popular imagery of the postcard is not a medium with a universally accepted meaning. It is a medium that provides subjective evidence of history—through the creation of a culturally fluid space ready to be appropriated—a space whose ideological meaning is only acquired through its reading and dissemination. As a result, postcards can mean different things to different readers, supporting and illustrating different arguments leading to different conclusions within different cultural contexts. The first step in theorizing postcards is the process of their collection. Collecting here should not be mistaken for the process of accumulation of apparently objective historical evidence. The collecting of postcards is both a conscious and an unconscious process, through which one's cultural identity and personal preferences are constructed and revealed. From there, a reinterpretation of history is constructed through externalization of those preferences, albeit within another kind of historical time. In her book *On Longing*, Susan Stewart writes:

The collection seeks a form of self-enclosure, which is possible because of its ahistoricism. The collection replaces history with classification, with order beyond the realm of temporality. In the collection, time is not something to be restored to an origin; rather, all time is made simultaneous or synchronous with the collection's world.[8]

The (re)construction of history as a new constellation of time/space[9] is only one of the processes that take place in the collection. The other processes include fetishization, the pleasure of possessing an object that is dependent upon others, and displacement, the removing of the objects of the collection from its original context and use value. Postcard collections remove objects from their original context of consumer tourism into a world of subjective spatial and temporal narrative, replacing everyday consumption with the production of history.

The collector abstracts everyday processes first through the miniature readymade format of postcards, and secondly through the de- and recontextualizing processes of new visual, spatial and temporal relationships of the collection as a whole. This reduces the complexities of the worlds around us—the public, the private, the architectural, the urban, the political, the economic—into a single two-dimensional sight. Finally, collections acquire their value only if compared to other collections and others' desires to possess things. Comparing collections to other collections is what generates their value. This value is in part economic, rational, measurable, and institutionalized through the art and antique market; but it is also derived from the less measurable world of personal fantasies. The collection therefore has a double function, extending the idea of value, or use value, into a much more subjective world of desires. Traditional collections are privatized worlds based on desires to possess things and to enclose them (and close them, so to speak) within the privacy of a domestic environment. This closeness and enclosure overshadow the use value of the object, especially in the case of inexpensive everyday objects, such as postcards or souvenirs.

Not to be overlooked here is the fact that the appropriation of postcards comes after the act of their collection. Unlike the single postcard, postcard collections represent a privatized view of an individual subject. If later externalized into the world of architectural culture, the appropriation process changes the value of the collection yet again. Authenticating distant traveling experiences, vintage postcards are also souvenirs that shockingly "*discredit* the present."[10] They embody an idea of a different past, something forgotten and more intimate; something to which we compare our alienated present. This critique of the present condition represents the beginning of Boyarsky's appropriation of postcards.

Postcards and Montage

The origin of the postcard is closely related to the development of photography, mechanical reproduction of the image and, in particular, to the development of montage as a new artistic technique after the First World War. Montage is a specific representational strategy first developed by Berlin Dadaists in which the *monteur* or the artist of montage produces, like the industrial steelworker (*monteur* in French), an assembled work of art. The Dadaists utilized industrial ready-mades, such as newspapers or photographs, and often thought of themselves as engineers rather than artists.[11] Montage practices thus bridged the worlds of art, design, cinema, and architecture, establishing a complexity of relations between high art, mass media, and everyday life. The art of montage aimed at the representation of an industrial world and, unlike traditional painting, was conceived from and for the very possibility of mechanical reproduction.

John Heartfield and Hannah Hoch were two of the most important representatives of the art of montage. Montage strategies in their work were based on working with altered photographs and newspaper cuttings, creating a new and stronger dialectical relationship between the parts and the whole through displacement of elements from their original context and, most important—communication of *meaning*. The art of montage usually communicated meaning through strong political messages, which were often associated with the political left. The art of Heartfield in particular aimed at the disruption of Nazi propaganda, revealing social injustice and political oppression. His montage *Sleeping Reichstag* embodies compositional devices of dramatic scale differences and displacement of elements from their original context in order to provide a social critique. This montage, like many others from the same period, encompasses one of the most important characteristics of montage—"shock effect." Through the use of shocking imagery, *monteurs* tried to mobilize the public around certain political agendas in order to confront social injustice.

The shock effect spread quickly from artistic montage into other fields of art, like cinema and architecture. Ludwig Mies van der Rohe, for example, used montage to advertise the progressive and shockingly simple character of his projects for Berlin. He superimposed the crystal-like forms of his office buildings for the Alexanderplatz over the dense city fabric of Berlin. In *Mechanization Takes Command,* Siegfried Giedion uses stills from Luis Bunuel's film *Un Chien Andalou* in order to drastically draw attention to changed notions of life and death in the context of industrialization.[12] Architect Stan Allen has republished the same stills and the same shocking scenes of the cut eyeball.[13] This continuous interest in the power of montage and its collision of different images demonstrates the contemporary architectural avant-garde's continued interest to define itself as socially progressive. In all cases, these strategies aim at addressing wider audiences—ideally the mass audience of the postcard. Both media—the postcard and the artistic/cinematic montage—shared the same visual vocabulary and at least two common goals: to find a visual means to represent the modern metropolis and to establish advertising precedents in the age of global consumerism and mechanical reproduction. It is also through the art of cinematic and artistic montage that the first active interchange between the historical avant-garde and mass culture took place, potentially bringing the avant-garde's social agenda closer to the public.

There is, however, an important difference between montage and postcards—an ethical distinction. The *monteur*'s aim is very close to that of the critical theorist and, in particular, the members of Frankfurt school, which typically assigned positive function to art only if it stood up against hegemony and domination. Obviously, such noble ethical goals were not associated with postcards, but it is precisely in the art of the postcard that photo-manipulation and photo-amusement for the masses was first widely exercised. Like architects and artistic *monteurs* themselves, the producers of postcards faced the challenge of establishing the postcard's relationship with social critique. While the art of montage criticized the position of art and the artist in a given society, it also criticized society at large. The art of the postcard is less socially engaged. Considering that its origins were in popular sensibility and mass media, some of the reasons for this disengagement are self-explanatory. Rather than being critical, postcards are more reflective of societies and their modes of production. Whilst they depict the division of labor and sites of production, they are designed to inspire and sell. They are just one of many aestheticized manifestations of the modernist division of time—they either represent sites of leisure or sites of labor. Postcards were introduced in order to record the site/sight of popular activities and imply that for the first time people are able to devote their leisure time to such activities—whether commercial travel, shopping, or entertainment.

The rise of postcards as a phenomenon meant that various sites could be advertised through the use of easily recognizable imagery and distributed globally for the first time. This imagery included photographs of shoppers on the streets of Paris and Chicago, or leisure activities at Coney Island in New York or London's Hyde Park. In order to compress the number of attractive images, the producers of postcards played with formatting images, altering, reducing, or retouching them in order to reach the desired effect. This effect was usually associated with the advertisement of certain site specificities, and the best way to achieve such effect was to use the most shocking images available. It is this strategy of shock, and the experimental use of ready-made texts and photographs, that bring together the art of the postcard with the art of montage. Both media communicate their messages directly and rely on the ready-made imagery of everyday culture.

The ideological agenda of montage strategies in postcards was achieved through the use of a new industrial imagery that stood in sharp contrast to the recent preindustrial past, still symbolized by the congested metropolis struggling to overcome problems with sanitation and manual modes of production. The modernist myth of the metropolis and its belief in science, technology, and industrialization were the messages delivered by postcards. Postcards with images of infrastructural networks and industrial machinery were not only aimed at representing Chicago as a site of leisure and shopping. Rather, their message was more complex, and conceptualized Chicago as an embodiment of modernity. The city was not only a good place to visit but also a good place to live and work. The working-class character of the city was idealized through its industrial sites such as the steel mills, stockyards or harbors. Sites of political unrest such as the Haymarket Affair and the iconography of workers movements were carefully avoided and omitted. Unlike the art of montage, postcards deny any kind of political activism, associating themselves with the market economy and the current social order.

Chicago's Mechanically Reproduced History

As the essays in this collection attest, the history of Chicago modernism is inseparable from the international economy of photographs through which it was popularized.[14] In the first instance, photographs of certain late nineteenth-century commercial buildings were juxtaposed with images of American industrial structures, grain elevators and the like, effectively implying a mythical Chicago origin for the modernist project. These deliberately shockingly juxtaposed images and the rhetorical implications they conveyed, were disseminated by European proponents of modernism such as Walter Gropius, Le Corbusier, and Siegfried Giedion.[15] Le Corbusier's images of ocean liners and Giedion's images of automatic hog-weighing devices conveyed ideas of interdependency between the market economy, mechanization, and architectural production. Furthermore, these often shocking images were deployed to rally architectural culture around the social and formal ideals of modern architecture. Eventually this work was embraced and further propagated by American critics, curators, and historians, most notably Phillip Johnson. The so-called second Chicago school, the work of Mies van der Rohe, his collaborators and contemporaries, championed by Johnson and others, mobilized photographic images in a very different way. These photographs, most notably the stylized high contrast black and white photographs produced by the Hedrich-Blessing firm, were disseminated internationally as rhetorical devices in the promotion of a modernism with decidedly different goals. They came to visually embody international style modernism and were read as equally demonstrative of Chicago's particular historical provenance over the field.[16] The subtle, yet enormously significant difference between these two regimes of image reproduction, roughly approximated by the crude terms first and second Chicago schools, can be read in the social (read political) agendas of their proponents.

This distinction in the social and political economy of images in Chicago modernism might be further illuminated by examining a third body of images, namely, Alvin Boyarsky's collection of popular picture postcards. Boyarsky was one of the most influential architectural educators of the twentieth century. He served as associate dean and professor at the University of Illinois at Chicago (UIC) College of Architecture and the Arts from 1965 to 1971, before becoming the chairman of the Architectural Association in London, a position he held until his death in 1990. He transformed the Architectural Association into one of the most prestigious architecture schools in the world. Although Boyarsky represents one of the most significant architectural educators in Europe, his role in U.S. architectural education and practice is yet to be examined. Chicago, the city where he began his career as an educational leader, almost seems to have forgotten him. His once-famous collection of Chicago postcards, an allegorical narrative of midwestern modernity, lives on in the memories of senior UIC faculty and holds mythical status among European academics associated with the Architectural Association, but for the current generation of Chicago architects both Boyarsky and his postcard collection hold little significance.

Boyarsky was a passionate collector and disseminator of images reminiscent of the iconic representations of technological progress so beloved by Le Corbusier and Giedion

18.1

18.2

and that accompanied the first Chicago school and its vision of modernism. A small part of his extensive postcard collection has appeared in Boyarsky's written body of work, which is scattered throughout many periodicals. His writings and, in particular, his images are yet to be excavated, pieced together, and interpreted. This essay forms a beginning.

Boyarsky's postcard collection encompasses a breadth and richness of depictions of architecture, urban space and landscape, and everyday life in Chicago, spanning one hundred years of Chicago history. He collected postcards systematically and made conscious decisions about what types of postcards were appropriate for the collection. Like Giedion before him, Boyarsky was particularly interested in those postcards that represented anonymous and unrecognized histories (architecturally speaking, at least). An absence of any kind of high art or high architecture objects is therefore evident in his collection. There are no postcards of heroic buildings designed by master architects. Instead, the collection is mostly composed of nineteenth-century and twentieth-century postcards of Chicago representing the city's most famous sites of labor, such as grain elevators, steel mills, slaughterhouses, highways, and airports.

Much of the collection stands as a critique of the corporate, depoliticized context of the second Chicago school, thus revealing and underlining the tensions between the first and second Chicago schools. Boyarsky's images of Chicago industry, infrastructure, and commerce recall the images first deployed by Giedion and other European proponents of modernism. However, they differ subtly in their source of origin as well as their context for reception. This parallel between the first deployment of images of Chicago modernism and Boyarsky's reappropriation of its techniques is a particularly important example, as it suggests a reading of Boyarsky's critical agenda within the context of a depoliticized culture of Miesian modernism. While the architecture and urbanism of the first Chicago school has come to be associated with the myth of technological and social progress of European modernism, the work of the second Chicago school substituted the idea of social change for the idea of pure and de-

18.1 Postcard—Most Beautiful Diner in Chicago.

18.2 Postcard—Armour Grain Elevator, S. Branch, Chicago River.

politicized form. This shift is evident in the postcards of the two periods and their relationship to official architectural imagery. The postcards in the Boyarsky collection that were printed at the time of the first Chicago school were very similar to the official imagery of early European modernists, depicting various industrial sites, including grain elevators and slaughterhouses. During the period of the second Chicago school, the postcards still enthusiastically represented images of progress—this time of Chicago's highways, airports, and large public works, but official architectural historiography did not, however, follow the same direction.

Architectural books and periodicals of the late 1960s shifted the discussion from the issues of economic, technological, and sociological change to a discussion about the purity of style and appropriateness of form. Rather than depicting technological and social invention through architecture, architectural representations of the city of Chicago became monuments to late modernism—primarily corporate skyscrapers and middle-class housing. This imagery, most notably represented in the architectural photographs of Hedrich-Blessing, became more and more distant from the predicaments of the everyday world and popular imagery of newspapers, magazines, and postcards. Images of production lines, factories, slaughterhouses, bridges, and canals were substituted with Hedrich-Blessing's melancholic photographs in which the beauty of architectural form is delineated and emphasized through the exceptional use of light and shadow. It comes as no surprise that in such an environment, dominated with corporate architect-artists, Boyarsky felt isolated; his activist ideas regarding social change, and particularly his concern with wars in third world countries, were not favorite topics in the architectural discourse of the time. Boyarsky turned to postcards as representations that could address crucial architectural questions: the detachment of architectural imagery from popular sentiment, the incomprehensibility of modernist monument-buildings to a broader audience, and the disappearance of the social program associated with the early modern ideal of architecture. It is with these questions in mind that Boyarsky embarked on the collection, research, and dissemination of popular picture postcards.

Postcards as Sites of Labor and Leisure

The earliest postcards of Chicago in the Boyarsky collection show streetscapes full of people and images of parks with pedestrians strolling in a calm preindustrial landscape. The images of urban *flaneurie* present congested streets of Chicago, with individuals engaged in shopping and the pursuit of leisure time (fig. 18.3). State Street in particular is a favorite subject, with images of curious customers gazing at department store windows. These images of streets full of human bodies are still based on early industrial notions of density, where the city is at the same time the site of production, leisure, and

18.3

18.3 Postcard—Looking North from Adams Street, Chicago, Illinois.

18.4 Postcard—Scene from Rustic Bridge, Washington Park, Chicago.

18.5 Postcard—Sheep in Washington Park, Chicago, Illinois.

18.6 Postcard—McKinley Park Swimming Pool, Chicago.

18.7 Postcard—Union Stock Yards, Chicago, Illinois.

housing. But it was precisely in the nineteenth century that this congestion was perceived as threatening and led to attempts to improve sanitary and infrastructural conditions in the early modern metropolis. Chicago was no exception. It is because of these conditions that the early images of a dense and busy downtown Chicago streets are supplemented by many postcards with images of public parks free of crowds and buildings. They show relaxed individuals, mostly women, strolling in an artificially cultivated but yet seemingly very natural landscapes (fig. 18.4). Compared to the images of streetscapes, the human body is much smaller and usually depicted as an integral part of nature (fig. 18.5). The images of human bodies relaxing on green meadows or sitting alongside irregularly shaped ponds are carefully retouched or blurred with an exaggerated presence of plants and even animals. The pastoral imagery is characterized by the disappearance and minimization of the human body, or at least its loss of domination within the image (fig. 18.6). This abstract character and absence of the centrality of the human body is, in fact, also a permanent feature of many postcards in the Boyarsky collection.

Many Chicago postcards from the Boyarsky collection use industrial imagery as their point of departure (fig. 18.2 above). They demonstrate an enthusiasm for industrial production, depicting stockyards, steel mills, and grain elevators. The postcards depict industrial machinery and technical inventions that rationalize the production line. They include images of hog-killing and hog-measuring devices intended for catching, weighing, and suspending hogs—proud inventions of nineteenth-century Chicago that provided a fast and efficient route from the abattoir to the dining table (fig. 18.7). In *Mechanization Takes Command* Giedion uses similar imagery of the Chicago stockyards and their technological advancements, commenting that union workers often received such innovations with hostility and skepticism.[17] Giedion recognizes that, fearing for his or her own job description and wages, the worker saw technological innovation and scientific management as a new means of exploitation. Giedion concludes:

Not to be overlooked are those aspects which have to do with the class struggle. They, however, lie outside the actual problems of this book, whose task is to describe the impact of a mechanized world on the human organism and on human feeling.[18]

Although he calls for the appreciation of the anonymous history of mechanization, Giedion does not seem to be interested in the social or cultural issues that underpin those processes, namely, class struggle. He sees culture as a mere product of such mechanization, evolving seamlessly in parallel with industrial revolution. The "industrial" postcards of Chicago are very similar—they convey the same socially and culturally neutral idea of progress, depicting modes of production but not referencing issues such as

18.4

18.5

18.6

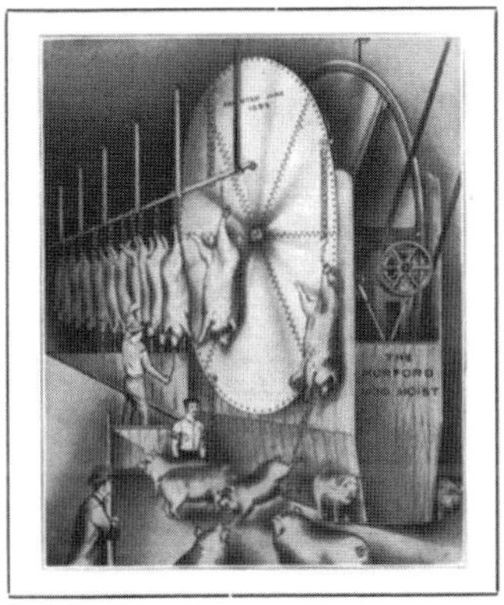

UNION STOCK YARDS
CHICAGO

18.7

class, race, gender, or ethnicity. The postcards of the Union Stockyards on the South Side of Chicago depict a city that believes in industrial progress and the pioneering nature of its inhabitants—a city dominated by a work ethic and belief that a better life is possible through the acceleration of capitalist development (fig. 18.8). Needless to say, these beliefs were not shared by the workers' movements of the late nineteenth century, whose ideas about a better life were not compatible with the existing social and economical order. It is worth noting that there are no references to sites of social and ethnic unrest, such as the Haymarket Affair—whether in the Boyarsky postcard collection or in the writings of modernist historiographers like Giedion.

Other postcards from the collection focus on Chicago public works, mostly networks of railroads, highways, and airports. Images of bridges, canals, underground passages, railroads, harbors, and airports encompass an early ideal of the working-class city as a site of large-scale public infrastructure (figs. 18.9, 18.10, 18.11). They also symbolize the national and international aspirations of Chicago to become a leader of the industrialized world.[19] Similar to some other midwestern cities, such as St. Louis and Cincinnati, Chicago is perceived as a site of innovation, but more than anything else, the postcards show it as a city in which "first nature" is conquered and from which a "second nature" is built. In *Nature's Metropolis: Chicago and the Great West,* William Cronon writes:

18.8

18.9

18.8 Postcard—Cattle Pens and Runways, Union Stock Yards, Chicago.

18.9 Postcard—Greetings from Chicago: Jack Knife Bridge over Chicago River.

18.10 Postcard—Eisenhower Expressway at the Chicago Circle Center.

18.11 Postcard—John F. Kennedy Expressway, looking toward the Chicago Loop.

18.10

18.11

A kind of "second nature," designed by people and "improved" towards human ends, gradually emerged atop the original landscape that nature—"first nature"—had created as such an inconvenient jumble. Despite the subtly differing logic that lay behind each, the geography of second nature was in its own way as compelling as the geography of first nature, so boosters and others often forgot the distinction between them. Both seemed quite "natural."[20]

This unique interplay of the natural and industrial landscape is highly visible in the postcards in the Boyarsky collection. A significant number depict the blending of the vast landscape of the prairie with Chicago's canals, cultivated lakefront, railroads, elevated trains, highways, and airports. These artifacts are overlaid onto the prairie landscape, suggesting that such infrastructural improvements will "naturally" lead to a better, cleaner, and more efficient life; technological progress will meet all human demand, ensuring no need to change existing social or power structures. The proud placement of highways and airports in the postcards of Chicago is telling; the celebration of public works efficiently shifts the discussion from political progress to economic progress through the existing political system. This attitude is very close to Le Corbusier's familiar dilemma (architecture or revolution), and it is also close to Giedion's plea in which he calls for a stronger bond between industry, art, culture, and everyday life:

Once historical consciousness is awakened, self-respect will awaken too, a self-respect that inspires every true culture. This renewed awareness will find means of preserving the key sources to American history.[21]

Clearly, historical consciousness for Giedion is not class consciousness. Rather, it is technological consciousness based on industrial inventions and their impact on everyday lives. It is no coincidence that this technological fetishization is inspired by American material culture, used as a progressive example for architectural modernism to reify images of the nation's high level of industrial development. Just as Russian constructivists, for example, and Kazimir Malevich in particular, looked at American skyscrapers as architectural ideals embodying all progressive as-

18.12 Postcard—entrance highway and plane overpass, O'Hare International Airport, Chicago.

18.13 Postcard—The Merchandise Mart, Chicago.

pects of labor and technology, Alvin Boyarsky was interested in a similar validation of material culture when he called O'Hare International Airport "Chicago's Versailles" (fig. 18.12).[22]

Another set of postcards depicts the city through aerial views. This is again inspired by new technologies—aerial photography in particular—which for the first time offered the possibility of accurate overhead surveillance. These postcards focus on the large scale of the modern metropolis and depict the city as an abstract composition of superstructures, infrastructure, and the horizontal plain of the prairie. The human dimension and its representation are completely lost, thus enabling these images to reinforce the modernist tradition of design for the abstract universal subject.

The postcards of large buildings such as the Merchandise Mart (fig. 18.13), the Main Post Office, or the Sears Tower demonstrate Chicago's fascination with large structures, which beyond a certain scale depart from their architectural features and start to acquire the characteristics of the city itself. Architectural Association alumnus Rem Koolhaas defines these buildings as belonging to "bigness"—a new species of architecture that obscures the relationship between the skin and the interior spaces and that depends on accelerated construction, the elevator, electricity, air conditioning, and steel.[23] Koolhaas further extends modernist optimism for technology by saying that such large structures and Chicago's many technological inventions have "potential for the reorganization of the social world."[24] It is here that we start to see a powerful continuity of ideas, stretching from Giedion and Le Corbusier to Boyarsky and Koolhaas. This continuity replaces the traditional redeeming power of beauty with the redeeming notion of technology and, in the case of Koolhaas, with the redeeming power of global capitalist development.

Postcard as a Vehicle for Architectural Criticism

Unlike most other architectural critics, Boyarsky used picture postcards and newspaper spreads—media available to and understandable by a broader public audience. In using the popular imagery of the postcard, an author like Boyarsky is faced with an almost impossible task: how to maintain a critical position with respect to visual depiction of the city through popular iconography and yet reach beyond mere criticism to address the complexities inherent in depictions of everyday life.

An amateur deltiologist and a member of the "Windy City Postcard Club," Boyarsky used several venues to discuss his postcard collection. His famous lecture, provocatively entitled "Animal City," talked about Chicago through its postcards. One of his most intriguing texts, "Chicago à la Carte: The City as an Energy System," was first published

18.12

18.13

in *Architectural Design* (1970) and again in *The Idea of the City*.[25] Rather than a conventional scholarly essay, "Chicago à la Carte" is a collection of lecture notes and fragmented theses in the manner of Walter Benjamin's *Passagenwerk* project. It examines Chicago as a context for architectural practice, and in particular, it examines Chicago modernism through images mechanically reproduced for mass audiences: picture postcards and newspaper articles. Most of the December 1970 issue of *AD* is occupied by Boyarsky's lengthy photo-essay, supplemented by two other essays on Chicago, "Map Guide: Chicago" by Joseph Griggs[26] and "Chicago Frame" by Colin Rowe.[27] In "Chicago à la Carte," Boyarsky constructs an urban history through postcards, some of which are presented in this essay. In doing so, he combines images of large structures and industrial sites with excerpts from Upton Sinclair's *The Jungle*,[28] producing a melancholic image of Chicago as a site of labor, inventions, and pioneering spirit. Although not sentimental about architectural forms, Boyarsky was very passionate about the social production of space, especially about the future of urban public spaces. Critical of the City's public art projects, Boyarsky displays images of the huge Picasso sculpture on Daley Plaza together with images of political protests, concluding that this public space is "not packed by restless demonstrators who remain dissatisfied with the symbolism offered."[29] The essay culminates with a visual metaphor, an epilogue composed of two sites: photographs of the political riots of 1968 and a cover page from the July 28, 1970, issue of the *Chicago Tribune* describing the casualties of riots in Grant Park: "seize 140 in riot; 25 hurt."[30] Just below these casualty numbers rises a soaring rendering of the future Sears Tower, announcing the construction of the tallest building in the world. It is through this careful juxtaposition of political and architectural images that Boyarsky chose to act primarily as a social critic.

Boyarsky not only appropriated postcards, he also designed them. The International Institute of Design (IID) was in many ways Boyarsky's pilot study for his future curricular initiatives at the Architectural Association. Located in Chicago and London, the IID was an intensive summer workshop that provided an international forum for discussions about architectural education and practice. Boyarsky was well aware that such global exchange of ideas was made possible by the advances in technology, such as the introduction of affordable jet travel. It was also the liberating and rebellious spirit of the sixties that defined the work and the imagery of IID, both well documented through postcards, posters, flyers, and journals. While the official IID letterhead features soaring images of jet liners, the IID postcards represent a more delicate montage of faces, words, and urban images. Represented on the postcards are Boyarsky, Peter Cook, other members of Archigram, Queen Elizabeth II, double-deckers, and images of London, Chicago, New York, and other cities. Boyarsky even produced stamps with his portrait and portraits of others involved in IID: James Stirling, Hans Hollein, Colin Rowe, Robin Middleton, Cedric Price, and Reyner Banham, to name a few.

Alvin Boyarsky's courageous ability to look at diverse sets of architecturally disturbing images, such as political protests and sites of industrial production, influenced his students at the Architectural Association. In his essay "Atlanta," Rem Koolhaas writes:

. . . Alvin probably influenced to some degree my subconscious, and I would like to dedicate this lecture to the lack of sentimentality he was displaying and to the evident pleasure with which he discussed dangerous situations in architecture.[31]

In *Delirious New York*, Koolhaas's most well-known use of postcards, he sees design possibilities in the dangerous condition of the *real* and explores operational strategies for the architectural profession within an increasingly globalized market economy. An interesting pairing of postcards published in the book is that of Coney Island Luna Park.[32] The first postcard shows the amusement infrastructure of Luna Park in daylight. "A pathetic dimension, an aura of cheapness" observes Koolhaas. The other postcard, published on the same page, represents Luna Park at night. Koolhaas writes:

For the price of one, Thompson has created two distinct cities, each with its own character, its own life, its own inhabitants. Now, the city itself, is to be lived in shifts; the electric city, phantom offspring of the "real" city, is an even more powerful instrument for the fulfillment of fantasy.[33]

In Koolhaas's work the postcards (and architecture) of Coney Island acquire meaning through the introduction of the effects of electricity and the phantasmagoric representation of the entertainment industry. Disinterested in social conflicts, he focused on a potential for architecture to be fed by the fantastic creations of the entertainment industry. He used the pairing of postcards and opposing sights to build an argument, thus reinforcing the idea that an image and a collection acquire meaning through comparison with other objects. But unlike Boyarsky, who juxtaposed postcards to newspaper clips and photos of political riots, Koolhaas juxtaposed two postcards from similar cultural contexts, thus presenting the postcard as a socially unproblematic medium. His historical context was different to the one in which Boyarsky developed as a critic: a global shift from manufacturing technologies to information and entertainment industries was taking place. Using similar historical evidence as Boyarsky, he created a very different subjective history of those industries, and a manifesto for his own architecture in the making:

If this infrastructure supports a largely cardboard reality, that is exactly the point. Luna Park is the first manifestation of a curse that is to haunt the architectural profession for the rest of its life, the formula: technology + cardboard (or any other flimsy material) = reality.[34]

This transition from Boyarsky's social activism to Koolhaas's interest in the realities of consumer capitalism speaks of a much larger shift—a process of intentional erasure and abstraction of labor processes in favor of postindustrial products that conceal any evidence of their own making.

Conclusion

The patterns of postcard appropriation in Boyarsky's work rely on two critical strategies. First, industrial and everyday imagery is invested retroactively with new significance; it is revalorized and aestheticized. Second, postcards derive meaning from the discourse around them, offering multiple readings and re-readings, providing critics with the possibility to make conscious decisions about the use value of the postcards. Through these strategies, and despite his apparent fascination with the icons of capitalist development, Boyarsky returned to the original social ideals of modernity. He used images of the sites of labor in order to revive a belief in the possibility of architecture *with* utopia—a society and architecture qualitatively different from the one he lived in. This ideal is very close to the social ideals of John Heartfield and other *monteurs*, who sought not only to represent reality through their ready-mades but also to extend that idea of reality to something new, unseen, and yet to be accomplished. Unlike traditional realist painting, the art of montage collapsed many opposing views into one reassembled message that encompassed all three horizons at the same time: the real, the desired, and the utopian. It is with these three critical horizons in mind that Boyarsky looked at postcards and their messages.

A passionate participant of the sit-ins for Cambodia (see fig. 18.14) and an active participant of the political debates of the 1960s, Boyarsky was a friend of civil rights activist Jessie Jackson and a sympathizer of the Black Panthers. He had no illusions—faced with

18.14

18.15

the rapid advancement of late capitalism and information technology—that the modernist project was rapidly losing its social energy. To use postcards with images of slaughterhouses and highways was an attempt at social criticism at a time when architects started to look (again) for historically beautified images of bourgeois society (thus abandoning any possibility of social change). Faced with the collapse of the modernist project, the "new" context of the 1970s engaged in irony rather than activism. It resonated with pessimism rather than social optimism. This new condition, which many call the condition of postmodernity, offered a series of fragmented formal options that were unable to provide real social or architectural alternatives. Faced with such a questionable notion of history, Boyarsky looked for other historical and formal models. He found them in his postcards, and like Giedion before him, he praised this anonymous history; unlike Giedion, he wondered how architects could benefit from the radical futuristic visions that postcards offered. Boyarsky wrote:

> **. . . they [postcards] appear relieved of the laws of historical continuity and purely compositional activities involving good taste, harmony and delicacy of expression. Plotted with a compass whose co-ordination is indefinitely future, these self-regulating models of empirical efficiency appear to glean immediate benefit from science and technology.**[35]

Although aware of the crisis of modern architecture, Boyarsky was still devoted to the "future" as an ultimate architectural horizon. He was critical of the role of architecture in society. His use of postcards was a voice of concern and criticism of a profession that had rejected the acceptance of the painful *reality* in which some tasks were taken away from architecture by capitalist development.[36] This ideological criticism of the architectural profession was part of the wider context of the critique of modernism in the 1970s. The most radical view was probably that of Manfredo Tafuri who contended that the social project of architecture collapsed under the deployment of capitalist development and its technologies, negating any possibility for a better world or architecture for the working class. Similarly, Boyarsky's criticism went beyond conventional (and formal) discourse, revisiting the issue

18.14 Alvin Boyarsky, sitting in for Cambodia, Chicago, May 1970. Photograph courtesy of the Alvin Boyarsky Memorial Trust.

18.15 Postcard—Marina City under construction, Chicago, Illinois.

of the future of the public realm, putting aside the question of style as less important or even irrelevant.

Through images of political protests at the Daley Plaza in Chicago, Boyarsky questioned the future of public space and architecture's ability to generate such spaces. He called the unveiling of the rusty steel Picasso sculpture at the Daley Plaza an "orgy"[37] and added that "today's generation has not the ability to make large plans to inspire the future,"[38] suggesting that spectacle had replaced architecture as a now conservative social force. But unlike Tafuri, Boyarsky was not completely pessimistic; he saw Goldberg's Marina City as a bright ray pointed toward the future—an architecture of the future based on progressive technology, labor and expanded and accessible public space (fig. 18.15). Boyarsky saw Marina City's layered infrastructural network as a true expression of Chicago's large public works—canals, harbors, and railroads—which are so clearly depicted in his postcards.

Boyarsky's article "Chicago à la Carte" might give a misleading stylistic impression of its author's devotion to everyday consumerism and pop culture commodities. This was not the case—instead his interest in the everyday was closer to that of Walter Benjamin, in which the everyday lived experience requires critical interpretation and search for alternatives, rather than being a formal role model. Boyarsky's two primary sources for his collection—picture postcards and newspaper spreads—were by definition available to a broader public audience. In these two ways, as well as in the acts of collection and juxtaposition, Boyarsky was working as a social critic, indicting mainstream modernism's ambivalence to its social origins. While many of the images in the collection reiterate the themes and topics of the first Chicago school, they are transformed by the social and cultural context of their particular time, and the fact that they come from inexpensive, equalitarian, and readily available sources. Boyarsky's Chicago narrative is based on labor and politics, defying the abstraction of labor processes and their separation from the production of urban spaces. It tells the history of "urban ghosts and shadows"[39]—a history of social conflict that moves beyond the traditional vision of modernism based solely on economic and technological progress.

Bertrand Goldberg: A Personal View of Architecture

19

Geoffrey Goldberg

Background

Bertrand Goldberg was a Chicago architect. Born in Chicago in 1913, he studied at Harvard College; in 1931, he went to the Bauhaus in Germany. Goldberg apprenticed briefly in Ludwig Mies van der Rohe's office in Berlin and, upon returning to Chicago, worked in the offices of the Keck brothers, Paul Schweicker, and others. In 1937, the young architect opened his own office. He practiced in Chicago until his death in 1997.

The Work: Early Period, 1937–50

Goldberg's early work can be understood in light of his Chicago origins and his training at the Bauhaus. He believed in a progressive social agenda coupled with a strongly American, and in some sense, Chicagoan sense of pragmatism. His work reflects an individualistic combination of this pragmatism with the social and formal ideas of the Bauhaus.

Houses

Goldberg's early work included many residential projects. They can be considered as part of a larger body of intriguing early modernist residential work built in America by a number of architects. These residences were modest in size and were formally impetuous in their interiors. In each, moments of architectural intensity were developed within otherwise calm and tranquil layouts (figs. 19.1–19.4).

19.1

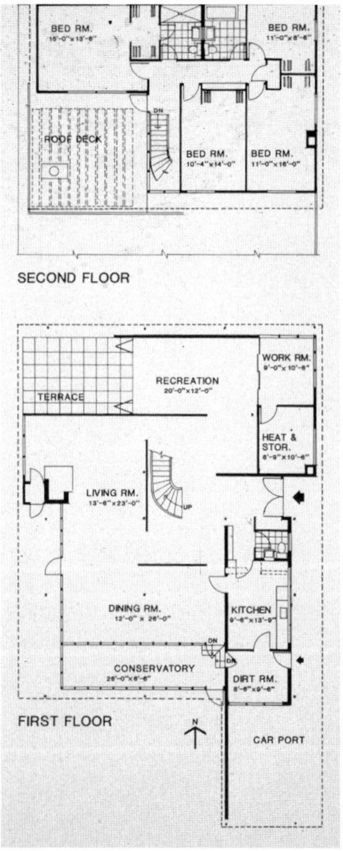

19.2

19.1 Abrams House, Glencoe, Illinois, 1936–37, Hedrich-Blessing Photo. Courtesy of the Hedrich-Blessing Collection, Chicago Historical Society.

19.2 Abrams House, plan, Hedrich-Blessing Photo. Courtesy of Bertrand Goldberg Associates.

19.3 Helstein House, Chicago, c. 1950, Hedrich-Blessing Photo. Courtesy of the Hedrich-Blessing Collection, Chicago Historical Society.

19.3

19.4

19.5

19.4 Helstein House, interior, Hedrich-Blessing Photo. Courtesy of the Hedrich-Blessing Collection, Chicago Historical Society.

19.5 Custom furniture, c. 1950, Hedrich-Blessing Photo. Courtesy of the Hedrich-Blessing Collection, Chicago Historical Society.

Goldberg detailed and furnished these early houses with a particular sensibility. For example, one kitchen was fitted with sprinklers to wash down stainless steel countertops; another house had limestone slabs, some 20' long, for entry walls; dressing mirrors were hinged to provide hidden jewelry storage behind. For many, custom furniture was also designed (fig. 19.5).

Prefabrication

Another body of Goldberg's early work was focused on industrial design and manufacturing processes. Here, the interest was in problems of constructability and sequencing. In 1938, Goldberg designed a movable ice cream store to fit in the back of a truck so that it could be driven to Florida in the winter and return to Chicago in the summer. The building was erected and suspended from a single (collapsible) mast (figs. 19.6, 19.7).

The same year, he also designed a gas station, suspended from two columns to minimize foundation work. During World War II, Goldberg designed a mobile delousing unit and a prefabricated mobile penicillin lab; postwar work included a prefabricated pressed steel bathroom unit and a stressed-skin plywood boxcar, which was even used in one installation for a single family residence (figs. 19.8–19.9).

The Work: Middle Period, 1950–64

After a brief partnership with Lee Atwood (who had worked with R. Buckminster

19.6

19.7

19.6 North Pole on a truck. Hedrich-Blessing Photo. Courtesy of the Hedrich-Blessing Collection, Chicago Historical Society.

19.7 North Pole Mobile Ice Cream Store, River Forest, 1938, Hedrich-Blessing Photo. Courtesy of the Hedrich-Blessing Collection, Chicago Historical Society.

19.8 Clark Maple Gas Station, Chicago, 1938, Hedrich-Blessing Photo. Courtesy of the Hedrich-Blessing Collection, Chicago Historical Society.

19.9 Snyder House, Shelter Island, New York, 1952. Courtesy of J. Alex Langley.

19.8

19.9

19.10

Fuller on the Dymaxion Car and whose father had been associated with Burnham years before), Goldberg started his own firm, Bertrand Goldberg Associates, in the early 1950s. Throughout the 1950s, the firm's work included office buildings, union halls, art centers, and some residential development. Goldberg attained modest success: he was published, and he won a *Progressive Architecture* design award in 1957 for Drexel Gardens, an affordable housing complex in Chicago.

Marina City

In 1959, Goldberg started work on Marina City. The project, completed in 1967, was the defining work of his career. He was involved in all areas of the project, including programming, financing and development, architecture, engineering, and construction management.

Marina City was one project with many buildings: it included two sixty-story residential towers, a sixteen-story office building with a recreational building for bowling below, and a freestanding theater. These buildings were all set atop a three-story base building that incorporated an ice-skating rink and a marina off the river (figs. 19.10, 19.11, 10.12).

Marina City was launched as a result of an interesting collaboration. A Chicago politician and labor leader named Bill McFetridge, head of the International Union of Building Maintenance Employees, asked Goldberg to find a site for a new union

19.10 Marina City promotional model, 1959, Hedrich-Blessing Photo. Courtesy of the Chicago Historical Society.

19.11 Marina City, c. 1967, Hedrich-Blessing Photo. HB-23215, courtesy of the Hedrich-Blessing Collection, Chicago Historical Society.

19.12 Marina City, site plan. Courtesy of Bertrand Goldberg Associates.

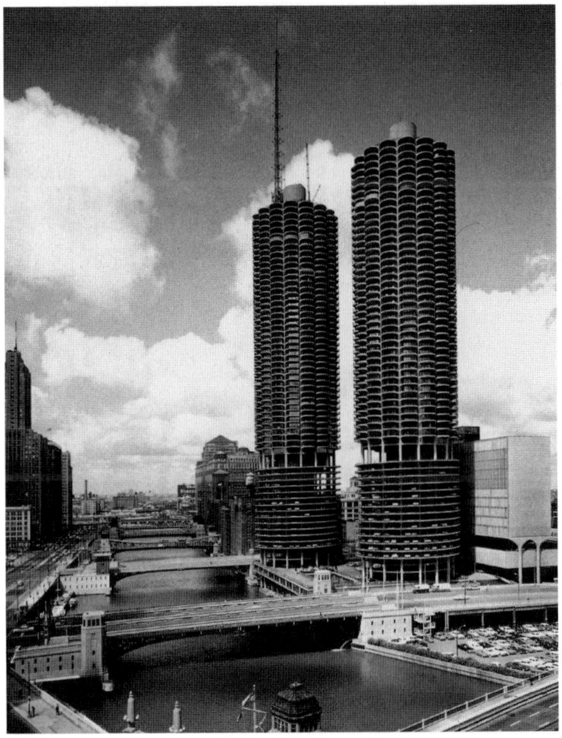

19.11

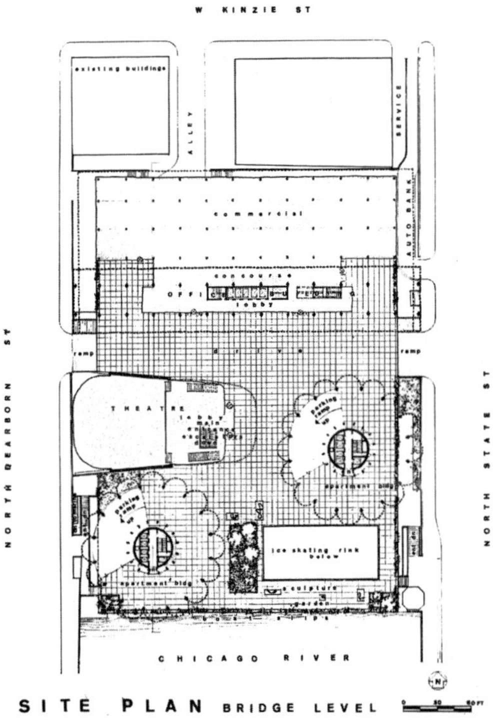

19.12

19.13

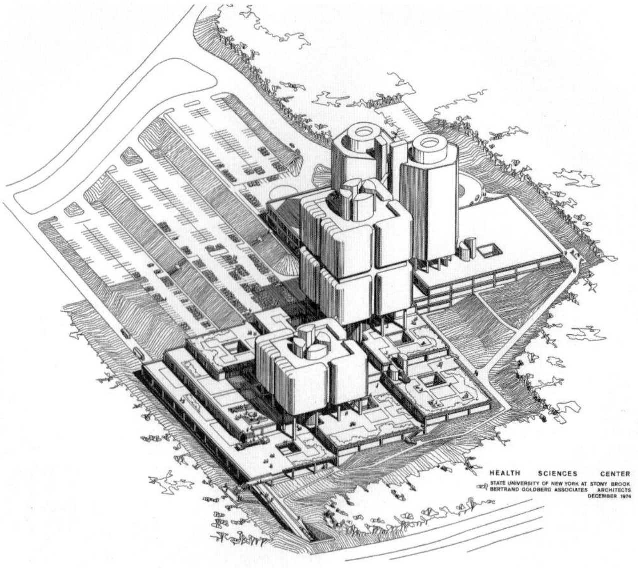

19.14

19.13 Drawing of Health Sciences Center, c. 1970. Courtesy of Bertrand Goldberg Associates.

19.14 Health Sciences Center, Stony Brook, New York, c. 1970, Hedrich-Blessing Photo. Courtesy of the Hedrich-Blessing Collection, Chicago Historical Society.

19.15 Prentice Women's Hospital, Chicago, 1974, Hedrich-Blessing Photo. Courtesy of the Hedrich-Blessing Collection, Chicago Historical Society.

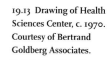

headquarters. Goldberg found an attractive site on the river in downtown Chicago, but the site was too expensive. Goldberg himself proposed other development to make the project viable and convinced the union leadership that their long-term needs would be served best by developing work and housing for their members in downtown Chicago. He proposed an entire complex as a "city within a city," a place where different functions reinforced each other. The whole was to be greater than the sum of its parts.

Construction started in 1960, and the popularity of Marina City was extraordinary. Marina City was a project choc-full of innovation, described by Carl Condit as a "staggering display of structural virtuosity." Chicagoans delighted in watching the towers grow beside the river; the exuberant new shapes captured something of Chicago's brash spirit. Even today, they maintain a lasting hold on the popular imagination.

The Work: Late Period, 1964–97

Marina City emerged as the culmination of Goldberg's earlier interests in people and their use of space. The project also embodied his interests in innovative use of systems building technologies and in the detailing that made those solutions workable. Developed outside of the mainstream, Marina City launched Goldberg's career; with its success, he was able to speak convincingly and obtain larger and more complex commissions. From the late

19.15

1950s, the office of Bertrand Goldberg Associates (BGA) grew from a modest size of ten people up to its maximum size, in the 1970s, of over one hundred people.

At its height, BGA had offices in Boston and Palo Alto and undertook major building and planning commissions on a national scale. Goldberg led the office, but it was run by a core group of dedicated staff that stayed with him from the early 1960s through the early 1990s.

Institutional projects

BGA received many commissions for educational and health care facilities. Over twelve major new hospitals were designed by BGA, and at both Health Sciences Center (Stony Brook, New York, 1967–74; fig. 19.13, 19.14) and Wright College (Chicago, 1985–92), BGA designed and planned entire educational campuses. Typically BGA was responsible for the programming, planning, architecture, and engineering. This integration permitted BGA to develop and execute its alternative solutions effectively; for example, the unique structural solutions of the office were informed by the close connections between design, engineering, and construction.

In the mid-1960s, the firm completed its first health care project, a hospital for the town of Elgin, Illinois. Clad in metal, this hospital was the firm's first round institutional structure. The firm's first major medical project was the Affiliated Hospital Center (Boston, 1970–84), a visionary ef-

19.16

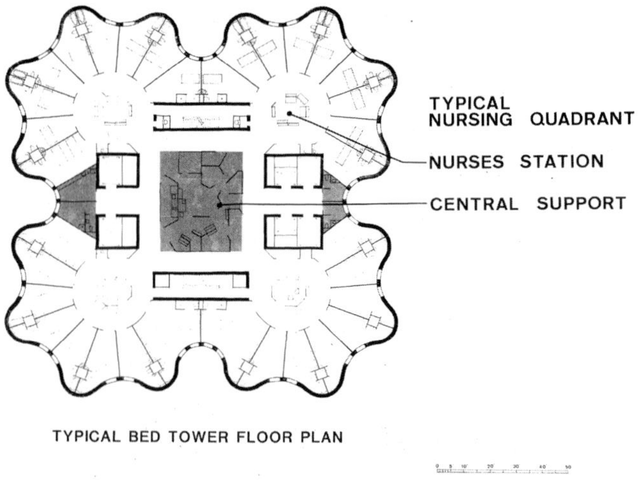

19.17

fort to combine several Harvard hospitals into one entity. Initiated under a comprehensive master plan in the 1960s, the project became a series of individual buildings (Dana Cancer Center, 1974; Brigham Hospital, 1980; and others). The firm designed other large hospitals in Chicago (fig. 19.15), Boston, Tacoma (Washington), Phoenix (Arizona), Milwaukee (Wisconsin), and Mobile (Alabama).

In all of these projects, BGA focused on the patient's environment by improving the patient-nurse relationship. Typically, hospitals had been designed for maximum space utility, with patient rooms laid out along long corridors. BGA developed radial solutions that provided direct visual connection from the patient to the nurse, creating clusters of patients around a central nurse's station (fig. 19.16). This concept challenged the basic organization of the hospital; consequently, the firm undertook studies of material handling, administrative organization, and a general reshuffling of priorities, so that innovative spatial and organizational arrangements could be realized.

Each of the hospital designs was similar in concept, but incorporated modest changes to the concrete form and structure. Each utilized concrete shell technology, providing both structure and form (fig. 19.17). The inherent economy of this approach was only achievable by the integration of unique notions of space and form with an appropriate construction methodology.

19.16 Plan of St. Joseph's Hospital, Tacoma, Washington, 1970–75. Courtesy of Bertrand Goldberg Associates.

19.17 Providence Hospital, Mobile, Alabama, 1985. Courtesy of Bertrand Goldberg Associates.

19.18 Raymond Hilliard Homes, Chicago, 1966. Photograph by Orlando Cabanban. Courtesy of Bertrand Goldberg Associates.

Urban buildings

Goldberg's burgeoning interest in social issues led to other, typically urban, projects, addressing housing or other social concerns. This interest had roots in the early BGA public housing project for Drexel Home and Gardens (Chicago, 1957), as well as the public housing complex of Raymond Hilliard Homes (Chicago, 1966; fig. 19.18). After Marina City and Hilliard, BGA developed a number of other visionary urban proposals. Most were not built.

Goldberg dreamed of building a tower using only a supporting core, without perimeter columns. First proposed for Denver, this concept was again proposed in New York as a corporate headquarters for ABC. Never built, this tower was also key for a large-scale development Goldberg proposed as River City in Chicago, a vast grouping of towers to be built along the river (1974–80; fig. 19.19). After years of effort, he redesigned the project in the 1980s as a medium-rise housing development of two snakelike forms (fig. 19.20). The result is one of Goldberg's last radical building forms: the exterior shapes are of two cast concrete serpentine shapes (fig. 19.21), and the resultant interior atrium is both tall and narrow and of an austere quality. This space is probably the most dramatic interior he ever designed (fig. 19.22).

19.18

Sculptural structures

Goldberg's structural and material inventiveness can also be seen in a series of

19.19

19.20

19.19 Model of River City I, Chicago, c. 1974, Hedrich-Blessing Photo. Courtesy of the Hedrich-Blessing Collection, Chicago Historical Society.

19.20 Aerial view of River City, Chicago, 1985. Courtesy of Bertrand Goldberg Associates.

19.21 Plan of River City as built. Courtesy of Bertrand Goldberg Associates.

19.22 Atrium at River City. Photography by Orlando Cabanban. Courtesy of Bertrand Goldberg Associates.

19.22

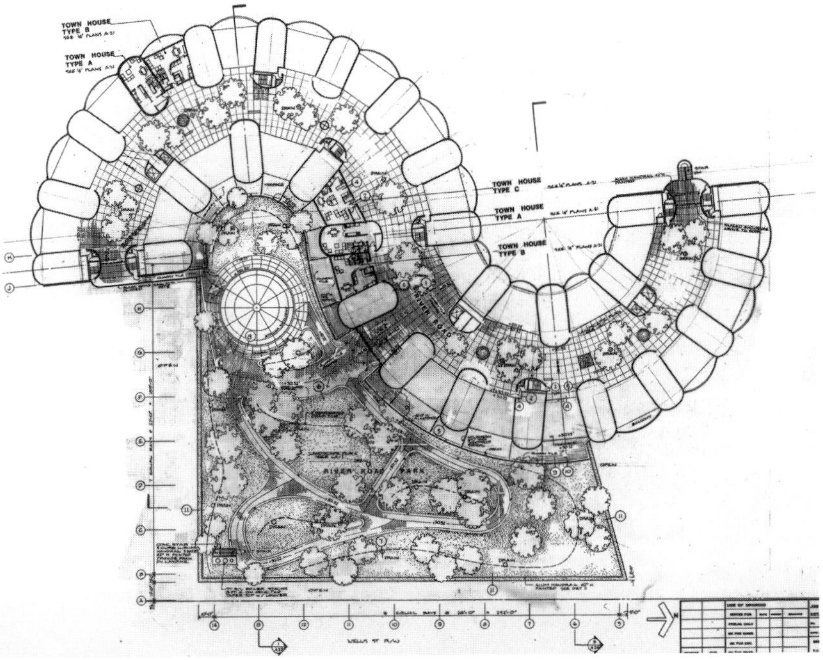

19.21

19.23 Joseph Brenneman School, Chicago, 1963, Hedrich-Blessing Photo. Courtesy of the Hedrich-Blessing Collection, Chicago Historical Society.

19.24 Model for San Diego Theater, 1968, Hedrich-Blessing Photo. Courtesy of the Hedrich-Blessing Collection, Chicago Historical Society.

smaller, unique projects undertaken by the office. These projects served as both research and inspiration for the more regular work of the office. They included the Menninger Clinic (1965, unbuilt), a combination research and patient care facility; the Brenneman School (Chicago, 1963), a public school with flaring sprayed concrete roofs over each classroom (fig. 19.23); the West Palm Beach Auditorium (West Palm Beach, Florida, 1967), a large domelike building with pre-cast concrete roofing rafters; the San Diego Theater (1968, unbuilt), proposed with sprayed concrete shells (see fig. 19.24); and Night World (1979, unbuilt) a proposed twenty-four-hour recreation center to be developed near Disneyworld in Florida, with a series of tent structures sited on a new lake.

The Vision: Cities and Social Progress

Goldberg believed in cities as special places. He saw in them a synthesis of physical form, political activity, and intellectual creativity. Goldberg also saw great potential in the ability of power to consolidate itself in cities and for progressive ideals to take hold.

These ideals were evident in the many master plans BGA produced during the 1960s and 1970s. Goldberg advocated comprehensive planning on a vast scale and attempted to plan for community formation, educational programming, recreation, and transportation systems. He engaged numerous community leaders and

19.23

19.24

specialists to provide a fuller vision of what urban development should and could entail.

Conclusion

Goldberg was an intellectual as well as an architect. An active propagandist, he spoke engagingly and often in public. He had studied with Whitehead at Harvard, with Mies and Albers at the Bauhaus. He was familiar with the Chicago intellects of his time and was a key part of the broader intellectual life in Chicago.

Goldberg's vision was a combination of technical knowledge and personal insights that cut across more traditional understandings. Belonging within a larger modernist agenda, his work was notable for its individualistic, unique solutions to complex planning and building problems. His work suggests a way in which broad social ideas and architectural solutions could be combined and, indeed were, if only for a brief moment.

Making Marina City: Men, Money, Masquerade, and Modernity

Katerina Rüedi Ray

20.1 Bertrand Goldberg, William McFetridge, and Charles Swibel with a model of Marina City, probably 1959–61, Hedrich-Blessing Photo. HB-23215 F, courtesy of the Hedrich-Blessing Collection, Chicago Historical Society.

20.2 Men posing the Marina City model office, probably 1959–61, Hedrich-Blessing Photo. HB job series 23215 courtesy of the Hedrich-Blessing Collection, Chicago Historical Society.

He loved the theatre. I think that he was a frustrated actor . . .

Ben Honda[1] on Bertrand Goldberg[2]

Bertrand Goldberg's architectural career is largely documented in two sources—his oral history commissioned in 1992 by the Art Institute of Chicago and the now out of print and almost impossible to obtain monograph, *Dans la Ville*. Numerous articles in architectural, planning, construction, and business magazines complement these two sources, but consist mainly of formal and technical commentaries. The Chicago Art Institute's oral history conducted by Betty Blum is currently the only major work locating Goldberg's work in the context of the political, economic, and social relationships that played such a powerful role in the unfolding of architectural modernism in Chicago.

Marina City is Bertrand Goldberg's most famous work. However, the paucity of Goldberg literature means that Marina City is understood mainly through the qualities identified thus far in professional magazines—its innovation in form, program, and structure. The reliance of Goldberg's current reputation on his formal and technical skills alone undervalues his considerable talents. It also affirms a false autonomy for architectural production and denies the specificity and complexity of Marina City's genesis and reception in a particular historical, geographical, economic, and social condition—the Chicago of the 1950s. In particular, the role of the alliance between finance and politics in enabling the very existence of the building remains hidden in the past and therefore unavailable to the purposes of the present.

I have chosen to revisit the history of Marina City and examine the alliance between architecture, finance, and politics in the form of a one-man play. Bertrand Goldberg, child thespian and student at the Bauhaus in Germany in the last days of the Weimar Republic, is the play's main actor and narrator and, in a sense, also its coauthor. His words follow the theater of money, politics, and marketing in the making of Marina City. In the spirit of the Bauhaus theater, Brechtian montage, and Goldberg's own interest in mass production and the assembly of "ready-mades," his words are quotations directly appropriated from his 1992 Art Institute oral history. Their combination cuts in and out of chronology and reality to construct a narrative whose content builds up through dialectical juxtaposition rather than linear continuity. In this way I hope to respect Goldberg's voice and provide historical wiggle room for the more rhetorical and mischievous of his apparently truthful statements, and use theatrical settings to add shades of allusion and illusion.

The play is divided into three parts, each emphasizing a key factor in the conception and execution of the Marina City project. In the first act, "Money," Goldberg shows us the

20.1

centrality of financial acumen shared by the client, realtor, lender, planner, and architect of Marina City in the success of the project. In the second act, "Masquerade," Goldberg affirms the equally powerful role of a theatrical consciousness in the marketing of Marina City. In the third and final act, "Modernity," he outlines the role of the psychosocial context of the Depression and his time at the Bauhaus in Berlin in defining the democratic industrial utopian ideals of Marina City. It is this vision—an idealism embedded within the alliance of money, theater, and modernity—that disappears in Marina City's afterlife, when the visionary use of men, money, and masquerade is replaced by the singular drive for profit and therefore no longer serves a larger urban, political and social vision.

20.2

Making Marina City: Men, Money, Masquerade, and Modernity

Background: Projected image of men in an office interior—a mock-up of Marina City.

ACT ONE / MONEY

Location: Bertrand Goldberg's office, downtown Chicago, in the late 1950s. In front and to the left of the image is a desk, two chairs, and a lamp. A flat file stands at the front left center of the stage with two rolls of drawings on top. A model of Marina City stands on a pedestal behind. A dining table set with linen, flatware, and three cocktail glasses stands at the front right center. A large camera on a tripod stands mid–center stage pointing toward the back of the stage. A placard lowered from above reads, in Bauhaus typeface: THE CLIENT.

Goldberg enters front stage left, turns to address the audience. McFetridge enters backstage right, stands with his back to the audience, looking up at the image.

GOLDBERG: Bill McFetridge . . . was the head of the janitors' union. Bill was . . . a great man, brilliant and sophisticated, and yet publicly he was a labor stiff; he was corrupt in many ways as the labor movement was corrupt. . . . He understood that he had a responsibility beyond that of simply being a labor stiff.[3]

. . . I designed a fairly large office for his union. He said to me on that occasion:

MCFETRIDGE, *turns, looks at Goldberg:* You know, I have always been concerned about my union and what is happening to the members of my union as the suburbs become more and more populous. My people cannot get jobs out in the suburbs. People move to the suburbs to avoid paying my people the wages we need to live. If I could persuade people to come back into town to live by showing them a desirable way of living in town, I would like to do that.[4]

Goldberg and McFetridge walk toward the dining table and sit down. Swibel enters stage right, also sits down. Goldberg turns to the audience.

GOLDBERG: Bill McFetridge and Charles [Swibel] were very close friends, and Chuck Swibel did Bill's real estate development for him.[5]

. . . Swibel, McFetridge, and I were having lunch at Fritzel's . . . I said to Bill McFetridge (*turns to Bill*) "You asked me to find you a piece of property. We have nine pieces of property, eight of which are within the budget that you suggested and the ninth of which is too rich for your blood."

MCFETRIDGE, *intrigued*: What one was that?

GOLDBERG, *with a smile*: We can walk out of Fritzel's here and I'll show it to you.

Turns back to the audience.

And we did. The three of us stood out there on the sidewalk and I said (*stands up, walks back towards the image, looks at the model, but points into the distance*), "There."

He looked at it and said to Chuck Swibel (*McFetridge turns to look at Swibel—*)

MCFETRIDGE: "See what you can buy it for." (*Turns and decisively leaves stage right, Swibel follows.*)

GOLDBERG: Chuck Swibel succeeded in buying it without any money until we had FHA approval . . . Today we would say Swibel got an option on the land for no money. That was his skill.[6]

. . . He [Bill McFetridge] paid, I think, three million dollars for that, and that was the last money he put into it. That was the first and last money he put into it.[7]

Swibel believed in other people's greed and he operated in that fashion . . . He understood more about other people's greed, perhaps, than McFetridge understood. Swibel had no illusions and he, in a sense, did the things that other people wanted to have done for them but wouldn't do themselves.[8]

Bill McFetridge, who was, after all, a labor leader, was under pressure to at least investigate why we had chosen concrete instead of choosing steel to build the building. So I agreed to design the building both in steel and in concrete to settle the argument, and we took bids on it both ways.[9]

A new placard lowered from above reads: THE FUNDER. Waner walks in, sits in front at the desk and begins signing papers, Goldberg picks up the first roll of drawings from the flat file, faces the audience.

GOLDBERG: I had to go to Washington and persuade the federal government that this project was appropriate for their regulations, because the regulations of the federal government said that the FHA was for family living . . . I pointed out to the federal government through the Department of Labor, which I had access to through Bill McFetridge, that there was a completely new family constituency, and that much older children were living at home on an independent basis who still considered themselves as part of an extended family composition. We persuaded the government, by those arguments, to change their regulations.[10]

The financing was made possible only by the existence of the Federal Housing Authority insurance program for mortgages. I had . . . to get the Federal Housing Authority in Washington to give us FHA approval—to insure the mortgages on these houses. . . . It took, I think, three trips to Washington. We persuaded the government, by those arguments, to change their regulations . . . The purpose of the FHA was to promote family with children, and children were always looked upon as sandbox children.

(*Turns and unrolls the first set of drawings.*) My early drawings on that building are for two rectangular towers—to show people that they were going to live downtown . . . When we wanted to have the land approved, I showed the rectangular forms. . . . The approval for the land came first, I got the land approved, but the approval of the project had to follow the approval of the land.[11]

I took it to Washington, and I showed it there and they liked it with some degree of hesitancy. The chief architect for the FHA loved the idea. He loved my design when I came to him with the circular design. He recommended it to the underwriter, and the underwriter said, "Well, if you are recommending it . . . ," you know.

(*Laughs.*) Almost six months after we broke ground they wrote to me and said they were beginning to question whether we should not reexamine our design and build a square building.[12]

(*Puts the first set of drawings in the flat file, closes it firmly, turns and with the second set of drawings walks towards Waner at the desk.*). . . . I got an approval for a certain amount of money, but it was a million dollars shy of what we needed. We had only until the next day at noon to get FHA approval. I went to John Waner, who was head of the FHA [in Chicago]. (*Sits down at the desk facing Waner, hands him a file of papers.*) . . . he thought the Marina City idea was just great. I went to John, and I said, "We are a million dollars shy, John, and at twelve o'clock today it will be too late. I either have your approval for another million dollars by twelve o' clock or the project is dead. John, analyzing that million dollars against the whole transaction amounts to the fact that you have to increase the rental income of each room in this project by fifty cents a month. John, is your judgment so accurate that you think you could not get fifty cents a month for each room as an increase in our rental income? That will produce the increased value for another million dollars." . . . I had done my homework. John called in his chief underwriter (*underwriter enters stage left, lighting on Waner, who opens the file and shows it to the underwriter*), and he relayed the whole thing to him. The two of them looked at me and said—

WANER AND UNDERWRITER: (*Waner stands up, both men turn, face Goldberg.*) "We'll give you the fifty cents a month."[13] (*Both exit stage right.*)

A new placard lowered from above reads THE PLANNER. Bach walks in stage left, sits in front at the desk and begins unrolling a set of drawings. Goldberg walks over to the desk, sits down on the other side, faces the audience.

GOLDBERG: . . . The building was against the building code, against the zoning code. But we had good people in government administration. Ira Bach, for example, who was the head of the planning department of the city. . . . Ira was not only a competent scholar of planning, but he was also an effective planner, assuming that planners look toward the future. Ira was very sympathetic with the idea I was proposing. Ira and I saw fit to create a district that required a minimum area of land. We complied with that minimum area, and we were off and running as far as the planning board was concerned.[14]

I knew I had to design something that had far greater efficiency than anything that had been done before, because I had to design for low rents. . . . the price for living there had to be a bargain. . . . In order to induce people to live downtown, I had to have an exciting environment—a total environment. As my mother-in-law said, it was like living above the store.

A new placard lowered from above reads THE ARCHITECT. An unnamed architect walks in with a roll of drawings under his arm, sits down at the desk, unrolls the drawings, and begins measuring.

GOLDBERG: I think that people who have money to invest are interested in new ideas . . . I think most of the people I have been with have always enjoyed that—the participation in new development.

During the war . . . one of the things we did was to build five prefabricated houses in Melrose Park . . . The houses . . . sold for $2,995 in Melrose Park—two bedrooms, completely equipped with bathrooms and kitchens and the rest of it . . . And we sold them in a day. We did not have a real estate salesman.

In the instance of our prefabrication, we had just banking groups who wanted to participate in this with the idea that they would make money.

In Marina City . . . I had a study commission by the Central Area Committee, a group I belonged to . . . It was a group of downtown businessmen. They had a study made by the Real Estate Research Corporation in 1952 or 1953, which showed that lots of people wanted to live downtown.

(*Ben Honda walks in with a roll of drawings under his arm, sits down at the desk, unrolls the drawings and begins measuring.*) We did some more study to see whether there was any increased efficiency in the fluidity of the structural forms, where the columns merge into beams and where beams move around in a flowing pattern rather than in a pattern that would be created by the juncture of sticks. We found that we could save a very substantial amount of reinforcing bars by using these forms and distributing the stresses in the pattern which you've seen here. That economy in reinforcing bars more than paid for the cost of the forming of the columns and beams.[15]

(*Frank Kornacker, Frank Severud, and Berthold Weinberg enter, sit down at the dining table, leaf through files.*) Inherent efficiencies of the circle over the square or rectangle are displayed in the apartment/parking towers. These efficiencies include a maximum enclosed area within the exterior periphery, an equal distribution of all communal services to living units, a minimalization of corridor area, and structural advantages of less wind resistance and elimination of traditional structural weak points. The repetitive employment of plastic concrete forms and the use of special climbing cranes enabled the towers to rise at the rate of one floor a day.[16]

I learned a great deal about public acceptance—what things give the public a sense of security. Comfort, perhaps, is a more understandable word. A comfort level. If one is too radical, the comfort level decreases and has to be compensated for in some other way, for example, in cost. If you build something inexpensively enough, people will build it no matter whether they approve of your style or not because they buy for economic reasons. Then if it works, it's fine, and if it works and is less expensive, then it's even better.

ACT TWO / MASQUERADE

Curtain rises. A new placard lowered from above reads THE SHOW APARTMENT.

Background: Projected image of janitors' wives at the exhibition of the Marina City Show Apartment. A new placard lowered from above reads A BOY AT THE PERFORMANCE. Goldberg enters front stage left and stands in front of the tripod camera, light on his face from below.

20.3 Visitors at the Marina City model, 1961, Hedrich-Blessing Photo. HB job series 23215, courtesy of the Hedrich-Blessing Collection, Chicago Historical Society.

GOLDBERG: My sister . . . made it possible for me to go down to the Goodman Theatre on Saturdays to learn how to do stage design, for example, and stage lighting, which was very attractive to me at that time . . . If it was 1925 I was twelve years old. So I was really allowed to become familiar with her Goodman theatrical world at a relatively early age.[17]

A new placard lowered from above reads THE BAUHAUS BALL.

GOLDBERG: I designed the invitations for the Bauhaus Ball that year. That was an annual festival—an annual celebration which was, I suppose, meant to clear you of all your inhibitions and to make the pursuit of happiness part of design and creativity.[18] . . . I think it was also for townspeople . . . because there wouldn't have been invitations otherwise, and I know the invitations went out because, as I said, I designed them . . . It was large, it was a big thing.[19]

. . . my memories are also of a lot of gaiety, a lot of just wild dancing and a shedding of inhibitions.[20]

(*Enter McFetridge. Goldberg moves so that each stands to one side of the camera tripod and faces the audience.*): Now, I said to Bill McFetridge (*turns to McFetridge*), "We've designed this unusual plan and it's been accepted. We are moving on, but I'm scared to death. This has not been done before. I don't know how people will receive it. I don't know how it will be marketed. I propose that we build a mock-up of this, a full-scale mock-up of this, and that we have it furnished. Not by us, because I can design the furniture that would make it look spiffy, but that we ask Marshall Field's to furnish it out of things they have in the store so that we know that in these unusual spaces, available furniture can be a practical installation."

MCFETRIDGE, *turns to face Goldberg:* How much will this cost?

GOLDBERG: "At least $50,000." (*Walks to the back of the camera tripod, turns it to point at the audience, and addresses the audience above the*

20.4

20.4 Marina City model apartment balcony, probably 1961, Hedrich-Blessing Photo. HB job series 23215, courtesy of the Hedrich-Blessing Collection, Chicago Historical Society.

20.5 McFetridge on the model apartment balcony, probably 1961, Hedrich-Blessing Photo. HB-23215N, courtesy of the Hedrich-Blessing Collection, Chicago Historical Society.

camera body.) Now, in the year 1959, $50,000 had a value today of probably several hundred thousand dollars . . . We did a one-bedroom and an efficiency apartment. We built the balconies, and I hired a helicopter to perch itself at about the height of the fortieth floor and to photograph the skyline at that point. Then we had large photomurals done from that.

We brought in people—lots of people. We brought in the whole janitors' union, invited them to come down with their wives . . . We took all the surveys as we went along. We invited bankers to come in. We invited the FHA to come down from Washington to see what they had insured.[21]

Background: Projected image of show apartment balcony showing photo panorama of Chicago skyline

HONDA, *enters stage left, stands to the side facing Goldberg:*

It was very cleverly done. You looked out of the windows and he had a huge photomural of the skyline of Chicago on the outside of it. So you were transported. Bud was a showman. He liked the theatre and he loved this sort of thing.[22] (*Exits stage right.*)

Close curtain.

ACT THREE / MODERNITY

Curtain rises. Background: Projected image of McFetridge in profile on the balcony of the show apartment. A new placard lowered from above reads USA, THE DEPRESSION. Goldberg enters and sits on the flat file.

GOLDBERG: . . . you must remember that when Mies came here it was 1937, and the world war had not occurred. But what had occurred was the Depression, and the Depression was our foretaste of war. A restudy of our value system—the superficial nonsense, the style, the decoration of the twenties, even in its so-called modern forms at that time—the Art Déco; the word *déco* is obviously the diminutive of "decorative"—but the sweeping away of all these things and the substitution of what is industrialized, the prefabrication of housing, and the seek-ing [*sic*] of simplicity in the use of more natural materials. All of that was a mirror of the social revolution that was occurring, which in turn was a mirror of the economic failures that we had gone through and the economic reevaluations we were having at that time.[23]

Very few people remember that the Depression was an exciting time. . . . Everything was reduced to such fundamentals that there was every attempt to find—the idea was that for everyone there would be a new world, and the new world became possible because the old world had failed.[24]

20.5

You have to remember that Harvard during the Depression was filled with all kinds of influences. In the political sciences, certainly there was a feeling that the world was going to change radically and that the concepts of the old world may not do for the new world.[25]

A new placard lowered from above reads WEIMAR REPUBLIC.

GOLDBERG: There was in Germany a sense of ferment. That same ferment that existed intellectually at Harvard existed sociologically in Germany. . . . at the Bauhaus I was immersed in an architecture that had really come out of the yeast of the Weimar Republic. The value system of modern architecture came from the value system of political rebellion.[26]

A new placard lowered from above reads POSTWAR CHICAGO.

People believed in themselves. Who was I for them to believe? I had no track record. People believed in themselves. I was not asking them to believe in something that I had done before. I had never done it before . . . I didn't dare show anybody the circular towers—I mean, to show people they were going to live downtown, which in itself was new, in two high rise towers, which was new.

. . . These were the highest apartment buildings in the world at the time.[27]

You must remember also that the time was vastly different than it is today. In spite of the fact that the meanest and most painful part of the Depression was over, the feeling that people wanted something new was prevalent. That seeking of a new world or new ideas was prevalent certainly right on up through 1960 when I designed Marina City.

Look at Marina City as an architectural concept. Certainly it not only was a new form from a viewpoint of design but was structurally vastly innovative. How would one have done that without other people around him, bankers and owners, feeling as if there could be a new world?[28]

Close curtain.

ACT FOUR / POSTSCRIPT

Background: Projected image of the laying of the foundation stone of Marina City, with Mayor Richard J. Daley, the archbishop of Chicago, and McFetridge.

Goldberg, McFetridge, Swibel, Waner, Bach, Myhrum, Honda, Kornacker, Severud, Weinberg, and the underwriter enter stage left and line up below the image facing the audience, with Goldberg at the center. Goldberg steps forward.

GOLDBERG: What condominiumizing Marina City did was to take a building that had been constructed very economically—ten dollars a square foot is what it cost to build the towers at Marina City—they took a building which had been built very economically, which had proven its market acceptability, and they sold it off for a new capital level which yielded a substantial profit for the developers. What happened was, then, that the new capital cost, had to be amortized and paid off by the people who lived in the building at a much higher level than it originally was renting for. The taxes therefore went up because the building now had a newly created value and tax is based upon value. This is an area where we have been disappointed—in the commercial exploitation of Marina City.[29]

Goldberg walks toward the camera, points it at the group, returns to the group and with the extension cord takes a picture.

The curtain falls quickly at the same time as the flash and lights out.

Walter Netsch: Field Theory

Martin Felsen and Sarah Dunn

21.1 Photograph of an Italian hill-town, 1975. Netsch viewed this image not as a hill-town but as an ordered, geometric (flat) field of optical information. Note the visual relationship to Netsch's buildings in figures 21.13, 21.14, and 21.15. Photograph by Robertson Ward, courtesy of Walter Netsch.

"We keep trying to find new ways to see things. We look at models and buildings through fish-eye lenses and other devices; we make films as other means of seeing things differently. Our Field Theory is a process of looking at things differently, and of ordering too." —Walter Netsch, quoted in C. Ray Smith, *Supermannerism*, 28.

If, like Walter Netsch, you build 800,000 square feet of space per year, you'd better have at your disposal a reliable design theory. Luckily, Walter Netsch did. He called it field theory, and he thought it would revolutionize the look and function of corporate architecture. "We keep trying to find new ways to see things," Netsch explained, "our Field Theory is a process of looking at things differently, and of ordering too" (fig. 21.1).[1] When Netsch began working at Skidmore, Owings & Merrill (SOM) in the mid-1950s, field theory was a behavioral science concept used to interpret events as "the resultant of dynamic interplay among sociocultural, biomechanical and motivational forces."[2] Netsch borrowed the concept, coupled it with his own ideas of organizational and spatial efficiency, and transformed it into a highly functional planning and visualization methodology. In terms of building design, field theory allowed Netsch to break the Miesian box by serving three primary functions in the design process: first, field theory provided aesthetic and psychological variety; second, field theory provided programmatic and structural flexibility in that it was used as an open-ended design system; and third, field theory allowed for economical change over time because it preestablished a unifying design objective. Under Netsch's guidance, field theory became a totalizing system of discovery and composition.

Essentially, field theory was a formal process of planning a site while simultaneously analyzing the programmatic and material intricacies of a building. Technically, the process involved manually manipulating sets of two-dimensional geometries to arrive at a plan-based design: from the structure and partition walls to wall/roof openings and furniture of a building. The process began with a grid printed on a sheet of transparent acetate (fig. 21.2). Two sheets of acetate with the same grid were then superimposed onto one another, creating/visualizing a lattice or moiré. Building plans were created by tracing the moirés—in the tracing came discovery. Netsch and his team made thousands of tracings by hand, employing a great number of nonmodular variable geometries (figs. 21.3–21.7). In an era before computer animation, they made films of models built from these tracings in an effort to accelerate the process of uncovering compositional solutions. Ostensibly, the field theory process was begun without preconceived ideas regarding building design. Ideally, the process itself was to create a different field within which each building program and structure was uniquely grown.

In practice, field theory relied heavily on the idea of the forty-five-degree angle. Recently Netsch was quoted as having said that "the rotated square was the way we broke the box, by rotation."[3] Netsch's first complete building to break the box was the Architecture and Arts Laboratories building at the University of Illinois at Chicago begun in 1965 (figs. 21.8–21.13). The structure of the Architecture and Arts Laboratories was conceived from fields of rotated squares based around geometries of circles. Netsch firmly believed

21.2 Acetate sheets superimposed to create moirés, lattices, and fields: manipulation to discovery. Courtesy of Walter Netsch.

"Lattices create a linear expansion of the progression of different activities and communications for which the building is used." —Walter Netsch, quoted in C. Ray Smith, *Supermannerism*, 30.

that the conventional rectangular grid would not create a complex enough environment. With field theory he was capable of cultivating a system of design that was iconic yet nonarbitrary, while simultaneously yielding efficient programmatic organizations and economical structures (fig. 21.14). Without this system of design, he would have been unable to communicate the rigors of the generative geometric process to his corporate colleagues and design team. And if the design methodology devolved into arbitrary pattern making, the resultant buildings would inevitably lose their organizational and functional efficiency in favor of simplistic visual aptitude. The self-organizing robustness of field theory solutions, Netsch said, "avoid the willful, cute angularities that are sometimes designed in for sculptural variety."[4]

At the scale of site planning in an urban context, field theory produced less compelling results. At the University of Illinois at Chicago campus, one of the larger projects accomplished with field theory, there was an inversion of the existing Chicago grid. Instead of instituting a method of assembling critical mass, (or intellectual concentration of bodies) field theory promoted the systematic dismantling of the urban field, a kind of artificiality without urbanism, or basically a bunch of buildings without relationship to one another (fig. 21.15). The idea of a field as a network capable of organizing either spatial or programmatic relationships between unique yet individual elements was lost. Movement was separated; the infrastructure of the cross street was cut, and pedestrian paths were displaced off the (public) ground and onto a second-story walkway system. Homogenous zones of program were created; lecture halls, classrooms, labs and offices were all separated as objects, without spatial/programmatic relationship to one another. Basically, field theory competently, even rigorously, devised a sprawling and purposefully incomplete set of landscapes and buildings. Ironically, the buildings were most beautiful when they were the most incomplete.

At SOM, Netsch was a maverick. He was given little respect from his partners, and he had his own autonomous studio away from SOM headquarters. But he remained tightly connected to the SOM establishment by way of his general urban assumption, even insistence that any project site/context be empty before design work begins: field theory can't or won't deal with existing context, it needs to makes its own fresh start. The operative ground condition of field theory is tabula rasa.

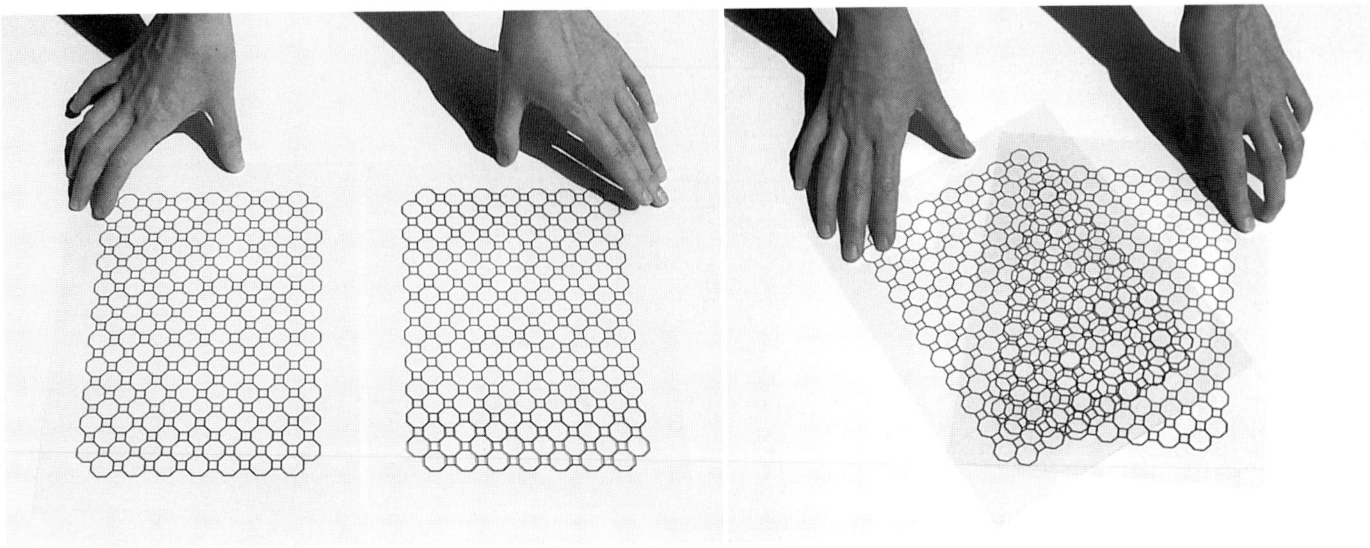

21.2

21.3

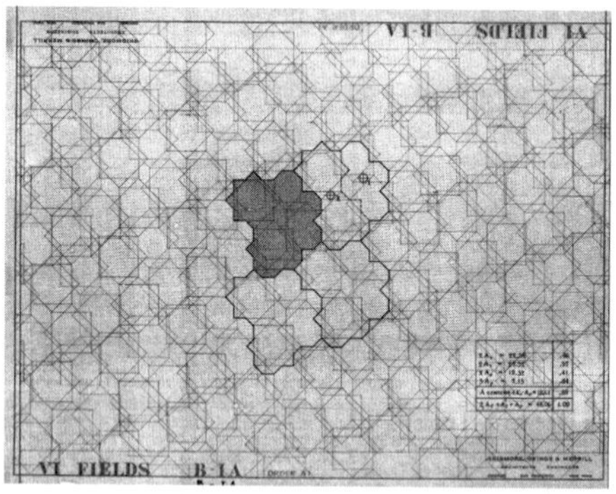

21.4

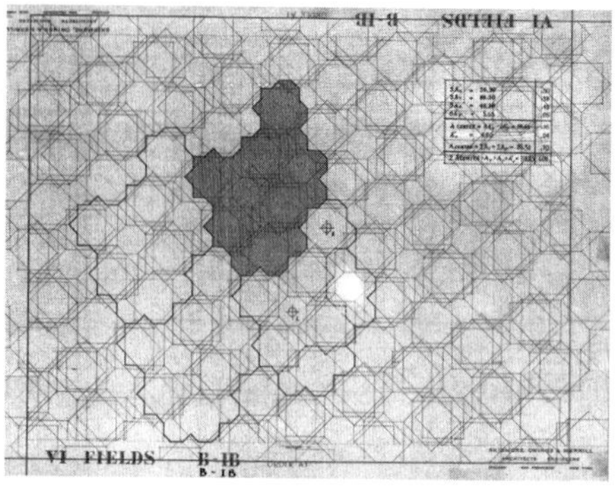

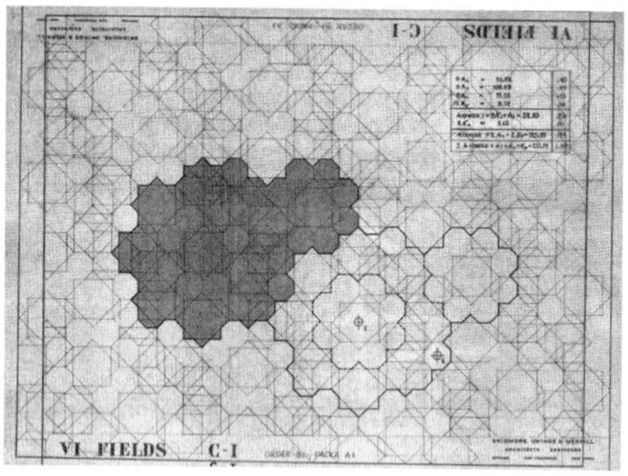

21.5

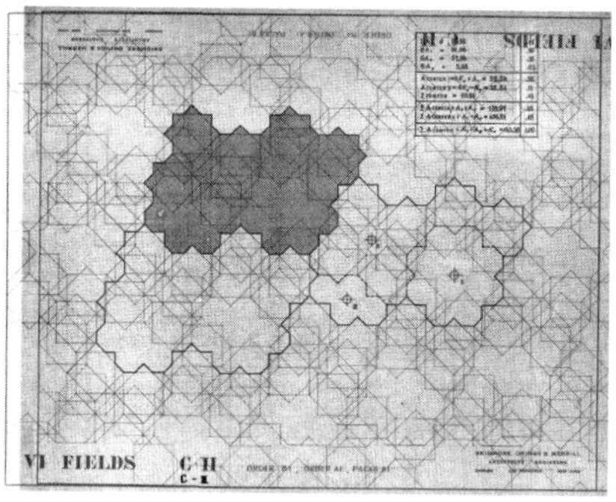

21.6

21.3 Field study: VI fields: B-IA, order A1, 1960. Courtesy of Walter Netsch.

21.4 Field study: VI fields: B-IB, order A1, 1960. Courtesy of Walter Netsch.

21.5 Field study: VI fields: C-I, order B1, pack A1, 1960. Courtesy of Walter Netsch.

21.6 Field study: VI fields: C-II, order B1, order A1, pack A1, 1960. Courtesy of Walter Netsch.

21.7 Field study: VI fields: D-II, order B-3, order A-3, pack-2/order A-1, pack A-1, 1960. Courtesy of Walter Netsch.

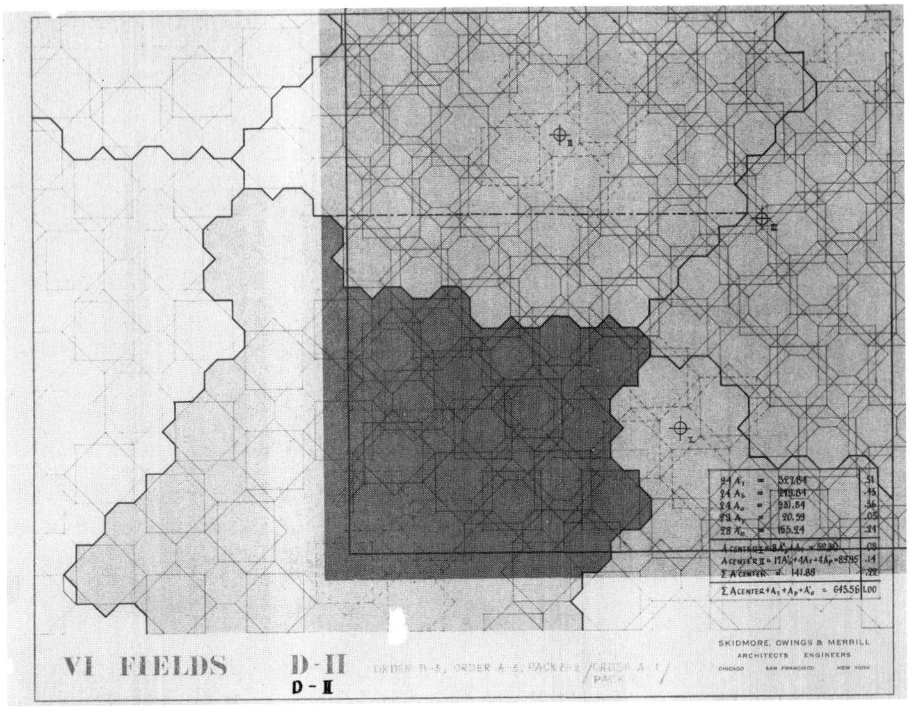

21.7

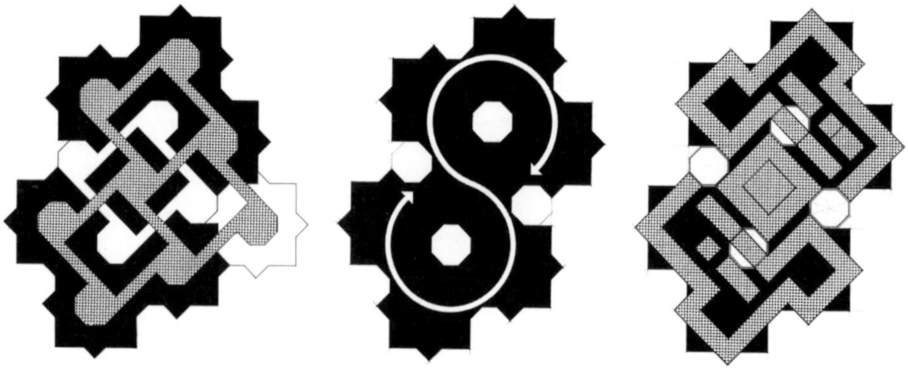

21.8

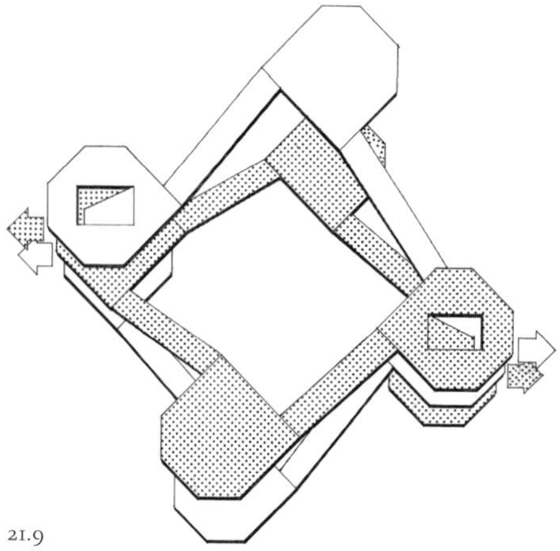

21.9

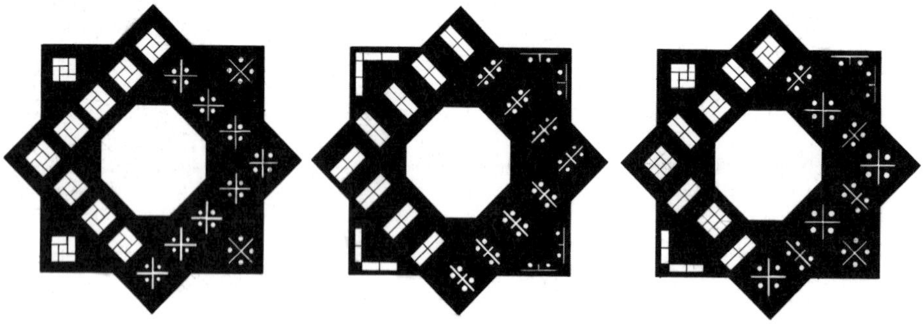

21.10

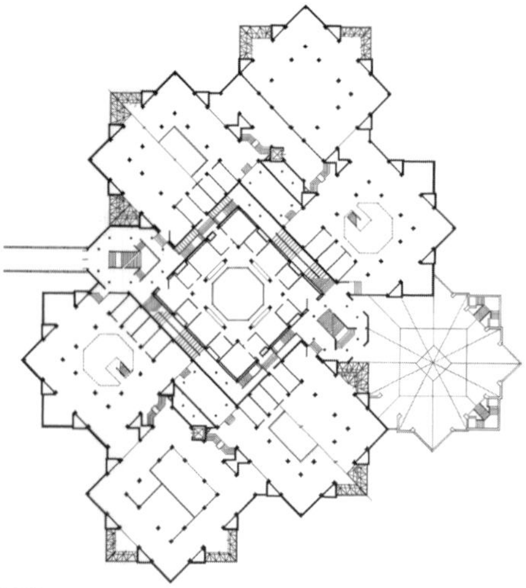

21.11

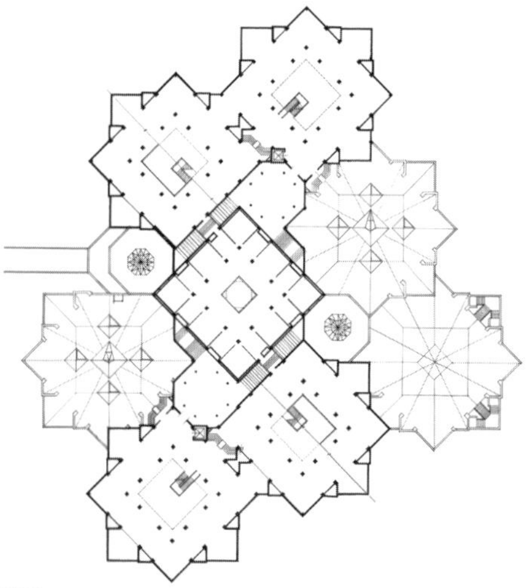

21.12

21.8 Lattice capability, spiral capability, and linear capability of field theory planning of the Architecture and Arts Laboratories, University of Illinois at Chicago, 1965. Courtesy of Walter Netsch.

"Field Theory is network oriented rather than structure oriented. It is iconic, volumetric and spatial." —Walter Netsch, *Progressive Architecture* (March 1969): 94.

21.9 Circulation system analogous to the double-helix structure of DNA; Architecture and Arts Laboratories, University of Illinois at Chicago, 1965. Courtesy of Walter Netsch.

"Field Theory is a self-organizing system in that it permits anyone who is responsive to it to participate." —Walter Netsch, *Progressive Architecture* (March 1969): 103.

21.10 Design and planning of interior environment including furniture for the Architecture and Arts Laboratories, University of Illinois at Chicago, 1965. Courtesy of Walter Netsch.

21.11 Design development of the second level of the Architecture and Arts Laboratories, University of Illinois at Chicago, 1965. Courtesy of Walter Netsch.

"Field Theory, as a system of a way of looking, assumes that all actions are not linear, that all forms must be additive, that plans need not be orthogonal to be useful or active." —Walter Netsch, *Progressive Architecture* (March 1969): 102.

21.12 Design development of the fourth level of the Architecture and Arts Laboratories, University of Illinois at Chicago, 1965. Courtesy of Walter Netsch.

21.13 Skylight and glass details of the Architecture and Arts Laboratories, University of Illinois at Chicago, 2003. Courtesy of Walter Netsch.

21.13

21.14

21.15

21.14 Behavioral Science Center, University of Illinois at Chicago, 1965. Photograph by Orlando R. Cabanban, courtesy of Walter Netsch and Skidmore, Owings & Merrill.

"Field Theory is a network oriented rather than structure oriented . . . a linear expansion of the progression of different activities and communications for which the building is used." —Walter Netsch, *Progressive Architecture* (March 1969): 94.

21.15 Behavioral Science Center, University of Illinois at Chicago, 1965. Photograph by Orlando R. Cabanban, courtesy of Walter Netsch and Skidmore, Owings & Merrill.

Despite rigorous elemental variety and variation in geometry, program and scale, field theory left the landscape (and other spaces between buildings) underplanned and therefore susceptible to insensitive contemporary redesign.

Systematic Genius: Walter Netsch and the Architecture of Bureaucracy

David Goodman

Support Service

The year is 1957. *L'Architecture d'aujourd'hui*, in an issue devoted to the work of promising young architects, includes a number of American designers in a volume filled with neo-Miesiana, Corbusian spinoffs, and a surprising number of projects that might well be described as Niemeyeresque. Among the young American designers selected are Ralph Rapson, I. M. Pei, Paul Rudolph, and Walter Netsch. Netsch, of Skidmore, Owings & Merrill (SOM), has recently completed a sober concrete-framed campus for the U.S. Naval Postgraduate School in Monterey, California, and guided the development of the Inland Steel Building in Chicago until pulled from the job to take charge of the U.S. Air Force Academy, a project that is in the late stages of development at the time of the issue's publication. The magazine includes photographs and drawings of all three projects, ending its section on Netsch with a somewhat detached and apparently dismissive appraisal of the work: "Here is an example," they write, "of a young architect whose work is greatly enhanced by all of the support services behind him."[1]

This assessment of Netsch's work might seem puzzling when we consider his later work: Netsch would, just seven years after the *L'Architecture d'aujourd'hui* article, achieve fame for his heroic, aluminum-clad Air Force Academy Chapel and would go on to pursue field theory, a complex system of geometry and programming analysis that produced oddly shaped, brightly painted buildings unlike anything in the SOM portfolio (fig. 22.1). Frequently at odds with the SOM partnership and at times operating at a distance from the firm, Netsch seems an iconoclast; a misfit in the corporate environment. To categorize his work primarily as the beneficiary of SOM's "support services" seems, with hindsight, to misrepresent Netsch as more reliant upon the corporate structure than he actually was.

Yet a deeper analysis of Netsch's work suggests that the French magazine's assessment of Netsch and his relationship to SOM remains useful, even prophetic, more than forty years later. Netsch's work, while apparently at odds with the ideology and aesthetic of SOM, is not only compatible with the corporate framework of a large firm like SOM, it is also—and perhaps more important—impossible without it. I will argue that Netsch's brand of individual genius relied heavily on the "support services" and resources of the corporate, bureaucratic firm around him. But more significantly, his is a genius born of the bureaucracy itself. It is a genius of processes, management, programming, and organizing just as much as it is a genius of form-giving, of authorial statement. This study of Netsch's work will suggest ways in which the auteur and the organization can coexist and, through this coexistence, produce mutations in both.

22.1 Wells College Library, Aurora, New York, 1968. Photograph by Walter Netsch.

22.1

Bureaucracy versus Genius

I borrow the terms "bureaucracy" and "genius" from Henry-Russell Hitchcock's 1947 article, "The Architecture of Bureaucracy and the Architecture of Genius."[2] Hitchcock applied the terms in neither a pejorative nor an especially laudatory sense. He defined bureaucratic architecture as "all building that is the product of large-scale organizations, from which personal expression is absent,"[3] using SOM and Albert Kahn, Inc., as examples of efficient, consistent, and anonymous production. These firms, Hitchcock argued, do not depend on "the architectural genius of one man" but instead rely on "the organizational genius which can establish a fool-proof system of rapid and complete plan production."[4] Hitchcock contended that this sort of firm can produce architecture with "a high level of amenity" but will rarely or never author "a major work of architectural art."

Hitchcock described the "genius," meanwhile, as "the sort of architect who functions as a creative individual rather than as an anonymous member of a team."[5] This sort of architect is unlikely to take on projects of extremely large scale because they necessarily require massive organization and bureaucracy. "For this," Hitchcock notes, "the 'genius' is rather unlikely to have either the taste or the special administrative and executive talent."[6]

Hitchcock concluded that "very little" architecture of genius will be built in the postwar era, declaring that the efficient and consistent "plan production" teams of the large corporate firms will (and should) come to dominate architectural production in the coming decades.

Walter Netsch collapsed Hitchcock's genius/bureaucracy dialectic onto itself. Certainly, his work bears a clearly legible mark of his authorship—with a brief glance through any SOM monograph, one can immediately pinpoint the Netsch buildings for their twisted geometry and swaths of applied color. The development of field theory set Netsch apart from the anonymous "plan production" teams, carrying him close to the realm of the genius architect. For reasons I will describe below, Netsch was in fact the first SOM designer to receive individual credit for a project, clearly a violation of Hitchcock's code of anonymity. Yet at no time did Netsch flee from the administrative and organizational aspects of practice. On the contrary, processes of group organization and dynamics played an integral part in his practice and would eventually be a crucial element in the development of field theory, itself the true masterwork of Netsch's career—a self-generating system that could, in theory, render genius institutional, mandatory, effortless. Netsch is the genius of the bureaucracy, within the bureaucracy. The overlap of these two apparently opposed positions suggests an architecture that mediates between anonymous process and authorial invention, an architecture of systematic genius.

The role of genius of and within the bureaucracy is not an easy one to play; such an architect must, in proper human resources parlance, be able to don many "hats," to "multitask." This paper will be divided according to five such "hats" worn by Netsch during his career with SOM. These five personae—the Idealist, the Programmer, the Specialist, the Auteur, and the Opportunist—combine, in occasionally contradictory ways, to describe the architect at home in the organization but still intent on challenging and questioning it from within. In the case of Netsch, each of these five personae is shaped or created by a significant biographical moment, a "creation myth" to which all further development will refer. I will use these biographical "myths" to assemble a roughly chronological narrative out of Netsch's work, a narrative that will leave us with a portrait of the architect for whom large-scale organization is both a vehicle for production and a source of artistic inspiration.

The Idealist

Creation myth: Firstborn son of the military-industrial complex

We all knew that because we were at MIT that we would probably finish. . . . They were doing radar domes on the roof. MIT was influential in the war.

Walter Netsch, 1995[7]

Walter Netsch left his home on Chicago's South Shore in fall of 1939; as war in Europe began, Netsch headed to MIT to begin his education as an architect. He chose MIT not because of any specific star faculty member but rather because there were no star faculty members. "I didn't want a god," he remarks. "I didn't want Gropius or anybody. Mies was really not a factor." Few students, apparently, felt that the dawning days of war offered an opportune time to begin a career in architecture—Netsch had just eight classmates at MIT, and young faculty were similarly hard to recruit. Lawrence Anderson and Herbert Beckwith, two young professors recently added to a program that had only recently departed from the Beaux-Arts model, contributed to the war effort by surveying bombing damage from aerial photographs. "As architects," Netsch later explained, "they could tell what happened."[8]

Netsch and his classmates were trained to be problem solvers, programmers, technicians—contributors to a war effort that only allowed them to complete their MIT degrees in a time of war because they were, upon graduation, expected to become the brain trust of the U.S. war machine. Students were assigned large-scale planning projects, infused, Netsch would later recall, with a "deep social commitment."[9] The class worked through summers to complete the program early and join the war effort as soon as possible. It was, Netsch remarks, "a very serious time."[10]

Netsch's mode of operation was fundamentally shaped during this period—MIT was deeply involved in the war effort, and to be educated under such a system meant being exposed not only to the evolving technologies of the day but also to the developing methods of managing and administering a mass public. "MIT didn't teach us a style," Netsch remarked, "they taught us Modern. Modern was supposed to be . . . a rational interpretation of social, physical, material needs."[11] This "rational interpretation" of needs would necessarily depend more on process and system than on individual inspiration. "This was not," Netsch remembers, "the time of form-giving."[12]

Organization

The Idealist was thus created. The stakes at MIT during the war were undeniably high, and Netsch and his classmates were at the epicenter of America's strategic and technological workshop. Netsch was taught to interpret needs and to respond to them efficiently. He was taught that his work could, and indeed must, aim at changing—or saving—lives. But perhaps most important, Netsch developed an unswerving faith in the power of large-scale organizations to solve the pressing problems of the day. Netsch the Idealist was conceived roughly at the same time and place as the military-industrial complex. As such, it should come as no surprise that Netsch saw large-scale organization (be it the state or the corporation) not as a necessary evil but as the proper vehicle to tackle current, large-scale problems. Netsch was the firstborn son of the military-industrial complex, his education shaped by its institutions and its fusion of technical innovation and mass administration. Netsch's idealism, bred in a time of crisis, understood bureaucratic organization as an opportunity and a resource, not as a threat.

Netsch's early experience with SOM was intimately linked to the military-industrial complex that had shaped his education. Already known for its ability to tackle large-scale planning and design projects, SOM had, at the time of Netsch's hiring in 1947, been awarded the job of planning the city of Oak Ridge, Tennessee, a city dedicated to the development and production of America's nuclear arsenal. At Oak Ridge, Netsch worked on the design of shopping centers, schools, and workers' housing, a project he describes as "the prize example of modern architecture done with a social conscience."[13]

Netsch's work at Oak Ridge was an affirmation of all he had learned at MIT. Here, the large-scale organization—SOM, acting under the aegis of the U.S. military—was granted unprecedented control over the built environment, and the task at hand demanded a "rational interpretation of needs." The job was perfect for Netsch, who accepted the challenge and perceived no contradiction between the social conscience of the affordable housing and the martial agenda that underlay it. Reared in the midst of war and a member of the U.S. Army for four years, Netsch saw the U.S. national interest as being in perfect agreement with the greater good. And as such, the provision of housing at "Atom Town" was another opportunity to attach his acute problem-solving skills to the mass mechanisms of planning and design available at the time.

Netsch followed his work at Oak Ridge with further jobs for the U.S. armed forces in Japan and North Africa before being awarded the commission for the U.S. Naval Postgraduate School in Monterey and the Air Force Academy in Colorado Springs. In each of these cases, Netsch's idealism—a faith in the power of the large-scale organization to produce good works—remained a powerful force in his work. "I had this naïve courage," he recalls, "the courage of having faith in architecture . . . I had such faith in Skidmore as a symbol of the Holy Grail . . . that I couldn't fail them."[14] Even in times of deep discord within the firm, Netsch remained a believer in SOM's potential and was committed to the idea of the firm as a coherent team: "I was," he remarks, almost wistfully, "very loyal to SOM."[15]

The Programmer

Creation myth: "Backwards research" and the program as object of design

After four years with SOM, Netsch was given a chance to head a design team. The job initially seemed disappointing: the U.S. Navy had developed plans for a barracks-like campus for its postgraduate school on the former grounds of the Del Monte Hotel in Monterey, California. It was SOM's job to produce working drawings for the Navy. Netsch examined the Navy's drawings, visited the site, and immediately refused to draw the scheme. The barracks, Netsch explained to Nathaniel Owings, would destroy much of the historic landscape of the hotel grounds. Furthermore, these buildings were identical to any set of military barracks, anywhere in the world. "We just can't do that," Netsch, ever the idealist, argued. "Skidmore can't do that."[16]

Netsch's arguments were persuasive. Owings allowed Netsch to prepare an original scheme for the campus to be presented to the Navy in hopes that the agency would abandon the barracks scheme for Netsch's improved version. Netsch went to work. But there was a hitch: he had no program, only the plans for the proposed barracks buildings given to him by the Navy. So Netsch constructed the program in reverse, analyzing the Navy's drawings in detail to determine the number of students expected, the number of disciplines to be taught, the number of laboratories and classrooms needed (fig. 22.2). With this preliminary program assembled, Netsch proposed a basic site plan of interconnected slabs, dodging the trees that dotted the campus.

The Navy approved the general scheme, and Netsch returned to work—intent on refining the program. Netsch, along with a team of SOM architects, moved to the Naval Headquarters in Annapolis, Maryland, and began to conduct intensive research on programming the new school. The group held interviews with faculty members, analyzing the written curriculum of the proposed school in order to develop a detailed breakdown of lab and classroom arrangement. Netsch's group produced an exhaustive set of graphic analyses, mapping the spatial requirements for each academic department, the number of hours students were expected to spend in classrooms and labs, the utilities needed to supply the lab spaces, and whether or not labs would require roof or ground access (figs. 22.3, 22.4). The group simultaneously began to map the needed adjacencies in plan, determining which departments would require access to the classroom wing, to the lecture auditorium, or to the electrical engineering laboratories.

Gradually, a solution began to appear—a solution based largely on the intensive construction of program undertaken by Netsch and his team (fig. 22.5): "The analytical procedure," Netsch wrote in a 1954 article on the programming of the college, "was so intensive and unremitting an effort to determine all the implications of the school's courses of instruction that the essential design, in the form of schematic space allocation studies, emerged simultaneously with the completed program."[17] Once the programming was completed, Netsch seemed to suggest, the development of buildings was more or less automatic.

Particularities

Netsch's experience at Monterey set the tone for much of his later work: consistently eschewing general, universally inhabitable spaces, Netsch instead searched out particularities, programmatic specifics that forced one space to be distinct from another. In order to achieve this sort of in-depth programming analysis, Netsch made skillful use not only of SOM's resources but also of his own talents as a master of process. At the U.S. Naval College, Netsch designed a system, a scientific method of analysis that, in producing a detailed program, made the design of buildings more or less a matter of creative packaging. The true invention was the program itself.

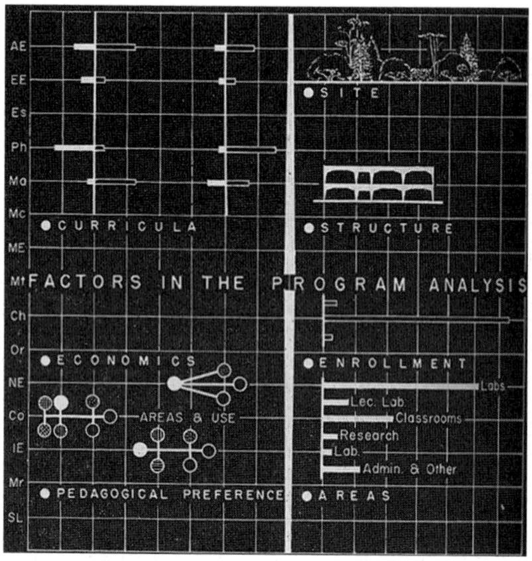

22.2

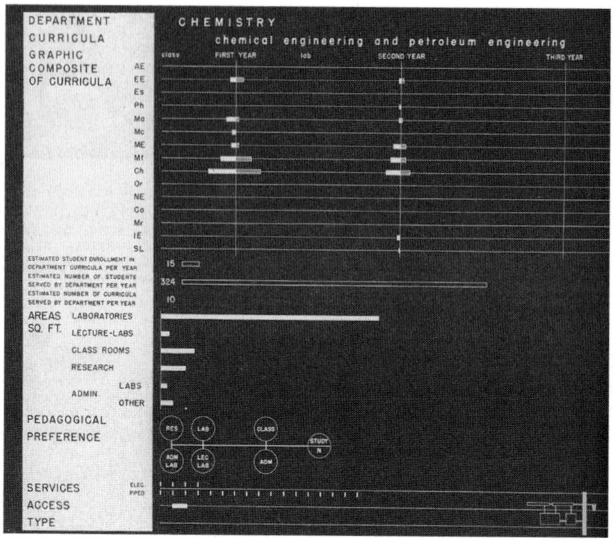

22.3

22.2 "Factors in the Program Analysis," chart prepared by Netsch and SOM for programming of U.S. Naval Postgraduate School, Monterey, California, 1951. Courtesy of Walter Netsch.

22.3 Analysis of chemistry department for programming of U.S. Naval Postgraduate School. Courtesy of Walter Netsch.

22.4 Diagram of plan adjacencies for programming of U.S. Naval Postgraduate School. Courtesy of Walter Netsch.

22.5 Plan of Laboratory Sciences Building, U.S. Naval Postgraduate School. Courtesy of Walter Netsch.

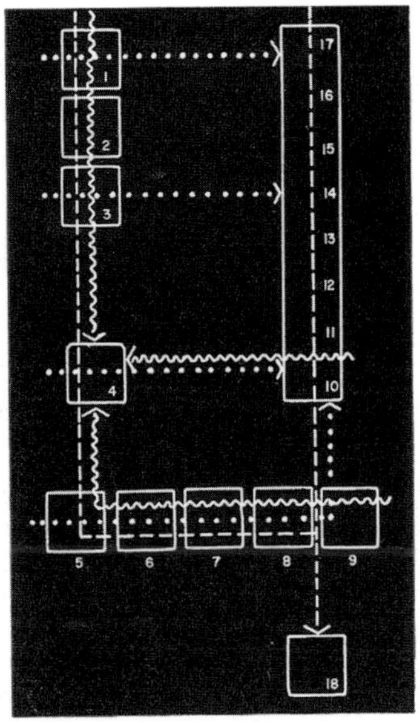

• • • •› *Departments requiring access to classroom building*

〰〰› *Departments requiring access to electrical engineering department*

– – –› *Departments requiring access to lecture auditorium*

1. Wind Tunnel Laboratory (Aeronautical)
2. Aeronautical Structural Laboratory
3. Mechanical Engineering Laboratory
4. Electrical Engineering Laboratory
5. Aerology
6. Electronics
7. Metallurgy
8. Chemistry
9. Physics
10. Mathematics and Mechanics
11. Electrical Engineering
12. General Classroom and Seminars
13. Mechanical Engineering
14. Ordnance
15. Communications
16. Naval Engineering
17. Aeronautical Eng.
18. Lecture Auditorium

22.4

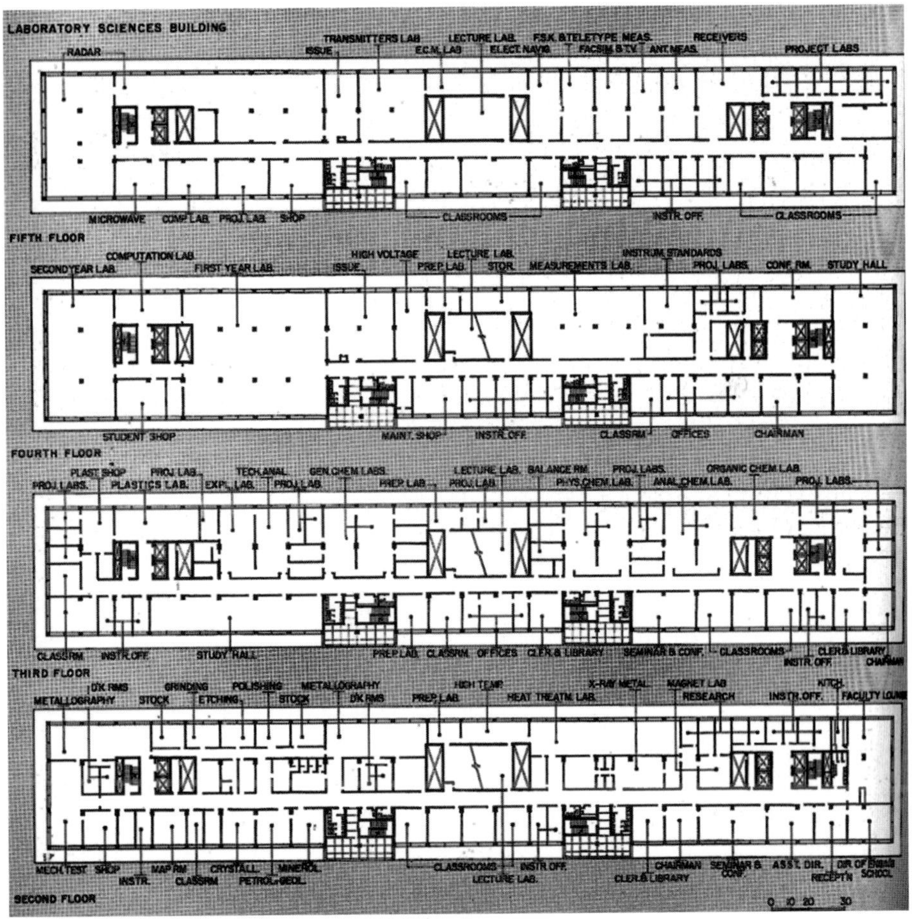

22.5

Netsch's devotion to programming in projects like Monterey or the Grinnell College Forum (1965; fig. 22.6) can, when viewed with his later output in mind, be understood as a definitive step in the direction of field theory. Field theory aimed at a systematic way to translate organizational and programmatic requirements into formal arrangements. This was precisely the kind of analysis begun in the Monterey project. Netsch ultimately based his design on an in-depth understanding of exactly how the building was to be occupied. Mies's "universal space" was, for Netsch, anathema; without specific functional requirements, he was unable (or unwilling) to arrive at a formal solution.

In his description of the Grinnell College Forum, a project in which a heavily triangulated geometry makes an early appearance, Netsch made quite clear the connection of plan geometry and specificity of program: advised by college administrators to construct specific, self-contained spaces instead of multipurpose halls, Netsch arrived at a building with a "strong geometry" in plan "because we could define the uses of the spaces and did not have to have a homogenous series of triple-purpose spaces such as is common in most union buildings."[18]

By insisting on the specific over the general and relying on particularities of program to provide novel formal strategies, Netsch would eventually find himself in conflict with the corporate framework around him. Although SOM prided itself on its ability to master any program or building size, it remained fundamentally a large-scale organization. And in order for such an organization to operate efficiently and, perhaps more importantly, profitably, it must take advantage of standardization and mass production. SOM's continued devotion to the tall office building can be understood as a way to maximize efficiency and profit; programs that allowed for "homogenous" space could reuse elements of other designs. Furthermore, there was no need to spend costly and difficult hours inventing the program if there existed no program beyond repetitive slabs of office space on unobstructed floor plates. Seen in this context, Netsch's devotion to particularity and to detailed programming appears to be in conflict with one of the most fundamental requirements of large corporate organizations: to show a profit sizeable enough to justify the expense of maintaining a large firm. In the 1970s, as SOM turned its attention almost exclusively to office towers, Netsch could not help but feel out of sync with the rest of the partnership: "I was still existing in the past," he remembers. "We were still hands-on. We were designing buildings for specific purposes. We were not doing anonymous office buildings."[19]

22.6 Plan of Grinnell College Forum, Grinnell, Iowa, 1965. Courtesy of Walter Netsch.

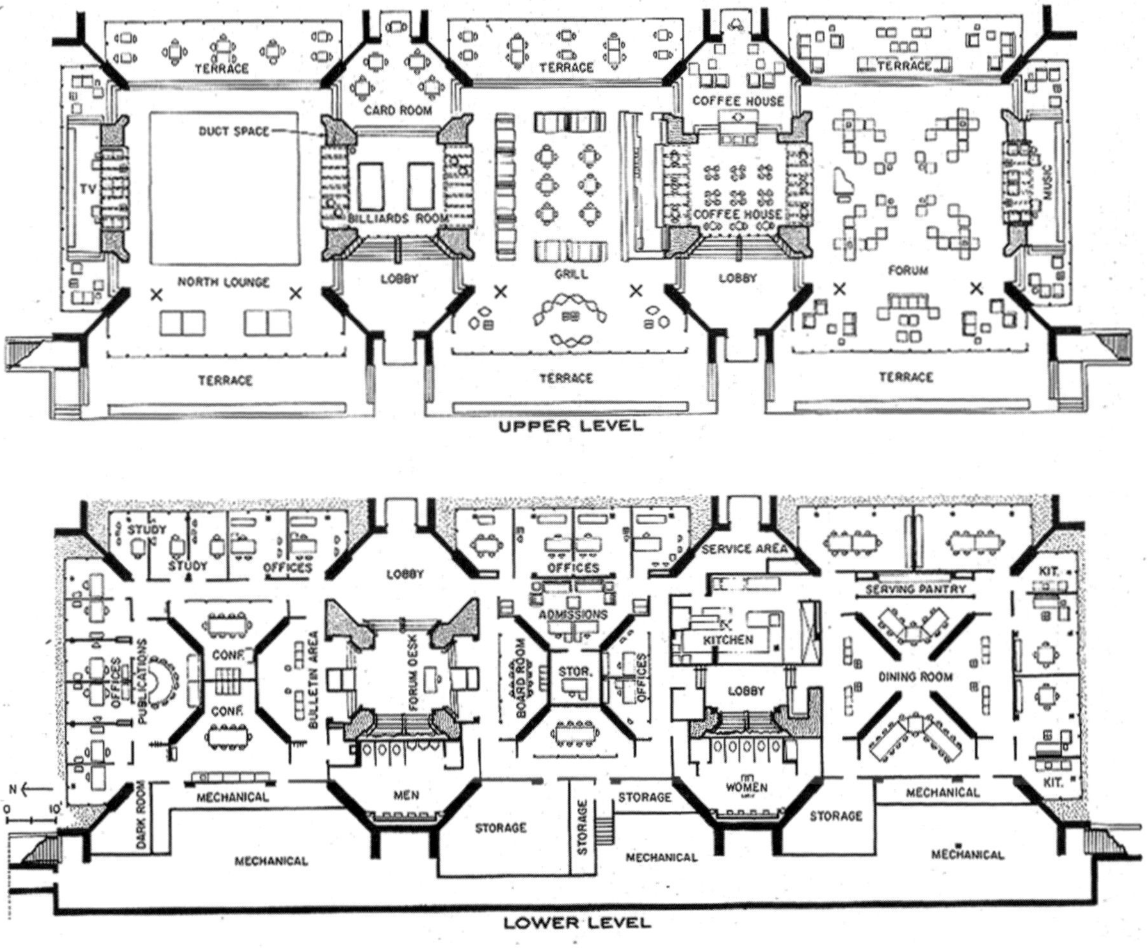

22.6

The Specialist

Creation myth: "Niche Netsch" and the winning of the Air Force Academy

It finally came down to two things: one, that we could get the work done on time; and two, we knew something about military education.[20]

Netsch's work on the Naval Postgraduate School had earned the architect a reputation: a master of complex programmatic demands. Increasingly identified as an expert in the planning of educational buildings, Netsch began to carve out his own territory within the SOM organization. He was the firm's education specialist and a master of creative organization. The Monterey project, Netsch remarked, "actually moved Skidmore into a new field, and it gave me my entrée into a noncommercial environment. So I was not competing with other designers in Skidmore to get the office building or to get this or get that."[21] Netsch opened a new, expanding market for SOM, and he was prepared to claim his own sphere of influence and expertise within that market. "I had, in a sense, made a niche for myself. No joke—'Niche Netsch.'"[22]

Asked to make a proposal for the enormous new U.S. Air Force Academy in Colorado Springs, SOM turned to "Niche Netsch," just thirty-four years old at the time. The commission was considered one of the most prestigious and important of the day, and Netsch—only recently made a partner in the firm—was placed solidly in control. His experience and expertise in the academic building type gave SOM a secret weapon in the unofficial competition for the job; Netsch's successful management of the Monterey project gave SOM a clear advantage over the other firms (including Frank Lloyd Wright—the consummate "genius" architect) in preparing schemes for the Air Force. The Air Force's final decision to hire SOM was made behind closed doors; Netsch later suggested that each of the competitors "knew somebody" in the government who was expected to pull strings in their favor. Ultimately, Netsch argued, these competing and overlapping connections neutralized one another: "It was a question of everybody knowing somebody . . . so the question is how do you make a decision when everybody knows everybody?"

SOM was awarded the job; Netsch's "niche" marketing garnered the firm its largest and most prestigious commission to date. Already known for his expertise in academic buildings, Netsch the Specialist was appointed to the biggest job of the decade primarily because his systematic invention of both the program and the campus of the Postgraduate School had been so impressive: "I got the golden palm for having done the Naval Postgraduate School because other architects had done a lot of military work, but none of them had done a school that had the reputation that the Naval Postgraduate School had."[23]

Part of the appeal of the Specialist is a guarantee of success. With the program-driven process established at Monterey, Netsch's systematic genius could not fail—it did not depend on unique inspiration. It was, instead, an easily replicable process with a predictably ingenious result. Hitchcock, in his discussion of bureaucracy and genius, described the typical architect of genius as an "architect-gambler" whose work "may or may not come off, but rarely just gets by."[24] The architect of bureaucracy, Hitchcock argued, is better suited to large-scale projects because consistency—even if a mediocre consistency—is crucial in such projects. Netsch, meanwhile, applied a quasi-bureaucratic system of analysis and teamwork in a way that was itself a deeply authorial work. The architectural process outlined by Netsch, especially in the later development of field theory, functioned with the predictable consistency of bureaucratic design, but the process and the resulting building both bore his signature.

The humanist angle

As a specialist in academic buildings, Netsch began to separate from the rest of the firm: "Our studio," he says, "became isolated from Skidmore simply because our clients were so different."[25] While it is clear that Netsch's early projects for academic institutions gave him valuable expertise in the academic building type, it is less clear why he chose to specialize almost exclusively in such projects and did not apply his organizational and programming skill to corporate projects. Clearly, Netsch's organizational analysis would have been as valuable, perhaps more valuable, to a corporation. Even during Netsch's field theory period, the sort of detailed programmatic analysis that led to geometrically complex, expressionist university buildings could easily have been applied to corporate organizations—the large corporation easily contains as much diversity of activity as an academic institution. Why, then, did Netsch's projects remain peripheral to SOM's corporate work? Why did Netsch become a specialist in programming and organizing academic buildings when the programming and organizing itself seemed to be his true specialty?

It is possible that the generic, unprogrammed floor slab—rather than Netsch's specifically programmed organization of rooms—simply might have been more appropriate and more appealing to SOM's corporate clientele. A more provocative explanation, however, is that Netsch's specialization on academic buildings allowed SOM to participate in a market otherwise off-limits to the firm: Netsch was unsullied by the vulgarity of commercial work. He was therefore an acceptable architect for the academy; his four honorary doctorates positioned him as a sort of Organization Man with one foot planted firmly in the academic world.[26] To college presidents, Netsch was "one of us"; to SOM, he was a ticket to prestigious academic commissions. There was no need to place the academic specialist in charge of the corporate project; the firm had no shortage of experts on that building type and doing so might risk Netsch's credibility as the "humanist" architect backed by a corporate organization. "So long as I was in the firm," Netsch observes, "there was something else to look at . . . Slides of my buildings would go along to a presentation in case someone was interested in the humanist angle."[27]

The Auteur

Creation myth: Building the chapel, casting the blame

Walter is doing a non-SOM building. Walter is doing a crazy building.[28]

When the plans for the Air Force Academy were publicly exhibited for the first time in May 1955, the response was generally positive. A number of U.S. senators attend the exhibition in Colorado Springs—the scheme depended on their approval, and as they examined the models and drawings of the cadet quarters, parade grounds, and classroom buildings, they seemed to like what they saw. And then they noticed the chapel. Elevated on a massive plinth, the chapel was composed of a series of folded triangular ribs, linked together to form a sort of accordion-shaped canopy (fig. 22.7). "Everything looks fine," one senator remarked, "except that chapel. I don't hear the rustle of angels' wings." Another senator agreed: "It looks like a bunch of tepees to me."[29] The academy was approved. The chapel was rejected. Netsch, determined to try again, was reduced to tears.

At the urging of Owings, Netsch traveled to Europe for the first time. Shocked to hear that Netsch has never seen Notre-Dame, and certain that he would be unable to design a proper chapel until he did so, Owings insisted that Netsch visit the great cathedrals of Europe. Netsch spent a month in Europe searching for inspiration and answers. He returned from the trip energized, determined to "create something that will be as inspiring and aspiring as Chartres, and with the light of Sainte-Chapelle."[30] He revised his earlier scheme, transforming what had been a squat structure into a soaring, aluminum-clad peak. An assemblage of interlocked tetrahedra, the chapel cut an enormous triangular profile at the foot of a neighboring mountain range. Netsch was enthusiastic: "We had something this time. We had Bucky Fuller, we had our geometry, our tetrahedra; we had technology . . . This was a very contemporary thing and in a sense it was Gothic in its form."[31]

22.7 Preliminary model of the cadet chapel, U.S. Air Force Academy, 1955. Courtesy of Walter Netsch.

Not everyone in SOM shared Netsch's enthusiasm. Convinced that Netsch's chapel was "crazy" and "non-SOM," Bruce Graham traveled to New York to persuade Gordon Bunshaft to overturn the design. Bunshaft refused to reject the design but arrived at a compromise with Graham: Netsch, not SOM as a group, would take credit—or blame—for the chapel. This would be the first time SOM's code of group anonymity would be broken. As Netsch explained, "there were some people in Skidmore who were partners who wanted to disown it. So Walter did the chapel, and Skidmore were the architects for the Academy. I was the designer for the whole damned thing, but what it did was break the recognition factor." Largely out of self-defense, then, Netsch was given individual credit for a work that was too strange, too *personal*, for the group to claim as its own. From this moment on, authorship within SOM would no longer be cloaked behind a screen of anonymity. "You'll find," Netsch remarked dryly, "that Gordon's buildings got identified as Gordon's buildings after that."[32]

Netsch's struggle with the Air Force chapel was, apparently, of Roarkian proportion. One could convincingly argue that at the moment his work was deemed too personal, too "crazy" to be produced anonymously, Netsch entered the terrain of the genius architect. This would certainly be in line with Hitchcock's bureaucracy/genius dialectic, and it would go a long way toward explaining Netsch's occasionally rocky relationship with the rest of the SOM partnership. Yet, as was frequently the case in Netsch's career, the situation was not quite that simple. While it is clear that the design of the Air Force chapel was a significantly more individual expression than is typical of a "bureaucratic" firm like SOM, it was nevertheless a project that depended in large part on the technical expertise of the organization. With its enormous aluminum-clad tetrahedra, the chapel required a level of technical expertise that would likely be outside the grasp of the genius architect working alone. Indeed, Netsch's genius lay not only in his ability to develop the scheme as an individual designer but also in his ability to mobilize SOM's institutional resources to construct the scheme as it was designed. Architects of the time seem to have understood this; Netsch notes that other designers—especially those without the resources of a firm like SOM—tended to discount Netsch's abilities primarily because of his willingness to rely on the firm's support services: "I . . . had to carry the burden of SOM along," he remarks, "because all of these other people would say, 'I'm the genius all alone, and here Walter has all of this support."[33]

Self-generating genius: The development of field theory

Although the project was not universally admired, the Air Force Chapel established Netsch as the resident auteur of SOM's Chicago office—he was the first to receive individual credit within the firm, and the mastermind of a controversial and iconic monument. Netsch the Auteur was under pressure to follow his Air Force triumph with similarly inventive and personal works: "I'm not going to just redo the Academy forever," he remarked to his partners, "I'm just not going to do it."[34]

In the years after the Air Force project, then, Netsch once again searched for inspiration, examining the work of Rudolph, Yamasaki, and Mies. He was not impressed, or at least not impressed enough to become a mimic. "The idea of adopting someone else's style—Corbu, Mies—that was not going to be it." Netsch instead turned to geometry: a tool that had been crucial in the development of the Air Force Academy Chapel. In the early stages of design for the University of Illinois at Chicago (UIC), Netsch began to "pursue the geometry of the rotated square. That was the next step from the tetrahedron."[35] Square columns at UIC are twisted along their length, terminating in triangulated capitals. After these hesitant first steps, Netsch combined his interest in programming and arranging human activity with his love of geometry. He formulated field theory: a fundamentally practical theory that would render his particular brand of genius automatic and self-generating.

Netsch borrowed the term "field theory" from the behavioral sciences—it refers to "a method of analysis . . . that describes actions or events as the resultant of dynamic interplay among sociocultural, biomechanical, and motivational forces."[36] It should at this point come as little surprise that Netsch's artistic theory had at its base a theory of social organization; the most logical source of inspiration for the genius of the bureaucracy is, it seems, the bureaucracy itself. Based largely on the analysis of program and activity, field theory proposed a set of aesthetic rules that, when applied to the sort of rigorous program analysis Netsch had conducted for the U.S. Naval Postgraduate School, would produce buildings that were not only functionally optimal but were also expressionist and apparently authorial in form.

Field theory is a proportional system based on matrices of overlapping squares—the resulting matrix is used to organize rooms and walls (figs. 22.8, 22.9). Netsch argued that this matrix produces "a linear expansion of the progression of different activities for which the building is used."[37] That is, the "field" created through Netsch's overlapping geometry is intended to provide an ideal site for each of the activities required by the program. It is not clear exactly why the geometry of the rotated square is ideally suited to the planning of laboratories, classrooms, and offices. In fact, Netsch made no claim that the system was a perfect tool for doing so. He did, however, contend that field theory's reliance on geometry ("I was rediscovering the way the Gothicists used geometry," he said) made it an efficient and eminently teachable method of planning buildings:

22.8

22.8 Field theory matrices, 1969. Courtesy of Walter Netsch.

22.9 Film stills from "Field Theory Film on Lab Planning: An Animated Color Movie Designed by Skidmore, Owings & Merrill, Architects." Produced and directed by Walter Netsch. Courtesy of Walter Netsch.

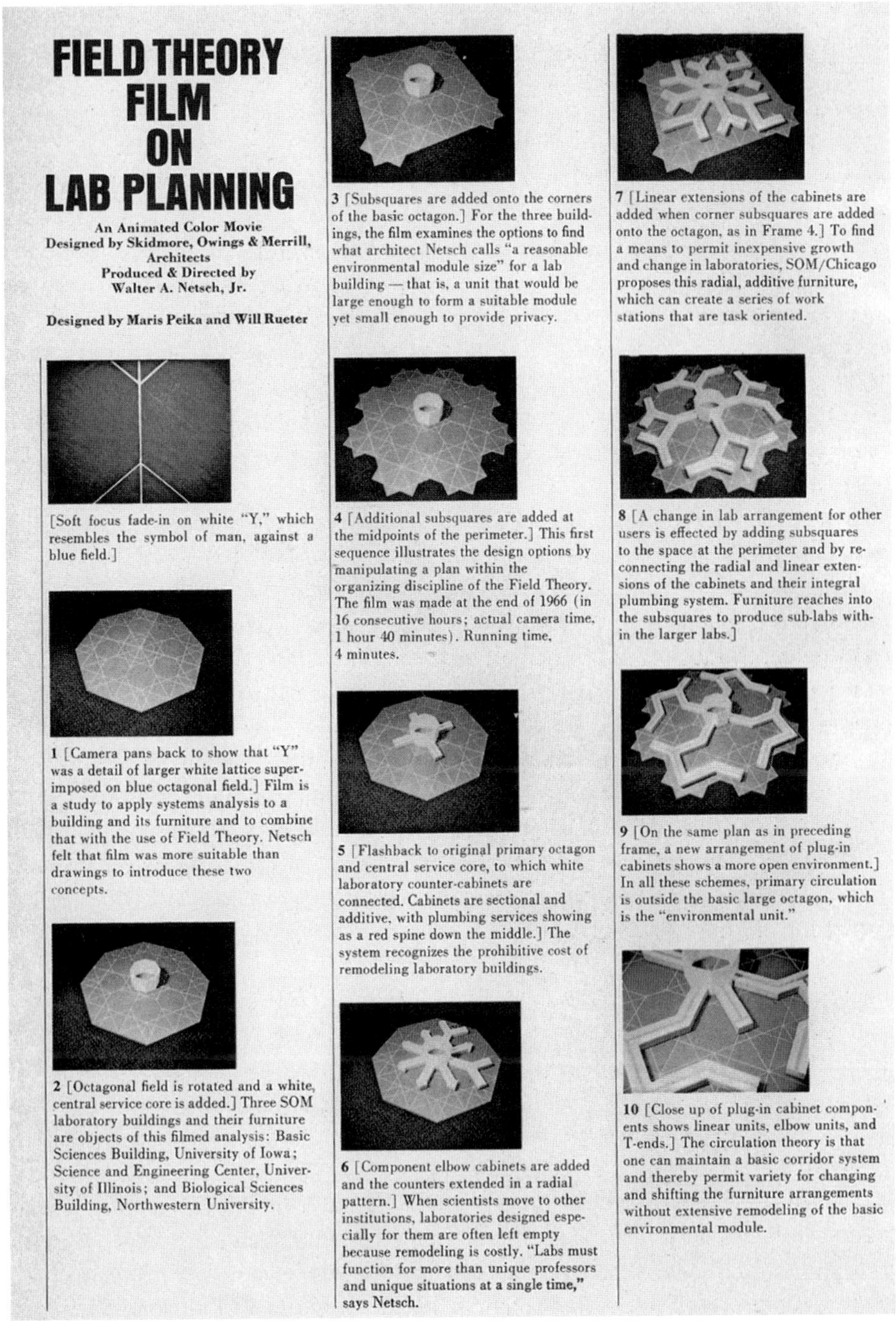

FIELD THEORY FILM ON LAB PLANNING

An Animated Color Movie
Designed by Skidmore, Owings & Merrill, Architects
Produced & Directed by
Walter A. Netsch, Jr.

Designed by Maris Peika and Will Rueter

[Soft focus fade-in on white "Y," which resembles the symbol of man, against a blue field.]

1 [Camera pans back to show that "Y" was a detail of larger white lattice superimposed on blue octagonal field.] Film is a study to apply systems analysis to a building and its furniture and to combine that with the use of Field Theory. Netsch felt that film was more suitable than drawings to introduce these two concepts.

2 [Octagonal field is rotated and a white, central service core is added.] Three SOM laboratory buildings and their furniture are objects of this filmed analysis: Basic Sciences Building, University of Iowa; Science and Engineering Center, University of Illinois; and Biological Sciences Building, Northwestern University.

3 [Subsquares are added onto the corners of the basic octagon.] For the three buildings, the film examines the options to find what architect Netsch calls "a reasonable environmental module size" for a lab building — that is, a unit that would be large enough to form a suitable module yet small enough to provide privacy.

4 [Additional subsquares are added at the midpoints of the perimeter.] This first sequence illustrates the design options by manipulating a plan within the organizing discipline of the Field Theory. The film was made at the end of 1966 (in 16 consecutive hours; actual camera time, 1 hour 40 minutes). Running time, 4 minutes.

5 [Flashback to original primary octagon and central service core, to which white laboratory counter-cabinets are connected. Cabinets are sectional and additive, with plumbing services showing as a red spine down the middle.] The system recognizes the prohibitive cost of remodeling laboratory buildings.

6 [Component elbow cabinets are added and the counters extended in a radial pattern.] When scientists move to other institutions, laboratories designed especially for them are often left empty because remodeling is costly. "Labs must function for more than unique professors and unique situations at a single time," says Netsch.

7 [Linear extensions of the cabinets are added when corner subsquares are added onto the octagon, as in Frame 4.] To find a means to permit inexpensive growth and change in laboratories, SOM/Chicago proposes this radial, additive furniture, which can create a series of work stations that are task oriented.

8 [A change in lab arrangement for other users is effected by adding subsquares to the space at the perimeter and by reconnecting the radial and linear extensions of the cabinets and their integral plumbing system. Furniture reaches into the subsquares to produce sub-labs within the larger labs.]

9 [On the same plan as in preceding frame, a new arrangement of plug-in cabinets shows a more open environment.] In all these schemes, primary circulation is outside the basic large octagon, which is the "environmental unit."

10 [Close up of plug-in cabinet components shows linear units, elbow units, and T-ends.] The circulation theory is that one can maintain a basic corridor system and thereby permit variety for changing and shifting the furniture arrangements without extensive remodeling of the basic environmental module.

22.9

"Field Theory can be done by anyone," he argued, "I'm not developing an idiom that could be used only by specialists."[38]

In the end, however, what was compelling about field theory was not only that it provided an easily replicable method to organize program; it is, in fact, arguable (and it has, in fact, been argued) that field theory buildings are frequently alienating, confusing, and difficult to navigate. Instead, the importance of field theory was that, through a process ostensibly based on logical and functionalist arrangement of activities, it produced iconic, expressionist works of architecture; authorial works that, Netsch suggests, could well have been designed without the intervention of the author himself. Field theory is thus an easily duplicated recipe for "signature" architecture: it is a system of self-generating genius.

Field theory was, despite the rhetoric, rarely employed outside Netsch's studio. Those who had worked under Netsch at SOM were, at the time of his retirement, warned that any mention of the theory would cost them their jobs, and few outside of SOM took the time to understand how the system actually worked.[39] It is ironic that a system that Netsch had intended to be universally applicable was, even within his own firm, considered so fundamentally linked to his individual signature that it could never be used in his absence. Yet the fact that field theory failed as a generally accepted tool for making architecture is ultimately less important than the fact that it was intended to be such a system—Netsch understood his creation to be a method, not a style. And in creating a program-based method that can simulate individual authorship, Netsch proposed an apparently effortless way to produce genius architecture through bureaucratic means. This system, it seems, suggested a new way to apply "genius" solutions to problems that would otherwise be too large or complex to sustain this type of highly wrought approach. "In a day when . . . we must think on a mammoth scale, a scale in which entire buildings must be considered as details were in the past," *Progressive Architecture* remarks in a 1969 article on Netsch, "the Field Theory design process may point a way."[40]

The Opportunist

Creation myth: "The corporate boiler"

Well, where are you going to get the computer? Where are you going to get the star HVAC?[41]

It is difficult to pinpoint the exact moment in which Netsch the Opportunist was created. In a sense, the Opportunist and the Idealist emerged simultaneously from the wartime environment at MIT. There, Netsch learned firsthand the ways in which large-scale organizations could serve as crucial resources for the architect. MIT's role in the war effort and the general tenor of the design assignments reinforced the message that the individual architect was no longer a viable or responsible option in the face of the challenges facing architects. While the Idealist therefore saw the role of the organization as a means to reach and serve a mass public, the Opportunist understood it primarily as a powerful tool with which to pursue a personal artistic agenda. Both of these descriptions, perhaps in equal measure, apply to Walter Netsch. Yet it was not until both Netsch and SOM began to view field theory as somehow incompatible with the corporate culture of the firm that Netsch's opportunism became clearly legible. "When you have a really original idea like I did with Field Theory," he notes, "it's very hard to put that into the corporate boiler."[42]

Whatever the explanation for Netsch's gradual estrangement from SOM, he remained with the firm until poor health forced his retirement in 1980. And, as Netsch freely admits, the relationship was a productive one: "One must understand that for many, Skidmore, Owings & Merrill represents the Establishment," he noted in a 1980 article in *Architectural Record*. "While our work in Field Theory should not flourish in such an environment, nevertheless it does flourish."[43] We can draw two conclusions from the fact that field theory could "flourish" within an organization that largely rejected it: first, it suggests that the theory might not be as foreign to the SOM system as both Netsch and the firm may have believed it to be; and second, it suggests that Netsch was especially adept at exploiting the resources of the firm to realize his unorthodox agenda. It is this second reading that effectively describes the workings of the Opportunist: Netsch was able to convert the conflict between himself and the rest of the firm into an advantage while simultaneously relying on the engineering and technical expertise of the firm to help realize his studio's work.

Cheaper space

"Netsch's studio" was not just a corner of the SOM Chicago office dedicated to his projects. For much of Netsch's time at SOM, he maintained a physically separate studio, located in an entirely different, and presumably less expensive, building than the SOM "front office." It is likely that financial considerations had something to do with the decision to move Netsch's studio out of SOM's main office in the Inland Steel Building: "They moved us out into cheaper space," Netsch explains, "because we were big, we were going to get bigger."[44] Yet, given the hostility between Netsch and Bruce Graham, who dominated the Chicago office, it seems more likely that the decision to expel Netsch's studio from the rest of the SOM office, as well as Netsch's apparent willingness to go, reflected a realization by both camps that a "trial separation" might be best for all involved. In his studio Netsch could, with the full backing of a large corporate firm, conduct extensive field theory research (his studio produced a series of films explaining the derivation and benefits of the theory) and could develop projects without the interference of a partnership that had little sympathy for Netsch's new direction.

Netsch spawned a satellite office of SOM—a sort of specialty brand that received no commissions from the "front office" but was free to develop an architectural system that, quite literally, had no home in the corporate mainstream. In establishing a studio distinct from the SOM office, Netsch sacrificed potential commissions but earned a degree of control over his studio that would likely have been impossible had he remained in the Inland Steel office space.

I began with a quotation that seemed to place much of the credit for Netsch's strong work on "all of the support services behind him." This comment is applicable to all phases of Netsch's career, even those during which he was physically and ideologically separated from the rest of SOM. Netsch was, at times, so distraught over his strained relationship with the rest of the firm that he often considered departing to establish his own practice. Yet, as his wife Dawn Clark Netsch counseled, leaving the firm would be disastrous for Netsch's ability to realize field theory projects: "Where are you going to get the computer? Where are you going to get the star HVAC?" she asked.

Netsch realized that he would be unable to operate without the backing of the rest of the firm: although his buildings rarely involved elaborate structural innovation, they were nevertheless so enormous that the execution of the project would likely be beyond the scope of a small office; academic buildings required technical expertise on laboratory planning and organization; and field theory made use of a million-dollar supercomputer purchased in the early 1970s, a computer that was used primarily to assist SOM engineer Fazlur Khan in calculating wind stresses on skyscrapers.[45] All of these demands could not be met by the genius architect acting alone. And Netsch was clearly aware of this; his continued loyalty to SOM was—at least in part—motivated by the knowledge that his architecture had become impossible to realize without it.

A theory of the purely practical, or "the infinity problem"

Perhaps the most significant result of Netsch's opportunism is that field theory was never confined to the realm of the theoretical. Netsch's involvement with SOM gave him access to large commissions and to the resources needed to realize them. Field theory was put into practice even as it was still being formulated; it was tested in an actual building before its author truly knew what he had created. There could be no other way of evaluating field theory, because it was a theory of the purely practical. That is to say,

Netsch established a theory whose success or failure could only be judged by the performance of the building produced. He made few claims for field theory beyond its ability to manage program efficiently and to produce "iconic" form.[46] A successful field theory building, judged on Netsch's own terms, was therefore one that accomplished these primary tasks, and not necessarily much more.

Field theory buildings were unleashed on the city before the theory itself had been tested or refined. The results are somewhat difficult to evaluate. The Art and Architecture Building at Netsch's UIC campus is the earliest built field theory experiment. Never fully completed, the building's proposed double-helix circulation system ends abruptly—a dead end, its proposed connections to adjacent buildings severed. An unfinished exterior wall, with exposed floor slabs and provisional-looking concrete block infill, marks the building's entrance. Although Netsch was disappointed by the disfigured state of the building, this unfinished project illustrates field theory's approach to the city more clearly than does any other Netsch building: it appears as a fragment of a larger system, a system that could expand indefinitely, engulfing neighborhoods, districts, cities. Netsch acknowledges that the idea of the "field" implies an endless expandability: "In this way," he says, "we are trying to tackle the infinity problem."[47]

The notion of the infinitely expandable building is not new; but Netsch's field theory projects, when placed in an urban context, always seem to be incomplete, waiting to colonize neighboring parking lots or office buildings, to extend their planning matrices over the entire city. Field theory thus represents an urban project fundamentally concerned with the network: with a continuous system extending far beyond the borders of the individual building. And like field theory, this urban project suggests a potentially self-generating urbanism: that is, once the matrix has been established, there exists little more than to fill in the blanks and continue the pattern. The triumph of the bureaucrat/genius architect would thus be complete—he would have created a city based on *process*, a process that he had authored and whose sheer brilliance would ensure that the entire city has the quality of a masterwork. The megalomania of this reading is, of course, absurd. Surely, Netsch had no such plans for absorbing the Chicago grid with an enormous "chrysanthemum field" of rotated squares. Yet the idea of the self-generating system, so clearly embedded in the individual field theory buildings, can hardly be ignored on the urban scale.

Postscript: Another Genius

In the mythic terms of genius and bureaucracy, Bunshaft looms as a superhuman presence; it is virtually impossible to avoid his work when attempting to address the issue of how individual authorship and the organization coexist. Bunshaft's buildings, like Netsch's, can frequently be identified as his even when they are attributed to SOM as a whole. And if it is difficult to distinguish his work from that of his peers, it is primarily because, more than any other SOM designer, he defined exactly how a SOM building should look. Like Netsch, Bunshaft also took advantage of the resources of the firm in order to execute his projects. Might we then consider Bunshaft, like Netsch, to be an architect who straddles the genius/bureaucracy divide?

While there is little question that Bunshaft was capable of works of signature "genius," that is, projects that clearly bear the mark of his authorship, it would be difficult to argue that his particular brand of genius had much at all to do with mastering the nuances of the bureaucratic organization and, in turn, using that understanding to enrich his architecture. Bunshaft described his position in rather plain terms: "[T]he architect is no artist who dreams up something," he says. "He guides the development so that it is aesthetically pleasing. The owner guides it so that it is functionally correct."[48] While Bunshaft's buildings were often both "aesthetically pleasing" and "functionally correct," there was little effort in these projects to collapse the two categories—the functional aspects of the program are largely independent of the authorial statement of the building as a whole.

Netsch, in comparison, seemed to relish the moment in which bureaucratic organization was rendered aesthetic. There could be, for Netsch, no easy division between "correct" functioning and aesthetics. This is not to say that Netsch was purely a functionalist—the decision to use matrices of overlapping squares and octagons was surely an arbitrary one, with little correspondence to the demands of the program. Yet there was in Netsch's work a very real attention to the specifics of program: like Netsch, field theory was fundamentally shaped by the bureaucracy—the expressionist exterior forms it created were ostensibly direct expressions of the organizational complexity within.

Postscript Two: A different kind of company, a different kind of car

For all Netsch's sympathy for and devotion to the structure of bureaucratic organizations—the military, the state university, the corporate design firm itself—his work hung in an uneasy tension with the SOM organization around him. The presence of the genius *of* the bureaucracy *within* the bureaucracy brought about mutations in the bureaucracy itself. First, and perhaps most obviously, Netsch's studio-in-exile represented a major modification of the SOM structure. Ideally composed of anonymous teams of problem solvers, SOM's structure was, after Netsch's separation, forced to absorb a new entity—the specialist and his atelier. While insisting that he remained "very loyal to SOM," Netsch pursued his own, noncorporate clients, developing an aesthetic system apart from SOM's "house style." SOM, however, did not entirely shun Netsch for this departure. While it is clear that he faced resistance from others within the firm, his projects were used in client presentations of the Chicago office's work—the organization apparently realized that "niche Netsch" offered a potentially lucrative and prestigious foothold in an academic, "humanist" market that might otherwise elude them. Although SOM did not continue the distinct studio arrangement after Netsch's retirement, the development suggested that the firm might develop a series of more individualized "brands" under the SOM corporate banner.

Netsch also illustrated how corporate resources might be creatively misused in order to pursue new design approaches. When Netsch appropriated Khan's million-dollar supercomputer to help develop new field theory matrices, he manipulated a tool that had originally been intended solely for the engineering of tall buildings. Netsch's creative misuse of this resource suggests a way in which the actions of free agents within the corporate environment might redeploy the tools of "the Establishment" to forge an avant-garde from within.

The mutations begun by Netsch are analogous to subsequent developments in the automobile industry. As late as the early 1980s, before the office tower slump threw the firm into crisis, it would not at all be an exaggeration to call SOM "the General Motors of Architecture": a dominant, if slightly dinosaurlike presence in the market. If SOM was the GM of architecture, then the studio of Walter Netsch might well be considered the Saturn brand within SOM.

Some explanation is required: in the mid-1980s, as GM watched Japanese imports claim the majority of the small car market, GM executives realized that as it currently existed, GM was unlikely to regain that lost market share. First, the cumbersome and hierarchical organization of the company made it difficult to conduct fast-paced, market-responsive product development. Second—and, perhaps more important—GM realized that young car buyers were repelled by the conformist, corporate culture that the company seemed to represent. No self-respecting, progressive twentysomething, they admitted, would dare be seen driving a Chevrolet. Instead of reorganizing the existing divisions of GM, a move that would be almost impossible given the entrenched interests of the existing brands, GM chairman Roger Smith proposed the creation of an entirely new brand, the Saturn Corporation. The new brand, which would make use of many elements from the GM parts bin and would have full financial and technical support from the parent company, would nevertheless be given a good deal of autonomy within the company itself. Product design, manufacturing, and marketing would be handled by Saturn with minimul interference from Detroit.

When the cars were introduced nearly a decade later, with a series of soft-focus, feel-good television ads, the brand was an immediate success. Although the cars were judged by critics to be slightly inferior to the Japanese competition, sales were brisk, and owners were rabidly loyal. Frequently unaware that the brand was in any way associated with GM, the young, upwardly mobile clientele that Detroit had initially hoped to attract now flocked to the company in droves, largely, it might be argued, due to the nonconformist, anticorporate marketing of the Saturn brand itself. The Saturn tag line, "A different kind of company, a different kind of car," is an outright attack on the big automakers, an attack on the corporate culture of GM itself. Saturn owners were invited to annual "homecoming" weekends at the manufacturing plant in Tennessee; the brand seemed to relish in its homespun, folksy image. And they were wise to do so, because their market is defined largely by those who rejected corporate culture. Not surprisingly, the directors of existing brands at GM were suspicious, even jealous of the upstart brand, working to limit funding for Saturn, attempting to ensure that the large car market would remain solidly in their hands.

The parallels to Netsch's work within SOM are clear: funded and given technical support by the parent firm, Netsch pursued an academic market that might otherwise reject a firm whose clientele consisted largely of multinational corporations. Yet, unlike executives at GM, the SOM partnership was never fully able to understand the potential value of having such a figure within the organization. Although SOM did not pursue this possibility, Netsch presented them with a model of target market branding within SOM. As I have suggested, this model, which allows for considerable innovation with tremendous corporate support, might lead a firm like SOM to develop a series of niche brands, each devoted to a specific market, each existing with relative autonomy. These niche brands might then be free, indeed encouraged, to produce research that challenges the nature of the parent organization itself. And it is ultimately this possibility—the potential for avant-garde research to be generated from deep within the corporate structure itself—that makes the case of Walter Netsch a valuable one.

23 Opposing Mies: The Triangular Constructs of Harry Weese

Leah Ray

Harry Weese envisioned a Chicago in which people lived, played, sailed, and celebrated amidst skyscrapers, seaways and parks. He wrote

> **Architecture as city is generated and shaped by movement systems: sea lanes, transit arteries, and streets, thronging conduits softened by green. . . . Stiletto spires, dome cupola, stacks, tanks and towers fret the sky's edge suddenly sundered at the core by the hard edge bar graph of downtown . . . . Architecture is the aggregate image of a city: dominant-recessive, chaste-vulgar, phlegmatic-mannered, unified or chaotic.[1]**

Weese's eclectic architecture reflects these words. While Mies van der Rohe designed projects for Chicago which enforced an orthogonal, minimal, orderly architecture in the International Style, Weese's humanist designs drew heavily upon Chicago and the lives of its inhabitants as distinct from other cities. He implemented triangular and circular forms in his designs to thematically resist an orthogonal urban grid, and embraced both historic preservation and adaptive reuse as viable architectural projects. Indeed, the dynamic opposition between the ideas of Mies and Weese set the stage for vibrant architectural debate in Chicago during the mid-twentieth-century. Weese's vision of Chicago is best represented in the design of two constructed works, the Metropolitan Correctional Center and River Cottages, and two unbuilt projects, the 1992 World's Fair (figs. 23.1, 23.2, 23.3) and renovation of Navy Pier (fig. 23.4), in which he reveals his desire to mix living, working and recreational spaces in the heart of the city.

While Weese designed a number of skyscrapers in Chicago, he warned of the problems that were inherent in a downtown populated by skyscrapers that took no notice of their natural surroundings or the scale of Chicago's urban street life. The Metropolitan Correctional Center, a building where federal prisoners are temporarily held while awaiting trial (figs. 23.5–23.10), is the best example of skyscraper design that Weese hoped Chicago would embrace. The building cuts through the Chicago skyline with its massive triangular concrete form punctuated by thin slotted windows that open directly to prisoners' cells. The width of the windows, a mere 5", is dictated by the need to prevent prisoners from escaping. In this way, the building's façade is a haunting reminder of its inhabitants' predicament. Passersby are often seen watching inmates exercising on the rooftop garden, while inmates atop the building gaze upon the city below. This dynamic between the incarcerated inhabitants of the jail and observers moving freely through the plaza below heightens the dramatic impact of the building's form. While the prisoners inside are forcibly retained, inhabitants of the original plaza were drawn by the cool shade of this urban garden's trees and two beds of tulips that sheltered the plaza from the street.[2] Attention to both the interior and exterior spaces of the building

23.1 Harry Weese's vision for the 1992 Chicago World's Fair, highlighting the relationship between the corporate and institutional spaces of skyscrapers framing the edge of the Chicago Loop in juxtaposition with the social and recreational spaces of Grant Park and Chicago's active lakefront. Uncataloged. Courtesy of the Harry Weese Associates Collection, Chicago Historical Society.

23.2 Rendering of Weese's vision for the lakefront design of the 1992 World's Fair, highlighting use of triangular form in design of docks. Uncataloged. Courtesy of the Harry Weese Associates Collection, Chicago Historical Society.

23.3 Lakefront plan for 1992 World's Fair showing Weese's desire to further integrate the lake, river, parks and the city. Uncataloged. Courtesy of the Harry Weese Associates Collection, Chicago Historical Society.

23.4 Perspective sketch of Weese's vision for Navy Pier. Uncataloged. Courtesy of the Harry Weese Associates Collection, Chicago Historical Society.

as well as the scale of the skyscraper in relation to the street and its surroundings are hallmarks of Weese's urban designs.

The use of triangular forms in projects such as the River Cottages at Wolf Point Landing can also be said to reflect Weese's love of sailing, which strongly influenced his civic designs. He aspired to link urban Chicago with Lake Michigan, and dreamed of incorporating nautical life into both residential and civic projects throughout the city. At Wolf Point Landing, Weese designed a residential community with direct access to the Chicago River and the River North Community. A schematic model of the River Cottages shows the use of triangular form as a thematic link to the sails of the boats harbored on docks along the river. The cottages were sited between the street and the river, and Weese envisioned their inhabitants as utilizing both means of transportation in their daily lives. Immediately adjacent to the River Cottages, Weese initiated the first loft conversion in Chicago (figs. 23.11–23.15) at Fulton House. Originally a cold storage building sited on the Chicago River, Fulton House became the first of many industrial warehouses to be converted into residential units along the Chicago River. Today, loft conversions have become some of the most popular residential building types in the River North area, and the area adjacent to the Fulton House and River Cottages has become populated with town houses and residential high rises as Weese foresaw in his initial designs for Wolf Point.

Weese saw the city center as a hub of infrastructure, entertainment and consumption and directed his work to that end. His architecture drew its inspiration from movement systems such as sea-lanes, transit arteries, and tree-lined streets. In the following pages, his visionary urban sketches are juxtaposed with images of his buildings, sailboats, parks and commercial strips. The following images will explore his works in terms of his fascination with certain dualisms expressed in the city, and these projects should be viewed as opposing impulses to the Miesian canon. Indeed, the dialogue and debate between these two architects was at the core of the dynamic architectural culture of Chicago in the mid twentieth century. Warning that Chicago could become populated with multiple "sunlit tombstones," Weese proposed an alternate vision of a city replete with carnivals, trolleys, riverside parks, and entertainment centers.

23.1

23.2

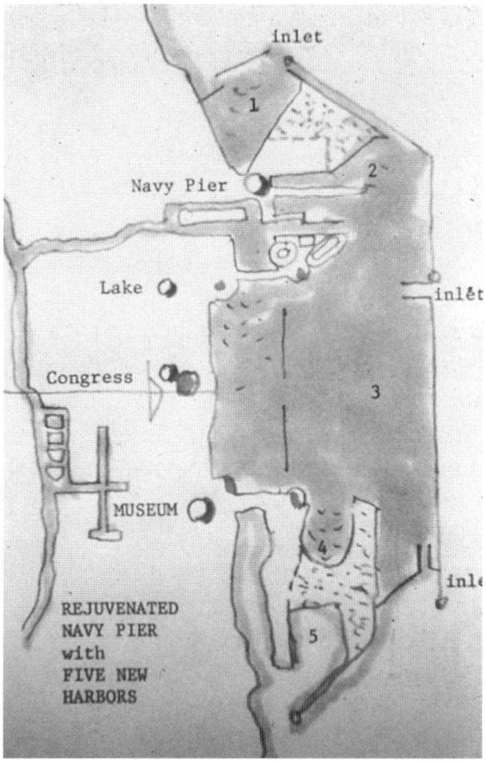

23.3

23.4

23.5

23.6

23.7

23.8

23.5 The Metropolitan Correctional Center (originally called the United States Courthouse Annex, Harry Weese and Associates, 1975) as photographed by Hedrich Blessing, portraying the jail's strong relationship to the street. Uncataloged. Courtesy of the Harry Weese Associates Collection, Chicago Historical Society.

23.6 View of the Metropolitan Correctional Center from the pedestrian's perspective, reflecting the strong triangular form of the building cutting across the predominantly orthogonal Chicago skyline. Uncataloged. Courtesy of the Harry Weese Associates Collection, Chicago Historical Society.

23.7 Interior view of the Metropolitan Correctional Center showing Weese's use of circular and triangular forms. Uncataloged. Courtesy of the Harry Weese Associates Collection, Chicago Historical Society.

23.8 Interior view of the Metropolitan Correctional Center showing its structure as a symbol of both containment and restraint. Uncataloged. Courtesy of the Harry Weese Associates Collection, Chicago Historical Society.

23.9 Sectional drawing of Metropolitan Correctional Center showing collection of internees' cells organized around communal double-height spaces. Uncataloged. Courtesy of the Harry Weese Associates Collection, Chicago Historical Society.

23.10 Metropolitan Correctional Center plan showing Weese's use of both triangular and circular themes. Uncataloged. Courtesy of the Harry Weese Associates Collection, Chicago Historical Society.

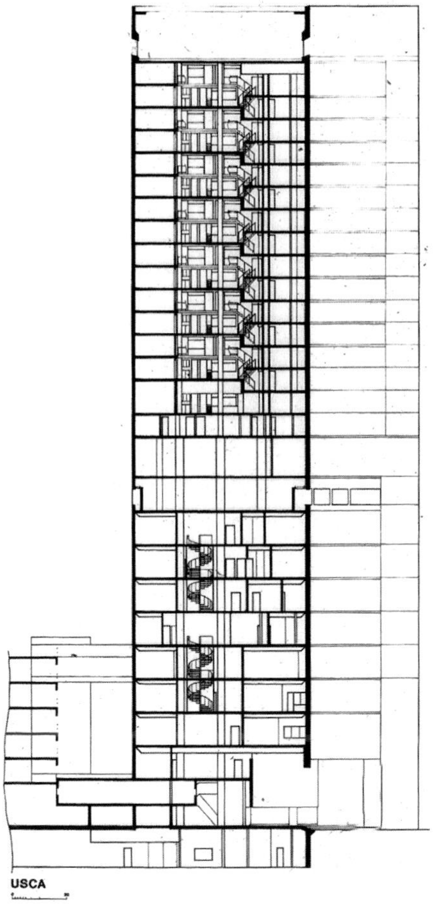

23.9

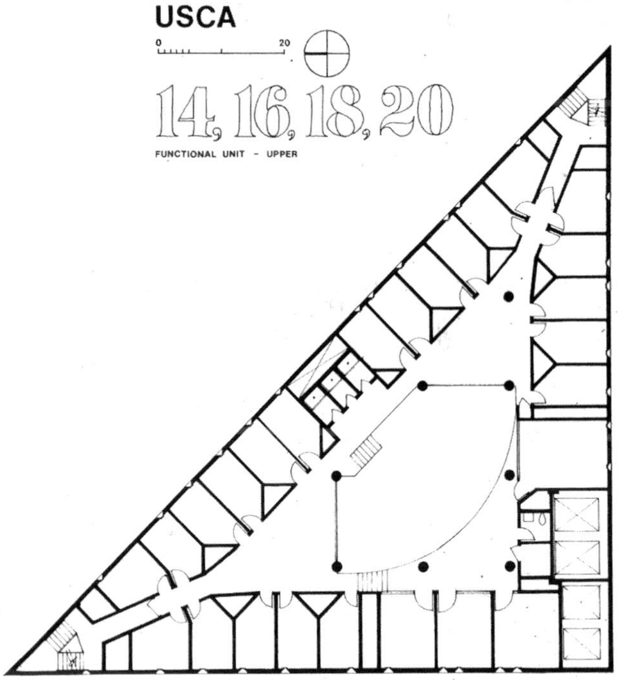

23.10

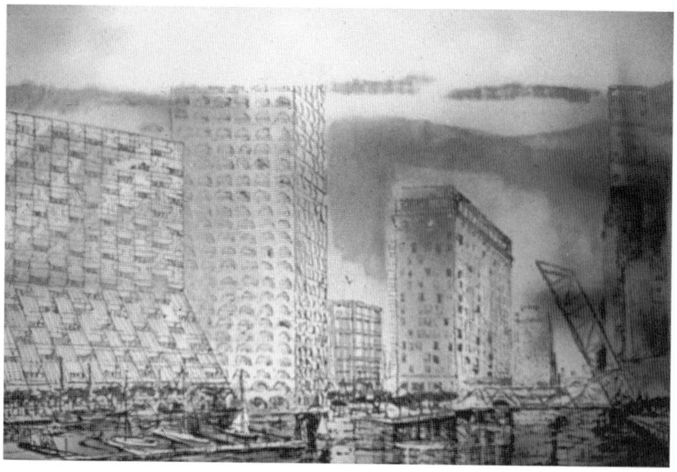

23.11

23.12

23.13

23.11 Rendering of Wolf Point Landing presenting Weese's vision for the north branch of the Chicago River. Uncataloged. Courtesy of the Harry Weese Associates Collection, Chicago Historical Society.

23.12 Sketch of Wolf Point Landing examining the relationship between the Chicago River and the city. Uncataloged. Courtesy of the Harry Weese Associates Collection, Chicago Historical Society.

23.13 Axonometric drawing of the River Cottages showing the building's relationship to infrastructure along the predominantly industrial Chicago River. Uncataloged. Courtesy of the Harry Weese Associates Collection, Chicago Historical Society.

23.14

23.15

23.14 Schematic model of the River Cottages showing triangular nautical form. Uncataloged. Courtesy of the Harry Weese Associates Collection, Chicago Historical Society.

23.15 View of the River Cottages as built. Uncataloged. Courtesy of the Harry Weese Associates Collection, Chicago Historical Society.

Diminishing High-Rise Public Housing

Janet L. Smith

Until recently, driving into Chicago on the Dan Ryan Expressway would bring you past "the projects"—some of the most famous architecture in the city and some of the most notorious public housing in the United States. Now, nearly all these high-rises are gone.

The Chicago Housing Authority (CHA), which erected these buildings, is transforming the architecture of poverty by demolishing fifty-one high-rise buildings. Most are of the "gallery style" design built between 1957 and 1968 on the city's South Side. While not old, the buildings are no longer of value to the CHA and the city—it is cheaper to tear them down than it is to maintain them.[1] Residents get a housing assistance voucher to relocate into the private rental housing market while they wait for replacement housing, if any, to be built.

By 2009, most buildings will be replaced by low-rise walk-ups and single-family houses, built at about the same density as fifty years ago before urban renewal cleared the "slums" to put up the high rises. Unlike the past, however, these new developments will be "mixed-income" communities, and the architecture will not distinguish who is poor or who is middle class, or that the government had anything to do with its design. This essay looks back to make sense of the role of high-rise public housing in the architecture of poverty then and now. While it has not gone entirely full circle, history appears to be in some ways repeating itself.

For many years, the experience of passing by public housing on the South Side was not unlike what Friedrich Engels described when walking through Manchester in the 1840s:

> The town itself is peculiarly built, so that a person may live in it for years, and go in and out daily without coming into contact with a working-people's quarter or even with workers; that is, so long as he confines himself to his business or to pleasure walks. This arises chiefly from the fact, that by unconscious tacit agreement, as well as with outspoken conscious determination, the working people's quarters are sharply separated from the sections of the city reserved for the middle class; or, if this does not succeed, they are concealed with the cloak of charity.[2]

While visible markers showing precisely where many poor people lived in Chicago, these developments, with names like Robert Taylor Homes and Stateway Gardens, were still "sharply separated from the sections of the city reserved for the middle class." An expressway and railroad right-of-way separated the middle class from the poor, keeping them under the government's large cloak of charity.

Even at a distance, the magnitude of these buildings was striking. Standing noticeably above the landscape, these monoliths tall and broad have no obvious scale without a tree

24.1 Stateway Gardens, 2000. Photograph by Birgit Kasper.

24.2 Dan Ryan Expressway, Robert Taylor Homes (foreground) and Stateway Gardens, looking north, 1964. Photograph by Bill Engdahl, Hedrich-Blessing Photo. HB-26129A, courtesy of the Hedrich-Blessing Collection, Chicago Historical Society.

24.3 Last standing building of Robert Taylor Homes A, 2003. Photograph by Bill Lerch.

24.1

24.2

24.3

24.4 Water carried from next door, frozen over at 533 East Thirty-sixth Place, 1950. Photograph by Mildred Mead. Courtesy of the Chicago Historical Society, ICHi-24628.

24.5 Alley between Cottage Grove Avenue and Ellis Avenue, 1951. Photograph by Mildred Mead. Courtesy of the Chicago Historical Society, ICHi 00809.

24.6 Dilapidated housing, 3559 South LaSalle Street, 1953. Copyright Chicago Daily News, DN-P4459, courtesy of the Chicago Historical Society.

or person as a referent. Rows of windows, once the eyes to the souls inside, are now covered with metal and wood, marking units no longer inhabited and waiting for demolition.

Build Up

Before 1951, the CHA had never erected an elevator building. By 1968, the CHA had built 15,591 new public housing units for families. Most were in high-rise buildings. Half of these units were in three developments on the South Side of the city:

1. Stateway Gardens: two ten-story buildings and six seventeen-story buildings containing 1,684 units. Designed by Holabird and Root and Burgee; completed in 1959.

2. Robert Taylor Homes: twenty-eight sixteen-story buildings mostly in u-shaped groups of three, with red or yellow brick veneers, containing 4,312 units. Designed by Shaw, Metz and Associates; completed in 1962. This was the largest single development of public housing in the United States.

3. Washington Park Homes: sixty row house buildings and seven sixteen-story buildings of the same design as the Robert Taylor Homes, containing 1,065 units. It was completed in 1962.

At peak occupancy, these buildings had hundreds of families living on top of each other with kids filling up the wide-open

24.4

24.5

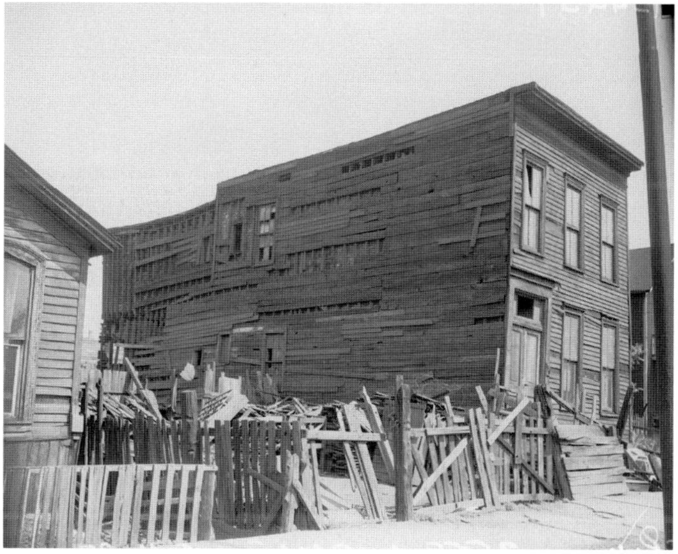
24.6

gallery hallways and the grassy open spaces down below. While the architecture itself was not significant, other than some interesting structural aspects of the design, these developments represented the architecture of modern public housing in the United States.

Based on what was there before, it is understandable why some considered these developments a better alternative. Despite such modern features as hot running water, the demise of the high rise was foreshadowed while still in the design stage. Housing expert Catherine Bauer condemned these "super tenements" for their lack of community scale. Similarly, the Chicago American Institute of Architects chapter concluded soon after the last unit was leased at the Robert Taylor Homes that high-rise buildings were the wrong format for housing families and children.

Despite these concerns, the city and the CHA obviously promoted the high rise as the means to "modernize" aging communities and house a growing postwar population. As a CHA official described:

Virtually all new construction in the city is high-rise. Families who either must or want to live in an urban area will have to learn to live with the high-rise building for all large centers of population must plan for accommodating an ever increasing number of people within a prescribed land area.[3]

Several reasons are often cited. From a design standpoint, building up meant more

24.7

24.8

24.9

24.10

24.7 Lake Meadows, circa 1960. Photograph by Betty Hulett. Courtesy of the Chicago Historical Society, , ICHi-25341.

24.8 Demolishing Mecca Flats, 1951. Photograph by Bernie R. Davis. Courtesy of the Chicago Historical Society, ICHi-24831.

24.9 Mecca Flats, 1951. Photograph by Ledward B. Dumetz, Jr. Courtesy of the Chicago Historical Society, ICHi-31789.

24.10 Crown Hall, Illinois Institute of Technology, 1955. Photograph by Bill Engdahl, Hedrich-Blessing Photo. HB-18506-Z4, courtesy of the Hedrich-Blessing collection, Chicago Historical Society.

units on the site and more open space, providing a park for families to congregate and children to play in. When compared to low-rise structures, the high rise was assumed to be cost-effective in terms of construction, because it could exploit new technology and materials (e.g., poured concrete framing). It also could save time and political capital acquiring land, since less was needed overall to produce more units of public housing.

Nationwide, the high rise also helped to solve a practical development problem created by the 1949 Housing Act, which included an ambitious plan to build 810,000 units of public housing in just five years. If for no other reason than meeting annual production quotas, erecting modernist "towers in the park" could help advance national policy goals. However, to build at such a speed, help from private sector developers was needed. This meant public housing production had to be profitable. In the end, these behemoths usually were profitable despite federal budget constraints. However, this profit came only after the overall per unit construction cost was reduced by scaling back room size, using shoddy materials, and skimping on basic construction practices (e.g., not insulating elevator shafts).[4]

The business community supported development of high-rise public housing but only because of the role it played in getting federal funding to help lure more of the middle class into the city and hopefully revitalize the city's downtown.[5] In other words, large urban renewal grants turned their gaze to the south where the "slum" was standing in the way of progress and encroaching on the central business district. Urban renewal was the solution to the problem because it created a means to contain poor people and to build up a buffer that could separate poor blacks from the downtown. Two new high-rise developments, Lake Meadows and Prairie Shores, were built up at the north end of the urban renewal site and were considered perfectly suitable for middle-income families.

In addition, urban renewal helped the Illinois Institute of Technology (IIT) expand after apartment buildings like Mecca Flats were demolished, despite resident protests, and replaced with buildings like Ludwig Mies van der Rohe's Crown Hall. So what made buildings like the Mecca Flats a slum in the first place? Some argue that middle-class "black flight" caused conditions to deteriorate as those left behind were without role models and economic stability.[6] However, this diminishes and even conceals the role played by deliberate disinvestment by public officials, banks, and private property owners—an important point to keep in mind as the wrecking ball is being swung again.[7]

Tear Down

The high rise changed the architecture of poverty on Chicago's South Side, making it more visible to the middle class driving by on their way downtown. As a resident of Robert Taylor Homes described in 1965: "The world looks on all of us as project rats, living on a reservation like untouchables."[8]

From today's vantage, residents feel a slightly different gaze as policymakers and politicians return their attention south again. For some, these homes in the sky are too visible now in a city trying to position itself as world-class. Following years of disinvestment, Chicago is making plans to transform public housing. This time, the idea is to return to the scale and architecture of fifty years ago, which means fewer units of public housing for current residents but also for poor people in the future.

Transforming public housing in Chicago—in the United States, for that matter—relies on an image of the high rise as an architectural villain of sorts; a menace that socially isolates the poor and prevents families from being exposed to the cultural norms and mores that induce the middle class to work and be responsible members of society. As victims of architecture, the scale and height of buildings have trapped them in a space that makes it hard to escape poverty.

While this image justifies demolition of family high-rise buildings, it does not really come up when the discussion turns to similar buildings occupied by older adults. Instead, these are being renovated. In Chicago, as in many other cities, the public housing high rise has a restricted use now: senior citizens only. Poor families can live nearby, but only in row houses or small multifamily buildings, and only if there is a mix of income groups and public housing residents are not the majority.

In Chicago, the high rise hasn't been eliminated from the architecture of public housing, it just has had its role diminished. In this sense, the occupants rather than the architecture have been transformed. And while the remaining senior citizen high rises keep poverty on the horizon, they also draw attention to the irony of demolishing fifty-one public housing buildings in a city where there is a shortage of affordable housing for families and an abundance of new luxury high-rise condominiums recently added to the skyline. Many of these new buildings are not designed for families, and those that are, generally market to middle- and upper-income people who have the resources to afford living in the now upscale neighborhoods nearby where high-rise public housing once stood.

24.11 Dearborn Street looking north to Stateway Gardens, 1959. Photograph by Clarence Hines. Courtesy of the Chicago Historical Society, ICHi-35845.

24.12 Clybourn Avenue looking south to Orchard Park with senior public housing, near Cabrini Green, 2003. Photograph by Janet Smith.

24.13 Waiting for demolition, Robert Taylor Homes, 2003. Photograph by Bill Lerch.

24.11

24.12

24.13

High-rise public housing made poverty both visible and invisible in Chicago. Clearly, it did not help people get out of poverty; however, it did guarantee that thousands of families had a home even when they had no money to pay rent. This has changed now. While the architecture of poverty has been diminished, poverty itself, especially among families, has not. The question now is, will the middle class remember that poor families exist on the South Side now that the visual referent has been removed? As longstanding activist and public housing resident Wardell Yotagan said when demolition was first proposed: "Once you tear these high-rise buildings down, you don't have to know I exist any more."[9]

25

Understanding Chicago's High-Rise Public Housing Disaster

D. Bradford Hunt

During their less than half century in existence, Chicago's high-rise public housing projects descended into a disaster of massive proportions. Projects such as Cabrini-Green and the Robert Taylor Homes are today internationally recognized symbols of concentrated poverty, national neglect, and policy failure. Moreover, the history of the creation of the Chicago Housing Authority's (CHA) elevator buildings has devolved into myth, with limited understanding of the ideas, forces, and incentives that led to their construction. Many observers blame modernist architecture and racial discrimination for the monstrous high-rise designs that blighted Chicago's neighborhoods. Yet a detailed look at the historical context and administrative decisions that shaped the CHA's projects tells a story that has far more to do with bureaucratic concerns than any other single explanation. Tragically, after a handful of early experiments, planners understood by the mid-1950s that high rises were a counterproductive choice for families with children. From 1955 to 1959, the CHA actively fought to use low-rise designs for future projects but was blocked by federal officials obsessed with cost considerations. Reluctantly, Chicago officials plodded ahead with high rises despite reservations and built the city's most ill-conceived housing complexes. Multiple factors contributed to the demise of these buildings, but primary among them was the inherent difficulty of housing unprecedented numbers of children in a high-rise environment. The resulting social chaos chased out working-class tenants, leaving public housing with the additional burden of concentrated poverty. Struck by two blows—chaotic youth densities followed by crushing poverty—Chicago's projects never recovered, and the city's poor paid a terrible price.

The historical context in which the CHA developed its public housing complexes after World War II included planning assumptions, political pressures, and bureaucratic incentives. The planning assumptions originated from a generation of progressive advocacy on behalf of low-income housing and urban redevelopment. First, progressive planners argued that the private market would never adequately serve the "bottom third" of the income scale with decent, safe, and affordable housing. The market failure involved both supply (not enough affordable apartments) and physical condition (too many dilapidated apartments). Serious housing shortages during the war confirmed for progressives that market failure was structural and could be remedied only with the construction of large amounts of publicly sponsored housing.[1] Although difficult to predict at the time, private construction actually rebounded rapidly in the postwar period (due in part to federal subsidies), and the extent of market failure receded significantly by the 1950s.[2]

A second planning assumption involved the desirability of rebuilding the city's slums. Chicago's progressives, supported by selected downtown business interests, agreed that large swaths of land surrounding the central business district—nearly ten square miles of Chicago—were "blighted" and beyond saving. These areas, they argued, would need wholesale clearance and large-scale rebuilding to rescue the city from stagnation (fig. 25.1).[3] The CHA, arguably the city's most progressive public agency between 1938 and 1951, expected to be the major player in this rebuilding. In 1949, as a first phase, the CHA proposed to build 25,000 apartments on cleared slum land in five years and another 15,000 on vacant land. The vacant land units were to be used as relocation housing to facilitate the rapid emptying, clearance, and rebuilding of the slums. Further, the CHA "conservatively" estimated in 1949 that 105,000 public housing units would be needed to replace slums and address market failure.[4] To give some perspective to these ambitious numbers, the CHA's entire postwar production of public housing on slum sites amounted to fewer than 20,000 units over twenty years.

Three additional planning assumptions shaped Chicago's postwar projects. First, given the belief in a perpetual housing shortage and given the rising cost of urban land, planners proposed that slum sites should be redeveloped at relatively high population densities. The Chicago Plan Commission's 1943 master plan envisioned 50,000 people per square mile on rebuilt land, a figure actually on par with the city's overcrowded slums.[5] Such densities would later restrict the CHA's design options. Second, given the perceived urgency for action, planners pushed for large-scale projects with thousands of units. In a 1945 speech, CHA Executive Director Elizabeth Wood (the city's leading housing progressive) argued that rebuilding "must be bold and comprehensive—or it is useless and wasted."[6] She rejected as unsound and uneconomical the suggestion that her agency carry out selective demolition and targeted renovation to address the slum problem.[7] To be fair, Wood suggested smaller projects would be "islands in a sea of blight," but fundamentally, housing progressives viewed large areas of the city as unsalvageable. Slum clearance and large-scale redevelopment became the CHA's primary mission in the postwar period, and the massive size of Cabrini-Green (3,600 units), the ABLA complex (Addams, Brooks, Loomis, and Abbott projects, 700 units), and the Wells group (3,500 units) were the vision of the CHA's progressive leadership.[8]

Political pressures—revolving almost entirely around issues of race—also played a significant but not all-determining role in influencing the shape of public housing in Chicago. The massive migration of African Americans escaping the Jim Crow South strained postwar race relations in the city to the breaking point. Whites used a variety of tools—including racial violence—to enforce segregated residential boundaries, but the increase from 278,000 African Americans in 1940 to 813,000 in 1960 put enormous pressure on housing markets. Panic peddling, white flight, and racial transition were the postwar norm in most (but not all) South and West Side neighborhoods as

25.1 Chicago's blighted areas, 1942. Courtesy of the Chicago Plan Commission.

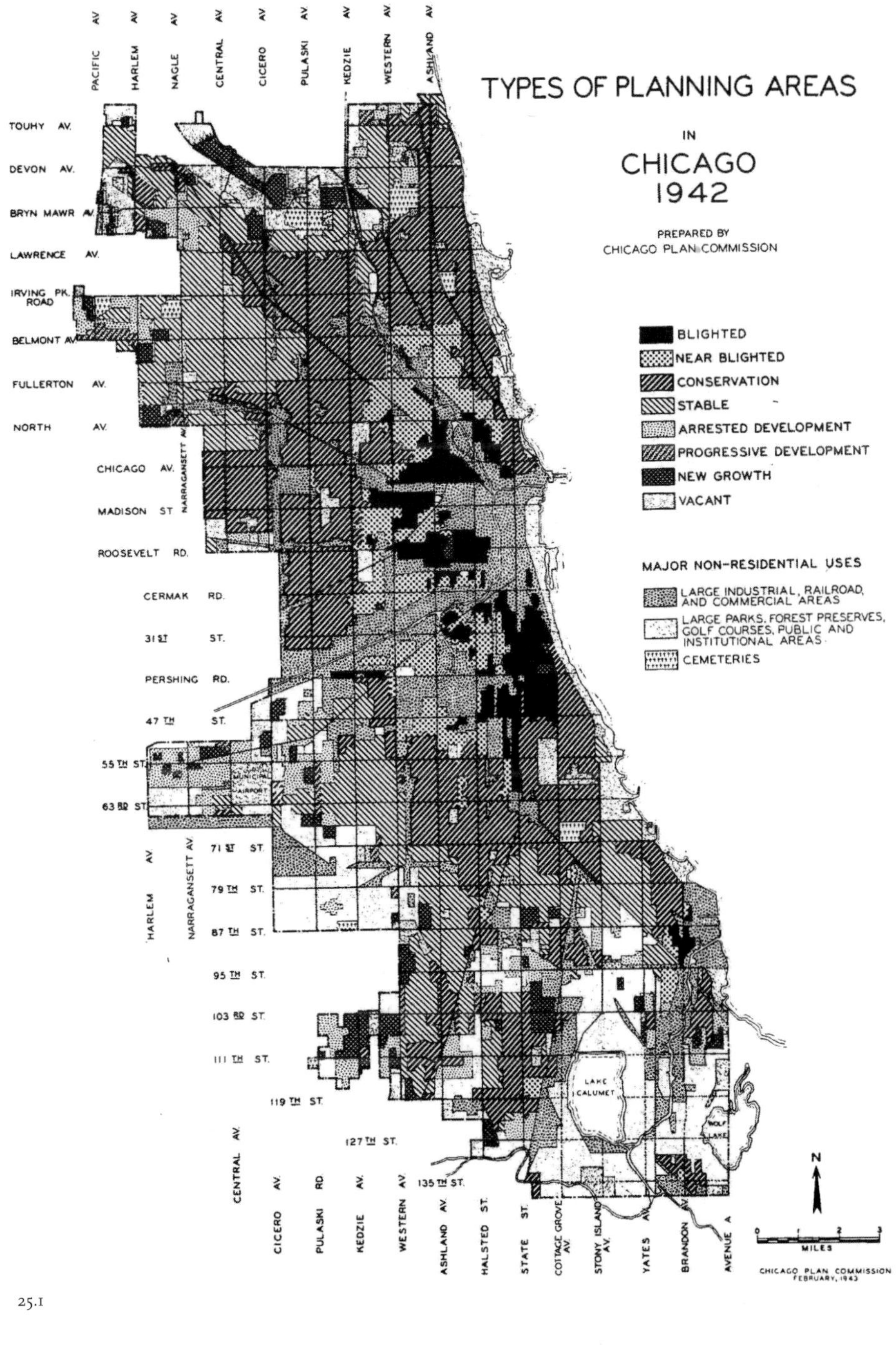

25.1

working- and middle-class African Americans desperately sought relief from overcrowded prewar ghettoes.[9] In this atmosphere, aldermen in white areas refused to support the construction of public housing in their neighborhoods, especially after 1946 when the CHA signaled its intention to racially integrate new projects. Meanwhile, most black aldermen embraced public housing as a vast improvement over slum conditions.[10] Between 1948 and 1951, reactionary whites in the city council clashed with the CHA over sites and integration, a battle that eventually cost Elizabeth Wood her job in 1954.[11]

As a result of these political forces, the CHA could not win significant relocation housing on vacant land in outlying white neighborhoods, nor could it be a force for residential integration, as Wood had hoped. But integration was only one part of Wood's agenda—her primary goal was to rebuild the city's slums with public housing. The fight with the city council was never over the mutually exclusive options of placing public housing entirely on vacant land or entirely on slum sites occupied by African Americans. The CHA wanted to rebuild slums, the worst of which were disproportionately occupied by blacks; it argued that vacant land housing was needed to expedite clearance. That is, even if the CHA had received the vacant land sites it wanted between 1948 and 1951, it would still have pursued the wholesale rebuilding of black slums.[12] Indeed, after the war, the first four sites picked by the CHA's progressive leadership were in slum neighborhoods housing African Americans.[13]

A final historical context influencing Chicago's postwar projects consisted of the incentives created by the 1937 Housing Act. Under the act, 90 percent of all costs—site clearance, design, and construction—was paid by the federal government, while cities could meet their 10 percent contribution through tax exemption.[14] This formula essentially offered free money to local housing authorities, and Chicago eagerly sought maximum allotments from Washington.[15] Even after Wood's ouster, Mayor Richard J. Daley (1955–1976), embraced public housing construction (though, again, not in white neighborhoods). His enthusiasm was in part due to his interest in rebuilding the city and in part because of the federal dollars the act brought to the city's builders and unions.[16]

Within this historical and planning context, the CHA still faced the challenges of designing successful public housing projects. Before World War II, the CHA had built low-rise projects exclusively, but in 1945, it turned on its own initiative to the multistory elevator building as the future for its slum clearance projects. Wood and her staff studied New York City's prewar high-rise projects, including the East River Houses, and came away impressed with the combination of high density and park space offered by the design. The CHA directed its architects to follow New York's lead.[17] While the Corbusian

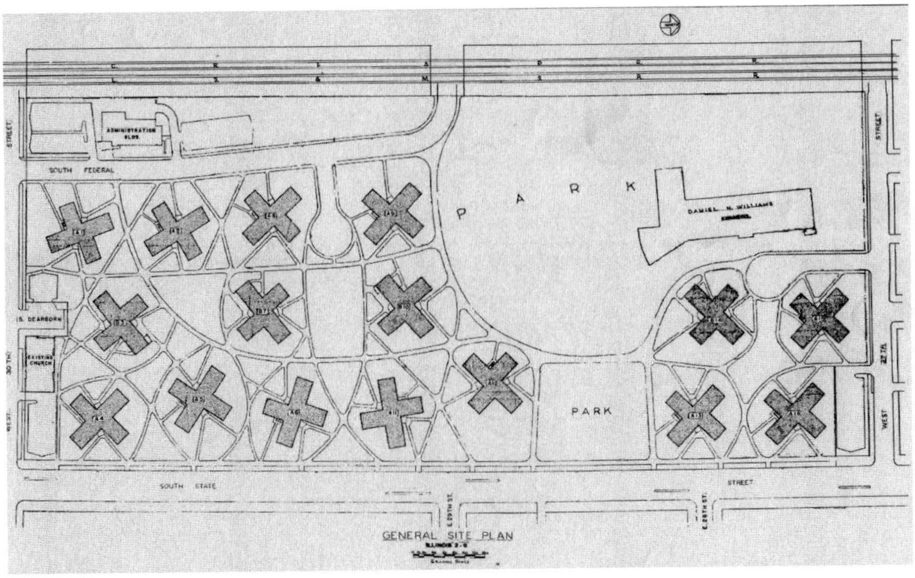

25.2 Dearborn Homes site plan, 1947. Courtesy of the Chicago Housing Authority.

term "tower in the park" does not appear in CHA literature, the high-rise form seemed to solve the dilemma of building large amounts of housing on scarce land without paving the entire space. In a letter to a friendly alderman explaining the CHA's 1945 decision to build its first high-rise development, the eight-hundred-unit Dearborn Homes (fig. 25.2), Wood explained that "high-rises allowed for more open park space" than earlier designs:

> The determination to construct six-story elevators instead of three-story walk-ups that the same density will permit was made on the same basis as our desire to achieve a more attractive pattern for the use of the land. The use of these elevator structures gives us wide-open spaces, larger playgrounds, and a general effect of a park that will not be possible if the land were developed as three-story walk-ups.[18]

While the choice to build mid-rises rather than equally viable low rises in 1945 suggested the influence of Corbusian modernism, Wood called Dearborn Homes "an experiment," acknowledging the risks in pushing the CHA toward high rises.[19]

But the CHA's desire to build as many units as possible overrode any concerns. Two years later it revised its Dearborn Homes plans and raised the height of several buildings from six to nine stories, thereby increasing the size of the complex to eight hundred units. The new design created a density even greater than that envisioned by the Chicago Plan Commission.[20] But the CHA argued that the in-

25.3

25.3 Loomis Courts, gallery, 1952. Courtesy of the Chicago Housing Authority.

25.4

25.4 Loomis Courts, 1950. Courtesy of the Chicago Housing Authority.

creased density would "change the picture of the future community little . . . and the present serious overcrowding in the Negro areas indicates the need for an augmented supply of housing for Negroes of the low-income group."[21] Given Chicago's housing shortage, particularly for African Americans, Wood and African American CHA Chairman Robert R. Taylor (1943–51) moved to maximize density and not waste the opportunity to expand the city's housing stock. The resulting projects were often built at a higher density than the surrounding neighborhoods.

The experimental phase of high-rise design continued between 1948 and 1950 in five City-State projects, named after their funding sources.[22] Again, the CHA could have developed low rises, as state and city laws placed few restrictions on cost or design. But the struggle between the city council and the CHA over sites produced only small parcels, and the CHA sought to make the most of the available space.[23] Still, the CHA approached its mid-rises cautiously and worked with such emerging Chicago architects as Harry Weese to develop a range of projects. Wood encouraged efforts to "humanize" the designs by using "gallery" arrangements that offered outdoor corridors as entryways to apartments. The gallery innovation is most clearly seen in Loomis Courts, a project singled out for praise by an architectural advisory board of the federal Public Housing Administration (PHA) (figs. 25.3, 25.4).[24] At the time, one architectural critic applauded the innovation as "sidewalks in the air," but these galleries would later be condemned as an unfortunate design decision.[25]

Still, even as these projects were being developed, doubts about their efficacy grew in Washington, D.C., and Chicago. In 1950, a major policy bulletin from the PHA labeled high rises the "least desirable" form of public housing and used a surprisingly strong tone in counseling against them:

The grave and serious problems incident to the rearing of children in such [high-rise] housing are too well known to warrant any comment, nor are the management difficulties which go with such projects subject to any complete remedy. All of these disadvantages are so great and so thoroughly understood that local housing authorities familiar with the problem would counsel this type of housing only because local conditions enforce it as the only solution for a specific neighborhood. In those localities where the cost of land would make other types prohibitive in total development cost, such housing is virtually the only solution.[26]

If high-rise designs have to be used, the PHA emphasized, "every conceivable device short of those involving extravagant expenditures should be utilized to mitigate the disadvantages of apartment living."[27]

The bulletin's warnings were issued as a preface to a set of revised rules on density and cost that further restricted design choices. The changes created limits that made it nearly impossible to build anything but high rises on land deemed "high-cost," which included all of Chicago's slum clearance sites. The new standard required fifty units per acre for projects built on high-cost slum land, and neither row houses nor walk-ups could be accommodated at this density.[28] The rationale for greater density related to cost and total public housing output. More units per acre would dilute fixed land costs to keep per-unit total costs within politically acceptable bounds. The bulletin came in response to alarmingly high costs per unit at the first postwar complexes. Truman administration officials, who had experienced ongoing fights in Congress over the public housing program's legitimacy, feared a public relations disaster if costs were not brought under control.[29] Ironically, this 1950 decision and the resulting high-rise designs did more to damage public housing's political image than any balance sheet on costs.

In Chicago by late 1951, Elizabeth Wood had also turned against high rises. In a January 1952 *Architectural Forum* issue devoted to the question of high-rise housing, Wood made "The Case for the Low Apartment." Taking a child-centered perspective, she argued:

25.5

The row-house solution is simple and natural. The indoor-outdoor activity takes place close to where the mother is at work. The child can keep in touch with her. . . . But in an apartment house project, where playgrounds are carefully arranged at some distance, vertical as well as horizontal, from the family supper table, there will be much less parent-child play. . . .[30]

Despite her defense of row houses, Wood stopped short of publicly criticizing the Truman administration or calling for a halt to the CHA's designs for large-scale public housing projects, then on the drawing board and awaiting PHA approval and funding.

In 1951, Chicago had five federally funded slum-clearance sites under development.[31] By 1953, costs in acquiring the sites by condemnation had exceeded estimates, and to keep costs per unit within acceptable boundaries, the PHA forced design changes at several projects.[32] The Cabrini Extension (1,921 units) project went through three iterations, rising from a collection of seven-, nine-, and sixteen-story buildings to its completed form of seven-, ten-, and nineteen-story buildings. Density increased only slightly, from 51 units per acre to 54, but most savings were found by deleting one entire building while adding floors to the remaining buildings at a relatively low marginal cost, helping drive down the all-important total development cost per unit.[33]

While these new plans were being negotiated, administrators in the early 1950s were experiencing serious problems in managing the CHA's early high rises. Elevator systems broke down frequently, involving considerable expense; children playing elevator tag were often blamed. Worse, several rapes in elevators in one project in 1956 fueled grave safety concerns. Small-scale vandalism created large problems. In 1958, the CHA reported replacing 18,000 light bulbs per month. In 1959, vandals turned on a fire hose on the ninth floor of one recently opened building at Stateway Gardens, flooding and severely damaging the eight floors below.[34]

With significant problems in existing high rises readily apparent, the CHA in 1955 made a dramatic change in its design program. It proposed developing its next wave of projects—which would include the Robert Taylor Homes and the William Green Homes (of Cabrini-Green)—as four-story buildings (fig. 25.6).[35] The CHA took this idea to Washington, which had the final say on designs. After much delay, Washington replied that the plans were too expensive, as each apartment would cost over $20,000 to build at a time when a new house in the suburbs could be purchased for around $15,000.[36]

For four years, the CHA pleaded with federal officials for approval of its low-rise design, with both sides arguing over costs. Federal officials pointed to weak bidding practices that stifled competition; the CHA commissioned a study that blamed federal red tape.[37]

25.5 Maplewood Courts, 1952. Courtesy of the Chicago Housing Authority.

25.6 Sketch of CHA's proposed four-story public housing, 1957. Courtesy of the Chicago Housing Authority.

25.6

Mayor Richard J. Daley traveled to Washington twice in 1959 to lobby on behalf of the CHA's new low-rise designs. He testified before the Senate: "We have constant harassment and difference of opinion on architectural plans in the desire to try to improve what is now public housing, in the desire to make it not only high rises but also walk-up and row houses."[38] But Daley's lobbying failed, and federal officials refused to budge in 1959. Washington offered Chicago only high rises.

The CHA never fully admitted the dilemmas that had brought it to this impasse. Its waiting lists were clogged with low-income African American families with five or more children.[39] Such large families needed apartments with three or more bedrooms, but large apartments cost more than smaller ones. Costs could be reduced if inexpensive vacant land sites were available, but the city council said "no" for racist reasons. Given this political reality, the only way to reduce costs was to increase density and build up. But the CHA knew that high rises and children did not mix. The only visible way out of this box was to get Washington to exempt the CHA from its cost rules and approve the expensive four-story design on slum sites, which would provide large apartments without elevators. As CHA Executive Director Alvin Rose explained in a letter to the PHA during the height of the battle in 1958:

(Your cost limits) left this authority and the city administration with one of the following decisions to make: (1) Should sound and sensible

25.7

planning concepts be ignored and site densities increased so that the reduction in land costs per dwelling could absorb the rise in construction costs, or (2) should low-income families living in unsafe and unsanitary buildings be left in this environment. . . .[40]

But Washington would not approve expensive low-rise designs, and in September 1959, with sites cleared and embarrassingly vacant, Chicago capitulated and agreed to redesign 9,000 units of housing as high-rise projects (fig. 25.7).[41] Almost 80 percent of these units were large apartments with three, four, and five bedrooms. Once filled with children, these projects proved to be impossible to manage and catastrophic to public housing.

The problem with high-rise buildings was not their modernist design, it was their unsuitability for large numbers of children. The staggering demographic fact of public housing in Chicago was that, by design, it contained unprecedented numbers of youth compared to the numbers of adults. Public housing was literally overrun by children, creating social chaos in high rises that quickly sent them spiraling downward. The decline was compounded by the lack of government intervention to support the social programs and additional maintenance so desperately needed in a child-centered environment.

A typical Chicago neighborhood has a mix of family types—single people, couples without children, families with children, and the elderly. In 1960, the average

25.7 Sketch of Robert Taylor Homes, 1960. Courtesy of the Chicago Housing Authority.

25.8 Concentration of youth: a comparison. Diagram by D. Bradford Hunt.

25.9 Robert Taylor Homes, playground, no date (1964?). Courtesy of the Chicago Housing Authority.

25.10 Elevators at Henry Horner Homes, 1967. Courtesy of the Chicago Housing Authority.

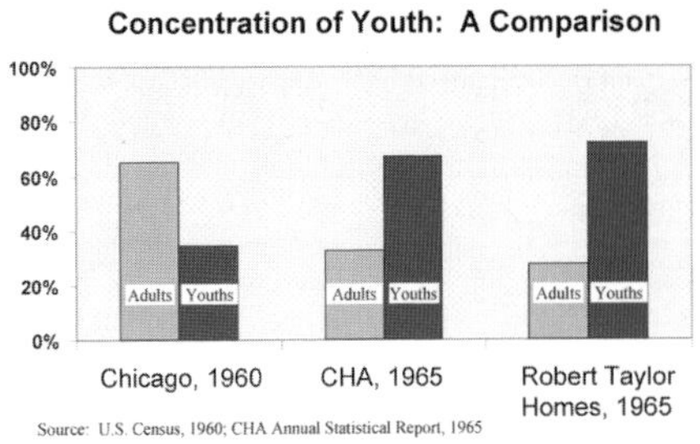

25.8

25.9

25.10

Chicago neighborhood had two adults for every minor, and no neighborhood had more youths than adults—except public housing complexes (fig. 25.8).[42] In high-rise projects, the CHA housed twice as many minors as adults—an inversion of the ratio in the rest of the city. The Robert Taylor Homes opened in 1963 as a predominantly working-class project with mostly two-parent families with employment income. But there were 21,000 youths, and 7,000 adults.[43] This demographic imbalance created an untenable social environment.

Compounding the problem, the CHA did not provide the social services, community facilities, or even the playgrounds necessary to deal with large concentrations of children. In 1964, less than a year after the Robert Taylor Homes opened, the CHA asked federal officials for more funds for playgrounds, reporting that "children often lined up seven and eight deep to use playground equipment and upwards of 2,000 children may be cramped into one or two relatively small play areas" (fig. 25.9).[44] Children also overwhelmed the inadequate branch libraries opened in several high-rise projects. The story was the same for other institutions such as the public schools, the park district, and the Boy Scouts.[45] The CHA and the city, in part for racist reasons and in part because of the overwhelming magnitude of the problem, simply did not dedicate the resources needed to handle the huge number of youths in the high rises.

As a result, the destructive impulses of youth were often directed on the buildings themselves. Breakdowns of major systems, including elevators, trash chutes, lighting, and plumbing, were connected to children looking for an outlet for their energy. Of these, elevator failure proved the most devastating, as elevators were the major arteries for high-rise buildings; tenants were willing to walk up stairs to upper floors for only so long (fig. 25.10).[46] The point here is not to blame families with many children or even the children themselves—that would be blaming the victims of an inappropriate housing policy. Instead, concentrating children at extraordinary densities was a crucial mistake in public housing management history.

These densities not only led to vandalism and infrastructure decay, they also drove out the working class from public housing. As a result, projects cascaded downward as increasingly concentrated poverty fueled budget crises and maintenance neglect. When a new building opened during the 1950s or early 1960s, whether low rise or high rise, the CHA was able to fill it with a majority of working-class, two-parent families. But these families did not stay long. Some were repelled by the social chaos in high-rise buildings, while others were asked to leave because their incomes had grown too high—a rule started in the 1930s and not modified until 1979. Finally, the increasingly affordable private housing market of the late 1960s gave working-class African Americans housing options, and working-class public housing residents were pulled back into the private market.

This exodus of the working class is shown in stark terms in figure 25.11, which measures the median income of public housing residents in inflation-adjusted terms. During the early 1960s, when large numbers of new apartments opened, average tenant income actually rose. But after 1966, with projects such as the Robert Taylor Homes only four years old, the flight of the working class started—and then accelerated. A small portion of tenants became impoverished and remained, but figure 25.11 points more clearly to a massive turnover in which the working class moved out, and those without jobs moved in.[47]

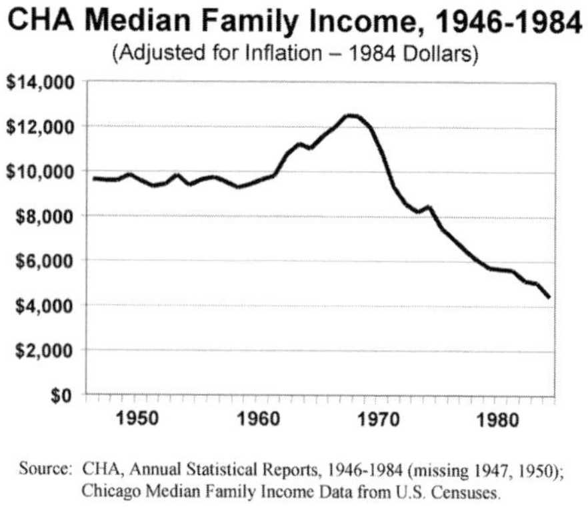

25.11 CHA median family income, 1946–84. Table by D. Bradford Hunt.

The loss of the working class dealt a shattering blow to the CHA's financial health. Per federal rules established in 1937, the CHA depended on income from tenant rents for its maintenance budget. But since rents were set as a percentage of tenant income, as average tenant income dropped, so did the CHA's budget—at precisely the time when the CHA needed more money to manage its increasingly poor clientele. With the CHA deferring maintenance because of budget problems and with poverty growing, it entered a tailspin. With each unfixed elevator, with each vandalized mailroom, with each broken garbage system, those with options sought housing elsewhere. The high rises suffered first and drained the CHA's budget, eventually dragging down conditions at the low rises as well. By 1974, the working class had fled, and only 15 percent of residents reported full-time work. In 1964, just ten years earlier, 65 percent of households had had a full-time wage earner.[48]

The tragic history of high-rise public housing in Chicago is a more complex story than previously suggested. Bureaucratic cost pressures, themselves shaped by a planning and political context, proved far more important than trends in architecture or outright racism in determining public housing's size, shape, and ultimate failure. The communities created were unsustainable because they placed enormous numbers of youths and few adults into a high-rise environment and because tenant rents were expected to support maintenance. This predictable formula for disaster was recognized—if never bluntly stated—by the city and federal administrators involved. Yet, despite the apparent disagreements between Chicago and Washington, stunningly few voices were raised in opposition to the overall shape of the program and the decisions being made.[49] Instead, bureaucratic cost considerations trumped reasonable planning, and benign neglect substituted for critical evaluation. The resulting high rises proved to be a disaster not only for Chicago but also for cities like St. Louis, Philadelphia, Newark, and

San Francisco. Moreover, the failure of large-scale public housing as executed in the postwar period undermined the entire validity of state-sponsored housing in the United States. Today, vouchers for private sector housing and mixed-income, privately managed, New Urbanist designs are the only form of acceptable public intervention. Slowly, cities like Chicago have recovered, but only by undertaking an ironic and expensive second wave of slum clearance—this time of public housing—to wipe clean the mistakes of a previous generation.

Bas-Relief Urbanism: Chicago's Figured Field[1]

Sarah Whiting

Even fans of Ludwig Mies van der Rohe's campus for the Illinois Institute of Technology (IIT, 1939–58) frequently describe the project as an autonomous island, a tabula rasa that disregards its physical and social context. Such an interpretation is only reinforced by Mies's presentation collages, which ruthlessly eliminated one hundred acres of the city's dense urban fabric in order to make way for the expansive, low-density campus (fig. 26.1). Architectural culture has itself played a significant role in isolating both Mies and IIT from their context and turning them into "absolutist black holes" or icons of modernism. While the campus has been recognized for its structural integrity and elegance as well as for its innovative approach to American campus design, it has yet to be recognized as a productive urban model. When studied in relation to Chicago's Near South Side during the 1940s, however, another, more effective reading of IIT emerges: rather than a singular black hole, the campus forms an integral component of a larger, more complex and multifarious field. Mies's plan for IIT initiated a new form of modern urbanism; at once figural and abstract, figure and ground, the IIT campus proffers what I propose to call a bas-relief urbanism. This new approach to urbanism was part of a larger reconceptualization of modernism that ultimately redefined the urban subject, creating a publicly empathetic subject: a member of a collective field who was simultaneously individualized by his or her particular experience within that field.

To understand IIT and the Near South Side of Chicago as a horizontal bas-relief of interconnecting and overlapping superblocks is to highlight Mies's empathetic urban project for the campus, which has been overshadowed both by the initial process of land clearance that made the project possible and by the architecture eventually installed there. The urban bas-relief inflects the horizontal ground plane, permitting the surface itself to exhibit its socioeconomic contours. It is a figural landscape, but not a figurative one: while the figures that it forms are not recognizable as typical urban forms, they are nevertheless differentiated, unlike the homogenous uniformity of a grid. The urban bas-relief ultimately unfolds the oppositional structure between modernism and its beaux-arts counterpart, for Mies's reintroduction of a figural urbanism does not represent a beaux-arts redemption or an overthrow of the modernist field, but a combination of the two that is itself parallel to the bas-relief's blending of figure and ground.

Although the trope of the bas-relief is most striking as a formal analogy, it additionally operates as a diagram of political overlaps and economic contingencies. Chicago's Near South Side Plan formed a gravitational field of interdependent urban influences, each emanating from one of the area's institutions. From the late 1930s through the early 1950s, the Near South Side, just south of the Loop, was developed into a collection of institutions whose frequently coincident corporate boards suggest that what might look to be separate superblocks in the urban fabric were in fact largely overlapping (fig. 26.2).

26.1 Illinois Institute of Technology Campus: photomontage aerial view showing model within Near South Side (detail). Mies van der Rohe office, 1947. Hedrich-Blessing Photo. HB-19232, courtesy of the Hedrich-Blessing Collection, Chicago Historical Society.

26.2 South Side Planning Board Redevelopment Plan for Chicago's Near South Side. In John McKinley, *Redevelopment Project, Number 1: A Second Report* (New York: New York Life Insurance Company, 1950). Courtesy of the Canadian Centre for Architecture.

26.1

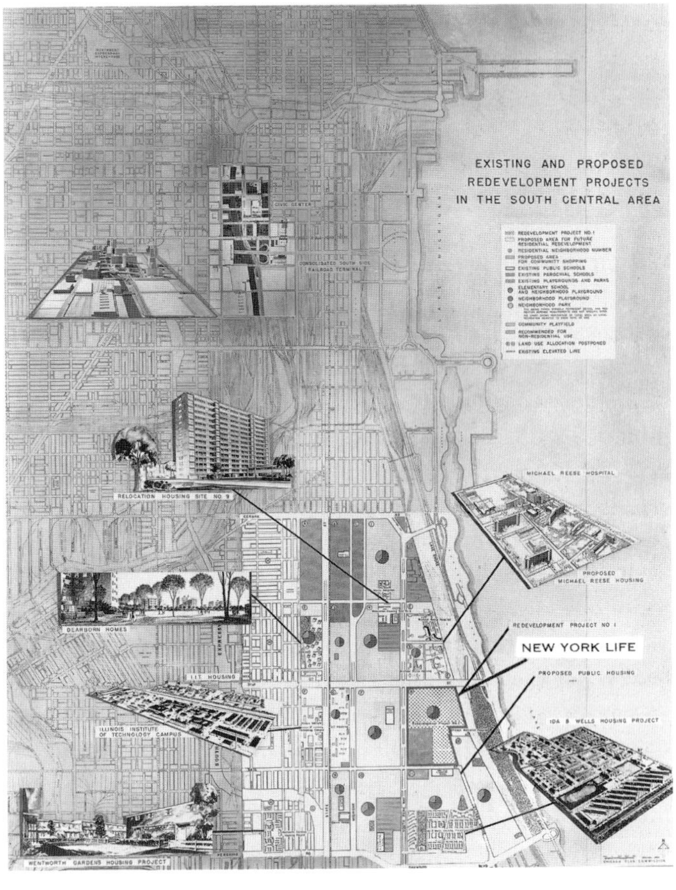

26.2

Beginning with IIT, and later including Michael Reese Hospital, the Chicago Housing Authority, Mercy Hospital, and several private housing developments, a group of institutions collaborated under the name of the South Side Planning Board to plan and execute one of the first large-scale modern urban plans in the United States. This seven-square-mile plan paved the way for the federal slum clearance, redevelopment, and urban renewal legislation, including the Housing Acts of 1949 and 1954. In addition to Mies and Ludwig Hilberseimer from IIT, key figures involved in the promotion of the Near South Side Plan included Walter Gropius, planners Reginald Isaacs and Walter Blucher, real estate developer Fred Kramer, IIT president Henry Heald, and University of Chicago sociologist Louis Wirth, among others.

Influenced by the British economist John Maynard Keynes, American urban policy became the foundation for a new form of architectural development that consciously sought to reflect this complex alliance of public and private domains. By reintroducing urban difference into modernism's urban field, this alternative planning strategy redefined metropolitan order, as can be seen in the example of Chicago's Near South Side. First, the formal terms of this plan's order were more field- than object-derived. Unlike modernism's field, however, this postwar field was not homogeneous, but variegated—it maintained rather than eliminated gravitational forces. Second, what could be called its foreground or monumental buildings were devoted not to civic or ecclesiastical programs but rather to private and semiprivate institutional ones that nevertheless actively engaged and redefined the postwar public realm.

Reflecting new economic alliances, the Near South Side Plan also projected a protean synthesis of otherwise autonomous social, political, and aesthetic tableaux. In so doing, the public-private plan offered a new visual and spatial language for America's postwar democracy. As the United States adopted a significant global role during the 1940s, it sought physical manifestations of its self-assigned status as the flag bearer of democracy as well as the engine of the world's economy. The appropriate means for depicting this role were not immediately obvious, however: in order to reinforce the country's future orientation, the representation of postwar America had to be contemporary and, therefore, could not rely upon classical democratic motifs. Further, architecture and urbanism had to promote collectivity without succumbing to the specter of totalitarian collectivism. This speculative image had to depict a flexible, variegated unity.

The gridded urban fabric of Chicago's Near South Side, untouched by the Great Fire of 1871, had constituted Chicago's original "Gold Coast," but by the 1920s the area was characterized more by its burgeoning industries, which took advantage of the area's rail and water access, than by its residential splendor.[2] Restrictive covenants made it diffi-

26.3 "Some of their Offspring." A cartoon by Joseph Parrish published in the *Chicago Tribune*, December 19, 1952. Reprinted in *Report to Chicagoans, 1947–52* (Chicago: Land Clearance Commission, 1952), inside cover. Courtesy of the *Chicago Tribune*.

cult for Chicago's rapidly increasing black population to purchase property other than on the South Side, which was how the narrow strip of land between the railroads and the industrial areas south of the Loop to Thirty-ninth Street acquired the nickname the "Black Belt."[3] Unbearable odors, sharply accentuated during Chicago's humid summers, wafted over the belt from the Keeley Brewery to the north and the stockyards to the west. As the neighborhood's elite moved out, many of the former mansions were divided into small flats, increasing the area's density. In contrast to the decline of the neighborhood's building stock was the rise of a vibrant social scene unique to the Black Belt. With the closing of New Orleans's Storyville in 1917, many jazz and blues musicians—including Louis Armstrong, Bessie Smith, and Leadbelly—had relocated to Chicago. In depicting this period, corporate histories of the institutions on the Near South Side romanticize the Black Belt's music scene for its exoticism but also criticize it for its influence on morals, claiming that many of the clubs violated Prohibition laws, were linked to bootlegging rings, and condoned drug use, gambling, and prostitution.[4] While a sincere desire to ameliorate slum conditions fuelled the drive for urban renewal, a genuine fear that this moral underbelly, combined with the deterioration of the area's building stock, would multiply and spread across Chicago, provided the immediate impetus to act (fig. 26.3).

While IIT's tabula rasa plan tends to be associated primarily with Mies, the school's expansion plan actually stemmed from decisions that predated Mies's arrival in Chicago in 1938. As early as 1933, the Armour Institute of Technology (AIT, which became IIT when it merged with the Lewis Institute of Technology in 1940) had begun looking to move away from the area. But by 1937 the Institute had decided to stay put. The decision to maintain the existing site was largely mandated by the much-publicized blighted condition of the neighborhood; the Institute could ill afford to purchase land elsewhere for what it would get from selling its holdings. Two initial campus schemes designed by AIT faculty members John Holabird and Alfred Alschuler were used by the development committee to raise funds for land purchasing. Both schemes adopt a City Beautiful, beaux-arts sensibility, complete with axes terminating in significantly programmed buildings. The awkwardness of inserting such a beaux-arts logic into the relentless grid reveals the primary challenge of IIT's design: how to give the campus an identity while making the design work with the urban layout of Chicago.

More of a third alternative than a mean between two extremes, the campus urbanism of Chicago's Near South Side combines the gravitational determinism of a baroque "point" urbanism with the dispersed logic of a modernist "field" logic. The "bas-relief" strategy inserts what one could call quasi figures into the field model, creating not points but overlapping zones of significance. The projects of the Near South Side are not singular, isolated, massive buildings and are not constructed of the materials and forms that underlie the codified vocabulary of traditional monumental civic architecture. Nor are they programmatically typical traditional monuments: the structures that comprise the Near South Side Plan are neither civic nor commemorative, but are instead private institutions that partially engage the public and thereby require a "public presence" within the city. In this particular example, a group of institutions—IIT, Michael Reese Hospital, Mercy Hospital, and the Chicago Housing Authority—worked together in an unusual form of voluntary political, economic, and urban collaboration in order to create overlapping influences over the entire Near South Side. IIT both initiated this collaborative, bas-relief urbanism and, simultaneously, was itself engendered by the new policy and planning legislation ushered in by this urbanism.

The potential for a bas-relief to engage a viewer had been theorized already in 1893 in Adolf von Hildebrand's book *Das Problem der Form in der bildenden Kunst* [The problem of form in the arts], which, as he stated in the text's introduction, "concerns the relation of form to appearance (*Erscheinung*), and its implications for artistic representation (*Darstellung*)." Hildebrand distinguished between two modes of perception: from far away, the viewer perceives an object as a two-dimensional surface, what Hildebrand calls "pure scanning," wherein the third dimension can be perceived only through contrasts, such as light versus dark. When close, the viewer cannot perceive the object in a single glance in this manner but has to move her eyes from point to point, reconstructing the entirety of the object in her mind—what Hildebrand refers to as "purely kinaesthetic eye activity."[5] Understanding IIT and the Near South Side projects within such a framework, there is similarly a global, aerial view that reveals each project to be a significant insertion within a larger context, and a close view, a kinaesthetic view, which is that of the individual within each campus. As indicated by an interview that appeared in the magazine *Modern Hospital* in 1945, Mies understood planning and architecture to be a combination of these two points of view. First, he saw the process as if he were looking down at a plan from far above, from whence he could get an objective, comprehensive view:

> The home has its various elements and the furnishings must be assigned to the elements in which they are to function appropriately. So it is with cities . . . ; they must be located by plan; nothing must be accidental. The various elements of community life must be composed in the plan and then all new buildings may rise unashamedly in the right places.[6]

But while Mies envisioned the world as a planar, fieldlike order where everything had its place, he also introduced a form of subjectivity into this composition. His desire for order reflected not simply a compositional drive but also a concern for the user's psychological well-being. Continuing his analogy, Mies noted the anxieties that can be brought on by a lack of order: "You are not really living in a house or an apartment on Moving Day, with the entire load of household effects dumped into a single room. . . . You plainly, if not silently, suffer there until furniture and equipment are put into their rightful places."[7] Everything has its rightful place, but urban order is experienced, not just surveyed. Mies's combination of objective and subjective siting techniques at IIT merged the ultraperspectival characteristics of the point city and the ultraplanar characteristics of the field city.

In contrast to the entirely abstract view of the high modernist plan diagram, Mies's bas-relief reintroduces a certain point of view, or subjectivity, though not the singular or constricted subjectivity that corresponds to the one-point perspective. While a plan view can be grasped immediately and does not depend upon a specific angle of vision, a reading of a bas-relief changes, even if only slightly, as the viewer changes position or as contextual conditions change, altering shadows, forms, and spatial relations. A bas-relief collapses distinctions between an abstract field and a figural object. In the friezes of the Parthenon, for example, figures emerge from the plane of the frieze, but still belong to that plane. In other words, because it introduces the z-axis, the bas-relief suggests subtle modulations, subtle differences across an otherwise even field. Depending on the observer's viewpoint, a figure can be seen emerging from the field, but the figure never separates completely from that field to become an independent object. Oftentimes, only the rendered shadows of Mies's axonometrics and perspectives offer any distinction between the campus's verticals and horizontals. Despite the very precise and mathematical determination of the campus grid and the scientific attention to programmatic requirements, it is the shadowy realm, the inexplicit, that conveys the most critical information—this shaded area is what turns the field into a figured field.

Upon the foundation of public and private investments, concerns, and speculations, a *modulated empathetic topography*—that is, a continuous but figured field—was put in place at IIT, which combined the perspectival and the planometric (fig. 26.4). The empathy of this bas-relief urbanism should not be confused with the humanism that was reappearing on the architectural stage at about the same moment. The figuration that the bas-relief introduced to the field was not related to the human scale or history, but to human vision and psychology—the "figures" were not legible representations, but differentiations in the abstract field that elicited differing and multiple visceral reactions to that field. This dispersed monumentality oscillated across multiple scales: beyond the built scale of the projects themselves, it included federal and local urban and economic policy as well as the network of relations that existed among urban institutions. A re-examination of the notions of collective engagement that are raised in the forms, pro-

26.4

26.5

26.6

26.4 Illinois Institute of Technology Campus: aerial view looking north, 1986. Photograph by John Hill. Courtesy of Tigerhill Studios.

26.5 Ludwig Mies van der Rohe and Ludwig Hilberseimer with a preliminary model for the Illinois Institute of Technology Campus (1941–45). Ludwig Hilberseimer papers. Couresty of the Burnham Library, Art Institute of Chicago.

26.6 Chemistry Building (Wishnik Hall), 1953. Photograph by Werner Blaser.

grams, and interconnections of these modernist yet monumental projects from the 1940s reveals a means of encouraging such engagement without programming it.

Once Mies was officially asked to design the campus, he began by studying the program, which was just being developed (and which would continue to be developed over the twenty years that Mies directed the project). After considering and testing various alternatives, he determined that a twenty-four-foot-square module could be used to accommodate the programs of classroom buildings, laboratory buildings, and office spaces. Rough volumes were established and wooden blocks were cut, with gridded elevations pasted on, and then Mies and his associates played with the blocks on the site: a large piece of paper, gridded with the same twenty-four-foot module (fig. 26.5).[8] Although Mies once claimed that he did not think that site was "that important,"[9] the combination of the gridded background and the gridded blocks gives the impression that the blocks protrude from the paper—that the figures of the buildings emerge from the field of the ground plane as the grid flips up ninety degrees from a horizontal to a vertical surface. While the decision to divide the school's program into several individual buildings predated Mies's arrival at IIT, and although this choice was probably driven largely by economic concerns (it was easier to raise money for individual departments and easier to proceed slowly if the process was broken down into pieces), this decision was also the mechanism that allowed the design of IIT to be as much the design of a campus (or quasi-urban) space as it was a design of buildings. Mies's method of moving blocks about rather than working only in plan demonstrates to what extent he recognized the problem of the campus design to be a three-dimensional spatial issue.

At the scale of the campus, the "ceremonial" or communal programs (the library and the student union) are given significant sites but do not serve to centralize or focus the campus as they would have had they been conceived along the lines of a traditional point-oriented city plan. Rather than occupying the center of the central courtyard space, these programs define its edge, as well as the edge of what is referred to as Mies Alley. Presentation drawings also reveal the campus's accessible institutional identity. Rather than converging onto one significant point or feature, Mies's perspectival views tend to draw the outsider into the campus; their multiple side axes promise endless possibilities lying just around the corners of the drawn buildings. In the earliest schemes, many of the buildings were on pilotis; it was Mies's dream that the entire ground plane could be one surface, interrupted only by the glass walls of the lobby spaces and stairs, smoothly taking people up into the buildings above. Each building would then have a transitional, public/private space between the exterior, public, world and the interior, private or academic world. Even if budget considerations eventually forced the elimination of the pilotis, the continuum was stressed: once the decision was made to put the buildings on the ground, Mies put them directly onto the ground, aligning the ground-floor slab with the ground itself. Even the detailing of the doors does not interrupt the flow of space between outdoors and indoors, as demonstrated by the centered, pivot-hinge doors to the Chemical Engineering and Metallurgy Building (now Perlstein Hall): the door handles are kept vertical and in alignment with the doorframe, avoiding any interruption of the view (fig. 26.6). Given that the campus plan was designed as if the field and the figures were one and the same—the gridded blocks emerging from the grid of the ground plane—it was not necessary for the "ground level" of the buildings and of the landscape to remain level zero: the "ground" is sometimes at grade and sometimes raised above grade, as with Crown Hall, where the main level is half a level above street level. Even the lower levels in use—Crown, the Commons, and Alumni Memorial Hall—are more like a ground plane that has dipped downward rather than a basement. The use of half-levels, high clerestory windows, ramps, and shallow, wide, and unenclosed stairways turn the experience of this modulated ground plane into that of a continuous horizontal surface.

In 1942, IIT president Henry Heald wrote a letter to Mies suggesting that, for aesthetic and security reasons, a wall be erected around the perimeter of the campus. In a particularly insensitive gesture toward those displaced by the demolition, Heald even suggested building the wall of recycled materials culled from former homes: "It has been suggested that a brick wall might be used, built from brick salvaged from some of our wrecking operations."[10] While no reply is documented, Mies's answer is suggested by the campus's permeability. Just as the courtyards are not closed off with four walls, as on traditional university campuses, the campus as a whole is open. The field upon which IIT's buildings sit extends out from the centermost courtyards to the very edges of the campus. With such moves, Mies deliberately redirected the city grid in a positive way and at two scales: that of IIT itself, where he replaced the tabula rasa of the land-clearance program with a modulated abstraction, and that of the entire Near South Side, which would follow Mies's design lead.

If the baroque city is best represented by the one-point perspective and the modernist city by the flat plan view, what modes of representation emerge from an urbanism that fit neither of these categories—an urbanism that tried to be simultaneously objective and subjective? That Mies constantly shifted between a larger, planar scale of order and a smaller, more immediate scale of personal experience can be seen from his design development drawings for the IIT campus. Plans, axonometrics, and models—all of which were used to organize the buildings by ordering them within the space of the campus—were complemented by perspectives that situated the user directly in the campus. Unlike the one-point perspectives of the point city model, Mies's are mostly two-point constructions that lead your eye off the page, away from any central focus (fig. 26.7). Foliage and people often frame the right and left sides, but rather than closing the image inward, they suggest its continuation ad infinitum. Clusters of buildings or clumps of trees are almost always cut off by the edges of the sheet, but the viewer completes them in her mind, thereby extending the composition. Adjacent buildings and surrounding trees also give depth to the campus design, defining multiple pathways heading off in different directions. These exterior "hallways" create a series of layers in the drawings, thereby rendering more visually complex the space foregrounding and surrounding the buildings, all the while suggesting multiple possibilities for experiencing that space. The asymmetrical campus plan, as conveyed through these representational devices, offers an urban type that is neither foreground nor background but both; when multiplied, it provides zones rather than points within the larger field of Chicago's grid.

Although Alan Colquhoun has argued that a superblock can never play a representational role within the city, the figured fields of the Near South Side, following IIT's lead, did forge a new form of symbolic urbanism.[11] The Near South Side Plan makes *space* rather than *buildings* representational. In the original scheme for Lake Meadows (fig. 26.8), a privately funded housing development designed by Skidmore, Owings & Merrill that similarly deployed a campuslike strategy for its combination of slabs, towers, and garden apartments, the street "facade" of the development resonates as a public front: a formal space is captured as a cube between the two large residential slabs (and further underscored by the more formal landscape treatment in this part of the project). In contrast, space flows freely around the lower-scaled, asymmetrically placed row houses, in the project's "backyard" area closer to the lake. Space can become symbolic without being turned into a literal metaphor along the classical lines of representation. The Near South Side's landscaped "new frontier" flows across the multiple campuses of the Near South Side Plan, representing "a new freedom" of accessibility and publicness and an implication of total flexibility and movement.

Despite the uneven politics between the residents and the institutions that so marked the Near South Side, Mies's understanding of the subject as being at once part of a collective—part of a planar logic—and also an individual—part of a perspectival logic—reveals the shift from the bourgeois public sphere to a consumerist mass subject, laying the groundwork, as it were, for the multiplied subjectivities of our contemporary understanding of the public realm. In an article entitled "The Mass Public and the Mass Subject," public sphere theorist Michael Warner reads consumer sovereignty as having been instrumental in the redefinition of the public sphere. If the "modern" public sphere, as theorized by Jürgen Habermas, was an abstract entity whose anonymity was one means of guaranteeing the citizens' disinterested concern for the public good, the

26.7 Amour Institute of Technology Campus, perspective sketch along 32d Street (1939). Mies van der Rohe office, George Danforth delineator: additions, Mies van der Rohe. Courtesy of the Museum of Modern Art, licensed by SCALA/Art Resource, NY.

26.8 Lake Meadows, Chicago, 1950–60: aerial photomontage. Skidmore, Owings and Merrill, architects. Courtesy of the Canadian Centre for Architecture.

postwar public realm is one that is mediated by the discourse of consumption: as individual and collective consumers, we make symbolic identifications in a field of choice. In other words, where the subject of the eighteenth-century public sphere cannot be differentiated, consumer capitalism made available an endlessly differentiated subject.[12] While some of the Near South Side Plan's components may strike us today as rather naïve responses to this transformation of the metropolitan or modern subject, and while the plan did not erase the iniquities between the area's residents and institutions, it nevertheless represents a collective attempt on the part of these institutions to foster a new public realm.

At its most successful, this new realm, as defined on the Near South Side, depended upon two forms of bas-relief, one formal and one programmatic. Ultimately, however, the spatial complexity and programmatic variety underlying the IIT campus (which had a library and student union, as well as laboratory and classroom buildings) or in the overall Near South Side Plan (which called for extensive shopping venues, as well as museums, community centers, and recreational facilities along the lakeshore) were compromised. The idealism that fuelled the vision of the new postwar realm was strong enough, in short, to tie the institutions together during their land acquisition period, but it began petering out once these parcels were fixed.

Between 1939 and 1958, when Mies retired from IIT, the Near South Side's urban bas-relief wove together the different institutions sited there, differentiating the seemingly neutral and totalizing traits normally ascribed to the Chicago grid or to canonical modernism. The topography that the early plan threw into relief included the multiple layers of networked relationships among the institutions, the architects, the planners, and the agencies involved, as well as the formal terms of the space itself.

If the bas-relief of the Near South Side failed in certain respects, that does not warrant a total abandonment of what was a prescient if naive urban strategy. Its prescience lies in its susceptibility to the complexities of urban space and its complicity in the different networks that it spun within that space: its effort to engage the collective and the individual simultaneously, to link institutions with institutions, local politics to federal politics, private economies to public ones. IIT works because it is like a minicity where mixed uses and scales figure space in order to provide for an empathetic, variegated, and animated public sphere. The figured fields of the campus superblocks provided a means of balancing the individualism of the real-estate parcel with the collectivity of the shared public realm. Beginning with IIT, the Near South Side Plan pulled the lakeshore's green belt inland, creating a nexus of semipublic open spaces funded by a Keynesian combination of municipal, state, and federal politics with private, local

26.7

26.8

institutions. The topography of this ground plan—the seemingly inert "park" of the "tower in the park"—became instead a charged, infrastructural carpet, reflecting the complex relations underlying the entire area.

In forging a partially figured field at IIT, Mies projected an urbanism that lacked the easy identity of the point or field approach—an urbanism that mirrored the complex topographies of postwar Chicago. The tabula rasa that resulted from the land clearance of the Near South Side was given formal, programmatic, political, economic, and social contours from what both constituted and surrounded it. For a short while, while the web of the South Side Planning Board was most intact, Mies's gravitational field turned the tabula rasa into a bas-relief of susceptible but provocative semi-figures, thereby transforming modernism's homogeneous field into an articulated, proactive network.

27 From Operational Anonymity to Brand Identity: Chicago O'Hare

Charles Waldheim

O'Hare is Chicago's Versailles. An inspiring diagram, speaking the poetry of flow, an unheralded masterpiece descended from such giant prototypical installations as the stockyards, the pier, the service tunnels, Soldiers Field, and so on, it recalls the generic style of the city itself. Open-ended, each with its own characteristic calm of geometry, scale, service and information, the automobile, the passenger and the aeroplane are linked. The built facility, idealized by Team X topologies, spare and laconic, traces the edge of their interface.[1]

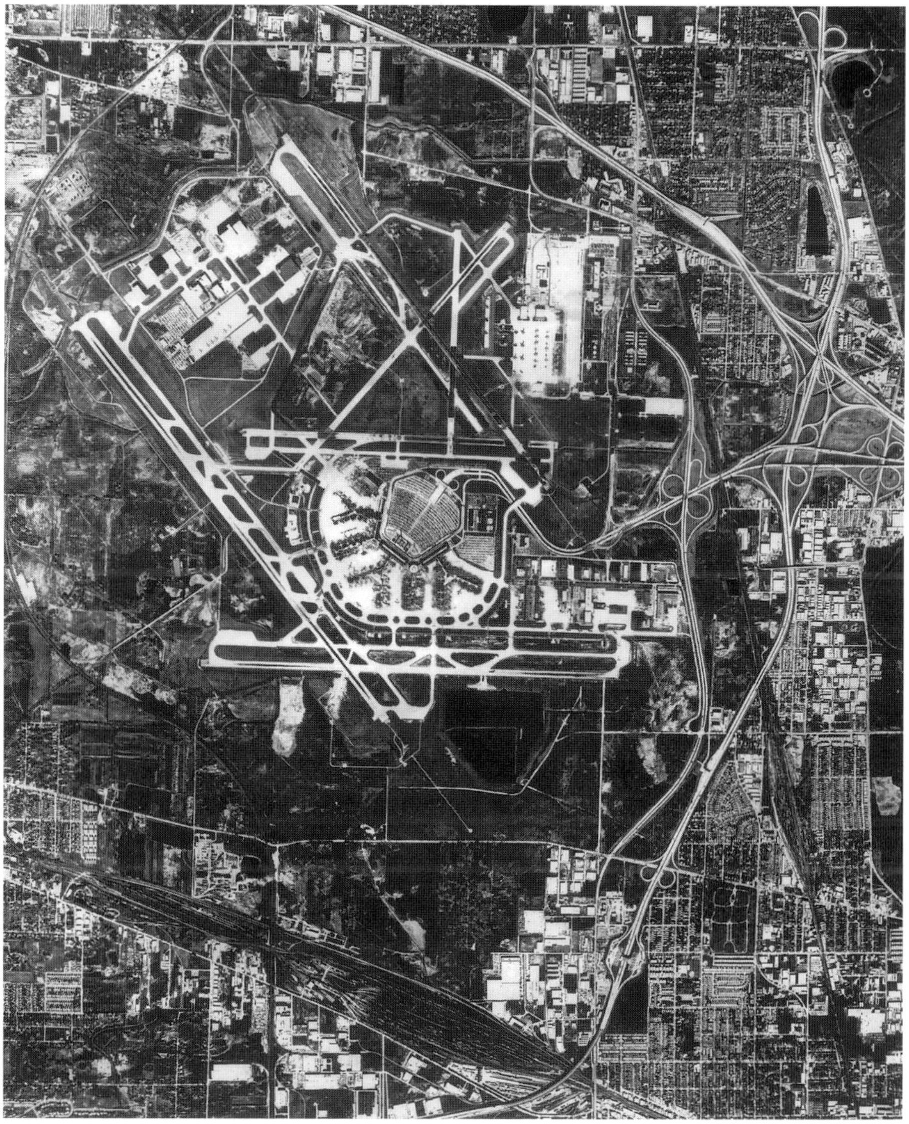

27.1

27.1 Chicago O'Hare International Airport (1957–63), aerial view, 1973. Courtesy of the Chicago Historical Society, ICHi 23502.

In the second half of the twentieth century, Chicago's O'Hare International Airport (C. F. Murphy Associates et al., 1957–63) was the biggest and busiest facility of its kind in the world. Remarkable for its seamless integration of transportation infrastructure and architectural expression, O'Hare served as an international model for modern airport planning and design as well as an example of a modern architecture nearly completely conditioned by optimized technology. An architectural ensemble at the scale of a small city, the scope and complexity of O'Hare's planning provided an unprecedented opportunity for the testing of modernist principles by generations of Chicago architects and engineers.[2]

Popular accounts of O'Hare's design and planning fit easily into the by now familiar Chicago school myths of size, technical innovation, and anonymous engineering efficiency. As an alternative to that narrative, this essay examines the architecture and urbanism of O'Hare in relation to the economic and political forces that have shaped it. This reading is most evident in the stylistic transformations from the original facility's "Team X topologies" to the mannered late modernism and historically alliterative postmodernism found in the most recently completed work at O'Hare. The purported autonomy of architectural culture in the narratives of Chicago modernism would suggest that this refutation of international style modernism was primarily a stylistic concern; these decisions, principally the domain of the architects commissioned for the work. A review of the politics, patronage, and economic power attendant to design and planning decisions at O'Hare affords a different reading altogether.

The vast majority of O'Hare has been designed by two Chicago architecture dynasties, C. F. Murphy Associates and Perkins and Will. These firms and their successor firms have consistently been awarded commissions for work based, at least in part, on their previous work at the site. This system of patronage for public works in the awarding of architectural commissions parallels the larger and well-documented history of patronage in the awarding of engineering and construction contracts in Chicago, especially as part of the Democratic machine politics that governed the city through much of O'Hare's planning and development. Charles (C. F.) Murphy secured the primary commission for O'Hare's design based on his relationship with Mayor Richard J. Daley and experience in Chicago public works patronage. Murphy, not formally trained as an architect, was first known to Daley as a fellow alumnus of the business program at the De La Salle Institute and fellow member of the Irish Fellowship Club, a meeting of which at the Palmer House provided the clubby context for Daley to offer Murphy the job.[3]

The mythical origins of modernism in 1880s Chicago commercial construction, as documented in this collection, were founded upon an idea of private speculative development with minimal involvement of the public sector. In striking contrast, much of the vaunted second Chicago school work could not have been conceived, much less implemented, absent a robust and fully deployed City machinery of patronage in the letting of public works at the local, state, and federal levels. From Mies van der Rohe's Chicago Federal Center (1959–74) to C. F. Murphy's Chicago Civic (Richard J. Daley) Center (1963–65); from Skidmore, Owings & Merrill's University of Illinois at Chicago Campus (1965–67), to O'Hare itself, the Second coming depended to a great extent upon political appointments and public funds. While these projects benchmark the often-cited successes of Mayor Richard J. Daley's administration, they are equally illustrative of the dependence of Chicago's modernist architects on a system of patronage delivered by the City's mythic machine politics. The stylistic shifts at O'Hare, from an anonymous and efficient international style modernism to distinctly identifiable postmodern historical references, read differently in this light. This shift tends, not coincidentally, to parallel precisely the shift of political and economic power away from the city machine and toward the airline companies themselves, and the competing airports and destination cities they service. This structural realignment manifested itself in a demand for greater visual identity for the various competing corporate and civic entities, demanding distinct and identifiable brands in the minds of constituents and consumers. The diffusion of power from the centralized control of city hall took place in a broader historical context in which the mobility of corporations and their capital, as well as the mobility of the markets they serve, tended to redistribute the economic power once concentrated in the industrial city. Ironically, O'Hare's development, and the transportation infrastructure that supported it, accelerated these shifts. In so doing, it catalyzed suburban development to the north and west of the city, simultaneously drawing population and resources from a shrinking city tax base, and ultimately hindering future expansion of the facility itself.

In 1963, the year of O'Hare's dedication, the airport was simultaneously the busiest passenger air facility in the world and the recipient of a design award from the American Institute of Architects. This rare convergence of popular and critical acclaim continued through much of the following quarter century as O'Hare was branded and exported globally as a seminal example of second Chicago school principles applied to one of the more pressing problems facing the modern city: the expanding importance of commercial aviation for the general public. This is evident in the conscious representation of those principles through high contrast black and white photographs already commissioned and reproduced in professional journals by the time of its official dedication (figs. 27.2–27.6).[4] The reproduction and dissemination of those images while the airport was still under construction helped to bolster O'Hare's legitimacy as heir to the fictional alliance between Chicago's architectural history and its great works of nineteenth-century engineering championed by the proponents of European modernism.

27.2

27.3

27.2 View, O'Hare terminal building and split-level entry drive, C. F. Murphy Associates (1957–63), Hedrich-Blessing photograph, 1963. Hedrich-Blessing Photo. HB-25500, courtesy of the Hedrich-Blessing Collection, Chicago Historical Society.

27.3 View, O'Hare terminal building and split-level entry drive, C. F. Murphy Associates (1957–63), Hedrich-Blessing Photo, 1963. HB-25500, courtesy of the Hedrich-Blessing Collection, Chicago Historical Society.

27.4 View, O'Hare terminal building interior, C. F. Murphy Associates (1957–63), Hedrich-Blessing Photo, 1963. HB-25500, courtesy of the Hedrich-Blessing Collection, Chicago Historical Society.

27.5 View, O'Hare terminal building interior, C. F. Murphy Associates (1957–63), Hedrich-Blessing Photo, 1963. HB-25500, courtesy of the Hedrich-Blessing Collection, Chicago Historical Society.

27.6 View, O'Hare terminal building interior, C. F. Murphy Associates (1957–63), Hedrich-Blessing Photo, 1963. HB-25500, courtesy of the Hedrich-Blessing Archive, Chicago Historical Society.

27.4

27.5

27.6

O'Hare afforded its architects the opportunity to literally construct a lineage of affiliation between their most recent addition to the pantheon of great modernist works and the engineering infrastructure that had been the mythical source of legitimacy for modernist accounts of Chicago's contribution to modernism internationally.[5]

The photographs of O'Hare's construction made by Hedrich-Blessing reveal the difficulties of isolating a particular architectural object from the infrastructural ensemble that is an airport. Ironically, the elements of architectural obsession most easily objectified through the formalism of modernist photography were the architectural housings of such discrete services as the telephone switching building, heating and cooling plant, and control tower. The public realm and spaces that constitute the experience of O'Hare appear as momentary glimpses along a continuous extrusion of movement space, differentiated only by mode of transport: automobile, train, or moving walkway. The endless infrastructural extrusion of public space evident at O'Hare, has come to embody much of the contemporary public realm in North American cities. This posthumanist public realm resists being photographed in the highly stylized manner that has come to stand for modern architecture in the wake of its use by the second Chicago school. Perhaps the most revealing and profound images are those of the airfield, the enormity and vacuity of O'Hare's ramps, aprons, and approaches standing for the posthumanist landscape of the modern world (figs. 27.7–27.8).

Irrespective of the cultural ideology implicitly embodied in the stylized photography of Hedrich-Blessing, O'Hare's development was, and continues to be, motivated by the conservative goal of maintaining Chicago's market share of national and international air travel. By the time of O'Hare's planning and design, Chicago's Metropolitan Airport (later Midway) was already the busiest airport in the world and had been so as early as the 1930s, the early days of commercial air travel. The construction of O'Hare by the City of Chicago was undertaken in the interest of maintaining Chicago's market share for transportation based on its privileged geographic position as linchpin of the national railroad network established in the nineteenth century. As the *Chicago Daily News* immodestly put it in 1922: "Chicago is destined to be the air center of the world." By 1950, Chicago already enjoyed the fees from over a thousand plane movements at Midway Airport annually, more than twice the volume of its nearest rival, New York.[6]

Nearly half a century of work at O'Hare illustrates the ongoing and pervasive role of consumer markets in the transformation of architectural and iconographic styles. The transformation of architectural imagery embodied in design decisions at O'Hare are typically explained as a form of superficial stylistic change from modernism to postmodernism to mannered neo-modernist revival. On closer reading, they represent a complex array

27.7 View, O'Hare Airfield apron and ramps, Hedrich-Blessing Photo. HB-32803, courtesy of the Hedrich-Blessing Collection, Chicago Historical Society.

27.8 View, O'Hare Airfield apron and ramps, Hedrich-Blessing Photograph. HB-32803, courtesy of the Hedrich-Blessing Collection, Chicago Historical Society.

27.7

27.8

of external forces brought to bear on what might otherwise be mistaken as the "purely" architectural decisions of taste culture and style. Principal among these forces was the impact of macroeconomic transformations at the end of Fordist production, and the concurrent collapse of the production economy in the United States in the mid-1970s. This era of oil crisis and recession coincides, not coincidentally, with the deepest crisis of modern architecture, the proclaimed "death of modern architecture" and the deregulation of markets, including the deregulation of the airline industry.[7] The subsequent post-Fordist reorganization of the airline industry had multiple repercussions on architectural culture, not least the increasing demand for a variety of architectural images for popular consumption by mass audiences. While the production of affordable mass-produced consumer goods for the middle class had been a principal tenet of the modern industrial age, subsequent growth could not be found in increased economies of scale given the relative affluence of the 1960s. Rather differentiation within and between consumer markets for multiplicity of choice demanded that stratification take place within mass-market goods and services. The shift away from an economy based on Fordist production paradigms to an economy based on services, information, and stratification of consumption is apparent in architectural production over this period through an increased dependence upon stylistic difference applied to essentially modernist containers, the products of optimized industrial production. This superficial surface of signification was understood in architectural culture of the postmodern era as a rejection of the so-called failures of modernism in favor of a semantic surface offering the potential for communication with multiple audiences, typified by Venturi's decorated shed. Interestingly, these transformations within architectural taste culture took the form of multiple scenographic surfaces wrapped as a thin veneer over an optimized and technologically driven container and its connective infrastructure. Revealingly, these efficiencies were folded seamlessly into the logic of consumer culture. The disposability of this imagery corresponded to the increased pace of changes within the marketplace while maintaining the utility and durability of the container, allowing architecture to morph efficiently in spite of stagnant technological and programmatic conditions.

The emergence of postmodern architecture and urbanism in the seventies, sweeping the market in the eighties, represents much more than a new aesthetic sensibility. The postmodern rejection of homogeneity, coherence, and completeness, and the explicit celebration of heterogeneity mark a radical departure from fifty years of modernist development. The force behind these developments, rather than emerging from within the architectural discipline itself, must be found on the socio-economic level."[8]

This understanding leads to a reinterpretation of postmodern architecture as the product of economic forces rather than cultural ones, and suggests renewed interest in the economic and social conditions underpinning the work that has come to be known as the second Chicago school. As a continuously constructed site planned by a small group of architecture and engineering firms, O'Hare International Airport offers an extraordinarily legible account of these transformations. Initially designed as one of Chicago's paradigmatic examples of a modern architecture shaped by technology and the rhetoric of infrastructural extrusion, O'Hare reveals in subsequent alterations and additions the economic and political impact of airline deregulation and Chicago's concurrent loss of market share to a range of increasingly indistinguishable competitor cities.

Position

The geographic position of Chicago gave rise to its development as a strategic geographic point in all manner of transportation networks as early as the first European colonial settlements. Grafting civic identity onto Chicago's geographical position as a pivot point between East and West at the continental scale was first manifest with the beginning of construction on the I & M canal in 1836, connecting the Great Lakes to the Mississippi River. By 1848, that proposed infrastructural improvement was open for business, and ready to be quickly rendered redundant by the introduction of the railroad, solidifying Chicago's pretensions as the crossroads of North America. This privileged position and the concomitant wealth produced from trade, transport, and real estate speculation fueled Chicago's growth and, as has been well documented, contributed to the financial basis of its growing reputation as a site for innovations in modern architecture. Chicago's identity as a transportation hub within a national and international network contributed to the association of Chicago's architectural culture with engineering, infrastructure and large-scale civic works. This reputation continued into the early days of commercial aviation, with civic leaders arguing as early as the 1920s that Chicago should invest public funds in securing its position as the center of what would become a national and international network of commercial airline travel, ultimately replacing the railroads as the principal means of public transport on a national scale.

By the dawn of the jet age in the 1950s, Chicago had been the busiest air travel destination for the previous two decades, and the construction of a World War II aircraft production facility northwest of Chicago was undertaken with an eye toward future peacetime expansion of Chicago's aviation capacity for larger aircraft. The postwar push to develop what had been known as Orchard Place Airport (hence O'Hare's designation ORD) for jet aviation was intensified by Metropolitan (Midway) Airport's physical constraints and inadequacy for the larger dimensions required for jet aircraft. This reflected economic imperative, as Chicago's civic and political leadership, especially its business community, keenly sensed the danger of losing the race for the jet age to competing

27.9 President John Kennedy and Mayor Daley placing a wreath on memorial monument to Butch O'Hare at one of several formal dedications of O'Hare Airport in 1960. Between 1960 and 1963, Daley dedicated portions of O'Hare on a variety of politically expedient occasions, several of which were timed to coordinate President Kennedy's availability in Chicago to maximum political and public relations effect. Courtesy of the Chicago Historical Society, ICHi. 32484.

27.10 Mayor Daley and Federal Aviation Administration (FAA) leaders preside over the dedication of O'Hare's new air traffic control tower in 1971. The FAA awarded the commission, an exception to local control of design patronage, to I. M. Pei Associates with Landrum and Brown Architects as part of a national system of new towers nationally. Courtesy of the Chicago Historical Society, ICHi. 32502.

cities. Promoted by a coalition of booster groups, military aviation officials, and political leaders, the development of O'Hare was motivated by a sense of Chicago's manifest destiny, the notion that this city, above all others, deserved to maintain its privileged birthright as the national transportation hub. Central to this initiative was the work of planner Ralphe Burke, who asserted the importance of the airfield to maintaining the city's historic market share: "The industrial leadership of Chicago depends upon its ability to remain a great center of travel."[9]

Politics

In spite of the economic imperative to develop a jet airport for Chicago, progress between the end of World War II and the first passenger flight in 1953 was slow and uneven. In the late 1940s the various airlines serving Chicago's Metropolitan (Midway) Airport organized a committee of executives from each company to negotiate with the city. By March 1949, this "Top" committee confirmed interest in the new airport. By June of that year, Mayor Kennelly renamed the airfield for a local war hero, "Butch" O'Hare, a naval aviator killed in action over the Pacific. In spite of this auspicious moment, progress on the airport was fundamentally hampered by a lack of construction financing, with both the City of Chicago and the airline companies refusing to take responsibility for the primary costs of construction. While some improvements at the airfield including the construction of an 8,000-foot runway for jet traffic were accomplished in the early 1950s, the airlines refused to shift flights to the facility unless its construction was financed publicly.

The airline industry in the 1950s was regulated by an agency of the U.S. Department of Commerce, the Civil Aeronautics Board, but granting access to gates at individual airports (and the markets they served) was the prerogative of the owner of the airport, in this case the city of Chicago. By 1955, with the election of Richard J. Daley as Mayor, work at O'Hare was languishing due to the airline industry's reluctance to bear the financial burden of shifting flights to the new airport site. Daley, convinced that Chicago's future depended upon expansion for jet-age air travel, immediately made the development of O'Hare a top priority and was in contact with the heads of each major airline company in the first weeks of his term. Daley's combination of skillful political pressure, relentless schedule of meetings, and scorn for the airline's individual self-interest in maintenance of the status quo, persuaded the airlines to increase their flights to and from O'Hare and share the financial burden of its development. This was accomplished with an unprecedented agreement that committed the airlines to support the cost of O'Hare, confirming the arrangement until 1970, and allowing Daley to claim the only major airport project in the country to be completely guaranteed by airline fund-

27.9

27.10

ing. During Daley's first term, the development of O'Hare was made a public works priority and linked to the construction of the Northwest Expressway (later renamed Kennedy Expressway) between the Loop and the airport. The completion of this vital piece of transportation infrastructure, connecting O'Hare directly to the Loop and the site of the new University of Illinois Chicago Circle campus, cemented the airport's unique status as the only major U.S. airport connected by highway (and ultimately elevated train) directly to the central business district. By the end of Daley's first term in 1959, O'Hare was on its way to replacing Midway Airport as the busiest commercial airport in the world (fig. 27.9).

Patronage

The mythical formulation of Chicago as "the city that works" is a testament to a culture of professional engineering and construction, organized along party lines, through which racial and ethnic groups were balanced in a regulated economy of patronage. The letting of public works contracts for specific projects on a regular and repeating basis was one of the elements that ensured the loyalty of various groups in Daley's Democratic machine. O'Hare was no exception, as one of the largest projects in the city's history.

In the years following World War II, Ralph Burke and Associates began preliminary planning of what would become O'Hare. Burke's 1948 plan featured a pentagonal central terminal building with radiating concourses and twelve radial runways tangent to the terminal. While construction began the following year, by 1957, Daley replaced Burke with fellow Irish Fellowship Club member and De La Salle alumnus Charles F. Murphy's firm Naess and Murphy (later renamed C. F. Murphy Associates). C. F. Murphy was later joined by Perkins and Will in preparing plans for O'Hare (fig. 27.10). The most significant changes to the Burke plan were based on the increased size of jet aircraft and increased estimates for numbers of passengers and their automobiles. The inadequately sized terminal was replaced with a linear series of connected terminal buildings in a modified horseshoe shape ringing a central transportation hub. The 1958 plan further described the three pairs of parallel runways that remain in use today (figs. 27.11, 27.12). The facility profited from a number of remarkable breakthroughs in airport design and planning first implemented by C. F. Murphy and Associates at O'Hare, as well as the adaptation of precedents from other airports internationally. Among these was the development of a two-tier roadway system bringing enplaning passengers to the upper level and carrying deplaning passengers away from the lower level of the two-story terminal buildings. The extensive system of "Y" finger concourses extending from the terminal buildings was augmented with the first large-scale installation of mechanically

27.11 Chicago O'Hare International Airport (1957–63), aerial view, 1973. Courtesy of the Chicago Historical Society, folio no. G80: 342.48.

27.12 Chicago O'Hare International Airport (1957–63), aerial view, 1973. Courtesy of the Chicago Historical Society, G80: 342.48.

27.11

27.12

telescoping jetways connecting passengers and crew from gate to plane on the same level. The basic premises of the 1958 C. F. Murphy plan, its integration of multiple infrastructures, its innovative dual level entry and exit roadway, and its forward-thinking use of telescoping jetways served the airport admirably over the course of its nearly continuous expansion and renovation (fig. 27.13). The airport's planning was derived from the spatial extrusion of its complex programmatic organization, while its architectural expression was unified though the application of a modernist enclosure system of steel and glass over a structural frame of reinforced concrete (fig. 27.14). Other notable and subsequently influential design innovations from the early 1960s at O'Hare included the Charles Eames/Herman Miller–designed Tandem Sling Seating and the O'Hare Cargo Scale, both of which were adopted internationally as industry standards for modern airport design.

By the time of its dedication in 1963, O'Hare was serving 13.5 million passengers per year, a volume of traffic exceeding even the most optimistic growth projections by nearly twenty years. The completion of the Northwest (Kennedy) Expressway in 1960 and the introduction of a Chicago Transit Authority train/bus connection from the city to O'Hare fueled this extraordinary growth. In addition to its efficient transportation infrastructure, the entire airport is serviced by a transparent utility building housing massive pumps, furnaces, and refrigeration equipment in a glass box. Intended as an image of the airport's (and the city's) modern aspirations and faith in technology, the mechanical systems of the airport were designed to be displayed to arriving and departing passengers, illuminated at night, prominently visible from plane, train, or automobile.

In 1963, the American Institute of Architects recognized C. F. Murphy Associates for their design work at O'Hare. Subsequent work at the site has consistently won awards and critical acclaim from the architectural, engineering, and planning communities. Subsequent work at the site reflects well on the initial site planning and architectural design decisions, even as growth threatens to overwhelm the airport. In the three decades following its dedication, the completion of infrastructural connections and the expansion of terminal facilities at O'Hare were executed without compromising the basic logic of its initial planning.

In 1971, construction was completed on a new air traffic control tower of slip-formed concrete construction designed by I. M. Pei Associates with Landrum and Brown Architects. In 1973, construction was completed on a new airport hotel and parking garage at the center of the terminal complex, designed by C.F. Murphy Associates. The convex curved hotel mirrors the steel mullions and glass panels of the terminal buildings while

27.13

27.14

27.13 Chicago O'Hare International Airport (1957–63), gate expansion through extrusion, Hedrich-Blessing Photo. HB-32005, courtesy of the Hedrich-Blessing Collection, Chicago Historical Society.

27.14 View, O'Hare Terminal building entrance road and walk, C. F. Murphy Associates (1957–63). Photograph by Glenn E. Dahlby, 1964. Courtesy of the Chicago Historical Society, ICHi 26515.

screening the massive concrete frame of the parking garage. Designed for a capacity of 9,300 vehicles, the garage was the largest of its kind in the world at its completion.

The deregulation of the airline industry in 1978, President Ronald Reagan's firing of Air Traffic Controllers in 1981, and ensuing competition between airlines fueled remarkable transformations in the organization and design of O'Hare, particularly as airlines sought to differentiate themselves (figs. 27.15, 27.16). This segmentation of the market produced a corporate search for brand identity, which prompted the design of signature terminal buildings by "star" architects for airlines' major hub airports. Revealingly, these transformations were not accommodated at O'Hare through the hiring of new architectural firms, but rather through the rehiring and rebranding of the very same architectural firms that had done the original design work. This was accomplished with the elevation to "star" status of the architect principals in charge of design for these firms, Helmut Jahn of Murphy/Jahn and Ralph Johnson of Perkins and Will. The repackaging of these established firms, the public profiles constructed for their star design partners, and the production of stylistically distinct architectural works at O'Hare followed a postmodern pattern of commodity-driven market diversification in the airline industry, generating unique brand identity for individual airlines within the increasingly competitive marketplace of commercial aviation.

In 1981, a consortium of firms led by the rebranded Murphy/Jahn, Envirodyne Engineers, Schal Associates, and Landrum and Brown, completed plans for further expansion of O'Hare and the addition of domestic and international gates. This plan specified the construction of several long-awaited transportation infrastructure improvements, including the completion of the CTA train connection to the city, a highway connection to the Northwest Tollway, and the construction of an intra-airport transit train or ATS system.

In 1987, construction was completed on a new domestic terminal building for United Airlines designed by Murphy/Jahn. The United Airlines Terminal One Complex appropriated the original terminal's modernist vocabulary of glass and steel enclosure for use as a structural frame but featured a postmodern arched section and other architectural devices as references to the extruded halls of nineteenth century trainsheds and gallerias. This historical allusion cloaked the modern, optimized, and efficient distribution of bodies and equipment in nostalgic imagery (figs. 27.17, 27.18).[10]

While work at O'Hare during the 1980s used postmodern architectural imagery and stylistic scenography for its principal tenant, United Airlines, subsequent economic and demographic shifts over the 1980s and 90s threatened Chicago's dominance of the

27.15

27.16

27.15 O'Hare terminal building overwhelmed with passengers during first holiday travel season following deregulation, 1978. Photograph by Neal Callahn. Courtesy of the Chicago Historical Society, ICHi 26528.

27.16 O'Hare terminal building overwhelmed with baggage during holiday travel season following deregulation, 1978. Photograph by Neal Callahn. Courtesy of the Chicago Historical Society, ICHi. 21676.

27.17 United Airlines terminal one complex, O'Hare International Airport, Murphy/Jahn et al., (completed 1987). Photograph by Timothy Hursley. Courtesy of Murphy/Jahn.

27.18 United Airlines terminal one complex, O'Hare International Airport, Murphy/Jahn et al., (completed 1987). Photograph by Timothy Hursley. Courtesy of Murphy/Jahn.

27.17

27.18

27.19 O'Hare international terminal, Perkins and Will et al., (completed 1993), Hedrich-Blessing Photo. Courtesy of Perkins and Will.

27.20 O'Hare international terminal, Perkins and Will, et al. (completed 1993), Hedrich-Blessing Photo. Courtesy of Perkins and Will.

commercial aviation market. The airlines that survived deregulation, United among them, found their leverage with their airport hosts substantially increased as cities competed for their own form of brand identity and market share of takeoffs and landings. Locating an airline's "hub" in a particular city gave airlines enormous negotiating power over host cities and their airports. Since most passengers in a hub and spoke system are changing planes at a geographically convenient point on the way toward their destination, airlines had increasing economic power to negotiate access to gates in host of cities such as St. Louis, Dallas, Detroit, Denver, and Atlanta. By the 1990s, Chicago's O'Hare International Airport had been replaced by Atlanta as the busiest airport for commercial aviation in the United States, while a host of other cities competed for increased market share, eroding Chicago's dominance. This paralleled the general trend in the 1980s and 1990s of large industrial cities losing population to the sunbelt cities of the south and west. With the disintegration of the production economy that had fueled Chicago's extraordinary growth from 1870 to 1970, the postmodern era in Chicago witnessed a loss of distinction between first-tier cities such as Chicago and formerly secondary markets. This shift gave rise in the 1980s and 1990s to the increasing importance of tourism, recreation, and entertainment as economic bases for U.S. cities. Chicago is presently pitted against a host of formerly second-tier cities nationally and internationally in competition for convention business, business travel, domestic recreation, and international tourist dollars. This places increasing pressure on the airport as the gateway and icon of the city in attracting visitors. The shift from an industrial economy of material production toward a service economy of tourism and leisure shaped developments at O'Hare in very specific ways and continues to affect design and planning decisions.

In 1993, construction was completed on a new international terminal designed by Ralph Johnson, of Perkins and Will in collaboration with Heard and Associates and Consoer, Townsend and Associates. Echoing the United Terminal's postmodern references to obsolete technological imagery, albeit in a more subtle language of mannered late modern quotation, the International Terminal obliquely references the international style origins of O'Hare. The International Terminal, while winking at the original language of O'Hare, is rendered as a kind of postmodernism lite, made readily consumable, and leavened with lighter colors, and curving forms, distinct from the sober steel mullions, dark glass, and concrete frame of the original terminals (figs. 27.19, 27.20).[11]

The World Gateway and On-Time O'Hare plans for expansion of the airport, proposed in 2001 by Mayor Richard M. Daley, continued these trends with the proposal of a second entrance to the airport from the west, to ease access for growing suburban populations. This work, combined with reconfigured and expanded runways, reconfigured

27.19

27.20

entryway drives and parking, as well as additional terminal gates, and decentralized customs for international arrivals are planned with the intention of regaining Chicago's strategic economic advantage. The public announcement of these improvements has been accompanied by the well worn argument that work at O'Hare will ensure Chicago's future economic viability in the face of increasing competition from other hub airport cities, implying the increasing importance of the airport in the fabrication of the city's own brand identity.

The Mayor's proposal [On-Time O'Hare] will help position Chicago as the national and international aviation center of North America. It will add enormous value to the region . . . ." Lester Crown, Chair, Civic Committee Aviation Task Force.[12]

Contemporary Chicago continues its transformation from a Fordist economy of production and consumption to a post-Fordist economy of service industries, tourism, recreation and leisure. Contemporary architectural work at O'Hare is programmed by these economic forces, just as it had been previously by the economic imperatives of industrial production. Rather than suggesting that postmodern architectural work at O'Hare contradicted the airport's modernist origins and Chicago school patrimony, this suggests that the history of Chicago modernism and its postmodern reprise were equally bounded by and founded upon a range of economic conditions that continue to affect cultural production. It is a reminder that the progressive architectural modernism of the late nineteenth and early twentieth centuries was itself a response to the broader social and economic transformations attendant to industrialized modernity and not the self-interested stylistic concern that it was reduced to in Chicago school mythology. This makes a close reading of the economic and social conditions corresponding to the city's rapidly evolving present imperative for those interested in the critical practice of architecture in Chicago today.

From Flesh to Fiberglass: Cows on Parade in Chicago

C. Greig Crysler

Introduction: Conversions and Renovations

I am standing on the side of a road that runs between empty lots scattered with broken glass and pieces of brick. To my right, spare parts of industrial machinery sit in an open service yard adjacent to a one-story warehouse. In the flat middle distance just beyond, there is a shipping terminal, the headquarters for a school bus company, a pharmaceuticals distributor, and other businesses that display nothing but street numbers on their blank facades. These extend for several acres across a gray horizon that is cut across by chainlink fences, withering trees, and an occasional passing truck. The skyline of Chicago looms in the background (fig. 28.1). The landscape is barely recognizable as Packingtown, once the vast stockyard operation on the South Side of the city, where, at its height, twenty million living animals per year were efficiently turned into packaged meat.[1]

The view suggests a partly transformed industrial hinterland, but the pungent, overpowering smell of chemicals and burning meat that hangs in the air insists that there are still active remnants of the past here. Behind me is an early twentieth-century warehouse, seven stories high, that was once a meatpacking plant. The windows are mostly boarded up now, but the building is connected by gleaming stainless steel pipes to a pair of industrial vats across the street, from which noxious steam is rising in billowing plumes. I drive around to the rear of the building, passing along Ashland Avenue, once the commercial center of the working-class neighborhood adjacent to the stockyards. A narrow residential road lined with a mixture of modest brick and timber frame buildings leads me to the other side of the building, which I view from the steps of the Back of the Stockyards Saloon (figs.28. 22, 8.3). This is one of the few remaining watering holes for those who work in what has now become the Stockyards Industrial Park, an attempt to diversify the economic base of a neighborhood that was almost destroyed by the closing of the packing houses in 1970.[2] The same overpowering aroma is here, too, but no one seems to notice it but me. The men entering the bar tell me that what I smell is the byproduct of a curing process for a plant that makes "a good smoked ham."

Most accounts of the history of the meat industry suggest that the closing of the Chicago stockyards anticipated more systematic changes across the U.S. economy in the late 1970s.[3] The oil shocks in 1973 and the deep global recession that followed through the mid-1970s prompted various sectors of industrial production to seek more "flexible" forms of profit accumulation.[4] In doing so, an industrial system that had relied on the "structural rigidities" of a well-paid, unionized work force and profits generated by standardization and economies of scale was gradually dismantled. When the centralized mass production of meat was "restructured" in the early 1970s, the large packing

28.1

28.1 Chicago Stockyards Industrial Park, Chicago, 2003. Photograph by C. Greig Crysler.

28.2

28.2 Meat processing plant, Chicago Stockyards Industrial Park, Chicago, 2003. Photograph by C. Greig Crysler.

28.3

28.3 The Back of the Stockyards Saloon, near the Chicago Stockyards Industrial Park, Chicago, 2003. Photograph by C. Greig Crysler.

houses of Chicago moved to locations adjacent to rural feedlots, completing a process that had begun as early as the 1880s.[5] Even as the Chicago stockyards were closed, working conditions that recall some of the worst excesses of the nineteenth century reemerged in a dispersed landscape of "ruralized" production. These remote locations continue to offer lower labor costs through a migrant work force made up largely of women and people of color.[6] They also isolate workers from remaining union strongholds in big cities, while further separating the consumers of meat from the unsavory conditions of its production.[7]

It is this displaced landscape of dispersion and intensification that is documented so effectively in Eric Schlosser's *Fast Food Nation*.[8] He describes a clandestine visit to an unnamed slaughterhouse somewhere in the "high plains," where up to four hundred cattle are slaughtered per hour, nearly eight times the number killed in Chicago at the height of the productivity of the stockyards. Arriving after dark, Schlosser renders the workers and cattle of the "kill floor" in a portrait of blood:

I see: A man reach inside cattle and pull out their kidneys with his bare hands, then drop the kidneys down a metal chute, over and over again. . . . For eight and half hours, a worker called a "sticker" does nothing but stand in a river of blood, being drenched in blood, slitting the neck of a steer every ten seconds or so, severing its carotid artery. He uses a long knife and must hit exactly the right spot to kill the animal humanely. He hits that spot again and again.[9]

Schlosser's account describes how both humans and animals are caught in a spiraling regime of mechanized exploitation that is spectacular in its hidden brutalities. Yet the geographical displacement of production (not only for the meat industry but for everything from cars to shoes) has also had dramatic, if less visceral, consequences in the urban contexts such movements of capital have left behind. One of the key issues in deindustrializing cities in the United States and elsewhere has centered on how to turn abandoned industrial infrastructure into profitable new uses. The problem is one of symbolic as well as functional "conversion." Thus the urban smokestack needs to be changed from a symbol of grimy production and class division to an indicator of lifestyle consumption, just as the former industrial loft needs to be redefined as a site of luxury housing.[10]

Such renovations in meaning and use are carried out in relation to individual buildings through the actions of investors, real estate agents, and financial institutions, as well as the through the operations of "symbolic analysts" such as architects, public artists, critics, preservationists and historians.[11] Increasingly, it is not only individual buildings but also the image of an entire city that is the subject of such signifying transactions.

28.4 Chicago stockyards, c. 1920. ON-0000985, courtesy of the Chicago Historical Society.

28.5 Interior of a slaughterhouse, Chicago stockyards, 1904. Photograph by William T. Barnum. Courtesy of the Chicago Historical Society, ICHi-70649.

These bring together and help to consolidate public/private partnerships through "city-building" projects (such as urban "regeneration" zones, museums, and ballparks), as well as events such as exhibitions, public art displays, and festivals for everything from Ping-Pong to "ethnic" cuisine.[12] Chicago has been particularly aggressive in deploying a wide array of cultural and beautification programs to reposition the city as a consumption artifact with an industrial "heritage."

The unlikely figure that stands at the center of this process is the cow. Cattle were central to the emergence of Chicago as an industrial powerhouse: their bodies were slaughtered by the millions and sold as part of an extensive chain of commodity relations that made Chicago an international center for industrial food production in the first half of the twentieth century. After the stockyards closed, cows disappeared both literally and figuratively from the city, only to return in "parade" formation in the summer of 1999. They were part of an urban spectacle orchestrated by the City's Department of Cultural Affairs, which initiated the project at the urging of a local businessman who had visited a similar event staged in Switzerland the year before.[13]

The three hundred fiberglass cows that occupied the city were not confined to the former sites of slaughter: instead, most inhabited the urban center, taking up strategic positions next to prominent public buildings and businesses. Each of the cows was sponsored by a local business or institution, and the artists who designed and decorated them were paid a fee by their patrons. In another ironic coda to the operations of the meat industry, 140 of the cows were purchased in an auction for Chicago charities held after the parade ended.[14] A small number remain on display throughout the city.

As cattle moved from periphery to center and from flesh to fiberglass in the official imagination of the city, so too did the meaning of the city's industrial past undergo symbolic and material transformations. This paradoxical conversion process invoked a figure of urban modernity (the industrial cow), while displacing the "other" side of modernization and its bloody consequences. It is this dimension of experience that I attempt to recover in what follows: a (de)tour through several sights/sites of Chicago's bovine urban history.

Bloody History

I am sifting through the photographic archives on the stockyards at the Chicago Historical Society. I quickly become aware of the inverse ratio of evidence to the scale of the stockyards and their significance. That something this immense, this solid, could

28.4

28.5

melt so completely into air is a testament to the power of Chicago's capitalist modernization. The disappearance was achieved through a ruthless pragmatism that (perhaps unlike anywhere else) immediately consigned the marginally efficient to the status of the completely disposable.

I extract two photographs from bulky green hanging files: The first image shows one of the more common views of the stockyards in the 1920s (fig. 28.4). Most of the frame is taken up by a vast arrangement of holding pens, a gigantic gulag that recedes into the horizon. In several pens, the massed bodies of cows are packed together so tightly that they become a single, undulating carcass contained in a tidy square by the timber fences that surrounds them. An elevated railway that brought the animals to the stockyards rises along one edge. Enclosed timber ramps lead from here to the pens. The words Swift and Armour hang in the background, and another set of ramps leads through a grimy haze to the interior of a slaughterhouse.

The second photograph was taken at ground level inside a slaughterhouse (fig. 28.5). It lacks the sense of control and distance of the first and brings the viewer forcefully inside the scene. In the darkness of the interior, a group of figures are gathered along the disassembly line. A row of carcasses, each turned upside down and split with a single cut from tail to head, is moving past them on hooks attached to a mechanized chain. The men are splattered with blood, and the floor is slick with shiny pools of "waste" that will later be collected and converted into fertilizer or soap.

The progressive disassembly of animals defined a racialized division of labor that placed black workers at the grisly beginning of the line or in the filthy and noxious departments where various products were made from reconstituted waste.[15] In the nineteenth and early twentieth centuries, the "clean" jobs in the stockyards were held by white workers; African Americans often gained access to skilled positions by first acting as strikebreakers.[16] The photo, taken in 1904, may well depict some of the hundreds of "Negro workers" who were enticed to Chicago from the South with offers of room, board, and guaranteed pay of $2.25 a day. The violence that accompanied the strike required many to sleep and eat inside the slaughterhouses during the sweltering summer heat.[17]

The growth of the stockyards was accompanied by the development of a symbolic universe to surround the marketing and consumption of food. At the turn of the century, the large food companies began to develop marketing themes and brand identities that separated the product to be consumed from its method of production. In the milk industry, for example, the early twentieth century marked a dramatic change in the mythic idea of milk as a consumer commodity. Advertising for milk from the mid- to late nineteenth-century constructed a pastoral landscape as the site of production, and introduced the cheerful, ruddy-faced milkmaid as the nurturing, motherly producer. This occurred at a time when cows were fed distillery swill and suspended in hoists to be milked as they died.[18]

At the beginning of the twentieth century, the conditions of production were scarcely more sanitary, but the scale of the milk industry was expanding rapidly. References to the milkmaid as producer disappeared altogether, and stress was placed more firmly on the consumer. As E. Melanie DuPuis has shown, the image of a bird watching over a plump and healthy baby in a nest became the dominant visual trope of the emergent milk industry: the bird was a metaphor for a female consumer who brought food to her infant-filled nest. Not only did the mythologized reference to the milkmaid as producer disappear; so too (with the single, monumental exception of Elsie the Cow) did any reference to the cow as the final source of production.[19] Milk was transformed into a vitamin-filled fluid that would enable the mother/bird to "grow" healthy babies, displacing the mechanization of production with the "natural" mechanization of consumption via the growth-inducing qualities of "scientifically" produced milk. Indeed, milk was associated by urban reformers with Christian "whiteness" and perfection, and its consumption was linked to the production of bodies that were not only healthy but morally pure.

A similar trajectory developed in relation to meat. Consumption increased dramatically with innovations in refrigerated railcars that allowed markets to expand to national and then international dimensions. New forms of marketing by companies such as Oscar Meyer and Swift developed ways to expand the appeal of their products. Like the sale of milk, the marketing of meat depended on its portrayal as a mythical body-enhancing commodity and its simultaneous detachment from the often grisly conditions under which it was produced. A parallel symbolic order emerged in which cows became "cuts" of beef, and the carcass became a topography of tough or tender culinary sensations.[20]

The appearance of meat at the point of sale was a vital part of this universe. But even more crucial than the marketing of chops, tips, and steaks as fleshy "jewels" in glass display cases was the expansion of byproducts built from the waste of the production process. The economies of scale achieved through the concentration of production in the stockyards allowed a "waste conversion" industry to emerge in which the droppings and drippings of the butchering process were converted to everything from combs and brushes to fertilizers and glue.[21] Each product had a shape and function that bore little or no discernible relationship to its animal source. As William Cronon writes, the animal died a second death:

> **Severed from the form in which it had lived, severed from the act which had killed it, [the cow] vanished from human memory as one of nature's creatures. Its ties to the earth receded, and in forgetting the animal's life, we also forget the grasses and the prairie skies and the departed bison herds of a landscape that seemed more and more remote in space and time . . . one hardly thought of the prairies or the plains while making one's purchase, any more than one thought of about Packingtown, with its Bubbly Creek and stinking air . . .[22]**

The commodification of meat is predicated on relations of distance that permit, as much as possible, the detachment of knowledge of production from consumption. This relationship has been transformed over time, together with the changing structure of capital itself. In retrospect, the ideological relations of distance constructed at the end of the nineteenth century were unevenly realized and subject to disruption by unplanned "penetrations" of the conditions of production into the spaces of consumption. In large cities like Chicago, where labor strife over working conditions was a nearly continuous feature of urban life, and where diseases stemming from rapid industrialization were commonplace, this separation was under constant pressure. At the beginning of the twenty-first century, the relations of distance (both symbolic and material) that define the gap between production and consumption have multiplied in scale and intensity, so that production is often located thousands of miles from the point of consumption. Ironically, these relationships have also granted the cow a new visibility in Chicago's urban space.

Flesh to Fiberglass

I was passing through the "Loop" of Chicago on a cold afternoon early in spring 1999 when I turned a corner and found myself standing in front of an empty storefront. A dim amber glow from the rear of the space illuminated a small herd of life-size cattle. The animals were completely, brilliantly white, with fine white dust gathered like silk around their feet. Their sugary state of abstraction was exaggerated by their benign fa-

28.6 **Heidi visits with a goat, while her Swiss dairy cows wander in the hills. Courtesy of the St. Moritz Tourist Office.**

cial expressions and relaxed posture. Each cow had both horns and udders. They were jammed together "naked," simultaneously evoking a ghostly apparition and a herd of unclothed animal mannequins. Some looked absently onto the street, while others had their heads turned shyly inward. The School of the Art Institute of Chicago was nearby, and I assumed the assembled herd must be part of an art installation. I later discovered that the unused shop was a holding pen for undecorated additions to the Cows on Parade.

Many of the urban ideas that have transformed the center of Chicago began as the dream-work of the comprador class—wealthy local capitalists who have sought in different ways to make Chicago legible on an imaginary stage of, first, national, and more recently, global, capital. The idea of Cows on Parade in the center of Chicago was transported from Zurich, Switzerland, where Peter Hanig, a Chicago shoe magnate, had been on vacation in 1998. The cow has a special place in Switzerland's quaint version of the global imaginary: the country is typically represented in postcards and travel advertisements as a giant alpine dairy farm, replete with goats and cows draped in garlands and bells. They are sometimes shown sauntering happily alongside the ur-matron of the national udder, a blonde Heidi who is dressed in a "Swiss Miss" lace and bonnet costume (fig. 28.6). The simulated cows that Hanig admired in Zurich shifted the image of the alpine cow into the city, urbanizing an international fantasy of Switzerland while also making it an object of "cultural tourism." He realized that a similar level of displacement could be achieved in Chicago, where cows had also figured in the global imaginary of the city, but in relation to a process of modernization that was much less benign than the pastoral idyll of rural Switzerland.

Hanig's initial moment of Swiss inspiration has become the subject of urban legend, and his apocryphal trip to Switzerland is recounted in the City's official history of Cows on Parade as the immaculate conception that brought to life Chicago's herd of fiberglass cows.[23] The meaning of the Cows on Parade project, now replete with its own manufactured history, is nevertheless intimately bound up with the brutal material history of cattle and livestock in Chicago. The project constructs a series of symbolic conversions and economic "renovations" that become meaningful when considered in the context of the larger spatial histories of industrialization and meat production in Chicago.

In the nineteenth-century model of meat production, the meat of the slaughtered animal was sold at a loss to the producer: it was the products generated from the waste materials of the production process that were the source of huge profits for the meatpackers. The death of cattle allowed the production of commodities to begin. With the Cows on Parade, the process is reversed: the metaphorical birth of the fiberglass cow leads to more fiberglass cows. These replications refer not to a living specimen, but to the original fiberglass simulation. It is possible to purchase miniature reproductions of the parading cows; the entire event has also been copied (with alterations in the "cast" of characters) in over twenty cities worldwide. There is a Cows on Parade Web site with books and merchandise departments, and the concept is now copyrighted.

Splice of Life

In the industrial reduction of cows to meat, soap, and shoes, the slaughtered animal is constituted as an equivalent part of an infinite series: a species category composed of more or less identical representative specimens. Cows that are slaughtered for meat production become an undifferentiated mass through their constructed opposition with humans: as animals they are defined by the meat industry, the animal science community, and much of popular culture as instinctually driven and lacking in the capacity for rational or emotional experience. Thus a human who behaves abnormally is sometimes described as beastly or as someone who acts "like a wild animal." The absence of human rationality is presumed to lead to a descent into wild and uncontrollable animal urges.[24]

The domesticated animal is one whose wildness has been tamed by human management and hence represents a particular conception of "trained" animal consciousness. Yet some animals are classified as both domesticated and dumb—a category that the cow has typically occupied. As a way to describe humans, comparison with a cow ("you stupid cow") is an index of stupidity or an inability to comprehend. In some situations this also acquires gender implications. For example, women and cows have been semantically equated as nurturers who are obedient, caring, and dewy-eyed in their milk-producing, maternal sweetness. In the context of Chicago, the cow has historically assumed the status of displaced coding for "woman," as exemplified by the story of Daisy, the cow that was reputed to have started the Great Fire of 1871 by "dumbly" kicking over a lantern. The cow became interchangeable with her owner, Mrs. O'Leary. Both were later absolved, but for over one hundred years "cow" acted as a bovine proxy for "woman" thus helping to keep the category of "woman-as-cow" active.

In the Cows on Parade, each cow had a distinctive "personality," which registered in its physical form and its decorated hide. The Cows on Parade therefore did not manifest a lack of "humanness," but rather, a plentitude of it. Many were human/animal hybrids. In some cases they joined the cow and the business that sponsored their creation together with a prototypical consumer. For example, the now-defunct Disney Quest (a multistory building in downtown Chicago filled with interactive games inspired by Disney's films and theme park attractions) commissioned a cow wearing a virtual reality visor (fig. 28.7). Here the cow merged with a generic participant in an urban attraction. In other cases, the cows were semiological mutations of famous humans. A good example is Cowileo—a cow version of Galileo that has remained on display after the end of the exhibition. Cowileo stands on his/her hind feet and looks at the stars through a telescope (fig. 28.8). We might assume that the cow has been invested with the ultimate powers of rational consciousness, since Galileo is credited with helping to establish Enlightenment science and the secular relativization of "man." Yet what has happened here is not so much the acknowledgement of the sensory and emotional potential of cows as the generalization of "humans" into animals. In another splicing, Mrs. O'Leary is merged with her famous cow, Daisy, and the hybrid figure reads about her absolution as a fire-starter in the morning paper (fig. 28.9). In this case, it is the category of woman that is joined with the cow, but with a subtle inversion: Mrs. O'Leary is still a cow, but no longer "dumb." In all three cases the birth of the human/cow marks the symbolic death of the animal/cow. The cow is assimilated to the human.

It is also worth noting that the Cows on Parade had both horns and udders. In the Swiss context, this species of female dairy cow is the norm, but in North America it is the exception, where gender distinctions associate horns with bulls and udders with cows. It is not surprising that in a midwestern city such as Chicago, which continues to attract many rural visitors, the Cows on Parade were regarded with some confusion as simultaneously male and female, as well as human and animal. How can we interpret the proliferation of multiple systems of cultural coding on the body of the parading cow, each of which contradicts the essentially "natural" meaning of the "real cow?"

One answer may be that the Cows on Parade, in all their anthropomorphic glory, are intended to represent and bring about a model of identity construction that is realized

28.7 "Virtual Cow in Reflective Moosaic," Chicago, 2003. Photograph by C. Greig Crysler.

28.8 "Cowileo," Chicago, 2003. Photograph by C. Greig Crysler.

28.9 Mrs. O'Leary's cow reads about her exoneration, Chicago, 2003. Photograph by C. Greig Crysler.

28.7

28.8

28.9

28.10

28.11

through consumption. Take, for example, the group of well-dressed women that gathered around a cow stationed outside a women's shoe store on North Michigan Avenue (fig. 28.10). The hide of this cow had been decorated to match the surface of the sequined shoes displayed in the store window, and admirers moved in what was presumably the intended manner, from gazing upon the surface of the cow to gazing upon the surface of a duplicate cow standing adjacent to shoes in the shop window, to actually entering the shop (fig. 28.11). This ritual underscores how the cows helped to instrumentalize the blurring of public and private realms by projecting the spectacular space of the shop window onto the city sidewalk. To mingle with the cows on Michigan Avenue was therefore to float temporarily in a suspended zone of consumption, one that reproduced the space of the traditional "sidewalk sale" without representing itself as such. The Cows on Parade reportedly viewed by 10 million people[25] and generated over $200 million dollars in additional tourist revenue during the four and half months of the event.[26]

Figures of Displacement

Various critics have argued that identity in the late capitalist United States is about performance: cultural identity is constructed through the appropriation and manipulation of code systems that we learn through repetition in specific (signifying) contexts. This model of identity construction is linked to the historical circumstances of capital in postindustrial societies. In the shift from an economy organized around production to one that is increasingly based on services and consumption, the "realization problem" of capital has become paramount.[27] What is purchased now is less a product with a specific use value than an emotion, an identity, or a theme. As Donald M. Lowe suggests, the result is the commodity that simultaneously refers to exchange values and represents a value to be consumed in and of itself: as Lowe describes it, the commodity becomes a "signifier of the signifier" of exchange value.[28]

The point is perhaps best illustrated through the recent advertisements for Nike shoes, which do not show the shoes or name the

28.10 "Rhinestone Cowgirl" outside 900 North Michigan Avenue, Chicago, 2003. Photograph by C. Greig Crysler.

28.11 A duplicate "Rhinestone Cowgirl" in the window of Stuart Weizman, Inc., Chicago, 2003. Photograph by C. Greig Crysler.

company but merely juxtapose the corporate logo with a particular experience, indirectly conflating possession of the product with access to a particular emotion. In this context, athletic shoes become "semiotic hybrids": the shoe is a tertiary support for a dreamscape of identity that is entered through the act of consumption, on terms that are defined in advance by the producer. Once the material props are purchased, such dreamscapes are not necessarily "performed" in the manner intended by their purveyors. In some cases the performance may directly contradict the manufacturer's intentions, but we nevertheless remain within the terms of the corporate dreamscape, thereby affirming its power as the primary frame of reference.[29]

Cows on Parade can be understood as part of an ongoing attempt to reposition Chicago in the global marketplace for tourism, jobs, and corporate investment. The success of this urban "makeover" depended on reestablishing an interchangeability between city and cow, so that to consume the cow (and the dreams attached to it) would be to also consume the remade city; and to consume the remade city would be to alter its meaning as a grimy old metropolis of industrial production. Thus the semiological magic of the parade revived the associative link between Chicago (once known as the "Great Bovine Capital of the World") and cows, while changing its meaning. The process was underscored by the many puns used to describe the event. These inserted "cow" into the name of the city, turning Chicago into "Chi-Cow-Go,"[30] and prominent public institutions into "Moo-seums." Tourists were asked to "moo" when visiting the Chicago Cultural Center.[31] But the symbolic revival and redefinition was also accomplished by positioning the cows on the streets, where, as human/animal hybrids, they provided evidence of Chicago not as a paradigm of industrial efficiency, but as a city of "paradox and surprises," in which everything old becomes new(ly profitable) again. As the breathless account in the official Cows on Parade book notes:

> **. . . Chicago is being rebuilt, remodeled, revamped, rehabbed and rerouted . . . a former working dock, Navy Pier, was made into a festival marketplace . . . the lakefront airport, Meigs Fields, will soon become a park. The neighborhood that runs along Madison to the United Center has gone from Skid Row to pricey condo lofts. The Reliance building, the crown jewel of the Chicago School of Architecture that had fallen into disrepair, is being restored to its former glory . . .**[32]

The conversion of living flesh into meat was (and continues to be) a locus for labor strife, racial inequities, and massive environmental degradation. The stories told by boosters, civic agencies, and the popular press in Chicago about the fabrication of the fiberglass cows are allegories of postindustrial production, shorn of labor conflict and varnished with the myth of a unified and playful city. Once complete, the cows were rhapsodized as emissaries from a collective urban imagination, the zeitgeist of Chicago's "spirit," and metaphors for a city transformed. The rhetoric extended the splicing of humans and animals to a metropolitan scale: the theatrical herd thus signified an idealized citizen/cow whose agency is expressed through spectacular acts of consumption.

The Cows on Parade not only gave form to a collective subject of civic consumption; they also helped to institute a collective space of consumption. Diaphanous and unstable, this space is perhaps best thought of as the twenty-first-century version of the endless rows of pens that enclosed cattle in the stockyards of the nineteenth century. The parade helped to articulate a "regime" of abstract space defined not by enclosing boundaries but by the erasure of boundaries: between public and private, art and commerce, subject and object, and indeed (if it pays) between humans and animals. The citizen/cows emerged whole from the slippery dreams of urban entrepreneurs, dipped in paint and scattered with sequins.[33] Their decorated hide became the surface upon which the dissolution of categories was rendered as a decorative urban motif; their hollow carcasses signified the bloody history they displaced.

Notes

Chapter 1

1. This modernist view was initiated by European criticism in the 1890s, written in the wake of the 1893 Chicago World's Columbian Exposition and continued in the writing of early twentieth-century avant-garde architects such as Erich Mendelsohn, Bruno Taut, Ludwig Hilberseimer, and Richard Neutra. Under their influence it entered American histories through texts such as Henry Russell Hitchcock's *Modern Architecture: Romanticism and Reintegration* (1929; reprint, New York: Arno, 1972); Museum of Modern Art, *Early Modern Architecture: Chicago, 1870–1910,* 2d rev. ed., exhibition catalog (New York: Museum of Modern Art, 1940); Sigfried Giedion, *Space, Time and Architecture: The Growth of a New Tradition*, 5th ed., rev. and enl. (1941; Cambridge, MA: Harvard University Press, 1973); Colin Rowe, "Chicago Frame" (1956) in "*The Mathematics of the Ideal Villa" and Other Essays* (Cambridge, MA: MIT Press, 1990), 89–117; and Carl Condit, *The Rise of the Skyscraper* (Chicago: University of Chicago Press, 1952), and *The Chicago School of Architecture: A History of Commercial and Public Building in the Chicago Area, 1875–1925* (Chicago: University of Chicago Press, 1964).

2. In particular, Daniel Bluestone, Robert Bruegmann, Narcisco Menocal, Joseph Siry, Theodore Turak, and David Van Zanten have (with differing methodological approaches) drawn attention to the intellectual aims and the economic, cultural, and social milieus of particular Chicago architects. See Daniel Bluestone, *Constructing Chicago* (New Haven: Yale University Press, 1991); Robert Bruegmann, *The Architects and the City: Holabird & Roche of Chicago, 1880–1918* (Chicago: University of Chicago Press, 1997); Narciso Menocal, *Architecture as Nature: The Transcendentalist Idea of Louis Sullivan* (Madison: University of Wisconsin Press, 1981); Joseph Siry, *Carson Pirie Scott: Louis Sullivan and the Chicago Department Store* (Chicago: University of Chicago Press, 1988); Theodore Turak, "William Le Baron Jenney, Teacher," *Threshold: Journal of the University of Illinois at Chicago School of Architecture* (fall 1991): 61–82, and "The Ecole Centrale and Modern Architecture: The Education of William Le Baron Jenney," *Journal of the Society of Architectural Historians* 29, no. 1 (March 1970): 40–47; and David Van Zanten, *Sullivan's City: The Meaning of Ornament for Louis Sullivan* (New York: W. W. Norton, 2000). The anthology, *Chicago Architecture, 1872–1922: Birth of a Metropolis* (New York and Munich: Prestel, 1987) edited by John Zukowsky, is also important in this respect.

3. This journal was named *Inland Architect and Building News* until 1887, when it was renamed *Inland Architect and News Record.*

4. Robert Bruegmann has deconstructed the term "Chicago school," situating it as a polemical term created by the European architectural avant-garde of the 1920s and examining its continued influence on the way the city has been planned into the late twentieth century. See Robert Bruegmann, "Myth of the Chicago School" in this collection and "The Marquette Building and the Myth of the Chicago School," *Threshold: Journal of the University of Illinois at Chicago School of Architecture* (fall 1991): 7–23.

5. Robert Prestiano has written the only comprehensive study, *The Inland Architect: Chicago's Major Architectural Journal, 1883–1908* (Ann Arbor, MI: UMI Research Press, 1973).

6. Mary Woods, "The First American Architectural Journals: The Profession's Voice," *Journal of the Society of Architectural Historians* 48 (June 1989): 117–38.

7. Arnold Lewis describes the European reaction to Chicago in comprehensive detail in *An Early Encounter with Tomorrow: Europeans, Chicago's Loop, and the World's Columbian Exposition* (Urbana: University of Illinois Press, 1997).

8. Jacques Hermant, "L'architecture aux États-Unis et à l'exposition universelle de Chicago," *L'Architecture* 7 (October 20, 1894): 341–46.

9. Montgomery Schuyler, "D. H. Burnham and Co.," part 2, no. 2, in the Great American Architects series published by *Architectural Record* (February 1896): 49–69. Reprinted in William Jordy and Ralph Coe, eds., *American Architecture and Other Essays* (Cambridge, MA: Harvard University Press and the Belknap Press, 1961), 405–18.

10. See Anthony Alofsin, "Tempering the Ecole: Nathan Ricker at the University of Illinois, Langford Warren at Harvard," in *The History of History in American Schools of Architecture, 1865–1975*, ed. Gwendolyn Wright and Janet Parkes (New York: Princeton Architectural Press, 1990); Alan K. Laing, *Nathan Clifford Ricker, 1843–1924: Pioneer in American Architectural Education* (Urbana: University of Illinois Press, 1973); and Mark L. Peish, "Nathan Clifford Ricker and the Beginnings of Midwestern Education," *The Chicago School of Architecture: Early Followers of Sullivan and Wright* (New York: Random House, 1965), 7–15.

11. George W. Maher, "Originality in American Architecture," *Inland Architect* 10 no. 4 (October 1887): 34–35.

12. See, in particular Condit, *The Chicago School of Architecture.*

13. On Viollet-le-Duc's ideas of the racial basis of human progress, see Martin Bressani, "Notes on Viollet-le-Duc's Philosophy of History: Dialectics and Technology," *Journal of the Society of Architectural Historians* 48 (December 1989): 327–50.

14. Eugéne Emmanuel Viollet-Le-Duc, *Habitations of Man in All Ages* (1875). Translated extracts were published in *American Architect* 1 (February 26, 1876), and as "The History of Habitations" in *Building Budget* [Chicago] 4, no. 12 (December 1888).

15. In his 1883 memoirs, John Mills Van Osdel, the first practicing architect in Chicago (he arrived in the town in 1841), showed an eagerness to justify Chicago architecture and its adherence to European principles by quoting the French theorist approvingly. John Van Osdel, "History of Chicago Architecture," *Inland Architect,* part 1, vol. 1, no. 2 (March 1883): 17–18.

16. William Le Baron Jenney, "Architecture," *Inland Architect* 1 (March 1883): 18–20; (April 1883): 33–34; (May 1883): 48–50; (June 1883): 63–63; (July 1883): 76–78; vol. 2 (September 1883): 105–6; (October 1883): 117; (November 1883): 130–32; (December 1883): 144–46; (January 1884): 158; and vol. 3 (February 1884): 3.

17. Jenney, "Architecture," *Inland Architect* 3 (February 1884): 49.

18. Jenney, "Architecture," *Inland Architect* 1 (March 1883): 20.

19. Thomas G. Dyer, *Theodore Roosevelt and the Idea of Race* (Baton Rouge: Louisiana State University Press, 1980).

20. Jenney, "Architecture," 1 (April 1883): part 2, 34.

21. See Kenneth Frampton, "Frank Lloyd Wright and the Text-Tile Tectonic," *Studies in Tectonic Culture: The Poetics of Construction in Nineteenth and Twentieth Century Architecture* (Cambridge, MA: MIT Press, 1995), 93–120; Joseph Rykwert, "Architecture Is All on the Surface: Semper and *Bekleidung,*" *Rassegna* 20, no. 73 (1998): 20–29: and Richard Pommer and Barry Bergdoll, "American Architecture and the German Connection," *Kunstchronik* 42, no. 10 (October 1989): 570–74.

22. On the sources of Semper's own ethnographic knowledge, see Harry Francis Mallgrave, "Semper, Klemm and Ethnography," *Lotus International* 109 (2001): 118–31.

23. On Baumann's life and influence, see Roula Geraniotis, "German Architectural Theory and Practice in Chicago, 1850–1900," *Winterthur Portfolio* 21 (winter 1986): 293–306.

24. Gottfried Semper, "Development of Architectural Style," translated by John W. Root and Fritz Wagner, *Inland Architect* part 1, vol. 14, no. 7 (December 1889): 76, 78; part 2, vol. 12, no. 8 (January 1890): 92–94; part 3, vol. 15, no. 1 (February 1890): 5–6; part 4, vol. 15, no 2 (March 1890): 32–33.

25. Semper's popularity was not confined to the Midwest, but appeared wherever German immigrants settled. In California a year later, Bernard Maybeck, whose father was German, announced his intention to translate some of Semper's writing in the *Architectural News* of San Francisco in January 1891. However, if this translation was made it was never published. Sally B. Woodbridge, *Bernard Maybeck: Visionary Architect* (New York: Abbeville Press, 1992), 15–27.

26. Semper, "Development of Architectural Style," part 1, 76.

27. Georges Teyssot, "Norm and Type: Variations on a Theme," in *Architecture and the Sciences: Exchanging Metaphors*, ed. Antoine Picoan and Alessandra Ponte (New York: Princeton Architectural Press, 2002), 140–73. I am grateful to Professor Teyssot for discussing with me the implications of the ethnographic approach in America.

28. Richard Slotkin, *The Fatal Environment: The Myth of the Frontier in the Age of Industrialization, 1800–1890* (New York: Atheneum, 1985).

29. Alan Colquhoun, "The Concept of Regionalism," in *Postcolonial Space(s)*, ed. G. G. Nalbantoglu and C. T. Wong (New York: Princeton Architectural Press, 1997), 13–23.

30. *Inland Architect* 4 (November 1884): 13.

31. Henry Van Brunt, "Architecture in the West," *Inland Architect* 14, no. 7 (December 1889): 78–80.

32. John Wellborn Root, "The City House in the West," *Scribner's Magazine* 8, no. 4 (October 1890): 416–34.

33. John Wellborn Root quoted in Harriet Monroe, *John Wellborn Root, A Study of His Life and Art* (Boston and New York: Houghton, Mifflin, and Co., 1896), 69.

34. Joachim Wolschke-Bulmahn has drawn parallels between the growing movement for "native" landscaping in Germany and America (including the work of Jens Jensen) and nineteenth-century theories of racial superiority. See "Ethics and Morality: Questions in the History of Garden and Landscape Design. A Preliminary Essay," *Journal of Garden History* 14, no. 3 (1994): 140–45. My thanks to Alessandra Ponte for drawing this to my attention.

35. Allen B. Pond, "The Evolution of an American Style," *Inland Architect* 10, no. 9 (January 1888): 98.

36. Irving K. Pond, "The Home," *Inland Architect* 10, no. 6 (November 1887): 63–65.

37. This view is seen most clearly in an 1887 symposium entitled "What Are the Present Tendencies of American Architecture?" The principle speakers were John Root, Dankmar Adler, and W. W. Boyington. Frederick Baumann and Louis Sullivan were in the audience. *Inland Architect* 9, no. 3 (March 1887): 23–26.

38. Prof. N. Clifford Ricker, "Possibilities for American Architecture," *Inland Architect* . 6, no. 5 (November 1885): 62–63.

39. Woods, "The First American Architectural Journals," 117–38.

40. Root, "The City House in the West," 430.

41. Index to the *New York Times*, 1880–1890.

42. *Inland Architect* 7, no. 10 (June 1886): supplement.

43. William Morris, "The March of the Workers" *Alarm* 1, no. 17 (April 4, 1885): 1, and "The Tables

Turned," *Alarm* 1, no. 29 (September 29, 1888): 3. Ruskin is also quoted approvingly as saying, "We Communists of the old school think that our property belongs to everybody and everybody's property to us," *Alarm* 1, no. 9 (November 22, 1884): 2.

44. James F. O'Gorman, "The Marshall Field Wholesale Store: Materials Toward a Monograph," *Journal of the Society of Architectural Historians* (October 1978): 175–94.

45. Carl Smith, *Urban Disorder and the Shape of Belief: The Great Chicago Fire, the Haymarket Bomb and the Model Town of Pullman* (Chicago: University of Chicago Press, 1995), 107. Mario Manieri-Elia has described the control of the building production in Chicago by "bosses" in "Chicago in the 1890s and the Idea of the Fair," in Giorgio Ciucci et al., *The American City: From the Civil War to the New Deal* (Cambridge: MIT Press, 1979), 1–20.

46. Elliott Shore, Ken Fones, and James P. Darby, eds., *The German-American Radical Press: The Shaping of a Left Political Culture, 1850–1940* (Chicago: University of Illinois Press, 1992).

47. "Chicago," *American Architecture* 46 (November 1894): 60.

48. *Alarm* 1, no. 5 (November 1, 1884): 1.

49. "Explosives: A Practical Lesson in Popular Chemistry. The Manufacture of Dynamite Made Easy," *Alarm* 1, no. 20 (April 4, 1885): 1.

50. Smith, *Urban Disorder*, 116.

51. Lucy Parsons, "Word to Tramps," *Alarm* 1, no. 1 (October 4, 1884): 1.

52. Thomas C. Hubka refers to the possible relationship between Richardson's defensive design and the unstable political climate of Chicago in "H. H. Richardson's Glessner House: A Garden in the Machine," *Winterthur Portfolio* 24, no. 4 (winter 1989): 209–30.

Chapter 2

1. The basic source for the history of the term has been H. Allen Brooks, "Chicago School: Metamorphosis of a Term," in *Journal of the Society of Architectural Historians* (May 1966): 115–18. In his admirable, concise essay, Brooks clearly presents the major lines of the story, but he did not mention the use of the term by Howells in literature or other nonarchitectural uses. Brooks also did not attempt to do much interpretation of what this piece of historiography might mean. A bibliography can be found in Jessie L. Poesch, *The Progressive Spirit in Architecture: The Chicago School in Contemporary Literature*, ed. Frederick D. Nichols, American Association of Architectural Bibliographers, 13 ([Chicago]: n.p., 1958, and idem, *The Chicago School in Print: An Annotated Bibliography*, ed. Frederick D. Nichols, American Association of Architectural Bibliographers, 13 ([Charlottesville]: American Association of Architectural Bibliographers, 1959).

2. "Certain of the Chicago School of Fiction," *North American Review* (1903): 734–36. The term was not picked up by subsequent writers, who were more likely to refer to the "Chicago Renaissance." See, for example, Bernard Duffey, *The Chicago Renaissance in American Letters: A Critical History* (East Lansing: Michigan State College Press, 1954).

3. "The Chicago School," *Architectural Review* (April 1908): 69–74. Both the use of the term "school" to mean a group of like-minded artists and the idea that Chicago was somewhat different from other cities in architecture were very common at the turn of the century. Writing in *Pall Mall* in 1899, Peter B. Wight stated, "I think it will be recognized that the work of Chicago architects has been less influenced by foreign schools and the fads and fashions that have prevailed in the United States from time to time than that of any other American city."

4. Ironically, Peisch's *The Chicago School* appeared in the same year that Carl Condit published a book with the same name but that discussed a different

set of buildings. Carl Condit *The Chicago School of Architecture: A History of Commercial and Public Building in the Chicago Area, 1875–1925* (Chicago: University of Chicago Press, 1964). On this, see discussion below. The efforts by Brooks to codify the meaning of Chicago School and Prairie School were ultimately fairly successful. While later books, for example, Hugh C. Miller, *The Chicago School of Architecture: A Plan for Preserving a Significant Remnant of America Architectural Heritage* (Washington D.C.: National Park Service, 1973), continued to use the term in both senses, the earlier meaning of "Chicago school" as the residential work of Sullivan and Wright has become much less common.

5. A particularly influential example of a European looking at the American landscape as a source of inspiration is Walter Gropius, "Die Kunst in Industrie und Handel" in *Jahrbuch des Deutscher Werkbunds* (1913). The photographs that Gropius had accumulated were apparently lent to Le Corbusier, who used them in his famous 1923 publication *Vers une architecture* (Paris: G. Crés) and elsewhere. Reyner Banham has demonstrated how Le Corbusier, determined to find pure geometric forms in works of engineering, applied an airbrush liberally to the photographs to remove historic details and other features he found offensive. The discovery by Europeans of Chicago's forgotten commercial architecture of the 1880s and 1890s is documented in Lewis Mumford, "New York vs. Chicago in Architecture" *Architecture* (November 1927): 241–44. It seems apparent that the reputation of the Chicago buildings was, like the contemporary enthusiasm for American grain elevators and dams, a kind of oral tradition among the avant-garde. The inaccuracies and confusion in the text and in the captions for buildings of the 1880s and 1890s in books like Erich Mendelsohn's *Russland, Europa, Amerika: Ein architecktonischer Querschnitt* (Berlin: R. Mosse, 1929) and Bruno Taut's *Modern Architecture* (London: The Studio, 1929) suggest they had little reliable information on the buildings they were traveling to see and that they were interested primarily in their visual qualities.

6. Mumford visited Chicago in 1927, lectured on the buildings in 1929, and presented his views on them to a wide audience in *The Brown Decades: A Study of the Arts in America* (New York: Harcourt Brace, 1931). He explicitly connected these buildings with the contemporary European *neue Sachlikeit*, as, for example, in his description of the Monadnock Building (62). According to the records of the Museum of Modern Art's Department of Architecture and Design, the show, Early Modern Architecture: Chicago, 1870–1910, was organized by Philip Johnson, and the short catalog was written by Henry-Russell Hitchcock. According to a press release put out by the museum, the two men spent summer 1932 in the Midwest collecting information. Undated press release in files of MOMA Department of Architecture and Design. The show opened at the museum in January 1933.

7. According to Martin Bulmer in *The Chicago School of Sociology: Institutionalism, Diversity and the Rise of Sociological Research* (Chicago: University of Chicago Press, 1984), 229, the earliest use of the term in this way was in L. L. Bernard, "Schools of Sociology," *Southwestern Political and Social Science Quarterly* (September 1930), referring to work that had been underway during the 1920s.

8. Terms like "French shool" or "Venetian school" had been frequently used in the nineteenth century and continue to be used into the twentieth to designate groups of artists working in a given place. "School" was also used to indicate atelier membership or stylistic affiliations, as in the "school of Titian." The term was similarly used in architecture, as, for example, in the 1896 edition of Sir Bannister Fletcher's monumental *History of Architecture on the Comparative Method*, where he referred to the Classic school and the Gothic school of nineteenth-century design. Hitchcock clearly loved such art historical labels, traditional or invented, for example, Schinkelesque (in the manner of Karl Friedrich Schinkel) or Ledolcian (in the manner of Claude-Nicolas Ledoux).

9. Museum of Modern Art, *Early Modern Architecture, Chicago*, 2d ed. (New York: Museum of Modern Art, 1940), 14.

10. A good introduction to the work of Giedion can be found in Spiro Kostof, "Architecture, You and Him: The Mark of Sigfried Giedion," in *Daedalus* (winter 1976): 189–204.

11. Not every term succeeds in this way. Probably the vast majority of them are forgotten almost as soon as they are coined. A good example of a term that has dramatically fallen in favor is "mannerism" as used in architecture.

12. Henry-Russell Hitchcock in his *Modern Architecture, Romanticism and Reintegration* (New York: Payson & Clarke, 1929), 108, stated that the Tacoma was perhaps the best expression of functional structure of the Chicago architects but that its ornament was second-rate Richardsonian Romanesque.

13. A good example of this kind of approach can be found, for example, in the recently published *L'Architecture de l'École de Chicago: Architecture functionaliste et idéologie américaine* by Claude Massu (Paris: Dunad, 1982). It is a theme that runs through the work of Manfredo Tafuri and his Italian colleagues. See, for example, the essay by Mario Manieri-Elia in Giorgio Ciucci et al., *The American City from the Civil War to the New Deal* (Cambridge, MA: MIT Press, 1979). A recent example of the same kind of view can be found in Heinrich Klotz, "The Chicago Multi-Story as a Design Problem" in *Chicago Architecture, 1872–1922: Birth of a Metropolis*, ed. John Zukowsky (Munich: Prestel, 1987).

14. Carl Condit, "The Chicago School and the Modern Movement in Architecture," *Art in America* (February 1948): 19–36.

15. Sigfried Giedion, *Space, Time and Architecture*, 3d ed. (Cambridge, MA: Harvard University Press, 1956), 368–93. On the second Chicago school, it appears that the term was made popular by an issue of *Architectural Forum* devoted to Chicago architecture published in May 1962.

16. Questions about the use of the term were raised from the beginning. See, for example, the penetrating review of Condit's book by William Jordy in *Perspectives in American History*, 1 (1967): 390–400. Still, for a number of years, many authors went along with Condit's presentation, even after Condit abandoned his position. For example, in his recent and, on the whole, splendid survey, *A History of Architecture, Settings and Rituals* (New York: Oxford University Press, 1985), 666, Spiro Kostof speaks of an "abnegation, the noncultural, nonhistorical drive forward" of late nineteenth-century Chicago architects.

17. The assertion that Jenney invented skeletal construction or that the skyscraper originated in Chicago has been refuted over and over again since the claims were first made around the turn of the twentieth century. On the Home Insurance Building the most complete and judicious assessment was made by the group appointed by the Western Society of Engineers in 1931. The conclusions contained in "The Home Insurance Building: A Report on the Type of Construction Observed in the Home Insurance Building As It Was Demolished," in *Journal of the Western Society of Engineers*, was almost certainly known to Condit. These findings have been restated more recently in Theodore Turak, "Remembrances of the Home Insurance Building," *Journal of the Society of Architectural Historians* (March 1985): 60–65; and in Gerald Larson and Roula Gerianotis, "Toward a Better Understanding of the Iron Skeleton Frame in Chicago," *Journal of the Society of Architectural Historians* (March 1987): 39–48.

18. This had long been a preoccupation of American scholarship as the controversies over the American origins of the log cabin testify. John McCoubrey's little volume, *American Tradition in Painting* (New York: G. Braziller, 1963), represents a particularly good example of the intensified post-

war effort to assert America's place in the context of the larger art historical scene. On this effort, see Wanda Corn, "Coming of Age: Historical Scholarship in American Art," in *Art Bulletin* (June 1988): 188–192. The same kind of effort characterizes *The Rise of an American Architecture* (New York: Praeger, 1970), edited by Edgar Kaufmann, Jr. In the first essay in this book, Henry-Russell Hitchcock attempted to demonstrate different kinds of American innovation and influence on Europe dating back to the eighteenth century. The fourth essay, by Vincent Scully, expanded on that author's famous book, *The Shingle Style: Architectural Theory and Design from Richardson to the Origins of Wright* (New Haven: Yale University Press, 1955), in which Scully attempted to prove that late nineteenth-century America pioneered several new modes of residential construction. Much of what these postwar historians tried to prove has subsequently been disputed as more is learned about contemporary events in Europe. Much of what Scully claimed to be peculiarly American, for example, has been shown to be part of a larger movement in Western culture in an interesting analysis by Sarah Bradford Landau, "Richard Morris Hunt, the Continental Picturesque, and the 'Stick Style,'" *Journal of the Society of Architectural Historians* (October 1983): 272–89. A recent and provocative analysis of the American need for cultural heroes can be found in Serge Guilbaut, *How New York Stole the Idea of Modern Art: Abstract Expressionism, Freedom and the Cold War* (Chicago: University of Chicago Press, 1983).

19. *Architectural Forum* (May 1962): 96.

20. Weisman's most developed statement can be found in "The Chicago School of Architecture: A Symposium. Part 1" in *Prairie School Review* 20 nos. 1–2 (1972): 6–30.

21. Full documentation of the Marquette Building will be found in my three-volume catalog, *Holabird and Roche/Holabird and Root: An Illustrated Catalog of Work* (New York: Garland, 1991). The initial structure was built in 1893–95, and a bay was added along Adams Street in 1905–6. The building originally had a projecting portico of Ionic columns at the entranceway but these were soon removed as was, considerably later, a heavy cornice. A good many other minor modifications were made over the years, but many of these were removed during a restoration in 1979–81 carried out to the designs of Holabird & Root, the successor firm.

22. Giedion, *Space, Time and Architecture*, 377.

23. Condit, *Chicago School*, 121–22.

24. Condit's books were *Chicago, 1910–29: Building Planning and Urban Technology* (Chicago: University of Chicago Press, 1973), and *Chicago, 1930–1970: Building, Planning and Urban Technology* (Chicago: University of Chicago Press, 1974). The article, "The Triumph and Failure of the Skyscraper," *Inland Architect* (January 1977), was a modification of "Trionfo tecnologico e fallimento architettonico" that appeared in *Casabella* (October 1976).

25. The best indication of this trend is the monumental catalog *Chicago Architecture, 1872–1922: Birth of a City*, edited by John Zukowsky, to accompany an exhibition in 1987 organized by the Art Institute of Chicago.

26. I am grateful to my colleague Thomas Gordon Smith at the University of Notre Dame for his insights on the classical ornamentation on the Marquette.

27. Joseph and Caroline Kirkland, *The Story of Chicago*, vol. 2, (Chicago: Dibble, 1892–84), 353.

28. *The Legend and Legacy of Père Marquette* (Chicago: [Aldis, Aldis & Northcote], 1894).

29. A good example of this process is the issue entitled "The Chicago School of Architecture," *Process Architecture* 35 (1983). The intent, according to editor Masami Takayama, was to present a comprehensive rather than "structuralist and functionalist"

point of view (4). On the pages that follow, even the Chicago Public Library and the Art Institute are included with the Monadnock and the Marquette. Another good example of the way the focus of what is perceived to be Chicago school has shifted from the 1880s to the 1890s and the turn of the century and beyond can be found in the popular pamphlet by John Poppeliers, Allen Chambers, and Nancy Schwarz, *What Style Is It?* (Washington, D.C.: National Trust for Historic Preservation, n.d.).

Chapter 3

This article was previously published in Threshold *5/6 (1991): 103–8.*

1. Lewis Mumford, "The Imperial Façade," in *Sticks and Stones: A Study of American Architecture and Civilization* (New York: Boni and Liveright, 1924), 273–74, 275.

2. Peter B. Wight, "Daniel Hudson Burnham," *Construction News* (15 June 1912), 19.

3. Vachel Lindsay, *Art of the Moving Picture* (New York: MacMillan Company, 1916). 273–79.

4. Harriet Monroe, *John Wellborn Root: A Study of His Life and Works* (Boston and New York: Houghton Mifflin, 1896).

5. Louis Sullivan, *Autobiography of an Idea* (New York: Press of the American Institute of Architects, 1924), 314.

6. Frank Lloyd Wright, *Autobiography* (New York: Longmans, Greene and Company, 1932), 123–24.

7. Paul Bourget, *Outre-mer: Notes sur l'Amérique* (Paris: A. Lemerre, 1894), 381, translation in Monroe, *John Wellborn Root,* 136–37.

Chapter 4

Earlier versions of this essay appeared in Threshold: Journal of the Chicago School of Architecture *[University of Illinois at Chicago] 5–6 (fall 1991): 39–59; and* Midwestern Landscape Architecture, *ed. William H. Tishler (Urbana and Chicago: University of Illinois Press, 2000), 57–79.*

1. Jenney's architectural innovations are celebrated in Sigfried Giedion's bible of modernism, *Space, Time, and Architecture* (Cambridge, MA: Harvard University Press, 1941), and have received fresh reassessment by Theodore Turak in *William Le Baron Jenney: A Pioneer of Modern Architecture* (Ann Arbor: UMI Research Press, 1986). Fortunately Turak's research has begun to restore the fading record of Jenney's accomplishments in landscape architecture, most of which occurred early in his long and productive architectural practice. The following biographical sketch of Jenney is based on Turak's *William Le Baron Jenney,* chapters 1–6.

2. "Process space" is a term coined by J. B. Jackson. Personal conversation with J. B. Jackson, February 1976. See also John Brinckerhoff Jackson, *American Space: The Centennial Years, 1865–1876* (New York: W. W. Norton, 1972), 85–86, where Jackson defines "process space" as one organized as "an orderly system of events leading up to a product."

3. Adolphe Alphand, *Les Promenades de Paris* (Paris, 1867–73); Frederick Law Olmsted, *Public Parks and the Enlargement of Towns* (Cambridge, Mass., 1870); Cynthia Zaitzevsky, *Frederick Law Olmsted and the Boston Park System* (Cambridge: Belknap Press, 1982); Daniel Walker Howe, "Victorian Culture in America," in *Victorian America,* ed. Daniel Walker Howe (Philadelphia: University of Pennsylvania Press, 1976), 3–28; and David Schuyler, *The New Urban Landscape: The Redefinition of City Form in Nineteenth-Century America* (Baltimore: Johns Hopkins University Press, 1986).

4. Despite Jenney's never having actually designed a park or boulevard, the West Chicago Park commissioners apparently had sufficient faith in his abilities to hire him. His local residency (no small consideration in Chicago appointments) and his recently coauthored book on architectural theory

may also have been factors in their decision. Turak, *Jenney*, chap. 6; Victoria Post Ranney, *Olmsted in Chicago* (Chicago: Donnelley, 1972); Alfred Theodore Andreas, *History of Chicago from the Earliest Period to the Present Time in Three Volumes* (Chicago, 1886), 3: 167–89; William Le Baron Jenney and Sanford E. Loring, *Principles and Practices of Architecture* (Chicago, 1869).

5. When Jenney submitted a plan for Douglas Park, the commissioners insisted that he modify the straight diagonal boulevard bisecting it into a more curvilinear drive. Jenney complied, although Ogden Avenue was finally built as a straight diagonal. This drama suggests that the design for the West Parks grew out of a lively dialogue between strong clients and their architect, a situation that often leads to innovative results. "Official Proceedings of the West Parks Commission, 1869–1893," 8 December 1870 (manuscript in Chicago Park District Archives, Chicago, Illinois); I am indebted to Mary O'Shaughnessy for calling this material to my attention. Jenney left the commission's service in 1877. Thereafter, his former employee O. F. Dubuis supervised the work along the lines of Jenney's original design, which remained the basis of all further work as affirmed by official vote of the West Park commissioners. There is no evidence that Jenney resigned because of difficulties with the commission, although some evidence suggests that they were not paying him promptly. Probably Jenney wanted to devote more time to his burgeoning architectural practice. He maintained a cordial relationship with the commission; he served occasionally as a consultant well in to the 1890s and later even designed several park buildings. In fact, it is difficult to separate Dubuis's work from Jenney's, and several of the modifications of the original 1871 plan, necessitated by a shrinking budget, may have been formulated by Jenney in consultation with Dubuis, until the commissioners terminated Dubuis's appointment as chief engineer in 1893.

6. Jenney described his idea for the park system in the *Second Annual Report of the West Chicago Park Commission* (Chicago, 1871). See also *First Annual Report* (1870), *Third Annual Report* (1872), *Fourth Annual Report* (1873), and Turak, *Jenney*, chap. 6. Jenney was not inclined to make elaborate written statements about his design intentions. His description of Central Park in the *Second Annual Report* is a succinct seven pages. Accompanying his statement was a quite elegantly drawn and finely detailed 250-scale plan of the park. In what follows, I have used Jenney's brief statements as a point of departure and supplemented them extensively with my own reading of his plan, taking care to distinguish between the two.

7. While Jenney adopted Alphand's preference for a subtropical planting scheme, he avoided two of what Robinson considered Alphand's "mistakes," carving up the parks with too many roads and ruining the lake edges by bringing pathways too near their shoreline. William Robinson, *The Parks, Promenades, and Gardens of Paris Described and Considered in Relation to the Wants of Our Own Cities* (London, 1869), and Alphand, *Les Promenades.*

8. Olmsted, *Public Parks*; Frederick Law Olmsted, letter to William Hammond Hall, 1874, Olmsted Papers, Library of Congress; Frederick Law Olmsted and Calvert Vaux, *Report Accompanying Plan for Laying Out the South Park*" (Chicago: South Park Commission, Chicago, 1871).

9. *Second Annual Report*, 62.

10. *First Annual Report, Second Annual Report*, and *Third Annual Report.*

11. Jenney, *Second Annual Report*, 52–72. Limited funds precluded sinking the roads below grade as in New York's Central Park.

12. Jenney probably consulted chapters 1–10.

13. A comprehensive history of the West Parks is yet to be written. Valuable preliminary research has been conducted by Julia Sniderman Bachrach. See her manuscripts, "Model Preservation Planning Project Survey Analysis, Humboldt Park" (1989),

Chicago Park District Archives; and "The Historic Resources of the Chicago Park District. United States Department of the Interior, National Park Service, National Register of Historic Places Multiple Property Documentation Form" (n.d.; copy in Chicago Park District Archives). See also the annual reports of the West Chicago Park Commission, 1870–73. According to Alfred Caldwell, who at one time worked for Jens Jensen, Jensen had deep respect for Jenney's ability as a park designer. Caldwell, personal communication to the author, 24 September 1990.

14. *Second Annual Report*, 52–68.

15. Jenney and Loring, *Principles and Practices of Architecture*, example c, pl. 2.

16. Turak, *Jenney*, chap. 4, esp. 50.

17. *Second Annual Report*, 62–68.

18. *Second Annual Report*, 64–68.

19. Early in the next century, Jens Jensen's major additions to the unfinished portions of Jenney's West Parks would transform Jenney's cosmopolitan planting plan into a regional one utilizing native plants and celebrating the prairie's beauty.

20. When Olmsted first saw tropical scenery while crossing the Isthmus of Panama in 1863, he immediately wrote to his chief gardener at Central Park and urged him to attempt to create "tropical character" in portions of the park by the profuse planting of vines and the special pruning of hardy native vegetation. Frederick Law Olmsted, letter to Ignaz Anton Pilat dated 26 September 1863, in *The California Frontier, 1863–1865*, ed. V. P. Ranney, G. J. Rauluk, and C. F. Hoffman, vol. 5 of *The Papers of Frederick Law Olmsted*, ed. C.C. McLaughlin and C. E. Beveridge (Baltimore: Johns Hopkins University Press, 1990), 85–92. Olmsted followed a similar strategy in the South Park lagoons.

21. *Fourth Annual Report* (1873), *Fifth Annual Report* (1874), and *Sixth Annual Report* (1875).

22. This matching of building style with landscape character was central to the work of Andrew Jackson Downing, whom Jenney greatly admired. *Second Annual Report*, 64–67; Turak, *Jenney*, 91–93.

23. Christian Norberg-Schulz, *New World Architecture* (New York: Princeton Architectural Press, 1988), 27–41.

24. Jenney to Frederick Law Olmsted, letter dated 15 September 1865, Olmsted Papers, Library of Congress.

Chapter 5

1. Donald L. Miller, *City of the Century* (New York: Simon & Schuster, 1996), 81–88.

2. Miller, *City of the Century*, 82.

3. Richard C. MacCormac, "The Anatomy of Wright's Aesthetic," in *Writings on Wright*, ed. H. Allen Broooks (Cambridge, MA: MIT Press, 1981), 163–74.

4. H. Allen Brooks, introduction to "The Anatomy of Wright's Aesthetic," in *Writings on Wright*, 165.

5. Colin Rowe, "*The Mathematics of the Ideal Villa*" *and Other Essays* (Cambridge, MA: MIT Press, 1976), 89–117.

6. Leonard K. Eaton, *Two Chicago Architects and Their Clients* (Cambridge, MA: MIT Press, 1969).

7. Frank Lloyd Wright, "The Art and Craft of the Machine," in *Frank Lloyd Wright Collected Writings* (New York: Rizzoli, 1992–95), 1: 58–69.

8. A. Rosenblueth and N. Weiner, "Purposeful and Non-purposeful Behavior," *Philosophy of Science* 18 (1951), quoted in Richard Lewontin, *The Triple Helix* (Cambridge, MA: Harvard University Press, 2000), 4.

9. Frank Lloyd Wright, in *Frank Lloyd Wright Monograph, 1951–1959*, ed. Bruce Brooks Pfeiffer (Tokyo: A.D.A. Edita, 1988), 269.

Chapter 6

This paper is a revised version of an article originally published in the Journal of Architectural Education *47 (May 1994): 197–207.*

1. See Susan Porter Benson, Stephen Brier, and Roy Rosenzweig, eds., *Presenting the Past: Essays on History and the Public* (Philadelphia: Temple University Press, 1986); Warren Leon and Roy Rosenzweig, eds., *History Museums in the United States: A Critical Assessment* (Urbana: University of Illinois Press, 1989); and Michael Frisch, *A Shared Authority: Essays on the Craft and Meaning of Oral and Public History* (Albany: State University of New York Press, 1990).

2. See Robert Bruegmann, "The Myth of the Chicago School," reprinted in this collection, and Daniel Bluestone, *Constructing Chicago* (New Haven: Yale University Press, 1991),105–51.

3. *Industrial Chicago*, vol. 1 (Chicago: Goodspeed Publishing, 1891), 168.

4. Bruegmann, "The Marquette Building," 7–18.

5. Museum of Modern Art, *Early Modern Architecture, Chicago 1870–1910*, typescript catalog (New York: Museum of Modern Art, 1933).

6. Hugh Morrison, *Louis Sullivan, Prophet of Modern Architecture* (New York: Museum of Modern Art and W.W. Norton Co., 1935), 270.

7. Sigfried Giedion, *Space, Time and Architecture: The Growth of a New Tradition* (Cambridge, MA: Harvard University Pres, 1941); Carl Condit, *The Rise of the Skyscraper* (Chicago: University of Chicago Press, 1952); and idem, *The Chicago School of Architecture: A History of Commercial and Public Buildings in the City Area, 1875–1925* (Chicago: University of Chicago Press, 1964). See also Reyner Banham, "A Walk in the Loop," *Chicago* 2 (spring 1965): 24–28; and Bluestone, *Constructing Chicago*, 105–8.

8. "The Shrinking Giant," *Newsweek* 52 (December 9, 1958): 76.

9. "An Encroaching Menace," *Life Magazine* 38 (April 11, 1955): 125–34.

10. "A New Rage to Reconstruct Central Chicago," *Architectural Forum* 116 (May 1962): 114–15.

11. "The Chicago School," *Inland Architect* 1 (October 1957): 15–16.

12. Ibid.

13. Daniel H. Burnham and Edward H. Bennett, *Plan of Chicago* (Chicago: Commercial Club, 1909), 87

14. Edward C. Logelin, "This Is Chicago Dynamic," *Inland Architect* 1 (October 1957): 9–10.

15. *Chicago Tribune*, October 31, 1957.

16. Quoted in *Chicago Sun-Times*, October 31, 1957.

17. *Chicago Sun-Times*, October 31, 1957.

18. "Forum of Formidables," *Inland Architect* 1 (April 1958): 14–17.

19. George E. Danforth, "Mies van der Rohe," *Inland Architect* 7 (November 1963): 6.

20. *Chicago Tribune*, March 19, 1957.

21. See Frederick T. Aschman to Van Allen Bradley, letter dated January 11, 1956, and Thomas B. Stauffer, memorandum, "Round Robin," dated April 24, 1956. Leon Despres Papers, box 40, Chicago Historical Society.

22. *Hyde Park Herald*, December 25, 1957.

23. Hyde Park–Kenwood Community Conference, "Questions and Suggestions of Kenwood Block Groups on Urban Renewal Planning," February 1956, Urban Renewal Demonstration Case Files, Housing and Home Finance Agency Records Record Group 207, box 17, National Archives, Washington, DC.

24. See Margaret M. Myerson, "Urban Redevelopment in Hyde Park" (master's thesis, University of Chicago, March 1959); and Peter H. Rossi and Robert H. Dentler, *Politics of Urban Renewal: The Chicago Findings* (New York: Free Press of Glencoe, 1961); on opposition, see Margery Frisbie, *An Alley in Chicago: The Ministry of a City Priest* (Kansas City, MO: Sheed & Ward, 1991), 94–110.

25. Hyde Park–Kenwood Community Conference, *Segments of the Past* (Chicago: The Conference, 1962).

26. Ruth Moore, "A Second Life for Landmarks," *Chicago* 2 (spring 1965): 28–31.

27. Historic American Building Survey Records, Prints and Photographs Division, Library of Congress, Washington, D.C.

28. See Richard Cahan, *They All Fall Down: Richard Nickel's Struggle to Save America's Architecture* (Washington, D.C.: National Trust for Historic Preservation, 1994), chap. 5. See also *Chicago Daily News*, August 29, 1956; and *Chicago Tribune*, February 23, 1964, and January 7, 1965.

29. *Journal of the Proceedings of the City Council of the City of Illinois, for the Council Year 1957* (Chicago: Fred Klein Co., 1957), 4187.

30. Earl H. Read to Preservation Officers, circular letter dated September 26, 1956. Committee on Historic Resources, box 1948–1969, American Institute of Architects Archives, Washington, DC.

31. Chicago *Sun Times*, October 9, 1955.

32. "Obsolescence Study of an Office Building in Chicago," *Engineering News-Record* 99 (July 28, 1927): 136–37; and Robert Craik McLean, "The Passing of the Woman's Temple," *Western Architect* 31 (January 1922): 13–14.

33. *Chicago Daily News*, June 21, 1939.

34. Cahan, *They All Fall Down*, chap. 4.

35. Mies's position quoted in *Chicago Sun-Times*, June 14, 1960; Corbusier quoted in "Corbu and Stauffer Comment on Garrick Theater," *Progressive Architecture* 42 (June 1961): 208.

36. *Chicago Sun-Times*, June 9, 11, 13, 14, and 18, 1960.

37. Quoted in Elinor Rickey, "What Chicago Could Be Proud Of," *Harper's Magazine* 223 (December 1961): 34–39.

38. Richard H. Howland to David B. Wallerstein, letter dated June 28, 1960, in Vertical Files, National Trust for Historic Preservation Library, University of Maryland, College Park, Maryland.

39. See Cahan, *They All Fall Down*, esp. chaps. 4 and 5.

40. Norman Ross, "Chicago Is Destroying Architectural Heritage," *Inland Architect* 6 (September 1962): 6.

41. *Chicago Sun-Times*, June 14, 1960.

42. Ruth Moore, "The Citizens Are Learning," *Inland Architect* 4 (April 1961): 9.

43. Ruth Moore, "A City Reborn," *Chicago Sun-Times*, October 14, 1958.

44. *Chicago Tribune*, January 25, 1895; see also Bluestone, *Constructing Chicago*, 174.

45. *Chicago Sun-Times*, January 16, 1959.

46. Noble W. Lee to Thomas B. Stauffer, letter dated March 11, 1963; Thomas B. Stauffer to Noble W. Lee, letter dated March 12, 1963. Chicago Heritage Committee Papers, box 1, Chicago Historical Society.

47. "News Press Release from the Office of Senator Paul H. Douglas," July 10, 1961, in National Historic Preservation Library, University of Maryland, College Park, Maryland.

48. *Chicago Sun-Times*, October 31, 1957.

49. Carl Condit, letter to the editor, *Chicago Sun-Times*, September 23, 1960. Nickel wrote to the developers of the Cable Building site and complimented them on the design of the new building, Richard Nickel to Ray Henson, Continental Assurance Co., letter dated February 12, 1962. Richard Nickel Papers, box 2, Chicago Historical Society.

50. Benjamin Weese, "The Republic Building," *Inland Architect* 4 (December 1960): 9.

51. Carroll W. Westfall, "Towards a New (Old) Architecture," *Modulus* 16 (1983): 78–97.

Chapter 7

Portions of the research for this essay were funded by a grant from the Graham Foundation. Special thanks to Richard Solomon and to Ben and Cynthia Weese for their support and personal reminiscences relevant to the project, and to Charles Waldheim for bringing it to publication. I would like to thank those other Chicago architects and engineers who agreed to be interviewed in 1997–99 for this study, Y. C. Wong, George Schipporeit, John Macsai, Ezra Gordon, and Larry Booth. Thanks also for their sharing their knowledge to Kevin Harrington, Robert Bruegmann, Jacques Sandberg, Heather Hootman, and Joan Pomaranc. For assistance with examining original plans and photographs, thanks to the archivists at Loebl, Schlossman and Bennett, the Chicago Landmarks Commission, and the Chicago Historical Society.

1. Sigfried Giedion, *Space, Time and Architecture*, 3d ed. (Cambridge, MA: Harvard University Press, 1954), 560; 5th ed. (1967), 607.

2. Daniel Bluestone, *Constructing Chicago* (New Haven: Yale University Press, 1991); Robert Bruegmann, *The Architects and the City: Holabird & Roche of Chicago, 1880–1918* (Chicago: University of Chicago Press, 1997); Carol Willis, "Light, Height and Site: The Skyscraper in Chicago," in *Chicago Architecture and Design, 1923–1993*, ed. John Zukowsky (Chicago: Art Institute/Prestel, 1993), 119–40. Willis makes it clear that financing, zoning, and technical developments continued to be the major elements in shaping the form of Chicago skyscrapers in the twentieth century. Mies himself rejected the idea that his work was an extension of the first Chicago school, telling one interviewer that he barely knew the famous late nineteenth-century Loop buildings, since he always took taxis to work at IIT (William H. Jordy, *American Buildings and Their Architects*, vol. 5, *The Impact of European Modernism in the Mid-twentieth Century* [New York: Oxford University Press, 1972], 223).

3. The first Chicago building definitely identified as a "flat" building rather than a working-class tenement was a stone-faced, four-story brick-and-timber structure constructed in 1878 on West Erie Street between State and Dearborn, close to the then-fashionable upper-class residential area along Rush and Wabash streets (Edith Abbott, *The Tenements of Chicago, 1908–1935* [Chicago, 1936], 44–48). This first Chicago flat came a few years after the first New York example, Richard Morris Hunt's Stuyvesant Apartments (1869), but any direct influence of Hunt's building is doubtful. A surviving example of an early Chicago multifamily building from this period is the Hotel St. Benedict Flats (James J. Egan, 1882) at the northeast corner of Wabash and Chicago avenues, which was designed to resemble a row of red brick Second Empire townhouses.

4. Many of these early high-rise apartment hotels are described and illustrated in Carl Condit, *The Chicago School of Architecture: A History of Commercial and Public Building in the Chicago Area, 1875–1925* (Chicago: University of Chicago Press, 1964), 149–53. The high-rise apartment hotel type as a national phenomenon is analyzed in detail in Paul Groth, *Living Downtown: The History of Residential Hotels in the United States* (Berkeley: University of California Press, 1994).

5. Herbert Croly, "Some Apartment Houses in Chicago," *Architectural Record* 21 (Feb. 1907): 119–30. One of the earliest examples is the neoclassical Pattington Apartments (D. E. Postle, 1903).

6. An excellent documentary source on luxury three- and six-flats is A. J. Pardridge and Harold Bradley, *Directory to Apartments of the Better Class along the North Side of Chicago* (Chicago, 1917; reprinted by Lisec and Klimek, 1979).

7. In planning the Century of Progress exhibition, East Coast architects Raymond Hood and Paul Cret asked Harvey Wiley Corbett, Ralph Walker, and Arthur Brown to join them, who then added Edward Bennett, Hubert Burnham, John A. Holabird, Louis Skidmore, and Nathaniel Owings to the fair's design commission. The commission eventually designated Skidmore as the chief of design (Carl Condit, *Chicago 1930–70* [Chicago: University of Chicago Press, 1974], 6–8).

8. A good example of streamlined moderne apartment design of this period is Andrew Rebori's Fisher Apartments (1936). See Terry Tatum, *Frank F. Fisher, Jr., Apartments* (Chicago: Commission on Chicago Landmarks, 1991); Stuart E. Cohen, *Chicago Architects* (Chicago: Swallow Press, 1976), 79–81.

9. Keck and Keck's House of Tomorrow in illustrated in Cohen, *Chicago Architects*, 84–85.

10. *Keck-Gottschalk-Keck Apartments* (Chicago: Commission on Chicago Landmarks, 1994); *Flats; George F. Keck* (*Architectural Review* 88 [December 1940], 175–77).

11. Devereaux Bowly, *The Poorhouse: Subsidized Housing in Chicago, 1895–1976* (London: Feffer and Simmonds, 1978); Wim de Wit, "The Rise of Public Housing in Chicago, 1930–1960," in *Chicago Architecture and Design, 1923–1993*, ed. John Zukowsky (Chicago: Art Institute/Prestel, 1993), 233–46.

12. Horatio B. Hackett, "How the PWA Housing Division Functions," *Architectural Record* 77 (March 1935): 148–66.

13. Former luxury apartment architects involved in early Chicago public housing included Ralph Huszagh at Jane Addams Homes, Robert DeGolyer and Israel Loewenberg at Lathrop Homes, and Philip Maher at Trumbull Park Homes. At the Ida B. Wells Homes (1941), Theilbar & Fugard were on the team, and at Cabrini Homes (1942), the design team included Loewenberg, Louis Solomon, Maurice Rissman, and Henry Holsman. Bowly, *The Poorhouse*, 20, 23, 25, 28, 35–36.

14. "Glass and Brick in a Concrete Frame," *Architectural Forum* (January 1950): 71–74.

15. Peter Blake, *Mies van der Rohe* (Baltimore: Penguin, 1964), 94.

16. Miles Berger, *They Built Chicago* (Chicago: Bonus Books, 1992), 247; the sonnet is Keats's "On First Looking into Chapman's Homer" (1816). A plan of the Darien is in Cohen, *Chicago Architects*, 52.

17. On the firm's history, see http://www.parker-holsman.com/.

18. "Pioneering Construction Ideas," *Architectural Forum* (January 1950): 79–83.

19. Y. C. Wong, interview by the author, July 14, 1997; "Atrium Houses by Yau C. Wong, Architect,"

Arts and Architecture 79 (April 1962): 12–13; "Return of the Atrium," *Architectural Forum* (March 1962): 86–88.

20. "Return of the Atrium," 86–88.

21. Harry Weese, "Housing Patterns and What Makes Them," *Architectural Record* 123 (July 1958): 171–74.

22. "High-Rise, Low-Rise and Shopping for Chicago Redevelopment," *Architectural Record* 131 (April 1962): 163–67.

23. *Architectural Forum* 120 (March 1964): 70 ff. Interviews with Ben Weese, 1997–2001.

Chapter 8

The author wishes to thank the Graham Foundation for Advanced Studies in the Arts for their financial support for the research underlying this essay.

1. Phyllis Lambert, ed., *Mies in America,* exhibition catalog ([New York]: H. N. Abrams, 2001).

2. Books dealing with architects and their buildings from the broader perspective include Sir John Summerson, *Georgian London* (New York, C. Scribner's Sons, 1946); Philippe Bourdon, *Lived-In Architecture: Le Corbusier's Pessac Revisited,* trans. Gerald Onn (London: Lund Humphries, 1972); Tim Benton, *The Villas of Le Corbusier,* **1920–1930** *: With Photographs in the Lucien Hervé Collection* (New Haven: Yale University Press, 1987); Joseph Connors, *Borromini and the Roman Oratory: Style and Society* (New York and Cambridge, Mass. : Architectural History Foundation and MIT Press, 1980), Diane Ghirardo, *Building New Communities: New Deal America and Fascist Italy* (Princeton: Princeton University Press, 1989); Iain Borden and David Dunster, eds., *Architecture and the Sites of History* (New York: Whitney Library of Design, 1996)*;* and Robert Bruegmann, *Holabird & Roche, Holabird & Root: An Illustrated Catalog of Works, 1880–1940* (New York: Garland in cooperation with the Chicago Historical Society, 1991), and idem, *The Architects and the City: Holabird and Roche of Chicago, 1880–1918.* Regrettably such efforts are swamped by considerably more works of connoisseurship and interpretation.

3. See Fritz Neumeyer, *The Artless Word: Mies van der Rohe on the Building Art* (Cambridge, Mass.: MIT Press, 1994).

4. On the occasion of the fortieth anniversary of the opening of 860/880 Lake Shore Drive, a symposium, 860/880 Lake Shore Drive: A 40 Year Retrospective, was held at the Arts Club of Chicago on September 19, 1992. The meeting was chaired by Franz Schulze and included tenants of the buildings, included those who had worked on the project in Mies's office: George Danforth, Myron Goldsmith, Ed Duckett, Bruno Conterato, and Joseph Fujikawa. For the purposes of this essay, the statements by Robert McCormick, and Mrs. Herbert Greenwald have been crucial. I am deeply indebted to Edward Windhorst, who transcribed the tapes and allowed me to take a copy. Hereafter all references are to the Windhorst transcript.

5. "Oral History of Charles Booher Genther," interview by Betty J. Blum on September 30, 1983, and contained in *Chicago Architects Oral History Project* (Chicago: Dept. of Architecture, The Art Institute of Chicago, 1995), 20. Available at http://www.artic.edu/aic/collections/dept_architecture/genther.htm l. In the interview, Genther explains that Promontory cost $11,000 while 860 cost $13,000 (both prices for a one-bedroom apartment).

6. Neumeyer, *The Artless Word.*

7. Not just these writers but also significant literary critics such as the new Criticism and the authors William K. Wimsatt, *The Verbal Icon: Studies in the Meaning of Poetry,* with the collaboration of Monroe C. Beardsley on two preliminary essays (New York: Noonday Press, 1958).

8. A. J. Liebling, *Chicago: The Second City* (New York: Knopf, 1952).

9. Giorgio Ciucci uses machine corruption as the explanation for the failure of planning in the American city. See *The American City: From the Civil War to the New Deal*, trans. Barbara Luigia La Penta (Cambridge, Mass.: MIT Press, 1979).

10. See Frank A. Randall, *History of the Development of Building Construction in Chicago* (Urbana: University of Illinois Press, 1949), 289. Randall describes the building as twenty-four stories high, the Field Office building at 135 La Salle was completed in 1932 and 1934. "The building is 23 stories high, with a nineteen-story tower and three basements."

11. Built over 1871 fire damage rubble, North Lake Shore Drive connected the Loop with the Gold Coast surrounding Oak Street Beach and the southern end of Lincoln Park, and continued as an embankment against the lake to Diversey Parkway, where it subsequently continued inland to Bryn Mawr Avenue and Hollywood Boulevard.

12. The Streeterville Collection in the Chicago Public Library at Archives STR details the court cases, which were effectively concluded only in the 1920s.

The issue at the center of the controversy was ownership of made land. The owners of shore property hastily banded together and struck a deal with the state and the Lincoln Park board of directors. By this agreement, the shore owners built a boulevard a half mile out in the Lake (now Lake Shore Drive), filled in the pool behind it, and continued the city streets across the new marshy land. The boulevard was presented to the state, and the state gave the shore owners titles to the reclaimed land. In the middle of this acreage sat Streeter's shack, successor to the Reutan as the couple's home.

Streeter's legal argument was that the state of Illinois had no jurisdiction in giving shore owners title to the land. This was based on the 1821 survey of the Chicago area authorized by Congress as part of a treaty with the Indians. Rather than giving "the shore of Lake Michigan" as a general eastern boundary, surveyor John Wall minutely described the shore line. Thus, when Robert Kinzie acquired a 103.27-acre tract north of the Chicago River, it had definite eastern boundary. Over the years, the courts had consistently ruled that the heirs of the Kinzie grant could never claim more than a total of 103.27 acres, and here lay the strength of Streeter's case.

Claiming the new land as his own, Streeter sold and gave away enough building lots to surround himself with a coterie of interested parties able to benefit materially from his ascendancy. Having established to his satisfaction that the land was not part of Illinois, he therefore set up the independent "District of Lake Michigan" with William H. Niles as Military Governor. Allegiance in the District was owed only to the Federal government. On both sides, land deeds were issued: the legal description of the land, according to the shore owners, was Cook County, Illinois; to George Street, it was the District of Lake Michigan.

Streeter was forcibly removed from his home by Chicago police on May 5, 1889, but soon returned. In 1900, open combat between the police and the defenders of the District erupted. Trespassing suits and countersuits went through the courts with tedious regularity. During World War I, the District of Lake Michigan declared neutrality and fought off attempts to plant war gardens in its sandy soil.

The opening of the Michigan Avenue Bridge in 1920 catapulted Streeterville into the most prime real estate in Chicago. Having been kept relatively vacant for decades because of the constant litigation, the land was still under dispute when the construction boom began. Captain Streeter's death on a riverboat in Calumet Harbor on January 22, 1921, occurred at the beginning of a decade of intensive development of Streeterville, described by the Chicago Daily News (April 14, 1928) as "a program of building activities unsurpassed by any district of similar size in the world."

The Streeter heirs continued to push their claims to the land. The Captain's widow was eventually ruled ineligible to inherit anyway due to the fact that she had not ever legally married George Streeter. The court ruled against a collection of nieces and nephews and in favor of Chicago Title and Trust in April, 1928.

See also Carl Condit, *Chicago, 1910–1929: Building, Planning, and Urban Technology* (Chicago: University of Chicago Press, 1973), 158–60. The Oak Street Condit refers to was earlier Hickory Street. The renaming of streets and renumbering began in 1908. See Don Hayner and Tom McNamee, *Streetwise Chicago: A History of Chicago Street Names* (Chicago: Loyola University Press, 1988), xiv–xv.

13. See the map drawn by John Stamper in his *Chicago's North Michigan Avenue: Planning and Development, 1900–1930* (Chicago: University of Chicago Press, 1991), xxi, fig. 1.11.

14. See Condit, *Chicago, 1910–1929*, 227. Note that the McCormick family donated the site.

By 1920, Northwestern University's professional schools were scattered in various locations throughout the city of Chicago. The medical school had long been located at Prairie Avenue and 26th Street, with its teaching hospitals nearby. In 1902, Northwestern had purchased the former Tremont House Hotel at Clark and Lake Streets to house the Schools of Commerce, Dentistry and Law.

In 1921, Northwestern University purchased nine acres of land along Lake Michigan in the rough, near-north-side Streeterville neighborhood, and architect James Gamble Rogers created a master plan for the major buildings to be erected there. Important funding came from several donors who lent their names to the buildings.

Ground was broken in May 1925, and dedication ceremonies for the new buildings and their campus were held in June 1927. The campus itself was named the Alexander McKinlock Memorial Campus in memory of donor George McKinlock's son, who had died in World War I. During the Depression, when McKinlock's financial losses prevented him from continuing his promised support, the University forgave his debt and, in 1937, officially changed the name to the Chicago Campus. Passavant Hospital's decision to move to Northwestern's Chicago Campus in 1927 paved the way for the development of the multi-institution medical center that now makes up a substantial portion of the Chicago.

From "Building History: Northwestern University. The Campuses," exhibit at the Northwestern University Library, University Archives Web site, http://www.library.northwestern.edu/archives/exhibits/building/campuses.html, accessed May 2002.

15. The Lake Shore Club of Chicago was a private athletic facility purchased in 1977 by Northwestern University and is now called the Lake Shore Center. The sixty-five-year-old building is located at 850 North Lake Shore Drive and now is set up with racquetball, squash and basketball courts, a twenty-five-meter swimming pool, a cardiovascular area, a free weight room, a steam room and sauna, and men's and women's locker rooms and the building has Graduate Housing for the Chicago campus of the University.

16. Among composers who performed at the Arts Club were Stravinsky, Prokofiev, Bartók, Schonberg; painters did not fare as well up to 1951. See *The Arts Club of Chicago, 75th Anniversary Exhibition, 1916–1991*, private circulation, 1991; and especially the well-documented essay therein by James B. Wells.

17. See James Sloan Allen, *The Romance of Commerce and Capital: Capitalism, Modernism, and the Chicago-Aspen Crusade for Cultural Reform* (Chicago: University of Chicago Press, 1983).

18. "In 1935, in the middle of the Depression, supreme optimist Leo Burnett founded the Leo Bur-

nett Company. The fledgling agency made its temporary headquarters in a suite of rooms at Chicago's Palmer House Hotel. The entire office staff could sit comfortably around a card table. Three accounts made up the client list (one of which, Green Giant, remains a client to this day)." Quoted from the Leo Burnett Web site, © 2000.

19. See Robin Kinross, *Modern Typography: An Essay in Critical History* (London: Hyphen Press, 1992), 110.

20. The others were Vance Packard's *The Hidden Persuaders* (New York, D. McKay Co., 1957); and Herbert Marcuse's *One-Dimensional Man: Studies in the Ideology of Advanced Industrial Society* (Boston: Beacon Press, 1964).

21. Ed Duckett, telephone conversation with author, 13 February 2002.

22. Frantz Schulze, personal communication, February 2002.

23. Miles L. Berger, *They Built Chicago: Entrepreneurs Who Shaped a Great City's Architecture* (Chicago: Bonus Books, 1992), 235.

24. Quoted from pamphlet in the Art Institute of Chicago, Ryerson and Burnham Libraries, Ed Duckett Archive, file 4, call number 1986.2.

25. Duckett, telephone conversation with author, 13 February 2002.

26. See Berger, *They Built Chicago*, 235.

27. The total cost on which the architects' fee was calculated at 2 percent for Mies was $5,475,000. Duckett Archive, file 10.

28. Windhorst transcript.

29. While the younger McCormick was heavily involved in the design and the assembly of the site, the guarantor of the loans appears to have been his father who exercised to the full his droits de seigneur.

30. See Mies volume for sketch of Mies's own apartment, *The Mies van der Rohe Archive: An Illustrated Catalog of the Mies van der Rohe Drawings in the Museum of Modern Art*, ed. Arthur Drexler (New York and London: Garland, 1986–92), 14: 221.

31. Kenneth Jackson, *Crabgrass Frontier: The Suburbanization of the United States* (New York: Oxford University Press, 1985), 243.

32. See William Whyte, *The Organization Man* (Harmondsworth: Penguin, 1963).

33. See Berger, *They Built Chicago*, 209–10.

34. On June 22, 1944, President Franklin D. Roosevelt signed the "Servicemen's Readjustment Act of 1944," better known as the "GI Bill of Rights. Major provisions included education and training, loan guaranty for a home, farm, or business, unemployment pay of $20 a week for up to fifty-two weeks, job-finding assistance, top priority for building materials for VA hospitals, and military review of dishonorable discharges.

35. See Berger, *They Built Chicago*, 236. 'The project at 5530 South Shore Drive was considered too innovative, too 'ultra-modern' with too much glass to suit public tastes. Lenders . . . feared 'highrise' meant high cost . . . The Greenwald solution was to offer the apartments on the mutual ownership plan, a cooperative investment concept that he had become familiar with during his university moonlighting years. To the astonishment of the real estate community, Greenwald sold more than half the apartments from plan. The other half were sold before the reinforced concrete frame went up.'

36. See A. Smithson and P. Smithson, *Ordinariness and Light; Urban Theories, 1952–1960 and Their Application in a Building Project, 1963–1970* (Cambridge, MA: MIT Press, 1970).

37. Robert Venturi, *Complexity and Contradiction in Architecture* (New York: Museum of Modern Art, 1966); Rosalind E. Krauss's famous essay on grids in *The Originality of the Avant-Garde and Other Modernist Myths* (Cambridge, MA: MIT Press, 1985); and the study of Mies by Juan Pablo Bonta, *Architecture and Its Interpretation: A Study of Expressive Systems in Architecture* (New York: Rizzoli, 1979).

38. Eric Hodgins, *Mr. Blandings Builds His Dream House*, first published in 1946 with acknowledgement to the designer George Nelson, who was then working on Architectural Forum. It was made into a film in 1948.

39. Mies was the subject of a profile in *Life* magazine in 1953. See Windhorst transcript.

Chapter 9

From 1991 to 1992, Janet Abrams lived at 880 Lake Shore Drive while working as director of the Chicago Institute for Architecture and Urbanism. She recalls living in apartment 22A as the most enjoyable part of that experience.

Chapter 10

The author wishes to thank the Chicago Historical Society and the Richard M. Daley Library at the University of Illinois at Chicago for their assistance, and Rhona Hoffman Gallery, Chicago, Illinois, and Christopher Grimes Gallery, Santa Monica, California.

1. The building was built in 1922 as designed by Theodore Steuben, architect. During the 1950s the Chicago Pure Milk Co. occupied the street-level storefront space.

Chapter 12

The completion of my essay "Only Girl Architect, Lonely," would not have been possible without the support and encouragement of many people. I thank Anthony May, for his patience and his photgraphic talents, Carol Crandall for reading and commenting on early drafts and providing images of the CARY exhibit, Lisa Kulisek for her reading of later drafts and providing the encouragement I needed to finish it, Katerina Rüedi Ray, my editor, for her patience and guidance, Environ Harley Ellis, my current employer, for their support, and lastly but of no less importance, the staff at the Architectural League of New York, specifically, Director Rosalie Gennevro and her assistant Rose Evans, for allowing me special access to the inactive archive on Women in American Architecture. This access practically doubled the amount of information I had been able to gather on Elisabeth Martini.

1. *Architrave* 2, no. 1 (July 1938): 1. The *Architrave* was a pamphlet occasionally published by the Women's Architectural Club of Chicago. The only surviving copies can be found at the Burnham Library, Art Institute of Chicago. The Martini story is also told in Doris Cole, "From Tipi to Skyscraper: A History of Women in Architecture," first published in 1973 and reprinted in *Women in American Architecture: A Historic and Contemporary Perspective*, ed. Susana Torre (New York: Whitney Library of Design, 1977), 88.

2. The Single Family Residence at 5637 North Newcastle Avenue, Norwood Park, was included, along with 17,300 other properties that are "considered to have some historic or architectural importance," in the *Chicago Historic Resources Survey* completed in 1996. Construction began in 1926, and Elisabeth A. (E. A.) Martini is credited as the architect. Martini is also the architect of record of Saint Luke's Lutheran Church in Park Ridge, Illinois, at 205 North Prospect Avenue. Martini stated in a letter to the AWA, dated November 12, 1974, that this church was her largest project. *Architrave* 3 (January 1942): 15, indicates that Martini left the Chicago area in 1932 and as far as is possible to tell she lived and continued to practice architecture in Bangor, Michigan, until 1961 when she officially retired and relocated once again to Uplands Retirement Center in Crossville, Tennessee. Attempts to contact local historical societies (Hartford Historical Society, as

Bangor does not have one) in Michigan regarding any further information on Martini have to date been unsuccessful.

3. Terry Tatum, director of almuni relations, Pratt Institute of Design, letter to author dated April 2002.

4. Hazel Ker, "South Haven Woman Top Architect," *News-Palladium* [Benton Harbor, Michigan], October 1954; and Marie Carney, "Profiles," *Cumberland County Times* [Crossville, Tennessee] October 6, 1971.

5. S. M. Franklin, "Elisabeth Martini, Architect," *Life and Labor* (February 1914): 235–36.

6. Office address for E. A. Martini listed on permit for the Norwood Park residence, for which Martini was architect of record.

7. Susan Faludi, *Backlash: The Undeclared War against American Women*, (New York: Anchor Books, 1991), 50.

8. Gertrude Lempp Kerbis, FAIA, and founder of Chicago Women in Architecture (CWA), was the first woman architect to serve as local chapter president of the AIA in 1980. Linda Searl, FAIA, currently serves as vice chair of the Plan Commission and is a member of the Chicago Central Area Plan Steering Committee. Searl honed her leadership skills as a past president of the local chapters of both the AIA and CWA.

9. Other early examples include Marion Mahony Griffin and Julia Morgan. It was naturally young women of affluence who would first be able to take advantage of this opportunity to enter the architectural profession through the academy. Morgan is probably the best example of this first generation of American professional women architects. Morgan led a prolific career in northern California after being the first woman in the world to graduate from the École des Beaux-Arts in Paris in 1902. In Illinois, the somewhat-famous Frank Lloyd Wright collaborator, Mahony Griffin, would become the first woman licensed in the state in 1897. By the time Martini would begin to seek out other women architects, Mahony Griffin had left the area for Australia with her second major collaborator, her husband Walter Burley Griffin. For more on Mahony Griffen, see chapter 14 in this volume.

10. Jeanne Madeline Weimann, *The Fair Women* (Chicago: Academy: Chicago, 1981), 150.

11. Ibid.

12. Ibid., 36.

13. Ibid., 31.

14. Ibid., 144.

15. Pamela Hill, "Ladies of the Corridor Series: Louise Bethune," *Muse* (September–October 1996), Chicago Women in Architecture bimonthly publication.

16. Ibid.

17. Weimann, *The Fair Women*, 142.

18. Louise Bethune, "Women and Architecture," *Inland Architect and News Record* (March 1891): 21.

19. Madeleine B. Stern, *We the Women: Career Firsts of Nineteenth-Century America* (University of Nebraska Press, 1962), 76.

20. Weimann, *The Fair Women*, 148.

21. Even Weimann claims that "it was not a particularly good sign that she had chosen to become a teacher of mechanical drawing rather than apply her degree to actual architectural work, as Lois Howe had done with less training" (ibid., 151–52). Third prize went to Laura Hayes, Bertha Palmer's secretary, who had no formal training except apparently in knowing Mrs. Palmer's personal stylistic tastes (149).

22. Bethune, "Women and Architecture," 20.

23. Franklin, Elisabeth Martini, Architect."

24. Weimann, *The Fair Women*, 153.

25. Ibid., 151–52.

26. Erik Larson, *The Devil in the White City* (New York: Crown, 2003), 84.

27. Bethune, "Women and Architecture," 21.

28. Stern, *We the Women*, 74 (implying melancholia); and Weimann, *The Fair Women*," 177 (suggesting brain fever).

29. Dolores Hayden, "Sophia Hayden," in *Notable American Women: The Modern Period: A Biographical Dictionary*, ed. Barbara Sicherman and Carol Hurd Green (Cambridge, MA: Belknap Press, 1980), 323.

30. Ibid.

31. Weimann, *The Fair Women*, 153.

32. Hayden, "Sophia Hayden," 323.

33. Bethune, "Women and Architecture," 21.

34. The Women's World Fairs were a series of fairs held in Chicago each year beginning in 1925 and ending in 1928. More than 200,000 people visited the first fair in 1925, which included over one hundred exhibitions of women in business. The first fair netted $50,000. Each of the three fairs was larger than the previous year's, according to the obituary of Helen Bennett, who was their organizer. See Bennett's obituary, clipping folder, "Expositions: Women's World Fair. First," Chicago Historical Society.

35. Marilyn Domer, "The Role of Women in Chicago's World's Fairs: From the Sublime to the Sensuous," in *1992 World's Fair Forum Papers*, vol. 2 (Evanston: Center for Urban Affairs and Policy Research, Northwestern University), 9.

36. After the death of Daniel Burnham, his sons formed an architectural practice called the Burnham Brothers in Chicago.

37. Domer, "The Role of Women," 23.

38. Ibid., 13.

39. *Women through the Century: A Souvenir of the National Council of Women Exhibit* (New York: National Council of Women of the United States).

40. Weimann, *The Fair Women*, 598.

41. Domer, "The Role of Women," 23.

42. *Architrave*, 1–2.

43. While sources on Whitman often cite the importance of the inclusion of her work at the Century of Progress World's Fair, unfortunately the Scheid Residence is not to be found in the brochure that accompanied the exhibit Houses of Tomorrow at the Home Planning Hall. All of the architects credited with the designs for the eleven houses in the brochure were men. Whitman was also a member and officer of the Women's Architectural Club of Chicago. Her experience with architectural education suggests that being admitted to a university and being welcomed were, at that time, not the same. According to Rita Rice in an article in the *Chicago Tribune*, September 27, 1974, titled "Architect Designs Her Own Life," when Whitman applied to the Architecture Department at the University of Michigan in 1914, she was told by the dean that "We don't want you, but since the school is coeducational and state owned, we have to take you if you insist." Whitman's determination to do what she loved, architecture, which she viewed as a combination of mathematics and art, would carry her through an inspirational career spanning over fifty years. Unlike Martini, Whitman not only carefully documented her work that, like Martini's, was pri-

marily residential, but also deposited her projects in several institutions. She recognized the historic value of her struggle to work as a woman architect in the early part of the twentieth century and that she could serve as a role model to other young women. There are at least fifty houses designed by Whitman in Evanston, Illinois, primarily examples of Tudor and Colonial revivalism. These were styles that she enjoyed and that her clients desired; they were also reflective of her training at the University of Michigan—like MIT and most architectural programs at this time, highly influenced by École des Beaux Arts methodology. Whitman's work was certainly not avant-garde. She is quoted in her 1984 obituary as saying "I'm not Shakespeare or Frank Lloyd Wright, but I enjoy what I do, and I enjoy showing men that we women are just as good as they are in whatever we do."

44. *Architrave* 2, no. 1.

45. This organization of women architectural students from Washington University in St. Louis and the University of Minnesota in Minneapolis was formed in 1917. See *Overview of Women Groups of Architects*, 1, a pamphlet published by the Association of Women in Architecture to accompany membership invitations, 1960. Predating Martini's Club by four years, by 1922 this group, in contrast to the Chicago Women's Drafting Club, was growing stronger, with chapters in Texas and California as well as the two in the Midwest. It held a convention in St. Louis in 1922 and established itself as a national sorority for women architecture students. Over the next decade, the alumnae began to outnumber the students, and in 1934 the alumnae formed a sister organization of professionals called the Association of Women in Architecture (AWA). The AWA continues to exist today through its Los Angeles chapter, with a membership of around two hundred women architects from that area and members at large throughout the country. See under "'Historical Note," at the Association for Women in Architecture Records at the International Archive for Women Architects (IAWA) Web site: http://spec.lib.vt.edu/IAWA/inventories/awa.htm, accessed April 7, 2002.

46. Ruth, letter to the Archive of Women in Architecture, Architectural League of New York, dated October 25, 1974. Perkins also states, "As you no doubt realize, our main concern was to earn our livings rather than to make history, but we were in fact trailblazers and I must say that I enjoyed every minute of it."

47. *Architrave* 2, no. 1.

48. "Oral History of Mary Ann Elizabeth Crawford," interviewed by Betty J. Blum, Art Institute of Chicago Oral History Project: Mary Ann Elizabeth Crawford, biographical summary, May 17, 1983. Available at http://www.artic.edu/aic/collections/dept_architecture/crawford.html.

49. Ruth Perkins, letter to the Archive of Women in Architecture dated January 30, 1975. Perkins goes on to state that in working with Weber she "performed every architectural service from interviewing clients through making full-size details. I did not supervise construction. The large houses that I did for Mr. Weber are located in every North-shore suburb of Chicago."

50. Ruth Perkins, letter to the Archive of Women in Architecture, Architectural League of New York, October 25, 1974.

51. Jack Hartray, conversation with the author, May 2, 2002.

52. Susan King, "Getrude Kerbis," *A Creative Constellation: Chicago Women in Architecture; Celebrating Twenty-Five Years* (Chicago: Chicago Historical Society, 1999), 123.

53. Blum, interview, 123.

54. Gertrude Lempp Kerbis, telephone conversation with the author, May 3, 2002.

55. "Oral History of Gertrude Lempp Kerbis," interviewed by Betty J. Blum, Art Institute of Chicago Oral History Project, May and June 1996. Available at http://www.artic.edu/aic/collections/dept_architecture/kerbis.html.

56. Ibid., 124.

57. Information from Oral Stories told by founding member Carol Ross Barney in September 1999 at the CWA Member's Reception.

58. Torre is a self-described feminist. In 1977, she served as project director for the exhibit, Women in Architecture, which opened at the Brooklyn Museum and then toured around the United States. She also edited and wrote the introduction and several parts of the book, *American Architecture: A Historic and Contemporary Perspective,* which accompanied the exhibition and continues to serve today as an invaluable resource of the history of women in American architecture.

Having received her architectural diploma from the University of Buenos Aires, she went on to study urban planning there and at Columbia University in New York. She has lived in the United States since 1968 and has held several top academic positions with architectural programs. Of particular note is her brief directorship for the graduate art program at Cranbrook Art Academy, a leading private school where top positions were once held exclusively by men.

Having served on the Board of Advisors for the International Archive of Women in Architecture from 1985 to 1995, today, Torre is an honorary member. It is rather ironic that she didn't bring the two archives together. See http://architecture.about.com/library/bl-torre.htm?terms=Torre (accessed February 22, 2004).

59. Other CARY members included, among others, Janet Abrams, Anita Ambriz, Ellen Browning, Susan Budinsky, Carol Crandall, Jason Feldman, Roberta Feldman, Bonnie Humphrey, Kay Janis, Sally Levine, Kathryn Quinn, John Ritzu, John Scully, and Amy Yurko.

60. Carol Crandall, *More than the Sum of Our Body Parts,* exhibition catalog (Chicago: CARY, 1993), 1.

61. It is not my intent to discredit Maxman's achievements in any way. Historically, Maxman's role in the AIA will be viewed as Bertha Palmer's role in the Columbian Exposition is viewed now. was a hundred years previously. The position of the AIA national president at that time required a non-controversial woman. Unfortunately, to date her achievement has not been surpassed, as no other women have yet to serve as AIA national president.

62. *More than the Sum of Our Body Parts,* 34.

63. According to an AIA member firms survey in 1997, 19 percent of AIA members were women, but only 10 percent were licensed architects and 31 percent were interns. Current information (2004) provided by the AIA indicates that of their licensed members, 11 percent are women, and of their associate members, 33 percent are women. However, there is no update on the total percentage of women members (regardless of level). Therefore it is difficult to discern the progress of women in the AIA in the past seven years.

64. The author was given special permission to access the archive in June 2002 for the purposes of this essay and is grateful to the Architectural League of New York for this opportunity. After my visit, the league was pleased to inform me that the archive would be submitted to the International Archive for Women Architects (IAWA), maintained by the Virginia Polytechnic Institute and State University (Virginia Tech). In this new location the archive will be more accessible to the public.

65. Kathryn H. Anthony, Designing for Diversity: Gender, Race and Ethnicity in the Architectural Profession (Urbana: University of Illinois Press, 2001), 181.

Chapter 13

1. For monographs on Walter Burley Griffin's life and work, see James Birrell, *Walter Burley Griffin* (Queensland: University of Queensland Press, 1964); Donald Leslie Johnson, *The Architecture of Walter Burley Griffin* (Melbourne: Macmillan Company of Australia, 1977); and Mati Maldre and Paul Kruty, *Walter Burley Griffin in America* (Urbana: University of Illinois Press, 1996). For discussions of both of the Griffins within the context of the Chicago school, see Mark Peisch, *The Chicago School of Architecture: Early Followers of Sullivan and Wright* (New York: Random House, 1954); and H. Allen Brooks, *The Prairie School: Frank Lloyd Wright and His Midwest Contemporaries* (Toronto: University of Toronto Press, 1972). A number of scholars have addressed the Griffins' work in Australia and India. For this later work, see Jeff Turnbull and Peter Y. Navaretti, eds., *The Griffins in Australia and India* (Victoria: Melbourne University Press, 1998); Anne Watson, ed., *Beyond Architecture: Marion Mahony and Walter Burley Griffin* (Sydney: Powerhouse Publishing, 1998); and Jenepher Duncan, ed., *Walter Burley Griffin: A Re-view,* (Clayton, Victoria: Monash University Gallery, 1988). For Marion Mahony Griffin. see Susan Fondiler Berkon and Jane Holtz Kay, "Marion Mahony Griffin, Architect," *Feminist Art Journal* 4 (spring 1975); Janice Pregliasco, "The Life and Work of Marion Mahony Griffin," *Museum Studies* 21, no. 2 (1995); Anna Rubo, "Marion Mahony Griffin: A Portrait," *Walter Burley Griffin - A Re-View,* ed. Jenepher Duncan (Victoria: Monash University, 1988); Anna Rubo, "Marion Lucy Mahony Griffin," in *Women Building Chicago, 1790–1990,* ed. Rima Lunin Schultz and Adele Hast (Bloomington: Indiana University Press, 2001): and Elizabeth Joy Birmingham, "Marion Mahony Griffin and the Magic of America" (Ph.D. diss., Iowa State University , 2000); James Weirick, "The Magic of America: Vision and Text," *Walter Burley Griffin: A Re-view,* ed. Jenepher Duncan (Clayton, Victoria: Monash University Gallery, 1988); and James Weirick, "Marion Mahony at MIT," *Transition* 25, no. 4 (1988): 49–54.

2. Paul Kruty has definitively established that Marion Mahony Griffin was the first woman to receive an architectural license. In 1897, Illinois became the first state to require licenses for architects; in 1898 Mahony Griffin was one of the twelve candidates to take the first licensing examination ever administered, receiving the third-highest score. See Paul Kruty, "A New Look at the Beginnings of the Illinois Architects Licensing Law," *Illinois Historical Journal* 90 (fall 1997): 154–72. Julia Morgan (1872–1957), whose lifetime paralleled Mahony Griffin's (1871–1961), did not become certified in California until 1904. For Morgan, see Sarah Holmes Boutelle, *Julia Morgan, Architect* (New York: Abbeville Press, 1988).

3. From the *1894 Class Book,* Massachusetts Institute of Technology, 1898, as quoted by Susan Fondler Berkon, "Marion Mahony Griffin," in *Women in American Architecture: A Historic and Contemporary Perspective,* ed. Susana Torre (New York: Whitney Library of Design, 1977).

4. Nancy Woloch, *Women and the American Experience* (New York: McGraw Hill, 1994).

5. For information on Mahony Griffin's role in the Wright Studio, see Grant Carpenter Manson, *Frank Lloyd Wright to 1910: The First Golden Age* (Random House, 1964); and Fran Martone, *In Wright's Shadow: Artists and Architects at the Oak Park Studio* (Oak Park: Frank Lloyd Wright Home and Studio Foundation, 1998).

6. This house, located at 1946 Estes in Chicago, is still standing. From its current exterior appearance, it would not seem to be the design of an architect who was active in the most progressive architectural movement of the time. Additional research on this home is required.

7. In 1997, due to the efforts of John K. Notz, Jr., a Graceland Cemetery Trustee, Mahony Griffin's cremated remains were moved to the Columbarium and the location designated with a custom-designed memorial plaque. A special dedication ceremony

and reception were held to commemorate the event; Janice Pregliasco also delivered a lecture on Mahony Griffin at the Art Institute. For a narrative of these efforts, see John K. Notz, Jr., "A Beginning, an End and Another Beginning (Marion Mahony Griffin, Architect)," paper delivered to the Chicago Literary Club, April 2001.

8. *Illinois Society of Architects Monthly Bulletin* (February–March 1937): 6.

9. Barry Byrne, "The Chicago Movement," transcript of papers prepared by Robert C. Spencer, George S. Elmslie, and Barry Byrne, delivered before the Illinois Society of Architects, Tuesday November 28, 1939, 3, Illinois Society of Architects Files, Chicago Historical Society.

10. Ibid.

11. Ibid.

12. Ibid., 5.

13. *Illinois Society of Architect's Monthly Bulletin* (August–September, 1940).

14. Anthroposophy, an outgrowth of theosophy, is a philosophical and religious movement founded by Rudolph Steiner in 1912 that emphasizes the creative and spiritual development of mankind. It is the philosophy upon which the Waldorf school system is based.

15. When Elizabeth Wood, Chicago Housing Authority secretary, attends a meeting of the Illinois Society of Architects and gives a presentation, it is specifically noted that *one woman* (author's italics) was among those in attendance.

16. Johnson, *The Architecture of Walter Burley Griffin,* 148 n. 28.

17. These two projects were first discussed in Berkon Kay, "Marion Mahony Griffin, Architect." Pregliasco also discusses these projects in "The Life and Work of Marion Mahony Griffin." They comprise the final two entries in the catalogue raisonné, Turnbull and Navaretti, *The Griffins in Australia and India.*

18. Formed at Hull House on October 2, 1897, the founding members of the Arts and Crafts Society also included Frank Lloyd Wright, Mr. and Mrs. Dwight H. Perkins (Mahony Griffin's cousin and his wife), Irving and Allen Pond, and R. C. Spencer. In the membership list, Mahony Griffin's address is listed as 1101 Steinway Hall.

19. For information on Lola Maverick Lloyd, see Melanie Gustafson's entry in *Women Building Chicago, 1790–1990,* ed. Rima Lumin Schultz and Adele Hast (Bloomington: Indiana University Press, 2001). The Henry Demarest Lloyd family home was in Winnetka, and Lloyd was a resident of Wilmette at the time Mahony Griffin worked with her to plan these two communities.

20. Marion Mahony Griffin to Estelle Burley Griffin, Walter Burley Griffin's mother, letter dated 12 March 1917. From "The Magic of America," section 2, "The Federal Battle," 197, microfilm no. 1988.3, Burnham Library, Art Institute of Chicago. Mahony Griffin spent much of the decade of the 1940s working on her autobiographical memoir, "The Magic of America." She was unable to obtain a publisher during her lifetime. There are two versions of the manuscript. One is in the possession of the Art Institute of Chicago (AIC), the other is held by the New York Historical Society (NYHS). The Burnham Library at the Art Institute of Chicago has both versions available on microfilm. The manuscript consists of typewritten text, magazine and newspaper clippings, personal photographs, and drawings and photographs of the Griffins' projects. The text between the two versions is similar. The NYHS version has some handwritten notations that are not included on the AIC copy. The illustrations are similar but not exactly the same. Only the NYHS version contains her entry to the Chicagoland Home Prize Competition.

21. Mahony Griffin, "Magic of America," section 2, 269, New York Historical Society, microfilm no. 1988.3, Burnham Library, Art Institute of Chicago.

22. Ibid., 273.

23. Ibid., 275.

24. Ibid., 296.

25. Ibid., 297.

26. Ibid., 297.

27. Ibid., 298.

28. H. Evert Kincaid, "New Homes for Old," *Illinois Society of Architects Monthly Bulletin* (October–November 1945).

29. See "William Tell Tells Program to Beautify, Improve City," *Chicago Herald American*, April 9, 1945, 1.

30. William Tell, "Iowan Turns Hobby into Better City Plan," *Chicago Herald American*, July 10, 1945, 7.

31. The Institute of Design merged with IIT in 1949.

32. *The American City* 60 (April 1945): 5.

33. *Chicago Herald American*, July 10, 1945.

34. This project was identified as a "Plan for South Chicago," see Berkon and Holtz, "Marion Mahony Griffin, Architect," 14. Pregliasco ("The Life and Work of Marion Mahony Griffin," 180) was the first to establish that these drawings were prepared as entries to a competition; however, she noted the paper as the "Chicago *Herald*" and the date as 1947. These drawings and this project are not included in the catalogue raisonne in Turnbull and Navaretti, *The Griffins in Australia and India*.

35. Mahony Griffin, "Magic of America," section 4, 425.

36. Ibid., 451.

37. Ibid., 422.

38. Ibid., 452.

39. Ibid., 440.

40. Ibid., 445.

41. Ibid., 447.

42. This octagonal organization of residential units with radial streets was also used in the Griffins' plan for Canberra. See Peter Muller, "The Esoteric Nature of Griffin's Design for Canberra," Walter Burley Griffin Memorial Lecture, delivered 24 November 1976.

43. Robert Anderson Pope, *City Residential Land Development* (Chicago: City Club of Chicago, 1916).

44. Mahony Griffin, "Magic of America," sect. 4, 422.

45. Ibid., 442.

46. First Prize was awarded to a joint entry of David S. Geer, Edward W. Waugh, and George Matsumoto, who were employed by Saarinen and Saarinen at the time. According to the *Architectural Forum* (March 1946): 168, the winning entry was based upon "the philosophy expounded in Eliel Saarinen's book, *The City*.

47. "Announcing the $24,000.00 Chicagoland Home Prize Competition," *Progressive Architecture* (October 1945).

48. *Progressive Architecture* (November 1945): 26.

49. Peter Y. Navaretti, "Catalogue Raisonne," in *The Griffins in Australia and India* , no. 2713-07, Multi-

ple Unit Knitlock Homes for Chicago, 263.

50. Navaretti, "Catalogue Raisonne," 263.

51. "Ten Prize Winning Houses," *Architectural Forum* (April 1946). This article featured homes by four Chicago-area designers: Ray Stuemer, D. Coder Taylor, Eric Wenstrand, and C. W. Schroeder. According to the author of this article, the *Tribune* houses were '(f)eatured for five weeks on the cover of its Sunday Color Graphic section and displayed a month at Chicago's Art Institute"; they "were enthusiastically received by the public—so much so that Sunday Editor Ardis M. Kennedy revised his original plan to limit publication to prize winners, will feature honorably mentioned houses throughout the year."

52. Mahony Griffin, "Magic of America," sect. 2, 11.

Chapter 14

This essay is revised from "We're from Oz: Marking Ethnic and Sexual Identity in Chicago," Environment and Planning. D, Society and Space *21, no. 4 (summer 2003): 425–40.*

1. Sarah Bradford Landau, "Coming to Terms: Architecture Competitions in America and the Emerging Profession," in *The Experimental Tradition*, ed. Hélène Lipstadt (New York: Princeton Architectural Press, 1989), 70–73; see also Robert Bruegmann, "When Worlds Collided: European and American Entries to the Chicago Tribune Competition," in *Chicago Architecture, 1872–1922*, ed. John Zukowsky (Munich: Prestel Verlag, 1987), 303–17.

2. On ethnicity in Chicago see *Ethnic Chicago*, ed. Melvin G. Holli and Peter d'A. Jones, 2d ed. (Grand Rapids: William B. Eerdmans Publishing, 1984); and John D. Buenker, "Chicago's Ethnics and the Politics of Accommodation," in *A Wild Kind of Boldness: The Chicago History Reader*, ed. Rosemary K. Adams (Chicago: Chicago Historical Society, 1998), 123–31. The importance of ethnic models to gay identity in Chicago is well described in Richard K. Herrell, "The Symbolic Strategies of Chicago's Gay and Lesbian Pride Day Parade," in *Gay Culture in America*, ed. Gilbert Herdt (Boston: Beacon Press, 1992), 225–52. Herrell, however, assuming older models of ethnicity, concludes by contrasting gay identity with ethnic identity derived from birthright.

3. Despite restricting itself to racial and ethnic identity, an excellent discussion of global trends toward the visualization of difference in urban planning is Jane M. Jacobs, "Staging Difference: Aestheticization and the Politics of Difference in Contemporary Cities," in *Cities of Difference*, ed. Ruth Fincher and Jane M. Jacobs (London: Guilford Press, 1998), 252–78. The primary limitation of the mosaic metaphor is its failure to capture the dynamic of the mobile viewer as being part of the spectacle, an ideal described in the mayor's comments on the Boys Town project (see note 13 below). In both the style and argument of this essay, I have tried to enact this sense of reciprocity, which is sadly at odds with the norms of much cultural geography, as Rosalyn Deutsche's critique of the voyeurism inherent in the work of one prominent practitioner makes clear (*Evictions: Art and Spatial Theory* [Cambridge: MIT Press, 1996], 209–15).

4. Comparable initiatives in other cities are cited in relation to tourism in Dereka Rushbrook, "Cities, Queer Space, and the Cosmopolitan Tourist," *GLQ: A Journal of Lesbian and Gay Studies* 8, nos. 1– 2 (2002): 183–206. Rushbrook notes the methodological shortcomings inherent in discussions of tourists "consuming" the "commodity" of exotic spectacle as it applies to spaces where "queerness is performed and visible but where it is not always evident who is the consumer and who is the consumed" (197); her call for more subtle research into these dynamics would apply, as well, to new-ethnic constructions of identity as something other than the essential verities she assigns to the terms "race" and "ethnicity." The lived complexity of identity performance in cities like Chicago is evident in the way the *Chicago Tribune* and the *Chicago Sun-Times*, on different days, broke the story of the "Boys Town"

development, juxtaposing articles on the first page of the local sections with coverage of neighborhood festivals clearly constructed to turn old-ethnic antagonism into new-ethnic equal-opportunity spectacle: Indian Independence Day on Saturday, the Pakistani parade on the same street the next day. These performances serve both performers and audiences. Indeed, as the costumed marchers pose for newspaper photographs they will themselves consume, categories of performer and consumer overlap in rituals that promote the productive paradox of identities affirmed both by their visual difference from and by their structural equivalence to other performances of identity recognized by the city's institutions with a specific day and/or place.

5. Officially titled the Division Street Gateways, this project received seven professional awards, including a 1995 Distinguished Building Award from the Chicago chapter of the American Institute of Architects. Architectural historian and critic Franz Schulze praised it, saying that "One could hardly imagine anything more symbolically at home on its site, or more successful in reaching the specific audience it was meant to address" ("Chicago Now," *Art in America* [September 1998]: 63).

6. In Windhorst's original plan, the Boys Town pylons were also conceived to be bracketed by symbolic gateways, though these were sacrificed in the ensuing controversy.

7. Mayor Richard M. Daley, open letter published in the *Windy City Times*, 18 December 1997, 20. Despite this rhetoric, the Boys Town project has little relevance to lesbian identity. Another district, Andersonville, is widely seen as inhabited by lesbians.

8. *Halsted Street, 1931* (Conrad O. Nelson, writer and editor), 15 min., Film and Photo League of Chicago; *Halsted Street U.S.A.*, 1998 (David E. Simpson, director, writer, and editor), 57 min., Panacea Pictures, Chicago, 1998. Because the latter film was shot before its release date, it does not feature the Boys Town pylons, though it concludes with footage of the annual Gay Pride Parade.

9. Greg Longhini, quoted in Mary Ellen Podmolik, "North Halsted Streetscape Plan Drawing Attention," *Chicago Sun-Times*, 26 August 1997, 43.

10. "Tolerance on Halsted Street," *Chicago Tribune*, 19 August 1997, sec. 1, 20.

11. Mary Schmich, "Gaytown Enters Gray Area of Community Naming," *Chicago Tribune*, 20 August 1997, sec. 2, 1.

12. Dennis Byrne, "Everybody On Board Halsted St. Express," *Chicago Sun-Times*, 17 August 1997, 31. As is often the case, this satire of identity politics is blind to the way dominant identities are routinely encoded in conventions that are taken for granted. Leaving aside the ubiquity of heterosexuality in urban street imagery, one might note an 1869 guide to the Chicago area that described suburban Evanston, known for its religiosity and strict temperance laws, as "laid out at right angles, as rigidly as Methodism itself could demand." (James B. Runnion, *Out of Town*, 1869, quoted in Michael H. Ebner, "The Result of Honest Hard Work: Creating a Suburban Ethos for Evanston," in *A Wild Kind of Boldness* (cited above), 177.

13. Steven Epstein, "Gay Politics, Ethnic Identity: The Limits of Social Constructionism," *Socialist Review* 17, nos. 93–94 (May–August 1987), 9–54. Epstein, seeking to intervene in debates between "essentialist" and "social-construction" understandings of sexual identity, relied for his analysis of ethnicity on extant sociological studies: see especially Stephen Murray, "The Institutional Elaboration of a Quasi-ethnic community," *International Review of Modern Sociology* 9 (1979): 165–77.

14. Arjun Appadurai, *Modernity at Large: Cultural Dimensions of Globalization* (Minneapolis: University of Minnesota Press, 1996).

15. The connection between the White and Emerald cities is made in Stuart Culver, "What Manikins Want: The Wonderful Wizard of Oz and the Art of Decorating Dry Goods Windows," *Representations*

21 (1988): 105; William R. Leach, "A Trickster's Tale: L. Frank Baum's The Wonderful Wizard of Oz," in The Wonderful Wizard of Oz by L. Frank Baum, ed. William R. Leach (Belmont, CA: Wadsworth, 1991), 164; and in Michael Riley, "The Great City of Oz: L. Frank Baum at the 1893 World's Fair," *Baum Bugle* 42, no. 3 (winter 1998), 32–38. I thank Diane Dillon for suggesting this connection and Dee Michel for introducing me to the *Bugle* and the International Wizard of Oz Club, which publishes it.

16. Recent theorization has supplanted Susan Sontag's 1964 "Notes on Camp." See Andrew Ross, "Uses of Camp," in *No Respect: Intellectuals and Popular Culture* (New York: Routledge, 1989), 135–70; and three anthologies: Fabio Cleto, ed., *Camp: Queer Aesthetics and the Performing Self—A Reader* (Edinburgh: Edinburgh University Press, 1999); Moe Meyer, ed., *The Politics and Poetics of Camp* (New York: Routledge, 1994); and David Bergman, ed., *Camp Grounds: Style and Homosexuality* (Amherst: University of Massachusetts Press, 1993), which reprints the extract from Newton's 1972 Mother Camp with its comparison of sexual and racial identity.

17. A number of publications challenge the incompatibility of gay and nonurban identity. Their self-presentation as outside—and often hostile to—mainstream gay culture, however, confirms the continuing centrality of narratives of urban escape in both the history of modern gay identity and the experience of individuals who identify as gay. See, for example, the newsletter *R.F.D.*; Neil Miller, *In Search of Gay America: Women and Men in a Time of Change* (New York: Atlantic Monthly Press, 1989); and Darrell Yates Rist, *Heartlands: A Gay Man's Odyssey across America* (New York: Dutton, 1992).

18. Richard Dyer's *White* (London: Routledge, 1997) begins with this kind of revised memory of a childhood incident "I don't myself remember," following this with a sensitive analysis of the links between his sense of his gay identity and ethnic and racial identities (5–8). Dyer's nuanced discussion supplants facile dismissals of the "ethnic identity model" as a racist "unitary gay identity" invested in "a drama of authentic embodiment" aimed at "a reification of identity" (Michael Warner, ed., *Fear of a Queer Planet* [Minneapolis: University of Minnesota Press, 1993], quotations on xix, 117. Such claims ignore that theorization of ethnicity is itself constructed and variable.

19. The significance of this line is discussed in Vito Russo, *The Celluloid Closet* (New York: Harper & Row, 1981), 65. Its applicability to the "new ethnicity" may be judged from a 1977 essay, cited by Epstein, in which the influential critic Irving Howe described how "ethnic groups now turn back—and as they nervously insist, 'with pride'—to look for fragments of a racial or national or religious identity that moves them to the extent that it is no longer available. Perhaps, also, because it is no longer available." "The Limits of Ethnicity," *New Republic*, 25 June 1977, 18.

20. On third cultures, see M. Featherstone, "Global and Local Cultures," in *Mapping the Futures*, ed. Jon Bird et al. (London: Routledge, 1993), 169–87.

21. Christopher Reed, "Imminent Domain: Queer Space in the Built Environment," *Art Journal* 55, no. 4 (winter 1996): 64–70. Analogous urban formations outside the United States have been analyzed as U.S. exports; see Alan Sinfield, *Gay and After* (London: Serpent's Tail, 1994), 103.

22. Although my analysis focuses on the historical context and debates over ideas behind the Boys Town markers, it should be noted that as they were installed according to designs revised through the period of controversy—that is, without the bracketing gates and with the colored lights replaced by a white floodlight—the pylons were dwarfed by the streetlights and engulfed in their radiance and, therefore, do not achieve the full nighttime effect claimed in the planning documents.

23. The *Chicago Tribune* reported about one "highly charged public hearing": "Audience members jeered one another, shouted profanities and made

obscene gestures at speakers with opposing points of view" (Stephanie Banchero, "Rift Threatens Unity of North Halsted," *Chicago Tribune,* 24 September 1997, sec. 1, 1ff). The *Tribune*'s coverage played to this divisiveness more than the supposedly tabloidy *Sun-Times.* From its first stories, the *Tribune* ignored comparable neighborhood projects and foregrounded arguments that, in the words of one pull-quote, "the project could scare away straight people" (Stephanie Banchero, "N. Halsted to Get $3.2 Million Face Lift," *Chicago Tribune,* 18 August 1997, sec. 2C, 1ff; compare Robert L. Kaiser, "Gays Only One Part of Halsted Mix," *Chicago Tribune,* 20 August 1997, sec. 1, 1ff; and Suzy Frisch, "Gay-Pride Theme on Halsted Is Protested," *Chicago Tribune,* 4 September 1997, sec. 2C, 1ff).

24. Quotations from Ernest Tucker, "Some Seeing Red over Plan for Pylons on North Halsted," *Chicago Sun-Times,* 13 October 1997, 21; and Tresa Baldas, "City Ends North Halsted Debate," *Chicago Tribune,* 20 November 1997, sec. 2C, 10. Regarding these quotations, it is important to note the impossibility of dividing quoted speakers into clear groups of insiders who "speak for" the community and outsiders who do not. Speakers identified as living or working in Boys Town are not necessarily gay: many straight residents and business owners complained about being identified with a gay neighborhood, and this anxiety may animate comments by those who did not speak explicitly to that issue. Conversely, some of those identified in the coverage as city officials are themselves lesbian or gay with strong ties to the neighborhood. Twenty years ago, Gordon Johnston's *Which Way Out of the Men's Room* (South Brunswick, N.J.: A. S. Barnes, 1979) condemned gay "ghettos" as "prisons." The special "Pride" issue of the *Windy City Times* for 26 June 1997 featured a cover story under the headline "Trailblazing" that focused on gay marriage, with highlighted pull-quotes, "It's hard to say whether there are more gay people living outside the city or whether they're just more visible" and "now I live in the suburbs, and all our straight neighbors threw us a baby shower"; as well as a feature article headlined "Love! Valour! Assimilation! Or How to Leave the Ghetto without Losing Your Caftan." Aaron Betsky asserts, without quantification, that this drive to assimilation characterizes current queer culture (*Queer Space: Architecture and Same-Sex Desire* [New York: William Morrow, 1997], 14, 44–45, 192). I read this assertion not as a statement of fact but as the rhetorical premise for Betsky's own repeated performance of the nostalgia for lost ways of life that is, I am arguing, a hallmark of gay identity.

25. John McCarron, "Gays Need to Confront Their Image Problem," *Chicago Tribune,* 8 September 1997, sec. 1, 11.

26. Quoted in Robert Sharoff, "Taking Sides on Neighborhood Pride," *Washington Post,* 29 November 1997, E12ff.

27. Undergirding such arguments is a body of academic writing belittling gay neighborhoods; see, for example, Lawrence Knopp's "Sexuality and Urban Space" and Tim Davis's "The Diversity of Queer Politics and the Redefinition of Sexual Identity and Community in Urban Spaces," both in *Mapping Desire: Geographies of Sexualities,* ed. David Bell and Gill Valentine (London: Routledge, 1995), 149–61, 284–303. Knopp dismisses the significance of "vibrant gay commercial and entertainment scenes" and areas of "gay gentrification" in cities as just episodes of capitalism "eager to colonise new realms of experience and to undermine potential threats to its power" (158). Davis sets up a false opposition between his promotion of the activist group Queer Nation's (short-lived) "new spatial tactics for social change" (demonstrations in shopping malls and homophobic neighborhoods) and the "isolation and continued oppression" of the "gay ghetto" (284–85), though he offers no evidence—apart from the somewhat dismaying standard that "fewer jeers [and] fewer projectiles" met a second demonstration in one nongay neighborhood—for the success of the new tactics in relation to the asserted failure of gay neighborhoods to provide a "safe space" or "liberated zone" (284, 301). For a comparison of perceptions of safety in gay versus nongay neighborhoods, see Wayne D. Myslik,

"Renegotiating the Social/Sexual Identities of Places," in *Bodyspace: Destabilizing Geographies of Gender and Sexuality*, ed. Nancy Duncan (London: Routledge, 1996), 156–69.

28. In Reed, "Imminent Domain," I critiqued such fluid definitions of "queer space" as articulated in installation projects by architects Brian McGrath (There Is No "Queer Space," Only Different Points of View, in Queer Space, put on at the Storefront for Art and Architecture in New York in 1994) and Benjamin Gianni and Scott Weir (Queers in [Single Family] Space, in *House Rules*, catalog published as *Assemblage* 24 (August 1994); see also project statement "Queerying (Single Family) Space," *Sites* 26 (1995): 54–57). John Ricco's "The Itinerancy of Erotic Uncertainty" (paper delivered at the Society of Architectural Historians conference, Los Angeles, 18 April 1998, and at the University of Chicago, 26 May 1998) offers an articulate exposition of this position; this material appears in revised form in Ricco, *The Logic of the Lure* (Chicago: University of Chicago Press, 2002). Ricco associates "visual-based modes of knowledge" with "positivizing logics of reification, commodification, and privatization," leading him to conclude that it is "difficult if not impossible to posit an architecture, or for that matter a particular space, that might be identified or objectified as queer." This ignores the ways queers have created spaces that suggest exactly the kind of dynamic, highly charged, mutable experiences his words claim as queer. The mobility that is implied in pedestrian access and display and the slippage between eras suggested by the renovation aesthetic are just two ways that gay neighborhoods create queer space (the latter might be compared to Ricco's linguistic penchant for the oxymoron "non-positive affirmation," "non-relational relation"). While disagreeing with his conclusions, I thank him for his collegial permission to cite them here.

29. The opposition of real estate interests to the Boys Town markers challenges the common wisdom that gays gentrify urban neighborhoods. Long-term sociological studies suggest that although gays often play an important role in opening up neighborhoods for gentrification, this population consisting largely of renters is then priced out by mainstream real estate interests targeting a generic upscale market; see Timothy Pattison, "The Stages of Gentrification: The Case of Bay Village," in *Neighborhood Policy and Planning*, ed. Phillip L. Clay and Robert M. Hollister (Lexington: Lexington Books, 1983), 77–92; Marc Stein's *City of Sisterly and Brotherly Loves: Lesbian and Gay Philadelphia, 1945–1972* (Chicago: University of Chicago Press, 2000) draws the same conclusion. Rapidly escalating property values in Boys Town and recent controversies over projects for expensive townhouse developments perceived as marketed to heterosexuals indicate that the neighborhood is in this second stage of gentrification.

30. Ricco claims that queerness is manifest in "anonymous places"—"alleyways, parked cars, tearooms, bathhouse labyrinths, cruising grounds"—which are "unnamable, unformalizable, unrepresentable places outside of the law." He is straightforward in acknowledging that fleeting, anonymous sex may be no more conducive to "social cohesion and political expression" than it is to architecture. See also his "Coming Together," *A/R/C* 1, no. 5 (1994–95): 26–31. For other examples of theorists celebrating these spaces, see David Bell, "One-Handed Geographies: An Archeology of Public Sex," in *Queers in Space: Communities, Public Places, Sites of Resistance*, ed. Gordon Brent Ingram et al. (Seattle: Bay Press, 1997), 81–87; Mark Robbins's installation Scoring the Park, exhibited in *Disappeared*, curated by John Ricco at the Randolph Street Gallery in 1996; and Henry Urbach, "Spatial Rubbing: The Zone," *Sites* 25 (1993): 90–95. Far from being outside the law, public bathrooms in particular may be the most mapped, explicated, and policed of the spaces associated with sexual identity: Laud Humphrey's *Tearoom Trade* (Chicago: Aldine, 1975) is a classic text in both the canon of sexology and sociological method (for the questions it raised about participant observation); for a more recent analysis of how the physical and social structures of men's rooms function to police homosexuality, see Lee Edelman, "Men's Room," in *Stud: Architectures*

of Masculinity, ed. Joel Sanders (New York: Princeton Architectural Press, 1996), 152–61.

31. Both contingents present themselves as progressive critiques of stereotyping, but as Richard Dyer argues in relation to film, campaigns to replace stereotypes with notions of individualism often overlook how typologies, including stereotypes, to solidify collective identities by conferring on them a roster of visual signifiers that, though they may be intended as pejorative, bond those who share them ("Stereotypes," in *Gays and Film* [New York: Zoetrope, 1984], 27–39). Midcentury homosexuals used the term "double life" for the status that gays after the Stonewall riots of 1969 termed the "closet" (George Chauncey, *Gay New York: Gender, Urban Culture and the Making of the Gay Male World, 1890–1940* [New York: Harper/Collins, 1994], 134, 273–80).

32. John Hollister, "A Highway Rest Area as a Socially Reproducible Site," in *Public Sex/Gay Space*, ed. William L. Leap (New York: Columbia University Press, 1999), 55–70.

33. In Frisch, "Gay-Pride Theme," 2C, 1ff.

34. Ernest Tucker, "'Gay Pride' Street Markers Get a Toning Down," *Chicago Sun-Times*, 1 November 1997, 1. Stephanie Banchero, "Gay Theme Toned Down in Halsted St. Plan," *Chicago Tribune*, 2 November 1997, sec. 4C, 4; "City Offers Toned-Down North Halsted Plan," *Chicago Tribune*, sec 2C, 1.

35. Quoted in Tucker, "Gay Pride' Street Markers." It should be noted that the architect rejects characterizations of the revised plan as "toned down": "It was just different. . . . We didn't really set out to 'tone it down.' We changed it, refined it, did more work on it, made it better, as we would do on any project when we had more time to think about it. Maybe the density of the architectural elements was reduced a bit, but we would have done that anyway, because the concept was very preliminary. . . . We changed them to make them perform their function better, we thought." Edward Windhorst, interview with the author, October 1998.

36. In the Chicago context, objections to the camp visibility of the Halsted Street designs echo objections to the Chicago-based 1991 presidential campaign of the fabulously named black drag queen, Joan Jett Blak (see Moe Meyer, introduction to *Politics and Poetics of Camp*, 5–7).

37. This case is made about Sullivan by Betsky, *Queer Space*, 93–95. On Sullivan's homosexuality, see Robert Twombly, *Louis Sullivan: His Life and Work* (New York: Viking), 1986.

Chapter 15

1. Galen Cranz, "The Reform Park in the United States (1900–1930)," in *The Architecture of Western Gardens*, ed. Monique Mosser and Georges Teyssot (Cambridge, Massachusetts: MIT Press, 1991), 466–68.

2. Chicago Park District, *Handbook of Chicago's Parks*, 16 (Chicago: Chicago Park District, 1936).

3. Ibid., 29.

4. Ibid., 32.

5. Chicago Park District, *You Can Have a Good Lawn* (Chicago: Chicago Park District, 1938).

6. David Farber, *Chicago '68* (Chicago: University of Chicago Press, 1988), facing 211.

7. Mitchel Levitas, Charles Harbut, and Lee Jones, *America in Crisis* (New York: Ridge Press/Holt Rinehart and Winston, 1969), 142–65.

Chapter 16

This text is an edited version of the author's introduction to The Architectural Photography of Hedrich-Blessing *(New York: Holt, Rinehart, and Winston, 1984), 1–13.*

1. Cf. Helmut Gernsheim, *Focus on Architecture and Sculpture* (London: Fountain Press, 1949), 15–28; and Peter Wilhelm, "The Physiognomy of Building: Photography and Architecture," *Vanguard* (May 1981): 18.

2. Cited in David Lowe, "Hedrich-Blessing," *Interior Design* (October 1980): 265.

3. Arthur Siegel, quoted in [Minor White], "Substance and Spirit of Architectural Photography," *Aperture* 6, no. 4 (1958): 170.

4. Nikolaus Pevsner, foreword to Gernsheim, *Focus on Architecture and Sculpture,* 11.

5. For more on Hedrich-Blessing's techniques, see Eastman Kodak Co., "Hedrich-Blessing: A Half Century of Towering Achievements," *Studio Light* 1 (1981): 1–7.

6. Joseph W. Molitor, *Architectural Photography* (New York: John Wiley & Sons, 1976), 148.

7. Bill Hedrich quoted in Paul Gap, "The Exacting Business of Shooting Buildings," *Chicago Tribune Magazine,* November 12, 1978, 74.

8. Cf. the Panoramic Photograph Collection, listing of Kaufmann & Fabry Co. as copyright claimant of a panorama of the Century of Progress where it is noted "Kaufmann–Fabry Official Photographers." See http://memory.loc.gov/pp/panAuthors06.html, accessed 2 August 2003. Also cf. Kaufmann-Fabry, *A Century of Progress International Exposition, Chicago, 1933–1934,* commemorative album of "Official Photographs," no. AC1997.240.5.1–51, photography collection of the Los Angeles County Museum of Art.

9. Cf. Ada Louise Huxtable, "Is Modern Architecture Dead?" *New York Review of Books,* July 16, 1981, 22.

10. Norman Carver, Jr., quoted in [Minor White], "Substance and Spirit of Architectural Photography," *Aperture* 6, no. 4 (1958): 158.

Chapter 18

The author wishes to thank Nicholas Boyarsky for his help, advice, and kind permission to publish materials from the estate of Alvin Boyarsky; Jonathan Hill and Jane Rendell for their guidance and insightful advice; Charles Waldheim and Katerina Ruedi Ray, the volume editors, for their unflagging support throughout the development of this essay; Maia Rigas, manuscript editor at the University of Chicago Press, for her help and invaluable editorial suggestions; and finally, to Jasna Marjanović, for her love and support of a lifetime.

1. This is an excerpt from Alvin Boyarsky's lecture on Chicago, delivered at the Architectural Association in London; undated transcription, courtesy of the Alvin Boyarsky Memorial Trust, London.

2. Alvin Boyarsky, "Chicago à la Carte," *AD* v. XL, no. 7/6 (December 1970): 595.

3. Dawn Ades, *Photomontage* (London: Thames and Hudson, 1976), 7.

4. Dean MacCannell, *The Tourist: A New Theory of the Leisure Class* (Berkeley: University of California Press, 1999), 14–15.

5. Mike Crang, "Envisioning Urban Histories," *Environment and Planning Research A* 28 (1996): 438.

6. Boyarsky, "Chicago à la Carte," 595.

7. Crang, "Envisioning Urban Histories," 439.

8. Susan Stewart, *On Longing: Narratives of the Miniature, the Gigantic, the Souvenir, the Collection* (Durham: Duke University Press, 1999), 151.

9. Walter Benjamin, "The Work of Art in the Age of Mechanical Reproduction," in *Illuminations,* ed. Hannah Arendt (New York: Shocken Books, 1969), 225.

10. Ibid., 139.

11. For more information on the origins of montage as an art medium, see Dawn Ades, *Photomontage* (London: Thames and Hudson, 1976). Ades discusses the origins of montage in relation to the industrial and technological revolution and gives etymological explanation for the word "montage," which is derived from the German word *montieren*, which means "fitting" or "assembly line."

12. Seigfried Giedion, *Mechanization Takes Command: A Contribution to the Anonymous History* (New York: Oxford University Press, 1948), 245.

13. Stan Allen, *Points + Lines: Diagrams and Projects for the City* (New York: Princeton Architectural Press, 1999).

14. See Joanna Merwood, "Western Architecture: Regionalism and Race in the *Inland Architect*" and R. Bruegmann "Myth of the Chicago School," in this volume.

15. See Seigfried Giedion, *Space, Time and Architecture: The Growth of a New Tradition*, 5th ed. (Cambridge, MA: Harvard University Press, 1967) as well as Reyner Banham's historical account of Le Corbusier's use of industrial images in Reyner Banham, *A Concrete Atlantis: U.S. Industrial Building and European Modern Architecture* (reprint; Cambridge, MA: MIT Press, 1989).

16. See Robert Sobieszek, "The Architectural Photography of Hedrich-Blessing," in this volume.

17. Giedion, *Mechanization Takes Command*, 123.

18. Ibid.

19. For discussion on Chicago's position in the world economy and its international status, see Saskia Sassen, *Cities in a World Economy* (Thousand Oaks: Pine Forge Press, 1991) and idem, *The Global City: New York, London, Tokyo* (New York: Princeton University Press, 2001).

20. William Cronon, *Nature's Metropolis: Chicago and the Great West* (New York: W.W. Norton & Company, 1992), 56.

21. Giedion, *Mechanization Takes Command*, vi.

22. Boyarsky, "Chicago à la Carte," 636.

23. Rem Koolhaas, "Bigness" in *S, M, L, XL* (New York: Monacelli Press, 1995), 498.

24. Ibid.

25. See Robin Middleton, ed., *The Idea of the City* (Cambridge, MA: MIT Press, 1996), 10–48. This publication grew from a symposium, The Idea of the City, held at the Architectural Association in London in memory of the achievements of Alvin Boyarsky as chairman of the Architectural Association School of Architecture from 1971 to 1990. The symposium was chaired by Dalibor Vesely and Charles Jencks, and included talks from John Hejduk, Peter Eisenman, Rem Koolhaas, Daniel Libeskind, Bernard Tschumi, Leon van Schaik, and Peter Cook. The collected volume includes all their talks, plus papers about Boyarsky from other authors, such as Zaha Hadid, Ben Nicholson, and Peter Wilson, among others.

26. Joseh Griggs, "Map Guide to Chicago," *AD* v. XL, no. 7/6 (December 1970): 623–31.

27. Colin Rowe, 1970 "Chicago Frame," *AD* v. XL, no. 7/6 (December 1970): 641–47.

28. Boyarsky, "Chicago a la Carte," 611.

29. Boyarsky, "Chicago à la Carte," 638.

30. Ibid., 640.

31. Rem Koolhaas, "Atlanta" in Middleton, *The Idea of the City*, 85. In his lecture, Koolhaas describes his first encounter with Boyarsky, while the latter was giving a lecture on Chicago.

32. Rem Koolhaas, *Delirious New York* (New York: Monacelli Press, New York, 1994), 40.

33. Koolhaas, *Delirious New York*, 42.

34. Ibid.

35. Boyarsky, "Chicago à la Carte," 638.

36. See Manfredo Tafuri, *Architecture and Utopia: Design and Capitalist Development* (1976; reprint, Cambridge, MA: MIT Press, 1999). Tafuri's analysis of modern architecture and its social goals resonates with pessimism and the belief that it is impossible to provide a socially progressive architecture in the current social or economic order. Unlike Fredric Jameson, he does not believe in the modernist power of utopia. For Jameson's analysis of Tafuri's critique of ideology, see Fredric Jameson, "Architecture and the Critique of Ideology," in *Architecture Theory since 1968*, ed. K. Michael Hays (Cambridge, MA: MIT Press, 1998), 440.

37. Boyarsky, "Chicago à la Carte," 638.

38. Ibid., 622.

39. Michael Crang, "Envisioning Urban Histories," *Environment and Planning Research A* 28 (1996): 447.

Chapter 19

1. Carl W. Condit, *Chicago, 1930–1970: Building, Planning, and Urban Technology* (Chicago: University of Chicago Press, 1974), 72.

Chapter 20

I wish to thank Geoffrey Goldberg for his tremendous knowledge and the Art Institute of Chicago for their kind permission to reproduce images from the Goldberg Archive and text from the Goldberg and Honda oral histories. I would also like to thank David Cholewiak, Public Historian at the Chicago Historical Society, for sharing his research about Bertrand Goldberg, and Karen Lukritz of the Marina City Condo Association for sharing her understanding of Marina City's later years. However, none of the above should be associated in any way with the opinions presented or suggested in this work.

1. Ben Honda, Ed Center, Dick Binfield, and Al Goers were the key associates of the office from roughly 1963 on. They worked closely with Bertrand Goldberg on every major project

2. "Oral History of Ben Honda," interviews by Betty J. Blum in July–August 1999 and contained in *Chicago Architects Oral History Project* (Chicago: Dept. of Architecture, The Art Institute of Chicago, 2001), 106. Available at http://www.artic.edu/aic/collections/dept_architecture/honda.html.

3. "Oral History of Bertrand Goldberg," interviews by Betty J. Blum in February–April 1992 and contained in *Chicago Architects Oral History Project* (Chicago: Dept. of Architecture, The Art Institute of Chicago, 2001), 171. Available at http://www.artic.edu/aic/collections/dept_architecture/goldberg.html.

4. "Oral History of Bertrand Goldberg," 173–74.

5. "Oral History of Bertrand Goldberg," 174.

6. "Oral History of Bertrand Goldberg," 175.

7. Ibid.

8. Ibid.

9. "Oral History of Bertrand Goldberg," 266.

10. "Oral History of Bertrand Goldberg," 178.

11. Ibid.

12. "Oral History of Bertrand Goldberg," 181.

13. "Oral History of Bertrand Goldberg," 177–78.

14. "Oral History of Bertrand Goldberg," 181.

15. "Oral History of Bertrand Goldberg," 167.

16. Concept description of Marina City by Bertrand Goldberg Associates, date unknown.

17. "Oral History of Bertrand Goldberg," 2.

18. "Oral History of Bertrand Goldberg," 32.

19. "Oral History of Bertrand Goldberg," 34.

20. "Oral History of Bertrand Goldberg," 33.

21. "Oral History of Bertrand Goldberg," 171–72.

22. "Oral History of Ben Honda," 115.

23. "Oral History of Bertrand Goldberg," 97.

24. "Oral History of Bertrand Goldberg," 68.

25. "Oral History of Bertrand Goldberg," 14.

26. "Oral History of Bertrand Goldberg," 15.

27. "Oral History of Bertrand Goldberg," 178.

28. "Oral History of Bertrand Goldberg," 37.

29. "Oral History of Bertrand Goldberg," 209.

Chapter 21

The authors acknowledge the contributions of Walter Netsch, Dawn Clark Netsch, Robin Goldsmith, Chandra Goldsmith, India Gray, and Christina Kuras.

1. C. Ray Smith, *Supermannerism* (New York: E. P. Dutton, 1977), 28.

2. "Forms as Process," *Progressive Architecture* (March 1969): 94.

3. Walter Netsch interviewed by Detlef Mertins, *SOM Journal* 1 (May 21, 2001), 44.

4. Smith, *Supermannerism*, 33.

Chapter 22

1. Gabriel Guevrekian, "Enseignement de l'architecture et conditions de travail des jeunes aux États-Unis," *L'architecture d'aujourd'hui* 28 (September 1957): 72–95.

2. Henry-Russell Hitchcock, "The Architecture of Bureaucracy and the Architecture of Genius," *Architectural Review* (January 1947): 3–6.

3. Hitchcock, "Architecture of Bureaucracy," 4.

4. Hitchcock, "Architecture of Bureaucracy," 4.

5. Hitchcock, "Architecture of Bureaucracy," 6.

6. Hitchcock, "Architecture of Bureaucracy," 6.

7. "Oral History of Walter Netsch," interviews by Betty J. Blum on May 8 and June 5–28, 1995, and contained in *Chicago Architects Oral History Project* (Chicago: Dept. of Architecture, The Art Institute of Chicago, 1997–2000), 20. Available at http://www.artic.edu/aic/collections/dept_architecture/netsch.html.

8. "Oral History of Walter Netsch," 20–21.

9. Ibid.

10. Ibid.

11. "Oral History of Walter Netsch," 53

12. "Oral History of Walter Netsch," 23.

13. Netsch, interview with the author, May 2000.

14. "Oral History of Walter Netsch," 84.

15. "Oral History of Walter Netsch," 165.

16. "Oral History of Walter Netsch," 84.

17. Walter Netsch, "Programming the U.S. Naval Postgraduate School," *Architectural Record* (June 1954): 150–57.

18. Walter Netsch, "Grinnell's Social Geometry," *Progressive Architecture* 46 (December 1965): 118–25.

19. "Oral History of Walter Netsch," 160.

20. "Oral History of Walter Netsch," 116.

21. "Oral History of Walter Netsch," 81.

22. "Oral History of Walter Netsch," 113–14.

23. Ibid.

24. Hitchcock, "Architecture of Bureaucracy," 6.

25. "Oral History of Walter Netsch," 160.

26. Netsch received honorary doctorates from Purdue University (1991), Northwestern University (1980), Miami University of Ohio (1979), and Lawrence University (1968).

27. "Oral History of Walter Netsch," 422.

28. Netsch, quoting Bruce Graham in "Oral History of Walter Netsch," 142.

29. "Oral History of Walter Netsch," 140.

30. Ibid.

31. "Oral History of Walter Netsch," 142.

32. "Oral History of Walter Netsch," 152.

33. "Oral History of Walter Netsch," 155.

34. Ibid.

35. Ibid.

36. Netsch, *Webster's Third New International Dictionary*, as quoted in "Forms as Process," *Progressive Architecture* (March 1969): 94–111.

37. Netsch, "Forms as Process," 94.

38. "Oral History of Walter Netsch," 165.

39. Netsch, interview.

40. "Forms as Process," 103.

41. Dawn Clark Netsch to Walter Netsch, quoted in "Oral History of Walter Netsch," 168.

42. "Oral History of Walter Netsch," 182.

43. Mildred F. Schmertz, "A New Museum by Walter Netsch of SOM Given Order by His Field Theory," *Architectural Record* (January 1980): 111–21.

44. "Oral History of Walter Netsch," 101.

45. "Oral History of Walter Netsch," 127.

46. "Forms as Process," 94.

47. "Forms as Process," 102.

48. As quoted in Carol Herselle Krinsky, *Gordon Bunshaft of Skidmore Owings & Merrill* (Cambridge, MA: MIT Press, 1988), 258.

Chapter 23

1. Harry Weese, "A Word about Architecture," *Process: Architecture*, no. 11 (Tokyo: Process Architecture Publishing Co., 1979), 6.

2. Sadly, in the 1990s, all of the trees in the plaza were removed. Wardens feared that the trees could serve as camouflage for criminals facilitating prisoner escapes.

Chapter 24

1. The U.S. Congress approved Section 202 of the Omnibus Consolidated Reconciliation Act (OCRA 1996) requiring all public housing authorities to assess the "viability" of any property with 300 or more units and a vacancy rate over 10 percent. As a result of this assessment, "non-viable" developments—sites where it would cost more to rehabilitate than it would to demolish and provide residents with vouchers to go into the private sector—are to be removed from the permanent inventory within five years. In 1998, this was extended, with a mandatory conversion of any development with 250 or more units that fails the viability test.

2. Friedrich Engels, *The Condition of the Working Class in England* (1845; New York: Oxford University Press, 1999).

3. In Devereux Bowley, *The Poorhouse: Subsidized Housing in Chicago, 1895–1976* (Carbondale: Southern Illinois University Press, 1978), 127.

4. Bowley, *The Poorhouse,* 110–32.

5. Arnold Hirsch, *Making the Second Ghetto: Race and Housing in Chicago, 1940–1960* (Chicago: University of Chicago Press, 1998).

6. For example, see William Julius Wilson, *The Truly Disadvantaged : The Inner City, the Underclass, and Public Policy* (Chicago: University of Chicago Press, 1987).

7. See Hirsh, *Making the Second Ghetto*; and Thomas Philpot, *The Slum and the Ghetto: Neighborhood Deterioration and Middle-Class Reform, 1880–1930* (New York: Oxford University Press, 1978).

8. As quoted in the *Chicago Daily News,* April 10, 1965.

9. Wardell Yotagan was cofounder of the Coalition to Protect Public Housing and a resident of Rockwell Gardens on Chicago's West Side. He died in June 1999.

Chapter 25

1. Catherine Bauer, *Modern Housing* (Cambridge, MA: Riverside Press, 1934); Edith Elmer Wood, *Recent Trends in American Housing* (New York: Macmillan, 1931); and Nathan Straus, *Seven Myths of Housing* (New York: Holt, 1944). For a readable description of housing progressives, see John F. Bauman, *Public Housing, Race, and Renewal: Urban Planning in Philadelphia, 1920–1974* (Philadelphia: Temple University Press, 1987).

2. A host of data from the U.S. Census confirms that by standard measures, housing conditions for the majority of Americans improved rapidly in the postwar period. For instance, the percentage of housing units without complete plumbing facilities dropped from 45 percent in 1940 to 1 percent in 1990. See U.S. Census, "Housing: Then and Now, 50 Years of Decennial Censuses," http://www.census.gov/hhes/www/housing/census/histcensushsg.html, revised August 22, 2002. Even Michael Stone, the most pessimistic scholar of private housing markets, concedes an improvement of conditions during the 1950s and 1960s. See Stone, *Shelter Poverty* (Philadelphia: Temple University Press, 1993), 108.

3. Chicago Plan Commission, *Master Plan of Residential Land Use of Chicago* (Chicago: Chicago Plan Commission, 1943), table 17. South Side Planning Board, "An Opportunity for Private and Public Investment in Rebuilding Chicago," 1947. Sarah Whiting has also written an insightful, if overly theoretical, history of the planning context of Chicago's Near South Side in the early postwar years. See Sarah Whiting, "Bas-Relief Urbanism: Chicago's Figured Field," in this collection and in *Mies in*

America, ed. Phyllis Lambert (New York: Harry N. Abrams, 2001), 643–91.

4. CHA, "Application for Reservation of Urban Low-Rent Public Housing and for a Preliminary Loan," August 12, 1949, CHA files, Chicago, Ill., folder IL 2–7; Chicago City Council, *Journal of Proceedings,* July 22, 1949, 4613–4616; CHA annual report, 1949, available at the Chicago Public Library, Municipal Reference Collection (hereafter CPL-MRC); CHA, "Chicago's Housing Need," July 1949, CPL-MRC; see also Martin Meyerson and Edward Banfield, *Politics, Planning and the Public Interest* (Glencoe: Free Press, 1955), 33.

5. Chicago Plan Commisson, *Master Plan of Residential Land Use of Chicago;* CHA Executive Secretary Elizabeth Wood to Alderman George D. Kells, letter dated September 21, 1945, CHA files, folder "City Council."

6. Elizabeth Wood, "Realities of Urban Development," *Journal of Housing* (January 1946): 11.

7. Chicago Housing Authority (CHA), "The Slum . . . Is Rehabilitation Possible?" 1946; CHA annual report, 1941.

8. The site for the fourth major CHA conglomeration–Stateway Gardens-Robert Taylor Homes (6,000 units)–was selected by the Chicago City Council to remove the notorious Federal Street Slum, long one of the worst housing areas of the city.

9. Arnold Hirsch, *Making the Second Ghetto: Race and Housing in Chicago, 1940–1960* (New York: Cambridge University Press, 1982).

10. Chicago City Council, *Journal of Proceedings,* December 3, 1940, 3607; *Chicago American,* February 20, 1956; *Chicago Tribune,* May 10, 1956; *Chicago Defender,* editorial, May 14, 1956.

11. Beginning in early 1952, Elizabeth Wood and the CHA Board—now no longer dominated by progressives—began to clash over introducing racial integration to four all-white projects planned before the war. The clash came to a head over the unplanned integration of Trumbull Park Homes on the city's Far South Side. After a year of racial turmoil that rocked the city, Wood was forced out by the CHA board in a coup likely orchestrated by Mayor Martin Kennelly. Her removal marked a sad end to progressive policies on racial integration, but little evidence suggests it had any effect on the decisions surrounding public housing's design. See Hirsch, *Making the Second Ghetto,* 235, and Arnold Hirsch, "Massive Resistance in the Urban North: Trumbull Park, Chicago, 1953–1966," *Journal of American History* (September 1995): 522–50.

12. Arnold Hirsch's valuable work on race and housing has been largely interpreted to place the entire blame for the location of public housing in the ghetto on the city council. Hirsch actually made a narrower claim. See Hirsch, *Making the Second Ghetto,* 254. The March 2003 issue of the *Journal of Urban History* is devoted to more recent views of Hirsch's second ghetto thesis.

13. CHA annual report, 1947, 1949, CPL-MRC.

14. Robert Moore Fisher, *Twenty Years of Public Housing* (New York: Harper & Brothers, 1959).

15. CHA, "Application for Reservation"; CHA official minutes, resolution 54-CHA-258, September 27, 1954, CHA files.

16. Several investigations looked for corruption at the CHA but found little evidence of any wrongdoing. Contracts were secretly bid and had to be cleared by federal officials in Washington. Mayor Daley didn't really need to control CHA contracts; he already had control over city contracts, and only a handful of contractors had interest in building public housing due to difficult federal rules. However, the city's unions, tightly bound to the Democratic Party, were pleased with the prevailing wages on federal contracts. For three investigations, see Federal Public Housing Authority, "Report on the

Operations of the Chicago Housing Authority, June 1946," Library of the Department of Housing and Urban Development, Washington, D.C.; Public Housing Administration, "Management Review, Chicago Housing Authority, January 1958," January 1958, CPL-MRC; Institute for Community Design Analysis, "Review and Analysis of the CHA and Implementation of Recommended Changes. Final Report of Phase 1: Recommended Changes and Resulting Savings," March 31, 1982, CPL-MRC.

17. CHA Chairman Robert R. Taylor to Alderman William J. Lancaster, chairman, City Council Housing Committee, letter dated October 28, 1948, CHA files, folder "City Council."

18. CHA Executive Secretary Elizabeth Wood to Alderman George D. Kells, letter dated September 21, 1945, CHA files, folder "City Council."

19. Wood to Kells, letter dated September 21, 1945. Julian Whittlesley, "New Dimensions in Housing Design," *Progressive Architecture* (April 1951): 57–68. Whittlesely explained: "It was with trepidation and with a deep understanding . . . that the executive secretary of the CHA, Elizabeth Wood, long experienced in public housing management, first assayed the elevator-type project."

20. The Chicago Plan Commission approved the CHA's use of the Dearborn site at "approximately" 50,000 persons per square mile; but the final CHA design produced an actual density of 68,000 persons per square mile. The 68,000 figure is a generous calculation, taking the gross area of the project (including the land of the adjacent elementary school) and dividing it by the number of residents. CHA, "Development Program for IL 2-9," CHA files, folder "IL 2-9."

21. CHA, "Development Program for IL 2-9."

22. The five projects are Loomis Courts, Ogden Courts, Harrison Courts, Maplewood Courts, and Archer Courts.

23. The struggle over sites for the City-State projects had been triggered by the CHA's ill-advised proposal to use half of McKinley Park for a new high-rise style project. Neighborhood residents, outraged at the potential loss of park space, mobilized in 1948 and drew the attention of the city council. This marked a turning point in relations between the council and the CHA. For the five sites eventually selected, even at high densities (averaging 44 units per acre), the CHA could still only build a disappointing 1,430 units on the available sites instead of the 2,000 hoped for when planning began in early 1948. See D. Bradford Hunt, "What Went Wrong with Public Housing in Chicago? A History of the Chicago Housing Authority, 1933–1982" (Ph.D. diss., University of California at Berkeley), 192–97.

24. "Experiment in Multi-Story Housing," *Journal of Housing* (October 1951): 367–69. The same review board that praised Loomis Courts noted that nationwide good public housing design was "hard to find" and expressed deep concern about the lack of innovative and interesting work. It concluded that the problem stemmed from "a combination of architects who take the easy way out and the inevitable sterility that comes from the imposition of too many and too detailed standards." "Architects Act as Editorial Board," *Journal of Housing* (October 1951): 338.

25. Whittlesley, "New Dimensions in Housing Design," 61.

26. Public Housing Administration (PHA) , "Low Rent Public Housing: Planning, Design, and Construction for Economy," December 1950, Catherine Bauer Wurster Papers, Bancroft Library, University of California at Berkeley, folder 7, carton 31. This quotation begs the question of how the problem of high rises and children became "so thoroughly understood." A search for literature on the subject yielded little on the subject before 1950.

27. PHA, "Low Rent Public Housing: Planning, Design, and Construction for Economy."

28. PHA, "Low Rent Public Housing: Planning, Design, and Construction for Economy."

29. "Address by John Taylor Egan, Commissioner, Public Housing Administration, at the 17th Annual Conference of the National Association of Housing Officials, Detroit, Michigan, October 16–19, 1950," box 10, "Miscellaneous Records of the Liaison Division," Record Group 196, National Archives II, College Park, Md.; Hunt, "What Went Wrong with Public Housing," 303–9.

30. Elizabeth Wood, "The Case for the Low Apartment," *Architectural Forum* (January 1952): 102.

31. The CHA had proposed three of the sites, the Chicago City Council the other two.

32. CHA Official Minutes, Resolution 53-CHA-63, April 13, 1953, CHA files.

33. CHA, "Addendum No. IV to Development Program for Project IL 2-20," CHA files, folder "IL 2-20." The PHA forced similar design changes in Baltimore in 1952 and Buffalo in 1953. Gilbert Rodier to Charles Slusser, letter dated December 18, 1953, and Rodier to John Taylor Egan, letter dated January 7, 1953, both in box 5, "Correspondence of the Commissioner of Public Housing," Record group 196, National Archives II.

34. *Chicago Sun-Times*, March 12, 1956; Chicago *Daily News*, March 8, 1958; *Chicago Tribune*, October 31, 1958; *Chicago Tribune*, undated clipping from 1958 in CHA clippings book, CHA files; *Chicago Sun-Times*, April 5, 1959.

35. CHA annual report, 1955; CHA to Public Housing Administration Commissioner Charles Slusser, February 5, 1959, CHA files, folder "IL 2-37."

36. CHA annual report, 1955; CHA to Slusser, February 5, 1959, CHA files, folder "IL 2-37." The correspondence between CHA and PHA is also included in the appendix to Congressional hearings. See United States Senate, Committee on Banking and Currency, "President's Message Disapproving S.57," 86th U.S. Congress, 1st session, July 23–31, 1959, 604–12.

37. "Comparison on bids received on Project IL 2-34, Chicago with Project NY 5-34, New York," June 11, 1958, "Chicago Development Dispute" folder, box 5, "Historical Publications," record group 196, National Archives II, "Report of the Special Committee to the Commissioners of the Chicago Housing Authority on the Subject of Project Illinois 2-34," August 3, 1959, in CHA files, folder "PHA Development Dispute."

38. "President's Message Disapproving S. 57," 329.

39. Elizabeth Wood to CHA Commissioners, "The Tenant Selection Process," December 22, 1952, in CHA files, folder "Gautreaux"; CHA, monthly report, April 1955, CPL-MRC; CHA to Mayor Richard J. Daley, July 19, 1957, in CHA files, folder "Mayor's file"; CHA official minutes, memorandum of record, December 6, 1957, CHA files; CHA to Daley, July 19, 1957; *Chicago Tribune*, November 28, 1957, January 10, 1958, and January 14, 1958; CHA Annual statistical report, 1960, CPL-MRC.

40. CHA to Slusser, February 5, 1959.

41. CHA to Slusser, September 2, 1959, in CHA files, folder "PHA Development Dispute."

42. Even in the baby-boom suburb of Park Forest in 1970, the number of adults outnumbered the number of youths. See U.S. Census of Population and Housing: 1960, Final Report PHC(1)-26, Census Tracts for Chicago, IL, Standard Metropolitan Statistical Area, Table P-1.; U.S. Census, 1970. The literature is extremely thin on youth densities in the urban environment. Mark Baldassare's extensive work on urban residential crowding makes no analysis of age demographics. See Mark Baldassare, *Residential Crowding in Urban America* (Berkeley: University of California Press, 1979). The issue is mentioned but unevaluated in one study of public housing tenants in Boston. See Richard S. Sco-

bie, *Problem Tenants in Public Housing: Who, Where, and Why Are They?* (New York: Praeger, 1975), 59–64.

43. CHA annual statistical report, 1964, CPL-MRC.

44. CHA Director of Management Harry J. Schneider to PHA Regional Director William Bergeron, letter dated August 25, 1964, CHA files, folder "IL 2-37." The federal response to the CHA's request for more playgrounds is unclear.

45. See D. Bradford Hunt, "What Went Wrong with Public Housing in Chicago? A History of the Robert Taylor Homes," *Journal of the Illinois State Historical Society* (spring 2001): 96–123.

46. CHA Executive Director Alvin Rose to Bergeron, letter dated January 6, 1959, CHA files, folder "IL 2-30"; CHA official minutes, memorandum of record, January 21, 1961, CHA files; CHA Director of Management Harry Schneider to Thomas A. Williams, 4352 S. State St., no. 1003, September 21, 1966, CHA files, folder "Manager's folder, Robert Taylor Homes."

47. Data from CHA, annual statistical reports, 1946–1984, CPL-MRC.

48. CHA annual statistical reports, 1964, 1974 CPL-MRC.

49. Hirsch and Meyerson and Banfield document the local opposition to the city council's racist site selection and tenant selection policies, but few voices questioned the general direction of public housing in the country. The most notable exception is Catherine Bauer, a leading progressive planner and foremost author of the Housing Act of 1937. Bauer published her dissatisfaction in 1957. See Catherine Bauer, "The Dreary Deadlock of Public Housing," *Architectural Forum* (May 1957): 140–42.

Chapter 26

1. A much longer version of this text appeared in Phyllis Lambert, ed., *Mies in America*, exhibition catalog (New York: Harry N. Abrams, 2001), 642–91. The exhibit appeared at the Whitney Museum of American Art, New York, 21 June to 23 September, 2001; the Canadian Centre for Architecture, Montreal, 17 October 2001 to 20 January 2002; and at the Museum of Contemporary Art, Chicago, 16 February to 26 May 2002. I appreciate the Canadian Centre for Architecture's permission to print this shortened version and their generous help in retrieving images from the original text.

2. For the South Side story, see Wim de Wit, "The Rise of Public Housing in Chicago, 1930–1960," in *Chicago Architecture and Design, 1923–1993*, ed. John Zukowsky (Chicago and Munich: Art Institute of Chicago and Prestel, 1993).

3. Daniel Bluestone, "Chicago's Mecca Flat Blues," *Journal of the Society of Architectural Historians* 57, no. 4 (December 1998): 391.

4. Irene Macauley, *The Heritage of Illinois Institute of Technology* (Chicago: IIT, 1978), 68–70. See also Sarah Gordon, *All of Our Lives: A Centennial History of Michael Reese Hospital and Medical Center* (Chicago: Michael Reese Hospital and Medical Center, 1981), 127–30. For an excellent discussion of this particular social milieu, see Mark Haller, "Policy Gambling, Entertainment, and the Emergence of Black Politics: Chicago from 1900 to 1940," *Journal of Social History* 24, no. 4 (1991).

5. Adolf von Hildebrand, "The Problem of Form," in *Empathy, Form and Space: Problems in German Aesthetics*, ed. Harry Francis Mallgrave and Eletherios Ikonomou (Santa Monica: Getty Center for the History of Art and the Humanities, 1994), 235.

6. Ludwig Mies van der Rohe and Mildred Whitcomb, "Only the Patient Counts," *Modern Hospital* 64, n. 3 (March 1945): 67.

7. Mies van der Rohe and Whitcomb, "Only the Patient Counts," 67.

8. "We then also, as Mies got the program from the various departments of the school, we made wood blocks of the volume of the building, and on a plot of the whole site I drew up, he would work those out in some arrangement within the spaces of the buildings, having had that plot from—what was it?—31st Street down to 35th, State Street over to the tracks to the west, drawn up in a modular system that he had found workable for the contents of the program." George Edson Danforth, interview by Kevin Harrington, April 23, 1996; transcriptions of tape 4, side 1. Canadian Centre for Architecture Institutional Archive, Mies and His American Colleagues Oral History Collection. Centre Canadien d'Architecture / Canadian Centre for Architecture, Montréal.

9. Ludwig Mies van der Rohe, interview with Katherine Kuh in Kuh, *The Open Eye: In Pursuit of Art* (New York: Harper & Row, 1971), 35.

10. Letter from Henry Heald to Ludwig Mies van der Rohe dated 30 July 1942, Heald papers, box 17, folder 4, IIT Archives, Paul V. Galvin Library. Thanks to Phyllis Lambert for kindly pointing me to this reference.

11. Alan Colquhoun, "The Superblock," (1971) republished in Colquhoun, *Essays in Architectural Criticism: Modern Architecture and Historical Change* (Cambridge, MA: MIT Press, 1981), 98.

12. Michael Warner, "The Mass Public and the Mass Subject," in Bruce Robbins, ed., *The Phantom Public Sphere* (Minneapolis and London: University of Minnesota Press, 1993): 234–56.

Chapter 27

1. Alvin Boyarsky, "Chicago à la Carte," in *Architectural Associations: The Idea of the City*, ed. Robin Middleton (Cambridge, MA: Architectural Association and MIT Press, 1996), 44.

2. See the "Oral History of Charles F. Murphy," interviewed in 1981 by Carter H. Manny; compiled under the auspices of the *Chicago Architects Oral History Project* (Chicago: Dept. of Architecture, The Art Institute of Chicago, 1995), 78–82. On the political and economic underpinnings of O'Hare's early development, see Richard P. Doherty, "The Origin and Development of Chicago-O'Hare International Airport" (Ph.D. diss., Ball State University, 1970); and Eugene Kirchherr, "The Changing Pattern of Airport Land Use in the Chicago Region, 1941–1975," *Bulletin of the Illinois Geographical Society* 25 (spring 1983): 32–47. On the contemporaneous history of airport design nationally, see David Brodherson, "An Airport in Every City: The History of American Airport Design," *Building for Air Travel*, ed. John Zukowsky (Chicago: Art Institute of Chicago, 1996), 67–95.

3. "Oral History of Charles F. Murphy," 81–82.

4. See, for example, "Our Two Largest Airports," *Progressive Architecture* 44 (August 1963): 102–11. In order to multiply the political benefits of O'Hare's successful operation, the Daley administration organized multiple dedications for various portions of the site as they were completed. Most notably, organizing a dedication for the opening of the airport restaurant timed to coincide with a visit by President Kennedy. For the national political context of O'Hare's development and Daley's orchestration of it, see Adam Cohen and Elizabeth Taylor, *American Pharaoh: Mayor Richard J. Daley; His Battle for Chicago and the Nation* (Boston and New York: Back Bay Books/Little Brown and Co., 2001), 234–38.

5. Remarkably, O'Hare patronage extends to architectural photography. The Hedrich-Blessing firm, responsible for some of the most iconic images of Chicago modernism including the polemic images of Mies's work on the IIT campus and other projects in the United States, was hired to produce the original photographs of O'Hare for the C. F. Murphy firm. These images have become the official record of O'Hare's candidacy for second Chicago school credentials. Hedrich-Blessing continues to

be retained by O'Hare architects to photograph their work at the airport, with their photographs representing the new International Terminal by Perkins and Will as recently as 1993–94.

6. Chicago Daily News (October 3, 1922). For an overview of the Daley machine, and patronage in public works, and O'Hare in particular, see Cohen and Taylor, *American Pharaoh*, 234–38.

7. On the "death of modern architecture" see Charles Jencks, *The Language of Post-Modern Architecture* (New York: Rizzoli, 1977). On the relation between airport design and urbanism after deregulation, see Robert Bruegmann, "Airport City," *Building for Air Travel*, ed. John Zukowsky (Chicago: Art Institute of Chicago, 1996), 195–211.

8. On the economic crisis of Fordism in the 1970s and its relation to postmodern architecture, see Patrik Schumacher and Christian Rogner, "After Ford," *Stalking Detroit*, ed. Daskalakis, Waldheim, Young, (Barcelona: ACTAR, 2001), 48.

9. Ralph H. Burke, *Report of Commercial Airport Requirements for Chicago* (Chicago, 1944), 1, as quoted in Brodherson, "An Airport in Every City," 75.

10. Deborah K. Dietsch, "High Tech Expansion," *Architectural Record* 173 (May 1985): 132–39.

11. Charles Linn, "Form Follows Flight," *Architectural Record* 182 (June 1994): 116–23.

12. Lester Crown, Chair, Civic Committee Aviation Task Force, *On-Time O'Hare Promotional Brochure* (Chicago: City of Chicago Department of Aviation, 2001).

Chapter 28

I would like to thank Greg Castillo, Grant Kester, Wanda Liebermann, Anna Williams, and the editors of this volume for their constructive comments on earlier drafts of this essay. Responsibility for the final version of the essay is entirely my own.

1. Total estimates of the maximum number of animals processed varies according to the source: William Cronon suggests that no fewer than 13 million animals were processed per year between 1880 and 1930 *Nature's Metropolis: Chicago and the Great West* (New York and London: W. W. Norton and Co., 1991), 259. In *Chicago As It Is: A Stranger's Guide to the City of Chicago* (Chicago: Reig. Philo. Pub. Association, 1866), the figure is eighteen million, while the brochure published by the stockyards in 1953 cites that year as the one in which the 1 billionth animal was processed there. M. S. Parkhurst, *History of the Yards* (Chicago: Chicago Union Stockyard, 1953), 1.

2. The redevelopment of the stockyards for other industrial uses began in the 1960s, as the stockyards entered a period of dramatic decline. The redevelopment of the area was accelerated in 1988, when the city declared it a "model industrial park" and was subsequently designated as eligible for tax increment financing, which uses tax revenues in the district to retire bonds sold to finance infrastructure improvements. Merrill Gozner, "City Picks Industrial Park Sites," *Chicago Tribune*, Februrary 19, 1988, 1. Four years later the Back of the Yards Neighborhood Council, which promoted the development, claimed that 94 companies and 15,000 new jobs were generated by the redevelopment. See Patrick T. Reardon, "Smell Now Is of Success," *Chicago Tribune*, March 12, 1992, 1. The stockyards industrial park initiative needs to be seen in the context of a broader decline in factory employment in Chicago, which fell by 59 percent between 1947 and 1982. See Gregory D. Squires, Larry Bennett , Kathleen McCour, and Philip Nyden, *Chicago: Race, Class and the Response to Urban Decline* (Philadelphia: Temple University Press, 1987), 23–61.

3. See, for example, the discussion of the meat industry in the context of industrial restructuring in Jimmy M. Skaggs, "Microcosm of the American Economy," in *Prime Cut: Livestock Raising and Meatpacking in the United States, 1607–1983* (College Station : Texas A&M University Press, 1986), 3–10. See also Frances M. Ufkes, "Lean and Mean: US

Meatpacking in an Era of Agro-Industrial Restructuring," *Environment and Planning. D, Society and Space* 13 (1995): 683–705.

4. David Harvey, "From Fordism to Flexible Accumulation" in *The Condition of Postmodernity: An Enquiry into the Origins of Cultural Change* (Cambridge, MA: Blackwell, 1989), 141–72.

5. Cronon, *Nature's Metropolis,* 257.

6. Tyson Foods, the largest meat processor in the United States, was indicted in December 2001 on charges that it conspired to smuggle illegal immigrants to work at its plants. See David Barboza, "Meatpakers' Profits Hinge on Pool of Immigrant Labor," *New York Times,* December 21, 2001. See also David Harvey, "Class Relations, Social Justice and the Political Geography of Difference," in *Justice, Nature and the Geography of Difference* (Cambridge, MA: Blackwell Publishers, 1996), 334–65.

7. Frances Ufkes notes that in the United States since the 1970s, Iowa Beef Producers (IBP), ConAgra, and Execl expanded share of the U.S. market for beef by building "high-volume plants in rural areas near large supplies of cattle, by using nonunion workers in meat fabrication, by de-skilling tasks, and by increasing line speeds." Ufkes, "Lean and Mean," 695.

8. Eric Schlosser, *Fast Food Nation* (New York: Harper Collins, 2001).

9. Ibid., 170–71.

10. The issue is discussed at length in Sharon Zukin, *Landscapes of Power* (Berkeley: University of California Press, 1991).

11. Robert Reich identifies the work of symbolic analysts as "one of the three jobs of the future" in postindustrial societies. Symbolic analysts, writes Reich, "solve identify and broker problems by manipulating symbols. They simplify reality into abstract images that can be rearranged, juggled, experimented with, communicated to other specialists, and then, eventually, transformed back into reality." See Robert Reich, *The Work of Nations* (New York: Vintage Books, 1992), 178.

12. As Harvey writes, "Imaging a city through the organization of spectacular urban spaces became a means to attract capital and people (of the right sort) in a period (since 1973) of intensified interurban competition and urban entrepreneurialism." David Harvey, *The Condition of Postmodernity* (Cambridge, MA: Blackwell Poublishers,1989), 92. See also John Hannigan, *Fantasy City* (London: Routledge, 1998); and Dennis R. Judd and Susan S. Fainstein, *The Tourist City* (New Haven, CT: Yale University Press, 1999).

13. Herbert and Rico Berchtold, *Cows on Parade in Chicago* (Kreuzlingen, Switzerland: Neptunart, 2000), 10.

14. One-hundred forty of the cows were auctioned, raising a total of $3.5 million for Chicago charities. Raoul V. Mowatt, "Cows Milked for All They're Worth," *Chicago Tribune,* November 10, 1999, 1–3.

15. In the period of rapid growth and consolidation of the meatpacking industry in Chicago in the late nineteenth and early twentieth centuries, attempts to unionize the stockyards resulted in labor disruptions and strikes. Blacks, who were excluded from the ranks of the union leadership, entered the work force at the stockyards as strikebreakers. They were often dismissed after the strikes were settled. See Alan. H. Spear's discussion of the 1904 strike in *Black Chicago: The Making of a Negro Ghetto, 1890–1920* (Chicago: University of Chicago Press: 1967), 38–40. By the late 1930s, significant advances had been made. In their pioneering study of "Negro life" in Chicago during and after the end of the Great Depression, St. Clair Drake and Horace R. Cayton cite the comments of a prominent but unnamed union organizer in 1937 who describes the increasing integration of the packing industry unions with the following reservation: "Negroes and whites in the same departments get practically

the same pay. Of course, cleaner jobs go to the white workers. There are more Negroes on the wool, glue and sausage departments because this is dirtier work. Negro women are in the dirtier departments too. These things will have to be ironed out after the union has agreements in all packing houses" See St. Clair Drake and Horace R. Cayton, *Black Metropolis: A Study of Negro Life in a Northern City* (Chicago: University of Chicago Press, 1993), 309.

16. Spear, *Black Chicago,* 36. At the turn of the century, the Chicago meatpacking unions were generally perceived by blacks as white institutions. As Spear notes: "From the packers point of view, Negroes were ideal strikebreakers. They generally had no scruples about working as scabs: those brought in from the south were almost totally ignorant of the principles of trade unionism, while those who had experience of unions generally found them discriminatory" (36–37).

17. Ibid., 37.

18. E. Melanie DuPuis, *Nature's Perfect Food: How Milk Became America's Drink* (New York: New York University Press, 2002), 67–89.

19. Ibid., 90–121.

20. Cronon, *Nature's Metropolis,* 256. See also David Goodman, "The Industrial Substitution of the Rural Product," in *From Farming to Biotechnology: A Theory of Agro-industrial Development,* ed. David Goodman, Bernardo Sorj, and John Wilkinson (Cambridge, MA: Blackwell Publishers, 1987), 6–56.

21. Cronon, *Nature's Metropolis,* 235–47.

22. Ibid., 256–57.

23. Berchtold and Berchtold, *Cows on Parade in Chicago,* 10.

24. See, for example, Steve Baker, "Mad Dogs and Half Human Beasts: The Rhetoric of Animality," in *Picturing the Beast: Animals, Identity, and Representation* (Urbana: University of Illinois Press, 2001), 11–119.

25. Berchtold and Berchtold, *Cows on Parade in Chicago,* 174. Chris Hedges of the *Chicago Tribune* reports a much higher figure of 40 million spectators. See "Is Nothing Sacred?" *Chicago Tribune,* June 2, 2000, 7.

26. "Farewell the Cows of Summer," *Chicago Tribune,* October 31, 1999, 18.

27. See, for example, Mark Gottdiener, "The Mirror of Production: The Realization Problem of Capital," in *The Theming of America; Dreams, Visions, and Commercial Spaces* (Boulder, CO: Westview Press, 1997), 43–67.

28. Donald M. Lowe, *The Body in Late Capitalist USA* (Durham: Duke University Press, 1995), 71–72.

29. Robert Goldman and Stephen Papson, "Just Metacommunicate It," in *Nike Culture* (London: Sage, 2000), 24–45.

30. See "Only in Chi—Cow-Go" in Berchtold and Berchtold, *Cows on Parade in Chicago,* 88.

31. Near the end of the parade, Louise Kiernan wrote in the *Chicago Tribune* that "The city's director of public art confesses that he can no longer pronounce museum without turning it into a pun (MOO-seum), a worker at the visitor center in the Chicago Cultural Center has begun asking visitors to moo, and at least one local executive, after seeing the same cow from his fifth floor window for 4-1/2 months, has come to the conclusion that he can't live without it." Louise Kiernan, "Now Chicago Must Begin to Brace for Life after Cows," *Chicago Tribune,* October 18, 1999, 1.

32. Berchtold and Berchtold, *Cows on Parade in Chicago,*138.

33. During Cows on Parade businesses "gave birth" to cows see, for example, Susan Chandler, "Shoppers Will Have a Hard Time Avoiding the Cows," Chicago Tribune, June 12, 1999: B2–5. Chandler wrote that "Crate and Barrel is having a cow, so are Kenneth Cole and Tiffany. Marshall Field is having two cows. And Nieman Marcus is outdoing them all: It has three cows," B2.

Contributors

JANET ABRAMS
Director, Design Institute,
University of Minnesota

LEE BEY
Director of Media and Governmental
Affairs, Skidmore, Owings & Merrill

DANIEL BLUESTONE
Professor of Architecture,
University of Virginia

ROBERT BRUEGMANN
Professor and Chair of Art History,
University of Illinois at Chicago

C. GREIG CRYSLER
Assistant Professor of Architecture,
University of California at Berkeley

SARAH DUNN
Assistant Professor of Architecture,
University of Illinois at Chicago

DAVID DUNSTER
Roscoe Professor of Architecture,
University of Liverpool

MARTIN FELSEN
Studio Professor of Architecture,
Illinois Institute of Technology

JULIA FISH
Professor of Art and Design,
University of Illinois at Chicago

GEOFFREY GOLDBERG
Principal, G. Goldberg and Associates

DAVID GOODMAN
Architect, Chicago

PAMELA HILL
Architect, Chicago and Past Vice President,
Chicago Women in Architecture

D. BRADFORD HUNT
Assistant Professor of Social Science,
Roosevelt University

SUSAN F. KING
Architect, Environ Harley Ellis, Chicago
and Past President, Chicago Women in
Architecture

IGOR MARJANOVIĆ
Director, Core Design Program and
Assistant Professor of Architecture,
Iowa State University

JOANNA MERWOOD
Director of Public Programs, Department
of Architecture, Interior Design and Lighting,
Parsons School of Design

ERIC MUMFORD
Associate Professor of Architecture,
Washington University in St. Louis

REUBEN M. RAINEY
Professor of Landscape Architecture,
University of Virginia

KATERINA RÜEDI RAY
Professor and Director, School of Art,
Bowling Green State University

LEAH RAY
Instructor, The School of the Art Institute of Chicago

CHRISTOPHER REED
Associate Professor and Chair, Department of Art, Lake Forest College

SIDNEY K. ROBINSON
Associate Professor of Architecture and Art History, University of Illinois at Chicago

MITCHELL SCHWARZER
Associate Professor of Architecture, California College of Arts and Crafts

JANET L. SMITH
Associate Professor of Urban Planning, University of Illinois at Chicago

ROBERT A. SOBIESZEK
Head Curator of Photography, Los Angeles County Museum of Art

RICHARD SOLOMON
Director, The Graham Foundation for Advanced Studies in the Fine Arts

DAVID VAN ZANTEN
Professor of Art History, Northwestern University

CHARLES WALDHEIM
Associate Dean, Faculty of Architecture, Landscape, and Design, University of Toronto

SARAH WHITING
Associate Professor of Architecture, Harvard University

JANE WOLFF
Assistant Professor of Architecture, Washington University in St. Louis

Index